CHILDREN AND EXERCISE XIX

CHILDREN AND EXERCISE XIX

Promoting Health and Well-Being

Neil Armstrong, Brian Kirby and Joanne Welsman

Children's Health and Exercise Research Centre
University of Exeter, UK

Proceedings of the XIXth International Symposium of the European Group of Pediatric Work Physiology, 16–21 September 1997

E & FN SPON
An Imprint of Chapman & Hall
London · Weinheim · New York · Tokyo · Melbourne · Madras

Published by E & FN Spon, an imprint of
Chapman & Hall, 2–6 Boundary Row, London SE1 8HN, UK

Chapman & Hall, 2–6 Boundary Row, London SE1 8HN, UK
Chapman & Hall GmbH, Pappelallee 3, 69469 Weinheim, Germany
Chapman & Hall USA, 115 Fifth Avenue, New York, NY 10003, USA
Chapman & Hall Japan, ITP-Japan, Kyowa Building, 3F, 2-2-1 Hirakawacho, Chiyoda-ku, Tokyo 102, Japan
Chapman & Hall Australia, 102 Dodds Street, South Melbourne, Victoria 3205, Australia
Chapman & Hall India, R. Seshadri, 32 Second Main Road, CIT East, Madras 600 035, India

First edition 1997

Printed in Great Britain by TJ International, Padstow, UK

ISBN 0 419 22100 X

A catalogue record for this book is available from the British Library

Publisher's Note
This book has been produced from camera ready copy provided by the individual contributors in order to make the book available for the symposium.

∞ Printed on permanent acid-free text paper, manufactured in accordance with ANSI/NISO Z39.48-1992 and ANSI/NISO Z39.48-1984 (Permanence of Paper).

CONTENTS

ACKNOWLEDGEMENTS

The XIXth International Symposium of the European Group of Pediatric Work Physiology would not have been possible without the support of the following members of the Organizing Committee: Michael Chia, David Childs, Mark De Ste Croix, Alison McManus, Juliet Mosney, Chris Potter, Nikki Sutton, Craig Williams, Margaret Williams, Michael Williams, Richard Winsley and Sue Vooght. Alison Husband made both the Symposium and the Proceedings possible through her devoted and tireless secretarial efforts.

The editors are grateful to the distinguished keynote speakers and to the contributors of free communications, not only for the excellence of their presentations, but also for their willingness to prepare written papers in advance to allow publication of this volume during the Symposium. A special thanks to the Physical Education Association of the United Kingdom for publishing the abstracts of all free communications in the European Journal of Physical Education Volume 2, Number 1, 1997.

No international symposium can function without significant financial support and we are indebted to the following sponsors for their patronage:

United Kingdom Sports Council	British Heart Foundation
The Royal Society	Polar Electro Oy
Oxenham Will Trust	University of Exeter
Bodycare	Mars Incorporated
Clinical and Scientific Equipment	Royal Devon and Exeter NHS Health Care Trust
Sensor Medics	

In addition, the Symposium enjoyed the support of the British Olympic Association, the British Association of Sport and Exercise Sciences, the National Institute of Sports Medicine and the Physical Education Association of the United Kingdom.

PREFACE

Children and Exercise XIX contains the Proceedings of the XIXth International Symposium of the European Group of Pediatric Work Physiology (EGPWP) held at the Manor House, Moretonhampstead, near Exeter, UK, from 16-21 September, 1997. The Symposium was hosted by the Children's Health and Exercise Research Centre, University of Exeter which was celebrating its 10th Anniversary.

The EGPWP which was conceived in 1967 has organized the following symposia:

Symposium	Date	Place	Chair
I	1968	Dortmund, Germany	J Rutenfranz
II	1969	Liblice, Czechoslovakia	VS Seliger
III	1970	Stockholm, Sweden	C Thorén
IV	1972	Netanya, Israel	O Bar-Or
V	1973	De Haan, Belgium	M Hebbelinck
VI	1974	Seč, Czechoslovakia	M Máček
VII	1975	Trois-Rivières, Canada	RJ Shephard
VIII	1976	Bisham Abbey, UK	CTM Davies
IX	1978	Marstand, Sweden	BO Eriksson
X	1981	Jousta, Finland	J Ilmarinen
XI	1983	Papendal, Netherlands	RA Binkhorst
XII	1985	Hardenhausen, Germany	J Rutenfranz
XIII	1987	Hurdal, Norway	S Oseid
XIV	1989	Leuven, Belgium	G Beunen
XV	1989	Seregélyes, Hungary	R Frenkl
XVI	1991	St Sauves, France	J Coudert/E Van Praagh
XVII	1993	Hamilton, Canada	O Bar-Or
XVIII	1995	Odense, Denmark	K Froberg
XIX	1997	Moretonhampstead, UK	N Armstrong

The XIX Symposium attracted delegates from 26 countries and followed EGPWP tradition with an emphasis on discussion of issues relating to young people and exercise. This volume reflects the formal programme and contains the 11 keynote presentations, 4 papers presented in a mini-symposium on cardiac risk factors in children, and 59 of the free communications.

The theme of the XIXth Symposium was the promotion of children's health and well-being and this book offers comprehensive reviews of key topics and reports of current research in paediatric health and exercise sciences. If it stimulates further interest in the exciting study of the exercising child and adolescent and encourages scientists and paediatricians to initiate research programmes devoted to the promotion of young people's health and well-being it will have served its purpose.

Exeter
September 1997

NA, BJK, JRW

THE JOSEPH RUTENFRANZ LECTURE 1997

In recognition of the outstanding contribution to paediatric exercise science of one of the founder members of the European Group of Pediatric Work Physiology it was agreed at the XVth Symposium in Seregélyses in 1989 that each subsequent Symposium should begin with the Joseph Rutenfranz Lecture delivered by a distinguished paediatric exercise scientist.

The Joseph Rutenfranz Lectures

1991 Children and adolescents: performance, measurements, education
P.O. Åstrand

1993 New horizons in pediatric exercise research
D.M. Cooper

1995 Safe exercise for the child with a chronic disease
O. Bar-Or

1997 A scientific voyage through research in children's health - from heart via muscle to bone
H.C.G. Kemper

THE 1997 RUTENFRANZ MEMORIAL LECTURE

A SCIENTIFIC VOYAGE THROUGH RESEARCH IN CHILDREN'S HEALTH - FROM HEART VIA MUSCLE TO BONE

Research in paediatric exercise physiology

H.C.G. KEMPER and T. TSAHALINA
AGGO Research Group, EMGO Institute, Vrije University, Amsterdam, The Netherlands

Keywords: Exercise, history, meta-analysis, paediatrics, physiology, training

Introduction

During the XVIIIth Pediatric Work Physiology (PWP) Conference held in Denmark, in September 1995, the organizer of the next PWP Conference, Professor Neil Armstrong invited HK to give the opening lecture at the XIXth PWP Conference, in the United Kingdom, in September 1997. HK was, of course, very honoured by Neil Armstrong's invitation to present the Rutenfranz Memorial Lecture, but after accepting, he was then posed a second question: What will be the title of the lecture, so that it can be announced at the end of the XVIIIth PWP Conference. HK came up with the idea of a meta-analysis, of PWP Conferences since the birth of the European Group of Pediatric Work Physiology 30 y earlier, and to examine the main interests and trends in paediatric research between 1967 and 1997.

Initially, HK suggested the subtitle "a voyage from heart via muscle to bone". As an exercise physiologist HK started to teach students in sport and physical education the limiting factors of physical performance. HK was fascinated by the question of the weakest link in the oxygen transport-chain: ventilation, circulation, diffusion or muscle? In the 1950s it became clear that ventilation at maximal exercise was only at 80% of maximal rate. In the 1960s the doctrine was that the heart and blood circulation and not the ventilatory system were limiting the oxygen transport system[1]. In the 1970s techniques were developed to measure the metabolic rate in muscles by analyzing muscle biopsies and it was revealed that the (an)aerobic capacity of muscles was dependent upon their fibre type. It was noted that training increased the metabolic capacity of muscles more than the transport capacity of oxygen by lungs and heart[2,3]. The debate is still alive, but within the perspective of health the skeletal system is now attracting great interest among physiologists. While the incidence of morbidity and

Children and Exercise XIX. Edited by Neil Armstrong, Brian Kirby and Joanne Welsman.
Published in 1997 by E & FN Spon, 2–6 Boundary Row, London, SE1 8HN.
ISBN 0 419 22100 X.

mortality of cardiovascular diseases is decreasing, osteoporosis is becoming an epidemic. Exercise seems to be an important factor in the prevention of osteoporosis and the attention of many exercise physiologists has been attracted to the study of bone. Even osteoporosis, although only prevalent during middle and late adult life has been characterized by Dent[4] as a paediatric disease. In our meta-analysis one of the goals was to investigate whether a parallel interest could be traced through the research presented to PWP Conferences.

First HK tried to get information from participants who were present in 1967 on the occasion of the Ergometry meeting in Berlin. Second, HK and TT collected all written material from the congress programmes, abstract books, and more importantly the proceedings (if available) of previous conferences. Third, HK and TT categorized all presentations with respect to first author, country, age group, sex of the subjects, and topic of research. In this meta-analysis HK will present quantitative figures of main interests and trends in research presentations over the last 30 years and he will conclude the lecture with the longitudinal development of his own research, as presented to PWP Conferences.

Foundations of Pediatric Work Physiology (PWP)

From verbal information provided by Gunther Koch and a letter from Milos Mácek, HK could reconstruct the birth of the European Group of Pediatric Work Physiology.

In 1967, now exactly 30 years ago, Professor Mellorowicz organized an Ergometry meeting in Berlin (Germany). At that time work physiology was very popular in Germany. Exercise tests were carried out in different places and results published in German journals (Zeitschrift fuer Angewandte Physiologie, Medizin und Sport and Zeitschrifft fuer Paediatrie). The books of Professors Hollman (Hochst-und-Dauerleistungsfahigkeit des Sportlers[5]), Reindell (Herz Kreislaufkrankheiten und Sport[6]), and Mellerowicz (Ergometrie[7]) were widely known at that time. Later the Scandinavian (Åstrand, Lange Andersen, Hermansen, Saltin) and North American countries (Rowell, Fox, Montoye, Wilmore, Costill and many others) became more prominent.

In a small café in Berlin eight persons met over a pint of beer, they expressed their disappointment in the content of the Ergometry conference and more particularly in the loss of respect for differences in responses to exercise, training and rehabilitation of children compared to adults. Further they disagreed with the short time that was reserved for discussion and the strict way it was controlled during the sessions. This group of eight men consisted of Rutenfranz, Koch and Mocellin (Germany), Thorén and Eriksson (Sweden), Mácek, Seliger and Vavra (CSSR).

Rutenfranz offered to organise a small conference in Dortmund in 1968, where the participants could present their ideas and results and of which the main aim would be to exchange and discuss their research.

Figure 1 shows a photograph which was taken at the first conference of the European Group of Pediatric Work Physiology, in Haus Daneberg. Of the 17 persons in the picture at least ten are recognizable to HK, Rutenfranz, Hebbelinck (Belgium),

Fig. 1. A picture from the first PWP conference held in Dortmund 1968 (provided by Professor Mácek)

Mácek, Thorén, Eriksson, Hartley, Mocellin, Degré (France), Seliger and Parizkova (CSSR).

Joseph Rutenfranz insisted on having a working group which was not officially connected to organizations or conference procedures, but consisted of a club-like society only regulated by the principles of friendship and fellowship without any written rules[8].

In the introduction to the Proceedings of the IXth PWP Conference, held in Marstrand (Sweden), Rutenfranz himself formulated the goals for these conferences in six basic statements[9]:

1. Symposia with special topics related to the development of physical performance capacity in childhood and youth are needed,
2. These symposia should being together paediatricians and physical educators experienced in the field of work physiology,
3. The number of participants should not exceed 30-40,
4. The time for each presentation should be limited to 10-15 minutes, with unlimited time for discussion following each,
5. All discussions should occur without regard to prestige or to furthering one's professional career,
6. The symposia should be organized by a group of scientists, but not by a formal society, and the organizers should annually or biennially invite a good mixture of experienced and young scientists, mostly from European countries.

HK joined the group during the IVth PWP conference in 1972 and can confirm that most of Rutenfranz's rules are still fulfilled. From discussions with Rutenfranz it was apparent that he was never in favour of publishing the papers in printed proceedings, especially when that could have consequences for the congress fee or for the number of participants. Nevertheless, the number of participants has increased steadily as can be seen from the number of contributions. In the IInd PWP Conference, in 1970, in Liblice (CSSR) 16 papers were presented, but by 1975 the number of papers had increased to 44. This European conference was held in North America and exceeded the maximal number of presentations as proposed by Rutenfranz. In the opinion of HK this was the reason the founder did not participate.

In the 1980s the number of presentations showed a further increase with 59 in 1983, 66 in 1987 and 61 in 1989. However in 1989 a second PWP with 45 papers was organised in Leuven, (Belgium).

In 1993 the European PWP group held a combined symposium with the North American Society for Pediatric Exercise Medicine (NASPEM). Little wonder that 121 presentations were given, and in the XVIIIth PWP Conference in Denmark 109 posters and papers were presented. In the present PWP symposium 110 papers and posters are expected.

In Papendal (The Netherlands) in 1983, for the first time, poster presentations were included in the programme and since then special poster sessions have been scheduled each time and discussed with the participants. The increasing number of posters made it possible to accept more than Rutenfranz's desired maximum of 40 papers, without adding more days to the conference than the usual three and a half.

Another, not documented rule of the group is that the symposium venues are chosen outside big cities and the buildings of universities. We have experienced over the years many picturesque and calm places in and outside Europe: we have used sport centres (Wingate, Bisham Abbey, Papendal), rehabilitation centres (De Haan, Hurdal), a former mansion (Seregélyes), an island (Marstrand), a summer holiday centre (St Sauves), and several conference centres (Sec, Joutsa, Hardehausen, Faaborg and Alliston).

The reason for bringing the participants to remote areas is obvious; cities are attractive for simple researchers abroad to visit shopping malls, museums, and nightlife. Although the sessions are usually not scheduled at night, they start early in the morning and they need an audience and presenters that are bright and vigilant. The total list of the PWP conferences, year, place and total number of presentations (incl posters) is provided in table 1.

Quantitative analysis of presented research

The proceedings of PWP conferences

The basis for this analysis is the written material available from past conferences. From the first Dortmund gathering in 1969 nothing is left but the above photograph (fig 1). The other conferences have all published books of the proceedings, with the exception of the papers presented in Sec (1974) and in Bisham Abbey (1976). However, later in 1978 Borms and Hebbelinck published a selection of these papers in the Medicine and Science Series, as volume 11 entitled Pediatric Work Physiology published by Karger,

Table 1. Total list of PWP conferences with year, place and total number of presentations

No.	Place	Country	Year	Number of presentations
0	Berlin	Germany	1967	?
1	Dortmund	Germany	1968	?
2	Liblice	CSSR	1969	16
3	Stockholm	Sweden	1970	35
4	Natanya	Israel	1972	31
5	De Haan	Belgium	1973	28
6	Sec	CSSR	1974	14
7	Trois Rivières	Canada	1975	44
8	Bisham Abbey	UK	1976	44
9	Marstrand	Sweden	1978	36
10	Joutsa	Finland	1981	36
11	Papendal	Holland	1983	58
12	Hardehausen	Germany	1985	44
13	Hurdal	Norway	1987	64
14	Leuven	Belgium	1989	45
15	Seregélyes	Hungary	1989	61
16	St. Sauves	France	1991	70
17	Alliston	Canada	1993	121
18	Faaborg	Denmark	1995	109
19	Moretonhampstead	UK	1997	110

Basel[10]. The papers, not included in that particular volume, are taken from the abstract books of these two conferences.

Twice the proceedings were published as a supplement of a paediatric journal: In 1975 the papers of PWP III were published by Thorén in Acta Paediatrica Scandinavia as volume 10[11] and in 1974 the papers of PWP V were published by Borms and Hebbelinck in Acta Paediatrica Belgica as volume 28[12]. The PWP Conference in Alliston in 1993 was a conference combined with the North American Society of Pediatric Exercise Medicine and the proceedings were published in a book with only the full papers of the invited lectures[13] and all the other abstracts were published in number 3 of volume 5 of the journal Pediatric Exercise Science in 1993[14].

In table 2 the proceedings of all conferences are listed including the names of the editors, the publisher and year of publication.

The total number of pages of the 15 proceedings books is 4361 and the number of pages differ from conference to conference: The first one is the proceedings edited by Mácek in 1970 and comprises 96 pages reflecting the relatively small number of 16 contributions.

Table 2. Total list of PWP conference proceedings with editors, publishers and years of publication

No.	Place	Country	Editors	Publishers	Year
1	Dortmund	Germany	---	---	---
2	Liblice	CSSR	Mácek	Univ. Karlova	1970
3	Stockholm	Sweden	Thorén	Acta Paed.Scand	1971
4	Natanya	Israel	Bar-Or	Wingate Inst.	1973
5	De Haan	Belgium	Borms, Hebbelinck	Acta Paed.Belgica	1974
6	Sec	CSSR	Borms, Hebbelinck	Karger	1978*
7	Trois Rivières	Canada	Lavallée, Shephard	Ed. du Pélican	1977
8	Bisham Abbey	UK	Borms, Hebbelinck	Karger	1978*
9	Marstrand	Sweden	Berg, Eriksson	Univ. Park Press	1980
10	Joutsa	Finland	Ilmarinen, Välimäki	Springer	1984
11	Papendal	Holland	Binkhorst, Kemper, Saris	Human Kinetics	1985
12	Hardehausen	Germany	Rutenfranz, Mocellin, Klimt	Human Kinetics	1986
13	Hurdal	Norway	Oseid, Carlsen	Human Kinetics	1989
14	Leuven	Belgium	Beunen, Ghesquiere, Reybrouck, Claessens	Enke	1990
15	Seregélyes	Hungary	Frenkl, Szmodis	NEVI	1991
16	St. Sauves	France	Coudert, Van Praagh	Masson	1992
17	Alliston	Canada	Blimkie, Bar-Or	Human Kinetics	1995
18	Faaborg	Denmark	Froberg		1996
19	Moretonhampstead	UK	Armstrong, Kirby, Welsman	Spon	1997

* Selection of papers from two conferences

As the conferences grew the proceedings comprised more pages: for example, the Stockholm-papers published in 1971 add up to 157 whilst the Natanya-papers reached 344 pages in 1973[15]. Since then the proceedings have contained more than 200 pages, with the exception of the selection of the Sec-Bisham Abbey papers published in 1978 (with 175 pages) and the extra PWP XIV in Leuven in 1990[16] with 175 pages.

The largest proceedings are the ones from Trois Riviéres[17], Hurdal (1989)[18], and Hardehausen (1986)[19] with each having more than 400 pages.

Publishers involved in these proceedings were occasionally from the university or the institute of the organizers (Univ Karlova, 1970[20]; Wingate Institute, 1973[15]; NEVI, 1991[8]) but also involved were official publishers from different countries: Switzerland, Karger, 1978[10]; Canada, Edition du Pélican, 1977[17]; Germany, Springer, 1984[21] and Enke, 1990[16]; France, Masson, 1992[22] and USA, University Park Press, 1980[9] and Human Kinetics, 1985[23], 1986[19], 1989[18] and 1995[13]).

Nationality of researchers that have presented to PWP conferences

Since the birth of the European Society of Pediatric Work Physiology in 1967 participants from at least 28 different countries have contributed.

In table 3 the number of first authors of presented papers are given for each conference. Therefore, not the total number of participants attending the conferences is used in this table, but only those that have produced one or more contributions in the form of a presentation or a poster. The United Kingdom (UK) included participants from England, Wales, Scotland and (Northern) Ireland. During the last 30 y countries have combined (DDR and FRG) or separated (CSSR into Czech Republic and Slovakia and USSR into Latvia, Estonia etc). For DDR and FRG we have used Germany, for Czech Republic and Slovakia we have remained with CSSR, because the papers were presented before the separation in 1993 and because there were no papers from the USSR before 1991, the new countries are noted separately.

Initially it appears that PWP Conferences were attended by participants from 21 different European countries. USA and Canada are the countries outside Europe that have attended the most over the years; researchers from South Africa, Japan and more recently from Brazil, Australia and Saudi Arabia have also presented.

The number of presenters from a host country, for obvious reasons is always relatively high compared to that number in other conferences. This phenomenon is further accentuated by the PWP policy of inviting excellent researchers from the hosting country to present invited lectures to the participants.

The number of presentations given by researchers in the three countries that started the European Society for Pediatric Work Physiology: Germany, Sweden and CSSR is 71, 54 and 52 respectively. From the other European countries Belgium, Holland and UK provided the highest number of presentations: 64, 70 and 75 respectively. From the Scandinavian countries, other than Sweden, Finland produced 32, Norway 24 and Denmark 22 presentations. Israel (25), France (32) and Hungary (42) are the other three European countries that have made a significant number of contributions over the years.

From countries outside Europe, Canada has provided the highest number of papers (103), followed by the USA (90). The high number of Canadian contributions can in part be explained by the fact that this country organised two of the PWP conferences in 1975 and in 1993.

Table 3. Overview of the number of papers presented at the 18 PWP conferences from different countries. The number of presentations from the organizing country are printed in bold

COUNTRY	PWP 11	PWP 111	PWP 1V	PWP V	PWP VI	PWP VII	PWP VIII	PWP IX	PWP X	PWP XI	PWP XII	PWP XIII	PWP XIV	PWP XV	PWP XVI	PWE XVI	PWP XVIII	TOTAL/ COUNTRY
Australia															1	3	5	10
Austria				1		1	1	1	1	1	1	1	1	1	1			11
Belgium		1	3	**4**	4	4	3	1	**3**	4	2	5	**11**	4	4	6	6	65
Brazil															3	2		5
Bulgaria						1												1
Canada		1	6	2	2	**14**	7	2	2	13	5	2	6		6	**24**	11	103
CSSR	**8**	5		5	**2**	4	1	3	2	3	7	4	3	5				52
Denmark		1					1	1		2	1	3		3		2	**8**	22
Estonia																2	7	9
Finland				1			1	3	**7**	1	7	4	1	3	3		1	32
France						6	1	1				3	1	3	**11**	6	3	35
Germany	4	5	2	5	2	5	4	6	2	4	**3**	7	1	6	4	6	5	71
Holland			1	1	1	1	3	4	5	**10**	7	4	**6**	3	11	6	7	70
Hungary							1		3	3	2	5	3	**13**	5	5	2	42
Israel			**9**			2	1	1	2	1	1	2		1		2	3	25
Italy												1	1	1	1	3	2	9
Japan										1	3	3		2	1	4	2	16
Latvia																	3	3
Norway		2			1		3	3		2	1	**8**		1	1		2	24
Poland											1	1	1	3	1		4	11
Portugal												1	1		3	1	4	10
Saudi Arabia																1		1
Spain							1									1		2
South Africa			1	2						1			1					5
Sweden	4	**13**	5	4	2	3	4	7	5	2		2		1	1		1	54
Switzerland																1	2	3
United Kingdom		3	1	1			**10**		4	6	1	3	5	4	6	15	16	75
USA		4	3	2		3	2	2		4	2	5	3	7	7	31	15	90
Total/Conference	16	35	31	28	14	44	44	36	36	58	44	64	45	64	70	121	109	

Also a trend over time can be discerned. At the first nine PWP Conferences (between 1969 and 1978) Sweden was very productive and delivered 42 out of the total of 54 Swedish papers. The same holds for CSSR whose participants were very active until PWP XV in 1989 (52) but thereafter there have been no further contributions. The opposite is true of Finland, in the 1960s and 1970s only 4 papers were presented, but in the 1980s and 1990s 28 Finnish presentations were made.

Age and sex of the subjects studied

All of the published articles or abstracts of the presentations are categorized with respect to the age and sex of the subjects that were studied. The following four age groups were formed:

1. calendar age between 4 and 8 y,
2. calendar age between 8 and 12 y,
3. calendar age between 12 and 18 y,
4. calendar age over the age of 18 y.

If there was overlap between age groups the paper was categorized in more than one age group.

Three sex groups were discerned:

1. males
2. females
3. males and females

Papers not dealing with humans but with animals were counted separately.

In table 4 the percentage of papers dealing with subjects in the different age groups (4a) and sex groups (4b) are given. If in the paper or abstract no clear age indication was given, and this was often the case, the paper was not included in our calculations.

Most of the research presented at PWP Conferences is concerned with the teenage population: between 28 and 46% deal with 8-12-year olds and between 33 and 48% of the papers deal with 12-18-year olds. The percentage of papers on young children is between 8 and 21%, while adult populations, as expected, form a minority (0-15%).

If the published research is categorised according to sex groups (table 4b), the majority (26-53%) of the papers have boys as their subjects and only between 0-22% of the papers have females as their population of interest. The 22% is from the PWP XVIII Conference in Denmark and is relatively high compared to all foregoing conferences with previous percentages never higher than 12%.

Depending on the conference, between 32 and 72% have carried out their research with both boys and girls.

Over the 30 y of PWP Conferences only four animal studies have been presented: two rat studies (by Kucera et al. in 1970 and by Bell in 1985), one monkey experiment (by Casaer in 1990) and one dog study (by Matthys et al. in 1993).

Table 4a. Percentage of papers dealing with the four selected age groups

No.	Place	Country	Age group (y)			
			0-8	8-12	12-18	>18
2	Liblice	CSSR	12	46	34	8
3	Stockholm	Sweden	16	32	37	15
4	Natanya	Israel	16	35	35	14
5	De Haan	Belgium	13	46	33	8
6	Sec	CSSR	16	28	48	8
7	Trois Rivières	Canada	21	37	36	6
8	Bisham Abbey	UK	23	32	45	0
9	Marstrand	Sweden	16	32	40	12
10	Joutsa	Finland	13	45	33	9
11	Papendal	Holland	19	32	42	7
12	Hardehausen	Germany	15	31	45	9
13	Hurdal	Norway	11	39	42	8
14	Leuven	Belgium	21	31	37	11
15	Seregélyes	Hungary	17	35	45	2
16	St. Sauves	France	8	37	44	11
17	Alliston	Canada	13	36	37	14
18	Faaborg	Denmark	8	40	39	13

Table 4b. Percentage of papers dealing with (human) sex groups and with animals

No.	Place	Country	Males Animal		Females	M/F
2	Liblice	CSSR	42	0	50	8 (rat)
3	Stockholm	Sweden	39	6	55	0
4	Natanya	Israel	29	5	67	0
5	De Haan	Belgium	53	4	43	0
6	Sec	CSSR	38	8	54	0
7	Trois Rivières	Canada	43	5	52	0
8	Bisham Abbey	UK	40	14	46	0
9	Marstrand	Sweden	41	10	49	0
10	Joutsa	Finland	29	12	59	0
11	Papendal	Holland	20	5	72	3 (rat)
12	Hardehausen	Germany	32	3	65	0
13	Hurdal	Norway	39	0	61	0
14	Leuven	Belgium	29	5	67	2 (monkey)
15	Seregélyes	Hungary	44	4	52	0
16	St. Sauves	France	42	12	46	0
17	Alliston	Canada	26	10	63	1 (dog)
18	Faaborg	Denmark	26	22	52	0

Topics of research interest on the PWP conferences

Studying the proceeding books initially the titles of chapters that were given to sets of presentations dealing with a certain domain of paediatric work physiology were collected. A total of 92 different chapter titles were found. Secondly, 23 headings were formulated to restrict the total number of topics and to avoid overlap between the titles. Thirdly, we constructed seven themes that covered more or less all aspects of research in paediatric physiology. This procedure is summarised in fig 2.

The seven themes cover the following aspects of paediatric work physiology research:

1. **Exercise physiology**, including circulo-respiratory system, musculoskeletal system and endocrine system,
2. **Growth**, including growth, maturation and body composition,
3. **Exercise intervention**, including therapy, sports training, leisure time physical activity and motor learning,
4. Measurements of **lifestyles** and exercise in different **environments**,
5. **Health**, including biologic and psychosocial risk indicators, injuries and physical performance aspects,
6. Research with **specific child populations** such as gifted, handicapped or children of different ethnic backgrounds,
7. **Methodological aspects** e.g. design, cross-sectional, longitudinal and methods of exercise testing.

Which of the 23 headings belong to the seven themes is given in table 5.

Each presentation was, after reading the full paper, the abstract and/or title, assigned to a maximum of 6 of the 23 available headings. For each conference the total number of articles dealing with any of the 23 topics was calculated as a percentage of the total number of presentations. In fig 3 the range of percentage of presentations to each PWP conference is given for the seven research themes.

As would be expected the majority of the papers (between 55 and 100%) deal with "Exercise Physiology". "Methodology" (research designs and exercise testing methods) and "Growth" are also important headings with percentages between 30 and 72% of the papers in the conferences. The number of presentations on specific child populations vary widely over the conferences with percentages from 9 to 60%. Exercise interventions provide over the years between 12 and 47% of the cases. No significant trends are apparent between 1968 and 1995. However, during the first 12 PWP conferences (1969-1983) between 0 and 22% of the papers were devoted to "Health". In the last six PWP Conferences (1985-1995) between 30 and 36% of the papers have been concerned with this research heading, showing that the participants attending the last 10 y have shown more interest in aspects related to the health of children.

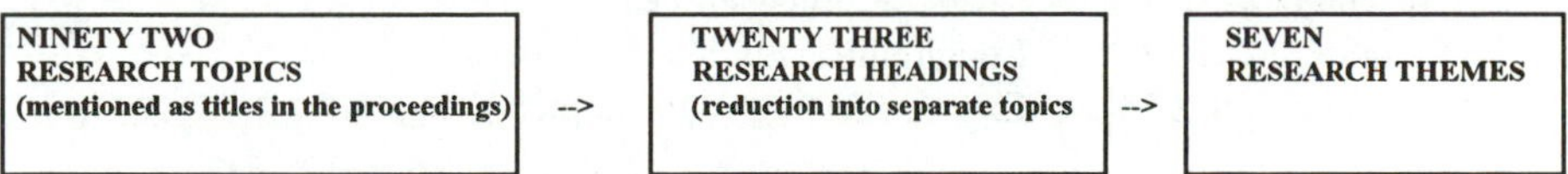

Fig. 2. Procedure of categorizing papers on research topics of interest

Table 5. Grouping of the 23 research topics over the 7 research themes

Theme 1:	EXERCISE PHYSIOLOGY		
headings:		1.1	Aerobic metabolism ($\dot{V}O_2$, $\dot{V}O_2$ max)
		1.2	Anaerobic metabolism (high energy phosphates, glyco lysis)
		1.3	Endocrinologic aspects
		1.4	Muscle metabolism
		1.5	Bone metabolism in skeleton, back
Theme 2:	GROWTH		
headings:		2.1	Body composition (fat, lean body mass, limb volume)
		2.2	Growth and maturation (height, weight, skeletal age, sexual)
Theme 3:	EXERCISE INTERVENTION		
headings:		3.1	Exercise therapy (disease, rehabilitation)
		3.2	Training effects (extra physical education, sport, physical activity)
		3.3	Motor development (neuromuscular, learning)
Theme 4:	LIFESTYLE AND ENVIRONMENT		
headings:		4.1	Environmental aspects (temp., altitude, socio-economic status)
		4.2	Habitual physical activity (questionnaire, interview, mo tion)
		4.3	Nutrition and exercise
Theme 5:	HEALTH		
headings:		5.1	Health/risk indicators (hypertension, overweight, hyper cholesterolemia)
		5.2	Physical performance (physical fitness)
		5.3	Psycho-social aspects
		5.4	Injuries
Theme 6:	CHILDREN		
headings:		6.1	Gifted children, young (top) athletes
		6.2	Handicapped children
		6.3	Clinical aspects (pathology)
Theme 7:	METHODOLOGY		
headings:		7.1	Cross-sectional studies
		7.2	Longitudinal studies
		7.3	Exercise testing (dynamometry, ergometry)

Because the majority of presentations were categorised within the theme "Exercise Physiology" (comprising the greatest amount of five headings) and within the theme "Methodology" (with three headings) further analyses were carried out into the distribution of these headings.

In fig 4 the range in percentage of presentations within the three methodology headings is shown.

Results from cross-sectional studies always form a small percentage of the papers varying from 0% to 26%. Longitudinal studies, however, are more frequently presented and include all studies that have more than one point of measurement over time and include both observational and intervention studies.

Papers presenting methods of exercise testing: instruments, protocols, analyzing methods, fitness batteries and performance testing, physical activity measurements etc. are very popular. Between 24% and 92% of the presentations over the years are involved with these aspects.

Within "exercise physiology" at each conference the presentations that study the (an)aerobic metabolism of the circulo-respiratory system are in the majority with percentages of at least 53% and at most 94%. The muscular system contributes between 5% and 35% of the presentations and bone metabolism is the least studied part of the body of youth, with percentages varying from 0 to 8% of the presentations. Moreover, there is a clear trend in the interest of bone. During the first nine PWP

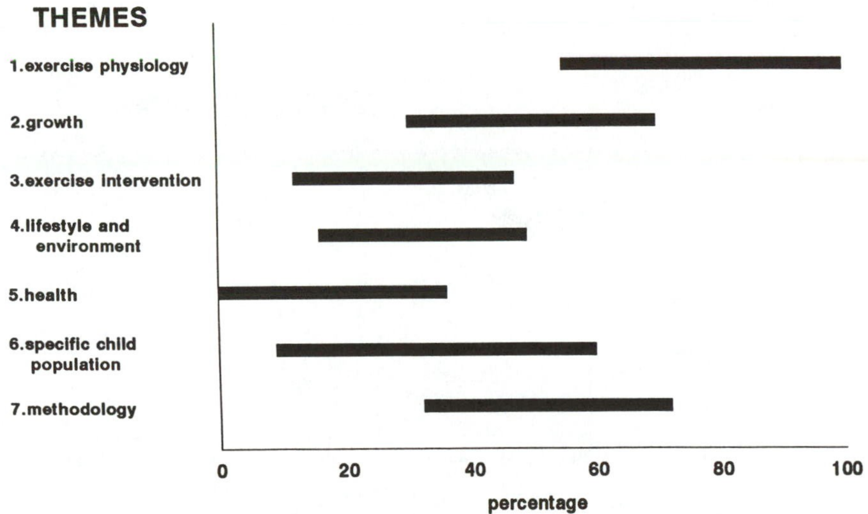

Fig. 3. Range in the percentage of papers dealing with each of the research themes

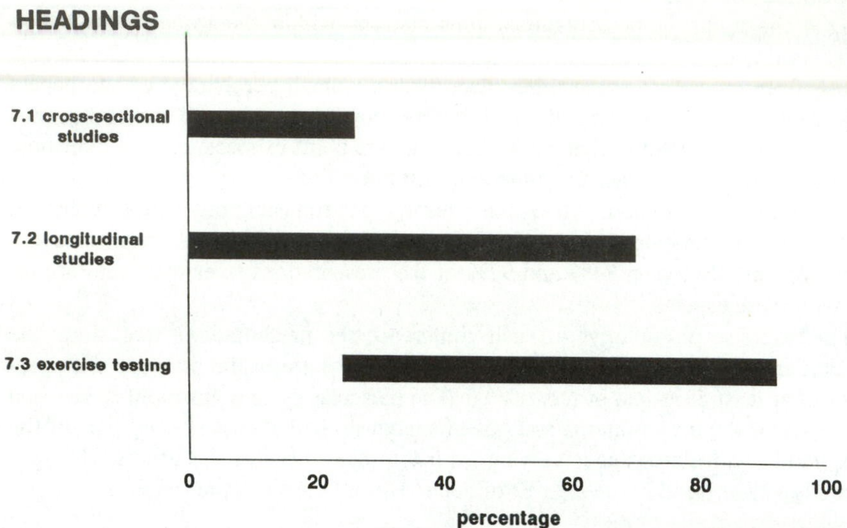

Fig. 4. Range in the percentage of papers within research theme: methodology

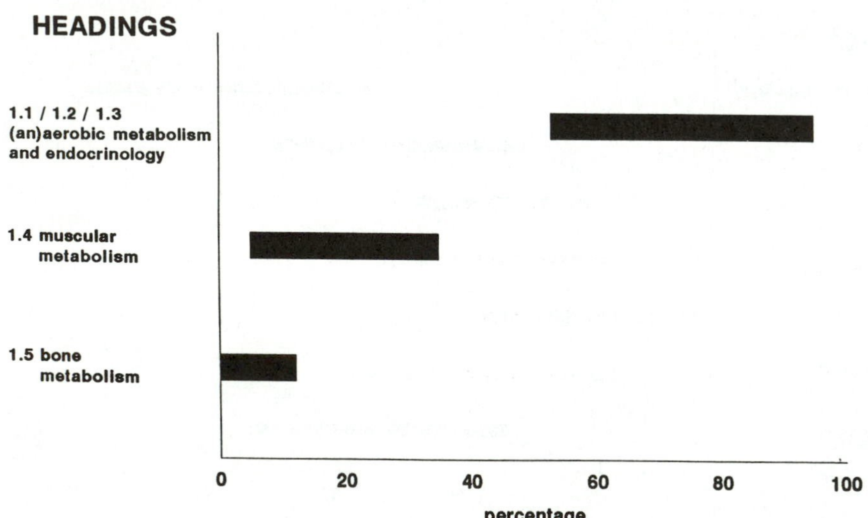

Fig. 5. Range in the percentage of papers within research theme: exercise physiology

Conferences (1969-1981) hardly any paper dealt with this topic, but since then in each conference between 4% and 12% of papers have been focused on "bone".

This quantitative analysis of course has its limitations. The material used is based on written publications, nothing can be said about the interest in research of the non-contributing participants and about the content of the discussions during the meetings. As mentioned before, these discussions after the presentations, during the poster sessions and all dialogue with the participants in between the sessions have had an important impact on the conference participants, as well as on those who did not present an oral or poster contribution. Another feature of PWP Conferences is that not only experienced and highly recognised researchers have contributed to the PWP proceedings but also young and/or inexperienced researchers are purposely encouraged to present papers. This policy of course is reflected in the quality of the research presented in the proceedings, however, it must be accepted that the scientific level is more diverse than that desired compared to scientific peer-reviewed journals.

Therefore, the educational aspect of this kind of conference cannot only be evaluated from the material analysed in this paper. Also, the percentages given in the tables can sometimes be influenced by the relatively small number of papers given in the first three conferences.

A final personal view

In 1972 Professor Rutenfranz invited HK personally to join the PWP group and to attend the IVth PWP Conference, organized by Professor Bar-Or at the Wingate Institute in Natanya, Israel. As a relatively young researcher HK enjoyed the conference but not particularly the experience of a presentation, although the atmosphere was stimulating, presenting a paper in English was stressful, and he was grateful that the questions and subsequent discussion did not take too long.

HK's research interest at that time was exercise testing of 12-year-old boys on a cycle ergometer and he studied a protocol of loading the subjects relative to their body weight (in $W \cdot kg^{-1}$).

In de Haan (Belgium), in 1973, with Robbert Verschuur we presented with much more confidence the results of the relation of biological age with physical activity and physical fitness in 12-year-old boys. The reason for working with 12-year-old boys was very simple, at that time HK had a part time job as physical educator in a secondary school for boys in Amsterdam and combined his research with teaching.

As physical educators and exercise physiologists Robbert Verschuur and HK were interested in the effects of regular physical education (p.e.) at school. So in the 1970s they conducted a 1 y research programme focusing on the physiologic and psychologic effects of 2 extra lessons of p.e. in circumpubertal boys over a whole school year. From this research papers were presented in 1974 (in Sec) and 1976 (in Bisham Abbey). One of the reasons that this intervention was not very successful (no significant increase in physical performance, character-building and school performance), seemed to be due to the population involved, very active 12-13-year-old boys with a wide range of biological ages.

Therefore they developed and evaluated instruments to measure physical activity (pedometers), interview based questionnaires and, together with Binkhorst and Saris, heart rate monitors. In 1975, calibration and validation of pedometers was presented in Trois Rivières.

In 1974, they planned a 4 y longitudinal study with boys and girls during their growth and development between 12 and 18-years-of-age. The aim was to monitor a whole school population by annual measurements at school with the collaboration of the p.e. teachers. Six year financial support was attracted for this project and a mobile laboratory built and placed near the schools to ensure a low attrition rate of the pupils.

In Marstrand the maximal treadmill test with automated oxygen uptake measurement was presented (1978). From that time on the Amsterdam Growth and Health Longitudinal Study (AGAHLS) was reported repeatedly to successive PWP Conferences.

In Papendal in 1983 presentations were given about the pros and cons of longitudinal research, the validity of the levelling-off concept in establishing a real $\dot{V}O_2$ max or peak value with children (Ritmeester) and heart rate measurement as a measure of daily physical activity (Verschuur).

In Hardehausen (1985) longitudinal data on skeletal age were presented to compare early and late maturers on the development of their $\dot{V}O_2$ max.

After finishing the school period we decided to continue our AGAHL study with an extra and fifth measurement at age 21 y. The same boys and girls were invited (after having left secondary school and spread out all over the country) to come back to the laboratory on a full day of their choice (including Saturdays).

In Hurdal (1987) the benefits of a longitudinal study to investigate the stability or "tracking" of coronary heart disease risk indicators in children between 12 and 22 y were demonstrated.

In 1989 (Hungary) the research group presented longitudinal data about the relationship between maturation and physical activity/nutritional intake (Post), physical fitness, and continued the analysis of levelling-off of $\dot{V}O_2$ and the relation with the active muscle mass.

In St Sauves (1991) the AGAHL research group was almost completely present and presented papers and posters about nutrient intake in Bolivian children (Post), Eurofit test (Van Mechelen), psychological characteristics (Snel) and, for the first time, about the measurement of bone mineral density at the age of 27 y in the longitudinal population.

This new measurement was added to the longitudinal measurements and demonstrates one of the problems of this kind of long term research, new techniques that become available later are not in the original protocol. The good thing however is that relations with the other longitudinal data, measured at young age (such as physical activity and nutrition) can be statistically modelled and related to the new health measurement taken at older age of the subjects.

In 1993 in Canada the tracking of physical fitness (van Mechelen) was reported as was the impact of calcium intake and physical activity on peak bone mineral density. During the last Faaborg conference in 1995 Van Mechelen and HK gave invited review papers about injury prevention and skeletal development respectively. Twisk (longitudinal data analysis of serum cholesterol), Van Lenthe (comparison of two methods of skeletal age), Post (nutrition and health) and Welten (nutrition of Bolivian boys and girls) presented posters and/or papers.

Even in this research programme the same "heart-muscle-bone" trend is discernible: The research group started with heart rate measurement during cycling and oxygen uptake measurement during treadmill running, continued with motor and neuromuscular fitness and the limitations of reaching peak $\dot{V}O_2$ by the amount of active muscle mass, and during the last two conferences the effects of calcium intake and physical activity on the peak bone mass have been addressed.

The research group has been encouraged in their work by participating in PWP Conferences over the past 20 y. It gave direction to research in terms of avoiding mistakes by the choice of a valid method or measure and it was encouraging to learn about similar problems experienced by colleagues. Last but not least it provided the opportunity to introduce younger members of staff and PhD students to the international forum of paediatric exercise scientists.

At last

This overview of research presented at PWP Conferences is in fact the main result of a self-organized network and may not be representative of the overall world wide interest in paediatric exercise physiology. The society never intended to gather all the research in this field and purposely kept meetings very informal and personal. During the last 10 y four of the founders and first participants of PWP Conferences have died: Seliger, Rutenfranz, Stoboy and Oseid. It is obvious that interests and trends in paediatric research have been stimulated by these people and it is sincerely hoped that this type of conference will help to increase the quality of paediatric work physiology research through international cooperation and friendship between researchers all over the world. We trust that it will continue to flourish in the near future and in the same spirit as was intended by the founders, even when the old teachers are not present anymore.

References

1. Shephard, R.J. (1971) *Frontiers of Fitness,* CC Thomas, Springfield, Il.
2. Pernow, B. and Saltin, B. (1971) *Muscle Metabolism During Exercise,* Plenum, New York.
3. Howald, H. and Poortmans, J.R. (1975) *Metabolic Adaptation to Prolonged Physical Exercise*, Birkhauser, Basel.
4. Dent, C.E. (1973) Cited in *Clinical Aspects of Metabolic Bone Disease*, (eds. B. Frame, M.A. Parfit and H. Duncan), Excerpta Medica, Elsevier, Amsterdam, p. 231.
5. Hollmann, W. (1963) *Hochst- und Dauerleistungsfaehigkeit des Sportlers*, J.A. Barth, Munchen.
6. Reindell, H. (1960) *Herz Kreislaufkrankheiten und Sport*, J.A. Barth, Munchen.

7. Mellerowicz, H. (1975) *Ergometrie, Grundriss der Medizinischen Leistungsmessung*, Urban and Schwarzenberg, Munchen.
8. Frenkl, R. and I Szmodis (1991) *Children and Exercise*, Pediatric Work Physiology XV, National Institute for Health Promotion, Budapest, Hungary.
9. Berg, K. and B.O. Eriksson (1980) *Children and Exercise IX*, International Series on Sport Sciences, Vol. 10, University Park Press, Baltimore.
10. Borms, J. and M. Hebbelinck (1978) Pediatric Work Physiology. *Medicine and Sport*, Vol. 11, Karger, Basel, Switzerland.
11. Thoren, K. (1971) Pediatric Work Physiology III. *Acta Paediatrica Scandinavica,* suppl. 214.
12. Borms, J. and M. Hebbelinck (1974) Children and Exercise Proceedings of the Fifth International Symposium. *Acta Paediatrica Belgica*, Vol. 28, (suppl), pp. 1-296.
13. Blimkie, C.J.R. and Bar-Or, O. (1995) *New Horizons in Pediatric Exercise Science*, Human Kinetics, Champaign, Il.
14. PWP/NASPEM Conference Abstracts (1993) *Pediatric Exercise Science*, Vol. 5, pp. 386-491.
15. Bar-Or, O. (1973) *Pediatric Work Physiology, Proceedings of the Fourth International Symposium*, Wingate Institute for Physical Education and Sports, Natanya, Israel.
16. Beunen, G., Ghequiere, J., Reybrouck, T. and Claessens, A.L. (1990) *Children and Exercise*, Schriftenreihe der Hamburg-Mannheimer-Stiftung fuer Informationsmedizin, band 4 Enke, Stuttgart.
17. Lavallée, H. and Shephard, R.J. (1977) *Frontiers of Activity and Child Health, Limités de la Capacité Physique Chez l'enfant, Collection Sciences de l'activité Physique*, Editions du Pelican, Quebec, Canada.
18. Oseid, S. and Carlsen, K-H. (1989) *Children and Exercise XIII, International Series on Sport Sciences*, Vol. 16, Human Kinetics, Champaign, Il.
19. Rutenfranz, J., Mocellin, R. and Klimt, F. (1986) *Children and Exercise XII, International Series on Sport Sciences*, Vol. 17, Human Kinetics, Champaign, Il.
20. Macek, M. (1970) *Proceedings of the Second Symposium of Pediatric Group of Working Physiology*, University Karlova, Praha CSSR.
21. Ilmarinen, J. and Valimaki, I. (1984) *Children and Sport, Paediatric Work Physiology*, Springer, Berlin.
22. Coudert, J.E. and van Praagh, E. (1992) *Pediatric Work Physiology, Children and Exercise XVI*, Masson, Paris, France.
23. Binkhorst, R.A., Kemper, H.C.G. and Saris, W.H.M. (1986) *Children and Exercise XII, International Series on Sport Sciences*, Vol. 15, Human Kinetics, Champaign, Il.

PART I

LIFESTYLE, HEALTH AND WELL-BEING

THE EFFECTS OF LIFESTYLE ON CHILDREN'S HEALTH AND WELL-BEING
Children's health and well-being

P-O. ÅSTRAND
Department of Physiology and Pharmacology, Karolinska Institute, Stockholm, Sweden
Keywords: Evolution, health and well-being, lifestyle, physical activity, risk factors

Evolutionary aspects

This century has been characterized by enormous advances in almost all aspects of human achievements. A person born at the end of the 20th century and still alive has witnessed more of technical evolution than occured during the preceding millions of years of the *Homo* family. During close to 100 % of this era the *Homo* species were hunters/food gatherers. Evolution of a species is a measure of the success of evolution in adapting an organism to particular environmental conditions. We became adapted to a life-style as hunters-gatherers. This also applies to our emotional and social lives and to our intellectual skills. Major adaptations for survival were consonant with habitual physical activity, including, e.g. endurance, muscle strength, and eventually peak efforts alternated with rest and socialization. Now, after a short spell in an agrarian culture, we have in some "priviledged" societies ended up in an urbanized, highly technologic society dominated by a sedentary life-style.

Our ancestors lived in small bands of perhaps 15-30 individuals as a cooperative society in which individuals and environments continuously interrelated and affected each other. An individual's age was not measured in years, but rather in terms of accumulated experience. Actually there was until quite recently no record with information about an individual's age, except for kings, emperors, people at the top of the hierarchy. Education began when a child had matured enough to understand the message of her/his teacher. Thus, the boys learned from a "retired" hunter, who thereby had entered a new niche in society, carrying out tasks that were still intellectually and physically demanding and of vital importance for the future of the

Children and Exercise XIX. Edited by Neil Armstrong, Brian Kirby and Joanne Welsman.
Published in 1997 by E & FN Spon, 2–6 Boundary Row, London, SE1 8HN.
ISBN 0 419 22100 X.

group. So, over millions of years the old person was very important and respected in society because she/he was credited with experience essential for the well-being and survival of the people. Now, in contrast to today: before "lecture hall" was outdoors and "curriculum" full of excitements very obvious and pertinant for successful hunting, collection of food from plants, fruits, roots, various sea foods..... In contrast, to-day there is an emphasis on chronological age more or less irrespective of maturity, body dimensions and functions, or intellectual potential. And, how can we in lecture halls explain for pupil/student and present in such an attractive and stimulating package in our educational system what is essential and of key importance for her/his future? [see 1]

Chronological versus biological age

Since maturation age differs markedly it is positive that research on adolescents more and more as a baseline tries to relate data to biological age, e.g. to Peak Height Velocity age (PHVage). That is particularly important in longitudinal studies. Certainly one problem is that one can not in advance predict when a child will reach PHVage. I often quote Lindgren's study[2] reporting that PHVage occured as early as at age 9.5 for some girls but not until 15 y for others. In boys the range was from 11 to 17 y. At chronological age 13 y we can face a boy with a body mass of 30 kg and a height 130 cm, and his classmate may weigh 80 kg and be 180 cm tall. It is a challenge to be a teacher in physical education: how to avoid accidents, e.g. in contact sports, how to stimulate the small pupil whose physical performance will inevitably be inferior in many activities to the large classmate. The "early bird" may dominate in a sport due to advantage with large body mass and thereby strength, body height, high aerobic power. She/he, coach, parents are happy because big money may wait around the corner. However, peers with real talent for that specific sport will mature, may catch up and pass. The "early bird" missed that talent and there is a risk that she/he, disappointed, loses interest in sports.

Selection of talents for sports

In 1985 five Swedish tennis players were ranked among the 15 top tennis players in the world. Actually they were engaged in many sports before age 14, at which time they started to specialize in tennis. They were compared with another group of players who were as good or better when 12 to 14 y old. Those players specialized much earlier in tennis, trained more, and matured earlier. However, they were apparently not gifted enough to reach world class[3]. May be they should have tried and been successful in another sport? One conclusion from the mentioned study of tennis players is that performance at age 12 to 14 y is not a good predictor of future elite performance. Malina[4] pointed out that with few exceptions, interage correlations for indicators of growth, fitness, and cardiovascular status are generally moderate to low and thus have limited predictive utility. A prepubescent boy who starts specializing in high jump or basketball and stops growing when 170 cm tall has definitely picked the wrong event.

I will give another example of sports with early selection based on chronological age. Junior players in soccer are often selected during phases of rapid growth and development. One of the problems faced by those responsible for the identification of elite players at junior level is to identify those who posess talent but who are still at a relatively low level of physical maturity. It may be difficult for the talented but less physically mature individuals to obtain selection for junior representative squads[5]. These authors report that the English Professional Clubs employ a limited number of junior players aged between 17 and 19 y, with an objective of them becoming future senior professional players. In England the selection year is consistent with the academic year, starting in September and ending in August. They noted that between 1992 and 1994 53% of these players were born between September and December, and only 16% between May and August! Identifying talent from an early age is a problem faced by many involved in sports. In view of the tendency to select physically mature individuals at a given chronological age, and the consequent large scale omission of equally talented but less mature individuals, it would seem sensible if procedures for selecting, e.g., junior squads were reviewed. It is best if children and young teenagers are stimulated to try many sports, they should taste a "smörgåsbord" of events, and they should not concentrate on one sport until after PHVage.

It is still debated whether high intensity and volume training may affect PHVage and time for menarche. Malina[4] after a review of the literature concludes that in the vast majority of athletes, intensive training for sports has no effect on growth and maturational processes. Menarche is to a higher extent affected by biological selective and social factors.

Risk factors in children

Boreham et al.[6] point out that while numerous adult epidemiological studies have clearly established relationships between antecedent risk factors and subsequent coronary endpoints, it is only more recently that the risk factor model has been extended to children. One rationale for this approach, according to these authors, is that the seeds of coronary heart disease (CHD) are sown in childhood, with postmortem studies demonstrating advanced atherosclerotic lesions as early as the second decade of life. In their studies of a randomly selected population of children aged 12 and 15 y in Northern Ireland, applying available criteria thresholds, they found that 15-23% displayed increased blood pressure, 12-25% had unfavourable lipid profiles, and 18-34% were overfat. In 15 y old children, 16-21% admitted being regular smokers, 26-34% displayed poor cardiovascular fitness, and 24-29% reported little physical activity in the previous week. Despite the exclusion of family history from the analysis, 16% of the older children exhibited three or more risk factors. Riddoch and Boreham[7] report that there are studies in the US and UK indicating that over 69% of children 12 y of age have at least one modifiable risk factor for CHD.

There is a general trend in industrial countries that the number of overweight young people increases. Body fatness is a risk factor for several diseases[8]. Armstrong[9] reports that about 13% of young people can be classified as overweight and that unfavourable blood lipid and lipoprotein profiles are common during childhood and adolescence.

According to WHO approximately 30% of all people with disabilities are children. At a recent meeting in Stockholm the message was that close to 70% of the total medical costs are spent on preventable disease. I am convinced that paediatric exercise physiology has an important role in prevention of accidents, and the improvement of rehabilitation programs.

How physically active are children and adolescents in the educational system and during leisure time?

In many industrial countries politicians and administrators have gradually reduced the compulsory time for physical education in schools and colleges, in some areas quite dramatically. In the UK the Department for Education advises that schools should provide a minimum of 2 h for physical exercise a week, yet a study published in March 1995 showed that the number of state schools where pupils are getting less than this amount has doubled since 1987[10]. Also in Sweden there has been a quite dramatic reduction for physical education in schools over the last decades. This trend is very unfortunate, particularly for individuals who do not choose sports and outdoor activities during their leisure time. Engström[11] found that between 1968 and 1984 there was an impressive increase in the percentage of 15 y olds who belonged to sports clubs (Sweden). The percentage for boys increased from 50 to 70% and for girls from approximately 17 to 50%. However, the total number of physically inactive young people had increased, from 4 to 26% for boys and from 10 to 32% for girls. The explanation was that in 1984 almost none were involved in sports during leisure time unless they were members of a sport club.

Riddoch and Boreham[7] have summarized data from large population studies. These data indicate that physical activity levels peak in children at around 13 to 14 y of age, and than markedly decline. Boys are normally reported to be more active than girls, but this difference is greatly reduced when moderate activity alone is compared, indicating that boys participate in more vigorous activities than girls. From a longitudinal study in Finland Telama et al.[12] concluded that physical activity had its peak at the age of 12, after which age it was reduced considerably. They also reported that physical activity during youth was a significant but weak predictor of the physical activity that takes place 9 y later. The best predictors were the school grade for physical education and participation in organized sports.

The curriculum in physical education is quite different in different countries, but the drop in sports participation after high school/college is relatively universal. Therefore, the key factor behind this reduced physical activity is probably not the experiences during lectures in physical education but simply a consequence of human nature!

What is optimal intensity, frequency, duration in programs we would like to recommend?

In their recent review Riddoch and Boreham[7] point out that the amount and type of physical activity undertaken during childhood that is appropriate for optimal health is unknown, although it has been suggested that, in the absence of such criteria, activity levels known to confer health benefits in adults are also appropriate for children.

Haskell[13] argues that quantity and quality of exercise to obtain health-related benefits may differ from what is recommended for physical fitness benefits. He points out that the view taken by advocates of the physical activity-health paradigm is that for many people, especially those inclined not to perform more vigorous exercise, and they are in majority, some benefit is better than none. "The greatest health benefits from an increase in physical activity appears to occur when very sedentary persons begin a regular program of moderate intensity, endurance type activity. Further increases in intensity and amounts of activity appear to produce further benefits in some, but not all, biological or clinical parameters. The magnitude of benefits becomes less for similar increase in intensity and/or amount of activity"[13]. A similar message is presented in the 1996 report of the Surgeon General in the USA "Physical Activity and Health"[14]. There it is pointed out that during the past few years the American College of Sports Medicine, the Centers for Disease Control and Prevention, the National Center for Chronic Disease Prevention and Health Promotion, the American Heart Association, the Presidents Council on Physical Fitness and Sports, and the National Institutes of Health have all recommended regular, moderate-intensity physical activity as an option for those who get little or no exercise. "All people over the age of 2 years should accumulate at least 30 minutes of endurance-type physical activity, of at least moderate intensity, on most - preferably all - days of the week". According to this 278-page report only about one-half of U.S. young people (ages 12-21 y) regularly participate in vigorous physical activity. One-quarter report no vigorous physical activity. Only 19% of all high school students report being physically active for 20 min or more in daily physical education classes.

This discussion is mainly based on studies on adults but is probably also relevant for children and adolescents. Malina[4] points out that there is no prospective work that can link, with any degree of certainty, health in adult years with childhood activity pattern. My viewpoint is that good prospective work in this area of research is so far not available.

One interesting area of research is the question whether there are future health gains when girls during adolescence invest in a "bone bank" by weight-bearing and muscle-strengthening activities, thereby increasing bone mass. Slemenda et al. (1991) showed a consistent positive association between physical activity and bone density in 118 children aged 5 to 14 y.

Prepubertal children are capable of responding to endurance training with improvements in maximal aerobic power. Such adaptations are qualitatively similar, but probably quantitatively less compared with those in adults[16]. There is a similar situation with training of muscle strength. Endurance training has a possible therapeutic value in common diseases of childhood such as asthma, cerebral palsy, cystic fibrosis, diabetes mellitus, hypertension, myopathies, and obesity [17].

Application of DNA technique on children

We have entered a new era in medicine. With DNA technique one has been able to identify defect genes which may trigger serious diseases like Huntington's disease, and specific types of cancer. From a research viewpoint that is very important but what about application of such knowledge? When will we have tools to prevent such diseases becoming real threats to health, and causing serious handicaps? Pessimists emphasize that it may take decades. With early diagnoses of such defect genes, what about the psychological trauma for the individual and the family? So far we know very little about how environmental factors and life style can prevent or in a positive - or negative - way modify the beginning and development of such diseases. What about false positive or negative diagnoses? These questions are extremely important to discuss and analyse, they involve serious ethical problems. To present one example, this technique has been applied to identify the "gender" of an egg from a mother with a husband with a family history of high incidence of serious disease only heritable in the male individual. Only an egg with two X chromosomes will be implanted in the uterus of the mother.

Another aspect of application of the DNA technique is that it may be possible at an early age to predict those individuals who may tolerate a high blood pressure, high level of blood lipids, obesity, smoking, a sedentary life style without serious health problems much better than others. Is that something we are looking forward to?

Concluding remarks

Many expressions of human behaviour, which were very appropriate adaptations to life in small bands, can be quite "catastrophic" when adapted by large and modern societies. If we transfer hominid history over a 4-million-year period into a 400 m distance, it has been very different during the last metre (10,000 y) and particularly during the last 10 millimetres (100 y). During those millimetres there have been more technical "evolutions" than during the preceding 399.99 metres! However, with adequate insight into our biological heritage, we may be able to modify our current partly self-destructive lifestyle. The human body has over millions of years adapted to the need of regular, moderate physical activity, as hunters and food gatherers, and a continuation of such activity is essential for its optimal functioning.

In this bizarre world, we notice overfeeding and the negative effects of a sedentary lifestyle in developed countries, but do little to help millions of children who are living under marginal or very poor conditions in the "Third World". It is impossible to follow the advice to exercise and be physically active in societies where there is not enough food to cover even the energy demand of basal/resting metabolic demand. Medical advances, including mass vaccinations, allow more and more children to survive in "Third World" countries, but what quality of life will they face as they become adults? How can we teach effective birth control to prevent over-population?

Open-air activities are an effective source of physical activity that is well anchored in our biological heritage. Once upon a time education in "fauna and flora" was essential for the children. Today, similar education is, unfortunately, very neglected. It could create an excellent, life-long hobby. There are those who do not like walking just for the sake of walking, but if a hobby like bird-watching demands some walking, they are prepared to walk! The message of enhanced physical activity, at any age, will seem more practical and realistic when we find ways to incorporate regular activity into our daily living.

References

1. Åstrand, P-O. and Rodahl, K. (1986) *Textbook of Work Physiology*, McGraw-Hill, New York, pp. 1-11.
2. Lindgren, G. (1978) Growth of school children with early, average and late ages of peak height velocity. *Annals of Human Biology*, Vol. 5, pp. 253-67.
3. Carlson, R. (1988) The socialization of elite tennis players in Sweden: an analysis of the players' backgrounds and development. *Sociology of Sport Journal*, Vol. 5, pp. 241-56.
4. Malina, R.M. (1994) Physical growth and biological maturation of young athletes. *Exercise and Sport Sciences Reviews*, Vol. 22, pp. 389-434.
5. Brewer, J., Balsom, P. and Davis, J. (1995) Seasonal birth distribution amongst European soccer players. *Sports Exercise and Injury*, Vol. 1, pp. 154-7.
6. Boreham, C., Savage, J.M., Primrose, D., Cran, G. and Strain, J. (1993) Coronary risk factors in schoolchildren. *Archives of Disease in Childhood*, Vol. 68, pp. 182-6.
7. Riddoch, C.J. and Boreham. A.G. (1995) The health-related physical activity of children. *Sports Medicine*, Vol. 19, pp. 86-102.
8. Williams, D.P., Going, S.B., Lohman, T.G., Harsha, D.W., Srinivasan, S.P., Webber, L.S. and Berenson, G.S. (1992) Body fatness and risk for elevated blood pressure, total cholesterol, and serum lipoprotein ratios in children and adolescents. *American Journal of Public Health*, Vol. 82, pp. 358-63.
9. Armstrong, N. (1995) Keynote speech: Children, physical activity and health, in *Children in Sport*, (ed. F.J. Ring), Centre for Continuing Education, University of Bath, Avon, pp. 5-16.
10. Smith, K. (1995) *Inquiries into Provisions of Physical Education in Schools 1994*, Aylesbury Grammar School.
11. Engström, L-M. (1990) Sports activities among young people in Sweden - trends and changes, in *Physical Activity and Life-long Physical Activity*, (eds. R. Telama, L. Laakso, M. Piéron, I. Ruoppila and V. Vihko), Report of Physical Culture and Health, Jyväskylä, Vol. 73, pp. 11-23.
12. Telama. R., Laakso, L. and Yang, X. (1994) Physical activity and participation in sports of young people in Finland. *Scandanavian Journal of Medicine and Science in Sports*, Vol. 4, pp. 65-74.
13. Haskell, W.L. (1994) Health consequences of physical activity: Understanding and challenges regarding dose-response. *Medicine and Science in Sports and Exercise*, Vol. 26, 649-60.
14. Department of Health and Human Services. (1996) *Physical Activity and Health: a Report of the Surgeon General, GA*. Superintendent of Documents, P.O. Box 371954, PA 15250-7954, S/N 017-023-00196-5.

15. Slemenda, S.W., Miller, J.Z., Hui, S.L., Reister, T.K. and Johnston, C.C. (1991) Role of physical activity in the development of skeletal mass in children. *Journal of Bone Mineral Research,* Vol. 6, 1227-33.
16. Rowland, T.W. (1992) Aerobic resposes to physical training in children, in *Endurance in Sports,* (eds. R.J. Shephard RJ and P-O. Åstrand), Blackwell Scientific Publications, London, pp. 381-9.
17. Schober, P. (1995) Effectiveness of endurance training in children, in *Children in Sport,* (ed. F.J. Ring), Centre for Continuing Education, University of Bath, Avon, pp. 101-13.

EXERCISE TOLERANCE AND QUALITY OF LIFE IN PAEDIATRIC LUNG TRANSPLANT RECIPIENTS

Exercise tolerance and lung transplantation

P.A. NIXON, D.M. ORENSTEIN, P.J. REBOVICH, B.E. NOYES, G. KURLAND, S.A. WEBBER and F.J. FRICKER
Department of Pediatrics, University of Pittsburgh, Pittsburgh, PA, USA
Keywords: Exercise, lung transplantation, pulmonary function, quality of life

Introduction

Heart-lung and lung transplantation have become acceptable interventions for paediatric patients with end-stage cardiopulmonary or pulmonary disease[1]. While transplantation may prolong life in many patients, exercise capacity has been shown to remain well below normal[2]. Furthermore, little is known about the effects of transplantation on aerobic fitness, pulmonary function, and quality of life in the extended months following surgery in paediatric recipients. Consequently, the purpose of this study was to make serial assessments of these variables at standard points in time, specifically 4, 12, 24, and 36 mo following transplantation.

Methods

Ten heart-lung and four double-lung recipients (aged 6-20 y) were able and consented to perform exercise and, pulmonary function testing, and answer a quality of life questionnaire at approximately 4, 12, and 24 mo post-transplantation. Nine of the 14 patients were also assessed 36 mo post-transplant. Four patients had died prior to the 36 mo assessment, and one patient refused testing at that time.

Aerobic fitness was assessed via the measurement of peak $\dot{V}O_2$ and physical work capacity (PWC) - the highest exercise intensity completed for 1 min. Progressive maximal exercise testing was conducted on a cycle ergometer following the Godfrey Protocol[3]. Pulmonary function was assessed via standard spirometric techniques, and expressed as % of predicted[4]. Pulmonary function testing included forced vital capacity (FVC) - a measure of lung capacity, forced expiratory volume in 1 s (FEV_1) -

Children and Exercise XIX. Edited by Neil Armstrong, Brian Kirby and Joanne Welsman.
Published in 1997 by E & FN Spon, 2–6 Boundary Row, London, SE1 8HN.
ISBN 0 419 22100 X.

a measure of larger airway flow, and maximal mid-expiratory flow rate (MMEFR) - a measure of smaller airway flow. Quality of life was assessed via the Bush Quality of Well-being Scale (QWB)[5], which is an interviewer-administered questionnaire with possible scores ranging from 0 (death) to 1 (optimal well-being).

Repeated measures analysis of variance (ANOVA) was used to detect significant differences in variables over time. Pearson correlational analysis was used to examine the relationships between % change in dependent measures from 4-12 mo ($T_{4\text{-}12}$), 12-24 mo ($T_{12\text{-}24}$), and 24-36 mo ($T_{24\text{-}36}$) time intervals.

Results

Subject characteristics at the initial assessment (T_4) are presented in table 1. Physical work capacity was below 60% of predicted in all but two patients. Nine of the 14 patients had an FVC less than 80% of predicted, and all but four patients demonstrated below normal larger airway function as reflected in a $FEV_1 < 80\%$ predicted.

Mean values of PWC and peak $\dot{V}O_2$ at T_4, T_{12}, and T_{24} were not significantly different. However, both PWC and peak $\dot{V}O_2$ showed significant initial increases (% change) during the first year, followed by significant decreases during the second and third years post-transplantation. As shown in fig 1, peak $\dot{V}O_2$ increased 9 $\pm$ 20% from $T_{4\text{-}12}$, but subsequently decreased 12 $\pm$ 22 % from $T_{12\text{-}24}$ ($p < 0.05$). Furthermore, the subgroup of 9 patients exhibited a significant decrease of 26 $\pm$ 20% in peak $\dot{V}O_2$ from $T_{24\text{-}36}$ ($p < 0.001$).

As shown in figs 2a-d, mean FVC, FEV_1, MMEFR, and QWB did not change significantly over the 24 and 36 mo following transplantation in the total group of 14 patients or in the subgroup of 9 patients.

Pearson product-moment correlation coefficients for the changes in aerobic fitness, pulmonary function, and quality of well-being are presented in table 2. From T_4 to T_{12}, the % change in FEV_1 correlated significantly with the % change in QWB. During the second year post-transplant ($T_{12\text{-}24}$), changes in FVC and FEV_1 correlated significantly with changes in PWC and peak $\dot{V}O_2$. In addition, changes in FEV_1 and MMEFR correlated with changes in QWB during the second year.

Table 1. Subject characteristics

Variable at 4 months	Mean ± SD	Range
Age (y)	13.9 ± 4.0	6 - 20
Weight (kg)	38.3 ± 13.2	22.0 - 67.5
Height (cm)	146.6 ± 16.5	115.6 - 172.7
FVC (% predicted)	78 ± 30	51 - 107
FEV_1 (% predicted)	72 ± 22	31 - 107
MMEFR (% predicted)	72 ± 33	9 - 131
PWC (% predicted)	39 ± 26	1 - 86
peak $\dot{V}O_2$ ($mL \cdot kg^{-1} \cdot min^{-1}$)	24.8 ± 6.7	14.6 - 37.7

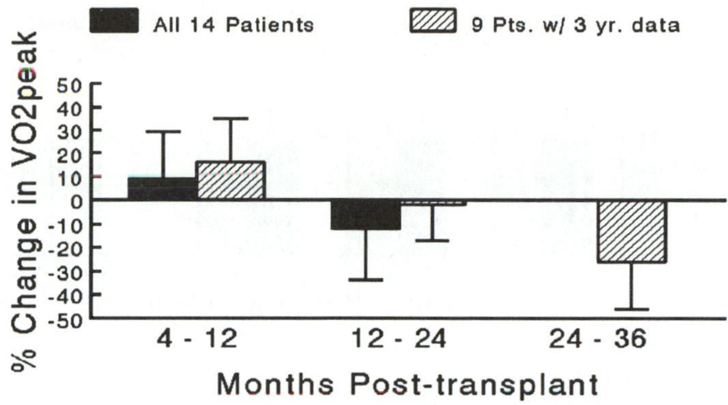

Fig. 1. Changes in peak $\dot{V}O_2$ over the 36 months following transplantation.

Discussion

The results of this study indicate that aerobic fitness improved during the first year following lung transplantation, but declined over the second and third years post-surgery in this relatively select group of paediatric patients who were able and willing to undergo exercise testing. These findings are in contrast to those reported for paediatric heart recipients who demonstrated no change in exercise capacity when tested 1 and 3 y after transplantation[6]. Following transplantation, many of these patients returned to active lifestyles and school, which may have helped to improve aerobic fitness. However, the subsequent decline in fitness observed during the second and third years post-transplantation may be attributed to several factors. During the second year post-transplant, the decrease in aerobic fitness was associated with a decline in pulmonary function. By the third year, many of these patients had developed obliterative bronchiolitis after chronic lung rejection which may have altered their ventilatory efficiency during exercise[7].

Exercise tolerance may also have been affected by long-term use of pharmacological agents. All patients were taking either tacrolimus (FK506) or cyclosporin for immunosuppression. Both agents have been shown to have haemolytic effects[8,9]. Cyclosporin has also been shown to alter muscle metabolism[10] and inhibit erythropoietin production[11] (resulting in lower serum haemoglobin levels and consequently, reduced oxygen transport capability). Furthermore, most of the patients were also taking corticosteroids for immunosuppression which may have induced skeletal muscle myopathy and, in turn, diminished aerobic fitness[12].

Changes in aerobic fitness were not significantly related to changes in quality of well-being throughout the study. However, failure to find significant relationships between fitness and quality of well-being may be attributed to the lack of statistical power associated with the relatively small sample size. In addition, the QWB questionnaire encompasses many other aspects of well-being including taking medications, being

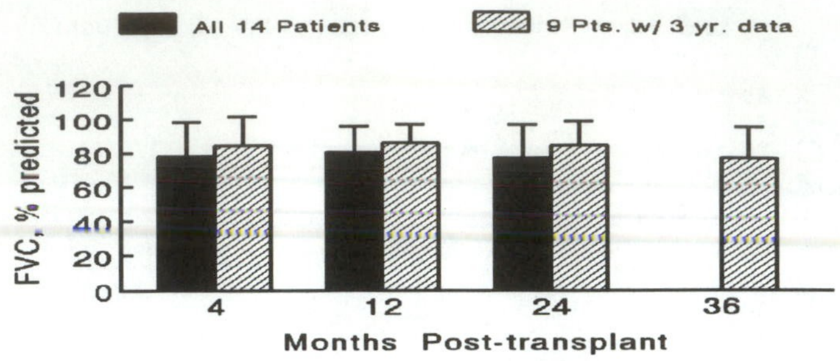

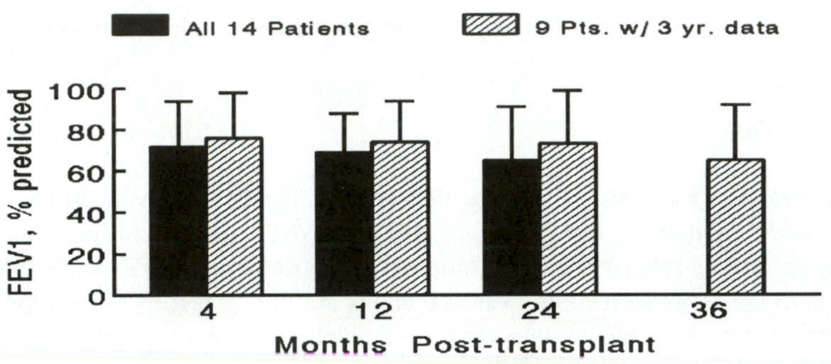

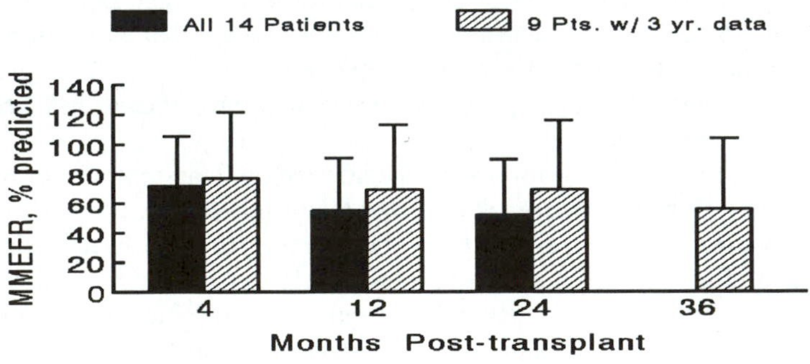

Figs. 2a-c. Pulmonary function and quality of well-being over the 36 months following transplantation

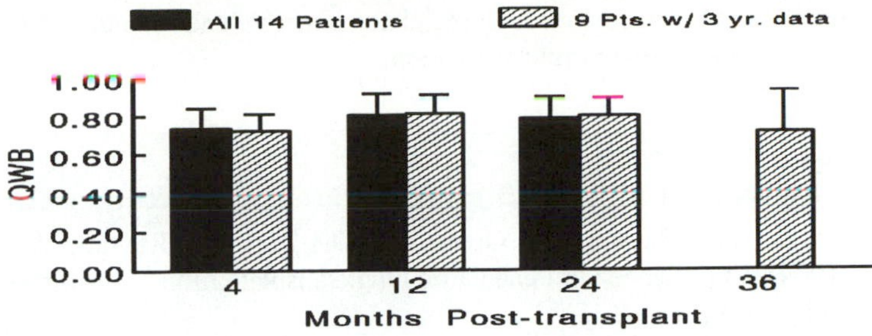

Fig. 2d. Pulmonary function and quality of well-being over the 36 months following transplantation

hospitalised, missing school for health reasons, all of which are common to these patients[5]. Consequently, while the patients subjectively reported better quality of life and improved functional capacity, their quality of well-being as assessed by the QWB scale may have been diminished by these other factors.

Conclusions

The results of our study show that paediatric heart-lung or lung recipients have diminished aerobic fitness that improves during the first year following transplantation, but declines progressively by 24 and 36 mo post-transplant. The decline in aerobic fitness may be attributed in part to impaired pulmonary function, but other factors such as infection, rejection, and pharmacological side effects (e.g. anaemia, altered skeletal muscle metabolism or myopathy) may also contribute to the long-term decrease in exercise tolerance in these patients. Future research is warranted to determine if exer

Table 2. Pearson product-moment correlation coefficients.

		Δ FEV_1	Δ MMEFR	Δ PWC	Δ peak $\dot{V}O_2$	Δ QWB
Δ FVC	$T_{4\text{-}12}$	0.62*	-0.11	0.21	0.02	0.35
	$T_{12\text{-}24}$	0.70*	0.43	0.66*	0.50*	0.33
Δ FEV_1	$T_{4\text{-}12}$	---	0.64*	0.10	0.06	0.65*
	$T_{12\text{-}24}$	---	0.85*	0.68*	0.56*	0.58*
Δ MMEFR	$T_{4\text{-}12}$	---	---	-0.11	0.20	0.27
	$T_{12\text{-}24}$	---	---	0.34	0.40	0.80*
Δ PWC	$T_{4\text{-}12}$	---	---	---	0.50*	-0.17
	$T_{12\text{-}24}$	---	---	---	0.80*	0.02
Δ peak $\dot{V}O_2$	$T_{4\text{-}12}$	---	---	---	---	-0.46
	$T_{12\text{-}24}$	---	---	---	---	0.20

Level of significance $^*p < 0.05$

cise training may help paediatric lung recipients improve and maintain their aerobic fitness over the years following transplantation.

References

1. Noyes, B.E., Kurland G., Orenstein, D.M., Fricker, F.J. and Armitage, J.M. (1994) Experience with paediatric lung transplantation. *Journal of Pediatrics*, Vol. 124, pp.161-8.
2. Nixon, P., Fricker, F.J., Noyes, B.E., Webber, S.A., Orenstein, D.M. and Armitage, J.M. (1995) Exercise testing in paediatric heart, heart-lung, and lung transplant recipients. *Chest*, Vol. 107, pp. 1328-35.
3. Godfrey, S. (1974) *Exercise Testing in Children,* W.B. Saunders, Philadelphia, p. 30.
4. American Thoracic Society. (1979) Snowbird workshop of standardization of spirometry. *American Review of Respiratory Disease*, Vol.119, pp. 831-8.
5. Kaplan, R.M., Atkins, C.J. and Timms, R.M. (1984) Validity of a quality of well-being scale as an outcome measure in chronic obstructive pulmonary disease. *Journal of Chronic Disease,* Vol. 37, pp. 85-95.
6. Hsu, D.T., Garafano, R.P., Douglas, J.M., Michler, R.E., Quaegebeur, J.M., Gersony, W.M. and Addonizio, L.J. (1993) Exercise performance after paediatric heart transplantation. *Circulation*, Vol. 88, pp. 238-42.
7. Sciurba, F.C., Owens, G.R., Sanders, M.H., Constantino, J.P., Paradis, I.L. and Griffith, B.P. (1991) The effect of obliterative bronchiolitis on breathing pattern during exercise in recipients of heart-lung transplants. *American Review of Respiratory Disease*, Vol. 144, pp. 131-5.
8. Abu-Elmagd, K.M., Bronsther, O., Kobayashi, M., Yagihashi, A., Iwaki, Y., Fung, J. Alessiani, M., Bontempo, F. and Starzl, T. (1991) Acute hemolytic anemia in liver and bone marrow transplant patients under FK 506 therapy. *Transplantation Proceedings*, Vol. 23, pp. 3190-2.
9. Faure, J.L., Causse, X., Bergeret, A., Meyer, F., Neidecker, J. and Paliard, P. (1989) Cyclosporine induced hemolytic anemia in a liver transplant patient. *Transplantation Proceedings*, Vol. 21, pp. 2242-3.
10. Higgins, R.M., Richardson, A.J., Endre, Z.H., Frostick, S.P. and Morris, P.J. (1990) Hypophosphataemia after renal transplantation: relationship to immunosuppressive drug therapy and effects on muscle detected by 31P nuclear magnetic resonance spectroscopy. *Nephrology, Dialysis, Transplantation*, Vol. 5, pp. 62-8.
11. Wolff, M. and Jelkmann, W. (1993) Effects of chemotherapeutic and immunosuppressive drugs on the production of erythropoietin in human hepatoma cultures. *Annals of Hematology*, Vol. 66, pp. 27-31.
12. Decramer, M. and Stas, J.K. (1992) Corticosteroid-induced myopathy involving respiratory muscles in patients with chronic obstructive pulmonary disease or asthma. *American Review of Respiratory Disease,* Vol. 146, pp. 800-2.

WEIGHT-BEARING PHYSICAL ACTIVITY AND BONE HEALTH IN PRE-PUBERTAL GIRLS

Physical activity and bone health

J.S. CARLSON and G.A. NAUGHTON
Centre for Rehabilitation, Exercise and Sport Science, Victoria University, Melbourne, Australia
F. MORRIS and J. WARK
Department of Medicine, University of Melbourne, Melbourne, Australia
Keywords: Bone density, girls, prepubertal, weight-bearing exercise

Introduction

Weight bearing physical activity has been advocated to be a major means of promoting the development and maintenance of bone mineral density[1]. The encouragement of activity which may optimise the development of a dense skeleton in the growing years may have future beneficial ramifications in the incidence of osteoporosis and cardio-vascular health in adulthood. Adult research has identified relationships between adult bone mineral status and the incidence of bone fracture in the aging population [2]. It is argued that practices which can optimise bone density in the growing skeleton could possibly prevent the onset of osteoporosis. Physical inactivity in the form of immobilisation or injury has been shown to result in bone loss[3,4]. This loss has been attributed to reduced mechanical loading[5]. The risk of osteoporotic fracture in women depends on bone mass attained in youth as well as the amount of bone loss which occurs in post menopausal years. Although genetic endowment determines an individual's upper achievable peak bone mass[6] there is still much to be learnt about the impact of intervention strategies, in particular exercise in early life. There is a lack of knowledge concerning the laying down of bone mineral during the growing years[5]. Factors such as genetics, nutritional sufficiency, hormonal status, lifestyle factors (eg. smoking and alcohol),and mechanical loading through physical activity have been recognised as some of the potential determinants of bone mass development during childhood and adolescence. Recker[7] has proposed that not attaining sufficient bone mass during childhood and adolescence may be a contributing factor to bone fragility in the elderly. As a consequence, it is recommended that attaining optimal bone mass during youth may be a significant factor in the prevention of osteoporosis in later life. The purpose of this study was to examine the influence of extra weight-bearing physical

Children and Exercise XIX. Edited by Neil Armstrong, Brian Kirby and Joanne Welsman.
Published in 1997 by E & FN Spon, 2–6 Boundary Row, London, SE1 8HN.
ISBN 0 419 22100 X.

activity on health related performance parameters and bone density of 9-11-year old girls.

Methods

This study assessed the status of bone health and a number of physical performance parameters in prepubertal females during a school based intervention programme involving a weight bearing physical activity programme. The programme utilised weight bearing physical activity based on existing physical education curriculum in 9-11-year-old females. The study of 10 mo duration involved four primary schools in Melbourne. Two schools comprised the activity group (n = 38) and two schools from a similar demographic status made up an age matched control group (n = 33). The activity group received three extra physical education classes a week of 30 min duration over three 10 wk school terms. The exercise programme included a variety of vigorous, high impact aerobic sessions including step and normal aerobics, ball games, modified sports, various forms of dance, circuits and weight training circuit unit. Sexual maturity was rated by parents based on the Tanner[8] scale. All subjects were tested for baseline data and at the completion of the school year. The descriptive data for the girls are presented in table 1. The groups were well matched as there were no significant differences between the girls on any of the descriptive characteristics both at baseline and following the programme.

Bone mineral density and body composition measurements were made by dual energy X-ray using the Hologic QDR 2000+ absorptiometer. Bone mass measurements were made at the neck of femur, lumbar spine and total body at both baseline and at the end of the school year. Bone mineral results are expressed as bone mineral density (BMD, $g{\cdot}cm^{-2}$) bone mineral content (BMC, g).

The physiological variables which were measured to quantify the changes in health-related fitness parameters resulting from participation in the physical activity programme were.

- Aerobic fitness assessed by the use of a continuous 20 m multi-stage shuttle run. This is a graded and incremental running speed test conducted to volitional termination.
- Muscular strength was tested using both isokinetic and dynamic muscular contractions. A Cybex Isokinetic dynamometer measured shoulder and leg strengths while contracting at a constant angular velocity of 60 $deg{\cdot}s^{-1}$ degrees per second. Hand grip strength was recorded for both dominant and non dominant sides using a Smedley grip dynamometer.
- Anaerobic performance was evaluated by having the young females run through a set of timing lights set 40 m apart.

Table 1 Descriptive characteristics of the activity and control groups

	Activity		Control	
	Baseline	Post	Baseline	Post
Age (y)	9.5 ± 0.9	10.3 ± 0.9	9.5 ± 0.9	10.3 ± 0.9
Height (cm)	139.7 ± 7.9	144.0 ± 8.7	138.6 ± 6.4	141.8 ± 6.6
Mass (kg)	33.4 ± 6.6	36.2 ± 7.1	34.8 ± 5.2	37.3 ± 5.5
Tanner Stage -breast	1.61 ± 0.6	1.81 ± 0.8	1.50 ± 0.6	1.97 ± 0.8
Tanner stage- pubic	1.26 ± 0.5	1.43 ± 0.6	1.13 ± 0.4	1.25 ± 0.5

Values are mean ± SEM

Data analyses

Data were analysed using ANOVA with repeated measures on time (SPSS PC). The α level of 0.05 was accepted as significant for all statistical analyses.

Table 2. Bone mineral density changes in selected sites of activity and control groups of girls

	Activity		Control	
	Baseline	Post	Baseline	Post
BMD ($g \cdot cm^{-2}$)				
Lumbar spine (a,b)	0.652 ± 0.01	0.683 ± 0.01	0.637 ± 0.02	0.645 ± 0.01
Femoral neck (a,b)	0.678 ± 0.01	0.750 ± 0.03	0.690 ± 0.07	0.702 ± 0.03
Leg (a,b)	0.561 ± 0.06	0.599 ± 0.08	0.563 ± 0.06	0.574 ± 0.03
Total body (a,b)	0.823 ± 0.01	0.852 ± 0.02	0.810 ± 0.01	0.820 ± 0.10
BMC (g)				
Lumbar spine (a,b)	24.90 ± 5.4	26.61 ± 3.6	22.85 ± 4.8	23.20 ± 2.9
Femoral neck (a,b)	2.93 ± 0.39	3.24 ± 0.28	3.06 ± 0.41	3.11 ±. 24
Total body (a,b)	1036 ± 32	1160 ± 56	1014 ± 24	1081 ± 34

Values are mean ± SEM
a= pre and post differences within groups; b=interaction between groups

Table 3. Selected health related fitness and performance changes following the intervention programme

	Activity		Control	
	Baseline	Post	Baseline	Post
Body Fat %	25.80 ± 1.06	26.31 ± 1.10	29.43 ± 1.24	29.91 ± 1.20
Endurance Run (level)	4.00 ± 0.23	5.76 ± 0.27ab	4.27 ± 0.26	4.40 ± 0.29
Anaerobic Sprint (s)	7.76 ± 0.09	7.72 ± 0.09	7.54 ± 0.29	7.82 ± 0.15
Strength				
Dominant Grip (kg)	18.09 ± 0.90	20.41 ± 0.68ab	16.97 ± 0.51	18.59 ± 0.52a
Non Dom Grip (kg)	14.70 ± 0.80	18.78 ± 0.74a	16.47 ± 0.59	17.21 ± 0.60
Leg Extension (Nm)	40.89 ± 1.60	44.42 ± 1.71a	39.29 ± 1.84	42.25 ± 1.72
Shoulder Flexion(Nm)	23.68 ± 0.90	35.74 ± 1.37ab	26.57 ± 1.16	30.75 ± 1.25

Values are mean ± SEM
a = pre and post differences within groups; b = interaction between groups

Results

Table 1 shows the two groups were well matched. Table 2 presents the changes that occurred in bone mineral accrual over the period of the study in both groups. The baseline bone mineral values were similar for both groups. At the completion of the programme the activity group had accrued significantly greater bone mass at total body, lumbar spine, leg, and femoral neck when expressed as BMC or BMD (table 2).

The results of selected health related fitness and performance parameters are presented in table 3. Cardiovascular fitness as measured by the level attained in the multistage shuttle run test showed a significant 30% improvement in the exercise group compared to a 2.9% improvement in the control group. Significant changes in strength following the programme were evident in the exercise group in leg, shoulder and non-dominant grip measures.

The measure of anaerobic performance in the timed 40m sprint showed no difference between groups nor between baseline and post testing.

Discussion

The results of this intervention programme have been most encouraging in providing evidence that a well designed weight-bearing exercise programme derived from physical education curricula, can enhance bone accrual and fitness performance in prepubertal girls. There have been a number of studies which have shown a relationship between BMD and physical activity. The nature of many of these studies has been either cross sectional observational or unilateral studies in which one limb is stressed[3,9]. There have been relatively few studies which have prospectively studied young children to examine the effects of physical activity on bone accrual[5,10]. The results presented in this study are most encouraging and imply a prime window of opportunity may be present for the growing bone to respond to mechanical loading during these years. Questions regarding the dose response or even potential decay or catch up are to be addressed with a larger cohort which will continue the study over the next few years.

The specificity of performance reflect the programme's aims and content in stressing both the aerobic and strength measures in the girls. These results clearly demonstrate that function and performance can be enhanced in this young age group.

References

1. Snow-Carter, C., Bouxsein, M.L., Lewis, B.T., Carter, D.R. and Marcus, R. (1992) Effects of resistance and endurance exercise on bone mineral status of young women: a randomised exercise intervention trial. *Journal of Bone and Mineral Research,* Vol. 7, pp. 761-9.
2. Kanis, J. and Pitt, F. (1992) Epidemiology of osteoporosis. *Bone,* Vol. 13, pp. S7-15.
3. Bailey, D., Daniels, K., Dzus, A., Yong-Hing, K., Drinkwater, D., Wilkinson, A., and Houston, S. (1992) Bone mineral density in the proximal femur of children with Legg Calve Perthes Disease. *Journal of Bone and Mineral Research,* Vol. 7, (suppl), p. S287.
4. Henderson, R., Kemp, G. and Campion, H. (1992) Residual bone mineral density and muscle strength after fractures of the tibia or femur in children. *Journal of Bone Joint Surgery,* Vol. 74, pp. 211-8.
5. Bailey, A.D., Faulkner, R.A. and McKay, H.A. (1995) Growth, physical activity and bone mineral acquisition. *Exercise and Sport Sciences Reviews,* Vol. 9, 233-67.
6. Wark, J.D. (1993) Osteoporosis; pathogenesis, diagnosis, prevention and management, in *The Menopause*, (ed. H.G. Burger), Baillière Tindall, London pp. 151-83.
7. Recker, R. (1987) Bone mass and calcium nutrition. *Nutritional Review,* Vol. 11, pp. 19-21.
8. Tanner, J.M. (1962) *Growth and Adolescence*, (2nd edition), Blackwell Scientific, Oxford.
9. Khan, K.M., Bennell, K.L., Crichton, K.J., Harcourt, P.R., Hopper, J.L.,and Wark, J.D. (1996) Ballet classes undertaken at age 11 predict augmented hip bone mineral density an average of 40 years later. *Journal of Bone and Mineral Research,* Vol. 11, (Suppl), p. S103.
10. Slemenda, C.W., Miller, J.Z., Hui, S.L., Reister, T.K. and Johnston, C.C. (1991) Role of physical activity in the development of skeletal mass in children. *Journal of Bone and Mineral Research,* Vol. 6, pp. 1227-33.

EXPERIENCED HEALTH: LONGITUDINAL RELATIONSHIPS WITH LIFESTYLE AND OBJECTIVE HEALTH PARAMETERS

Lifestyle, objective and experienced health

J.W.R. TWISK, H.C.G. KEMPER, W. VAN MECHELEN, J. SNEL, G.B. POST and F.J. VAN LENTHE

Institute for Research in Extramural Medicine, Vrije Universiteit, Amsterdam, The Netherlands.

Keywords: Amsterdam Growth and Health Study, experienced health, generalised estimating equations, lifestyle, longitudinal studies, objective health.

Introduction

In preventive medicine one of the main topics is the analysis of the relationships between lifestyle parameters and health. These analyses are mostly limited to objective health parameters. More recently, there has been a tendency towards using subjective health parameters like experienced health or quality of life as outcome variables in epidemiological studies[1,2]. In the Amsterdam Growth and Health Study (AGHS), longitudinal data are available not only on lifestyle parameters and objective health parameters, but also on experienced health. The purpose of this study was firstly to analyse the relationships between lifestyle parameters and experienced health. Because it is questionable whether experienced health is related to objective health, the second purpose of this study was to analyse the relationships between experienced health and objective health parameters.

Methods

The AGHS is an observational longitudinal study, which started in 1976 with boys and girls initially aged 13 y. Over a period of 15 y seven repeated measurements were carried out (at 13-16, 21, 27 and 29 y). The population in the present study consists of 98 females and 83 males who remained in the study at the age of 27/29 y.

Experienced health

Experienced Health was measured, from the age of 21 y only, by the Check-list on Experienced Health, which was based on an original list of Dirken[3]. The list contains

Children and Exercise XIX. Edited by Neil Armstrong, Brian Kirby and Joanne Welsman.
Published in 1997 by E & FN Spon, 2–6 Boundary Row, London, SE1 8HN.
ISBN 0 419 22100 X.

13 dichotomous questions and the total score on the questionnaire is an index of long-term health, physical malaise and general well-being[4].

Lifestyle parameters
At each longitudinal measurement dietary intake was measured by a modification of the cross-check dietary history, in which subjects recalled their usual food intake during the previous month. Total energy intake (MJ) and alcohol consumption (g) were obtained. Daily physical activity was measured by a structured interview which combined the total time spent on different activities with the intensity of those activities to form a weighted activity score (expressed in METs). Smoking behaviour was measured by a questionnaire.

Objective health parameters
Total serum cholesterol (TC) and high density lipoprotein cholesterol, were determined in venous blood. External quality control took place with samples from a WHO reference laboratory. Systolic blood pressure (SBP) and diastolic blood pressure (DBP) were measured indirectly with a sphygmomanometer. SBP and DBP were measured twice with a standard pressure cuff on the left upper arm and the lowest value was recorded. Body mass index (weight/height^2) and the sum of skinfolds (biceps, triceps, subscapular and suprailiac) were measured. Maximal oxygen uptake ($\dot{V}O_2$ max) was determined during a treadmill test to exhaustion. For information regarding the methods used in the AGHS see ref[5].

Data analyses

At the age of 29 y, not all variables used were measured. If possible the average value of the measurements at 27 and 29 y was used as value at 27/29 y. If this was not possible only the value at 27 y was used. Because the score on the experienced health questionnaire was skewed to the right, at each measurement the population was divided into two groups. Firstly based on the median score and secondly based on tertiles (i.e., lowest versus highest tertile). The lower the score on the questionnaire, the better the experienced health. Both dichotomous variables were used as outcome variables in all analyses. To investigate the relationships between lifestyle parameters and subjective health, two approaches were used: 1) The relationships between 'long term exposure' to certain lifestyle parameters and experienced health at the age of 27/29. 'Long term exposure' was measured over two time periods, the adolescent period, which included the first four annual measurements and the total longitudinal period, which covered the age period of 13 to 27/29 y. For the first period 'long term exposure' was calculated as the average value of the first four measurements. This value was added to the value at the age of 21 y and to the value at 27/29 y to form an indicator for 'long term exposure' over the total age period of 13 to 27/29 y. On the basis of the median value of alcohol consumption the population was categorised as 'non/low drinkers' and 'heavy drinkers'. Smokers versus non-smokers was also defined. The relationships between experienced health and 'long term exposure' to certain lifestyle parameters were analysed with logistic regression analysis. 2) In the second approach the longitudinal development of the lifestyle parameters was related to the longitudinal development of experienced health. This was done with generalised estimating equations (GEE)[6]. The advantages of using GEE in observational longitudinal studies is described elsewhere[7,8]. The longitudinal approach however was limited to the age period between 21 and 27/29 y, because experienced health was only measured from the age 21 y onwards. Besides the relationships between lifestyle parameters and experienced health, the longitudinal relationship between experienced health and some objective health parameters was analysed. After assessing the main effects of the two different statistical models, for each predictor variable its interaction with gender was added to the model to investigate whether or not different relationships exist for males and females. Logistic regression analyses were carried out using SPSS/PC, and the GEE analyses by the Statistical Package for Interactive Data Analysis (SPIDA).

Results

In Table 1, the results of the logistic regression analyses regarding the relationships between 'long term exposure' to certain lifestyle parameters and experienced health are shown. When 'long term exposure' was defined over the adolescent period as well as over the total longitudinal period, smoking behaviour was related to negative experienced health. However, this was only found when experienced health was divided into tertiles. Daily physical activity was related to a positive experienced health but only in the highest and lowest tertiles when 'long term exposure' was defined over the adolescent period.

Table 2 shows the results of the GEE-analyses regarding the relationships between the development of experienced health from 21 to 27/29 y and the development of certain lifestyle and objective health parameters. Smoking behaviour was related to a negative experienced health only in the extreme tertiles. The same relationship was found for energy intake. Regarding the objective health parameters, no significant relationships were found.

Discussion

This study analysed the relationships between lifestyle parameters and subjective health. From the different analyses, the main conclusion was that smoking behaviour is related to a more negative experienced health. This was found in the analysis relating 'long term exposure' to smoking behaviour and experienced health as well as in the longitudinal analysis. However all relationships were only found when the more extreme tertiles of the experienced health score were compared to each other. It is difficult to compare our results to other studies, because experienced health is often neglected as an outcome variable in epidemiological studies. When experienced health (or quality of life) is used as outcome variable it is measured with different questionnaires[1,2] and it is questionable whether or not a particular questionnaire is suitable for measuring experienced health. The second purpose of this study was to analyse the relationship

Table 1. Odds ratios (OR) and 95% confidence intervals regarding the relationships between the score on a experienced health questionnaire (dichotomized regarding the median [$OR_{(dich)}$] and the extreme tertiles [$OR_{(tert)}$] and 'long term exposure' to certain lifestyle parameters.

	$OR_{(dich)}$	$OR_{(tert)}$
Adolescent period		
Energy intake	0.99 (0.69-1.42)	0.91 (0.58-1.42)
Daily physical activity	0.78 (0.56-1.08)	0.64* (0.42-0.99)
Smoking behaviour	1.63 (0.82-3.23)	3.14** (1.36-7.27)
Alcohol consumption	1.17 (0.65-2.12)	1.14 (0.56-2.34)
Total longitudinal period		
Energy intake	1.24 (0.87-2.50)	1.22 (0.81-1.83)
Daily physical activity	0.87 (0.64-1.18)	0.83 (0.59-1.19)
Smoking behaviour	1.45 (0.79-2.65)	2.97** (1.40-6.30)
Alcohol consumption	1.86 (0.99-3.49)	2.10 (0.97-4.57)

Level of signficance *p < 0.05, **p < 0.01

Table 2. Odds ratios (OR) and 95% confidence intervals regarding the longitudinal relationships between the score on a experienced health questionnaire (dichotomized regarding the median [$OR_{(dich)}$] and the extreme tertiles [$OR_{(tert)}$] and certain lifestyle and objective health parameters.

	$OR_{(dich)}$	$OR_{(tert)}$
Lifestyle parameters		
Energy intake	1.20 (0.91-1.59)	1.42* (1.03 - 1.96)
Daily physical activity	0.94 (0.76 - 1.18)	0.98 (0.76 - 1.25)
Smoking behaviour	1.63 (0.97 - 2.72)	3.26** (1.73 - 6.15)
Alcohol consumption	1.23 (0.78 - 1.95)	1.28 (0.75 - 2.17)
Objective health parameters		
Total cholesterol (TC)	1.01(0.81 - 1.27)	1.16 (0.88 - 1.51)
High density lipoprotein (HDL)	1.10 (0.86 - 1.41)	1.19 (0.86 - 1.63)
TC:HDL ratio	0.94 (0.74 - 1.21)	0.96 (0.71 - 1.30)
Systolic blood pressure	0.97 (0.78 - 1.21)	0.93 (0.73 - 1.20)
Diastolic blood pressure	0.97 (0.78 - 1.20)	0.95 (0.74 - 1.21)
Body mass index	1.07 (0.85 - 1.35)	1.02 (0.76 - 1.37)
Sum of four skinfolds	1.11 (0.87 - 1.41)	1.07 (0.77 - 1.47)
Maximal oxygen uptake	0.83 (0.56 - 1.23)	0.87 (0.87 - 1.47)

Level of significance *p < 0.05, **p < 0.01

between experienced health and objective health parameters. Surprisingly it was shown that experienced health was not related to any of the objective health parameters. So, in the relatively healthy and young population of the AGHS, experienced health and objective health parameters seem to be different issues. From this, the probably unsolvable problem arose, which of the two health indicators is the most important? We believe that when one is interested in the relationship between lifestyle parameters and health in young populations one should focus on both objective and experienced health. And although the latter is difficult to measure accurately it should not be neglected as an outcome variable in epidemiologic studies.

References

1. Hellénius, M.L., Dahlof, C., Aberg, H., Krakau, I. and Faire, U. de. (1995) Quality of life is not negatively affected by diet and exercise interventions in healthy men with cardiovascular risk factors. *Quality of Life Research*, Vol. 4, pp. 13-20.
2. Li, J. and Fielding, R. (1995) The measurement of current perceived health among Chinese people in Guangzhou and Hong Kong, southern China. *Quality of Life Research*, Vol. 4, pp. 271-8.
3. Dirken, J.M. (1967) *Arbeid en Sress (in Dutch)*, Wolters-Noordhof, Groningen, The Netherlands.
4. Jansen, M.E. and Sikkel, D. (1981) Verkorte versie van de VOEG-schaal (in Dutch). *Gedrag and Samenleving*, Vol. 2, pp. 78-82.
5. Kemper H.C.G. (1996) *The Amsterdam Growth Study. A Longitudinal Analysis of Health Fitness and Lifestyle*. Human Kinetics, Champaign, Il.
6. Zeger, S.L. and Liang, K-Y. (1986) Longitudinal data analysis for discrete and continuous outcomes. *Biometrics*, Vol. 42, pp. 121-30.
7. Twisk, J.W.R., Kemper, H.C.G., Mellenbergh, G.J. and Mechelen, W. van. (1996) Relation between the longitudinal development of lipoprotein levels and biological parameters from 13 to 27 years of age. *Journal of Epidemiological and Community Health*, Vol. 50, pp. 505-11.
8. Twisk, J.W.R., Kemper, H.C.G., Mellenbergh, G.J. and Mechelen W. van. (1996) Relation between the longitudinal development of lipoprotein levels and lifestyle parameters from 13 to 27 years of age. *Annals of Epidemiology*, Vol. 6, pp. 246-56.

LONGITUDINAL RELATIONSHIPS BETWEEN RESTING HEART RATE, MAXIMAL OXYGEN UPTAKE AND ACTIVITY

Heart rate, $\dot{V}O_2$ max and activity

W. VAN MECHELEN, H.C.G. KEMPER, J.W.R. TWISK, F.J. VAN LENTHE and G.B. POST

Institute for Research in Extramural Medicine, Faculty of Medicine, Vrije Universiteit, Amsterdam, The Netherlands

Keywords: Heart rate, maximal oxygen uptake, physical activity

Introduction

In exercise physiology it is a widely observed phenomenon that in healthy individuals regular physical training leads to a lower resting heart rate[1,2]. Also high levels of aerobic endurance are associated with lower levels of resting heart rate[1]. Most of the knowledge on this topic comes from either bed rest and training studies, or from studies comparing elite with non-elite athletes.

In some epidemiological studies resting heart rate is used as a proxy measure of habitual physical activity[3,4]. It should be noted however that it has been shown that physical activity and resting heart rate are two independent prognostic factors for cancer mortality and for other noncardiovasular diseases[5]. It is also suggested by some that resting heart rate can be used in epidemiological studies as a proxy measure of cardiovascular fitness status[6], whereas other authors have questioned this[7]. Most of this information comes from studies in adults, with either a cross-sectional design or with a longitudinal design with a relatively short period of follow-up. Little is known about long-term relationship between resting heart rate, habitual physical activity and maximal oxygen uptake ($\dot{V}O_2$ max) in a relatively young population, including multiple measurements.

The purpose of this study was to investigate the longitudinal relationship between resting heart rate and $\dot{V}O_2$ max, controlling for levels of habitual physical activity, in healthy males and females measured 6 times between 13 and 27 years of age.

Children and Exercise XIX. Edited by Neil Armstrong, Brian Kirby and Joanne Welsman.
Published in 1997 by E & FN Spon, 2–6 Boundary Row, London, SE1 8HN.
ISBN 0 419 22100 X.

Subjects

This study was part of the Amsterdam Growth and Health Study (AGHS). The AGHS started in 1977 with four annual measurements on boys and girls with an initial age of 13 y. All subjects were pupils in the same form of an Amsterdam secondary school. The study continued in 1985 with a 5th measurement at the age of 21 y. The subjects returned in 1991 for a 6th measurement (age 27 y). Drop out over this period was low (about 23%) and was not selective[8]. In 1991 full data sets were available from 83 males (height 1.83 ± 6.5 m, weight 75.6 ± 8.3 kg) and 98 females (height 1.70 ± 6.1 m, weight 63.2 ± 7.8 kg).

Methods

At each year of measurement resting heart rate, $\dot{V}O_2$ max and habitual physical activity were measured. Resting heart rate was measured telemetrically (Telecust 36 and Sirecust BS1, Siemens, The Netherlands) with the subjects seated after about 5 min of rest, prior to the $\dot{V}O_2$ max test. No attempts were made to obtain basal conditions. Throughout the study this measurement was carried out in the mornings shortly after arriving at the laboratory. $\dot{V}O_2$ max was measured by means of a treadmill test. Running speed throughout the test was 8 $km \cdot h^{-1}$ with increases in slope every second minute of 2.5% or 5% (depending on the heart rate). Oxygen uptake was measured directly every minute using an Ergoanalyser (Mijnhardt B.V.). In order to obtain a fitness index independent of body weight $\dot{V}O_2$ max was expressed as millilitres of oxygen uptake per minute per kilogram body weight$^{2/3}$ ($ml \cdot kg^{-0.67} \cdot min^{-1}$). Daily physical activity was measured by a structured interview, which covered a period of the previous 3 mo. The interview concerned sports activities (organised and non organised), leisure time activities, activities with regard to work (including housekeeping) and/or education, active transportation (walking/cycling) and stair climbing. The total time spent on all daily physical activities was combined with the intensity of the different activities to form a total weighted activity score (expressed in $METs \cdot wk^{-1}$). For extensive information on the methods of measurements one is referred to Kemper and van Mechelen[9].

Data analyses

Generalised estimating equations (GEE) were used to investigate the association between the longitudinal development of resting heart rate and $\dot{V}O_2$ max, correcting for habitual physical activity[10,11]. This technique, previously described by Twisk et al.[12], has the advantage that all longitudinal data are included in one analysis. The relationships at the different time points are tested simultaneously, leading to one standardised 'longitudinal' regression coefficient (β). The multiple regression model applied includes, next to the dependent ($\dot{V}O_2$ max) and the independent (resting heart rate) variables, a time dependent covariate (habitual physical activity), a time independent covariate (gender) and time. After assessing the main effect, the interaction between resting heart rate and gender was added to the model by multiplication of the two parameters involved. The GEE analysis was carried out using SPIDA[13]. A 5 percent significance level was set.

Results

In figures 1-3 the mean values over time of resting heart rate, $\dot{V}O_2$ max and habitual physical activity are shown, for males and females separately.

The result of the GEE analysis showed, after adjustment for habitual physical activity a negative and highly significant association between $\dot{V}O_2$ max and resting heart rate, with a β-value of -0.09 (95% (C)onfidence (I)nterval: [-0.06;-0.13], p = 0.000). No significant interaction with gender was observed, indicating that the longitudinal associations were of the same magnitude in both males and females.

Discussion

The purpose of this study was to investigate the longitudinal relationship between resting heart rate and maximal oxygen uptake, controlling for habitual physical activity, in healthy males and females measured 6 times between 13 and 27 years of age. To our knowledge no other study has been performed with a similar design and in a similar age group. This makes it hard to make direct comparisons of our data with findings in the literature.

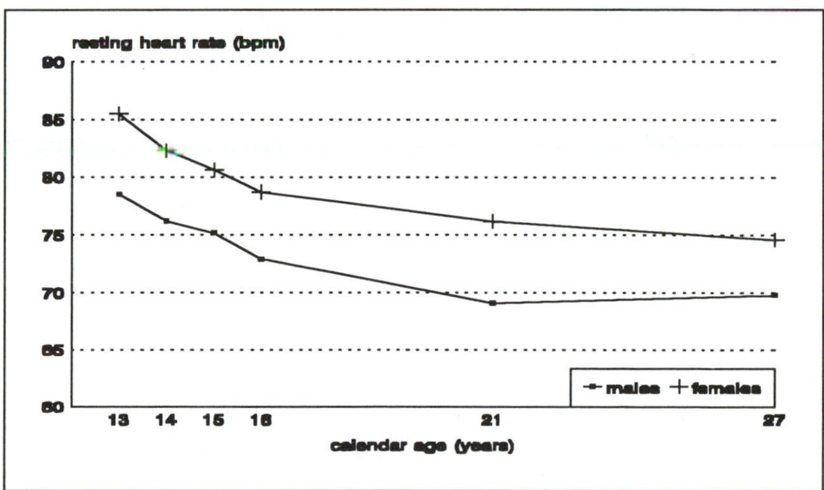

Fig. 1. Mean resting heart rate (beats·min^{-1}) by age

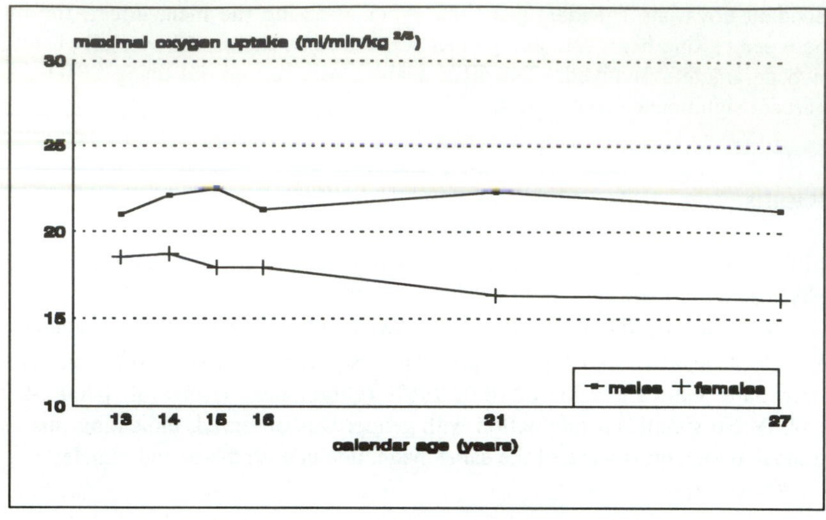

Fig. 2. Mean maximal oxygen uptake ($mL{\cdot}kg^{-0.67}{\cdot}min^{-1}$) by age

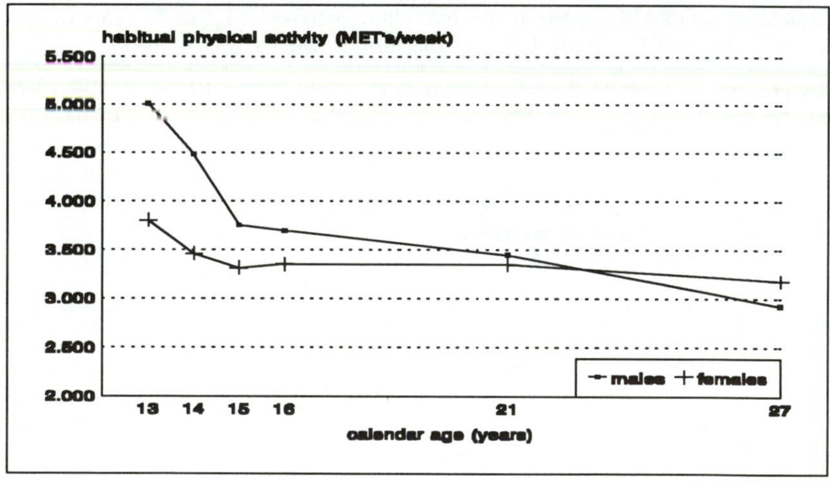

Fig. 3. Mean habitual physical activity ($METs{\cdot}wk^{-1}$) by age

In this 15 y follow-up study in 181 young people a low (β = -0.09), though highly significant negative association was found between resting heart rate and maximal oxygen uptake, after adjustment for habitual physical activity. The direction of this association is as expected and our finding is in line with those of others. For instance Whaley et al.[7] found in a cross-sectional study in 2350 adult men and women, after multiple regression analysis, a significant standardised regression coefficient of -0.15 between directly measured maximal oxygen uptake and resting heart rate, after adjusting for age, sex, cigarette smoking status, percentage of body fat and physical activity status. A similar relationship was found between resting heart rate and $\dot{V}O_2$ max by Jackson et al.[14] in a cross-sectional study in 2009 adult male and females, after adjusting for sex, age, body composition and habitual physical activity (standardised regression coefficient β = -0.13; p <0.001).

One may question the magnitude of the influence of habitual physical activity on the observed association. Therefore a univariate GEE-analysis was carried out between resting heart rate and $\dot{V}O_2$ max, not adjusting for habitual physical activity. This analysis hardly altered the observed association, resulting in a β-value of -0.10 (95% CI: [-0.06;-0.14]). This suggests that habitual physical activity, as measured in our study, had no meaningful independent influence on the association between resting heart rate and $\dot{V}O_2$ max. This finding is in contrast to previous results from cross-sectional studies[7,14].

To conclude, our findings support the notion that in longitudinal epidemiological studies similar to ours, resting heart rate can be seen as an independent proxy measure of $\dot{V}O_2$ max, independent of habitual physical activity.

References

1. Åstrand, P.O. and Rodahl, K. (1986) *Textbook of Work Physiology*, McGraw-Hill, Singapore, p. 440 and 452.
2. Marti, B., Suter, E., Riesen, W.F., Tschopp, A., Wanner, H.U. and Gutzwiller, F. (1990) Effects of long-term, self-monitored exercise on serum lipoprotein and apolipoprotein profile in middle aged men. *Atherosclerosis*, Vol. 81, pp. 19-31.
3. Severson, R.K., Nomura, A.M., Grove, J.S. and Stemmermann, G.N. (1989) A prospective analysis of physical activity and cancer. *American Journal of Epidemiology*, Vol. 130, pp. 522-9.
4. Klesges, R.C., Eck, L.H., Isbell, T.R., Fulliton, W. and Hanson, C.L. (1991) Physical activity, body composition and blood pressure: a multimethod approach. *Medicine and Science in Sports and Exercise*, Vol. 23, pp. 759-65.
5. Wannamethee, G., Shaper, A.G. and MacFarlane, P.W. (1993) Heart rate, physical activity and mortality from cancer and other noncardiovascular diseases. *American Journal of Epidemiology*, Vol. 137, pp. 735-48.
6. Shephard, R.J. and Bouchard, C. (1994) Principal components of fitness: relations to physical activity and lifestyle. *Canadian Journal of Applied Physiology*, Vol. 19, pp. 200-14.

7. Whaley, M.H., Kaminsky, L.A., Dwyer, G.B. and Getchell, L.H. (1995) Failure of predicted $\dot{V}O_2$-peak to discriminate physical fitness in epidemiological studies. *Medicine and Science in Sports and Exercise,* Vol. 27, pp. 85-91.
8. Twisk, J.W.R. and Kemper, H.C.G. (1995) Design of the Amsterdam Growth study, in *The Amsterdam Growth Study. A Longitudinal Analysis of Health, Fitness and Lifestyle*, (ed. H.C.G. Kemper), Human Kinetics, Champaign, Il, pp. 6-16.
9. Kemper, H.C.G. and van Mechelen W. (1995) Methods of measurement used in the longitudinal study, in *The Amsterdam Growth Study. A Longitudinal Analysis of Health, Fitness and Lifestyle*, (ed. H.C.G. Kemper), Human Kinetics, Champaign, Il, pp. 28-49.
10. Zeger, S.L. and Liang, K.Y. (1986) Longitudinal data-analysis for discrete and continuous outcomes. *Biometrics,* Vol. 42, pp. 121-30.
11. Zeger, S.L., Liang, K.Y. and Albert, P.S. (1984) Models for longitudinal data: a generalized estimating equation approach. *Biometrics,* Vol. 44, pp. 1049-60.
12. Twisk, J.W.R., Kemper, H.C.G., Mellenbergh, G.J. and van Mechelen, W. (1996) Relation between the longitudinal development of lipoprotein levels and biological parameters during adolescence and young adulthood in Amsterdam, the Netherlands. *Journal of Epidemiology and Community Health,* Vol. 50, pp. 505-11.
13. Gebski, V., Leung, O., McNeil D. and Lunn, D. (1992) *SPIDA User Manual, Version 6,* Macquarie Uni., NSW Australia.
14. Jackson, A.S., Blair, S.N., Mahar, M.T., Wier, L.T., Ross, R.M. and Stuteville J.E. (1990) Prediction of functional aerobic capacity without exercise testing. *Medicine and Science in Sports and Exercise,* Vol. 22, pp. 863-70.

BIOLOGICAL MATURATION IN RELATION TO LIFESTYLE FROM ADOLESCENCE INTO ADULTHOOD

Amsterdam Growth and Health Study

G.B. POST, H.C.G. KEMPER and J.W.R. TWISK
Institute for Research in Extramural Medicine, Vrije Universiteit, Amsterdam, The Netherlands

Keywords: Lifestyle, longitudinal, maturation, nutrition, physical activity

Introduction

Biological development of teenagers of the same calendar age shows large individual differences in timing during the age of puberty; the age of peak height velocity and sexual development differs widely. In the literature it is indicated that the rate of maturation is related to fatness, especially in women. Most of these studies were of a cross-sectional design. Also in longitudinal studies[1,2] associations are found between fatness and a rapid maturation. However, the reason for this maturation effect is not clear.

The Amsterdam Growth and Health longitudinal study covers a period of almost 15 y, in a group of about 180 males and females, from 12 until 28 y. Therefore the data from this population were used for the purpose of this paper, namely to find out if a different rate of biological maturation is accompanied with a different lifestyle, such as eating behaviour and activity level.

Subjects

A group of 84 males and 98 females were studied longitudinally from 1977 until 1991. Annual measurements were made between 1977 and 1980, in subjects aged 13-16 y. Additional measurements were made in 1985 and 1991 in the same subjects with a mean age of 21 and 27 y, respectively.

Of the original 307 subjects in 1977, the total drop-out percentage is 43% in males and 38% in females. No significant drop-out effects could be demonstrated in the parameters relevant for this paper[3].

Children and Exercise XIX. Edited by Neil Armstrong, Brian Kirby and Joanne Welsman.
Published in 1997 by E & FN Spon, 2–6 Boundary Row, London, SE1 8HN.
ISBN 0 419 22100 X.

Methods

Biological maturation

Biological maturation was estimated as skeletal age from radiographs of the left hand and wrist. By comparing the ossification stage of 20 bones, according to the Tanner-Whitehouse II method[4], the classification of skeletal maturity was made. In principle four annual measurements were taken during the teenage period, or less if subjects had already reached full skeletal maturity. Full maturity was reached in girls at skeletal age 16 y, and in boys at skeletal age 18 y.

Nutrient intake

Individual food intake was assessed with a modified cross-check dietary history interview method[5]. At each year of measurement the entire range of foods and drinks came under review. Only foods eaten at least once a fortnight were recorded.

The total daily energy intake, the contribution of the macro-nutrients (protein, fat and carbohydrate), and the daily calcium intake were calculated using a national Dutch computerized food composition table and were related to body weight (kg).

Physical activity

Individual physical activity was obtained from a structured interview[6].

All habitual physical activities, covering a period of 3 mo prior to the interview, were taken into consideration limited to activities with a minimal metabolic intensity level of approximately 4 times the basal metabolic rate (4 MET) and with a duration of at least 5 min. For each physical activity the metabolic equivalent (MET) was calculated. Total weekly physical activity of each individual was estimated as a weighted activity score (METTOT).

Data analyses

Over the adolescent period, at each of the 4 y of measurement, for each subject the calendar age was subtracted from the biological age (in months). The differences between the two ages are summed and considered as the rate of maturation. If full maturity was reached before the end of the 4 measurement years during adolescence, only the concerning years are taken into account. A univariate linear regression analysis was used to assess the relationship between the rate of maturation (independent variable) and several lifestyle parameters (dependent variables): i.e. the intake related to body weight of energy (Energy/BW), protein (Prot/BW), fat (Fat/BW) and carbohydrate (Carb/BW), calcium (Calc/BW), and METTOT. Also body fat (sum of 4 skinfolds,mm), body weight (kg) and body height (cm) were used as dependent variables. A critical region with a probability level of 5 percent was used to test the significance of the maturation effects. Two ages are considered in the regression analysis, namely the results at the mean age 21 y and age 27 y, separately for males and females.

Table 1. Regression coefficients (Beta) between maturation and nutrient intake, body composition, and physical activity for two age periods for males and females.

Age (y)	21		27		21		27	
	males (n=84)		males (n=84)		females (n=98)		females (n=98)	
	Beta	Sign.	Beta	Sign	Beta	Sign	Beta	Sign
Energy/BW	-0.301	p=0.008*	-0.152	p=0.175	-0.216	p=0.038*	-0.318	p=0.001*
Protein/BW	-0.255	p=0.026*	-0.055	p=0.624	-0.250	p=0.015*	-0.247	p=0.014*
Fat/BW	-0.209	p=0.069	-0.057	p=0.613	-0.190	p=0.068	-0.244	p=0.015*
Carb/BW	-0.299	p=0.008*	-0.172	p=0.122	-0.190	p=0.067	-0.322	p=0.001*
Calcium/BW	-0.200	p=0.082*	-0.005	p=0.962	-0.231	p=0.026*	-0.225	p=0.027*
METTOT	-0.232	p=0.043*	-0.125	p=0.266	-0.814	p=0.438	-0.171	p=0.094
Skinfolds **	+0.264	p=0.020*	+0.266	p=0.016*	+0.234	p=0.023*	+0.178	p=0.079
Body weight	+0.095	p=0.414	+0.149	p=0.183	+0.120	p=0.249	+0.094	p=0.357
Body height	-0.109	p=0.349	-0.997	p=0.376	-0.242	p=0.019*	-0.221	p=0.029*

Level of significancc *p <0.05
** Sum of four skinfolds (biceps, triceps, subscapular, suprailiac)

Results

The results, presented in table 1, show a significantly negative correlation between maturation and energy and nutrient intake per kg body weight in males at age 21 y, in other words the more mature the lower is the energy intake. In males also a negative association is demonstrated in relation between maturation and physical activity at age 21 y. At age 27 y in males no associations are found.

Females with a rapid maturation consumed less energy and nutrients per kg bodyweight at both ages. Only females of 27 y show a negative trend between physical activity and maturation. Significant associations could be demonstrated for the sum of four skinfolds in both sexes indicating that rapid maturation results in a higher fat mass at age 21 y and age 27 y. In females a negative relation was found between maturation and body height. No relationships were found for bodyweight.

Discussion

In earlier publications[2,7] biological maturation was used to find out if slow or rapid maturation was related to changes in body composition as a result of differences in nutrient intake or physical activity. In these articles the study population was reduced to groups of early or late maturers. Although the misclassification of early and late maturers was reduced to a minimum[2], the disadvantage however was the small numbers in the comparisons (about 25-30 in each sex). Therefore we changed the approach and used the data of all the longitudinal subjects and calculated the difference between the individual biological age and chronological age at each point of measurement during the adolescent period. The mean (± standard deviations) of these differences during adolescence appear to be +0.04 (± 0.85 y) in boys and -0.10 (± 0.89) y in girls. This demonstrates that on the average the biological age of these boys and girls corresponded quite well with the British children that acted as reference[4].

The presented longitudinal associations confirm that until the age of 27 y early maturation coincides with significantly lower energy and nutrient intakes, especially in females, and a trend (not significant), in lower physical activity. In both sexes this results in higher body fatmass (skinfolds) in rapid maturers. The regulation of energy intake seems no longer functional at a certain low level of habitual physical activity.

References

1. Beunen, G.P., Malina, R.M., Lefevre, J.A., Claessens, A.L, Renson, R. and Vanreusel, B. (1994) Adiposity and biological maturity in girls 6-16 years of age. *International Journal of Obesity and Related Metabolic Disorders*, Vol. 18, pp. 542-6.
2. van Lenthe, F.J., Kemper, H.C.G. and van Mechelen, W. (1996) Rapid maturation in adolescence results in greater obesity in adulthood: the Amsterdam Growth and Health Study. *American Journal of Clinical Nutrition*, Vol. 64, pp. 18-24.
3. Kemper, H.C.G. (1995) *The Amsterdam Growth and Health Study: a Longitudinal Analysis of Health, Fitness and Lifestyle. HK Sport Science Monograph Series*, Vol. 6, Human Kinetics, Champaign, Il.
4. Tanner, J.M., Whitehouse, R.H., Marshall, W.A., Healy, M.J.R. and Goldstein, H. (1975) *Assessment of Skeletal Maturity and Prediction of Adult Height (TW2 Method)* Academic Press, London.
5. Post, G.B. (1989) *Nutrition in Adolescence - a Longitudinal Study in Dietary Patterns from Teenager to Adult,* PhD Thesis, SO16, Haarlem, De Vrieseborch.
6. Verschuur, R. (1987) *Daily Physical Activity and Health; Longitudinal Changes During the Teenage Period,* PhD Thesis, SO12, Haarlem, De Vrieseborch.
7. Post, G.B. and Kemper, H.C.G. (1993) Nutrient intake and biological maturation during adolescence. The Amsterdam Growth and Health Study. *European Journal of Clinical Nutrition*, Vol. 47, pp. 400-8.

THE LONGITUDINAL ASSOCIATION BETWEEN PHYSICAL FITNESS AND FAT DISTRIBUTION

Physical fitness and fat distribution

F.J. VAN LENTHE, H.C.G. KEMPER, W. VAN MECHELEN and J.W.R. TWISK
Institute for Research in Extramural Medicine, Vrije Universiteit, Amsterdam, The Netherlands

Keywords: Adolescence, fat distribution, fitness, lean body mass, longitudinal

Introduction

Prospective studies have shown that a central pattern of body fat, with relatively more fat stored on the trunk compared to the extremities, is associated with an increased risk for coronary heart diseases (CHD), independent from total body fatness[1,2]. The development of a central pattern of body fat starts in adolescence[3]. Many studies on the distribution of body fat have been carried out in adults and mainly used a cross-sectional design. Longitudinal studies from adolescence into adulthood, investigating factors associated with the development of a central pattern of body fat, are limited.

Physical fitness, as indicated by the maximum oxygen uptake ($\dot{V}O_2$ max) is associated with all-cause mortality and mortality due to CHD[4]. The development of the $\dot{V}O_2$ max, relative to body weight, reduces from adolescence into adulthood in both sexes[5].

In the Amsterdam Growth and Health Study (AGHS), an observational longitudinal study which started in 1977, a healthy population of males and females was followed between the mean ages of 13 and 27 y[6]. The study is unique in that both indicators of body composition and physical fitness were measured longitudinally over this period of time. In the present study, the association between the development of the $\dot{V}O_2$ max and a central pattern of body fat was investigated in males and females between 13 and 27 y.

Subjects

The Amsterdam Growth and Health Study was initiated to describe the growth and biological maturation of adolescents[6]. Therefore, physiological, anthropometrical,

Children and Exercise XIX. Edited by Neil Armstrong, Brian Kirby and Joanne Welsman.
Published in 1997 by E & FN Spon, 2–6 Boundary Row, London, SE1 8HN.
ISBN 0 419 22100 X.

psychological and behavioural indicators were measured longitudinally. All pupils in the first and second form of a secondary school in Amsterdam (the Netherlands) were invited to participate in the study. Informed consent was obtained from the pupils and their parents. None of the subjects refused to participate and the initial population consisted of 148 boys and 159 girls.

At the first period of measurements in 1977, subjects were at a mean age of 13 y. In the next 3 y, follow-up measurements were performed annually, yielding data between 13 and 16 y. Additional follow-up measurements were carried out in 1985 and 1991 at the mean ages of 21 and 27 y. Only those subjects, who participated at all six periods of measurement, were included in the analyses. Consequently, the population under study consisted of 84 males and 98 females. No selective drop-out was found in any of the variables included in this study.

Methods

A central pattern of body fat

As an indicator of a central pattern of body fat, the (subscapular/triceps) skinfold ratio (S/T ratio) was used. Triceps and subscapular skinfold thicknesses were measured with a Harpenden caliper to the nearest 0.1 mm, according to guidelines of the International Biological Programme[9]. A coefficient of reproducibility of the skinfold measurements, estimated by the correlation coefficients when the time between two measurements is assumed 0, was above 0.80.

Physical fitness

$\dot{V}O_2$ max was measured during a running test on a treadmill (Quinton 18-54). Subjects started with a submaximal test in which they ran at a constant speed of 8 $km{\cdot}h^{-1}$. The slope of the treadmill increased from 0 to 2.5 to 5% in two minute intervals. After a short period of rest, the maximal test started. Subjects ran at a constant speed of 8 $km{\cdot}h^{-1}$. Every two minutes the slope increased 2.5% or 5% (depending on the heart rate) until exhaustion. $\dot{V}O_2$ max was expressed in $mL{\cdot}kg^{-.67}{\cdot}min^{-1}$, because this measure was almost independent from body weight.

Data analyses

To investigate the association between the development of the $\dot{V}O_2$ max and the S/T ratio, a generalised estimating equations technique (GEE) was used[8]. A major advantage of this longitudinal data analysis technique is that data obtained at several periods of measurement can be used simultaneously. The following formula was used to analyse the data:

$$Y_{it} = \beta_0 + \sum_{j=1}^{J} \beta_{1j} X_{ijt} + \beta_2 t + \varepsilon_{it}$$

where:

Y_{it} = observations of individual *i* from t_1 to t_m (where *m* = the number of measurements).

t = time

β_0 = intercept

J = number of independent variables

β_{1j} = standardized regression coefficient of the independent variable *j*

X_{ijt} = independent variable *j* of subject *i* at time *t*

β_2 = regression coefficient of time.

ε_{it} = measurement error of individual *i*.

The inclusion of all available data in the analysis required a correction for within-subject correlation. Based on the actual correlation coefficients between the S/T ratio at all periods of measurement, a stationary *m*-dependent correlation structure was used to correct for within-subject correlation. In this structure correlations between maximally *m* periods of measurements have different values (> 0) and correlations between data obtained more than *m* periods of measurement apart are 0. In this study, data of six periods of measurement were used in the analysis, and a stationary 5-dependent correlation structure was chosen. Prior to the analysis, all data were z-converted. Consequently, the coefficients of interest (β_1), indicating the association between the dependent (S/T ratio) and the independent variable ($\dot{V}O_2$ max), could be interpreted as a standardized longitudinal regression coefficients, varying between -1 and 1.

Results

Figs 1 and 2 present the development of the mean (± SD) $\dot{V}O_2$ max and S/T ratio between 13 and 27 y in males and females respectively. In males, the S/T ratio increased almost linearly from 0.71 (± 0.02) at the mean age of 13 y to 1.39 (± 0.04) at the mean age of 27 y. From 13 to 16 years of age the mean $\dot{V}O_2$ max increased from 210.0 $mL \cdot kg^{-.67} \cdot min^{-1}$ (± 2.0) to 232.7 $mL \cdot kg^{-.67} \cdot min^{-1}$ (± 2.5). From the mean age of 16 y a decrease was found, resulting in a mean $\dot{V}O_2$ max of 212.3 $mL \cdot kg^{-.67} \cdot min^{-1}$ (± 2.4) at the mean age of 27 y. In females, the S/T ratio almost remained constant over the entire period of study with values of 0.70 (± 0.02), 0.73 (± 0.02) and 0.85 (± 0.02) at the mean ages of 13, 16 and 27 y respectively. $\dot{V}O_2$ max decreased from 185.0 $mL \cdot kg^{-.67} \cdot min^{-1}$ (± 1.8) at the mean age of 13 y to 179.2 $mL \cdot kg^{-.67} \cdot min^{-1}$ (± 1.5) at the mean age of 16 y and to 160.8 $mL \cdot kg^{-.67} \cdot min^{-1}$ (± 2.0) at the mean age of 27 y.

Table 1 presents the results of the GEE analysis. In males, the development of the $\dot{V}O_2$ max was positively associated ($\beta = 0.10$, $p = 0.00$) with the development of the S/T ratio. No significant interaction-effect was found, which indicated that the association between

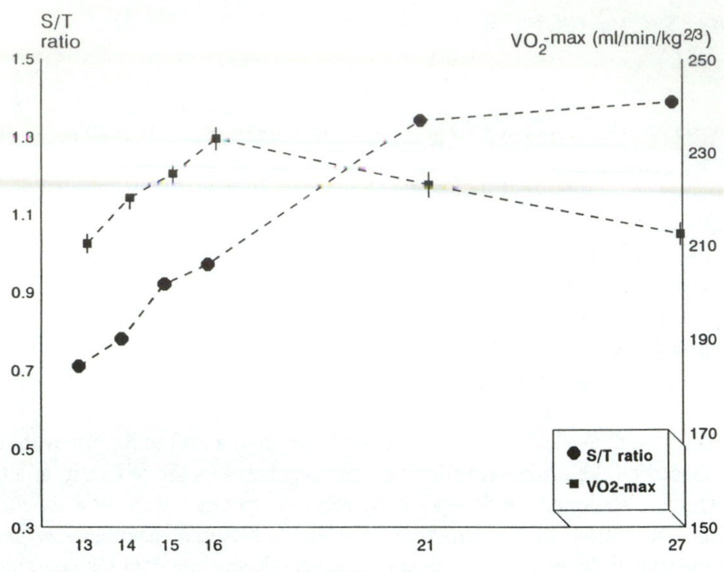

Fig. 1. Development of the $\dot{V}O_2$ max and the subscapular/triceps ratio between 13 and 27 year old males

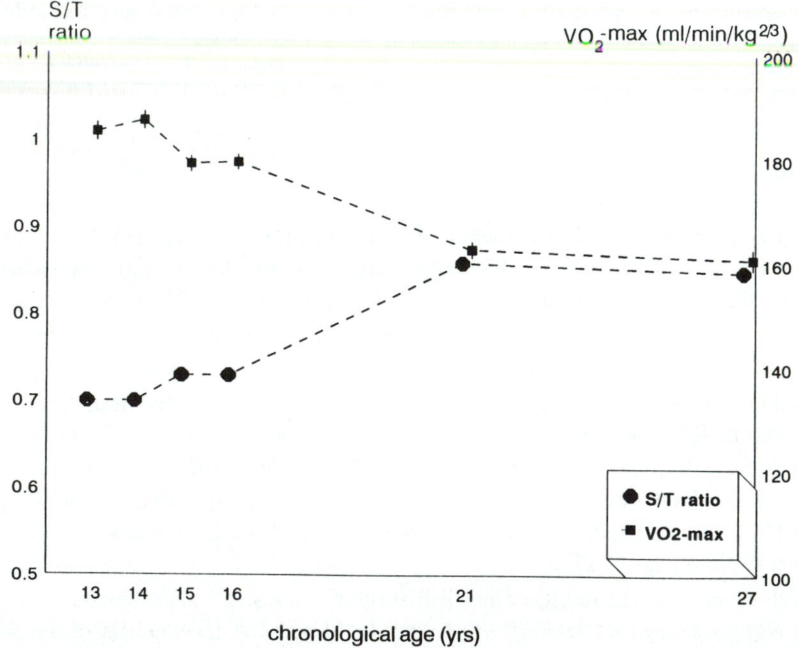

Fig. 2. Development of the $\dot{V}O_2$ max and the subscapular/triceps ratio between 13 and 27 year old females.

Table 1. The association between the development of the $\dot{V}O_2$ max and (components of) the S/T ratio between 13 and 27 y in males and females

	Males (n=83) $\dot{V}O_2$ max			Females (n=98) $\dot{V}O_2$ max		
	ß	95% c.i.	p	ß	95% c.i.	p
Triceps	-0.18	[-0.28;-0.10]	0.00	-0.04	[-0.10;0.03]	0.23
Subscapular	---	---	---	-0.06	[-0.11;-0.01]	0.03
S/T ratio	0.10	[0.02;0.18]	0.00	-0.05	[-0.12;0.01]	0.12

* did not converge in 50 iterations

$\dot{V}O_2$ max and the S/T ratio did not differ over time. GEE-analysis with the components of this ratio as the dependent variable showed a negative association between the development of $\dot{V}O_2$ max and triceps skinfold thickness. In females, no significant association was found between the development of the $\dot{V}O_2$ max and the S/T ratio, despite the negative association between the development of the $\dot{V}O_2$ max and the subscapular skinfold thickness (ß = -0.06; p = 0.03).

Discussion

In this study the association between the development of the $\dot{V}O_2$ max and the S/T ratio was investigated in males and females between 13 and 27 y. In males, the development of the $\dot{V}O_2$ max was negatively associated with the development of the triceps skinfold thickness, but not with the thickness of the subscapular skinfold. Probably, as a result, the $\dot{V}O_2$ max was positively associated with the S/T ratio. In females, only a negative association was found between the $\dot{V}O_2$ max and the subscapular skinfold thickness.

In our study, correlations between lean body mass (LBM) and the S/T ratio are significantly positive at most periods of measurements. Therefore, LBM could potentially confound the relationship between the $\dot{V}O_2$ max and the S/T ratio. In males, $\dot{V}O_2$ max and the S/T ratio remained positively associated (ß = 0.09, p = 0.02) after adjustment for LBM. Physical activity, energy intake, smoking and alcohol intake were not associated with the S/T ratio and could not, therefore, confound this relationship.

Conclusions

The development of the $\dot{V}O_2$ max, expressed relative to body weight$^{0.67}$, is positively associated with the S/T ratio in males between 13 and 27 y, probably due to a negative association between the $\dot{V}O_2$ max and the triceps skinfold thickness. In females, no association was found between the development of the $\dot{V}O_2$ max and the S/T ratio, despite a negative association between the $\dot{V}O_2$ max and the subscapular skinfold thickness.

References

1. Ducimetiere, P., Richard, J. and Cambien, F. (1986) The pattern of subcutaneous fat distribution in middle-aged men and the risk of coronary heart disease: the Parish Prospective Study. *International Journal of Obesity,* Vol.10, pp. 229-40.
2. Donahue, R.P., Abbott, R.D., Bloom, E., Reed, D.M. and Yano, K. (1987) Central obesity and coronary heart disease in men. *Lancet,* Vol. 1, pp. 821-4.
3. van Lenthe, F.J., Kemper, H.C.G., van Mechelen, W. and Twisk J.W.R. (1996) Longitudinal development and tracking of central patterns of subcutaneous fat in adolescence and adulthood: the Amsterdam Growth and Health Study. *International Journal of Epidemiology,* Vol. 25, pp. 1162-71.
4. Blair, S.N., Kohl, III H.W., Paffenbarger, R.S., Clark, D.G., Cooper, K.H. and Gibbons, L.W. (1989) Physical fitness and all-cause mortality. A prospective study of healthy men and women. *Journal of the American Medical Association,* Vol. 262, pp. 2395-401.
5. van Mechelen, W. and Kemper, H.C.G. (1995) Body growth, body composition and physical fitness, in *The Amsterdam Growth and Health Study: a Longitudinal Analysis of Health, Fitness and Lifestyle,* (ed. H.C.G. Kemper), Human Kinetics, Champaign, Il., Vol. 6, pp. 52-85.
6. Kemper, H.C.G. and van Mechelen, W. (1996) Methods of measurement used in the longitudinal study, in *The Amsterdam Growth and Health Study: a Longitudinal Analysis of Health, Fitness and Lifestyle,* (ed. H.C.G. Kemper), Human Kinetics, Champaign, Il., Vol. 6, pp. 28-49.
7. Weiner, J.S. and Lourie J.A. (1969) *Human Biology, a Guide to Field Methods. IBP Handbook No. 9*, Blackwell, Oxford.
8. Zeger, S.L. and Liang, K.Y. (1986) Longitudinal data-analysis for discrete and continuous outcomes. *Biometrics,* Vol. 42, pp. 121-30.

AEROBIC FITNESS AND FAT PATTERNING IN ADOLESCENT BOYS

Fitness and fat patterning

W. BELL
University of Wales Institute Cardiff, Cardiff, UK
Keywords: Adolescence, aerobic fitness, fat patterning

Introduction

A recent study[1] using dual energy x-ray absorptiometry (DXA) found elite young soldiers to have a smaller proportion of fat located at the abdomen, compared with less well-trained soldiers of the same average fatness. Even with increasing fatness, the fittest soldiers were found to have a greater proportion of fat in the arm, rather than the trunk. The mechanisms responsible for this difference were thought to be related to hormonal and lifestyle factors. The conclusions were that a different fat placement may be associated with active young men, and that a high level of training, or fitness, may predispose individuals to a different type of fat placement.

Whilst there are a number of reports describing fat patterning during adolescence[2, 3] the discourse on the relationship between aerobic fitness and fat patterning in children is limited. The aim of the present analysis, therefore, was to identify the longitudinal nature of fat patterning in adolescent boys with contrasting levels of aerobic fitness.

Subjects

Subjects were boys who participated in a longitudinal study between the mean ages of 12.3 $\pm$ 0.3 and 15.3 $\pm$ 0.3 y[4]. Multistage cluster sampling was used to provide a sampling frame from which subjects, a mixture of competitive and control boys, were recruited (n = 48). To maintain consistency in deriving and comparing variables, analyses were carried out using pure longitudinal data only (n = 32).

Children and Exercise XIX. Edited by Neil Armstrong, Brian Kirby and Joanne Welsman.
Published in 1997 by E & FN Spon, 2–6 Boundary Row, London, SE1 8HN.
ISBN 0 419 22100 X.

Methods

All measurements were recorded annually by a single observer at the same time each year. Stature was measured to the nearest 0.1 cm using a fixed Harpenden stadiometer and body mass to the closest 0.1 kg with a beam balance. Skinfold thickness was measured at the biceps, triceps, subscapular, suprailiac, thigh and calf sites using a Holtain caliper[5]. Duplicate measurements were taken and the mean used. Whole-body density was determined by hydrostatic weighing with simultaneous measurement of residual volume. Relative and absolute amounts of total body fat (TBF) and fat-free mass (FFM) were derived from body density using modified equations for age and gender[6].

Aerobic fitness was determined using a Monark cycle ergometer in an on-line system. Ventilation was measured on the input side of the respiratory circuit with a modified CD4 dry gas meter. Expired air was sampled from a mixing chamber and fed directly into regularly calibrated O_2 and CO_2 gas analysers. Heart rate was monitored using an electrocardiograph, the exploring electrode placed at the V_5 position. An intermittent protocol, employing a minimum of three progressive workloads, was used to span the heart rate 120-180 beats·min^{-1}. Peak oxygen uptake (peak $\dot{V}O_2$) was estimated from submaximal values extrapolated to a heart rate of 195 beats·min^{-1} [7].

Data analyses

Contrasting fitness groups were compiled by ranking individuals on the basis of peak $\dot{V}O_2$ and dividing into upper (n = 16) and lower (n = 16) halves. For descriptive purposes peak $\dot{V}O_2$ was expressed as a ratio standard (mL·kg^{-1}·min^{-1}) and a power function (mL·kg$^{-0.67}$·min^{-1})[8]. Subsequent analyses, however, were carried out using peak $\dot{V}O_2$ expressed as a power function. Since rank position changed with age, the composition of groups varied from year to year; each fitness group therefore comprised the highest and the lowest sixteen peak $\dot{V}O_2$ values respectively, at a given age. All data were re-aligned with peak $\dot{V}O_2$ at each age.

Principal components analysis (PCA) was used to identify fat patterning[9]. The advantage of this particular technique is that it removes individual differences in fatness before analysis. Each skinfold thickness was transformed to its natural log equivalent. A regression of each transformed skinfold thickness was made on the mean log skinfold thickness for an individual. The residuals were then analysed to produce components of fat patterning. Only those components with eigenvalues greater than unity were considered meaningful.

Table 1. Descriptive data for age, stature, body mass and total body fat

Age (y)	12.3 ± 0.3	13.3 ± 0.3	14.3 ± 0.3	15.3 ± 0.3
Stature (cm)	150.5 ± 5.9	156.7 ± 7.0	164.3 ± 8.3	171.4 ± 7.1
Body mass (kg)	37.8 ± 5.1	42.4 ± 6.6	49.6 ± 8.8	56.5 ± 8.8
TBF (%)	11.8 ± 4.6	12.3 ± 5.2	11.7 ± 5.3	11.3 ± 4.5

Values are mean ± SD

Results

The descriptive data for age, stature, body mass and % TBF for the entire group (n = 32) are given in table 1. The group as a whole followed the 50th centile line for stature and body mass, and had average levels of % TBF.

The mean values for upper (n = 16) and lower (n = 16) fitness groups are presented in table 2. Peak $\dot{V}O_2$ was estimated to be above average in the upper fitness group and below average in the lower fitness group[10]. Differences between groups were significant ($p < 0.0001$) at each age using both the ratio standard and the power function.

Unrotated principal component results for upper and lower fitness groups are summarised in tables 3 and 4. Only the first principal component is given. When interpreting components, loadings of approximately 0.3 were considered relatively unimportant, since they account for less than 10% of the variance.

In the upper fitness group at age 12+y (table 3), the first principal component accounted for 37% of the total variance. This discriminated the subscapular and suprailiac skinfolds with the biceps, triceps and calf skinfolds, and was interpreted as a trunk-extremity contrast. Similar interpretations were made at each of the other ages. Thus the first component at each age in the upper fitness group exhibited a trunk-extremity contrast.

Table 2. Peak $\dot{V}O_2$ in upper and lower fitness groups

Age (y)	Peak $\dot{V}O_2$ ($mL \cdot kg^{-1} \cdot min^{-1}$)		Peak $\dot{V}O_2$ ($mL \cdot kg^{-0.67} \cdot min^{-1}$)	
	upper fitness group (n=16)	lower fitness group (n=16)	upper fitness group (n=16)	lower fitness group (n=16)
12+	48.5 ± 3.3*	41.8 ± 3.0	161 ± 8.9*	137 ± 9.0
13+	53.0 ± 3.6*	43.7 ± 2.9	182 ± 7.8*	149 ± 8.6
14+	52.5 ± 4.0*	44.5 ± 3.3	188 ± 9.3*	161 ± 14.1
15+	52.1 ± 4.7*	44.1 ± 3.5	197 ± 14.7*	166 ± 13.6

Values are mean ± SD
Level of significance * $p < 0.0001$

Table 3. First principal component for upper fitness group

Age (y)	12+	13+	14+	15+
Eigenvalue	2.20	2.42	2.44	2.18
% variance	36.6	40.3	40.7	36.3
Biceps	0.44	0.01	-0.26	-0.01
Triceps	0.15	-0.23	0.02	0.15
Subscapular	-0.47	0.56	0.57	-0.59
Suprailiac	-0.52	0.56	0.58	-0.52
Thigh	-0.18	-0.17	-0.36	0.28
Calf	0.51	-0.53	-0.38	0.52

At age 12+y in the lower fitness group (table 4), the first principal component accounted for 42% of the total variance, and contrasted the skinfolds of the trunk (subscapular and suprailiac) with those of the extremities (biceps, triceps and calf). Similar configurations occurred at other ages, therefore the dominant component for the low fitness group was also a trunk-extremity contrast.

Since both fitness groups displayed a trunk-extremity contrast in the first principal component, individuals were assigned to sub-groups, using principal component scores, to reflect dominance in trunk and extremity fat patterning. Comparisons were made of peak $\dot{V}O_2$ at each age between these two contrasting fat patterns. The only significant difference occurred at age 15+y in the upper fitness group, where boys with a dominant extremity fat pattern had a higher peak $\dot{V}O_2$ than boys with a dominant trunk fat pattern (205±12 vs 189±8 $mL \cdot kg^{0.67} \cdot min^{-1}$, $p < 0.05$).

Correlations between peak $\dot{V}O_2$ and % TBF (range, r = -0.60 to +0.14) and peak $\dot{V}O_2$ and principal component scores (range, r = -0.20 to +0.46) were generally weak to moderate. The correlation between peak $\dot{V}O_2$ and % TBF at age 12+y in the low fitness group, was the only one found to be significant ($r = -0.60$, $p < 0.05$).

Table 4. First principal component for lower fitness group

Age (y)	12+	13+	14+	15+
Eigenvalue	2.53	2.24	2.46	2.59
% variance	42.1	37.4	41.0	43.2
Biceps	0.50	-0.38	0.03	0.14
Triceps	0.57	0.14	-0.12	-0.06
Subscapular	-0.46	0.55	0.58	0.56
Suprailiac	-0.32	0.50	0.53	0.47
Thigh	-0.29	0.09	-0.35	-0.46
Calf	0.18	-0.53	-0.49	-0.48

Discussion

The first principal component of fat patterning which emerged with contrasting levels of aerobic fitness at each age was a trunk-extremity contrast. Whilst details of the second principal component have not been given, it was found to be an upper-lower configuration in both groups at all ages. In the upper fitness group, the first two components accounted for an average of 66.3% of the total variance, and in the lower fitness group 72.8% of the total variance.

The finding of a trunk-extremity contrast at different levels of aerobic fitness is consistent with results based on chronological age[11,12]. In adolescents, Hattori et al.[2] identified three components of fat patterning; these were trunk-extremity, upper-lower trunk, and medial-lateral abdominal. Allometric analysis[3] subsequently confirmed the trunk as a primary site of fatness during this period.

At age 15+ y in the upper fitness group, boys dominant in extremity patterning had a significantly larger peak $\dot{V}O_2$ than boys dominant in trunk patterning. Although this was not a consistent finding, a similar result has been found in older males[13]. Where this circumstance arises, the advantage will favour those individuals who are active.

In prepubescent boys, greater amounts of centrally distributed fat have been shown to inhibit motor fitness tasks requiring speed, power and co-ordination[14]. At a more elite level, Olympic short-distance runners, jumpers and weight lifters, are seen to have the most centrally distributed fat, while those competing in acquatic events the most peripheral fat[15]; the benefits arising from these fat patterns in these particular events remain ambiguous.

Correlations between % TBF and peak $\dot{V}O_2$ were, in general, negative, and most fell below the level required for significance. Principal component scores had low and non-significant correlations with peak $\dot{V}O_2$. Whilst fat patterning is significantly related to aerobic fitness in adult men, it is considered secondary in importance to fatness[13].

Bearing in mind the genetic influences on both fitness[16] and fat patterning[17], and the distinction between fitness and physical activity, the current analysis has shown that adolescent boys with contrasting levels of fitness exhibited the same primary component of trunk-extremity fat patterning at each age. Limited evidence suggests that boys dominant in extremity fat patterning may have higher levels of aerobic fitness than those dominant in trunk fat patterning. In comparison with the findings in elite young soldiers, it may be that DXA fat is more sensitive in assessing and classifying fat distribution than skinfold thickness. Other confounding factors will include differences in age, level of fitness, and extent of physical activity.

References

1. Nindl, B.C., Friedl, K.E., Marchitelli, L.J., Shippee, R.L., Thomas, C.D. and Patton, J.F. (1996) Regional fat placement in physically fit males and changes with weight loss. *Medicine and Science in Sports and Exercise*, Vol. 28, pp. 786-93.

2. Hattori, K., Becque, M.D., Katch, V.L., Rocchini, A.P., Boileau, R.A., Slaughter, M.H. and Lohman, T.G. (1987) Fat patterning of adolescents. *Annals of Human Biology*, Vol. 14, pp. 23-8.
3. Becque, M.D., Hattori, K., Katch, V.L. and Rocchini A.P. (1992) Fat patterning of adolescents: allometery of fatfolds. *American Journal of Human Biology*, Vol. 4, pp. 521-5.
4. Bell, W. (1993) Body size and shape: a longitudinal investigation of active and sedentary boys. *Journal of Sport Sciences*, Vol. 11, pp. 127-38.
5. Cameron, N. (1984) *The Measurement of Human Growth*, Croom Helm, London.
6. Lohman, T.G. (1989) Assessment of body composition in children. *Pediatric Exercise Sciences*, Vol. 1, pp. 19-30.
7. Rowland, T.W. (1993) Aerobic exercise testing protocols, in *Pediatric Laboratory Exercise Testing*, (ed. T.W. Rowland), Human Kinetics, Champaign, Il, pp. 19-41.
8. Nevill, A.M., Ramsbottom, R. and Williams, C. (1992) Scaling physiological measurements for individuals of different body size. *European Journal of Applied Physiology*, Vol. 65, pp. 110-7.
9. Healy, M.J.R. and Tanner, J.M. (1981) Size and shape in relation to growth and form. *Symposium Zoological Society London*, No. 46, pp. 19-35.
10. Armstrong, N. and Welsman, J.R. (1994) Assessment and interpretation of aerobic fitness in children and adolescents. *Exercise and Sport Sciences Reviews*, Vol. 22, pp. 435-76.
11. Baumgartner, R.N., Roche, A.F., Guo, S., Lohman, T.G., Boileau, R.A. and Slaughter, M.H. (1986) Adipose tissue distribution: the stability of principal components by sex, ethnicity and maturation stage. *Human Biology*, Vol. 58, pp. 719-35.
12. Malina, R.M. and Bouchard, C. (1988) Subcutaneous fat distribution during growth, in *Fat Distribution During Growth and Later Health Outcomes,* (eds. C. Bouchard and F.E. Johnston), A.R. Liss, New York, pp. 63-84.
13. Mueller, W.M., Deutsch, M.I., Malina, R.M., Bailey, D.A. and Mirwald, R.L. (1986) Subcutaneous fat topography: age changes and relationship to cardiovascular fitness in Canadians. *Human Biology*, Vol. 58, pp. 955-73.
14. Malina R.M. and Reyes, M.E.P. (1994) Relative fat distribution: relationship to skeletal maturation, growth status, and motor fitness of boys 8-11 years of age. *American Journal of Human Biology*, Vol. 6, pp. 19-23.
15. Malina, R.M., Mueller, W.H., Bouchard, C., Shoup, R.F. and Lariviere, G. (1982) Fatness and fat patterning among athletes at the Montreal Olympic Games 1976. *Medicine and Science in Sports and Exercise*, Vol. 14, pp. 445-52.
16. Bouchard, C., Dionne, F.T., Simoneau, J-A. and Boulay, M.R. (1992) Genetics of aerobic and anaerobic performances, in *Exercise and Sport Sciences Reviews*, Vol. 20, pp. 27-58.
17. Bouchard, C. and Tremblay, A. Genetics of body composition and fat distribution, in *Fat Distribution During Growth and Later Health Outcomes,* (eds. C. Bouchard and F.E. Johnston), A.R. Liss, New York, pp. 176-88.

AEROBIC FITNESS, PHYSICAL ACTIVITY AND BODY FATNESS IN ADOLESCENTS

Adolescent fitness, fatness and activity

C.A.G. BOREHAM and J.J. STRAIN
Departments of Sports Studies and Human Nutrition, University of Ulster, Newtownabbey, Northern Ireland, UK
J.W.R. TWISK and W. VAN MECHELEN
EMGO Institute, Vrije Universiteit, Amsterdam, The Netherlands
J.M. SAVAGE and G.W. CRAN
Department of Child Health, The Queen's University of Belfast, Belfast, Northern Ireland, UK
Keywords: Adolescents, aerobic fitness, fatness, physical activity

Introduction

In adult populations, aerobic fitness has been shown to be strongly associated with all-cause and coronary heart disease (CHD) mortality[1] and with CHD risk status[2]. Furthermore, the association between aerobic fitness and CHD mortality appears to be independent of a host of potential confounding factors, including physical activity level and body fatness[3]. In children, however, the relationships between fitness and health status are less clear cut. Some authors maintain that any associations are primarily due to the influence of confounding variables, notably body fatness[4,5,6], while others[7] have shown strong relationships between fitness and CHD risk status of children, independent of body fatness. Furthermore, the relationship between habitual physical activity and aerobic fitness remains contentious, with some authors confirming such an association[8,9,10] and others questioning it[2,11].

Given the widespread promotion of physical activity and fitness testing in children [13] and the reported increase in the prevalence of paediatric obesity[14] it is clearly of some importance to clarify how physical fitness, activity and fatness are related in children. The purpose of this study was to examine such relationships in a large, representative sample of adolescent schoolchildren.

Subjects and methods

This study was part of the "Young Hearts Project" - a study of CHD risk factors in a sample of young people from Northern Ireland. The cross-sectional survey was completed in 1990, and a full description of methods is available elsewhere[15].

Children and Exercise XIX. Edited by Neil Armstrong, Brian Kirby and Joanne Welsman.
Published in 1997 by E & FN Spon, 2–6 Boundary Row, London, SE1 8HN.
ISBN 0 419 22100 X.

Briefly, the study population consisted of 1015 schoolchildren (251 boys age 12 y, 258 girls age 12 y, 252 boys age 15 y, and 254 girls age 15 y) selected from 16 schools in a random stratified sample representative of each of the five regional school boards throughout Northern Ireland. For each child, the test protocol involved a medical examination which included anthropometric measurements of height, weight and skinfold thicknesses taken at four sites (biceps, triceps, subscapular and suprailiac). A physical activity score computed for each subject based on self-reported information on everyday activities (for example, method of transportation to and from school, activities during breaks in the school day, and so on). Children were 'cued' with a time-based framework using the structure of a typical school day. Answers were coded according to frequency, intensity and duration, appropriately weighted and the activity score (from 1 to 100) computed[16]. Aerobic fitness was determined by the 20-m endurance shuttle run and scored as the total number of 'laps' completed at volitional exhaustion. Socio-economic status was determined from occupational information provided from the parent or guardian of each child, and was classified according to the Office of Population Census and Surveys[17]. All procedures were approved by the Medical Research Ethical Committee of The Queen's University of Belfast.

Data analyses

Statistical analyses were carried out using SPSSX. For each age and gender group, two analyses were undertaken: (1) univariate linear regression analysis between aerobic fitness and physical activity, and (2) multiple linear regression analysis between fitness as the independent variable and physical activity and body fatness (sum of skinfolds) as dependent variables. These latter analyses were carried out correcting for social class, height and weight.

Results

Table 1 displays the subject characteristics.

Table 1. Subject characteristics

	Boys		Girls	
	12 y	15 y	12 y	15 y
Sample size	251	252	258	254
Age (y)	12.5 (0.3)	15.5 (0.3)	12.5 (0.3)	15.5 (0.3)
Height (cm)	150 (7.9)	169 (7.2)	151 (7.5)	161 (5.9)
Weight (kg)	43 (9.4)	59 (9.4)	44 (9.0)	57 (8.5)
Sum skinfolds (mm)	37.9 (20.6)	32.9 (17.9)	43.6 (15.8)	49.9 (16.4)

Values are mean ± SD

Table 2. Standardized regression coefficients (β) regarding the univariate relationship between aerobic fitness and physical activity in 12 and 15-year-old boys and girls.

	β	p-value
Boys (12 y)	0.24	< 0.001
Girls (12 y)	0.19	0.003
Boys (15 y)	0.26	<0.001
Girls (15 y)	0.24	<0.001

Table 2 shows the standardised regression coefficients (β) for the univariate relationships between aerobic fitness and physical activity in 12 and 15-year-old boys and girls. All groups displayed a significant and consistent relationship.

Table 3 shows the standardised regression coefficients (β) for the multivariate relationships between aerobic fitness on the one hand and physical activity and body fatness on the other. It can be seen that the significant relationships between activity and fitness remain, even after controlling for body fatness, social class, height and weight, and that there is a very strong independent relationship between aerobic fitness and the level of body fatness.

Discussion

The results of this study not only indicate that children's habitual physical activity levels are significantly and positively related to their levels of aerobic fitness, but also that this relationship is independent of body fatness. Previous investigations into these relationships have been inconclusive, with some authors[11,12] claiming no association between habitual physical activity and fitness in children, and others[8,9,10] showing

Table 3. Standardized regression coefficients (β) regarding the relationships between aerobic fitness on the one hand and physical activity and body fatness on the other hand in 12 and 15-year-old boys and girls.*

	Activity	Body fatness
Boys (12 y)	0.23 (p<0.001)	-0.72 (P<0.001)
Girls (12 y)	0.20 (p<0.001)	-0.64 (p<0.001)
Boys (15 y)	0.22 (p<0.001)	-0.55 (p<0.001)
Girls (15 y)	0.15 (p=0.02)	-0.49 (p<0.001)

* Correcting for social class, body height and body weight.

the converse. This discrepancy is likely to be partly methodological in origin, and may depend on the techniques used to record physical activities and aerobic fitness. Furthermore, unlike the situation with adults, where even moderate intensities of habitual activity are associated with greater aerobic power[18], it is likely that more vigorous regular activity is necessary in children to induce an improvement in aerobic fitness[19,20].

The strong and independent negative association displayed between aerobic fitness and body fatness (table 3) is in keeping with previous reports[5,21]. Thus, at the very least, aerobic fitness and fatness seen to be inextricably linked both with each other and with the health status of children. Furthermore, the reported associations between habitual physical activity and fitness and between activity and fatness[22] particularly in very young children[23] point strongly to the existence of a fitness, fatness and activity triad, or what Gutin and colleagues[21] have termed, the "fit kid syndrome".

In conclusion, the results of the present analysis indicate that in adolescent schoolchildren, physical activity and aerobic fitness are related independently, and that strong relationships exist between fitness and body fatness in this population.

Bearing in mind the complexity of these relationships, and recent evidence that (a) children are not as active as they should be[24] and are becoming fatter[14], and (b) such problems in childhood and adolescence may lead to severe adult health consequences[25,26], it seems prudent to stress primary prevention strategies in childhood aimed at controlling obesity and promoting aerobic fitness. Such strategies should include regular testing of fatness and fitness as well as the promotion of habitual, vigorous physical activity.

Acknowledgments

This study was supported by the Northern Ireland Chest, Heart and Stroke Association.

References

1. Blair, S.N., Kohl, H.W., Paffenbarger, R.S., Clark, D.G., Cooper, K.H. and Gibbons, L.W. (1989) Physical fitness and all-cause mortality. A prospective study of healthy men and women. *Journal of the American Medical Association,* Vol. 262, pp. 2395-401.
2. Eaton, C.B., Lapane, K.L., Garber, C.E., Assaf, A.R., Lasater, T.M. and Carleton, R. A. (1995) Physical activity, physical fitness and coronary heart disease risk factors. *Medicine and Science in Sports and Exercise,* Vol. 27, pp. 340-6.
3. Sandvik, L., Erikssen, J., Thaulow, E., Erikssen, G., Mundal, R. and Rodahl, K. (1993) Physical fitness as a predictor of mortality among healthy, middle-aged Norwegian men. *New England Journal of Medicine,* Vol. 328, pp. 533-7.

4. Gutin, B., Basch, C., Shea, S., Contento, I., DeLozier, M., Rips, J., Irigoyen, M. and Zybert, P. (1990) Blood pressure, fitness and fatness in 5- and 6-year old children. *Journal of the American Medical Association,* Vol. 264, pp. 1123-7.
5. Hager, R.L., Tucker, L.A. and Seljaas, G.T. (1995) Aerobic fitness, blood lipids and body fat in children. *American Journal of Public Health,* Vol. 85, pp. 1702-6.
6. Hansen, H.S., Hyldebrandt, M., Froberg, K. and Nielsen, J.R. (1990) Blood pressure and physical fitness in a population of children - the Odense schoolchildren study. *Journal of Human Hypertension,* Vol. 4, pp. 615-20.
7. Hoffman, A. and Walter, H.J. (1989) The association between physical fitness and cardiovascular disease risk factors in children in a five-year follow-up study. *International Journal of Epidemiology,* Vol. 18, pp. 830-5.
8. Boreham, C.A.G., Twisk, J., Savage, J.M., Cran, G.W. and Strain, J.J. (in press) Physical activity, sports participation and coronary heart disease risk factors in adolescents. *Medicine and Science in Sports and Exercise.*
9. Dennison, B.A., Straus, J. H., Mellits, E.D. and Charney, E. (1988) Childhood physical fitness tests: predictor of adult physical activity levels? *Pediatrics,* Vol. 82, pp. 324-30.
10. Sallis, J.F., Patterson, T.L., Buono, M.J. and Nader, P.R. (1988) Relation of cardiovascular disease risk factors in children and adults. *American Journal of Epidemiology,* Vol. 127, pp. 933-41.
11. Andersen, L.B. (1994) Changes in physical activity are not reflected in changes in fitness during late adolescence: a 2 year follow-up study. *Journal of Sports Medicine and Physical Fitness,* Vol. 34, pp. 390-7.
12. Armstrong, N., Williams, J., Balding, J., Gentle, P. and Kirby, B (1991) Cardiopulmonary fitness, physical activity patterns and related coronary risk factors variables in 11 to 16 year olds. *Pediatric Exercise Science,* Vol. 3, pp. 219-28.
13. Kemper, H.C.G. and van Mechelen, W. (1996) Physical fitness testing of children: a European perspective. *Pediatric Exercise Science,* Vol. 8, pp. 201-14.
14. Troiano, R.P., Flegal, K.M., Kuczmarski, R.J., Cambell, S.M. and Johnson, C.L. (1995) Overweight prevalence and trends for children and adolescents - The National Health and Nutrition Examination Surveys, 1963 to 1991. *Archives of Pediatric and Adolescent Medicine,* Vol. 149, pp. 1085-91.
15. Boreham, C.A.G., Savage, J.J., Primrose, D., Cran, G.W. and Strain, J.J. (1993) Coronary risk factors in schoolchildren. *Archives of Disease in Childhood,* Vol. 68, pp. 182-6.
16. Riddoch, C., Savage, J.M., Murphy, N., Cran, G.W. and Boreham, C.A.G. (1991) Long term health implications of fitness and physical activity patterns. *Archives of Disease in Childhood,* Vol. 66, pp. 1426-33.
17. Office of Population Censuses and Surveys. (1990) *A Publication of the Government Statistical Service Standard Occupational Classification.* Vols. 1, 2, 3.

18. Marrugat, J., Elousa, R., Covas, M-I., Molina, L. and Rubies-Prat, J. (1996) Amount and intensity of physical activity, physical fitness and serum lipids in men. *American Journal of Epidemiology,* Vol. 143, pp. 562-9.
19. Hansen, H.S., Froberg, K., Hylderandt, N. and Nielsen, J.R. (1991) A controlled study of eight months of physical training and reduction of blood pressure in children: the Odense schoolchildren study. *British Medical Journal,* Vol. 303, pp. 682-5.
20. Rowland, T.W. (1985) Aerobic response to endurance training in prepubescent children: a critical analysis. *Medicine and Science in Sports and Exercise,* Vol. 17, pp. 493-7.
21. Gutin, B., Islam, S., Manos, T., Cucuzzo, N., Smith, C. and Stachura, M.E. (1994) Relation of percentage of body fat and maximal aerobic capacity to risk factors for atherosclerosis and diabetes in black and white seven to eleven-year old children. *Journal of Pediatrics,* Vol. 125, pp. 847-52.
22. Fontvieille, A.M., Kriska, A. and Ravussin, E. (1993) Decreased physical activity in Pima Indian compared with Caucasian children. *International Journal of Obesity,* Vol. 17, pp. 445-52.
23. Moore, L.L., Nguyen, U.D.T., Rothman, K.J., Cupples, L.A. and Ellison, R.C. (1995) Pre school physical activity level and change in body fatness in young children. *American Journal of Epidemiology,* Vol. 142, pp. 982-8.
24. Sleap, M. and Warburton, P. (1996) Physical activity levels of 5-11 year-old children in England: cumulative evidence from three direct observational studies. *International Journal of Sports Medicine,* Vol. 17, pp. 248-53.
25. Lauer, R.M., Lee, J. and Clarke, W. R. (1988) Factors affecting the relationship between childhood and adult cholesterol levels: the Muscatine Study. *Pediatrics.* Vol. 82, pp. 309-18.
26. Must, A., Jacques, P.F., Dallal, G.E., Bajema, C.J. and Dietz, W.H. (1992) Long-term morbidity and mortality of overweight adolescents. A follow-up of the Harvard Growth Study of 1922 to 1935. *New England Journal of Medicine,* Vol. 327, pp. 1350-5.

A BIOPSYCHOSOCIAL APPROACH TO FAMILY-BASED MANAGEMENT OF OBESE CHILDREN

A biopsychosocial approach to obesity

G. BILTZ, J. SIEGAL, T. DAVIS, K. PFAFFINGER and T. RONDEAU-AMBROSE
Department of Pediatrics, Mental Health and Center for Health Promotion
HealthPartners Inc., Minneapolis, Minnesota, USA
Keywords: BMI trend, cardiorespiratory fitness, family-system, interdisciplinary team, obesity

Introduction

Obesity in children and adolescents is an increasing problem in many countries especially in the United States[1]. Obesity in youth is a multifactorial problem with significant medical concerns[2] and a high rate of recidivism[3].

The purpose of this study was to evaluate the impact of an interdisciplinary team approach to obesity management in a managed care setting. Our team applied a biopsychosocial approach that emphasized a process for lifestyle change rather than a weight loss programme. Patients and their families were helped to adapt principles of energy balance, behavioral change and family communications to their individual situations and resources. It was hypothesized that providing an intervention focused on the patient within the family system could improve individual patient fitness level, weight trend, and dietary balance[4], and also contribute to positive changes in psychosocial measures of self-perception and family functioning. This study specifically addressed the question: can a biopsychosocial model[5] for obesity management be effective within the time and resource constraints of both the medical practice setting and the family environment?

Methods

The study population was referred to the Center for Exercise and Nutrition Therapy (CENT) clinic from a managed care population of over 250,000. Criterion for referral was the diagnosis of problematic obesity by the primary physician. This referral selection process resulted in a study population with an average BMI at initial

Children and Exercise XIX. Edited by Neil Armstrong, Brian Kirby and Joanne Welsman.
Published in 1997 by E & FN Spon, 2–6 Boundary Row, London, SE1 8HN.
ISBN 0 419 22100 X.

encounter of 31.95 kg·m^{-2}, which was 179% of the BMI at the 50th percentile adjusted for age and sex. The average z score for BMI at the initial encounter was 5.6.

Inclusion criteria for the study was a newly referred patient 8-18 years old as of October 1, 1995. Eight is the minimum standardized age for the Harter's Self-Perception Scales[6]. Decision to enter the study was made at the initial visit. Families that entered completed the Family Environment Scale (FES)[7] in addition to CENT eating and activity assessments. Consecutive participants were included until twenty-five subjects completed a minimum of four visits in 6 mo. Subjects with less than four visits in 6 mo were excluded due to insufficient contact time.

The age and adiposity characteristics of the study population are seen in table 1.

The CENT clinic team consisted of a paediatrician, nutritionist, and a health psychologist. Clinic was held every Monday with schedules that permitted two new patient evaluations per day and eight follow-up visits during the day per provider.

The initial visit consisted of a 30 min group evaluation with the team. This was followed by a 40 min individual session with each provider that day for a total of 150 min. Follow-up visits were 30 min with each provider sequentially. The minimum time between clinic visits was 1 mo due to scheduling constraints.

The team had evolved a set of standard questionnaires and handouts compiled from their respective literature. They also agreed on theoretical models for behavioral change[5,8]. Standard principles emphasized balancing eating and activity habits, becoming more physically fit rather than focusing on weight loss, and feeling in control. The message was tailored to patient and family context and function. The implementation of lifestyle change was the responsibility of the patient and family. This was shaped by feedback on weight trend, skinfolds, treadmill walk performance, eating habits, and family problem solving.

Measures

At each visit the study participant's height and weight were measured by the same nurse using a standard medical office scale (Health-O-Meter) and a stadiometer (model S 100 Ayrton Corp). Skinfold calipers (Harpenden British Indicators) were used to measure triceps and subscapular skinfolds. All measures were performed by the same paediatrician using standard techniques.

The Harter's Self-Perception Scale for Children and Adolescents was obtained at the initial and final visits. The Child's Scale was used for ages 8-13 y and the Adolescent's Scale for ages 14-18 y. The participants reported self-perceptions in specific domains such as scholastic competence, social acceptance, physical appearance, etc., as well as global self-worth.

The Family Environment Scale (FES) was also obtained at the initial and final visits as a measure of the quality of family functioning. The FES measures the social environment of families along three dimensions: nature of interpersonal relationships, directions of goal orientation and organizational characteristics of family. Parents were included at all visits.

A 3d prospective food record was used primarily to assess the reported fat and fibre content in the participant's diet. Records were mailed to prospective participants before the initial visit and again before the last visit in the study.

Table 1. Study population

	n	Age (y)	BMI ($kg \cdot m^{-2}$)	Triceps sf (mm)	Subscapular sf (mm)
Female	7	11.0 ± 2.2 (8-15)	29.3 ± 5.4	28.8 ± 6.4	29.5 ± 9.0
Male	16	11.8 ± 2.9 (8-15)	33.2 ± 6.55	34.6 ± 8.3	41.6 ± 11.4
All	23	11.5 ± 2.7 (8-15)	31.9 ± 6.36	32.8 ± 8.1	37.9 ± 12.0

Values are mean ± SD (range)

Cardiorespiratory fitness was assessed using a modified Balke protocol for treadmill walking (Quinton Q-50). The protocol consisted of a 3 min warm-up at 2.5% grade followed by five 1.5 min stages with 2.5% grade increase per stage. After the gradual warm up phase in stage one, a speed of either 4 $km \cdot h^{-1}$ or 3 $miles \cdot h^{-1}$ was selected depending on age and observed exercise response in stage one. Retest at the same speed occurred at least once during the study. Cardiorespiratory fitness was defined by heart rate response.

Table 2. Clinical outcomes

	Pre-Study	Post-Study	D Score		Pre-Study	Post-Study	D Score
BMI ($kg \cdot m^{-2}$)	31.9	31.8	-0.1	Cohesion FES	46.1	50.3	+4.2
Tricep (mm)	32.85	31.8	-1.05	Expression FES	54.1	58.2**	+4.1**
Subscap (mm)	37.93	34.50	-3.43*	Conflict FES	50.3	49.9	-0.4
Fat (%) diet	31%	30%	-1%	Recreation FES	49.6	54.3*	+4.7*
Fibre (g)	9.49	14.17*	+4.68*	Organized FES	48.5	46.8	+1.7
Resting bpm	79.13	79.09	-0.04	Control FES	51	52.05	+1.05
Stage I bpm	122.4	113.5*	-8.9*	Social Harter	2.67	2.87	+0.2
Stage IV bpm	147.5	136.1*	-11.4*	Physical Harter	2.19	2.5*	+0.31*
Stage VI bpm	162.4	150.9*	-11.5*	Athletic Harter	2.69	2.76	+0.07
Recovery bpm	104.4	94.4*	-10.0*	Global Harter	2.95	3.2*	+.25*

Level of significance * $p < 0.05$, ** $p < 0.10$

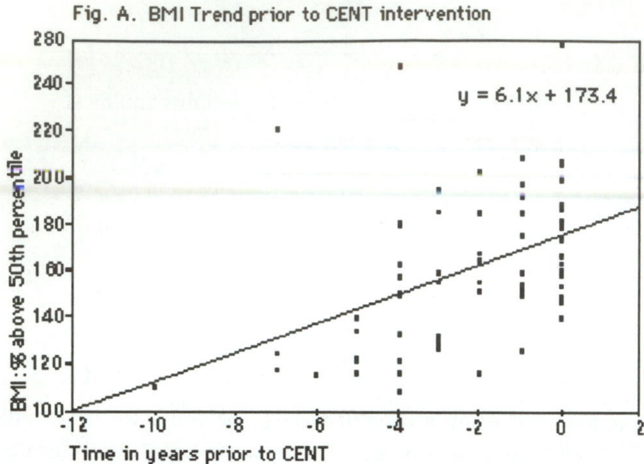

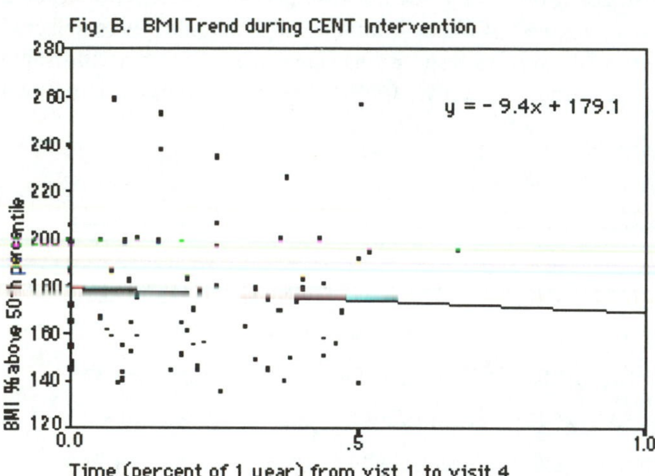

Pulse was obtained using a Polar Favor (Polar Electro Inc.) heart monitor in an initial resting position (in chair with feet up), standing on the treadmill at start, at the end of all six stages and 2 min post-exercise in the resting position.

Results

An overview of clinical outcomes is presented in table 2. Significance of pre-post results was determined by two-tailed t tests.

The mean BMI stabilized during the study period. The impact of this stabilization is more dramatic when seen in the context of the participants pre-study BMI trend.

Participants pre-study heights and weights were obtained from their medical records and used to project a BMI trend line prior to CENT intervention (fig A). The BMI is expressed as a percent of the 50th percentile adjusted for age and sex. The slope of BMI trend (regression line) changed from +6.1 pre-study (fig A) to -9.4 post-study (fig B).

As a comparison group we used a cohort of previously referred patients who were only seen once in our clinic and dropped out. There were no statistical differences between the study group and this cohort in terms of initial BMI, gender composition, or average age. Available records were reviewed for subsequent height and weight data to calculate BMI. The BMI trend for that cohort is described by the regression line $y = 5.22x + 171.1$. The slope of 5.22 is very similar to the pre-intervention BMI trend of the study population.

Significant pre-post study differences were seen in subscapular skinfold, fibre content of diet, family orientation toward planned recreational activity, self-perception of physical appearance and global self worth.

The post-study heart rate during modified Balke treadmill walk was lower at all six stages. The mean decrease ranged from 8-11 beats·min^{-1} and was statistically significant. (Stage I, $t(22) = 5.29$, $p <0.01$; Stage II, $t(22) = 5.02$, $p <0.01$; Stage III, $t(22) = 6.09$, $p <0.01$; Stage IV, $t(22) = 5.69$, $p <0.01$; Stage V, $t(21) = 5.74$, $p <0.01$; Stage VI, $t(18) = 4.38$, $p <0.01$; Recovery, $t(21) = 4.06$, $p <0.01$). The mean resting heart rate prior to testing was 79.1 for pre- and post-study walks.

During the study 14 children dropped out. A comparison between participants and dropouts on both demographic and baseline measures showed only one significant difference: the CENT study group felt less popular than dropouts.

Discussion

In traditional obesity studies independent variables such as caloric intake and quantity of exercise are usually controlled by the study specifications. Unfortunately, specified behaviors during the study typically fail to generalize beyond it. For the obese youth controlling eating and activity habits is the essential behavioral problem.

The dramatic change in the slope of BMI trend suggests successful intervention. Our goal was weight stabilization through lifestyle change, not weight loss per se. This philosophy of balance and control is consistent with current literature[9].

Significant improvement in fibre content from 9 to 14 g indicates that participants were eating more fruits, vegetables, and whole grains. Fat content in the diet was reportedly already at the target level of 30%. This is likely an under reporting of true dietary fat intake.

Improvements in self-perception (physical appearance and global self-worth) and family participation in recreational activity support our hypothesis that individual outcomes can be achieved through family-based changes. Families were able to incorporate activity principles and goals into specific actions with sufficient consistency to achieve both physiologic and psychosocial changes.

The significant lowering of heart rate throughout the treadmill walk represent an improvement in cardiorespiratory capacity. Although we have no direct measure of daily exercise, the results are consistent with increased activity. The mean resting heart rate pre-study and post-study was the same. Yet, the post-study heart rate at all six stages was consistently lower by 8-11 beats·min^{-1}. We believe the observed pulse change was not just a practice effect, but represents a true change in exercise capacity.

Conclusion

This study shows that our team approach to the obese child within the context and function of the family was effective without controlling the independent variables. This was accomplished with relatively infrequent visits over 6 mo. Individualized lifestyle changes based on principles of energy balance, behavioral change, and family communication can achieve and sustain both physiologic and psychosocial improvements.

References

1. Gortmaker, S.L., Dietz, W.H., Sobel, A.M. and Wehler, C.A. (1987) Increasing pediatric obesity in the United States. *American Journal of Diseases in Children*, Vol. 141, pp. 535-40.
2. Rosenbaum, M. and Liebel, R.L. (1989) Obesity in childhood. *Pediatrics in Review*, Vol. 11, pp. 43-55.
3. Brownell, K.D. and Wadden, T.A. (1992) Etiology and treatment of obesity: Understanding a serious, prevalent and refractory disorder. *Journal of Consulting and Clinical Psychology*, Vol. 60, pp. 505-19.
4. Hecker, L., Martin, D. and Martin, M. (1986) Family factors in childhood obesity. *American Journal of Family Therapy*, Vol. 14, pp. 247-53.
5. Engel, G.L. (1977) The need for a new medical model: A challenge for biomedicine. *Science*, Vol. 196, pp. 129-35.
6. Harter, S. (1988) *Issues in the Assessment of the Self-concept of Children and Adolescents, in Childhood Assessment: Through the Eyes of a Child.* (ed. A. LaGreca), Allyn and Bacon, New York, pp. 292-325.
7. Halvorsen, J.G. (1991) Self-report family assessment instruments: An evaluative review. *Family Practice Research Journal*, Vol. 11, pp. 21-55.
8. Prochaska, J.O., DiClemente, C.C. and Norcross, J.C. (1992) In search of how people change. *American Psychologist*, Vol. 47, pp. 1102-14.
9. Satter, E.M. (1996) Internal regulation and the evolution of normal growth as the basis for prevention of obesity in children. *Journal of the American Dietetic Association*, Vol. 96, pp. 860-4.

SECULAR TREND CHANGES IN HUNGARIAN SCHOOLBOYS

Secular changes in boys

A. FARKAS and R. FRENKL
Department of Health Science and Sport Medicine, Hungarian University of Physical Education, Budapest, Hungary

Keywords: Height, metric index, plastic index, secular changes, weight

Introduction

The secular trend as a phenomenon means all the measurable and registrable changes by which we can control the existence and evidence of human biological regularity in subsequent generations. It manifests itself in different aspects of the development of the human organism. For example, positive change/increase in the parameters of the body parts and the physique. In newborns and in later developmental stages, the earlier occurrence of bodily, hormonal and biochemical maturation of the organism, the greater body height of children and teenagers at the same age, the higher final stature of younger generations, and changes of the proportions of the body, etc. These changes are well-known and well-demonstrated[1-10]. On the basis of reports about the secular trend changes some differences in the essence and the rate of the manifestation can be seen in different societies. Since the root of the secular trend changes originated also from the social and economic development of populations it seems natural to accept the evidence of the special characteristics in magnitude and in velocity, nevertheless the direction of these changes is similar.

In some of our previous studies we have reported the secular changes in young adults in Hungary[8], and in students applying for admission to the Hungarian University of Physical Education[9,10].

In the present study we report on the secular trend changes registered in the school-age boys, aged between 7 to 14 years, formerly called the elementary school period.

Children and Exercise XIX. Edited by Neil Armstrong, Brian Kirby and Joanne Welsman.
Published in 1997 by E & FN Spon, 2–6 Boundary Row, London, SE1 8HN.
ISBN 0 419 22100 X.

Table 1. The number and the distribution of the subjects

Calendar age (y)	1976 (1.5%)	1983 (2.5%)	1991 (4%)		Σ
6.51- 7.50	228	391	469		1088
7.51- 8.50	268	337	404		1009
8.51- 9.50	312	293	352		957
9.51-10.50	388	283	339		1010
10.51-11.50	316	283	340		939
11.51-12.50	277	290	348		915
12.51-13.50	278	286	343		907
13.51-14.50	241	279	335		855
Σ	2308	2442	2930	ΣΣ	7680

Subjects

Subjects were healthy schoolboys attending elementary schools from 11 districts of the Hungarian capital Budapest, and the schools were randomly chosen. Table 1 describes the number of subjects in the age-groups at each time of data collection with a summary in the last column and on the bottom line.

Methods

We took body measurements three times over a 15 y period in 1976, in 1983 and in 1991, in altogether 7680 boys. The pecentage values in the brackets designate the number of boys representing their age groups of the population measured at each time of the cross-sectional study.

Body measurements were taken according to the specifications of the International Biological Program[11] and we calculated Conrad's growth type indices[12]. Conrad characterized the body build from two aspects and he called it growth type. The metric index describes the body proportions and the linearity while the plastic index characterizes the skeleto-muscular developmental level of individuals. For calculating the metric index we took three measurements: the chest width, chest depth and the stature. The diameters of the chest corrected by the linear function of stature would be valid to describe the body build between the extremes of picnomorphic and leptomorphic nature. The value of the metric index varies from negative to positive domain where in the positive range the more picnomorphic physique is embraced and the negative range contains the more leptomorphic body constitution. The transitional or so called metromorphic feature belongs to the slightly negative range.

The equation used for calculating the metric index value for the boys:

MIX = 0.16 (chest depth - 0.20 stature + 0.80 chest width - 2.61)

The plastic index describing the developmental level of the musculo-skeletal system is calculated from three measurements:

PLX = shoulder width + forearm circumference + hand circumference

With the two indices the growth type could be demonstrated in a right angle coordinate system for the individuals and also for the population with a characteristic age trend.

The means and standard deviations for each data collection were analyzed by ANOVA then with F-test using the 5% level of significance. The statistical significances are designated in the tables but the interpretation of the results follows anthropometric practical aspects, as well.

Results and conclusions

Stature is one of the most frequently measured morphological traits of the secular trend changes (table 2). In our present study we compared the age differences of the stature in the subsequent samples and significant differences ($p < 0.05$) were found in the age dependent mean values at the time of the first (1976) and the third (1991) data collection. But there was no significant difference ($p > 0.05$) between the means of the subsequent measurements (1976-1983 and 1983-1991),

Table 2. Stature at the time of each data collection

Age (y)	Stature(cm) 1976	1983	1991
7	123.29 ± 4.49	124.67 ± 5.42	125.51 ± 5.46
8	128.46 ± 5.46	128.49 ± 5.28	131.01 ± 6.08
9	133.67 ± 5.72	134.16 ± 5.51	135.53 ± 5.72
10	138.94 ± 5.57	139.02 ± 6.01	139.97 ± 6.18
11	144.45 ± 6.81	144.78 ± 6.20	145.43 ± 6.42
12	149.20 ± 6.43	150.00 ± 7.24	150.33 ± 7.55
13	156.96 ± 6.78	156.78 ± 7.76	157.69 ± 7.82
14	163.08 ± 6.14	163.46 ± 8.46	164.21 ± 7.06

Values are mean ± SD
Significant differences ($p < 0.05$) at all ages between 1976 and 1991

Table 3. Body weight at the time of each data collection

Age (y)	Body weight (kg) 1976	1983	1991
7	23.99 ± 2.73	23.71 ± 3.39	23.99 ± 4.05
8	26.88 ± 4.24	26.89 ± 4.18	28.06 ± 5.26*
9	29.14 ± 4.80	30.68 ± 5.52	30.94 ± 6.69*
10	32.47 ± 4.26	33.30 ± 3.09	33.76 ± 5.27*
11	36.45 ± 6.30	37.02 ± 6.88	36.80 ± 8.18
12	41.15 ± 7.02	41.32 ± 8.56	41.44 ± 10.04
13	44.83 ± 7.92	46.35 ± 10.19	46.73 ± 10.47*
14	51.44 ± 7.44	53.37 ± 9.63	53.33 ± 11.66*

Values are mean ± SD
*Significant differences ($p < 0.05$) between 1976 and 1991

though the values were slightly increasing. Besides, as shown by the standard deviations, the samples of the boys became more heterogeneous with time.

The secular changes of the stature could be characterised by a linearly increasing trend.

The means of the body weight (table 3) at the age-groups of 7, 11 and 12 y were not signficantly different ($p > 0.05$) at the time of the three observations. In the other age-groups the mean values were significantly ($p < 0.05$) higher in 1991 than in the middle of the 1970s. The standard deviations were also higher in the subsequent investigations and they also were increasing by age. With these results the phenomenon of the increasing secular trend changes of body weight in children and in prepubertals could be confirmed.

In the row of the metric index mean values (table 4) a "positive" trend of moving toward a more linear body build - a higher gracility - can be observed. This trend could be proved by age and by the subsequent observations, too. The increasing gracility is the result of the inevitable developmental changes of the body proportions during adolescence. There were no relevant changes in the standard deviations.

The means of the developmental level of the skeleto-muscular system described by the plastic index (table 5) were not significantly different ($p > 0.05$) at different age-groups. By the evidence of the slightly but significantly ($p < 0.05$) correlated stature and plastic index[14] further differences between the means may have been expected.

The slightly increasing gracility and the unchanged/constant skeleto-muscular developmental level is a disadvantageous consequence of the secular trend changes that is not only a characteristic of the Hungarian, Budapest children.

Table 4. The metric index at the time of each data collection

Age (y)	1976	1983	1991	p
7	-0.88 ± 0.24	-0.89 ± 0.21	-0.99 ± 0.26	<0.05
8	-0.97 ± 0.28	-0.98 ± 0.25	-1.08 ± 0.26	<0.05
9	-1.00 ± 0.24	-1.02 ± 0.30	-1.13 ± 0.30	<0.05
10	-1.11 ± 0.29	-1.14 ± 0.31	-1.21 ± 0.33	<0.05
11	-1.13 ± 0.30	-1.15 ± 0.26	-1.22 ± 0.29	<0.05
12	-1.13 ± 0.29	-1.17 ± 0.20	-1.29 ± 0.26	<0.05
13	-1.20 ± 0.30	-1.21 ± 0.30	-1.31 ± 0.30	<0.05
14	-1.23 ± 0.25	-1.25 ± 0.28	-1.35 ± 0.34	<0.05
p	<0.05	<0.05	<0.05	

Values are mean ± SD

Table 5. The plastic index at the time of each data collection

Age (y)	1976	1983	1991
7	59.14 ± 2.46	59.77 ± 2.79	59.62 ± 3.51
8	61.96 ± 3.00	62.44 ± 3.23	62.42 ± 3.62
9	63.80 ± 3.19	64.13 ± 3.44	63.93 ± 3.94
10	66.18 ± 3.32	66.54 ± 3.52	65.99 ± 3.35
11	68.19 ± 3.69	68.91 ± 3.78	67.91 ± 3.23
12	70.69 ± 3.75	71.02 ± 3.31	70.38 ± 3.51
13	73.97 ± 3.21	74.16 ± 3.92	73.87 ± 3.34
14	77.90 ± 3.65	78.31 ± 3.48	78.07 ± 3.20

Values are mean ± SD
No significant differences ($p > 0.05$) between means at any age

Summarizing our results we can state that:

- In the metric index values no peak velocity of the changes could be found, as could be seen in the case of height and body weight. By the means of the metric index in the 7 to 14-year-old boys the gracility had been linearly increasing - the absolute value decreasing in the negative domain - that would be followed by changes toward the less negative range[14], so the body proportions of the boys by the age of 18 y would be similar to that of the 7- year-old boys.
- The row of metric index values show us the hereditary traits of the universally changing body proportions. The leptomorphic modification of the body build during adolescence is one of these enforcing tendencies in most of the children in spite of the possible individual variability.

- By the (absolute) values of the plastic index slower and faster developmental periods could be distinguished. In our sample it shows an accelerating development by age so the magnitude of the changes are increasing up to 14 years of age.
- The tendency of secular trend changes in body build described on one hand by the metric index and on the other hand by the apparently constant age values of the plastic index - as the indicator of the skeleto-muscular system - there could be cause for anxiety about the physical capability of future generations. Does it really indicate such an alarming situation?

Our last personal information about the recent unpublished results of a Budapest study: no further secular changes could be observed in body dimensions. The causes could be many-sided containing the temporary measurable effects of the disadvantageous changes as a consequence of the transitional political and economic situation from the beginning of the 1990s. It could be a faulty evaluation of the secular trend changes if we speculate the end of the development of our population. We believe that future human biological studies will show us that this period is only a disadvantageous period of our modern history and a transitional one in our long-term future.

References

1. Van Wieringen, J.C. (1978) Secular growth changes, in *Human Growth 2: Postnatal Growth*, (eds. F. Faulkner, J.M. Tanner), New York, Plenum Press, pp.445-73.
2. Malina, R.M. (1978) Secular changes in growth, maturation and physical performance, *Exercise and Sport Sciences Reviews,* Vol. 6, pp. 203-55.
3. Malina, R.M. (1979) Secular changes in size and maturity: causes and effects, in *Secular Trends in Human Growth, Maturation and Development,* (ed. A.F. Roche), Monographs of the Society for Research in Child Development, Vol. 44(3-4), pp. 59-102.
4. Wolanski, N. (1978) Secular trend in man: evidence and factors. *Collegium Anthropologicum,* Vol. 2, pp.69-86.
5. Wolanski, N. and Siniarska, A. (1983) Environment and secular changes in modern man, *Ecology of Disease*, Vol. 2, pp.107-16.
6. Wolanski, N. (1984) Secular trend in man: bibliography, (Special issue on the occasion of the 4th Congress of the European Anthropological Association, Rome-Florence, September 2-8).
7. Prokopec, M. (1984) Secular trends in body size and proportions and their biological meaning, in *Secular Trend* (Studies in human ecology 6), (eds. N. Wolanski, and M. Szemik), Polish Scientific Publishers, pp. 37-61.
8. Gyenis, Gy. and Till, G. (1986) Secular changes of body measurements in Hungarian University students between 1976-1985. *Anthropológiai Közlemények,* Vol. 30, pp. 147-50.

9. Mohácsi, J., Mészáros, J., Sabir, A.R., Farkas, A., Szmodis, I. and Frenkl, R. (1989/90) Study on the secular trend among the male applicants to the Univeristy of Physical Education, Budapest, *Anthropológiai Közlemények*, Vol. 32, pp. 175-7.
10. Farkas, A., Mészáros, J. and Mohácsi, J. (1991) A study on the secular trend in young adults, *Anthropológiai Közlemények,* Vol. 33, pp. 171-5.
11. Weiner, J.E.S. and Lourie, J.A. (eds) (1969) *Human Biology. A Guide to Field Methods,* IBP Handbook, No. 9, Blackwell, Oxford.
12. Conrad, K. (1963) *Der Konstitutionstypus*, *2 Aufl,* Springer, Berlin.
13. Mészáros, J. and Mohácsi, J. (1983) *A Biológiai Fejlettség Meghatározása és a Felnõttkori Termet Elõrejelzése a Városi Fiatalok Fejlõdésmenete Alapján* (The determination of the biological developmental level and the prediction of the adult height by the development of the urban children), Candidate Thesis, MTA, Budapest.

PHYSICAL CHARACTERISTICS AND FITNESS MEASUREMENTS OF INTELLECTUALLY IMPAIRED BOYS

Measurements of intellectually impaired boys

A. BARABÁS
Department of Biomechanics, Hungarian University of Physical Education, Budapest, Hungary
J. BUDAY
Department of Pathophysiology, Bárczi G, College of Special Education, Budapest, Hungary

Keywords: Eurofit, intellectual impairment, physical characteristics, physical fitness

Introduction

There are several studies dealing with determining biological development of youth. In Hungary the Hungarian National Growth Study gave us comprehensive data on biological development and physical fitness of Hungarian children[1]. The representation of this growth study was 1.5% of the whole population. The investigated sample consists of healthy but not selected children.

There are some studies on mentally handicapped people to investigate their biological development and fitness[2]. Some of the growth characteristics of mentally disabled children were clarified by several cross-sectional studies[3,4,5,6]. There are no longitudinal studies in this field.

Adults with mental disability are employed as physical workers, and the work is very important for the quality of their life. Therefore, physical fitness and suitable physique for this kind of work are important issues for them[7]. In addition, physical training has a positive effect on growth and development[8].

The Homok Growth Study of institutionalised children has been in place for more than 20 y.

There are several difficulties in the investigation of physical performance of mentally handicapped children, first of all in understanding the tasks. These investigations need special tools and there are always different testing problems. These kind of investigations have to be carried out in very safe surroundings. The investigators require patience and usually work under medical direction.

The aim of this paper is to present selected results from a mixed-longitudinal growth study of mentally disabled boys in relation to their physical performance abilities.

Children and Exercise XIX. Edited by Neil Armstrong, Brian Kirby and Joanne Welsman.
Published in 1997 by E & FN Spon, 2–6 Boundary Row, London, SE1 8HN.
ISBN 0 419 22100 X.

Methods

During the last 5 y in addition to collecting biological development data from mentally handicapped boys we have carried out a mixed longitudinal investigation on physical performance abilities. Subjects were boys, aged 9 to 18 y, with mild mental disability.

The number of subjects varied each year in the range 100-200. Two hundred and fifty four boys were investigated between 1992-1996. In this paper we report the results of those children who were examined at least 3 times. Seventy nine to 46 boys participated in performance tests but the number participating in each different test depends on different, special tasks.

A detailed anthropometrical programme has been carried out[9]. Body height and weight are reported here.

To assess the physical fitness of boys the Eurofit test battery was used[10]. These tests are simple and understandable. There were difficulties with the balance and flexed arm hang tests, mainly because the children were afraid to perform them. Therefore we had to select the following tests from the Eurofit test battery: hand grip strength, standing broad jump, sit-ups, 20 m shuttle run, 10 x 5 m run, and sit and reach flexibility test.

Results and discussion

Table 1 illustrates the body height and weight of the investigated sample. Analysis of body height and body weight (table 1) reveals that the mentally handicapped children are shorter and lighter than national reference mean values. Values of the standard deviations in anthropometrical measurements are much higher than the standard deviations of national reference values because of the specialities of the examined sample. The aetiologic factors are different, these groups are not homogenous from a biological point of view.

The height and weight mean values are around 25% in the reference scale from the Hungarian National Growth Study[1].

Three of the Eurofit tests are comparable with the 1980 Hungarian reference values, based on the Hungarian National Growth Study. These are: hand grip strength, standing broad jump and sit-ups [tables 2,3,4].

Performances in the hand grip (right hand) strength test (kp) are less than the 10th percentile of national reference values except 18-year-old boys whose performance is around 25%. P10 are in corresponding age-groups: 12, 14, 17, 20, 22, 26, 32, 37, 40, 41. Standard deviation values of 1980s national cross-sectional study are: 4.12, 4.54, 4.68, 5.24, 6.30, 7.58, 7.89, 7.90, 8.21, 8.09.

The mean performance values of handicapped children in the standing broad jump test (cm) are remarkable poor. The results in the standing broad jump test are less than the 3rd percentile for 9-13-year-old boys (P3 are: 90, 100, 110, 120, 125) and around the 10th percentile of national norms for 14-18-year-old boys (P10 are: 140, 150, 160, 170, 180).

Table 1. Distribution and physical characteristics of the sample in the mixed longitudinal investigation (Homok, 1992-1996)

Age (y)	n	Body height (cm)	Body weight (kg)
9	11	127.01 ± 5.39	23.09 ± 2.11
10	18	130.78 ± 6.17	25.58 ± 3.27
11	17	137.88 ± 6.44	31.68 ± 7.80
12	31	142.93 ± 8.61	34.48 ± 8.91
13	31	151.56 ± 9.73	41.10 ± 9.35
14	41	156.98 ± 9.97	46.07 ± 10.13
15	32	162.86 ± 8.96	52.27 ± 10.77
16	37	166.77 ± 8.49	56.82 ± 10.06
17	21	167.31 ± 7.38	61.33 ± 13.50
18	11	174.64 ± 7.69	66.26 ± 12.84

Values are mean ± SD

Table 2. Hand-grip strength results of mentally handicapped boys

Age (y)	n	Hand grip strength (kp)	
9	11	8.91 ± 4.46	(1-14)
10	19	11.95 ± 6.23	(2-23)
11	17	14.06 ± 5.53	(2-22)
12	31	15.06 ± 6.62	(2-26)
13	31	19.32 ± 7.19	(4-32)
14	41	24.73 ± 7.69	(12-40)
15	31	29.29 ± 9.93	(3-46)
16	37	36.84 ± 11.83	(2-60)
17	19	38.32 ± 14.13	(8-60)
18	11	46.63 ± 12.09	(28-64)

Values are mean ± SD (range)

The results in sit-up tests fall generally between the 10th and 50th percentile although in some age groups around P50 of national norms. (P50 values are: 14, 15, 16, 17, 18, 19, 20, 20, 20, 20) Performances in the sit-up test depend on mental condition and these abilities of the investigated sample are different. (Standard deviations of reference mean values are: 3.73, 3.78, 3.89, 3.64, 3.69, 3.46, 3.38, 3.53, 3.51, 3.46)

In the case of disabled children the standard deviations in every measurement and test are higher than the standard deviation of reference values. These reflect the specialities of the investigated sample.

Table 3. Standing broad jump results of mentally handicapped boys

Age (y)	n	Standing broad jump (cm)	
9	7	83.43 ± 35.95	(40-127)
10	15	87.53 ± 35.07	(20-140)
11	14	103.50 ± 42.86	(20-160)
12	30	112.30 ± 33.69	(30-160)
13	31	118.48 ± 24.44	(60-180)
14	40	135.65 ± 29.69	(70-200)
15	30	155.13 ± 31.51	(60- 211)
16	36	163.75 ± 37.90	(70-215)
17	19	169.47 ± 26.95	(110-220)
18	11	182.09 ± 15.14	(150-200)

Values are mean ± SD (range)

Table 4. Sit-ups in 30 s test results of mentally handicapped boys

Age (y)	n	Sit ups	
9	6	14.33 ± 6.71	(6-24)
10	12	14.00 ± 7.47	(1-24)
11	10	13.60 ± 7.53	(2-24)
12	19	15.95 ± 7.01	(3-28)
13	22	17.77 ± 4.74	(8-26)
14	33	18.30 ± 3.57	(12-28)
15	27	17.67 ± 6.02	(3-28)
16	20	19.65 ± 6.60	(7-34)
17	11	17.36 ± 10.75	(2-38)
18	4	20.00 ± 2.83	(16-22)

Values are mean ± SD

Conclusion

The strength and some motor performance values of mentally handicapped boys are acceptable. During their institutionalised life they are taking part in intensive physical education and training. they are involved in physical work. It is very important for these children to have good physical abilities because they are likely to become physical workers.

From analysis of the values of body height and body weight the boys seem to have a late or longer puberty period[11]. In those physical fitness tests where the performance depends on practice and age the disabled children show a late development e.g. in the standing broad jump and sit-ups tests.

The importance of this examination is reinforced by the fact that most of these people will do physical work in their adulthood. An essential element of the quality of life is occupation, even in the cases of people with modest retardation. Body build and physical fitness are fundamental questions of success at work and in life.

References

1. Eiben, O.G., Barabás, A. and Pantó, E. (1991) *The Hungarian National Growth Study I,* Reference data on the biological developmental status and physical fitness of 3-18 year-old Hungarian youth in the 1980s. Humanbiologia Budapestinensis 21, Budapest.
2. Shephard, R.J. (1990) *Fitness in Special Populations*, Human Kinetics, Champaign, Il.
3. Moiser, H.D., Grossman, H.J. and Dingman, H.F. (1965) Physical growth in mental defectives, a study in an institutionalised population. *Pediatrics,* Vol. 36, pp. 465-84.
4. Katoda, H. (1991) *Health and Sex Education of Schoolchildren with Intellectual Handicaps,* Almqvist and Wiksell International, Stockholm.
5. Buday, J. (1974) Anthropometrische Untersuchung oligophrener Kinder. *Acta Paediatrica Scientiarum Hungariae,* Vol. 15, pp. 255-74.
6. Göncziné, Sz.T. (1985) Main results of mentally handicapped children's human biological examination in Szabolcs-Szatmár-Bereg County (Hungary). *Proceedings of International Scientific Conference,* BGYTF, Budapest, pp. 157-76.
7. Buday, J. (1992) Some aspects of human biological studies in disabled. *Anthropologiai Közlémenyek,* Vol. 32, pp. 19-23.
8. Blair, S. (1995) Physical activity leads to fitness and pays off. *The Physician and Sportmedicine,* No.11, pp. 87-94.
9. Buday, J. and Kaposi, I. (1986) Body development of mentally retarded boys - a mixed longitudinal study. *Anthropolpgiai Közlémenyek,* Vol. 29, pp. 97-105.
10. EUROFIT *European Tests of Physical Fitness*. (1993) Council of Europe. Committee for the Development of Sport, (CE CDDS), Strasbourg.
11. Buday, J. and Kaposi, I. (1992) Puberty of intellectually impaired boys, in *Studies in Human Biology,* (eds. E. Bodzsár and Ch. Susanne), Eötvös University Press, Budapest, pp. 241-5.

DEVELOPMENTAL COORDINATION DISORDER: EXPLORING THE CONDITION THROUGH SINGLE CASE STUDY

DCD - Single case study

J. HAMMOND
Faculty of Education, Health and Professional Studies, University of New England, New South Wales, Australia
A. PHILPOTT
Trinity Grammar School , Sydney, New South Wales, Australia

Keywords: Developmental coordination disorder, motor development, movement difficulties, visuo-motor tracking

Introduction

Children with Developmental Coordination Disorder (DCD)[1] account for 5-15% of the population. Teachers can expect that, in their classroom, there will be two or three children who are considered to be clinically clumsy, motor impaired or uncoordinated [2]. The multi-dimensional nature of DCD makes it difficult to give a concise or definitive statement of its characteristics. Hulme and Lord[3] adopted a definition for motor clumsiness seeing it as impaired motor performance of a degree sufficient to interfere seriously with many activities of daily life, including tasks involving motor activity and physical play activities. Although there is no observable physical impairment to the untrained eye, as soon as children with DCD start to move, they appear awkward and ungainly. In addition, close scrutiny of the child's background often reveals accompanying disadvantages physiologically, socially or neurologically.

Reports in the literature of group trends, do not allow for an in-depth analysis of the individual. Given the diverse nature of DCD, value can be gained from examining individual cases. Previous closely analysed single cases have revealed causes of DCD, such as: difficulties at birth[4,5]; movement deprivation[6]; and, the family environment[7]. Only when individual information is available, analysed and interpreted diagnostically, is it that individuals can be assisted with their difficulties. Using a single case study, this paper expands the knowledge available about children with DCD, elaborating on the heterogeneity of the problems associated with the condition.

This is an individual case study of a 9-year-old child with motor difficulties who may benefit from having an individualised adaptive physical education programme.

Children and Exercise XIX. Edited by Neil Armstrong, Brian Kirby and Joanne Welsman.
Published in 1997 by E & FN Spon, 2–6 Boundary Row, London, SE1 8HN.
ISBN 0 419 22100 X.

The case study describes how the child was identified and what conclusions may be made as a result of the identification and assessment process.

Background

Ben is one of triplets, born 10 wk prematurely. Post-natally, he was given only a 50% chance of surviving beyond 48 h and required a blood transfusion and phototherapy for hyperbilirubinaemia, and ventilation for 2 wk after birth. Other neonatal medical complications included pneumothoraces on both lungs and fluid build-up around the heart, both of which were successfully treated.

As an infant, Ben had colic between 6 and 9 months of age and has suffered from mild asthma since the age of 18 mo. He underwent corrective surgery for a bilateral squint at ages 1 and 3 y and lacks central binocular vision, although he may have some peripheral binocular vision, visual activity in each eye is satisfactory. Ben does not require glasses for these difficulties. With the exception of toilet training, developmental milestones (walking and talking) were reported to be slightly delayed compared to his brothers. Ben's mother describes him as accident prone, saying that he has a tendency to fall over and run into things.

As part of a long-term New South Wales study of infants requiring neonatal intensive care, Ben has been assessed by a team of health professionals (including neonatalogists, opthamologists, psychologists, occupational therapists and speech pathologists), at the Growth and Development Clinic at Westmead Hospital in Sydney, continuously from birth to 7 years of age. In 1992 he underwent intensive weekly occupational therapy sessions to overcome difficulties with poor gross motor skills (particularly difficulty with balance and general coordination), eye-hand coordination and visual motor integration tasks (specific delays in pen/paper skills), and perceptual skills (a particular difficulty with problem solving/puzzle strategies).

A coordinated approach between the pre-school, home and therapy setting was established to work on these areas. Vision difficulties have caused significant problems for Ben in completing tasks that require visuo-motor integration and, in his early school years, he had major difficulty with tasks requiring fine motor skills, such as handwriting. He had not established hand preference during kindergarten but appears to have settled on his left hand for dominance since then. By the end of year 2 his handwriting and fine motor skills had improved markedly. Educational intervention from kindergarten to year 2 included 3 h of group work per week with an itinerant support teacher who works with children with vision impairment.

Ben's overall intellectual functioning was assessed to be in the low to average range on the Stanford Binet - FE (September, 1995)[8]. This is consistent with the results of a previous psychological assessment conducted in 1992 and indicated that his level of intellectual functioning has remained relatively stable over this period. Ben's hearing was tested at Westmead Hospital in May 1992 and the result indicated normal bilateral hearing. Ben's vision difficulties appear to have improved but he still experiences difficulty with visuo-motor integration (approx. 2 y delayed).

Methods

Ben was identified and assessed as having motor difficulties by :

- Referral from his classroom teacher - teacher had observed the early signs of DCD.
- Consultation with parents and teachers - the classroom teacher established an interview in January 1996 with his parents, the school principal and the special education teacher. The meeting involved Ben's parents sharing information about his vision difficulties and the problems he had with motor skills in early childhood.
- Systematic follow-up observation - observation was made of Ben both in and outside the classroom environment, including the playground and in physical education (PE) lessons. This included using formalised checklists[9] in PE lessons.
- Standardised Testing - two screening tests for gross motor coordination[10,11].

Observations

The classroom teacher's knowledge of Ben's background history gave him an understanding of his motor development and skill acquisition potential. The teacher's general observations of Ben's movement around the school and in the classroom showed that his gross motor development was well behind children of similar age. Some of the problems observed included, collisions and loss of balance in the playground and classroom, difficulty in the control of direction of movement when throwing a ball, difficulty in coordinating arms and legs when running, hopping and throwing/catching a ball, difficulty in walking down and upstairs, frequently dropping things and knocking into equipment, poor organisational and motor planning skills.

Obviously, these gross motor difficulties and poor coordination problems are linked to the vision difficulties that Ben experiences. The teacher assessed Ben's fine motor skills more positively, particularly pen/paper handwriting skills which had improved over the last few years. The teacher concluded that Ben would benefit more from intervention for the gross motor area rather than for fine motor skills. Ben's movement skills were also observed in PE lessons (taught by a specialist teacher). Ben was observed using a 19-item checklist designed by Revie[9]. The 19 items were divided into two sections: a fundamental movement skill rating, which focused on rating gross motor skills; and, movement behaviour characteristics, which provided the opportunity to rate the fine motor skill of writing along with a number of movement behaviours which are seen to be characteristic of poorly coordinated children[12].

To assess Ben's gross motor skills, two screening tests were administered, providing quantitative data that would place his development against some previously established standards. A test to screen for gross motor coordination problems[10] was administered. This screening device also has a movement checklist which was used in conjunction with the screening analysis. In addition, the screening test designed for kindergarten to year 2 children[11] was given to Ben. Although he was then in year 3, it was thought appropriate to use this test because observations suggested Ben's movement skill and motor development was well behind his age-peers.

Results

Results of the test 'Screening For Gross Motor Co-ordination Problems In Primary School Children'[10] can be seen in table 1.

Average scores for children with coordination problems for both 8 and 9-year-olds are included in table 1 as Ben had just turned 9 y when the test was administered.

Results of the screening test 'Stay In Step - A Gross Motor Screening Test For Children K-2"[11] can be seen in table 2.

The movement checklist 'Fundamental Movement Skill Rating', saw Ben gain a ranking of two for five of the checklist items and a ranking of three on four items, where the rankings ranged from: one - not close to achieving; two - almost achieving; three - Okay; through to four - Good. These items mainly reflected achievement with hand/foot-eye coordination and hopping or skipping tasks.

The second movement checklist 'Movement Behaviour Characteristics', saw Ben rate at: a ranking of three for seven of the checklist items; a ranking of two on two items; and, a ranking of four on two items. The rankings ranged from: one - rarely characteristic of the child; two - occasionally characteristic of the child; three - sometimes characteristic of the child; through to four - often characteristic of the child. These items mainly referred to behaviours which indicated a lack of coordination and avoidance of physical activity.

General observations of Ben by the classroom teacher led to the following list of characteristics which are seen as typical, often falls over and is slow on moving down and up stairs, generally poor PE skills, (i.e. especially ball handling and problems with balance), poor involvement in playground activities and often the last to be picked in teams, often bumps into desks, chairs and people, and short concentration span with movement activities.

Conclusions and recommendations

The methodology adopted in appraising the extent of Ben's motor difficulties has used a variety of assessment approaches and dimensions, including both quantitative and qualitative procedures. This approach incorporates a more holistic view of the child [13], in that the knowledge gained about Ben's motor difficulties was obtained through a broad range of input modes. Through discussion, testing and observation of Ben it was realised that a great deal of progress had been made on his fine motor skills.

Therefore, a concentration on and analysis of the gross motor area seemed more appropriate. For this and other practical reasons, screening tests which concentrated on analysing gross motor development, avoiding more complex assessment batteries[14, 15] which incorporate fine motor skill/dexterity tasks as well as gross motor analysis, were used. Ben's parents were also very happy that there was a concentration on the gross motor area as they could see that intervention in this area would be of more benefit to Ben, given his past history of intervention and the progress that has been made in the fine motor skill area.

Table 1. Comparison of Ben's scores on the 'Hoare' test with age standards

Test Item	Ben's Score	Mean Score for Children with DCD at 9 y	Mean Score for Children with DCD at 8 y
Stationery hop (no)	24	57	51
Static balance (s)	26	48	32
Run (s)	11.5	11.7	12.2
Catch (no)	5	12	10
Stand. broad jump (cm)	110	117	115

Table 2. Rating scores on the "Stay in Step" test - seven years' age standards

Test Item	Ben's Score	Percentile Rank for 7 y	Descriptive Rating at 7 y
Single leg balance (s)	26	5	Very low
V/ball bounce and catch (no)	17	15	Very low
Hop for distance ($\sum$R / L legs)	165	40	Medium
Run (s)	11.5	35	Medium

In analysing the results, it can reasonably be assumed that Ben's physiological restrictions have caused his motor difficulties, in the main part by depriving him of unrestricted physical activity. The areas of gross motor coordination that are the weakest and require the most assistance are those of balance, ball skills and activities which involve the transference of weight such as hopping, jumping and skipping. Work on visual tracking and visual discrimination would also be needed to be incorporated into any programme of activities designed to help Ben develop his motor skills. However, although Ben has obvious motor difficulties, his difficulties are not so severe that they preclude him from participating in the regular PE and sporting programme at school. It is important that Ben continues to attend and follow the regular PE programme for his class, to enhance his social integration with his peers. Along with participation in the regular programme, Ben would benefit from an individualised gross motor programme, which concentrates on developing his balance, ball skills, locomotor and visual skills. The programme ought to be an intensive one-to-one programme designed to assist the development of these skills to a level which would allow increased participation in the regular PE programme with more confidence and success. Ben's concentration span and endurance is quite limited, thus making revision and practice necessary. The programme should be structured to allow for graduated progression of skill development and enhancement of some fitness parameters.

References

1. American Psychiatric Association. (1994) *Diagnostic and Statistical Manual of Mental Disorders* (DSM-IV-R), Washington.
2. Larkin, D. and Hoare, D. (1991) *Out of Step: Coordinating Kids' Movement*, Active Life Foundation, Western Australia.
3. Hulme, C. and Lord, R. (1986) Clumsy children: a review of recent research. *Child Care, Health and Development*, Vol. 12, pp. 257-69.
4. Johnston, O., Short, H. and Crawford, J. (1987) Poorly co-ordinated children: a survey of 95 cases. *Child Care, Health and Development*, Vol. 13, pp. 361-76.
5. Stephenson, E., McKay, C. and Chesson, R. (1990) An investigative study of early developmental factors in children with motor/learning difficulties. *British Journal of Occupational Therapy*, Vol. 53, pp. 4-6.
6. Hammond, J. and Sprinkle, J. (1995) Movement deprivation of children with developmental coordination disorder. *Australian Association for Research in Education - Annual Conference*, Hobart.
7. Sprinkle, J. and Hammond, J. (1994) Family relationships of motor impaired children: a case study. *Australian Association for Research in Education - Annual Conference*, Newcastle.
8. Terman, L. and Merrill, M. (1973) *Stanford-Binet Intelligence Scale:1972 Norms Edition*, Houghton Mifflin, Boston.
9. Revie, G. and Larkin, D. (1993) Looking at movement: problems with teacher identification of poorly coordinated children. *The ACHPER National Journal*, Vol. 142, pp. 4-9.
10. Hoare, D. (1992) Screening for gross motor problems in primary school children. *Sports Coach*, April, pp. 13-5.
11. Larkin, D. and Revie, G. (1994) *Stay in Step: a Gross Motor Screening Test for Children K-2*, University of New South Wales, Sydney.
12. Henderson, S. and Hall, D. (1982) Concomitants of clumsiness in young schoolchildren. *Developmental Medicine and Child Neurology*, Vol. 24, pp. 448-60.
13. Hammond, J. (1996) *Investigation into the Characteristics of Children with Motor Difficulties: an Holistic Approach*, PhD Thesis, University of New England.
14. Bruininks, R. (1978) *Bruininks-Oseretsky Test of Motor Proficiency - Examiner's Manual*, American Guidance Service, Minnesota.
15. McCarron, L. (1982) *McCarron Assessment of Neuromuscular Development: Fine and Gross Motor Abilities*, McCarron Dial Systems, Dallas.

PHYSICAL AND MOTOR STRUCTURE CHARACTERISTICS OF 11 TO 17 YEAR OLDS

Physical and motor structure characteristics

T. SZABÓ and J. PÁPAI
Central School of Sports, Budapest, Hungary
Keywords: Motor scores, multivariate analysis, somatotype

Introduction

One of the main fields of interest in our research work is the description and interpretation of changes in the motor performance of children in relation to their development.

Two basic factors have been assumed to affect the development of physical abilities in the child: growth and development of the body as a whole, and such specific effects that might arise from the repetition of motor actions (physical training and habitual activity).

Studies in adult athletes have shown that sports performance and body build are related, specific physique nearly always being associated with elite performance[1,2]. This aspect raises a number of as yet unanswered questions when applied to the growing child[3]. To witness how the relationship observed in adults develops has always been a stimulating task for us since - beyond the values of human biology proper - any knowledge acquired in this respect can be of practical importance for daily training activity[4].

The present study reports on our attempts to clarify the relationships between the anthropometric somatotype and some basic motor performance measures with a special interest in the effect of relative attributes of physique on physical abilities.

Methods

The subjects were children who applied for admission to Central School of Sports, altogether 1445 girls and 3529 boys aged between 6 and 17 y.

Children and Exercise XIX. Edited by Neil Armstrong, Brian Kirby and Joanne Welsman.
Published in 1997 by E & FN Spon, 2–6 Boundary Row, London, SE1 8HN.
ISBN 0 419 22100 X.

Body measurements were taken in accordance with the recommendations of the International Biological Programme. These measurements were used to calculate the three components (endomorphy, mesomorphy and ectomorphy) of the Heath-Carter somatometric somatotype[5] and estimate percent body fat[6].

Motor performance were measured using the 30m dash to the nearest 0.1 s (running speed), the 1200 m flat race to the nearest 1.0 s (general endurance), standing long jump to the nearest 1.0 cm (leg power) and fistball throw to 0.5 m (explosive power of the arms and trunk). The tests were performed according to existing athletic rules.

In addition to basic descriptive statistics, interrelationships between variables were examined using correlation and factor analysis followed by rotations of the factor loadings according to the varimax criterion. Significant coefficients above r = 0.60 were regarded as practically important. The number of factors to be extracted was chosen in reliance on the eigenvalues.

Results and discussion

Tables 1 and 2 contain the basic statistics of the studied variables for the boys and girls, respectively. As shown, somatotype components had a very wide range in both the boys and girls, endomorphy having the greatest one. This arose from the fact that the age range was broad.

Of the motor scores, variability was greatest in fistball throw, a test requiring considerable skill in addition to explosive strength. These children although displaying a positive attitude to sports, had mostly not yet taken part in regular intense physical training so their scores were scarcely better than those of their less athletic peers.

Correlations between the variables are summarised in tables 3 and 4 for the two genders. No significant relationships were found between the somatotype

Table 1. Basic statistics of the girls (n=1446)

Variables	Mean	SD	Var %	Min	Max	Range
Age (y)	10.60	1.58	14.9	6.59	16.21	9.6
Endomorphy	3.80	1.77	46.7	0.65	11.01	10.5
Mesomorphy	3.64	0.90	24.9	0.25	7.35	7.1
Ectomorphy	3.51	1.27	36.1	0.25	7.83	7.6
Body fat (%)	19.55	5.54	28.4	5.23	36.73	31.5
30 m dash (s)	5.83	0.53	9.0	4.60	8.40	3.8
1200 m run (s)	394.38	57.51	14.6	268.00	675.00	407.0
Standing long jump (cm)	172.22	19.89	11.6	100.00	265.00	165.0
Fistball (m)	19.22	6.83	35.5	5.00	53.00	48.0

Table 2. Basic statistics of the boys (n=3529)

Variables	Mean	SD	Var %	Min	Max	Range
Age (y)	10.55	1.70	16.1	5.81	17.07	11.3
Endomorphy	3.29	1.85	56.5	0.38	11.68	11.3
Mesomorphy	4.63	0.91	21.1	0.25	8.41	8.2
Ectomorphy	3.31	1.26	37.9	0.25	11.03	10.8
Body fat (%)	17.50	6.10	34.9	3.09	37.72	34.6
30 m dash (s)	5.78	0.51	8.9	4.30	8.00	3.7
1200 m run (s)	357.93	54.20	15.1	242.00	736.00	494.0
Standing long jump (cm)	173.00	21.61	12.5	90.00	260.00	170.0
Fistball (m)	29.22	8.71	29.8	7.00	70.00	63.0

components and the performance scores, but some of the interperformance and, in particular, some of the intercomponent relationships were considerably close. The overall pattern of correlations was very similar in the two genders.

Taking these facts also into account, a further step was taken to approach the interrelationships of measured and estimated variables, namely, factor analysis, the heuristic techniques of disclosing possible uncorrelated hidden background variables. On the basis of eigen values magnitude three factors each were extracted for the girls and boys alike. Tables 5 and 6 contain the factor loadings after varimax rotation applied to achieve a simple structure[7].

It could be stated that, despite considerable differences in the respective mean values for variables in the two genders and some slighter ones in the correlation matrices, the factor patterns for the boys and girls were similar, the factor loadings being comparable almost to the second decimal place.

Table 3. Correlation matrix, girls

Variables	2	3	4	5	6	7	8	9
Age (y)	0.06	-0.22	0.07	0.18	-0.49	-0.36	0.52	0.57
Endomorphy		0.54	-0.76	0.96	0.28	0.38	-0.29	-0.10
Mesomorphy			-0.83	0.46	0.17	0.26	-0.22	-0.10
Ectomorphy				-0.71	-0.23	-0.32	0.26	0.10
Body fat (%)					0.21	0.33	-0.19	-0.02
30 m dash (s)						0.54	-0.63	-0.54
1200 m run (s)							-0.47	-0.47
Standing long jump (cm)								0.54

Table 4. Correlation matrix, boys

Variables	2	3	4	5	6	7	8	9
Age (y)	0.05	0.08	0.14	0.15	-0.53	-0.42	0.60	0.67
Endomorphy		0.52	-0.74	0.96	0.27	0.43	-0.24	-0.05
Mesomorphy			-0.86	0.51	0.13	0.26	-0.15	-0.03
Ectomorphy				-0.68	-0.26	-0.39	0.27	0.13
Body fat (%)					0.19	0.37	-0.16	0.03
30 m dash (s)						0.56	-0.63	-0.58
1200 m run (s)							-0.50	-0.48
Standing long jump (cm)								0.62

Table 5. Rotated factor matrix, girls

Variables	Factors F1	F2	F3
Age (y)	0.73	0.41	-0.33
Endomorphy	-0.16	0.88	0.35
Mesomorphy	-0.10	0.25	0.92
Ectomorphy	0.11	-0.56	-0.76
Body fat (%)	0.06	0.93	0.26
30 m dash (s)	-0.82	0.20	0.00
1200 m run (s)	-0.69	0.36	0.04
Standing long jump (cm)	0.80	-0.12	-0.12
Fistball (m)	0.81	0.07	-0.04

Table 6. Rotated factor matrix, boys

Variables	Factors F1	F2	F3
Age (y)	0.83	0.29	-0.18
Endomorphy	-0.09	0.88	0.39
Mesomorphy	0.04	0.24	0.93
Ectomorphy	0.17	-0.46	-0.83
Body fat (%)	0.00	0.90	0.34
30 m dash (s)	-0.80	0.26	0.01
1200 m run (s)	-0.66	0.45	0.08
Standing long jump (cm)	0.82	0.14	-0.08
Fistball (m)	0.85	0.08	-0.03

Factor F1 contains loadings exceeding 0.60 of calendar age and all the four motor scores and near zero for the somatotype components. This fact was interpreted as showing that behind the motor scores there was a common background variable that was related with progressing age. The factor loading of age was much higher than the coefficients in the correlation matrix.

The observation that every motor performance concentrated to F1 was a surprise, because these tests are recognised as being largely independent of each other. The correlation matrices fully corroborated this assumption so this fact needs some additional comment. It should be noted that physical abilities as entities behind motor test scores are independent by principle. Motor test performances may combine, however, two or more abilities despite the effort taken to design pure tests. This is evident in the correlation matrix which also shows that the change with progressing age in somatotype components is negligible while that in the absolute scores is considerably larger.

Factor F2 was defined by the large loadings of body fat per cent and endomorphy. The two other components mesomorphy and ectomorphy turned up in Factor F3 with opposite signs, a fact to be considered by research workers interested in other fields than athletic youth, because it suggests that the more linear children become the less strong they will be provided that urbanisation continues to combine with habitual inactivity.

The results of the factor analysis have thus shown that functional characteristics and descriptors of physique are actually unrelated in the age group studied here. This observation is apparently in contradiction with that found in elite athletes. This paradox can be received by remembering that high-level sport performances are assumed to rely on highly developed physical abilities. This assumption is, however, a simplification, because basic physical abilities merely allow excellent sport performance, but they do not bring them about spontaneously. In our present sample of children sports orientated selection had not taken effect yet.

Summarising the obtained results it was concluded that,

- in the athletically-minded but still untrained children the basic physical abilities were still far from the level at which they could be influenced by physique,
- when a same level of skill is assumed, performance scores are very closely related with absolute body dimensions at all ages and for this reason - by being relative expressions - somatotype components in this period of life cannot reflect the subtle differences so important between elite athletes of the same event,
- similar indices of physique may occur at any age, but motor performance shows a well-defined time course of development in childhood and adolescence.

References

1. Borms, J., Ross, W.D., Duquet, W. and Carter, J.E.L.(1986) Somatotypes of World class body builders, in *Perspectives in Kinanthropometry*, (ed. J.A.P. Day), Human Kinetics, Champaign Il., pp. 81-90.

2. Claessens, A.M., Beunen, G.P., Simons, J.M., Wellens, R.I., Geldof, D. and Nuyts, M. (1986) Body structure, somatotype and motor fitness of top class Belgian judoists, in *Perspectives in Kinanthropometry*, (ed. J.A.P. Day), Human Kinetics, Champaign Il., pp.155-64.
3. Olgun,P. and Gurses, C. (1986) Relationship between somatotypes and untrained physical abilities, in *Perspectives in Kinanthropometry*, (ed. J.A.P. Day), Human Kinetics, Champaign Il., pp.115-22.
4. Bale, F. (1986) The relationship of somatotype and body composition to strength in a group of men and women sport science students, in *Perspectives in Kinanthropometry*, (ed. J.A.P. Day), Human Kinetics, Champaign Il, pp.187-98.
5. Carter, J.E.L.(1975) *The Heath-Carter Somatotype Method*, San Diego State University, San Diego CA.
6. Parizková, J. (1961) Age trends in fatness in normal and obese children. *Journal of Applied Physiology*, Vol.16, pp.173-4.
7. Thurstone, L.L. (1954) An analytical method for simple structure. *Psychometrika*, Vol.19, pp.173-82.

LIPIDS AND LIPOPROTEIN(a) AS ATHEROSCLEROSIS FACTORS IN YOUNG ATHLETES

Lipids and physical activity

S. CLAVEL, S. LEAUTE, P. JOUANEL and E.VAN PRAAGH
Laboratoire de la performance motrice, and Laboratoire de biochimie, Clermont-Ferrand, France

Keywords: Atherosclerosis factors, genotype, lipids, lipoprotein(a), young athletes

Introduction

Regular physical activity alters plasma lipoprotein profiles and thereby decreases the risk of coronary heart disease (CHD). It is well known that there is a direct relationship between cholesterol, triglycerides and atherosclerosis. Regular and intensive exercise training induces a reduction of plasma triglycerides and a redistribution of total cholesterol from the atherogenic particles (Very Low Density Lipoprotein (VLDL), Low Density Lipoprotein (LDL)) to the High Density Lipoprotein (HDL)[1,2]. Lipoprotein(a) (Lp(a)) has a lipid composition that is nearly identical to LDL, and like LDL, it contains a single copy of apolipoprotein B100 (Apo B). In addition, Lp(a) contains a large glycoprotein called apoprotein(a) (Apo(a)) which is attached to Apo B by a disulpher bond[3].

Lp(a) appears to be involved in the atherosclerotic process by inducing cholesterol deposits in the arterial wall and interfering with coagulation[4,5]. When Lp(a) levels are greater than 0.30 $g \cdot L^{-1}$, this particle represents an independent risk factor for coronary atherosclerosis[6]. Previous studies have demonstrated that Lp(a) concentrations are strongly genetically determined, with at least 90% of the variation determined by the variation within the gene for Apo(a)[7]. Results from the few published cross-sectional and intervention studies on the influence of exercise on Lp(a) have been inconsistent. To our knowledge, no study has reported any information about the genetic status of their subjects.

The purpose of the present study was to determine elite young athletes' Apo(a) genotypes and thereby check the correlation between genetic determinism and Lp(a) concentration. In addition, we were able to observe the effects of regular training on plasma Lp(a) level and on other lipids involved in the atherosclerotic process.

Children and Exercise XIX. Edited by Neil Armstrong, Brian Kirby and Joanne Welsman.
Published in 1997 by E & FN Spon, 2–6 Boundary Row, London, SE1 8HN.
ISBN 0 419 22100 X.

Subjects

Thirty elite young athletes (girls n = 8; boys n = 22), aged 15-18 y, were recruited to participate in this study. The subjects selected were involved in specific athletic training programmes (Sports classes which combine education and sports training). Their physical characteristics are presented in table 1. With respect to their athletic specializations, athletes were divided into two equal groups (n = 15) matched for sex differences: endurance athletes (long distance runs) and power athletes (jumping, throwing, sprint events). All participants consumed a normal European diet and completed a medical history form, in order to assess CHD risk factors, use of medication or smoking habits. A sedentary control group was formed by 21 healthy volunteers (girls n = 5, boys n = 16, mean age, 21.6 ± 1.5 y). Informed consent was obtained from each participant (or parents).

Methods

Anthropometric measurements and biochemical analyses

Height (cm), body mass (kg) and body fat (%) were recorded at the sport medicine centre in Clermont-Ferrand. Venous blood samples were drawn the morning after an overnight (12-14h) fast. Serum lipids and apolipoprotein determinations were conducted by an accredited laboratory (Laboratoire de biochimie médicale, Hôtel Dieu CHU, Clermont-Ferrand). Total cholesterol, triglycerides, phospholipids and cholesterol of fractioned lipoproteins were determined using an automated procedure, by enzymatic methods on fresh serum (BM HITACHI 717, Boerhinger Mannheim, France). HDL-cholesterol (HDL-C) and LDL-cholesterol (LDL-C) were quantified after selective precipitation by reagents (Biomérieux). Serum apolipoprotein AI (Apo AI) and apolipoprotein B (Apo B) were determined immunoturbidimetrically (Turbitimer, Behring) using specific antibodies to the apoprotein (Turbiquant, Behring). Quantification of lipoprotein AI particles (Lp AI) and Lp(a) were performed by an electroimmunodiffusion technique in agarose gel (Hydragel particles, Sébia).

Pulsed field analysis of the Apo(a) gene

15 mL of blood were collected from each individual in vacutainer tubes containing EDTA anticoagulant. Lymphocytes were isolated and embedded in agarose plugs before being treated and subjected to pulse field gel electrophoresis as described by Lackner[8]. Apo(a) alleles were revealed by a specific P^{32} radiolabeled probe.

Data analyses

All anthropometric and lipid variables were tested using non parametric statistics to compare the different groups. Because plasma Lp(a) levels were not distributed normally, a non parametric rank sum test was used to compare median Lp(a) levels. Futhermore, the Spearman rank correlation coefficient was calculated as a measure of the association between apo(a) DNA fragment size and Lp(a) levels.

Results

Anthropometric data and lipid profiles

There was no significant difference ($p > 0.05$) between the power ($n = 15$) and endurance ($n = 15$) athletes in age (16.8 ± 0.8 vs 16.8 ± 1.1 y), height (174.5 ± 9.9 vs 173.4 ± 7.2 cm) or % body fat (14.6 ± 2.1 vs 14.0 ± 3.3). The power athletes were significantly ($p < 0.05$) heavier (67.5 ± 8.1 vs 61.8 ± 7.4 kg). The $\dot{V}O_2$ max of the endurance athletes was 58.2 ± 10.5 $mL \cdot kg^{-1} \cdot min^{-1}$.

Comparision of the lipid profiles of the control group, endurance athletes and power athletes confirmed that the endurance athletes had the least atherogenic profile (table 1). The latter group had statistically significant higher levels of HDL-C and Apo AI compared to power athletes (HDL-C: $p = 0.01$; Apo AI: $p = 0.004$) and sedentary controls (HDL-C: $p = 0.01$; Apo AI: $p = 0.05$). Although their level of LDL-C was significantly lower than controls ($p = 0.01$). Lipid risk profile can be expressed by the ratio HDL-C to LDL-C. Comparison of this ratio between the three groups revealed that endurance athletes were favoured the most (table 2). This result was verified statistically (power athletes/endurance athletes: $r=-2.1$, $p=0.04$; control subjects /endurance athletes: $r = -3.5$, $p = 0.002$). It is interesting to note that this lipid index was not significantly different between the control group and power athletes. The same trend was observed when the ratio Apo AI (primarily associated with HDL) to ApoB (95% of apolipoprotein content of LDL) was used instead of HDL-C/LDL-C (power athletes/endurance athletes: $r = -2.3$, $p = 0.02$; control subjects/endurance athletes: $r = -2.5$, $p = 0.01$). Despite the differences in HDL-C, LDL-C, Apo AI, HDL-C/LDL-C and ApoAI/ApoB, no intergroup differences in other lipid parameters could be discerned. No significant lipid metabolism adaptation was observed in power athletes compared to control subjects.

Lp(a) distribution

As expected, in the control group the distribution of Lp(a) concentration was skewed with 62% of the population having Lp(a) levels ≤ 0.10 $g \cdot L^{-1}$. Plasma Lp(a) measure-

Table 1. Lipid profiles of the three groups

	Control subjects (n=21)	Power athletes (n = 15)	Endurance athletes (n = 15)
Cholesterol ($mmol \cdot L^{-1}$)	4.6 ± 1	4.2 ± 0.8	4.4 ± 0.7
Triglycerides ($mmol \cdot L^{-1}$)	1 ± 0.4	0.9 ± 0.5	0.8 ± 0.4
HDL-C ($mmol \cdot L^{-1}$)	1.2 ± 0.2	1.2 ± 0.2	1.4 ± 0.3
LDL-C ($mmol \cdot L^{-1}$)	2.6 ± 0.5	2.3 ± 0.7	2.2 ± 0.7
Apo AI ($g \cdot L^{-1}$)	1.2 ± 0.2	1.1 ± 0.2	1.3 ± 0.2
Apo B ($g \cdot L^{-1}$)	0.8 ± 0.2	0.8 ± 0.2	0.8 ± 0.2
HDL-C/LDL-C ratio	0.5 ± 0.1	0.6 ± 0.2	0.8 ± 0.3
ApoAI/ApoB ratio	1.5 ± 0.3	1.5 ± 0.4	1.9 ± 0.5

Values are mean ± SD

ments were neither significantly different between boys and girls, nor between the two training groups. Therefore, results shown in fig 1 represent the distribution of Lp(a) in the pooled population (endurance athletes + power athletes). Surprisingly, the levels of Lp(a) were skewed towards those of higher levels. Forty seven percent of this population had a concentration above 0.30 $g \cdot L^{-1}$ which is considered as a critical threshold for CHD risk.

Because Lp(a) levels of athletes and control groups were not distributed normally, based on either raw or logarithmic transformed values, only median values were reported. Lp(a) values were significantly different between athletes and control subjects. Comparison of the 75th percentile and median between control subjects and athletes demonstrated that Lp(a) levels were more elevated in the athletic group (control group: 75th percentile = 0.2, median=0.1; athletes: 75th percentile = 0.5, median = 0.2. Median comparison: $r = -3.2$, $p = 0.001$).

Athletes Apo(a) genotypes, relationship between Apo(a) genotype and Lp(a) level
Pulse field gel electrophoresis was performed to assess the size of the Apo(a) alleles in each subject of the athletic population previously defined (27 athletes had been genotyped). A total of 17 Apo(a) alleles were identified. Twenty four individuals were heterozygous and three were homozygous. The most common allele comprised 33% of the total Apo(a) alleles in the sample. The rank correlation coefficient between the size of Apo(a) alleles and plasma Lp(a) level was $r = -0.5$ ($p = 0.008$). Hence, in this young athlete population, there was an inverse relationship between the size of the Apo(a) allele and the plasma level of Lp(a).

Discussion

This study gives additional evidence that endurance athletes, even in young subjects, had a significantly better ratio of cardioprotective HDL-C to atherogenic LDL-C than power athletes or the sedentary control subjects[9]. Moreover, these data were confirmed by ApoAI/ApoB ratio, which is considered as a new atherogenicity index with a higher predictive value than ApoAI, ApoB separately or HDL-C/LDL-C ratio

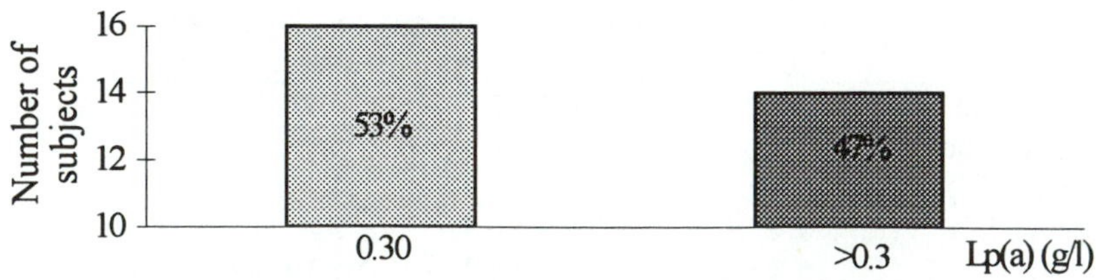

Fig. 1. Distribution of Lp(a) above and below 0.30 $g \cdot L^{-1}$ in young athletes (n =30)

[10].Consequently, it appears that regular aerobic exercise at a young age, contributes to the prevention of CHD.

Previous studies have reported that exercise tends to lower LDL-C. Because of the structural homology between Lp(a) and LDL particles, one might therefore expect that the atherogenic Lp(a) particle would be influenced by physical activity in a similar way. However, published results are inconsistent. Hellsten et al.[11] found that Lp(a) may significantly decrease in well trained individuals, whereas, a study investigating a long term effect of exercise in sedentary individuals demonstrated that Lp(a) levels rose almost twofold over a period of 9 months[12]. Hubinger reported higher Lp(a) serum concentation in adult long distance runners compared to non-athletic controls[13]. A similar trend was observed in our study. Athletes presented significantly higher Lp(a) levels compared to controls. Moreover, median Lp(a) concentration was higher in endurance athletes than in power athletes, but this difference was not statistically significant. Halle et al.[14] suggested that higher serum concentration of Lp(a), in endurance athletes, could be due to greater physical demands which cause muscular or systemic stress reaction. This condition may be associated with raised Lp(a) values, as Lp(a) has been shown to share characteristics of inflamatory parameters.

Some severe dyslipemias have a genetic origin (e.g. lack of B/E receptors of type IIa or lack of lipoprotein lipase type I), their detection by molecular biology facilitate early substitutive treatment of patients from childhood. Because Lp(a) level appears to be primarily genetically determined, Lobo et al.[15] suggested a similar genetic approach to give further information about Lp(a). In the present study, genotype analysis of the athletic population revealed an inverse relationship between the size of the Apo(a) allele and the Lp(a) plasma level ($r = -0.5$; $p = 0.008$), as previously described in a non athletic population. High Lp(a) level can, therefore, be explained by the genetic status of the athletes: elevated frequency of small size Apo(a) allele, associated with elevated Lp(a) levels. However, exceptions to this correlation do exist, suggesting that Lp(a) level can be explained by other phenomena. Determination of the Apo(a) genotypes of individuals can be used as a starting point for a follow up study in order to observe long term physical activity effects on Lp(a) levels. Possible Lp(a) concentration variations observed during years of physical activity could be attributed to the direct effect of exercise.

References

1. Haskell, W.L. (1986) The influence of exercise training on plasma lipids and lipoprotein in health and disease. *Acta Medica Scandinavica,* Vol. 711, (suppl), pp. 25-9.
2. Tran, Z.V. and Weltman, A. (1986) Differential effects of exercise on serum lipids and lipoprotein levels seen with changes in body weight. A meta analysis. *Journal of the American Medical Association,* Vol. 254, pp. 919-23.
3. Scanu, A.M. and Fless, G.M. (1990) Lipoprotein(a). Heterogeneity and biological relevance. *Journal of Clinical Investigations,* Vol. 85, pp. 1709-15.
4. Lawn, R.M. (1992) Lipoprotein(a) in heart disease. *Scientific American,* Vol. 266, pp. 26-32.

5. Loscalzo, J. (1990) Lipoprotein(a) a unique risk factor for atherothrombotic disease. *Atherosclerosis,* Vol. 10, pp. 672-9.
6. Armstrong, V.W., Cremer, P., Eberle, E., Manke, A. and Schulze, F. (1986) The association between serum Lp(a) concentrations and angiographically assessed coronary atherosclerosis. *Atherosclerosis,* Vol. 62, pp. 249-57.
7. Boerwinkle, E., Leffert, C.C., Lin, J., Lackner, C., Chiesa, G. and Hobbs, H.H. (1992) Apolipoprotein(a) gene accounts for greater than 90% of the variation in plasma lipoprotein(a) concentrations. *Journal of Clinical Investigations,* Vol. 90, pp. 52-60.
8. Lackner, C., Boerwinkle, E., Leffert, C.C., Rahmig, T. and Hobbs, H.H. (1991) Molecular basis of apolipoprotein(a) isoform size heterogeneity as revealed by pulse-field gel electrophoresis. *Journal of Clinical Investigations,* Vol. 87, pp. 2153-61.
9. Smith, B.W., Methrey, W.P. and Sparrow, A. (1986) Serum lipid and lipoprotein profiles in elite age group runners. in *Sport for Children and Youths,* (eds. M.R. Weiss and D. Gould), (1984 Olympic Scientific Proceeding Congress vol 10), pp.269-73.
10. Jacotot, B. (1996) Le HDL: role fondamental dans la regulation de 'atherosclerose. *Risques,* Vol 2, pp. 1-5.
11. Hellsten, G., Boman, K., Hallmans, G. and Dahlen, G. (1989) Lipids and endurance physical activity (letter). *Atherosclerosis,* Vol. 75, pp. 93-4.
12. Ponjee, G.A., Janssen, E.M. and Van Wersch, J.W. (1995) Long term physical exercise and lipoprotein(a) levels in a previously sedentary male and female population. *Annals of Clinical Biochemistry,* Vol. 32, pp. 181-5.
13. Hubinger, L., Mac Kinnon, L.T. and Lepre, F. (1995) Lipoprotein(a) levels in the middle-aged male runners and sedentary controls. *Medicine and Sciences in Sports and Exercise,* Vol. 27, pp. 490-6.
14. Halle, M., Berg, A., Frey, I., Konig, D., Keul, J. and Baumstark, M.W. (1995) Relationship of the obesity with concentration and composition of the LDL subfraction particles in normoinsulinemic men. *Metabolism,* Vol. 44, pp. 1384-90.
15 Lobo, R.A., Notelovitz, M., Bernstein, L., Khan, F.Y., Ross, R.K. and Paul, W.L. (1992) Lp(a) lipoprotein: relationship to cardiovascular disease risk factors, exercise, and estrogen. *American Journal of Obstetrics and Gynecology,* Vol. 166, pp. 1182-9.

SELECTED PREDICTOR VARIABLES AND LIPID-LIPOPROTEIN PROFILE IN PREPUBERTAL CHILDREN

Lipids in prepubertal children

K. TOLFREY and A.M. BATTERHAM
Department of Exercise and Sport Science, Manchester Metropolitan University, Alsager, UK
I.G. CAMPBELL
Division of Sport, Health and Exercise, Staffordshire University, Stoke-on-Trent, UK
Keywords: Body composition, cardiopulmonary fitness, habitual physical activity, heart rate monitoring, lipid-lipoprotein profile

Introduction

It is now well recognised that the process leading to atherosclerosis has paediatric origins[1]. Furthermore, a number of studies have indicated that a paediatric propensity for adverse lipid-lipoprotein concentrations, a primary risk factor for coronary heart disease (CHD), may be carried into adulthood[2]. The studies that have attempted to examine the independent effect of variables such as % body fat, cardiorespiratory fitness, diet and habitual physical activity (HPA) on the blood lipid-lipoprotein profile have not always reported consistent findings[3,4,5]. Whilst some studies have identified an association between cardiorespiratory fitness and lipid-lipoprotein profile[6,7], others have not[5]. Moreover, it has been reported[3] that age may be regarded as a confounding variable when attempting to quantify independent contributions to lipid-lipoprotein variability. By studying a narrow age range of children this problem may be controlled. The purpose of the present study was to examine the relationship between prepubertal children's lipid-lipoprotein profile, and cardiorespiratory fitness, HPA and % body fat. It was hypothesised that a higher HPA pattern would be related to a more favourable lipid-lipoprotein profile.

Subjects

From a pool of 108 volunteers recruited for two separate longitudinal training studies, 92 children were classified as prepubertal[8]. The pre-training data for these children were included in the current cross-sectional analysis. Prior to testing, all subjects, and a parent, gave their informed consent to participate in the study. The test procedures

Children and Exercise XIX. Edited by Neil Armstrong, Brian Kirby and Joanne Welsman.
Published in 1997 by E & FN Spon, 2–6 Boundary Row, London, SE1 8HN.
ISBN 0 419 22100 X.

Table 1. Subject characteristics

	Boys (n=51)	Girls (n=41)
Age (y)	10.6 ± 0.6	10.6 ± 0.6
Stature (cm)	143.1 ± 6.7	143.7 ± 7.5
Body Mass (kg)	35.4 ± 6.1	37.2 ± 7.2
% Body Fat	15.9 ± 5.4	19.7 ± 6.2**
peak $\dot{V}O_2$ (mL·kg^{-1}·min^{-1})	48.1 ± 5.3	40.9 ± 6.7**
HR > 140 bpm (%)	7.3 ± 2.7	6.2 ± 3.3*
HR >25% above resting	75.8 ± 15.9	75.2 ± 16.6

Values are mean ± SD
Level of significance *$p < 0.05$, **$p < 0.01$

were approved by the Departmental Ethics Committee. Subject characteristics are presented in table 1.

Methods

Lipid-lipoprotein profile

Following an overnight fast (12 h), venous blood samples were drawn using standard clinical procedures. Plasma total cholesterol (TC) and triglycerides (TG) were determined enzymatically (Boehringer Mannheim). HDL-C was similarly assayed after precipitation of LDL-C and VLDL-C by phosphotungstic acid and Mg ions. LDL-C was estimated according to Friedewald[10]. The ratios, TC:HDL-C and LDL-C:HDL-C were derived from these concentrations.

Cardiorespiratory fitness

Subjects completed a modified McMaster[10] cycle ergometer test to volitional exhaustion. Peak oxygen uptake (peak $\dot{V}O_2$) was determined during this test via open circuit spirometry and heart rate was continuously monitored using short-range telemetry (PE4000 Polar Sport Tester, Kempele, Finland). For inclusion in the analysis subjects had to satisfy at least one of the maximal effort criteria, $HR_{max} \geq 195$ and $RER_{max} \geq 1.00$[11].

Body composition

Stature was determined to the nearest 0.1 cm (Seca stadiometer 208) and body mass to the nearest 0.1 kg (Seca beam balance 710) with subjects dressed in minimal clothing. Skinfold measurements were taken on the right side of the body using a Harpenden (John Bull, England) calliper and recorded to the nearest 0.1 mm. The mean of three measurements was used as the representative value for the triceps and subscapular sites. Percent body fat (%BF) was then estimated using maturity and gender appropriate equations[12].

Habitual physical activity

Habitual physical activity was assessed using daily heart rate monitoring. Although it is recognised that heart rate provides a quantitative measure of relative cardiovascular stress, this method has received increasing support over recent years[4,13]. Heart rate was recorded each minute between 0900 and 2100 for two school days and one weekend. Four full days were selected in accord with recent recommendations[13]. The heart rate variables examined were the percentage time spent with the heart rate (i) ≥ 140 bpm (P140) and (ii) ≥ 125% of resting (PAHR-25). Complete HPA data were collected for 41 boys (78%) and 34 girls (83%).

Data analyses

Descriptive means and standard deviations (SD) were computed for boys and girls separately. None of the variables showed significant differences to a normal distribution following a Kolmogorov-Smirnov Goodness-to-Fit test ($p > 0.05$). However, where the distribution of the data was significantly skewed, Spearman rank order correlation coefficients were calculated to examine the relationship between predictor variables and lipid-lipoprotein profile. Pearson product moment correlations were determined for non-skewed data. Where inter-relationships were found between predictor variables, partial correlations were conducted to ascertain the independent relationship between predictor and lipid-lipoprotein variable. Mann-Whitney U or independent t-tests were used to examine differences between the group means of the boys and girls.

Results

The boys were collectively leaner and fitter (peak $\dot{V}O_2$) than the girls in this study ($p < 0.01$). No other sex differences in the listed physical characteristics were apparent

Table 2. Plasma lipid-lipoprotein concentrations

	Boys (n=51)	Girls (n=41)
Total Cholesterol ($mmol \cdot L^{-1}$)	4.14 ± 0.61	4.25 ± 0.64
Total Triglycerides ($mmol \cdot L^{-1}$)	0.58 ± 0.24	0.78 ± 0.33**
HDL-C ($mmol \cdot L^{-1}$)	1.28 ± 0.26	1.29 ± 0.37
LDL-C ($mmol \cdot L^{-1}$)	2.59 ± 0.55	2.59 ± 0.62
Total Cholesterol: HDL-C	3.36 ± 0.90	3.46 ± 0.98
LDL-C:HDL-C	2.14 ± 0.82	2.18 ± 0.85

Values are mean ± SD; Level of significance **$p < 0.01$

Table 3. Significant correlation coefficients between predictor variables and plasma lipids-lipoproteins

Boys					
PAHR-25	vs.	TC:HDL-C	(n=40)	r = -0.31	p=0.052*
PAHR-25	vs.	LDL-C:HDL-C	(n=40)	r = -0.35	p=0.028
P140	vs.	TG	(n=40)	r = -0.35	p=0.028
Girls					
peak $\dot{V}O_2$	vs.	TC	(n=41)	r = -0.33	p=0.033
peak $\dot{V}O_2$	vs.	TG	(n=41)	r = -0.38	p=0.013
peak $\dot{V}O_2$	vs.	HDL-C	(n=41)	r = 0.30	p=0.054*
peak $\dot{V}O_2$	vs.	LDL-C	(n=41)	r = -0.39	p=0.011
peak $\dot{V}O_2$	vs.	TC:HDL-C	(n=41)	r = -0.45	p=0.003
peak $\dot{V}O_2$	vs.	LDL-C:HDL-C	(n=41)	r = -0.42	p=0.006
% Body Fat	vs.	TC	(n=41)	r = 0.32	p=0.044
% Body Fat	vs.	LDL-C	(n=41)	r = 0.36	p=0.021
% Body Fat	vs.	TC:HDL-C	(n=41)	r = 0.37	p=0.018
% Body Fat	vs.	LDL-C:HDL-C	(n=41)	r = 0.37	p=0.018
PAHR-25	vs.	LDL-C	(n=34)	r = -0.36	p=0.038
PAHR-25	vs.	TC:HDL-C	(n=34)	r = -0.44	p=0.009
PAHR-25	vs.	LDL-C:HDL-C	(n=34)	r = -0.41	p=0.017

peak $\dot{V}O_2$ is expressed in $mL \cdot kg^{-1} \cdot min^{-1}$
*Included to demonstrate strong trend although $p > 0.05$

($p > 0.05$). Using P140 as an indication of levels of 'moderate' habitual physical activity, the boys were significantly more active than the girls ($U = 483$, $p < 0.05$).

Discussion

The range of plasma lipid-lipoprotein concentrations reported in this study are comparable with values reported from larger scale epidemiological studies[14] although they are lower than those reported in another European study[15]. Peak $\dot{V}O_2$ values are comparable for children of this age using a cycle ergometer[16]. Skinfold data (mm) compare favourably with other studies of healthy children, as do the converted %BF values[17]. When analysing the HPA data, it is difficult to classify the children because there do not appear to be well defined criteria on which to base this assessment. With this in mind, it is noted that the percentage of time spent above previously employed "thresholds" is similar to that reported elsewhere[4,13].

The study confirmed some of the associations between HPA, body composition, and lipid-lipoprotein profile generally described in the literature[3,18]. A main finding in this study was the favourable relationships between HPA and some of the lipid-lipoprotein variables studied in both the boys and girls. One of the associations includes the ratio LDL-C:HDL-C which has been suggested as the best predictor of future coronary heart disease[19]. Although the correlation coefficients (r = -0.31 to -0.44) and explained variances (r^2 = 10 to 19%) are relatively small, they do provide some indication that HPA may have a role to play in shaping children's lipid-lipoprotein profiles. This finding is in contrast to other studies that have employed continuous heart rate monitoring to assess HPA[4]. These differences may be attributed to alternative means of expressing the heart rate data collected. Current thinking regarding health and activity indicates that cumulative periods of activity totalling 30 minutes per day, every day, may be more appropriate than sustained periods of exercise for long-term health gains[20]. For this reason, expressing the heart rate data as total percentages above chosen "thresholds" rather than looking for sustained periods was deemed to be more appropriate.

In line with other studies, %BF may have a modulating effect on the relationship between cardiorespiratory fitness and lipid-lipoproteins[5]. This said, it may indicate that a means for favourably altering a child's lipid-lipoprotein profile could be best achieved by determining the activity required to change %BF. To conclude, this study has demonstrated a weak, but significant relationship between HPA and some of the lipid-lipoprotein variables commonly measured in children.

Acknowledgements

This study was supported by Sunday Best.

References

1. Kannel, W.B. and Dawber, T.R. (1972) Atherosclerosis as a pediatric problem. *Journal of Pediatrics*, Vol. 80. pp. 544-54.
2. Freedman, D.S., Shear, C.L., Srinivasan, S.R., Webber, L.S. and Berenson, G.S. (1985) Tracking serum lipids and lipoproteins in children over an 8-year period: the Bogalusa Heart Study. *Preventive Medicine*, Vol. 14. pp. 203-16.
3. Suter, E. and Hawes, M.R. (1993) Relationship of physical activity, body fat, diet, and blood lipid profile in youths 10-15 yr. *Medicine and Science in Sports and Exercise*, Vol. 25. pp. 748-54.
4. Armstrong, N., Williams, J., Balding, J., Gentle, P. and Kirby, B. (1991) Cardiopulmonary fitness, physical activity patterns, and selected coronary risk factor variables in 11 to 16-year-olds. *Pediatric Exercise Science*, Vol. 3. pp. 219-28.
5. Kwee, A. and Wilmore, J.H. (1990) Cardiorespiratory fitness and risk factors for coronary artery disease in 8- to 15-year-old boys. *Pediatric Exercise Science*, Vol. 2. pp. 372-83.
6. Sady, S.P., Berg, K., Beal, D., Smith, J.L., Savage, M.P., Thompson, W.H. and Nutter, J. (1984) Aerobic fitness and serum high-density lipoprotein cholesterol in young children. *Human Biology*, Vol. 56. pp. 771-81.

7. Tell, G.S. and Vellar, O.D. (1988) Physical fitness, physical activity and cardiovascular disease risk factors in adolescents: the Oslo Youth Study. *Preventive Medicine*, Vol. 17, pp. 12-24.
8. Tanner, J.M. (1962) *Growth at Adolescence*, (2nd ed.), Blackwell Scientific Publications, Oxford.
9. Friedewald, W.T., Levy, R.I. and Frederickson, D.S. (1972) Estimation of the concentration of low-density lipoprotein cholesterol in plasma, without use of the preparative ultracentrifuge. *Clinical Chemistry*, Vol. 18, pp. 499-502.
10. Rowland, T.W. (1993) Aerobic exercise testing protocols, in *Pediatric Laboratory Exercise Testing*, (ed. T.W. Rowland), Human Kinetics, Champaign, Il., pp. 19-42.
11. Rivera-Brown, A.M., Rivera, M.A. and Frontera, W.R. (1992) Application of criteria for $\dot{V}O_2$ max in active adolescents. *Pediatric Exercise Science*, Vol. 4, pp. 331-9.
12. Slaughter, M.H., Lohman, T.G., Boileau, R.A., Horswill, C.A., Stillman, R.J., Van Loan, M.D. and Bemben, D.A. (1988) Skinfold equations for estimation of body fatness in children and youth. *Human Biology*, Vol. 60, pp. 709-23.
13. DuRant, R.H., Baranowski, T., Davis, H., Rhodes, T., Thompson, W.O., Greaves, K.A. and Puhl, J. (1993) Reliability and variability of indicators of heart-rate monitoring in children. *Medicine and Science in Sports and Exercise*, Vol. 25, pp. 389-95.
14. Berenson, G.S. (1986) Evolution of cardiovascular risk factors in early life: perspectives on causation, in *Causation of Cardiovascular Risk Factors in Children*, (ed. G.S. Berenson), Raven Press, New York, pp. 1-26.
15. Kromhout, D., Van Der Haar, F. and Hautvast, J.G.A.J. (1977) Coronary heart disease risk factors in Dutch schoolchildren - results of a pilot-study. *Preventive Medicine*, Vol. 6, pp. 500-13.
16. Armstrong, N. and Welsman, J. (1994) Assessment and interpretation of aerobic fitness in children and adolescents. *Exercise and Sport Sciences Reviews*, Vol. 22, pp. 435-76.
17. Lohman, T.G. (1992) *Advances in Body Composition*, Monograph Number 3, Human Kinetics, Champaign, Il.
18. DuRant, R.H., Linder, C.W. and Mahoney, O.M. (1983) Relationship between habitual physical activity and serum lipoprotein levels in white male adolescents. *Journal of Adolescent Health Care*, Vol. 4, pp. 235-40.
19. Castelli, W.P. (1984) Epidemiology of coronary heart diseases: the Framingham Study. *American Journal of Medicine*, Vol. 76, pp. 4-12.
20. Haskell, W.L. (1994) Health consequences of physical activity: understanding and challenges regarding dose-response. *Medicine and Science in Sports and Exercise*, Vol. 26, pp. 649-60.

PLASMA FIBRINOGEN, PHYSICAL ACTIVITY AND AEROBIC FITNESS IN CHILDREN

A.D. MAHON, C.C. CHEATHAM, K.Q. KELSEY and J.D. BROWN
Human Performance Laboratory, Ball State University, Muncie, USA
Keywords: Activity, fitness, fibrinogen

Introduction

The conversion of fibrinogen (FG) to fibrin is part of a cascade of events that leads to blood thrombus formation[1]. Elevated FG levels have been linked to increased risk for coronary artery disease (CAD) and stroke[2,3,4]. Although high levels of physical activity and aerobic fitness have been associated with decreased risk for CAD[5], the influence of these parameters on FG levels has not been established clearly[3,6,7,8]. In children and adolescents CAD risk factors, including elevated FG levels[9,10], are evident as early as the prepubertal years[11,12]. To what extent FG level is related to physical activity and aerobic fitness in children is unknown. As exercise, activity, and aerobic fitness appear to have a positive influence on risk for CAD in adults[5], it would seem worth studying these relationships in children. Thus, the purpose of this study was to test the hypothesis that physical activity and aerobic fitness ($\dot{V}O_2$ max) are inversely related to FG levels in prepubertal and adolescent children.

Methods

Forty-seven children (29 male and 18 female) 10 to 16 years of age were subjects in this study. Each child was required to report to the laboratory on three separate days. The first day served as an orientation session; on a second day $\dot{V}O_2$ max was measured, and on a third day a resting venous blood sample was obtained in order to measure plasma FG.

Upon entering the laboratory on the first day, an explanation of the study was given and written informed consent was obtained. Height, weight and skinfold thickness were then

Children and Exercise XIX. Edited by Neil Armstrong, Brian Kirby and Joanne Welsman.
Published in 1997 by E & FN Spon, 2–6 Boundary Row, London, SE1 8HN.
ISBN 0 419 22100 X.

measured. A graded exercise test to near maximal effort was then performed to familiarize the child with the procedures used to measure $\dot{V}O_2$ max. In addition, the child and parent were given a copy of the Minnesota Leisure Time physical activity survey[13] along with verbal and written instructions for completing it. Pubertal status (pubic hair)[14] also was assessed on this day via parental report.

On a second day, a graded exercise test to maximal effort was administered on a motor driven treadmill. The protocol consisted of 2 min walking at 1.34 $m{\cdot}s^{-1}$, 2 min jogging at 2.01-2.46 $m{\cdot}s^{-1}$, and 2 min running at either 2.23, 2.46 or 2.68 $m{\cdot}s^{-1}$ depending on age. Thereafter the speed remained constant, but the elevation increased 2.5% per min until maximal voluntary effort was achieved. The slowest speeds were used with children 10-11 y, the intermediate speeds with children 12-13 y and the fastest speeds with children 14-16 y. During the exercise test expired gases were collected into a mixing chamber and analyzed by an Applied Electrochemistry S-3A O_2 and a Sensormedics LB2 CO_2 analyzer which were calibrated prior to each test. Pulmonary ventilation was measured during inspiration using a Parkinson-Cowan dry-gas meter. The gas analyzers and dry-gas meter were interfaced to an IBM compatible computer which recorded respiratory gas exchange measures at 30 s intervals. Heart rate was monitored continuously using a Polar HR monitor.

On a third day, the child reported to the laboratory following an overnight fast, and assumed a supine position for 10 min after which a 4.5 mL blood sample was obtained from an antecubital vein using a vacutainer containing 0.105 M sodium citrate. The sample was then centrifuged at 3250 rpm for 10 min and the plasma extracted and stored at -70°C until later analysis. FG concentration was measured in duplicate using a Diagnostica Stago reagent kit and analysed on either a Diagnostica Stago ST-4 or MLA 1600C analyser by an independent medical laboratory accredited by the American College of American Pathologists.

Physical activity was assessed using the Minnesota Leisure Time survey in a manner modified slightly from the procedures described by Aaron et al.[15]. The child and parent were instructed to record all physical activities that were performed by the child a minimum of five times over the preceding 12 mo. From the survey estimated energy expenditure was calculated as the average $kcal{\cdot}kg^{-1}{\cdot}week^{-1}$ for each activity[16]. The energy expenditures from each activity were then summed to provide an average total weekly energy expenditure.

A two-way (gender by maturation) ANOVA and Pearson-product moment correlations were used to analyse the data. A Tukey-Kramer post-hoc test was used to establish significant differences among maturational groups.

Results

The physical characteristics and plasma FG concentration of the children are presented in table 1. It should be noted that due to the small number of children classified as Tanner

Table 1. Physical characteristics and FG levels in children by Tanner stage and gender

Variable	Gender	T1 (n = 15)	T2 (n = 11)	T3 (n = 8)	T4/5 (n = 13)
Age (y)	B	11.0 (0.8)	11.4 (1.2)	13.2 (1.2)	14.7 (1.0)
	G	10.8 (0.6)	11.6 (1.2)	12.5 (0.7)	14.3 (1.8)
Ht (cm)	B	145.6 (9.4)	150.7 (5.4)	157.9 (11.5)	173.3 (6.2)
	G	144.6 (5.1)	147.2 (6.4)	154.0 (6.9)	164.1 (2.1)
Wt (kg)	B	39.6 (10.4)	48.5 (12.5)	51.7 (9.7)	63.8 (7.7)
	G	37.4 (4.6)	34.8 (3.7)	47.7 (2.3)	55.8 (6.9)
BSA (m^2)	B	1.26 (0.20)	1.42 (0.21)	1.50 (0.20)	1.75 (0.12)
	G	1.22 (0.10)	1.19 (0.09)	1.43 (0.01)	1.59 (0.11)
SS (mm)	B	76.5 (37.9)	91.1 (37.0)	68.9 (9.6)	70.3 (24.1)
	G	66.1 (17.5)	45.9 (12.5)	71.6 (13.5)	90.0 (26.7)
FG ($mL{\cdot}dL^{-1}$)	B	280.6 (43.5)	261.8 (38.2)	284.2 (21.0)	281.8 (50.1)
	G	255.7 (9.5)	262.8 (59.7)	293.7 (58.1)	265.5 (40.3)

Values are mean $\pm$ SD
B = Boys (n = 29); G = Girls (n = 18); SS = sum of six skinfolds

stage 4 and 5, these two groups were combined into one group. The two-way ANOVA revealed that body surface area and weight were lower ($p < 0.05$) in girls compared to the boys, but age, height and sum of skinfolds were similar ($p > 0.05$). There was a significant maturation effect for age, weight, height, and body surface area, but not for the sum of skinfolds. Post-hoc analyses revealed that Tanner stage 4/5 children were significantly different than the other three groups with respect to these variables. Tanner stage 3 children were older than the two youngest groups and also were taller, heavier, and had a larger body surface area than Tanner stage 1 children ($p < 0.05$). No other maturation differences for any of the physical characteristics were observed, nor were there any significant interactions among these variables. Plasma FG concentrations across each group are also displayed in table 1. There were no significant main effects or interaction with respect to FG concentration.

The physiological responses at maximal exercise and the average amount of physical activity across maturation groups and gender are outlined in table 2. There was a significant gender by maturation interaction for $\dot{V}O_2$ max regardless of whether it was expressed in $L{\cdot}min^{-1}$, relative to body weight or relative to body surface area. In absolute terms, $\dot{V}O_2$ max in boys increased across maturation stages more so than in girls. When expressed relative to body surface area, $\dot{V}O_2$ max increased steadily in boys across the four maturational groups while in girls an initial increase from Tanner stage 1 to stage 2 was followed by a decline through Tanner stage 3 and 4/5. When expressed relative to body weight, a similar trend was noted for the girls, whereas $\dot{V}O_2$ max tended to remain stable in boys. $\dot{V}O_2$ max also was higher in boys versus girls regardless of how it was expressed. Significant maturation effects were noted for $\dot{V}O_2$ max in $L{\cdot}min^{-1}$ and relative to body

Table 2. Physiological responses at maximal exercise and physical activity by Tanner stage and gender

Variable	Sex	T1	T2	T3	T4/5
$\dot{V}O_2$ ($L \cdot min^{-1}$)	B	2.02 (0.33)	2.41 (0.31)	2.92 (0.73)	3.47 (0.28)
	G	1.87 (0.27)	1.91 (0.31)	2.27 (0.17)	2.31 (0.22)
$\dot{V}O_2$ ($mL \cdot kg^{-1} \cdot min^{-1}$)	B	52.1 (8.5)	51.8 (5.4)	55.7 (5.0)	54.4 (3.9)
	G	49.2 (3.5)	54.3 (4.7)	48.1 (2.6)	41.5 (6.0)
$\dot{V}O_2$ ($mL \cdot m^{-2} \cdot min^{-1}$)	B	1612.2 (206.1)	1698.2 (71.5)	1918.8 (268.1)	1985.2 (80.6)
	G	1523.0 (122.2)	1605.8 (173.6)	1591.7 (101.2)	1453.3 (164.8)
HR ($beats \cdot min^{-1}$)	B	200.3 (5.8)	202.2 (4.7)	203.4 (6.4)	202.4 (6.9)
	G	201.2 (7.7)	203.2 (5.5)	202.7 (2.5)	202.5 (7.6)
RER	B	1.11 (0.08)	1.15 (0.07)	1.17 (0.07)	1.17 (0.05)
	G	1.14 (0.06)	1.14 (0.08)	1.06 (0.06)	1.17 (0.03)
Physical activity	B	55.2 (49.6)	57.5 (22.9)	62.8 (20.8)	84.9 (39.8)
($kcal \cdot kg^{-1} \cdot week^{-1}$)	G	33.6 (28.7)	76.7 (29.1)	44.6 (33.5)	70.2 (49.3)

Values are mean ± SD

body surface area, but not when $\dot{V}O_2$ max was expressed relative to body weight. $\dot{V}O_2$ max ($mL \cdot m^{-2} \cdot min^{-1}$) was greater in Tanner stage 3 and 4/5 children compared to stage 1 children. $\dot{V}O_2$ max ($L \cdot min^{-1}$) was significantly greater in Tanner stage 3 and stage 4/5 children versus the two younger groups. There were no significant differences with respect to HR and RER at maximal exercise, nor were there any significant differences with respect to physical activity.

The correlations between plasma FG, aerobic fitness, physical activity and selected anthropometrical measurements are detailed in table 3. As can be seen, there were no significant correlations among any of the measures when related to plasma FG. When these same analyses were performed using a partial correlation to factor out the influence of body fat, no significant relationships were noted. Physical activity was moderately related to aerobic fitness when $\dot{V}O_2$ max was expressed relative to body weight ($r = 0.45$; $p < 0.05$), or relative to body surface area ($r = 0.42$; $p < 0.05$), but not when it was expressed in $L \cdot min^{-1}$ ($r = 0.28$; $p > 0.05$).

Discussion

An elevated FG level has been identified as an independent risk factor for CAD and stroke [2,3,4]. Despite the fact that the symptoms of CAD do not manifest themselves until adulthood, it is generally accepted that risk factors such as obesity, hypertension, hyperlipidemia and physical inactivity have paediatric origins[9,10,11,12]. Furthermore, the finding that elevated FG levels are evident in children, and that FG in children is correlated

Table 3. Zero-order correlations between FG concentration and $\dot{V}O_2$ max, physical activity, selected anthropometrical variables

Variable	r	p-value
$\dot{V}O_2$ ($L \cdot min^{-1}$)	0.13	0.39
$\dot{V}O_2$ ($mL \cdot kg^{-1} \cdot min^{-1}$)	0.02	0.88
$\dot{V}O_2$ ($mL \cdot m^{-2} \cdot min^{-1}$)	0.09	0.54
PA ($kcal \cdot kg^{-1} \cdot week^{-1}$)	0.04	0.82
Wt (kg)	0.16	0.30
SS (mm)	0.12	0.42
BSA (m^2)	0.14	0.36

with several blood lipid variables is in agreement with several adult studies[9,10]. Although the potential impact of physical activity on FG is uncertain[3,6,7,8], it is generally agreed that exercise training has a positive affect on reducing the risk for CAD[5]. Whether this same influence applies to children is not entirely clear[10], but certainly deserving of further study since childhood may be an optimal time to develop positive habits and attitudes towards physical activity and exercise and possibly lower the risk for future development of CAD.

The results of this study indicate that neither aerobic fitness nor physical activity has an impact on plasma FG levels in children of this age. These results are in contrast to the data reported by Rosengren et al.[7] who reported that FG concentration was inversely related to physical activity in non-smokers. Similarly, Stratton et al.[8] found that 6-months of endurance training increased $\dot{V}O_2$ max and decreased plasma FG concentration in older males (60-82 y), whereas there was no change in FG level in younger males despite a significant increase in $\dot{V}O_2$ max as a result of the training. El-Sayed and Davies[6] also reported no significant changes in FG levels in young adults following 12 wk endurance training despite a significant increase in $\dot{V}O_2$ max. Several factors may influence the discrepancies noted with this literature including the age of the subjects and the FG concentration at the time of study. It is possible that when FG concentrations are in the normal range, physical training may have little influence on the degree of change.

The fact that both physical activity and aerobic fitness were not related to plasma FG concentration may not be that surprising. A number of reports that have examined the relationship of fitness and/or activity to a variety of CAD risk factors in children have reported generally inconsistent results. For instance Armstrong et al.[17] reported significant correlations between $\dot{V}O_2$ max and body fatness and blood pressure in girls (mean age, 13.2 y). For boys (mean age, 13.2 y) these authors reported significant correlations between $\dot{V}O_2$ max and body fatness and some serum lipid measures. However, in both groups of children the significant relationships were lost when body fatness was factored out using partial correlations. No relationships were reported in either sex when habitual level of physical activity was examined. Suter and Hawes[18] examined fitness, activity and blood lipid profiles in 10- to 15-year-old children and found that estimated $\dot{V}O_2$ max was unrelated to any blood lipid parameter. In contrast, physical activity was related to some lipid measures, but not all.

In summary, this study examined the relationship of aerobic fitness ($\dot{V}O_2$ max) and physical activity measured by a 12-month recall survey on plasma FG concentration in 10- to 16-year-old children. The results indicated that there was no relationship between either aerobic fitness or physical activity and plasma FG concentration. Physical activity was moderately, but significantly correlated to $\dot{V}O_2$ max when expressed relative to body size. Although physical activity and aerobic fitness were not related to plasma FG concentration in this age-group, developing and maintaining desirable levels of activity and fitness may have an positive impact on other risk factors for cardiovascular disease.

Acknowledgments

Supported by a grant received from the National Association of Sport and Physical Education

References

1. Vick, R.L. (1984) *Contemporary Medical Physiology*, Addison-Wesley Publishing Company, Reading, MA, pp. 393-4.
2. Kannel, W.B., Wolf, P.A., Castelli, W.P. and D'Agostoin, R.B. (1987) Fibrinogen and risk of cardiovascular disease: the Framingham Study. *Journal of the American Medical Association*, Vol. 258, pp. 1183-6.
3. El-Sayed, M.S. (1996) Fibrinogen levels and exercise: Is there a relationship? *Sports Medicine*, Vol. 21, pp. 402-8.
4. Wilhelmsen, L., Svardsudd, K., Korsan-Bengsten, K., Larsson, B., Welin, L. and Tibblin, G. (1984) Fibrinogen as a risk factor for stroke and myocardial infarction. *New England Journal of Medicine*, Vol. 311, pp. 501-5.
5. Haskell, W.L., Leon, A.S., Caspersen, C.J., Froehlicher, V.F., Hagberg, J.A., Harlan, W., Holloszy, J.O., Regensteiner, J.G., Thompson, P.D., Washburn, R.A. and Wilson, P.W.F. (1992) Cardiovascular benefits and assessment of physical activity and physical fitness in adults. *Medicine and Science in Sports and Exercise*, Vol. 24, pp. S201-20.
6. El-Sayed, M.S. and Davies, B. (1995) A physical conditioning program does not alter fibrinogen concentration in young healthy subjects. *Medicine and Science in Sports and Exercise*, Vol. 27, pp. 485-9.
7. Rosengren, A., Wilhelmsen, L., Welin, L., Tsipogianni, A., Teger-Nilsson, A.C. and Wedel, H. (1990) Social influences and cardiovascular risk factors as determinants of plasma fibrinogen concentration in a general population sample of middle aged men. *British Medical Journal*, Vol. 300, pp. 634-8.

8. Stratton, J.R., Chandler, W.L., Schwartz, R.S., Cerqueira, M.D., Levy, W.C., Kahn, S.E., Larson, V.G., Cain, K.C., Beard, J.C. and Abrass, I.B. (1991) Effects of physical conditioning on fibrinolytic variables and fibrinogen in young and old healthy adults. *Circulation,* Vol. 83, pp. 1692-7.
9. Bao, W., Srinivasan, S.R. and Berenson, G.S. (1993) Plasma fibrinogen and its correlates in children from a biracial community: the Bogalusa Heart Study. *Pediatric Research,* Vol. 33, pp. 323-6.
10. Sanchez-Bayle, M., Cocho, P., Baeza, J., Vila, S. and the Nino Jesus Group (1993) Fibrinogen as a cardiovascular risk factor in Spanish children and adolescents. *American Heart Journal,* Vol. 126, pp. 322-6.
11. Baranowski, T., Bouchard, C. Bar-Or, O., Bricker, T., Heath, G., Kimm, S.Y.S., Malina, R., Obarzanek, E., Pate, R., Strong, W.B., Truman, B. and Washington, R. (1992) Assessment, prevalence, and cardiovascular benefits of physical activity and fitness in youth. *Medicine and Science in Sports and Exercise,* Vol. 24, pp. S237-47.
12. Vaccaro, P. and Mahon, A.D. (1989) The effects of exercise on coronary heart disease risk factors in children. *Sports Medicine,* Vol. 8, pp. 139-53.
13. Taylor, H.L., Jacobs, D.R., Schucker, B., Knudsen, J., Leon, A.S. and Debacker, G. (1978) A questionnaire for the assessment of leisure time physical activities. *Journal of Chronic Diseases,* Vol. 31, pp. 741-55.
14. Tanner, J. M. (1962) *Growth at Adolescence,* Blackwell Scientific Publications, Oxford, pp. 32-3.
15. Aaron, D.J, Kriska, A.M., Dearwater, S.R., Anderson, R.L., Olsen, T.L., Cauley, J.A. and Laporte, R.E. (1993) The epidemiology of leisure physical activity in an adolescent population. *Medicine and Science in Sports and Exercise,* Vol. 25, pp. 847-53.
16. Katch, V.L., Katch, F.I. and McArdle, W.D. (1996) *Calorie Expenditure Charts for Physical Activity,* Fitness Technologies Press, Ann Arbor, Mi.
17. Armstrong, N., Williams, J., Balding, J., Gentle, P. and Kirby, B. (1991) Cardiopulmonary fitness, physical activity patterns, and selected coronary risk factor variables in 11- to 16-year-old children. *Pediatric Exercise Science,* Vol. 3, pp. 219-28.
18. Suter, E. and Hawes, M.R. (1993) Relationship of physical activity, body fat, diet, and blood lipid profile in youths 10-15 yr. *Medicine and Science in Sports and Exercise,* Vol. 25, pp. 748-54.

PART II

PHYSICAL ACTIVITY PATTERNS

VALIDITY OF TWO PHYSICAL ACTIVITY MONITORS IN CHILDREN AND ADOLESCENTS

Laboratory analysis of two accelerometers

P.S. FREEDSON, J. SIRARD and N. DEBOLD
Department of Exercise Science, University of Massachusetts, Amherst, USA
R. PATE and M. DOWDA
Department of Exercise Science, University of South Carolina, Columbia, USA
J. SALLIS
Department of Psychology, San Diego State University, San Diego, USA
Keywords: Accelerometers, Caltrac, CSA monitor, physical activity, Tritrac

Introduction

Assessment of physical activity in youth is a complex problem. Typically, questionnaires or activity check lists are used to characterize physical activity among youth. Numerous concerns arise with this type of evaluation including inaccurate recall of activity and the inability of these measures to capture all types of physical activity in this population. Accelerometer based motion sensors appear to be attractive alternatives as they can be used to directly measure movement. The first generation of this type of motion sensor was the Caltrac which is a single plane accelerometer that accumulates counts or kilocalories over time. Total activity is quantified as counts or kilocalories resulting in a generalized measure of physical activity. This monitor has been validated in both laboratory[1,2] and field settings[3,4].

Recent advances in motion sensor technology include the development of the Tritrac and Computer Science and Applications, Inc (CSA) accelerometers. The Tritrac contains three accelerometers that assess motion in the vertical, horizontal, and mediolateral planes. The CSA monitor is a single plane accelerometer. Both monitors also contain a memory that permits storage of data where user specified time intervals permit quantification of patterns of physical activity. A few studies have examined this new generation of monitors in studies of instrument validity in the laboratory[5] and in the field[6-8]. Janz et al.[8] have used the CSA monitor for assessment of physical activity in children.

No studies have examined the validity and reliability of these instruments simultaneously using measured energy expenditure as the criterion measure. This type of comparison is useful for assisting researchers in deciding which monitor may be best suited for assessment of physical activity in children. Therefore, the aims of this study

Children and Exercise XIX. Edited by Neil Armstrong, Brian Kirby and Joanne Welsman.
Published in 1997 by E & FN Spon, 2–6 Boundary Row, London, SE1 8HN.
ISBN 0 419 22100 X.

were: a) to evaluate inter-instrument reliability for each monitor and b) to examine how each accelerometer differentiates exercise intensity.

Subjects

The original sample for this investigation included 81 volunteers from 1st through 12th grade (40 males and 41 females). There were approximately 20 children (10 males and 10 females) from each of the following grade groups: Group A - 1st and 2nd, Group B - 3rd, 4th and 5th, Group C - 7th, 8th and 9th, and Group D - 11th and 12th. Parental or guardian and participant written informed consent was obtained in compliance with the university policy on the use of human subjects. Table 1 presents descriptive data for the subjects.

Methods

The Computer Science and Applications, Inc. (Shalimar, FL) Model 7164 is a vertical plane accelerometer (5.1 x 4.1 x 1.5 cm, 43 g) that assesses vertical accelerations ranging from 0.05 - 2.0 G's and is bandlimited with a frequency response from 0.25 - 2.5 Hz. These parameters detect normal body motion and filter high frequency vibrations. The acceleration signal is filtered by an analog bandpass filter and is digitized by an 8 bit A/D converter at 10 samples per second. Each digitized signal is summed over a user specified time interval and at the end of each epoch, the activity count is stored internally and the accumulator is reset to zero.

The Tritrac-R3D (Hemokinetics, Inc., Madison, WI) is a triaxial accelerometer (11.0 x 6.9 x 3.3 cm, 170 g) that assesses motion in the vertical, horizontal, and mediolateral planes. Acceleration counts for each plane are sampled at a user specified interval and are stored as counts for each plane separately and for the combined motion in all planes (vector magnitude). The vector magnitude is calculated as the square root of the sum of the squared activity counts in each plane. Activity kilocalories and total kilocalorie expenditure are also calculated for the Tritrac but will not be reported in this paper.

Subjects reported to the Human Performance Laboratory on one occasion. Following completion of the informed consent document, height and body mass were measured and subjects were introduced and familiarized with the equipment. For all four grade groups two CSA monitors were attached to an elastic belt that was securely fitted around the waist, next to the skin, with monitors positioned above the right and left iliac crest. For grade groups C and D, two Tritrac monitors were placed in Neoprene hip pouches and firmly secured directly above the CSA monitors. Only the CSA monitor was tested in the younger children (groups A and B) because the two Tritrac monitors were too large and affected the younger children's gait patterns. A 5-6 min treadmill practice period was subsequently completed where subjects walked and jogged on the treadmill at the three test speeds.

Subjects completed 5 min of walking or jogging at each of the following velocities: 4.4, 6.4, 9.7 $km \cdot h^{-1}$. The order of conditions was balanced across subjects and a 5 min

Table 1. Descriptive characteristics

Variable	n=81	
Age (y)	11.6 ± 3.97	(6.0 - 18.0)
Mass (kg)	46.0 ± 17.63	(19.6 - 104.6)
Height (cm)	149.3 ± 20.05	(111.8 - 190.5)

Values are mean ± SD (range)

rest period separated the conditions. Treadmill speed was verified with the subject on the treadmill by applying a high precision digital Biddle tachometer (Plymouth Meeting, PA) to the surface of the treadmill. Respiratory gas exchange was monitored minute-by-minute using an on-line data acquisition system. $\dot{V}O_2$ Plus software (Exeter Research, Exeter, NH) computed metabolic measures and the average of minutes four and five represented the metabolic cost for each condition. The average of the five, 1 min count values for the Tritrac and CSA monitors were used for subsequent analysis.

Results

Table 2 presents the inter-unit reliability data for the CSA and Tritrac monitors. The Pearson and intraclass correlation coefficients for the CSA monitor were all greater than r = 0.84 indicating good inter-unit reliability for all three treadmill speeds. Although the Tritrac unit intraclass reliability coefficients were high for the two walking speeds, the intraclass r was only 0.41 for the jogging speed. The intraclass and Pearson correlation coefficients for the Tritrac were quite different indicating that when total variance for the activity monitor is partitioned into between subjects and between instruments for the intraclass model, the inter-unit variation causes a large decrease in the correlation coefficient. Mean differences between units ranged from 3.8 - 6.4% for the Tritrac and 5.1 - 8.9% for the CSA monitor.

Right hip activity monitor data were used for subsequent analyses. The average (± SD) intensities for the three conditions (2 walking, 1 jogging) were: 4.6 (± 0.87), 6.8 (± 1.12), and 10.4 (± 1.04) METS. It was necessary to use a multiple regression approach rather than simple correlations between METS and monitor counts because

Table 2. Inter-unit reliability

Velocity		CSA			Tritrac	
($km{\cdot}h^{-1}$)	n	Pearson r	Intraclass r	n	Pearson r	Intraclass r
4.4	71	0.84	0.99	39	0.44	0.97
6.4	70	0.91	0.99	39	0.59	0.95
9.7	69	0.94	0.96	38	0.32	0.41

both body size and age affect the dependent variable (METS) during walking and running exercise. For the CSA monitor, the significant predictors of METS were counts per minute and age ($R^2 = 0.86$). For the Tritrac monitor, a multiple regression equation with Tritrac counts per minute, mass, and height as the independent variables yielded an R^2 of 0.90.

Figure 1 displays the relationship between METS and counts per minute for the CSA and Tritrac activity monitors. Both monitors appear to differentiate walking and jogging exercise intensities between the 4 and 10 MET range reasonably well.

For the 2.2 MET increase between the two walking speeds, there was a 1912 count increase for the CSA monitor. The 3.6 MET difference between the faster walking speed and the jogging speed of 9.7 km·h^{-1}, resulted in a 2998 count increase. Thus it appears that the rate of increase in CSA counts is linear between 4.6 and 10.4 METS for walking and jogging. For the Tritrac, a 2.2 MET change corresponded to a 795 count difference between the walking speeds and the 3.6 MET difference between the faster walking and jogging speeds yielded a 2156 count difference. The count increase per MET averaged 846 counts and 547 counts for the CSA and Tritrac monitors, respectively.

Discussion

The inter-instrument reliability for the CSA monitor is excellent for both moderate and high intensity exercise. Although the between Tritrac unit means differed by less than 6.5%, it appears that the variability between Tritrac units is sufficiently high to indicate poor inter-unit stability. One factor that may have contributed to this high inter-unit variation is that we were unable to stabilize these units as securely as the CSA monitor because of the size of the device. The Tritrac is nearly 3 times as large as the CSA monitor and we had to place these units in a fanny pack that was secured around the waist with a belt. At the higher jogging speed, it appeared that the pack was not totally secure around the waist causing some extraneous pack movement that may have resulted in inconsistent readings. This was not a problem with the smaller CSA units which remained securely in place on the hip for all exercise conditions. When monitoring physical activity in small children, it may be desirable to select the smaller device to

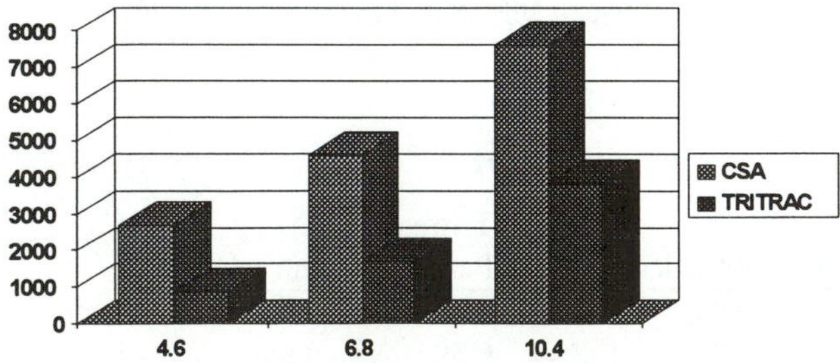

Fig. 1. Relationship between METs (x axis) and counts per minute (y axis)

eliminate the possibility of picking up motion that is not directly related to physical activity.

Use of accelerometry during level walking and jogging appears to differentiate exercise intensity in a consistent manner within the range of 4.6 to 10.4 METS. The R^2s were high for both monitors and are similar to data reported by others in studies using the Caltrac[1,2] and an earlier model CSA monitor in children[6] and adults[7]. Additional research is needed examining the use of this monitor in a field setting with children to objectively determine total activity and patterns of activity with consideration for time spent in different exercise intensities.

Acknowledgments

Funded by Cowles Media Foundation

References

1. Maliszewski, A.F., Freedson, P.S., Ebbeling, C.J., Crussmeyer, J. and Kastango, K.B. (1991) Validity of the Caltrac accelerometer in estimating energy expenditure and activity in children and adults. *Pediatric Exercise Science*, Vol. 3, pp.141-51.
2. Sallis, J.F., Buono, M.J., Roby, J.J., Carlson, D. and Nelson, J.A. (1990) The Caltrac accelerometer as a physical activity monitor for school-age children. *Medicine and Science in Sports and Exercise*, Vol. 22, pp. 698-703.
3. Klesges, L.M. and Klesges, R.C. (1987) The assessment of children's physical activity: a comparison of methods. *Medicine and Science in Sports and Exercise*, Vol. 19, pp.511-7.
4. Danner, F.M., Noland, M., McFadden, K., Dewait, K. and Kotchen, J.M. (1991) Description of the physical activity of young children using movement sensor and observation methods. *Pediatric Exercise Science*, Vol. 3, pp.11-20.
5. Melanson, E.L. and Freedson, P.S. (1995) Validity of the Computer Science and Applications, Inc. (CSA) activity monitor. *Medicine and Science in Sports and Exercise*, Vol. 27, pp.934-40.
6. Janz, K.F. (1994) Validation of the CSA accelerometer for assessing children's physical activity. *Medicine and Science in Sports and Exercise*, Vol. 26, pp. 369-75.
7. Matthews, C. E. and Freedson, P.S. (1995) Field trial of a three dimensional activity monitor: Comparison with self report. *Medicine and Science in Sports and Exercise*, Vol. 27, pp.1071-8.
8. Janz, K.F., Witt, J. and Mahoney, L.T. (1995) The stability of children's physical activity as measured by accelerometry and self-report. *Medicine and Science in Sports and Exercise*, Vol. 27, pp.1326-32.

VALIDATION OF THE TRITRAC-R3D™ ACTIVITY MONITOR DURING TYPICAL CHILDREN'S ACTIVITIES

TRITRAC-R3D™ activity monitor validation

R.G. ESTON, A.V. ROWLANDS and D.K. INGLEDEW
School of Sport, Health and Physical Education Sciences, University of Wales, Bangor, UK

Keywords: Accelerometry, heart rate, oxygen uptake, physical activity

Introduction

There is increasing concern about the level of physical activity in children. As children lack the cognitive ability to recall details about their activity patterns[1], objective methods, such as heart rate monitoring, have been used. However, this is subject to several well documented limitations[2].

Conceptually, the measurement of movement as a measure of physical activity is preferred. As this occurs in more than one plane, a comprehensive picture of total activity may be more accurately assessed by three dimensional accelerometry. This has been reported to be a valid physical activity assessment tool in children when heart rate is used as the criterion[3]. However, there are problems with the use of heart rate as a criterion measure.

The purpose of this study was to compare the accuracy of heart rate monitoring and three dimensional accelerometry for estimating the oxygen consumption (energy expenditure) of a number of typical childhood activities. These results are taken from a larger study involving the use of other accelerometry techniques (e.g., WAM, Computer Science Applications, Shalimar, Florida) and simple uniaxial pedometers, which will be reported elsewhere.

Methods

Subjects were 30 children (15 boys and 15 girls) aged between 8.2 and 10.8 y (mean = 9.3 ± 0.8 y, mass 29.8 ± 5.9 kg, height 133.7 ± 8.1 cm) from a local primary school in

Children and Exercise XIX. Edited by Neil Armstrong, Brian Kirby and Joanne Welsman.
Published in 1997 by E & FN Spon, 2–6 Boundary Row, London, SE1 8HN.
ISBN 0 419 22100 X.

the Bangor area of North Wales. Written informed consent was obtained from parents or guardians.

The relationship between accelerometry, heart rate (HR) and oxygen uptake ($\dot{V}O_2$) was assessed during two walking speeds (4 and 6 km·h^{-1} i.e. 1.11 and 1.67 m·s^{-1}) and two running speeds (8 and 10 km·h^{-1} i.e. 2.22 and 2.78 m·s^{-1}) on an electronically driven treadmill. In addition, three non-regulated activities were also performed; playing catch, hopscotch and sitting and crayoning.

Heart rate was measured using a BHL 6000 Medical heart rate monitoring system and stored for later analysis. The Tritrac™ monitor was programmed with the child's height, mass, age and sex and set to record activity data on a min by min basis. The unit was taped securely to a belt positioned on the right hip during all activities. The $\dot{V}O_2$ was measured by on-line gas analysis every 30 s during each activity (Biokinetics, Bangor, U.K.), using a very lightweight, low resistance mouthpiece. Samples of the expired air were drawn through 4mm tubing and breath-by-breath volumes were monitored continuously. All measurements were referenced to the same watch so data could be matched temporally.

After 5 min habituation to the Powerjog treadmill, the child walked at 4 km·h^{-1} and 6 km·h^{-1} and ran at 8 km·h^{-1} and 10 km·h^{-1} for 4 min at each speed. After a rest period to allow HR to return to resting levels, the subject played hopscotch for 4 min. This involved alternately hopping and jumping on a hopscotch grid at the subject's preferred pace (knowing they would be required to keep it up for 4 min). The subject rested again to allow HR to return to baseline, then played catch with an assistant. A football was used and the pace was not regulated, however, it was constant throughout the 4 min. The subject then sat and relaxed. After resting HR was reached the child sat down and crayoned for 10 min.

Data analyses

All analyses were performed on steady-state $\dot{V}O_2$ and HR data and expressed per min. Oxygen uptake was expressed as a ratio of body mass raised to the power 0.75, which has been reported to be the most valid when comparing prepubertal children to adults performing similar activities[4]. This exponential scaling factor of body mass is also the same as reported in the comparative zoology literature[5].

The output from the Tritrac™ provides separate activity count values for each of the three dimensions (tritrac x = mediolateral, tritrac y = anterior-posterior and tritrac z = vertical) and a three-dimensional vector [tritot = $(x^2 + y^2 + z^2)^{0.5}$] representation of the count. Each output was analysed to assess whether the assessment of three-dimensions offered any advantage over the assessment of any one dimension.

Pearson product-moment correlations were used to assess the concurrent validity of the Tritrac™ and HR monitoring. Simple linear regression equations were computed to predict $\dot{V}O_2$ from each measure. A one-way repeated measures ANOVA with Tukey post hoc tests was used to compare the percentage errors from the prediction of $\dot{V}O_2$ using tritot, tritrac x, y, z and heart rate.

Results

All correlations between the scaled $\dot{V}O_2$ measurements ($S\dot{V}O_2$) and measured variables were significant ($p < 0.001$) (table 1). All Tritrac™ variables (tritot, x, y, z) correlated more highly with $S\dot{V}O_2$ than with HR when all or non-regulated activities were considered. However, when only treadmill activities were considered, HR showed a better relationship with $S\dot{V}O_2$ than the anterior-posterior and mediolateral vectors from the Tritrac™.

When the Tritrac™ measures were correlated with HR as opposed to $S\dot{V}O_2$ a different trend in scores was shown (table 2). For example, when all activities were considered, the mediolateral component (x) was the best predictor, as opposed to the worst when $S\dot{V}O_2$ was the criterion.

Table 1: Correlations with $S\dot{V}O_2$

Activity	Tritrac total	Tritrac x	Tritrac y	Tritrac z	Heart rate
All	0.907	0.845	0.858	0.890	0.797
Treadmill	0.881	0.760	0.740	0.862	0.780
Unregulated	0.926	0.865	0.892	0.925	0.858

Table 2: Correlations with heart rate

Activity	Tritrac total	Tritrac x	Tritrac y	Tritrac z
All	0.791	0.816	0.750	0.756
Treadmill	0.855	0.835	0.760	0.805
Unregulated	0.876	0.864	0.849	0.867

All correlations are significant ($p < 0.001$)

During all activities, except crayoning and catching, the major acceleration component was in the vertical plane (z), followed by the anterior-posterior (y) with accelerations in the medio-lateral plane (x) having the smallest value (fig 1). During crayoning and catching, y was the dominant acceleration component, followed by x for crayoning and z for catching.

Regression equations were computed to predict $S\dot{V}O_2$ from tritot, x, y, z and heart rate for all activities together (tritot and HR are illustrated in figs 2 and 3).

$$S\dot{V}O_2 = 0.012\text{tritot} + 25.697$$

$$S\dot{V}O_2 = 0.624\text{hr} - 32$$

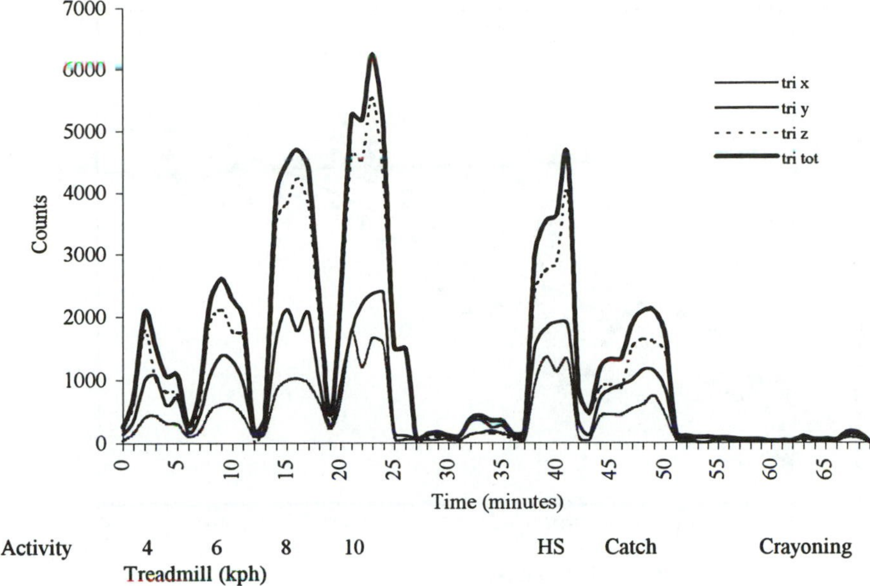

HS = hopscotch

Fig.1. A typical plot of the Tritrac™ output.

All prediction equations overestimated $S\dot{V}O_2$, though differences between actual $S\dot{V}O_2$ and predicted values were not significant ($F_{5,840} = 0.26$, $p=0.937$). However, significant differences were present in the percentage of predicted error between measures ($F_{4,672} = 4.39$, $p= 0.002$). These differences were between the Tritrac™ total activity count (tritot) and HR, y and HR, z and HR. The difference in percentage prediction error remained when a treadmill specific regression equation was used to predict $S\dot{V}O_2$ for treadmill activities only, and when an unregulated activity specific regression equation was used for unregulated activities only (fig 4). The greater scatter of the data around the regression line when heart rate is used as the predictor is also indicated in figs 2 and 3.

Discussion

This study examined the validity of the Tritrac™ against $S\dot{V}O_2$ during several regulated and non-regulated activities. Both the Tritrac™ and HR had a linear relationship with $S\dot{V}O_2$. The Tritrac™ was superior to HR as a predictor of $S\dot{V}O_2$ when raw HR values were used, although there is still a large standard deviation around the percentage error for the Tritrac™ (fig 4).

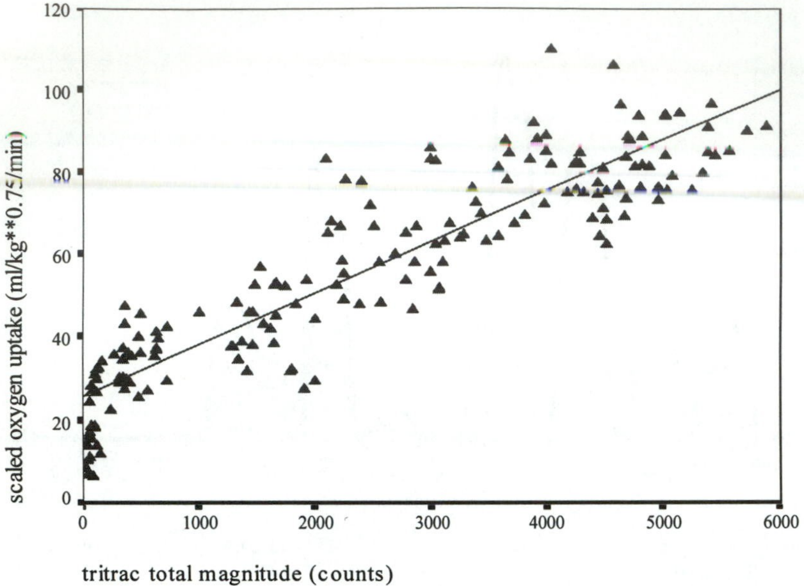

Fig. 2. Relationship between Tritrac™ total activity (tritot) and the scaled oxygen uptake measurements ($S\dot{V}O_2$).

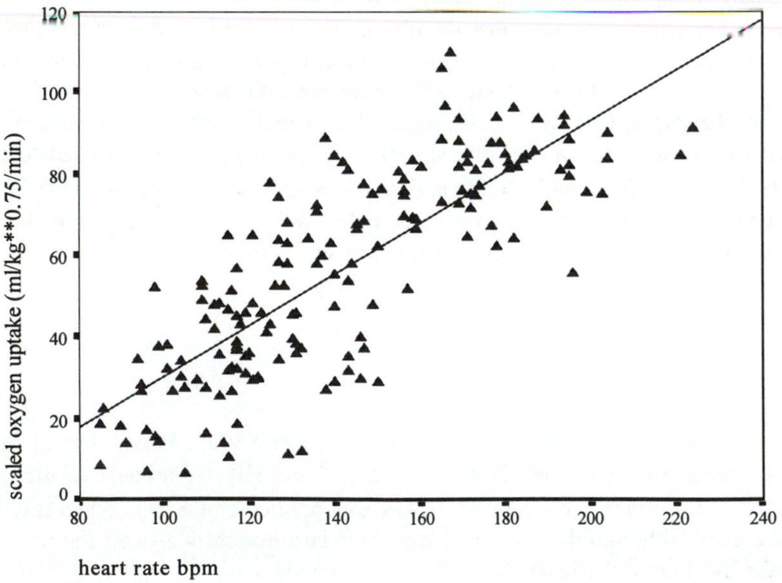

Fig. 3. Relationship between heart rate and scaled oxygen uptake measurements ($S\dot{V}O_2$).

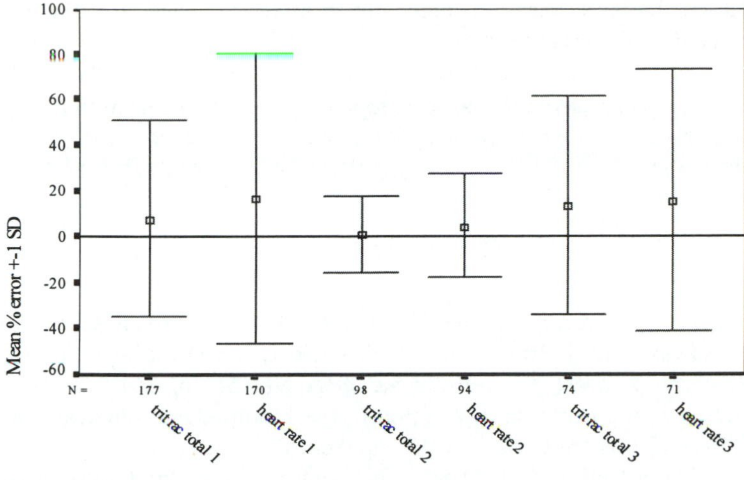

1=all activities predicted from overall regression equation
2=treadmill activities predicted from treadmill specific regression equation
3=unregulated activities predicted from unregulated activity specific regression equation

Fig. 4. Percentage error in prediction of $S\dot{V}O_2$ from Tritrac™ and heart rate. The error of the Tritrac™ total activity count (tritot) was lower.

Accelerometry tended to over estimate $S\dot{V}O_2$, particularly during sedentary activities, which supports some[6], but contradicts other previous research[7,8]. Underestimations of activity by accelerometers is sometimes attributed to their inability to detect load-carrying or uphill walking situations[8], although neither was used in this study. Unpublished work, cited in the latter study, indicated that the Tritrac™ is a good estimate of level walking, but tended to overestimate running energy expenditure by 68%. In the present study $S\dot{V}O_2$ for running and walking were overestimated by $0.5 \pm 17.0\%$ when a treadmill specific regression equation was used, and $3.8 \pm 17.0\%$ when the overall regression equation was used.

Time spent in each activity was well recorded for Tritrac™ (fig 1). This conflicts with previous studies which observed that Tritrac™ overestimated time spent in inactive pursuits and underestimated time spent in light, moderate and hard pursuits[8], although the time scale in the present study was much shorter.

The results indicate that more information is gained from triaxial accelerometry than uniaxial accelerometry. However, uniaxial accelerometry in either the vertical or anterior-posterior axis showed a significantly lower percentage prediction error than HR.

The higher correlations between $S\dot{V}O_2$ and Tritrac™ or HR during unregulated activities are not surprising. During treadmill running the activity levels of the children were more homogenous, which would most likely lead to lower correlations. As dren's habitual activity levels vary, it is important to assess the validity of the instrument across as many activities as possible.

In conclusion, either triaxial or uniaxial accelerometry exceeds the ability of HR to predict $S\dot{V}O_2$. Triaxial accelerometry appears to have greater potential in free ranging activities where the dominant movement is not along the vertical axis (for example, catching and crayoning).

References

1. Wallace, J.P., McKenzie, T.L. and Nader, P.R. (1985) Observed vs. recall exercise behaviour: a validation of a seven day exercise recall for boys 11-13 year old. *Research Quarterly for Exercise and Sport*, Vol. 56, pp.161-5.
2. Riddoch, C.J. and Boreham, C.A. (1995) The health-related physical activity of children. *Sports Medicine*, Vol. 19, pp. 86-102.
3. Welk, G.J. and Corbin, C.B. (1995) The validity of the Tritrac-R3D activity monitor for the assessment of physical activity in children. *Research Quarterly for Exercise and Sport*, Vol. 66, pp. 202-9.
4. Rogers, D.M., Olson, B.L. and Wilmore, J.H. (1995) Scaling for the $\dot{V}O_2$-to-body size relationship among children and adults. *Journal of Applied Physiology*, Vol. 79, pp. 958-67.
5. Schmidt-Nielsen, K. (1984) *Scaling: why is Animal Size so Important?* Cambridge University Press, Cambridge, U.K.
6. Meijer, G.A., Westerterp, K.R., Koper, H. and Hoor, F.T. (1989) Assessment of energy expenditure by recording heart rate and body acceleration. *Medicine and Science in Sports and Exercise*, Vol. 21, pp. 343-7.
7. Bouten, C.V., Westerterp, K.R., Verduin, M. and Janssen, J.D. (1994) Assessment of energy expenditure for physical activity using a triaxial accelerometer. *Medicine and Science in Sports and Exercise*, Vol. 26, pp. 1516-23.
8. Matthews, C.E. and Freedson, P.S. (1995) Field trial of a three dimensional activity monitor: comparison with self report. *Medicine and Science in Sports and Exercise*, Vol. 27, pp. 1071-8.

PHYSICAL ACTIVITY PATTERNS OF 5 TO 11 YEAR OLD CHILDREN

Young children's physical activity patterns

J.R. WELSMAN and N. ARMSTRONG
Children's Health and Exercise Research Centre, Institute of Clinical Science, University of Exeter, Exeter, UK
Keywords: Heart rate monitoring, physical activity

Introduction

In adult life, the effect of regular physical activity in promoting aerobic fitness, increasing muscular strength, lowering blood lipids, reducing high blood pressure, countering obesity, retarding osteoporosis, improving blood glucose control, and increasing psychological well-being is extensively documented[1]. Evidence is accumulating to support the view that adults' health and well-being has its origin in behaviour established during childhood[2] and there is general agreement that young people should be encouraged to adopt active lifestyles[3]. However, relatively little is known about young children's physical activity patterns.

The measurement of adults' habitual physical activity is one of the most difficult tasks in epidemiological research and the assessment of the habitual physical activity of children is even more problematic. The technique used must be socially acceptable, it should not burden the subject with cumbersome equipment, and it should minimally influence the subject's normal physical activity pattern. Ideally the intensity, frequency and duration of activities should be monitored and if a true picture of habitual physical activity is required a minimum monitoring period of 3 d is necessary[3].

Only two studies have satisfied these criteria and investigated the habitual physical activity of British primary school children[4,5]. Both of these involved 10 and 11-year-old children and objective data on younger children appear to be non-existent. The present study was, therefore, designed to investigate the physical activity patterns of children aged 5 to 9 y using continuous, minute-by-minute heart rate monitoring and to compare their results with 10 to 11-year-old children.

Children and Exercise XIX. Edited by Neil Armstrong, Brian Kirby and Joanne Welsman.
Published in 1997 by E & FN Spon, 2–6 Boundary Row, London, SE1 8HN.
ISBN 0 419 22100 X.

Methods

All children in years 1, 3 and 4 of four Exeter First and Middle schools were invited to participate in the project and the subject sample was randomly selected from those who returned signed parental consent forms. Forty children were selected from year 1 and 40 from years 3 and 4 combined. Equal numbers of boys and girls were chosen. The sample of 10 to 11-year-olds was drawn from our existing database of children's physical activity patterns. The frequency, duration and intensity of physical activity was measured using continuous minute-by-minute heart rate monitoring (Sport Tester 3000/Vantage NV). Each child was monitored from 0900 until bedtime (approximately 1900) for five consecutive school days. All children were monitored between the months of May to July inclusive.

Previous work with children aged 11 to 12 y has shown a brisk walk (6 $km \cdot h^{-1}$) and a jog (8 $km \cdot h^{-1}$) to elicit mean steady-state heart rates of 146 $beats \cdot min^{-1}$ and 164 $beats \cdot min^{-1}$ respectively[6]. Consequently, heart rate data have been analysed at thresholds of ≥140 and ≥160 $beats \cdot min^{-1}$[7,8]. To examine whether or not these thresholds were equally applicable to younger children, 38 of the 5 to 9-year-olds in the present study had their heart rate responses recorded during treadmill walking and jogging. Although treadmill speeds were necessarily reduced to accommodate these smaller children, mean heart rates at brisk walking and jogging of 136 and 161 $beats \cdot min^{-1}$ respectively were obtained, confirming that heart rate thresholds of ≥140 and ≥160 $beats \cdot min^{-1}$ were also appropriate for this age group.

Only children with data for 3 d, each of at least 450 min were included in the analyses. For each child the mean accumulated time (min) and mean % time at the thresholds of ≥140 and ≥160 $beats \cdot min^{-1}$ were computed. The number of 5 and 10 min periods with heart rate sustained above the two heart rate thresholds were totalled over the three days.

Descriptive statistics (means and standard deviations) by group and sex were computed for physical characteristics and activity variables. Within and between group differences were examined using group by sex (3 x 2) analysis of variance (ANOVA).

Table 1. Physical characteristics of children

	Group 1		Group 2		Group 3	
	Boys (n=11)	Girls (n=13)	Boys (n=15)	Girls (n=16)	Boys (n=44)	Girls (n=52)
Age (y)	6.3 ± 0.4	6.1 ± 0.2	8.9 ± 0.7	8.9 ± 0.6	11.2 ± 0.5	11.2 ± 0.5
Stature (m)	1.22 ± 0.04	1.14 ± 0.05	1.33 ± 0.06	1.35 ± 0.06	1.45 ± 0.06	1.46 ± 0.08
Mass (kg)	22.4± 2.2	20.5 ± 2.1	28.7 ± 4.5	31.7 ± 9.8	36.5 ± 5.6	38.8 ± 8.1

Values are mean ± SD

Table 2. Activity variables by group

Activity variable	Group 1 Boys	Girls	Group 2 Boys	Girls	Group 3 Boys	Girls
% ≥ 140	12.9 ± 3.4	10.3 ± 4.5	9.7 ± 4.6	7.4 ± 3.4	8.1 ± 4.1	6.9 ±3.9
% ≥ 160	5.2 ± 2.2	3.9 ± 2.3	4.4 ± 3.2	2.8 ± 1.7	3.3 ± 2.2	2.5± 1.9
5 @ ≥140	11.7 ± 4.7	7.9 ± 5.2	8.3 ± 4.6	5.6 ± 3.8	7.8 ± 5.5	6.5± 6.3
5 @ ≥160	3.0 ± 4.1	2.0 ± 2.2	1.9 ± 1.9	1.2 ± 1.4	3.2 ± 3.0	2.5 ±3.0
10 @ ≥140	2.7 ± 3.0	2.1 ± 2.1	2.1 ± 1.6	1.4 ± 1.3	2.5 ± 2.5	1.9 ± 2.5
10 @ ≥160	0.8 ± 1.0	0.2 ± 0.4	0.3 ± 0.6	0.2 ± 0.5	1.0 ± 1.6	0.5 ±1.0

Values are mean ± SD

%≥140 and % ≥160 indicate the % of time spent with HR ≥140 or ≥160

5 @ ≥140 and 5 @ ≥160 indicate the number of 5 min periods with HR ≥140 or ≥160

10 @ ≥140 and 10 @ ≥160 indicate the number of 10 min periods with HR ≥140 or ≥160

Results

Physical characteristics of the children for whom 3 days of heart rate data were available are presented in table 1. Mean values for physical activity variables are presented in table 2. ANOVA revealed a significant ($p<0.01$) decline across the three age groups in the % time spent with the heart rate ≥ 140 beats·min^{-1} and ≥ 160 beats·min^{-1}. Girls spent significantly ($p<0.01$) less time than boys with heart rates ≥ 140 beats·min^{-1} and ≥ 160 beats·min^{-1}. Despite a trend towards a decline in the number of 5 min periods ≥140 beats·min^{-1} with increasing age, this was not significant ($p>0.05$). Sex differences were, however, significant ($p<0.05$). Mean values for the number of 10 min periods ≥ 140 beats·min^{-1} and 5 and 10 min periods

Table 3. Number of 5 min periods with the heart rate ≥140 beats·min^{-1} and ≥160 beats·min^{-1} during three school days

No of periods	Group 1 Boys	Girls	Group 2 Boys	Girls	Group 3 Boys	Girls
≥140 beats·min^{-1}						
0	----	----	----	12.5	2.3	13.5
1	----	15.4	6.7	----	6.8	9.6
2	----	----	13.3	6.3	11.4	5.8
3 or more	100	84.6	80.0	81.2	79.5	71.2
≥160 beats·min^{-1}						
0	36.4	38.5	26.7	50.0	25.0	28.8
1	9.1	15.4	26.7	12.5	13.6	17.3
2	18.2	15.4	13.3	12.5	9.1	26.9
3 or more	36.3	30.8	33.3	25.0	52.3	27.0

Values are percentages of children

Table 4. Number of 10 min periods with the heart rate sustained ≥ 140 beats·min^{-1} and ≥160 beats·min^{-1} during three school days

No of periods	Group 1		Group 2		Group 3	
	Boys	Girls	Boys	Girls	Boys	Girls
≥140 beats·min^{-1}						
0	36.4	30.8	13.3	31.3	34.1	38.5
1	9.1	23.1	33.3	25.0	11.4	25.0
2	18.2	7.7	13.3	18.8	6.8	11.5
3	36.3	38.4	40.1	24.9	47.7	25.0
≥160 beats·min^{-1}						
0	54.5	76.9	80.0	87.5	61.4	67.3
1	9.1	23.1	13.3	6.3	15.9	21.2
2	36.4	----	6.7	6.3	9.1	3.8
3	----	----	----	----	13.6	7.7

Values are percentages of children

≥ 160 beats·min^{-1} were very low and no sex or group differences were observed. Tables 3 and 4 show the % of children within each age group achieving 5 and 10 min periods of activity above the two thresholds.

Discussion

Few studies have characterised the habitual physical activity patterns of children below the age of 10 y and their conclusions have been somewhat contradictory. Observational studies from America[9,10] have provided evidence which contrasts with the notion that young children are continually on the move or very active. The very detailed observation study by Bailey et al.[11], although involving only 15 children, demonstrated that 6 to 10-year-old children typically engage in very short (<15s) periods of intense activity interspersed with low to moderate activity. In none of these children was a continuous period of intense activity lasting 10 min observed. Observational data from British children[12,13] suggested much higher levels of activity, with 5 to 11 year olds engaging in moderate to vigorous activity for 30% of the observation time. However, these findings must be interpreted cautiously as they focused on physical activity during school break times, lunch times, and physical education lessons. "Classroom time", during which children were presumably inactive, was not observed. The present study is the first to measure British children's physical activity patterns in the age range 5 to 9 y using heart rate monitoring over several days.

The mean percentage times spent with heart rates raised above the two activity thresholds, although declining between the ages of 5 to 11 y, are higher than observed in our previous studies of older children and teenagers for both boys and girls[8].

The data presented in tables 2 and 3 demonstrate that 5 min bouts of moderate intensity activity are frequent in young children with the majority demonstrating at least 3 periods. By the age of 13 y, the percentage of boys and girls achieving three, 5 min periods ≥ 140 beats·min^{-1} has dropped to around 70% and 50% respectively[8]. Similarly, 10 min bouts at this intensity are far more frequent in the 5 to 11-year-old children studied here (table 4) compared with teenagers, where only 25% of boys and 14 % of girls achieve 3 or more 10 min periods of activity equivalent to a brisk walk [8]. In common with older children, and previous indications from observational studies[11] however, extended, sustained periods of moderate activity and 10 min periods of vigorous activity were rarely observed in 5 to 11-year-olds.

Significantly higher levels of physical activity in boys compared to girls in older children and adolescents are extensively documented[3], but previous observational studies have indicated no sex differences in the physical activity patterns of 5 to 11-year-old British school children[12,13]. In contrast, American studies have suggested that sex differences exist as young as 3 to 4-years-old[9,14]. The present study is the first to indicate using objective heart rate monitoring that sex differences in physical activity are indeed present in British children from the age of 5 y.

We have previously demonstrated that boys' activity levels do not decline significantly during secondary education whereas girls' activity decreases progressively[8]. The present data suggest that primary school boys' activity patterns are considerably higher during their initial primary education although a decline is observed as they approach secondary education. The decline in girls' physical activity appears to be a continuous process which has been initiated at least by the early years of primary education.

Acknowledgements

This study was supported by Persil Funfit.

References

1. Femtem, P.H., Bassey, E.J. and Turnbull, N.B. (1988) *The New Case for Exercise*, Sports Council and Health Education Authority, London.
2. Activity and Health Research (1992) *Allied Dunbar National Fitness Survey*, Sports Council and Health Education Authority, London.
3. Armstrong, N. and Welsman, J. (1997) *Young People and Physical Activity*, Oxford University Press, Oxford.
4. Armstrong, N. and Bray. S. (1991) Physical activity patterns defined by heart rate monitoring. *Archives of Disease in Childhood*, Vol. 66, pp. 245-7.
5. McManus, A. and Armstrong, N. (1995) Patterns of physical activity among primary schoolchildren, in *Children in Sport*, (ed. F.J. Ring), University Press, Bath, pp. 17-23.
6. Armstrong, N., Balding, J., Gentle, P. and Kirby, B. (1990) Estimation of coronary risk factors in British schoolchildren. *British Journal of Sports Medicine*, Vol. 24, pp. 61-6.
7. Armstrong, N., McManus, A., Welsman, J. and Kirby, B. (1996) Physical activity patterns and aerobic fitness among prepubescents. *European Physical Education Review*, Vol. 2, pp. 19-29.

8. Armstrong, N., Balding, J., Gentle, P. and Kirby, B. (1990) Patterns of physical activity among 11 to 16 year old British children. *British Medical Journal*, Vol. 301, pp. 203-5.
9. Baranowski, T., Thompson, W.O., DuRant, R.H., Baranowski, J. and Puhl, J. (1993) Observations on physical activity in physical locations: age, gender, ethnicity and month effects. *Research Quarterly for Exercise and Sport*, Vol. 64, pp.127-33.
10. Baranowski, T., Tsong, Y., Hooks, Pl, Cieslik, C. and Nader, P.R. (1987) Aerobic physical activity among third to sixth grade children. *Journal of Developmental and Behavioural Pediatrics*, Vol. 8, pp. 203-6.
11. Bailey, R.C., Olson, J., Pepper, S.L., Porszasz, J., Barstow, T.T. and Cooper, D.M. (1995) The level and tempo of children's physical activities: an observational study. *Medicine and Science in Sports and Exercise*, Vol. 27, pp. 1033-41.
12. Sleap, M. and Warburton, P. (1992) Physical Activity levels of 5-11 year old children in England determined by continuous observation. *Research Quarterly for Exercise and Sport*, Vol. 63, pp. 238-45.
13. Sleap, M. and Warburton, P. (1994) Physical activity levels of preadolescent children in England. *British Journal of Physical Education Research Supplement*, Vol. 14, pp. 2-6.
14. DuRant, R.H., Baranowski, T., Rhodes, T., Gutin, B., Thompson, W.O., Carroll, R., Puhl, J. and Greaves, K.A. (1993) Association among serum lipid and lipoprotein concentrations and physical activity, physical fitness and body composition in young children. *Journal of Pediatrics*, Vol. 123, pp. 185-92.

THE FREE-LIVING PHYSICAL ACTIVITY OF SCHOOLCHILDREN: A LONGITUDINAL STUDY.

Longitudinal study of physical activity

S. ATKINS, and G. STRATTON
Centre for Physical Education, Sport and Dance, Liverpool John Moores University, Liverpool, UK
L. DUGDILL
Centre for Health Studies, Liverpool John Moores University, Liverpool, UK
T. REILLY
Centre for Exercise and Sport Sciences, Liverpool John Moores University, Liverpool, UK

Keywords: Heart rate monitoring, physical activity, tracking

Introduction

An appropriate physical activity prescription, for the optimal health and fitness benefits of children, is unknown. Whilst such criteria have been provided for adolescents[1], the free-living habitual physical activity (HPA) of young children is often assessed using guidelines from these older populations. Additionally, the attainment of these standards are confounded by the lack of a recognised criterion measurement of free-living HPA[2], creating difficulty in the establishment of an appropriate HPA prescription for children.

In British schoolchildren, the quantification of free-living HPA has frequently been performed using heart rate monitoring techniques[3,4,5,6], with results commonly describing the sedentary nature of children. Whilst such data may have implications for health in later life, the classification of sedentary is determined from children's failure to attain the recognised 3 times 20 min of sustained HPA activity prescription[1].

Recent evidence has suggested that children's free-living HPA does not conform to such a rigid structure[7], with the majority of such activity lasting less than 15 s. A second guideline[1] suggests that adolescents should accumulate 30 min, or more, of moderate to vigorous physical activity on most days of the week. With the variable nature of children's HPA, and the prevalence of short-duration activities[7], a cumulative measurement of activity may be more applicable to younger populations. Using the "cumulative minutes" guideline children have been shown to attain such activity prescription more readily than the more common "3 x 20"[8,9]. Whilst reported studies have emphasised the sedentary nature of children's HPA, the lack of data examining a, seemingly, more appropriate activity prescription represents a gap in current understanding.

Children and Exercise XIX. Edited by Neil Armstrong, Brian Kirby and Joanne Welsman.
Published in 1997 by E & FN Spon, 2–6 Boundary Row, London, SE1 8HN.
ISBN 0 419 22100 X.

Children and adolescents are generally accepted as being sedentary, yet studies investigating changes in HPA behaviours, during growth and ageing, are uncommon. Evidence supporting the tracking of physical activity, during the growth period, remains equivocal[10,11,12]. Heart rate monitoring techniques have rarely been used to study changes in free-living activities, yet evidence does support the tracking (r = 0.81 over 3 y) of HPA in very young (3-4 y) children[12].

Despite such promising evidence, changes in free-living HPA must be considered a behavioural factor, and subject to great change during the lifespan. Literature suggests that levels of HPA "peak" at around 13-14 y and then markedly decline[2], yet such findings are greatly complicated by the lack of comparative, longitudinal data examining these changes, and the aforementioned problems associated with interchangeable methodologies.

Accordingly, the major aims of the current study were twofold. Firstly, to determine the degree of tracking of free-living physical activity behaviours of Liverpool schoolchildren, as measured by heart rate monitoring, during the circumpubertal period. Secondly, to assess the differences in attainment of physical activity guidelines[1], provided for adolescents and applied to younger children, during the growth period. Longitudinal data, examining objective measurements of HPA, are especially rare for British children, representing a large gap in current knowledge.

Methods

Twenty four boys (10.18 $\pm$ 0.83 y), and twenty seven girls (9.95 $\pm$ 0.83 y), gave written informed consent to take part in this study, part of a larger study examining the prevalence of chronic disease risk factors in Liverpool schoolchildren. Children were assessed for morphological maturity using the non-invasive estimation of percentage of adult stature[13].

Subjects were fitted with a short range radio telemeter (Polar Sportstester, Polar, Kempele, Finland) set to record data minute by minute, prior to attending school on three consecutive days. Fitting of HRM systems occurred between 0730 and 0845. Children were tested on two occasions, separated by 1 y, with all testing occurring between September and March of each year. Data were analysed each day, in the subject's home, using Polar HR Analysis Software 4.0 (Polar, Kempele, Finland), interfaced through a portable computer (Powerbook, Apple MacIntosh).

Heart rate thresholds were set at 139 beats.min^{-1}, a threshold espoused as providing health benefits[3,4,5,10], and at the heart rate reserve thresholds, estimated for the 60 and 75% HRR. The 75% HRR has been postulated to confer cardiorespiratory fitness benefits for adolescents[1], whilst the 60% HRR is an arbitrary value approximating the 150 beats·min^{-1} threshold assessed in previous HRM studies[5,9]. Maximal heart rate was determined during maximal treadmill running, and lowest recorded heart rate during sleep was used as a direct baseline measure. Continuous 5, 10, 15 and 20 min periods were identified at all heart rate thresholds, together with cumulative time spent with elevated heart rate.

Descriptive data were assessed for all variables. Tracking of physical activity behaviours was assessed using Pearson product-moment correlation coefficients.

Table 1. Descriptive data for estimated heart rate thresholds

	Boys		Girls	
	Visit 1	Visit 2	Visit 1	Visit 2
60% HRR	143 (13)	143 (5)	147 (13)	147 (8)
75% HRR	164 (9)	165 (8)	167 (13)	168 (6)

Values are mean ± SD

Differences in cumulative minutes HPA, between test occasions, were assessed using paired samples t-tests, with level of significance set at the 5% level.

Results

Estimated 60% HRR and 75% HRR did not differ significantly ($p > 0.05$), between gender groups (table 1).

Sustained duration physical activities, at pre-determined heart rate thresholds, are shown in table 2. No child attained the recommended "3 x 20" minute physical activity guidelines[1], during either test occasion. Data indicate that shorter duration periods of activity (5-10 min), at all thresholds, are more readily attainable by children in the current study, yet results also show that 41.6 - 84.6% of children did not attain a single 5 min period with heart rate elevated at any intensity.

Analysis of descriptive heart rate data reveal the attainment of the recommended cumulative minutes, with elevated heart rate[1], for boys and girls, at 139 beats$\cdot$min^{-1} and 60% HRR (table 3).

No significant gender differences ($p > 0.05$), are reported for cumulative minutes, with elevated heart rate, for any heart rate threshold.

Table 2. Descriptive data for number (percentage) of children attaining one or more sustained periods of activity at pre-determined thresholds (mean)

		>139 beats$\cdot$min^{-1}		>60% HRR		>75% HRR	
Period		Boys	Girls	Boys	Girls	Boys	Girls
5 min	Visit 1	14 (58)	13 (47)	6 (24)	6 (22)	3 (12)	2 (7)
	Visit 2	2 (15)	8 (41)	3 (23)	3 (15)	1 (8)	2 (11)
10 min	Visit 1	5 (21)	3 (11)	2 (8)	3 (11)	1 (4)	0 (0)
	Visit 2	3 (23)	1 (5)	0 (0)	3 (16)	0 (0)	1 (5)
15 min	Visit 1	1 (4)	0 (0)	1 (4)	3 (11)	0 (0)	0 (0)
	Visit 2	1 (8)	1 (5)	0 (0)	1 (5)	0 (0)	1 (5)
20 min	Visit 1	2 (8)	3 (11)	0 (0)	1 (4)	0 (0)	1 (4)
	Visit 2	1 (8)	3 (16)	5 (38)	2 (11)	1 (8)	0 (0)

Table 3. Descriptive data for cumulative minutes of physical activity with elevated heart rate

Heart rate intensity	Boys		Girls	
	Visit 1	Visit 2	Visit 1	Visit 2
>139 beats·min^{-1}	55 ± 53	45 ± 27	57 ± 54	46 ± 37
>60% HRR	40 ± 41	36 ± 25	40 ± 39	33 ± 28
>75% HRR	10 ± 15	6 ± 10	9 ± 11	7 ± 8

Values are mean ± SD

Paired samples t-test revealed no significant differences in cumulative minutes in elevated heart rate, or number of periods of activity with elevated heart rate, between test visits ($p > 0.05$). No differences were identified between any pre-determined heart rate thresholds.

Tracking correlations, between number of sustained periods (5, 10, 15 and 20 min), at pre-determined intensities, during both test occasions were poor. Of all variables only one correlation was determined, between number of 5 min periods at 139 beats·min^{-1} for girls ($r = 0.22$; $p < 0.05$). Poor to moderate correlations were identified between cumulative minutes of activity at specified intensities of activity ($r = -0.01$ to 0.18; $p < 0.05$), with significant relationships only identified for cumulative minutes at 75% HRR in boys ($r = 0.65$; $p < 0.01$).

Discussion

Results from the current study provide evidence for the low attainment of commonly espoused physical activity guidelines (3 x 20 min weekly), for adolescents[1], by younger children. Current data confirm previous British studies[3,4,5,6,], by recognising the relatively sedentary nature of children from these age groups when assessed using the "3 x 20" criteria at those thresholds recognised as providing health and fitness benefits. However, when assessed using the cumulative minutes of physical activity criteria, children do attain recommended guidelines at lower (>139 beats·min^{-1} and 60% HRR), heart rate thresholds (table 3).

The greater prevalence of short duration (5 min), physical activities support previous investigations[7], that children's participation in free-living HPA is characterised by intermittent elevations in heart rate. At greater heart rate thresholds (>75% HRR), activity participation is less marked, emphasising important limitations of the heart rate monitoring technique in assessing free-living HPA. Minute-by-minute heart rate recording is not sensitive enough to accurately assess heart rate responses of less than 15 s, a period recognised as encompassing the majority of children's higher intensity HPA[7]. The Polar Sportstester system is unable to collect data for periods in excess of 7 h, with system set to record heart rate every 15 s, considerably below previously reported 12 h recording intervals[3,4,5,6,]. This methodological issue further emphasises the inherent problems associated with accurate, and valid, measurement of free-living HPA. The cumulative time with elevated heart rate, assessed at durations below 60 s, may provide unique evidence for the contribution of intermittent duration activities to daily HPA, yet without multiple telemetry system protocols, such findings must remain equivocal.

Changes in patterns of free-living HPA are difficult to identify. The lack of attainment of sustained periods of HPA prevented accurate analysis of change in these variables between test occasions. Using cumulative minutes data no significant differences were identified between test occasions ($p > 0.05$), or gender groups, further emphasising the non-structured pattern of children's HPA behaviour.

Attainment of sustained periods of HPA, and subsequent tracking of these variables, were difficult to identify in the current study. The lack of attainment of 10, 15 and 20 min periods with elevated heart rate made the creation of tracking coefficients highly problematic, with only a low correlation shown between 5 min periods, with heart rate >139 beats·min^{-1} for girls ($r = 0.22$). The use of cumulative minutes criteria would provide a basis for the estimation of tracking between test occasions, due to each subject being given a numerical expression of activity, irrespective of number of minutes attained. Results from this study do not support the tracking of cumulative minutes HPA for these children, in contrast to previously reported data[12]. Again the choice, behavioural nature of free-living HPA must be considered influential in determining the activities of children.

In conclusion, results from the current study do not support the tracking of free-living HPA during early adolescence, using either cumulative minutes or sustained period criteria for assessing activity behaviours. These data may provide evidence for the changes in choice behaviour of children during the important early adolescent period, importantly characterised by the transition from primary to secondary school education. Results from the current study also emphasise the inappropriateness of the commonly used "3 x 20" activity prescription, especially when children do appear to attain recommended levels of HPA using cumulative minutes criteria. Further study is required to assess longer-term changes in HPA, during this important transitory period, and appropriate dose-response of physical activity in providing health and fitness benefits.

References

1. Sallis, J.F. and Patrick, K. (1994) Physical activity guidelines for adolescents: consensus statement. *Pediatric Exercise Science,* Vol. 6, pp. 302-14.
2. Riddoch, C.J. and Boreham, C.A.G. (1995) The health-related physical activity of children. *Sports Medicine,* Vol. 19, pp. 86-102.
3. Armstrong, N., Balding, J., Gentle, P. and Kirby, B.J. (1990) Patterns of physical activity among 11-16 year old British schoolchildren. *British Medical Journal,* Vol. 301, pp. 203-5.
4. Armstrong, N., Balding, J., Gentle, P., Williams, J. and Kirby, B.J. (1991) Cardiopulmonary fitness, physical activity patterns and selected coronary heart disease risk factor variables in 11-16 year old children. *Pediatric Exercise Science,* Vol. 3, pp. 219-28.

5. Armstrong, N., McManus, A., Welsman, J. and Kirby, B..J. (1996) Physical activity patterns and aerobic fitness among prepubescents. *European Physical Education Review,* Vol. 2, pp. 19-29.
6. Riddoch, C.J., Mahoney, C., Murphy, N., Boreham, C. and Cran, C. (1991) The physical activity patterns of Northern Irish schoolchildren. *Pediatric Exercise Science,* Vol. 3, pp. 300-9.
7. Bailey, R.C., Olson, J., Popper, S.C., Porszasz, J., Barstow, T.J. and Cooper, D.M. (1995) The level and tempo of children's physical activity: observational study. *Medicine and Science in Sports and Exercise,* Vol. 27, pp. 1033-41.
8. Simmonds, G., Aznar, S., Barnes, K., Goldberg, J. and Riddoch, C.J. (1995) The health related physical activity of children. Paper presented to the *XVIIIth Symposium of the European Group of Pediatric Work Physiology*, Odense, Denmark.
9. Gilbey, H. and Gilbey, M. (1995) The physical activity of Singapore primary school children as estimated by heart rate monitoring. *Pediatric Exercise Science,* Vol. 7, pp. 26-35.
10. Sallis, J.F., Berry, C.C., Broyles, S.L., McKenzie, T.L. and Nader, P.R. (1995) Variability and tracking of physical activity over 2 yr in young children. *Medicine and Science in Sports and Exercise,* Vol. 27, pp. 1042-9.
11. Malina, R.M. (1996) Tracking of physical activity and physical fitness across the lifespan. *Research Quarterly for Exercise and Sport,* Vol. 67, pp. S48-53.
12. Pate, R.R., Baranowski, T., Dowda, M., Trost, S.G. (1996) Tracking of physical activity in young children. *Medicine and Science in Sports and Exercise,* Vol. 28, pp. 92-6.
13. Roche, A.F., Tyleshevski, F. and Rogers, E. (1983) Non-invasive measurements of physical maturity in children. *Research Quarterly for Exercise and Sport,* Vol. 54, pp. 364-71.

MODERATE TO VIGOROUS PHYSICAL ACTIVITIES IN PRE-ADOLESCENT CHILDREN

Physical activity in preadolescent children

M. SALLO and J. HARRO
Department of Public Health, University of Tartu, Tartu, Estonia
A. VIRU
Department of Exercise Biology, University of Tartu, Tartu, Estonia
Keywords: Preadolescents, physical activity, questionnaires

Introduction

Regular appropriate physical activity (PA) is beneficial to health both in adults and children[1]. More active or fit adults tend to develop less chronic diseases than their inactive counterparts[2]. The public health concern about PA in children is great, since early childhood is a critical period in forming lifelong PA habits[3]. Several studies[4, 5] have provided evidence that PA in childhood is a determinant of PA in adulthood. Recently Pate et al.[6] showed that the level of PA tends to track during early childhood, and that less active children tend to remain less active than the majority of their peers. If the children with low levels of PA can be determined, intervention programs elevating PA in these children can be organized.

Nevertheless, the amount and type of PA necessary to promote health during childhood is unknown[7]. No age-specific guidelines are available for preadolescent children[8]. PA guidelines based on the meta-analysis of age-specific data on the effects of PA on health are available for adolescents (aged 11 to 21 y)[9]. According to these guidelines children should, firstly, be physically active daily or nearly every day as a part of their lifestyle, and secondly, they should engage in three or more sessions per week of physical activities of moderate to vigorous intensity (MVPA), lasting 20 minutes per session. Some authors believe that if children seldom undergo PA of high enough intensity and long enough duration (shown to have the greatest health benefits for adults and adolescents), this type of exercise does not continue into adulthood[10]. These activities include moderate to vigorous, continuous activities such as brisk walking, swimming, aerobic dance, bicycling, and jogging[11].

The information available about MVPA levels of preadolescents is limited since the assessment of children's habitual physical activity (HPA) is difficult[12]. In order to

Children and Exercise XIX. Edited by Neil Armstrong, Brian Kirby and Joanne Welsman.
Published in 1997 by E & FN Spon, 2–6 Boundary Row, London, SE1 8HN.
ISBN 0 419 22100 X.

develop PA guidelines for preadolescents more information about the PA of this age group is necessary. The aim of this study was to assess preadolescents' MVPA using 7 d simultaneous questionnaires for the parents and teachers.

Subjects

Teachers of all Estonian-speaking kindergartens and first grades located in Tartu were asked to participate in the study. In addition two second grades and two third grades from different locations of Tartu were also involved in the study. Teachers from two of the 18 kindergartens refused to participate because of the amount of work required to complete the questionnaires. From 1156 questionnaires given to the parents 558 (i.e. 48%) were returned. MVPA was assessed in 558 preadolescent children (263 boys and 295 girls) from Tartu. The mean age (± SD) of studied children was 6.5 ± 1.8 y, range 2 to 11 y.

Methods

MVPA was assessed for 7 d simultaneously with two questionnaires, one for the parents and another for the children's teachers. These questionnaires have been validated against heart rate monitoring and Caltrac accelerometer data[13]. The parents reported the duration of MVPA (the activities that made the child breathe hard) indoors and outdoors during the time the child was at home. The teachers reported the duration of MVPA of the children while at kindergarten or at school. From both questionnaires the total time of MVPA per day was calculated. The assessment of MVPA was carried out during the last week in May. Mean ± standard deviation (SD) and median ± median absolute deviation (MAD) values for MVPA of children were calculated. Mann Whitney test for nonparametric data was used to study gender-based differences.

Results

The mean time awake was 790 ± 42 min, the time spent in kindergarten or at school was 390 ± 50 min and at home 408 ± 93 min. No gender differences were found in total waking hours or the time in the kindergarten/school or at home. Total duration of MVPA per day (the mean of 7 d), during weekdays (the mean of 5 d), and weekends (the mean of 2 weekend-days), in kindergarten/school, and at home was significantly higher in boys ($p < 0.01$) (tables 1 and 3).

If MVPA was studied separately indoors and outdoors, the girls were found to demonstrate significantly higher values of MVPA indoors ($p < 0.05$) and the boys were significantly longer engaged in MVPA outdoors ($p < 0.01$) (table 1). No gender difference was found in MVPA while indoors at home, but the girls were significantly longer engaged in MVPA while indoors in kindergarten or at school ($p < 0.05$) (table 1). Total time per day spent outdoors and the time outdoors while in kindergarten/school

Table 1. Gender differences in moderate to vigorous physical activities

Variable	All children	Boys	Girls
Sample size	558	263	295
Total MVPA (min):			
The mean of schooldays	112 ± 41	122 ± 44	102 ± 36**
In kindergarten/ school	50 ± 18	54 ± 18	45 ± 18**
At home on a schoolday	48 ± 30	58 ± 34	42 ± 28*
MVPA (min) indoors:	34 ± 17	32 ± 18	37 ± 16*
At home	12 ± 12	10 ± 10	13 ± 13
In kindergarten/ school	16 ± 11	13 ± 11	18 ± 11**
MVPA (min) outdoors:	66 ± 31	81 ± 33	52 ± 28***
At home	25 ± 23	36 ± 26	21 ± 19***
In kindergarten/ school	29 ± 18	36 ± 20	24 ± 16****

Values are median ± MAD
Level of significance *p <0.05, ** p <0.01, ***p <0.001, **** p <0.0001

was longer in boys (237 ± 58 and 120 ± 53 min respectively) than in girls (209 ± 59 and 106 ± 48 min respectively) (p <0.01) (Median ± MAD). No difference between the boys and girls was found in the time spent outdoors while at home (119 ± 52 and 99 ± 46 min respectively).

In order to follow age-dependent differences in MVPA the children were divided into 6 age groups (table 2.). A significant increase in the duration of waking hours was found with increasing age. Thus, the percent of MVPA of the time awake was used to compare the duration of MVPA in different age groups. Children from the oldest group engaged in significantly more MVPA while at school, but no increase with age was found in total MVPA or in MVPA while at home. The duration of MVPA was longest in the oldest children both in time spent outdoors and indoors. But when outdoor and indoor MVPE were compared separately at school and at home, an increase with age was obvious in MVPA while outdoors at home and indoors at school. A decrease with age was found in MVPA while indoors at home and outdoors at school (table 2).

The differences in MVPA between schooldays and weekend-days were also followed (table 3). The total time with MVPA and MVPA outdoors in all children, and separately in boys and girls was significantly longer on weekend-days than on schooldays (p <0.05). Boys but not girls also spent more time in MVPA indoors during the weekends than on schooldays (table 3).

Table 2. Age-related differences in moderate to vigorous physical activities

Variable	Age groups of children (y)					
	≤4.5	4.6-5.5	5.6-6.5	6.6-7.5	7.6-8.5	≥8.6
n 63	117	119	64	70	87	
Age (y)	3.9 ± .6	5.1 ± .2	6.0 ± .2	7.0 ± .3	8.0 ± .3	9.6 ± .6
% of MVPA of per day	17 ± 8	15 ± 8*	16 ± 10	16 ± 8	16 ± 8	18 ± 10
% of MVPA in kindergarten/school	13 ± 9*	13 ± 8*	15 ± 8*	15 ± 8*	14 ± 8*	22 ± 10
% of MVPA at home	16 ± 12	12 ± 11	14 ± 13	14 ± 11	14 ± 12	13 ± 12
% of MVPA outdoors of the total time outdoors:	29 ± 15*	29 ± 15*	35 ± 18*	36 ± 18	33 ± 19*	44 ± 26
from that: in kindergarten/ school	57 ± 26*	65 ± 29*	65 ± 28*	55 ± 27*	37 ± 36	30 ± 35
at home	43 ± 26*	35 ± 29*	35 ± 28*	45 ± 27*	63 ± 36	70 ± 35
% of MVPA indoors of the total time indoors:	7 ± 6*	5 ± 5*	7 ± 6*	5 ± 4*	7 ± 4*	10 ± 6
from that: in kindergarten/ school	38 ± 35*	48 ± 38*	52 ± 36*	66 ± 37	62 ± 32*	80 ± 25
at home	62 ± 35*	52 ± 38*	48 ± 36*	34 ± 37	38 ± 32*	20 ± 25

Values are mean ± SD
Level of significance *$p < 0.05$ (ie groups significantly different from ≥ 8.6 y children)

Discussion

Moderate to vigorous physical activities cause a child to breathe hard and elevate the heart rate approximately above 140 beats·min^{-1}[14]. Total median time spent in MVPA in our study was 112 ± 41 min per ordinary schoolday and 120 ± 81 min per weekend-day. This study was carried out at the end of May, when the weather was warm and sunny. In another study (performed from October till April) in which the same questionnaire was used[15], children of the same age were involved in MVPA for 60 ± 32 minutes per day. Thus, seasonal and climatic differences have a great influence on MVPA in Estonian preadolescent children. In May the difference in MVPA was obvious between schooldays and weekend-days, such a difference was not seen during the winter.

Table 3. School and weekend days differences in moderate to vigorous physical activities

Variable	All children	Boys	Girls
Duration of MVPA (min):			
During schooldays	112 ± 41	122 ± 44	102 ± 36**
During weekends	120 ± 81	150 ± 83	100 ± 70***
MVPA indoors:			
During schooldays	34 ± 17	32 ± 18	37 ± 16*
During weekends	30 ± 30	30 ± 30	30 ± 30
MVPA outdoors:			
During schooldays	66 ± 31	81 ± 33	52 ± 28****
During weekends	63 ± 63	90 ± 78	45 ± 45****

Values are median ± MAD
Level of significance * $p < 0.05$; ** $p < 0.01$; *** $p < 0.001$; **** $p < 0.0001$

Boys were shown to be involved in more MVPA than girls. Several authors have found primary school boys to be physically more active than girls[14,16], although gender differences in PA in infancy are reported to be minimal[17]. Some studies have demonstrated[14,16] and some have not found[18,19] gender-based differences in activity level of preschool children. In our study, the girls were reported to experience more MVPA indoors in kindergarten or school than boys. This can be explained by the fact that more girls than boys were involved in aerobic and dancing lessons in addition to physical education classes. The parents and teachers expect these lessons to contain MVPA. According to the previous study[15] heart rate monitoring did not confirm the longer duration of MVPA indoors in girls. It can be suggested that, if those aerobic and dancing lessons are organised so that they contain MVPA, it would be possible to increase the real duration of MVPA in girls.

The duration of MVPA at school (specially indoors at school) and outdoors at home was greater in older children. Increased MVPA indoors at school can be explained by the greater involvement of older children in organised sports.

References

1. Powell, K.E., Caspersen, C.J., Koplan, J.P. and Ford, E.S. (1989) Physical activity and chronic disease. *American Journal of Clinical Nutrition*, Vol. 49, pp. 999-1006.
2. Berlin, J.A. and Colditz, G.A. (1990) A meta-analysis of physical activity in the prevention of coronary heart disease. *American Journal of Epidemiology*, Vol. 32, pp. 612-28.

3. Simons-Morton, B.G., Parcel, G.S., O'Hara, N.M., Blair, S.N. and Pate, R.R. (1988) Health-related physical fitness in childhood. *Annual Review of Public Health*, Vol. 9, pp. 403-25.
4. Paffenbarger, R.S.Jr., Hyde, R.T., Wing, A.L. and Steinmetz, C.H. (1984) A natural history of athleticism and cardiovascular health. *Journal of American Medical Association*, Vol. 252, pp. 491-5.
5. Dennison, B.A., Straus, J.H., Mellits, E.D. and Charney, E. (1988) Childhood physical fitness tests: predictor of adult physical activity levels? *Pediatrics*, Vol. 82, pp. 324-30.
6. Pate, R.R., Baranowski, T., Dowda, M. and Trost, S.G. (1996) Tracking of physical activity in young children. *Medicine and Science in Sports and Exercise*, Vol. 28, pp. 92-6.
7. Riddoch, C.J. and Boreham, C.A.G. (1995) The health-related physical activity of children. *Sports Medicine*, Vol. 29, pp. 86-102.
8. Sallis, J.F., Patrick, K. and Long, B.J. (1994) Overview of the international consensus conference on physical activity guidelines for adolescents. *Pediatric Exercise Science*, Vol. 6, pp. 299-301.
9. Sallis, J.F. and Patrick, K. (1994) Physical activity guidelines for adolescents: consensus statement. *Pediatric Exercise Science*, Vol. 6, pp. 302-14.
10. Sallis, J.F. (1987) A commentary on children and fitness: a public health perspective. *Research Quarterly for Exercise and Sport,* Vol. 58, pp. 326-30.
11. Stephens,T., Jacobs, D.R. and White, C.C. (1985) A descriptive epidemiology of leisure-time physical activity. *Public Health Reports*, Vol. 100, pp. 147-58.
12. Cale, L. and Almond, L. (1992) Physical activity levels of young children: a review of the evidence. *Health Education Journal*, Vol. 51, pp. 94-9.
13. Sallo, M. (In press) Validation of questionnaires filled in by the parents and teachers to assess physical activity of 4 to 10 years old children.
14. Gilliam, T.B., Freedson, P.S., Geenen, D.L. and Shahraray, B. (1981) Physical activity patterns determined by heart rate monitoring in 6-7 year old children. *Medicine and Science in Sports and Exercise*, Vol. 13, pp. 65-7.
15. Sallo, M. and Silla, R. (1997) Physical activity with moderate to vigorous intensity in preschool and first-grade schoolchildren. *Pediatric Exercise Science*, Vol. 9, pp. 44-54.
16. Saris, W.H.M., Elvers, J.H., van't Hof, M.A. and Binkhorst, R.A. (1986) Changes in physical activity of children aged 6 to 12 years, in *Children and Exercise, XII*. (eds. J. Rutenfranz, R. Mocellin and F. Klimt), Human Kinetics, Champaign, Il, pp. 121-30.
17. Eaton, W. O. and Enns, L.R. (1986) Sex differences in human motor activity level. *Psychological Bulletin*, Vol. 100, pp. 19-28.
18. Noland, M., Danner, F., Dewalt, K., McFadden, M. and Kotchen, J.M. (1990) The measurements of physical activity in young children. *Research Quarterly for Exercise and Sport,* Vol. 61, pp. 146-53.
19. Janz, K.F., Golden, J.C., Hansen, J.R. and Mahoney, L.T. (1992) Heart rate monitoring of physical activity in children and adolescents: the Muscantine Study. *Pediatrics*, Vol. 89, pp. 256-61.

DOES THE PERSONALITY OF PARENTS INFLUENCE THE PHYSICAL ACTIVITY OF THEIR CHILDREN?

Parental personality and physical activity

J. HARRO, M. SALLO, N. JAANIMÄGI, A. PÄEVLOO and I. VILLA
Division of Health Promotion, Department of Public Health, University of Tartu, Tartu, Estonia
H. RIMM
Department of Psychology, University of Tartu, Tartu, Estonia
Keywords: Parental report, perceived stress, physical activity, psychological measures, self-efficacy, state anxiety, teacher report, trait anxiety

Introduction

Several investigators have expressed concern that the levels of physical activity (PA) in children may be too low, even to the extent that this is detrimental to health[1-2]. Furthermore, PA in early childhood may be tracking to more mature ages[3]. Previous studies in Estonia have indicated, consistent with studies in other countries, that pre-adolescent children spend most of their day in sedentary activities[4]. Among the various variables which influence the level of habitual physical activity (HPA) in adults, personality factors, coping strategies and motivation seem to affect exercise adherence [5,6]. Enduring personality characteristics of children appear not to influence strongly their PA[6], but there is little information concerning the related family influence. Indeed, concern has been expressed that the sedentary lifestyle that many of today's adults have adopted has spilled over to the lives of their children[3], and family aggregation in PA has been reported[7], but the mediating factors of sedentary lifestyle still need to be identified. Physically active parents have physically more active young children, but there are multiple possible explanations for this[8]. For example, even though it is frequently hypothesized that significant others act as role models for exercising, little evidence supports this assumption directly. It has been shown that the child's perception of parental exercise is not associated with their own habits[9]. Neither do parental attitudes toward exercise determine children's activity levels[10]. We have attempted to test the hypothesis that certain personality characteristics of parents may be associated with their children's lifestyle with regard to PA.

Children and Exercise XIX. Edited by Neil Armstrong, Brian Kirby and Joanne Welsman.
Published in 1997 by E & FN Spon, 2–6 Boundary Row, London, SE1 8HN.
ISBN 0 419 22100 X.

Subjects

First-year schoolchildren of three classes of two schools in Tartu, Estonia and their parents were asked to participate in an intervention programme aimed at increasing the PA of children and the health awareness of their parents and teachers. The subjects, their parents, and their teachers were informed about the nature of the study and were free to decide whether they were willing to participate in all or selected investigations. Physical fitness data, parental psychological data, and both (parental and teachers) reports about HPA were available for 45 children from a total of 97. Only the data of these 45 children (26 girls, 19 boys) were analysed. No significant difference between data obtained from the children/parents of the three classes was detected.

Methods

Subjects were tested for their performance in various physical fitness tasks modified for younger children from Eurofit recommendations[11]. Combined parent+teacher's structured questionnaire, validated previously against heart-rate monitoring and accelerometry for use in 4 to 8-year-old children[12], was used to obtain data about the HPA of the children. Parents and teachers reported during 1 wk the duration (in min) of several activities indoors and outdoors. The activities were divided into two groups by their intensity: PA with low to moderate intensity where heavy breathing was not expected and PA with moderate to high intensity (MVPA). The teachers were asked to report separately the duration of physical education (PE) classes and the duration of MVPA in these classes. Psychological questionnaires were administered during a gathering of parents at the respective schools. One parent of each child filled in the approbated Estonian versions of the State-Trait Anxiety Inventory (STAI)[13], Perceived Stress Scale (PSS)[14], and Generalized Self-Efficacy Scale (SES)[15]. State-Trait Anxiety Inventory was used in the short versions (5-items STAI-S form; Cronbach alpha 0.83; 7 items STAI-T form, Cronbach alpha 0.89). Perceived Stress Scale for assessing the stress tolerance was in this study used in its short, 4-items version (Cronbach alpha 0.80). The Self-Efficacy Scale (SES), a self-report measure of sense of competence and control over one's environment, was adopted from the original 10 items version (Cronbach alpha 0.86).

Data analyses

The parental psychological measures and children's physical fitness data followed normal distribution. Parametric statistical analysis was therefore used for data evaluation and data expressed as mean ± SD. Pearson correlation coefficients were calculated to measure associations between variables. For group comparisons, one-way analysis of variance was used. For each psychological measure separately, parents' (and their children's) data were divided into a high or low scoring group on the basis of mean value. Some measures of PA did not follow a normal distribution and thus all PA data were treated with non-parametric statistics (Spearman correlations (SRC) and Mann-

Whitney U-tests (MWU)). All PA data were adjusted per day and expressed in min (median ± MAD). Due to the multiple correlation analyses, $p < 0.01$ was set as a significance level.

Results

The mean (± SD) age, body weight, and height of the sample were 7.02 ± 0.32 y, 25.6 ± 4.2 kg, and 126.4 ± 5.9 cm, respectively. Body weight and height were not significantly different between the sexes, but the girls (6.92 ± 0.31 y) were significantly ($p < 0.01$) younger than the boys (7.17 ± 0.28). Of the parents, there were 31 mothers and 14 fathers in the sample.

Median time spent in MVPA per day was 107 ± 55 min for the whole week, 100 ± 45 per school-day, and 120 ± 105 per weekend-day. At school, the corresponding value was 23 ± 12 $min \cdot d^{-1}$. From that 10 ± 6 min were obtained during breaks, and 11 ± 3 during PE classes. On average, children had also 5.3 min of MVPA outdoors, but less than half of the children had any MVPA outdoors. At home, the median of time spent in MVPA on schooldays during the school-free time was 71 ± 41 min. During this time MVPA was carried out equally indoors and outdoors (25 ± 24 vs 22 ± 22 min per day, respectively), but during the weekends much more time was spent with MVPA outdoors compared to indoors (88 ± 79 vs 25 ± 25 $min \cdot d^{-1}$, respectively). Thus, children were generally more active when outdoors.

The median of the total time spent outdoors was 213 ± 81 $min \cdot d^{-1}$ for the whole week, whereas more time was spent outdoors on a weekend-day compared to a week-day (270 ± 114 vs 159 ± 81 $min \cdot d^{-1}$, respectively). These data reflect the relatively pleasant weather during the observation period (September 1996), since the MVPA level is similar to the late spring period of our previous investigations and considerable higher than the autumn-winter period[12].

The time the children spent in MVPA correlated with standing broad jump performance ($r = 0.48$, $p < 0.005$) but not with other physical fitness tests. However, MVPA in school and during the week-days correlated significantly with the performance in endurance shuttle run (SRC $r = 0.76$; $p < 0.0001$ and $r = 0.50$; $p < 0.005$ respectively), but adding the weekend data rendered these associations nonsignificant. MVPA in school correlated with sandbag throw (SRC $r = 0.44$; $p < 0.01$) and with shuttle run (SRC $r = -0.48$; $p < 0.005$, negative correlation shows higher running speed in more active children), but the significance of these associations was lost when the teachers' and parental reports were combined.

The parental psychological measures were not associated with any children's performance indicators in physical tasks.

Parental psychological measures on average corresponded well to the values obtained in a general population with the same scales, being slightly in the direction of lower state and trait anxiety and perceived stress and higher self-efficacy. Resting heart rate was found to be correlated positively with the parental scores in state anxiety ($r = 0.58$; $p < 0.001$), trait anxiety ($r = 0.53$; $p < 0.005$), and perceived stress ($r = 0.53$; $p < 0.005$). The parents were divided by the mean values into low and high score subgroups for group analysis (STAI-S: 7.5 ± 1.2 vs 11.6 ± 2.0; STAI-T: 12.4 ± 2.0 vs

Table 1. Selected measures of children divided on the basis of their parents' state or trait anxiety, perceived stress, and self-efficacy into high or low group

Psychological measure	Group	Age (y)	Body weight (kg)	Height (cm)	RHR (beats·min^{-1})
STAI-S	Low	7.03 ± 0.38	27.0 ± 4.1	128 ± 5	63.1 ± 3.8
	High	7.02 ± 0.24	23.7 ± 3.9*	124 ± 5**	68.2 ± 6.5**
STAI-T	Low	6.99 ± 0.33	27.3 ± 4.9	128 ± 7	63.0 ± 3.3
	High	7.07 ± 0.31	23.8 ± 2.5**	124 ± 5*	67.5 ± 6.7*
PSS	Low	7.03 ± 0.27	25.5 ± 3.6	127 ± 6	61.9 ± 2.8
	High	7.02 ± 0.37	25.7 ± 4.8	125 ± 5	68.1 ± 5.8***
SES	Low	7.09 ± 0.19	24.7 ± 2.9	124 ± 5	66.4 ± 6.7
	High	6.97 ± 0.37	26.4 ± 5.0	128 ± 6*	64.1 ± 4.4

Values are mean ± SD
Level of significance *p <0.05; **p <0.01; ***p <0.001

19.3 ± 2.7; PSS: 3.4 ± 1.7 vs 8.1 ± 2.4; SES: 24.5 ± 3.2 vs 31.3 ± 2.5, mean ± SD, all low vs high p <0.0001). Resting heart rate was significantly higher in children of parents with high state anxiety scores, high trait anxiety scores, and high perceived stress scores. It was also found that even though children of parents scoring high or low in psychological tests were of the same age, children of parents with high state anxiety scores and high trait anxiety scores had lower body weight and height on average, whereas children of the parents with higher self-efficacy were taller.

Children of parents with high trait anxiety had significantly more MVPA (136 ± 77 vs 64 ± 44 min·d^{-1}; p <0.05). These children were reported by their parents to be significantly more active both on week-days and at weekends, but only at home.

Children of parents with low self-efficacy spent less time outdoors during the week (185 ± 47 vs 261 ± 50 min·d^{-1}; p <0.05), but no difference in PA was detected.

Discussion

This study is preliminary due to the small number of subjects, which is related to the difficulties of obtaining data about multiple measures from different sources and under standard and optimized conditions. Besides that limitation, several other methodological issues should be considered in further investigation. The socioeconomic variables were not included in data analysis, since the sample is relatively small, but all three subsamples were from a middle class living area. The role of the HPA of parents was not studied. Freedson and Evenson[7] have reported that in a study on thirty 5 to 9-year-old children, family aggregation was present in about 70% of the families.

The associations between time spent in MVPA and certain measures of fitness probably indicate that more fit children tend to be more active, since the objectively measured level of activity under similar conditions[4] should not be sufficient to increase fitness significantly. It is notable that weekdays and weekend-days seem to differ with this regard, although it may be related to the different reporting of teachers and parents[12].

Associations between resting heart rate in children, and state and trait anxiety and perceived stress in parents may possibly be explained by the partly hereditary balance of sympathetic/parasympathetic nervous activity. Differences in body weight and height in children of parents with different personality characteristics are difficult to interpret and require further analysis. These differences were not brought about by differences in sex or age between groups.

Associations of parental personality measures and the components of their children's lifestyle may have methodological implications for studies using parental reports of children's physical activity. The finding that parents with high trait anxiety have more physically active children deserves further study. At present, it might be hypothesized that since the difference was found on the basis of parental and not teachers' reports, this may reflect differences in reporting by psychologically different people rather than differences in children's behaviour. The children are generally more active outdoors, but there was no difference between the groups in time spent outdoors. However, it may be easier to report adequately the time when the child was indoors or outdoors, compared to reporting the level of intensity of PA. Thus, parents with high trait anxiety may overestimate the activity level of their children. Teachers' evaluation of children's physical activity levels seems to be more reliable than the parents' opinion[16,17]. The influence of the changeable personality measure, self-efficacy in parents on time their children spend outdoors should probably be interpreted as lifestyle-based, but requires detailed analysis. Probably the children of parents with high self-efficacy have more opportunities to be physically active spending more time outdoors, but whether this would influence reporting of their PA requires further study.

Acknowledgments

This study was supported by a grant from the Estonian Science Foundation (No 2467). We would like to thank Professor Atko-Meeme Viru for his comments.

References

1. Cale, L. and Almond, L. (1992) Physical activity levels of young children: a review of the evidence. *Health Education Journal*, Vol. 51, pp. 94-9.

2. Armstrong, N. and Bray, S. (1991) Physical activity patterns defined by continuous heart rate monitoring. *Archives of Disease in Childhood*, Vol. 66, pp. 245-7.
3. Pate, R.R., Baranowski, T., Dowda, M. and Trost, S.G. (1996) Tracking of physical activity in young children. *Medicine and Science in Sports and Exercise*, Vol. 28, pp. 92-6.
4. Sallo, M. and Silla, R. (1997) Physical activity with moderate to vigorous intensity in preschool and first-grade schoolchildren. *Pediatric Exercise Science,* Vol. 9, pp. 44-54.
5. Biddle, S.J.H. (1995) Exercise motivation across the life span, in *European Perspectives on Exercise and Sport Psychology*, (ed. S.J.H. Biddle), Human Kinetics, Champaign, Il., pp. 1-25.
6. Shephard, R.J. (1994) Determinants of exercise in people aged 65 years and older, in *Advances in Exercise Adherence*, (ed. R.K. Dishman), Human Kinetics, Champaign, Il., pp. 343-60.
7. Freedson, P.S. and Evenson, S. (1991) Familial aggregation in physical activity. *Research Quarterly for Exercise and Sport*, Vol. 62, pp. 384-9.
8. Moore, L.L., Lombardi, D.A., White, M.J., Campbell, J.L., Oliveria, S.A. and Ellison, R.C. (1991) Influence of parents' physical activity levels on activity levels of young children. *Journal of Pediatrics*, Vol. 118, pp. 215-9.
9. Godin, G., Shephard, R.J. and Colantonio, A. (1986) Children's perception of parental exercise: influence of sex and age. *Perceptual and Motor Skills*, Vol. 62, pp. 511-6.
10. McMurray, R.G., Bradley, C.B., Harell, J.S., Bernthal, P.R., Frauman, A.C. and Bangdiwala, S.I. (1993) Parental influences on childhood fitness and activity patterns. *Research Quarterly for Exercise and Sport*, Vol. 64, pp. 249-55.
11. Oja, L. and Jürimäe, T. (1993) *Scoring of Physical Fitness in Pre-School Children*, Tartu University Press, Tartu.
12. Sallo, M. (1997) Studies on habitual physical activity and aerobic fitness in 4 to 10 years old children. *Dissertationes Medicinae Universitatis Tartuensis*, Vol. 28, Tartu University Press, Tartu.
13. Spielberger, Ch. D., Gorsuch, R.L., Lushene, R., Vagg, P.R. and Jacobs, G.A. (1983) *State-Trait Anxiety Inventory (STAI-Form Y): Self-Evaluation Questionnaire,* Consulting Psychologists Press, Palo Alto.
14. Cohen, S., Kamarck, T., and Mermelstein, R. (1983) Perceived stress scale (PSS): A global measure of perceived stress. *Journal of Health and Social Behavior*, Vol. 24, pp. 385-96.
15. Wegner, M., Schwarzer, R. and Jerusalem, M. (1993) *Measurement of Perceived Self-Efficacy: Psychometric Scales for Cross-Cultural Research,* Forschung an der Freien Universität Berlin, Berlin.
16. Pate, R.R., Douda, M. and Ross, J.G. (1990) Association between physical activity and physical fitness in American children. *American Journal of Diseases of Childhood*, Vol. 144, pp. 1113-29.
17. Sallo, M. and Viru, A. (1996) Aerobic capacity and physical activity in 4 to 10 year-old children. *Biology of Sport*, Vol. 13, pp. 211-9.

FAMILIAL INFLUENCES ON ADOLESCENTS' PHYSICAL ACTIVITY

Family influences on activity

S. AZNAR, K. BARNES, A. PAGE, J. McKENNA, C. RIDDOCH, M. CHRISTOPHER, J. GOLDBERG and G. SIMMONDS
Exercise and Health Research Unit, University of Bristol, Bristol, UK

Keywords: Adolescents, encouragement, family, physical activity, social influence, social support

Introduction

Physical activity is an important health-related concern, and guidelines for adolescents' health-related physical activity have been suggested[1]. An age-related decline in physical activity levels among youth has been identified[2], particularly during adolescence[3], and during childhood and adolescence most individuals develop and establish a range of health behaviours. The family can be considered a major initial socialising influence through which the framework of health behaviours develops. Perceived support from the family, peer group and teachers, as well as the opportunity to participate in organised sport from an early age, might be considered as reasonable conditions for the creation and continuation of an active lifestyle into the adult years[4]. However, there is little research into the specific components of family supportive behaviour for physical activity changes in children, from which types of support which are most, and/or least, effective can be determined. Relationships between family support and physical activity behaviour[5,6], as well as family support and a high level of fitness[7] have been reported. Moreover, evidence suggests an association between parents' and children's physical activity levels[8,9].

A first attempt to develop a measure of perceived family support for physical activity behaviour in adults[10] described three dimensions of social support: a) the quantity of social relationships, b) the structure of relationships and c) the functional content of relationships. The first two are aspects of the social network while the latter refers to behaviours through which one person actually supports another. A more recent measure by Taylor et al.[11] has described three components of family influences on behaviour. The first component is "modelling", which represents family members' current or past physical activity patterns as well as exercising with a family member. In

Children and Exercise XIX. Edited by Neil Armstrong, Brian Kirby and Joanne Welsman.
Published in 1997 by E & FN Spon, 2–6 Boundary Row, London, SE1 8HN.
ISBN 0 419 22100 X.

a modelling process "the significant others" constitute available and powerful models. Secondly, "social influence", which involves encouragement provided by the family together with persuasion, pressure, expectations and sanctions. Thirdly, "social support" which includes giving information about physical activity, and providing material, transport and emotional support. Social support has been identified as an important determinant of success in changing health habits[10,12].

Some studies have reported that parental modelling was more effective in influencing physical activity behaviours in children than parental encouragement[13,14]. Andersen and Wold[15] on the other hand emphasised the importance of encouragement and emotional support. They also reported that girls and boys respond to family support in different ways, girls requiring a stronger social support network compared to boys[16]. A potential decline in parental influences on health behaviours as children get older has been reported by Horn and Weiss[17], who indicate that during adolescence the influence of parental health behaviour on children can be modified by the influence of peers. In contrast, Rossow and Rise[18] reported no differences in perceptions of parental influences from the age of 16-20 y.

The purpose of this study was to examine the nature of parental and sibling influences on adolescents' physical activity behaviour. The importance of "perceived", rather than "received" influences is stressed.

Methods

Questionnaires were distributed to children in five high schools in a large city in the South West of England. The schools represented urban, rural, public and private school populations. The sample consisted of 970 students (589 males and 381 females) representing two separate year groups [year 7 (12.2 ± 0.5 y) and year 12 (17.3 ± 0.5 y)] to represent early and late adolescence. A 25-item familial influences on physical activity questionnaire based on Taylor et. al.[11] and McMurray et. al.[19] was administered. The items represented the concepts of modelling, social influence, social support and encouragement. Each item was applied independently to different family members[14].

Physical activity was measured by a self-reported 7-day recall[20]. Children were asked to recall their activity for the previous seven days, how long each activity lasted and whether they felt breathless during the activity. Each day was separated into specific parts of the day, for example, morning break, lunch break, after school. From these data, achievement/non-achievement of each of the health-related physical activity guidelines were calculated. Guideline 1 recommends that children should accumulate 30 min of moderate activity on most days of the week. Guideline 2 recommends 3 or more sessions per week of moderate to vigorous activities that last 20 min or more at a time.

Data analyses

Principal components factor analysis with oblique rotation was carried out separately by gender to evaluate the structure of familial influences (the 25 items on the questionnaire). Factors with eigenvalues greater than 1 were extracted and any item values above 0.4 were considered to be significant. Cronbach's Alpha was used to assess internal reliability for the items representing the different constructs: modelling, social influence and encouragement. Mean subscale scores based on the factors were entered into stepwise discriminant analysis to assess their ability to discriminate between children who achieved the physical activity guidelines compared to those who did not.

Results

Descriptive analyses indicated that all possible scores were represented for each item and the mean for the majority of the items was centred around the median for the scale [3]. Reported internal consistency from the questionnaire was $\alpha = 0.87$ for modelling items (11 items) $\alpha = 0.71$ for social influence (3 items) and $\alpha = 0.90$ for encouragement (10 items). For the factor analysis for males, five factors emerged, explaining 69.3% of the variance in family influences. Seven factors emerged for females explaining 75.4% of the variance. For both males and females, the first factor was labelled 'parental encouragement'. This factor explained 40% and 38.9% of the variance for males and females respectively. The items (loadings 0.56-0.86) related to the level of encouragement children felt they received from parents for both getting started and continuing to participate in physical activities or sports.

For males only, a second 'encouragement' factor, representing support from siblings, emerged explaining 10.8% of the variance (factor 2). The factor comprised four items (loading 0.72-0.83), related to the level of encouragement received from both brother and sister. Two further factors were labelled 'brother(s)' modelling (factor 3) and 'mother/sister(s)' modelling (factor 4). The remaining factor (factor 5) was related to personal motivation ("yourself"). For females, 'sister(s)' modelling and 'parental modelling', represented two separate factors (factors 2 and 3). Factor 3 was labelled 'sister's modelling' and factor 6 for represented "sibling encouragement". Factor 5 labelled "yourself", represented self motivation for getting involved in physical activities. The remaining factors (4 and 7) for females were difficult to interpret due to multiple cross loadings. In terms of the health-related activity guidelines, 71.6% of boys and 59.4% of girls achieved Guideline 1 and 31.8% of boys and 22.1% of girls achieved Guideline 2. The five factors for males and seven factors for females were then entered into stepwise discriminant analyses in order to determine the practical utility of familial factors in classifying those who did, and did not, meet the guidelines. Analyses were conducted separately by gender.

For males achieving guideline 1, two factors, factor 3 ("brother modelling") and factor 5 ("yourself") were entered to produce one significant discriminant function ($\chi^2_{(2).} = 25.49$, $p < 0.001$). These factors correctly classified 70.51% of those males who achieved guideline 1. For females achieving guideline 1, one factor, Factor 5 ("yourself") was entered into the analysis to produce one significant discriminant function ($\chi^2_{(1)}$ = 9.98, p <0.01), correctly classifying 64.86% of girls who achieved guideline 1. For males achieving guideline 2, no significant function emerged which may have been due to insufficient numbers in the analysis because only subjects with a perfect family unit (mother, father, sister(s) and brother(s)) were entered into the analysis. For females achieving guideline 2, one factor, factor 6 ("sibling encouragement") was entered producing one emergent significant discriminant function ($\chi^2_{(1)}$ = 5.53, p <0.05), correctly classifying 63.48% of subjects.

Discussion

Factor analyses supported independent constructs of modelling, social influence, social support and encouragement with respect to familial influences on adolescent physical activity behaviour. These constructs appeared to group independently on separate factors. The grouping emphasised family members across a range of concepts rather than concepts dominating family groups. For example, "parental modelling" and "sister modelling" correspond to factors 2 and 3 for females and "brother modelling" corresponds to factor 3 for males. 'Parental encouragement' seems to be the dominant factor for all children. However, for both males and females the construct 'encouragement' was split between two separate factors: parent(s) and sibling(s). The 'modelling' items for females loaded on separate factors when referring to parents or sister(s), whereas for males the items represented brother(s) modelling and mother and sister modelling. The fact that a sister modelling factor emerged in females and a brother modelling factor emerged in males supports distinct gender roles for influence on physical activity. Family general support such as: 'family talking about physical activity', 'receiving positive comments about you as an exerciser from your family', 'family showing interest in physical activity', and 'perceiving that the family think the child is good at sport', did not emerge as an individual factor, which in turn support the fact that individual family members are seen as distinct and separate influences.

Different gender sources of modelling were evident, particularly for siblings, with brother(s) more relevant for males and sister(s) more apparent for females. A single factor for both males and females represented 'adolescent self-motivation' for physical activity. This is the only factor that does not reflect a social and/or environmental influence for physical activity, and suggests that individuals draw upon intrinsic tools (values) to participate in physical activity. The relationship between achieving guideline 1 and the "yourself" factor in both males and females may highlight the importance of intrinsic motivation for activity, which may be as powerful as the social and environmental influences which this study has identified. However, there is the possibility of a strong relationship between the "yourself" factor and the other family influences, which may be especially strong during the adolescent period. Adolescence is considered an "ego-emergent" period in which personality, values and attitudes are consolidated. It is interesting that females who achieved guideline 2 found encouragement from both brothers and sisters, a gender preference not being evident. This implies that encouragement from brother to sister as well as sister to sister is favourable to engage in or maintain vigorous physical activity.

In conclusion, our data support the validity of a questionnaire approach to assessing family influences on adolescents' physical activity behaviour. Moreover, some clear patterns of family influence have emerged. However, further investigation is necessary using different social groups, cultures and demographic areas, before a complete picture of the structure of family influences on physical activity can be seen. Future studies might identify alternative styles of family units, as our study has assumed a "traditional" family unit (father, mother, sister(s), brother(s)).

Acknowledgements

This study was supported by a research scholarship from the Sports Council.

References

1. Sallis, J.F. and Patrick, K. (1994) Physical activity guidelines for adolescents: consensus statement. *Pediatric Exercise Science* Vol. 6, No. 4, pp. 302-14.
2. Sallis, J.F. (1994) Determinants of physical activity behaviour in children, in *Health and Fitness Through Physical Education,* (eds. R.R.Pate and R.C. Hohn), Human Kinetics, Champaign, Il., pp. 31-43.
3. Armstrong, N., Balding. J., Gentle, P. and Kirby, B. (1990) Patterns of physical activity among 11 to 16 year old British children. *British Medical Journal,* Vol. 301, pp. 203-5.
4. Stucky-Ropp, R.C. and DiLorenzo, T.M. (1993) Determinants of exercise in children. *Preventive Medicine,* Vol. 22, pp. 880-9.
5. Dishman, R., Sallis, J. and Orenstein, D. (1985) The determinants of physical activity and exercise. *Public Health Reports,* Vol. 100, pp. 158-71.
6. Sallis, J.F., Patterson, T.L., Buono, M.J., Atkins, C.J. and Nader, P.R. (1988) Aggregation of physical activity habits in Mexican-American and anglo families. *Journal of Behavioural Medicine,* Vol. 11, pp. 31-41.
7. Ferguson, K.J., Yesalis, C.E., Pomrehn, P.R. and Kirkpatrick, M.B. (1989) Attitudes, knowledge and beliefs as predictors of exercise intent and behaviour in schoolchildren. *Journal of School Health,* Vol. 59, No.3, pp. 112-5.
8. Freedson, P.S. and Evenson, S. Familial aggregation in physical activity. *Research Quarterly for Exercise and Sport,* Vol. 62, pp. 384-9.
9. Moore, L.L., Lombardi, D.A., White, M.J., Campbell, J.L., Oliveria, S.A. and Ellison, R.C. (1991) Influence of parents' physical activity levels on activity levels of young children. *Journal of Pediatrics,* Vol. 118, pp. 215-9.
10. Sallis, J.F., Grossman, R.M., Pinski, R.B., Patterson, T.L. and Nader, P.R. (1987) The development of scales to measure social support for diet and exercise behaviours. *Preventive Medicine,* Vol. 16, pp. 825-36.
11. Taylor, W.C., Baranowski, T. and Sallis, J.F. (1994) Family determinants of childhood physical activity: A social-cognitive model, in *Advances in Exercise Adherence,* (ed. R.K. Dishman), Human Kinetics, Champaign, Il., pp. 319-42.

12. Price, R.H., Cioci, M., Penner, W. and Trautlein, B. (1993) Webs of influence: School and community programs that enhance adolescent health and education. *Teachers College Record,* Vol. 94, pp. 487-521.
13. Godin, G., Shephard, R.J. and Colantonio, A. (1986) Children's perception of parental exercise: influence on age and sex. *Perceptual and Motor Skills,* Vol. 62, pp. 511-6.
14. Wold, B., Øygard, L., Eder, A. and Smith, C. (1994) Social reproduction of physical activity. *European Journal of Public Health,* Vol. 4, pp. 163-8.
15. Andersen, N. and Wold, B. (1992) Parental and peer influences on leisure-time physical activity in young adolescents. *Research Quarterly for Exercise and Sport,* Vol. 63, pp. 341-8.
16. Lewko, J.H. and Greendorfer, S.L. (1988) Family influences in sport socialisation of children and adolescents, in *Children in Sport,* (eds. F.L. Smoll., R.A. Magill. and M.J. Ash), Human Kinetics, Campaign, Il., pp. 287-300.
17. Horn, T.S. and Weiss, M.R. (1991) A developmental analysis of children's self-ability judgements in the physical domain. *Pediatric Exercise Science,* Vol. 3, pp. 310-26.
18. Rossow, I. and Rise, J. (1994) Concordance of parental and adolescent health behaviours. *Social Science Medicine,* Vol. 38, pp. 1299-305.
19. McMurray, R.G., Bradley, C.B., Harrell, J.S., Bernthal, P.R., Frauman, A.C. and Bangdiwala, S.I. (1993) Parental influences on childhood fitness and activity patterns. *Research Quarterly for Exercise and Sport,* Vol. 64, pp. 249-55.
20. Riddoch, C.J. (1990) *Report of the Northern Ireland Health and Fitness Survey,* The Queen's University of Belfast, Belfast.

DO ADOLESCENTS ACHIEVE APPROPRIATE LEVELS OF PHYSICAL ACTIVITY?
Activity assessed by diary

U.M. EKELUND, A. YNGVE and M. SJÖSTRÖM
Department of Physical Education and Health, University of Örebro, Örebro and Department of Medical Nutrition and Department of Bioscience, Karolinska Institute, Stockholm, Sweden
Keywords: Activity diary, body composition, disease prevention, energy expenditure, physical activity

Introduction

The scientific evidence supporting the health benefits attained from physical activity are clearly established in the adult population[1]. Less is known about that relationship in youth. Physical activity provides protection from chronic diseases and improves quality of life in adulthood, and the behaviour of being physically active seems to track from adolescents into adulthood[2]. Guideline One in the recently published physical activity guidelines for adolescents states that all adolescents should be physically active daily, or nearly every day, as part of play, games, sports, work, transportation, recreation, physical education, or planned exercise, in the context of family, school, and community activities[3]. The guideline also states that it is reasonable to recommend the same minimal amount of physical activity for adolescents as for adults [3], which is described as accumulation of 30 min of moderate (i.e. 3-6 METs) physical activity daily or nearly every day[4].

In Sweden, indirect evidence indicates a gradual decline in physical activity over the past few decades although only participation in competitive sports and recreational exercise were taken into account[5]. No direct measures of physical activity or total daily energy expenditure (TDEE) were made.

The Örebro Youth Activity Study was designed as a prospective study examining adolescents' health with particular emphasis on physical activity. This paper reports the TDEE data and physical activity levels assessed using a 7 d activity diary[6].

Children and Exercise XIX. Edited by Neil Armstrong, Brian Kirby and Joanne Welsman.
Published in 1997 by E & FN Spon, 2–6 Boundary Row, London, SE1 8HN.
ISBN 0 419 22100 X.

Subjects

In order to provide a representative population from various residential areas (i.e., city, suburb and rural) as well as various socio-economic levels, subjects were selected through two-stage cluster sampling. Six schools were randomly selected from a total of 13 in the municipality of Örebro, Sweden. The number of students from each school was representatively proportional to the size of the school. The random sample of students (n = 241) thus chosen to participate were similar in age (14.8 y ± 0.3). Four students were not able to complete the questionnaire and five had moved to another school. Thus, 232 subjects participated in the questionnaire section of the study. Despite two written reminders, 20 of the students who had completed the questionnaire did not respond to their invitation to participate in the rest of the study. Reasons for not participating in the complete study were obtained from 25 students. The main reasons for not participating were lack of time (n = 15) and objections to blood sampling (n = 5). Four of the adolescents were under medical supervision and one stated previous participation in a research project as a reason for not participating. The rest of the students (n = 37) who declined to take part in the complete study did not provide a reason. The remaining 150 students agreed to participate in the complete study, including the 7 d activity diary.

There were no significant differences between participants and non-participants in gender, age, weight or height, which were measured by school nurses that same school-year, or in participation in competitive sports or in physical education marks.

The study protocol was approved by Örebro County Council Research Ethics Committee and all participants and their parents provided written informed consent.

Methods

Height was measured to the nearest 0.5 cm by a wall-mounted stadiometer and body mass was measured to the nearest 0.1 kg in shorts and T-shirt. From these measurements Body Mass Index (BMI) was calculated as weight·height^{-2}. Body composition (i.e. body fatness) was determined in two ways: (I) The sum of four skinfold thickness measurements (triceps, biceps, subscapular and suprailiac) which was completed using Harpenden skinfold calipers on the right side of the body as described by Lohman[7]; (II) Relative body fatness (%) was calculated from triceps and subscapular skinfolds according to Slaughter et al´s. method[8]. Body fat mass (FM) was obtained by multiplying the percentage of body fat by body weight. Fat-free mass (FMM) was calculated by subtracting body fat from body weight.

Physical activity and TDEE were assessed using the activity diary method developed by Bouchard et al.[6]. Thus, each of the 7 record days was divided into 96 15 min periods. The subjects were instructed to record the main activity completed in that 15 min period, and rate it on a scale from 1 to 9 (table 1). Each number on the scale represented a different activity category. Each ranking of activity category referred to different levels of energy expenditure and could be converted to the metabolic energy turnover (MET) classification, i.e., multiples of basal metabolic rate (BMR). Category

Table 1. Seven day activity log classification and the MET values used for energy expenditure calculations (from Bouchard et al[6])

Categorical value	Examples	MET value
1	Sleeping, lying, watching television	1
2	Sitting, eating, writing, listening, reading, playing board games	1.5
3	Light activity standing, washing, cooking	2.3
4	Slow walk (<4 $km{\cdot}h^{-1}$)walking indoors, music playing general	2.8
5	Light manual work, house chores, sweeping, cleaning, walking the dog, walking moderate	3.5
6	Leisure activities, golf, volleyball, cycling (<15 $km{\cdot}h^{-1}$), horse riding	4.5
7	Manual work, carrying goods, gardening, skateboarding	5.5
8	Leisure and sport activities, dancing, swiming, tennis, downhill skiing, cycling (>15 $km{\cdot}h^{-1}$), skateing, aerobics, badminton	6.0
9	High intensity sport activities and sport competition, running, cross country skiing, soccer, ice hockey, aerobics, badminton	8.0

1 represented inactivity (for example sleep, lying down, watching television) and was assumed to equal BMR.

BMR was calculated for each subject on the basis of sex, age, height and weight by using the predictive equations from Schofield[9] and converted to $MJ{\cdot}h^{-1}$. To calculate the TDEE from the 7 d diary, the number of 15 min periods in each activity category was summed and converted to hours. Time in a given activity category was multiplied by the appropriate MET intensity as described by Ainsworth et al.[10], and by the estimated BMR to calculate energy expenditure ($MJ{\cdot}h^{-1}$) in the different activity categories. The sum of the $MJ{\cdot}h^{-1}$ for each activity category provided a total energy expenditure for that time period and that was then divided by 7 to calculate TDEE ($MJ{\cdot}d^{-1}$). The physical activity level (PAL) was calculated as TDEE/BMR.

Frequency of participation in moderate and vigorous physical activity was calculated as the sum of 15 min periods equal to or more than 4.5 METs (activity categories 6-9). The sum was divided by 7 to obtain the number of periods per day of moderate and vigorous physical activity. Subjects who had two or more periods (30 $min{\cdot}d^{-1}$) of moderate and vigorous physical activity were considered to have met Guideline One in physical activity guidelines for adolescents[3].

All statistical analyses were performed using t-tests.

Table 2. Physical characteristics and body composition of subjects

	Boys (n=60)	Girls (n=67)
Age (y)	14.8 ± 0.3	14.7 ± 0.3
Height (m)	1.72 ± 0.09***	1.64 ± 0.06
Weight (kg)	61.9 ± 12.3***	55.2 ± 8.8
BMI ($kg \cdot m^{-2}$)	20.9 ± 2.8	20.6 ± 3.1
Sum of four skinfolds (mm)	41.3 ± 21.8	47.2 ± 20.1
FM (%)	17.4 ± 8.5**	21.5 ± 6.3
FM (kg)	11.3 ± 8.2	12.3 ± 5.3
FFM (kg)	50.4 ± 7.2***	43.0 ± 6.1

Values are mean ± SD
Level of significance **p <0.01, ***p <0.001

Results

Twenty-three of the students failed to complete a full week of activity registration and therefore, the results presented here are data from the 127 students who completed the 7 day activity diary. Those students (13 boys and 10 girls) who failed to complete the activity diary did not differ from those who completed it in levels of physical activity assessed by the questionnaire. Physical characteristics of the participants are shown in table 2.

Estimated BMR averaged 7.4 ± 1.0 and 6.0 ± 0.4 $MJ \cdot d^{-1}$ for boys and girls respectively (p <0.001). TDEE was significantly higher (p <0.001) in boys compared to girls whether expressed in absolute values (12.8 ± 1.7 vs 10.3 ± 1.1 $MJ \cdot d^{-1}$) or in relation to kg body weight (0.210 ± 0.03 vs 0.188 ± 0.02 $MJ \cdot d^{-1}$). However, when TDEE was expressed per kg of fat free mass ($MJ \cdot kgFMM^{-1} \cdot d^{-1}$) there was no significant difference between the gender groups (0.252 ± 0.05 vs 0.240 ± 0.02 $MJ \cdot d^{-1}$ for boys and girls respectively). PAL did not differ significantly between boys and girls (1.74 ± 0.2 vs 1.72 ± 0.2).

Fifteen percent of the boys and 18% of the girls were not physically active for at least 30 $min \cdot d^{-1}$ at an intensity level corresponding to ≥ 4.5 METs. This intensity level was equal to an energy expenditure of 5.5 ± 0.7 $kcal \cdot min^{-1}$ for boys and 4.5 ± 0.3 $kcal \cdot min^{-1}$ for girls based on estimated BMR. Thirty eight percent of boys and 36% girls were categorised as physically inactive at an intensity level of ≥ 5.5 METs. This intensity level was equal to an energy expenditure of 6.8 ± 0.8 $kcal \cdot min^{-1}$ for boys and 5.5 ± 0.3 $kcal \cdot min^{-1}$ for girls. Those who were defined as not physically active for at least 30 min at a ≥ 4.5 METs per day level had a lower PAL value then those who met the desired activity level (1.57 ± 0.1 vs 1.76 ± 0.2, p <0.001). There were no significant differences in any of the body composition measurements between the groups. Neither was there any significant difference in body composition when those who were defined physically inactive were compared with the 15% most active (i.e. those with the highest PAL values).

There was no significant difference between the gender groups in time spent at two different intensity levels. Mean time spent at an intensity level of ≥ 4.5 METs was 81.8 ± 49.1 min·d^{-1} for boys and 66.7 ± 39.4 min·d^{-1} for girls and mean time spent at an intensity level of ≥ 5.5 METs was 49.3 ± 37.2 min·d^{-1} for boys and 47.1 ± 30.9 min·d^{-1} for girls.

Discussion

The average value for height and median values for weight and BMI measurements for girls were similar to those recently published in Sweden[11].

In this study, TDEE and physical activity were assessed by a 7 d self administered diary. The advantages and disadvantages of this method have been discussed by others[12]. We have found, as described elsewhere[13], the activity diary comparable to min-by-min heart rate (HR) recording for both the assessment of TDEE and for time spent in moderate physical activity in this age group of adolescents. Furthermore, the activity diary method has been validated against the doubly-labelled water technique in 15-year-old adolescents[14].

Comparisons of physical activity data from different studies are difficult to make, mainly because of different methodologies used and different definitions of activity levels. The results of TDEE from this study are similar to those found in a comparative study between the diary and min-by-min HR recording[13]. The TDEE and PAL values found here seem to be higher than those from studies using activity diaries in the same age group[15]. Furthermore, the observed values of TDEE in this study are higher then the average, but within the distribution, according to the estimated Nordic reference values for energy intake[16].

It has recently been proposed that a PAL-value of 1.80 for boys and 1.65 for girls could be considered as moderate habitual physical activity in 14-18-year-olds[14]. These values are higher then the FAO/WHO/UNU factorial estimates for energy requirements, which are 1.65 and 1.57 in boys and girls[17]. The PAL values (1.74 and 1.72 for boys and girls respectively) found in the present study, indicate moderate physical activity in this group of boys and girls.

To examine whether the Swedish adolescents in this study met the first recommendation in physical activity guidelines for adolescents[4] we defined Guideline One as 30 min·d^{-1} of physical activity at an intensity level ≥4.5 METs. From this it seems obvious that at least 15% of the youths are not physically active enough to enhance future health. On the other hand, this group of physically inactive adolescents did not differ in any of the body composition measurements compared to the most active group.

Since we could not find any difference in TDEE when it was expressed in relation to fat free mass we conclude that the difference between the gender groups is due to a difference in body size and/or body composition and not in physical activity. These findings are in accordance with our previous findings[13], but opposed to the findings of Armstrong et al.[18] and Livingstone et al.[19]. However, it should be pointed out that different methodologies were used.

In conclusion, results from the present study suggest that there are no significant differences between the gender groups in either TDEE related to fat free mass or in PAL values. Furthermore, there is no difference in time spent at different intensity levels of physical activity. The results for TDEE and PAL are similar to our previous findings and indicate moderate habitual physical activity in this group of adolescents. It is a matter of concern, however, that 15% to one third of Swedish adolescents do not seem to achieve appropriate levels of physical activity according to established physical activity guidelines for adolescents.

References

1. Bouchard, C., Shephard, R.J. and Stephens, T. (eds.) (1994) *Physical Activity, Fitness, and Health: International Proceedings and Consensus Statement*, Human Kinetics, Champaign, Il.
2. Kuh, D.J.L. and Cooper, C. (1992) Physical activity at 36 years: patterns and childhood predictors in a longitudinal study. *Journal of Epidemiology and Community Health*, Vol. 46, pp. 114-9.
3. Sallis, J.F. and Patrick, K. (1994) Physical activity guidelines for adolescents: Consensus statement. *Pediatric Exercise Science*, Vol. 6, pp. 302-14.
4. Pate, R.R., Pratt, M., Blair, S.N., Haskell, W.L., Macera, C.A., Bouchard, C., Buchner, D., Ettinger, W., Heath, G.W., King, A.C., Kriska, A., Leon, A.S., Marcus, B.H., Morris, J., Paffenbarger, R.S., Patrick, K., Pollock, M.L., Rippe, J.M., Sallis, J. and Wilmore, J.H. (1995) Physical activity and public health, a recommendation from the Centres for Disease Control and Prevention and from the American College of Sports Medicine. *Journal of American Medical Association*, Vol. 273, pp. 402-7.
5. Engström, LM. (1989) *Idrottsvanor i Förändring*, HLS förlag, Stockholm, Sweden.
6. Bouchard, C., Tremblay, A., Leblanc, D., Lortie, G., Savara, R. and Theriault, G. (1983) A method to assess energy expenditure in children and adults. *American Journal of Clinical Nutrition*, Vol. 37, pp. 461-7.
7. Lohman, T.G., Roche, A.T. and Martorell, R. (eds.) (1991) *Anthropometric Standardization Reference Manual*, Human Kinetics, Champaign, Il.
8. Slaughter, M.H., Lohman, T.G., Boileau, R.A., Horswill, C.A., Stillman, R.J., Van Loan, M.D. and Bemben, D.A. (1988) Skinfold equations for estimation of body fatness in children and youth. *Human Biology*, Vol. 60, pp. 709-23.
9. Schofield, W.N. (1985) Predicting basal metabolic rate, new standards and review of previous work. *Human Nutrition and Clinical Nutrition*, Vol. 39C, (suppl), pp. 5-41.
10. Ainsworth, B.E., Haskell, W.L., Leon, A.S., Jacobs jr, D.R., Montoye, H.J., Sallis, J.F. and Paffenbarger jr, R.S. (1993) Compendium of physical activities: classification of energy costs of human physical activities. *Medicine and Science in Sports and Exercise*, Vol. 25, pp. 71-80.

11. Lindgren, G., Strandell, A., Cole, T., Healy, M. and Tanner, J. (1995) Swedish population reference standards for height, weight and body mass index attained at 6 to 16 years (girls) or 19 years (boys). *Acta Paediatrica*, Vol. 84, pp. 1019-28.
12. Montoye, H.J., Kemper, H.C.G., Saris, W.H.M. and Washburn, R.A. (1996) *Measuring Physical Activity and Energy Expenditure*, Human Kinetics, Champaign, Il.
13. Ekelund, U.M. and Sjöström, M. (1997) Total daily energy expenditure and patterns of physical activity in adolescents: a comparison between two field methods. *Medicine and Science in Sports and Exercise*, Vol. 28, (suppl), p. 41.
14. Bratteby, L.E., Sandhagen, B., Fan, H. and and Samuelson, G. (in press) A 7-day activity diary for assessment of daily energy expenditure validated by the doubly labelled water method in adolescents. *European Journal of Clinical Nutrition*.
15. Durnin, J.V.G.A. (1971) Physical activity of adolescents. *Acta Paediatrica Scandinavia*, Vol. 217, (suppl), pp. 133-5.
16. Nordic Nutrition Recommendations 1996 (1996) *Scandinavian Journal of Nutrition*, Vol. 40, pp. 161-5.
17. Food and Agricultural Organisation/World Health Organisation/United Nations University. (1985) *Energy and Protein Requirements*, WHO Technical Report Series. No. 724, pp. 1-175.
18. Armstrong, N., Balding, J., Gentle, P. and Kirby, B. (1990) Patterns of physical activity among 11 to 16 year old British children. *British Medical Journal*, Vol. 30, pp. 203-5.
19. Livingstone, M.B.E., Coward, W.A., Prentice, A.M., Davies, P.S.W., Strain, J.J., McKenna, P.G., Mahoney, C.A., White, J.A., Stewart, C.M. and Kerr, M.J.J. (1992) Daily energy expenditure in free living children: comparison of heart rate monitoring with the doubly labelled water ($^2H_2{}^{18}O$) method. *American Journal of Clinical Nutrition*, Vol. 56, pp. 343-52.

PART III

AEROBIC PERFORMANCE

THE DEVELOPMENT OF AEROBIC FITNESS IN CHILDREN

Aerobic fitness in children

T.W. ROWLAND
Department of Pediatrics, Baystate Medical Center, Springfield, USA

Keywords: Aerobic fitness, allometric scaling, arteriovenous oxygen difference, exercise, heart rate, oxygen uptake, stroke volume

Introduction

Maximal oxygen uptake ($\dot{V}O_2$ max) identifies the greatest rate at which the metabolic machinery of skeletal muscle cells can utilize oxygen in the provision of energy for locomotion. At submaximal levels of exercise $\dot{V}O_2$ is established by the aerobic demands of muscle contraction. Current evidence suggests, however, that the upper limit of $\dot{V}O_2$ during progressively intense exercise (i.e. $\dot{V}O_2$ max) is defined by oxygen delivery rather than muscle uptake. That is, it appears that factors such as maximal cardiac output, oxygen carrying capacity of the blood (i.e. haemoglobin concentration), and vascular supply to muscles are responsible for the "ceiling" of aerobic metabolic expenditure during exercise.

Performance in endurance exercise events is contingent upon an adequate supply of oxygen to contracting muscle. Successful endurance athletes are characterized by their high levels of $\dot{V}O_2$ max compared to non-athletes, and increases in $\dot{V}O_2$ max that occur with aerobic training are linked to improvements in endurance performance. Similarly, a decline in $\dot{V}O_2$ max is associated with a diminished ability to tolerate exercise.

Mathematically, $\dot{V}O_2$ max can be expressed simply as the product of cardiac output (heart rate x stroke volume) and arteriovenous (AV) oxygen difference (the Fick equation). From a physiologic/biochemical perspective, however, the determinants of $\dot{V}O_2$ max--the components of the oxygen delivery chain--are extraordinarily complex. This finely-tuned mechanism of ventilatory, cardiac, haematologic, vascular, and cellular biochemical factors must work in concert to provide oxidative energy

Children and Exercise XIX. Edited by Neil Armstrong, Brian Kirby and Joanne Welsman.
Published in 1997 by E & FN Spon, 2–6 Boundary Row, London, SE1 8HN.
ISBN 0 419 22100 X.

necessary for sustained muscular activity. Disease states which weaken individual links in this chain (i.e. anaemia, heart disease) result in a decline in $\dot{V}O_2$ max.

There is no reason to expect that these basic principles differ in children compared to adults. Still, several important issues have stimulated considerable interest in understanding the normal development of $\dot{V}O_2$ max during the course of childhood: A) Promoting life-long habits of aerobic activities is expected to reduce risk of chronic diseases such as hypertension, obesity, and coronary artery disease. Understanding how aerobic fitness can be maximized in childhood may have long term salutary benefits. B) An increasing number of endurance child athletes are becoming involved with intensive training regimens. Optimal safe levels of participation in such sports prior to puberty needs to be identified. C) The effectiveness and proper construction of exercise rehabilitation programmes for children with heart and lung disease is dependent on knowledge of the normal responses of children to aerobic exercise. D) The normal developmental changes of $\dot{V}O_2$ max with growth in children in many ways parallels alterations in aerobic fitness observed in adults with endurance training. Understanding how aerobic fitness normally improves in children with age may provide insights into mechanisms for such changes with training.

This review will address our current understanding of the normal development of aerobic fitness as indicated by changes in $\dot{V}O_2$ max as children grow. While certain aspects appear evident, the answers to many questions regarding the development of $\dot{V}O_2$ max remain obscure. How does $\dot{V}O_2$ max change with age relative to body size? To what extent are improvements in $\dot{V}O_2$ max with age related to development of function (i.e. myocardial contractility) rather than size? How do changes in the components of the oxygen delivery chain contribute to changes in $\dot{V}O_2$ max with growth? How can we explain differences in $\dot{V}O_2$ max between boys and girls?

In this brief discussion, the focus will be narrowed to the development of $\dot{V}O_2$ max in healthy, non-athletic children. Ignored, then, will be a number of other intriguing issues surrounding aerobic fitness in children, including the plasticity (trainability) of $\dot{V}O_2$ max, the relationship between mass-relative $\dot{V}O_2$ max and endurance performance during growth, population changes in $\dot{V}O_2$ max over time, and the aerobic characteristics of child endurance athletes. The author has also chosen not to address important issues of measurement, reproducibility, and identification of $\dot{V}O_2$ max in children. The interested reader is referred elsewhere for a discussion of these critical issues[1-4].

The facts

The course of childhood is accompanied by dramatic increases in the size of the "motor" consuming oxygen during exercise (i.e. skeletal muscle) as well as each of the components of the oxygen delivery chain. Average heart weight, for instance, rises from 119 to 169 g between the ages of 8 and 12 y, while lung weight increases from 290 to 459 g. During this time span estimated left ventricular volume at rest enlarges by 52% and lung vital capacity increases from 1890 to 2800 mL (a 48% rise).

Not surprisingly, then, maximal oxygen uptake increases as the child grows. Several authors have performed the task of amassing data from large numbers of cross-sectional and longitudinal studies of $\dot{V}O_2$ max values in children, and all demonstrate virtually the same pattern[1,3,4]. In boys, $\dot{V}O_2$ max expressed as $L{\cdot}min^{-1}$ rises in a gradual curvilinear fashion with age. This amounts to an annual increase of about 225 $mL{\cdot}min^{-1}$ from the age of 6-8 y on. The average 6-year-old boy has a $\dot{V}O_2$ max of about 1.2 $L{\cdot}min^{-1}$, while that of a 15-year old is 2.7 $L{\cdot}min^{-1}$. The greatest rate of increase in $\dot{V}O_2$ max in boys happens at or near the time of peak height velocity, presumably reflecting acceleration in the size of determinants of $\dot{V}O_2$ max at the time of puberty.

Values of $\dot{V}O_2$ max are, on the average, about 200 $mL{\cdot}min^{-1}$ lower in girls than boys at the same chronological age. Moreover, the increase with age in females reaches a plateau at puberty and remains stable at a mean level of about 2.0 $L{\cdot}min^{-1}$ throughout the teen years.

When $\dot{V}O_2$ max is related to body mass (the ratio standard), a different pattern emerges in the two sexes. $\dot{V}O_2$ max per kg remains stable throughout childhood in boys, with a typical value during treadmill testing of about 50-52 $mL{\cdot}kg^{-1}{\cdot}min^{-1}$. Girls, on the other hand, display a steady decline from age 8 years on. An average value for a 15 year old girl, for instance, is about 42 $mL{\cdot}kg^{-1}{\cdot}min^{-1}$.

The development of $\dot{V}O_2$ max closely parallels other markers of biological maturation. The correlation between $\dot{V}O_2$ max and skeletal age in boys is reported to be r=0.89[5]. Body weight bears a modest relationship to $\dot{V}O_2$ max, with typical correlation coefficients of r=0.60 to 0.80[4].

It is important to recognize the limitations of these data, particularly as they may be interpreted as representing normative values for the paediatric population. Few studies have been performed on children under the age of 8 y, different laboratories with varying protocols are included, and most investigations describe findings only in males. Moreover, as most involve volunteer subjects, it can be expected that these data reflect mainly the characteristics of fit, motivated, non-obese children. Normative, non-selective, population-wide information on $\dot{V}O_2$ max values during childhood are not yet available.

The questions

Beyond the recognized increase in absolute $\dot{V}O_2$ max with growth, a great deal of uncertainty persists in understanding the factors which establish this rise, the most appropriate means of "normalizing" $\dot{V}O_2$ max to body size, and the explanation for gender differences. Space permits only a limited discussion of these intriguing issues, which are dealt with in more detail elsewhere[1-3].

What factors influence the normal pattern of development of $\dot{V}O_2$ max during childhood?

It is intuitively obvious that the development of $\dot{V}O_2$ max in children is largely--if not entirely (more on this later)--related to growth in body size. It follows, then, that the principal determinants of the rise in $\dot{V}O_2$ max during childhood must be those factors which are responsible for somatic growth. Prior to the age of puberty, growth hormone and its mediators, the somatomedins, are the predominant factors effecting body growth, along with contributing influences of other hormones such as insulin and parathormone. At puberty, these endocrinological influences become supplemented by the actions of the reproductive hormones, particularly the anabolic effects of testosterone in the male.

These hormones dictate the shape, or slope, of the $\dot{V}O_2$ max curve with growth, an influence which is predominantly under genetic control. The extent that this curve can be modified--shifted to the right or left--by environmental influences is uncertain. While no long-term studies are available, cross-sectional investigations and some longitudinal data suggest that the effect of physical activity on the developmental rate of $\dot{V}O_2$ max is limited. Extremes of increased or decreased activity--endurance training and complete bed rest--alter $\dot{V}O_2$ max in children by only about 5-15%[6,7]. Nutrition, socioeconomic status, geography, race, and climate are all recognized as potential influences on the rate of biological maturation[8]. The effect of these factors on the development of aerobic fitness, however, is largely unknown.

How does gender influence the development of aerobic fitness during childhood?

Distinctive gender-related differences in maximal aerobic power are observed in adults. The average adult male demonstrates 15-20% greater values of $\dot{V}O_2$ max per kg than the typical female, a difference which has been attributed to a) greater body fat content and less muscle mass in females, b) a greater blood haemoglobin concentration in males, and c) gender differences in habitual activity and sports participation. Still, even when these factors are considered, $\dot{V}O_2$ max values remain somewhat greater in males, leading to the suggestion that unknown "inherent biological differences" might exist between adult males and females in the components of the oxygen delivery system[9].

Similar gender differences in $\dot{V}O_2$ max, albeit to a lesser extent, are observed in prepubertal children. Average values for absolute $\dot{V}O_2$ max are 5-10% greater in males, beginning at the youngest ages that maximal testing can be performed. This difference widens at the age of puberty. Part of the gender-related variability in $\dot{V}O_2$ max can be explained by differences in body composition. Boys typically have a greater percentage of lean body mass and lower body fat than girls, although differences are not nearly as dramatic as those observed following puberty. An 8-year- old boy can be expected to have about 15% body fat, while that of a girl the same age averages 23%. Amount of fat-free mass per unit of height is typically about 6% greater in boys than girls. When $\dot{V}O_2$ max is expressed relative to lean body mass in children gender differences decrease but do not disappear[10].

Blood haemoglobin concentrations are similar in boys and girls prior to puberty, so there are no gender differences in oxygen carrying capacity in children. Most studies identify greater levels of habitual physical activity in boys compared to girls, and boys are more likely to participate on organized sports teams. The potential of daily activity to improve $\dot{V}O_2$ max has been questioned, however, and it is not clear if gender differences in activity can explain similar differences in aerobic fitness.

The possibility remains, then, that biological factors beyond body composition, haemoglobin concentration, and physical activity patterns may contribute to gender-related differences in $\dot{V}O_2$ max in children. One possibility would be gender variations in left ventricular size. Nagasawa et al recently described longitudinal changes in left ventricular diastolic dimension (which is expected to be related to stroke volume) relative to body size and gender in 437 children with a past history of Kawasaki disease but normal echocardiograms[11]. Subjects were studied an average of 3.7 times over an mean duration of 6.7 y. Males showed a significantly greater rate of development of left ventricular size than females when height was used as an index, but no gender differences were seen when data were related to body surface area or weight. Information from other echocardiographic studies regarding possible gender differences in heart size have been conflicting.

Future studies controlling for body composition, haemoglobin concentration, and habitual physical activity will be needed to provide insight regarding the influence of gender on $\dot{V}O_2$ max in children.

What is the most appropriate means of relating $\dot{V}O_2$ max to body size?

If one is to compare $\dot{V}O_2$ max between individuals, or values in the same child over time, it is necessary to express maximal oxygen uptake relative to some measure of body size. Traditionally, this has been accomplished by relating $\dot{V}O_2$ max to body mass, a logical approach considering that whole body metabolic rate should be expected to correspond to the tissue mass of that organism. It has long been recognized, however, that metabolic rate is not directly related to body mass; in fact, $\dot{V}O_2$ max per kg body mass is inversely related to body mass. Consequently, expressing $\dot{V}O_2$ max per kg may provide misleading information, causing values to be falsely inflated in small subjects and underestimated in larger individuals. A more "proper" denominator for relating $\dot{V}O_2$ max to body size has generally been considered mass raised to an exponent somewhat less than 1.0, a conclusion based on both theoretical considerations and empirical observation[1].

An understanding of this search for a proper denominator for expressing $\dot{V}O_2$ max with growth is perhaps best understood in the historical context of a similar quest by comparative biologists for a means of normalizing metabolic rate to size among animals[12]. For over 100 y it has been recognized that an inverse relationship exists between animal size and resting metabolic rate per kg body mass. That is, the smaller animal will demonstrate a much greater resting $\dot{V}O_2$ per kg than a larger one. Given the marked diversity of body size in the animal kingdom (by a factor of 10^7) this difference in mass-specific metabolic rate can be quite dramatic. The resting metabolic rate of a mouse relative to its body mass, for example, is ten times that of a whale.

When resting metabolic rate (Y) of animals of diverse size is related to body mass (X) by the allometric equation $Y = aX^b$, the scaling exponent b has been identified as approximately 0.75. The consistency of this finding in different animal populations suggests the expression of a basic biological principle. But the identification of that principle--and the explanation for the 0.75 scaling exponent--continues to be debated to this day. The most popular idea for explaining the inverse relationship between body size and mass-relative resting metabolic rate in animals has been the "surface law". This holds that heat is lost from the body from its surface, and smaller animals have a greater surface/body mass ratio than larger ones. If true, however, the surface law would dictate that resting $\dot{V}O_2$ should relate to body mass by the exponent 0.67, a value also predicted by dimensionality theory, instead of 0.75.

Maximal oxygen uptake in animals of various sizes relates to body mass by the equation $\dot{V}O_2$ max = $1.92M^{0.81}$, a relationship similar to that observed at rest. This information is of interest to exercise physiologists studying children, since these resting and maximal exponents obtained among adult animals should be indicative of the isolated effect of size (as opposed to function). How do they compare to those observed in children? If the exponents are similar, it would suggest that $\dot{V}O_2$ max develops solely as a function of increasing body size. Differences in exponents in children and those observed in these animal studies would suggest, on the other hand, that other factors, particularly alterations in function, might be important in the development of $\dot{V}O_2$ max in children.

An examination of such relationships, however, provides no "neat" answer to the question. Allometric analysis of resting metabolic rate versus mass in children has demonstrated that the relationship of the two varies during the course of childhood. Holliday et al.[13] indicated that basal metabolic rate relates to mass by the exponent of 1.02 up to the weight of 10 kg, and by the exponent 0.58 thereafter. That is, these curves do not conform to either exponents of 0.67 or 0.75. Holliday et al.[13] suggested that this observation could be explained by changes in the relative decline in the size of the most metabolically active organs (brain, liver, heart, kidneys) with increasing body size.

Scaling exponents for $\dot{V}O_2$ max relative to body mass in both boys and girls have been identified in several cross-sectional and longitudinal studies (table 1). Almost all have been less than 1.0, with values ranging from 0.37 to 1.10. We recently compared scaling exponents obtained from a 5 y longitudinal study of 20 children from ages 8 to 13 y to those observed in cross-sectional analyses of the same children[20]. The mean longitudinal scaling exponent for $\dot{V}O_2$ max relative to body mass was 1.10 (SD 0.30) in the boys and 0.78 (0.28) in the girls. Respective cross-sectional values were 0.53 (0.08) and 0.65 (0.03). $\dot{V}O_2$ max expressed relative to $M^{1.00}$, $M^{0.75}$, and $M^{0.67}$ rose during the 5 y in the boys but not the girls. Significant gender differences in scaling exponents remained when $\dot{V}O_2$ max was related to lean body mass. These findings suggest that factors other than body size alone--particularly gender and body composition--may influence scaling exponents for $\dot{V}O_2$ max during childhood.

It is obvious that our understanding of the relationship between body size and $\dot{V}O_2$ max during the growing years is far from clear. In respect to the above discussion, it is not easy to interpret differences in scaling exponents for both resting and maximal energy expenditure observed in children and those reported in animal studies. However, perhaps two tentative conclusions emerge from the available information. First, so far there seems to be no single allometric scaling factor that is useful for "normalizing"

Table 1. Scaling exponent b in the allometric equation $\dot{V}O_2$ max = kMass^b in studies of children.

Study	n	Sex	Age (y)	Mass exponent
	Cross-Sectional Studies			
Cooper et al (14)	51	F	6-17	0.79, 0.91
	58	M		1.01, 1.02
Astrand (15)	68	M,F	6-17	0.95
Welsman et al (16)	29	M	10-11	0.92
	34	F		0.84
Rogers et al (17)	21	M	7-9	0.37
	21	F		0.68
Batterham et al (18)	30	M,F	10	0.66
Rowland et al (20)	11	M	8-13	0.53
	9	F		0.65
	Longitudinal Studies			
Beunen et al (19)	47	M	11-14	0.88, 0.97, 0.52
	31	F		0.23, 0.28, 0.42
Rowland et al (20)	11	M	8-13	1.10
	9	F		0.78

$\dot{V}O_2$ max across different populations of children. It is likely that factors such as body composition and somatotype, athleticism, relative contribution of muscle bulk to body mass, and gender may alter the relationship of mass to $\dot{V}O_2$ max. This confounds the search for a simple means of comparing aerobic fitness between children of different size and levels of biological development.

Second, current evidence suggests that aerobic fitness appropriately related to body size may actually improve over the course of childhood. This idea is counter to the traditional concept that aerobic fitness is closely coupled to body dimensions during growth, at least in boys (i.e. $\dot{V}O_2$ per kg remains stable over age). Given that most data indicate that the true mass exponent is less than unity, it follows that $\dot{V}O_2$ max expressed to such a denominator would be expected to increase in the growing male. Whether this is also true in females, who have a decline in $\dot{V}O_2$ per kg with age, is uncertain.

Also, whether the magnitude of any increase in aerobic fitness during childhood is sufficient to have physiological/performance implications is likewise problematic.

How do the components of the oxygen delivery chain change with growth?

Further insight into the development of aerobic fitness in children may be gained from examining the changes in the principal determinants of $\dot{V}O_2$ max--heart rate, stroke volume, and arteriovenous (AV) oxygen difference--as children grow. Unfortunately, much of our understanding of these changes is "sketchy", limited by methodologies of uncertain validity as well as ethical constraints on experimental procedures in children (i.e. muscle biopsy).

Heart rate

Among the uncertainties surrounding developmental exercise physiology, one observation seems clear: maximal heart rate plays no role in the improvement observed in $\dot{V}O_2$ max during childhood. Maximal heart rate varies with the mode and protocol of exercise, but given the same testing procedure, cross-sectional and longitudinal studies of children ages 6 to 16 y show no substantive changes over time[20,21]. Mean values are typically 195-205 beats·min^{-1}, with lower rates for cycle testing and higher for treadmill running. This lack of change in maximal heart rate with age suggests a stability of autonomic function (particularly sympathetic nervous input) during childhood.

During the growing years, however, the resting heart rate progressively declines. Consequently, the heart rate reserve, or number of beats that are "available" for increasing $\dot{V}O_2$ in a maximal test, increases with age. For example, the average boy increases his heart rate reserve from 120 to 133 beats·min^{-1} between the ages of 6 and 12 y. Just how this translates into possible changes in physiological or performance fitness is unclear.

Stroke volume

Given a stable maximal heart rate with age, increases in maximal stroke volume must be the sole factor responsible for the improvements in maximal cardiac output in growing children. That stroke volume would increase as the child ages is, of course, not surprising, given the concomitant progressive growth in heart size. Studies utilizing radionuclide angiography and echocardiography have suggested that increases in left ventricular size are, in fact, entirely responsible for the development of stroke volume during childhood; i.e. there is no good evidence that functional changes in myocardial performance play a role in these changes[22-24].

Some evidence has suggested, however, that stroke volume responses to exercise may be dampened compared to that in adults. This comes from the observation that at any given level of oxygen uptake during exercise, stroke volume is lower in children [3]. This stroke volume is only partially compensated by a higher heart rate, and this causes cardiac output (Q) at a given $\dot{V}O_2$ to be somewhat smaller in children compared to adults. Values of $Q/\dot{V}O_2$ increase during the course of childhood; Godfrey et al.[25] found that cardiac output increases by 0.020 L·min^{-1} for every cm increase in height of children working at the same $\dot{V}O_2$. It has been suggested that the lower $Q/\dot{V}O_2$ in young children might reflect a "hypokinetic" cardiac response to exercise[3].

Other lines of investigation, however, have failed to reveal any evidence that left ventricular size, myocardial contractility, or stroke volume during exercise in children differs from adults when values are expressed relative to body size. We recently compared cardiovascular responses to maximal upright cycle exercise in a group of 15 prepubertal boys and 16 young men using Doppler echocardiography[24].

Patterns of change in stroke volume were similar in the two groups. Average values for maximal stroke index, cardiac index, and peak aortic velocity were 59 (11) mL·m^{-2},

11.33 (2.32) $L \cdot min^{-1} \cdot m^{-2}$, and 152 (30) $cm \cdot s^{-1}$ for the boys. No significant differences were seen from those recorded in the men, who had respective values of 61(14) $mL \cdot m^{-2}$, 11.08 (2.52) $L \cdot min^{-1} \cdot m^{-2}$, and 144 (24) $cm \cdot s^{-1}$.

Evaluation of left ventricular ejection fraction by radionuclide exercise testing as well as shortening fraction by echocardiography indicate that myocardial contractility during exercise is independent of age[22]. Our study showing no differences in peak aortic ejection velocity at maximal exercise in children and adults supports this concept.

Consolidating these findings, the following construct appears tenable: Increases in maximal cardiac output are a key determinant of the development of $\dot{V}O_2$ max in children. Heart rate does not contribute to the rise in maximal cardiac output, as maximal values are stable during childhood. The increase in peak stroke volume with age is due entirely to the growth of left ventricular volume, as there is no evidence for changes in myocardial functional capacity during exercise as children grow. It follows that recognizing the "proper" relationship between left ventricular volume and body size--mass, surface area, height, or lean body mass--would presumably improve our understanding of similar relationships between $\dot{V}O_2$ max and body size, given the importance of maximal stroke volume as a determinant of the growth of $\dot{V}O_2$ max in children.

Unfortunately, this relationship remains uncertain. Cross-sectional resting echocardiographic studies in children have indicated that left ventricular diastolic diameter relates closely to the cube root of body surface area[26]. Since left ventricular volume approximates a cube function of diastolic diameter, it follows that left ventricular volume relates to body surface area, or $mass^{0.67}$, during childhood. Nagasawa et al.[11] found in their longitudinal study that left ventricular diastolic diameter was related linearly to height, suggesting that ventricular volume might be associated with $height^{3.0}$. Cardiac catheterization studies with small numbers of subjects have indicated that correlation coefficients between stroke volume and body weight and surface area are almost identical[27,28]. Some have suggested that heart size is best related to lean body mass[29].

Arteriovenous oxygen difference

In the adult, the oxygen content of arterial blood is approximately 19 $mL \cdot 100mL^{-1}$. At rest, venous oxygen content is about 14 $mL \cdot 100mL^{-1}$, indicating an AV oxygen difference of 5 $mL \cdot 100mL^{-1}$. At maximal exercise, the venous content may fall as low as 2-3 $mL \cdot 100mL^{-1}$ (i.e. a maximal AV oxygen difference of 16 $mL \cdot 100mL^{-1}$), indicating that the extraction of oxygen from blood perfusing exercising muscle can increase as much as three-fold.

Children demonstrate the same pattern of change, and some data suggest that values for maximal AV oxygen difference are the same in children and adults[30-32]. Nonetheless, there is at least one theoretical reason to expect that AV oxygen difference might be less in children, and several studies support this construct. Blood haemoglobin concentration, an important determinant of arterial oxygen content, is lower in children than in adults, particularly in males. As a result, a 10-year old boy will have an arterial oxygen content about 2 $mL \cdot 100mL^{-1}$ less than a young adult male. This lower "ceiling" in the child might compromise maximal AV oxygen difference, given that the limits of the "floor" (the venous oxygen content) reach very low levels in adults.

In our comparison of prepubertal boys and adult men, the latter had a maximal AV oxygen difference of 17.2 $mL \cdot 100mL^{-1}$ compared to 13.9 $mL \cdot 100mL^{-1}$ in the boys ($p < 0.05$)[24]. Others have also described lower AV oxygen difference in children compared to adults[33,34].

These data would suggest that even if maturity related differences in maximal AV oxygen difference exist, the magnitude of the discrepancy is relatively small. Thus, is appears unlikely that increases in AV oxygen difference during childhood, if they do in fact exist, contribute in any significant way to the rise in $\dot{V}O_2$ max during growth.

In summary, reasonably convincing evidence indicates that an increases in maximal stroke volume is the predominant factor causing a rise in $\dot{V}O_2$ max with age, an increase which is due exclusively to heart growth. It follows that recognizing the relationship between left ventricular volume and body size will provide information regarding the proper means of "normalizing" $\dot{V}O_2$ max to body size. Likewise, it can be anticipated that influences of factors such as gender, habitual activity, and athletic training on $\dot{V}O_2$ max in children may be expressed through their effects on stroke volume. Further research focusing on cardiac changes with growth is thus likely to provide useful insights into the normal development of $\dot{V}O_2$ max in children.

References

1. Armstrong, N. and Welsman, J.R. (1994) Assessment and interpretation of aerobic fitness in children and adolescents. *Exercise and Sport Sciences Reviews,* Vol. 22, pp. 435-76.
2. Rowland, T.W. (1996) *Developmental Exercise Physiology,* Human Kinetics Publishers, Champaign, Il.
3. Bar-Or, O. (1983) *Pediatric Sports Medicine for the Practitioner,* Springer-Verlag, New York.
4. Krahenbuhl, G.S., Skinner, J.S. and Kohrt, W.M. (1985) Developmental aspects of maximal aerobic power in children. *Exercise and Sport Sciences Reviews,* Vol. 13, pp. 503-38.
5. Hollman, W. and C. Bouchard (1970) Relations between chronological, skeletal age, ergometric characteristics, heart volume, anthropometric dimensions, and muscle strength in 8 to 18 year old boys. *Zeitscrift fur Kreislaufforschung,* Vol. 59, pp. 160-76.
6. Rowland, T.W. (1992) Trainability of the cardiorespiratory system during childhood. *Canadian Journal of Sport Sciences,* Vol. 17, pp. 259-63.
7. Rowland, T.W. (1994) Effect of prolonged inactivity on aerobic fitness of children. *Journal of Sports Medicine and Physical Fitness,* Vol. 34, pp. 147-55.
8. Malina, R.M. and Bouchard, C. (1991) *Growth, Maturation, and Physical Activity,* Human Kinetics Publishers, Champaign, Il.
9. Perrault, H. (1996) Cardiorespiratory function. *Perspectives in Exercise Science and Sports Medicine,* Vol. 9, pp. 215-44.

10. Kemper, H.C.G., Verschuur, R. and DeMey, L. (1989). Longitudinal changes of aerobic fitness in youth ages 12 to 23. *Pediatric Exercise Science,* Vol. 1, pp. 257-70.
11. Nagasawa, H., Arakaki, Y., Yamada, O., Nakajima, T. and Kamiya, T. (1996) Longitudinal observations of left ventricular end-diastolic dimension in children using echocardiography. *Pediatric Cardiology,* Vol. 17, pp. 169-74.
12. Schmidt-Nielsen, K. (1984) *Scaling. Why is Animal Size So Important?* Cambridge University Press, Cambridge.
13. Holliday, M.A., Potter, D., Jarrah, A. and Bearg, S. (1967) The relation of metabolic rate to body weight and organ size. *Pediatric Research,* Vol. 1, pp. 185-95.
14. Cooper, D.M., Weiler-Ravell, D., Whipp, B.J. and Wasserman, K. (1984) Aerobic parameters of exercise as a function of body size during growth in children. *Journal of Applied Physiology,* Vol. 56, pp. 628-34.
15. Astrand, P.O. (1952) *Experimental Studies of Physical Working Capacity in Relationship to Sex and Age,* Munksgaard, Copenhagen.
16. Welsman, J., Armstrong, N., Winter, E. and Kirby, B.J. (1993). The influence of various scaling techniques on the interpretation of developmental changes in peak $\dot{V}O_2$. *Pediatric Exercise Science,* Vol. 5, p. 485.
17. Rogers, D.M., Turley, K.R., Kujawa, K.I., Harper, K.M. and Wilmore, J.H. (1995) Allometric scaling factors for oxygen uptake during exercise in children. *Pediatric Exercise Science,* Vol. 7, pp. 12-25.
18. Batterham, A.M. and Tolfrey, K. (1996) Intraspecific allometry of aerobic performance in prepubescent children. *Medicine and Science in Sports and Exercise,* Vol. 28, (suppl), p. S103.
19. Beunen, G.P., Rogers, D.M., Malina, R.M. and Woynarowska, B. (1995) Longitudinal study of ontogenetic allometry of oxygen uptake in boys and girls grouped by maturity status. *Medicine and Science in Sports and Exercise,* Vol. 27, (suppl), p. S113.
20. Rowland, T.W., Vanderburgh, P. and Cunningham, L. (in press) The growth of maximal aerobic power in children: A longitudinal analysis. *Pediatric Exercise Science.*
21. Bailey, D.A., Ross, W.D., Mirwald, R.L. and Weese, C. (1978) Size dissociation of maximal aerobic power during growth in boys. *Medicine in Sport,* Vol. 11, pp. 140-51.
22. DeSouza, M., Schaffer, M.S., Gilday, D.L. and Rose, V. (1984) Exercise radionuclide angiography in hyperlipidemic children with apparently normal hearts. *Nuclear Medicine,* Vol. 5, pp. 13-7.
23. Vavra, J., Sova, J. and Macek, M. (1982) Effect of age on systolic time intervals at rest and during exercise on a bicycle ergometer. *European Journal of Applied Physiology,* Vol. 50, pp. 71-8.
24. Rowland, T.W., Popowski, B. and Ferrone, L. (in press) Cardiac responses to maximal upright cycle exercise in healthy boys and men. *Medicine and Science in Sports and Exercise.*
25. Godfrey, S. (1974) *Exercise Testing in Children,* Saunders, London.

26. Henry, W.L., Ware, J., Gardin, J.M., Hepner, S.I., McKay, J. and Weiner, M. (1978) Echocardiographic measurements in normal subjects. *Circulation,* Vol. 57, pp. 278-85.
27. Krovetz, L.J., McLoughlin, T.G., Mitchell, M.B. and Schiebler, G.L. (1967) Hemodynamic findings in normal children. *Pediatric Research,* Vol. 1, pp. 122-30.
28. Sproul, A. and Simpson, E. (1964) Stroke volume and related hemodynamic data in normal children. *Pediatrics,* Vol. 33, pp. 912-8.
29. Cureton, K.J. (1982) Distance running performance tests in children. What do they mean? *Journal of Physical Education, Recreation, and Dance,* Vol. 53, pp. 64-6.
30. Yamaji, K. and Miyashita, M. (1977) Oxygen transport system during exhaustive exercise in Japanese boys. *European Journal of Applied Physiology,* Vol. 36, pp. 93-9.
31. Johnson, R.L., Taylor, H.F. and Lawson, W.H. (1965) Maximal diffusing capacity of the lung for carbon monoxide. *Journal of Clinical Investigation,* Vol. 44, pp. 349-55.
32. Eriksson, B.O. (1972) Physical training, oxygen supply, and muscle metabolism in 11-13 year old boys. *Acta Physiologica Scandinavica,* Vol. 384, (suppl), pp. 1-48.
33. Miyamura, M. and Honda, Y. (1973) Maximum cardiac output related to sex and age. *Japanese Journal of Physiology,* Vol. 23, pp. 645-56.
34. Gilliam, T.B., Sady, S., Thorland, W.G. and Weltman, A.C. (1977) Comparison of peak performance measures in children ages 6 to 8, 9 to 10, and 11 to 13 years. *Research Quarterly,* Vol. 48, pp. 695-702.

INTERPRETING YOUNG PEOPLE'S EXERCISE PERFORMANCE: SIZING UP THE PROBLEM

J.R. WELSMAN
Children's Health and Exercise Research Centre, Institute of Clinical Science, University of Exeter, UK
Keywords: Allometry, analysis of covariance, exercise performance, maturation, ratio standards

Introduction

The assessment and interpretation of the physiological and metabolic responses to exercise of healthy, untrained young people in relation to age, sex, and maturity have been a major focus of the research programme of the Children's Health and Exercise Research Centre's in the 10 y since its inception in 1987. A major consideration in these endeavours has been the problem of how to partition out, or scale, exercise performance for differences in body size. This paper describes, in broadly chronological order, how our interest in scaling issues was initiated and has progressed, and summarises the results of our studies which have applied various scaling techniques to the interpretation of young people's exercise performance.

Scaling peak oxygen uptake

In a paper describing British children's peak oxygen uptake (peak $\dot{V}O_2$) in relation to age, sex and sexual maturity[1], the convention of expressing peak $\dot{V}O_2$ in simple ratio with body mass (i.e. as $mL \cdot kg^{-1} \cdot min^{-1}$) to normalise peak $\dot{V}O_2$ for body mass differences was accepted. Using this traditional analysis, it was evident that the progressive increase in absolute peak $\dot{V}O_2$ ($L \cdot min^{-1}$) with increasing age and maturity was essentially negated in boys once values were divided by body mass, whereas in girls a decline in mass-related values was observed. Throughout the maturational range studied, boys demonstrated significantly higher values of peak $\dot{V}O_2$ than girls.

Children and Exercise XIX. Edited by Neil Armstrong, Brian Kirby and Joanne Welsman.
Published in 1997 by E & FN Spon, 2–6 Boundary Row, London, SE1 8HN.
ISBN 0 419 22100 X.

Linear modelling of peak oxygen uptake

That this approach to removing the effects of body size from exercise performance measures might be both over-simplistic and misleading was first brought to my attention by Dr Edward Winter of de Montfort University, UK. He had been exploring the use of an alternative scaling method, described by Tanner in 1949[2], to interpret sex differences in anaerobic performance in adults[3]

Tanner's paper clearly described the theoretical and statistical caveats associated with the use of per body mass "ratio standards" and presented convincing arguments to demonstrate problems with their use to compare groups and in correlational analyses, stating that they "involve some statistical difficulties and are neither as simple nor as informative as they seem"[2]. A discussion of these issues is available elsewhere[4-6] and so will not be reiterated in detail here.

Dr Winter introduced me to the intricacies of analysis of covariance (ANCOVA), the statistical procedure used to generate and compare the slopes and intercepts of regression lines describing the relationships between body size and performance in different subject groups, for example by age or sex. Using this linear regression technique to partition out body size effects from exercise data, Winter et al.[3] had demonstrated sex differences in peak anaerobic power relative to upper leg volume which were masked when a ratio standard formed the basis of the analysis. I was, therefore, keen to explore whether this alternative and, arguably, more appropriate scaling technique would influence the interpretation of young people's peak $\dot{V}O_2$ data.

The results of this initial study "Changes in peak oxygen uptake with age and sexual maturation in boys: physiological fact or statistical anomaly?" were presented to PWP XVI in 1991. This simple comparison of peak $\dot{V}O_2$ in 10 and 15-year-old boys produced some surprising results[7]. As expected, mass-related peak $\dot{V}O_2$ did not differ significantly between the younger and older boys, but linear ANCOVA separated the boys into two distinct groups (see fig 1) and demonstrated that a 15-year-old boy would be predicted to have a higher peak $\dot{V}O_2$ than a 10-year-old boy *of the same body mass*, thus challenging previous findings based upon a traditional per body mass comparison[1].

These findings emphasised that removing the influence of body size from the interpretation of exercise performance was not as simple as it appeared and that here was an issue which would require further investigation in subsequent studies.

Allometric modelling of peak oxygen uptake

Although linear regression scaling can be demonstrated to provide a better statistical fit for performance data than the simple ratio standard, e.g. by a reduction in the residual error associated with the analysis[6] the method has well-documented limitations. For a detailed discussion see[4,5,6], but to summarise these briefly, positive intercept terms are common, suggesting that a physiological response exists for zero body size - an obvious impossibility. Thus, regression lines should not be extrapolated beyond the range of data points they describe[8]. Perhaps of greater consequence, is the poor fit linear regression analyses represent for performance data derived from subject groups ranging widely in age and body size. Such data are almost invariably heteroscedastic,

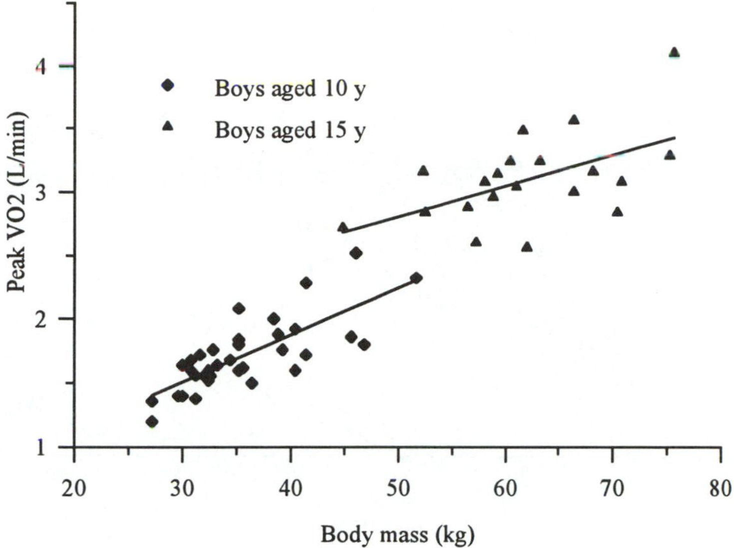

Fig. 1. Relationship between peak oxygen uptake and body mass in 10 and 15-year-old boys

i.e. as body size increases the greater the spread in the data points around the regression line[6,9]. This phenomenon is clearly evident in the data, from our laboratory for 12 year old subjects, presented in fig 2. Expressed another way, a significant correlation will exist between the body size variable and the regression residuals. Linear regression scaling models assume that the residual error is additive, i.e. will not increase with increasing body size, and therefore cannot represent an appropriate statistical fit for heteroscedastic data.

Dr Alan Nevill of Liverpool John Moores University, UK, encouraged me to investigate the use of allometric models to interpret exercise data, given the limitations that accompany straightforward linear models. He demonstrated how, by the use of ANCOVA on log-transformed data, the understanding of size/performance relationships could be further refined. This allometric approach to scaling exercise performance for body size has several advantages over the linear method. In addition to providing a better statistical fit for comparisons of exercise performance in different subject groups, the parameters a and b in the allometric relationship $y = a.x^b$ can be determined, enabling the identification of the body size exponent which appropriately normalises the performance measure in question.

Our next major study to employ alternative scaling techniques was an extension of the study described in fig 1, in which the aerobic fitness of groups of prepubertal, circumpubertal and adult males and females was examined. The results were initially presented to PWP XVII in 1993[10,11]. Sex and age group differences were compared using conventional mass-related ratio standards, linear ANCOVA and log-linear ANCOVA. The mass-related data confirmed conventional interpretation of the growth of

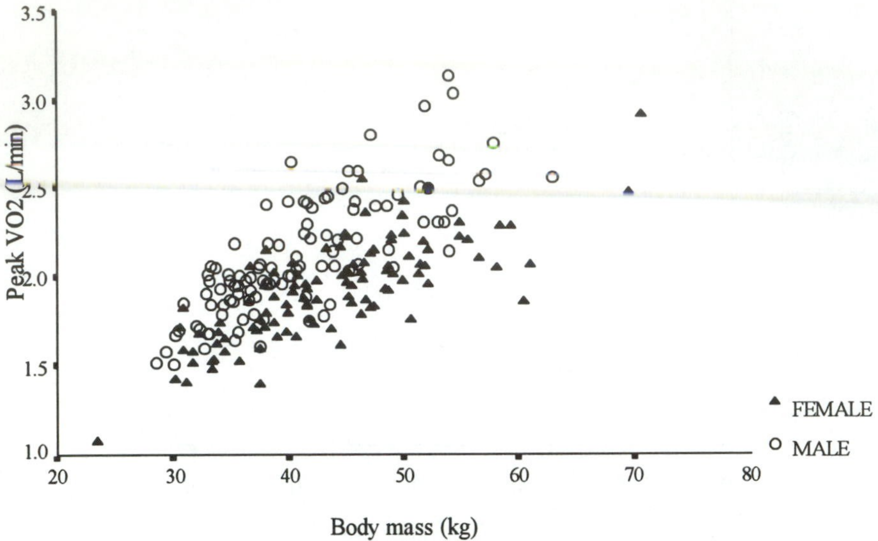

Fig. 2. Peak oxygen uptake and body mass data demonstrating heteroscedasticity

peak $\dot{V}O_2$, i.e. no significant change in males between prepuberty and adulthood, and indications of a decline in females' aerobic fitness between puberty and adulthood. In direct contrast, the results of the log-linear (allometric) model (which was demonstrated to provide the best statistical fit for the data) revealed significant increases in peak $\dot{V}O_2$ from prepuberty through to adulthood in males, whilst in females, significant increases in fitness were evident into puberty, with a subsequent maintenance of these levels into adulthood. These data provided a further indication that the inappropriate use of ratio standards may have clouded the understanding of changes in aerobic fitness with growth and maturation and that there is a need to investigate allometric relationships in future studies of young people's exercise performance.

Mass exponents for peak oxygen uptake

Having been encouraged to search the literature for previous studies using allometry to interpret size-related function it became evident that, although a new technique for me, this was by no means a contemporary approach to controlling for body size effects - investigators in the biological sciences have for many years routinely applied allometric scaling techniques to the understanding of structure/function relationships[12]. However, exercise scientists appear to have, almost exclusively, accepted the convention of normalising exercise performance data by computing simple ratio standards. Why should this be? Earlier studies had started to address allometric relationships in exercise performance in both adults[13] and children[14,15] but until recently, very few studies had employed anything other than a traditional ratio scaling approach to partitioning out body size differences from paediatric exercise data.

Exponents for normalising peak oxygen uptake

Perhaps one reason for the resistance to a more widespread use of allometry (aside from, perhaps, the more complex statistics involved) derives from studies using allometry to determine exponents for peak $\dot{V}O_2$ whose data appeared to suggest that there was, in fact, no reason to abandon conventional scaling methods. Table 1 summarises some of these data and it is immediately apparent that, almost invariably, exponents close to 1.0 have been identified supporting continued use of the simple per body mass ratio.

There are, however, compelling theoretical arguments based upon theories of geometric similarity or surface law[12,13,20] for expressing peak exercise performance in relation to mass raised to the power 0.67. Empirical data from large scale studies support this hypothetical relationship for peak aerobic and anaerobic performance in adults[6]. It is likely that the deviation of the exponents derived in young people from this theoretical value has hindered acceptance of allometry and has discouraged further investigations into its utility.

As discussed in previous publications[6,11,21] the mass exponent will be inflated if, in subject groups heterogeneous for body size, differences in stature are not considered. It has been suggested that disproportionate increases in muscle mass relative to increases in overall body size will distort the body mass/performance relationship and that this can be controlled for by incorporating stature, in addition to mass, into the allometric equation[9,21].

This problem was explored in a comparison of changes in peak $\dot{V}O_2$ with age and maturation[11]. When modelled for mass alone, an exponent of 0.80 was obtained common to all groups. When stature was incorporated into to the analysis, it made a significant contribution to the prediction of peak $\dot{V}O_2$ and the independent mass exponent was shown to be 0.71, a value not significantly different from the theoretical value of 0.67. Indeed, the flexibility of this scaling technique, i.e. allowing other variables to be incorporated into the allometric equation, is one of its advantages [9,21]. For example in our recent examination of resting lung function in subjects aged 10 to 16 y

Table 1. Mass exponents for peak $\dot{V}O_2$ in children and adolescents

Study	Age (y)	Sex	n	Mass exponent
McMiken[14]	7-13	M	50	0.88
McMiken[14]	12-16	F	30	0.97
McMiken[14]	10-15	M	14	1.07
Ross et al.[16]	8-16	M	25	0.95
Sjodin and Svedenhag[19]	12-19	M	8 untrained	0.78
		M	4 trained	0.75
Paterson et al.[18]	11-15	M	18	1.02
Rogers et al.[19]	8.9	MandF	42	0.52
Cooper et al.[20]	6-18	MandF	109	1.01

Data extracted from Armstrong and Welsman[5]

[22] we were able to demonstrate that age, stature and mass were all significant co-variates in the analysis of FVC and FEV.

It is also important to realise that theoretical mass exponents are only likely to be confirmed when modelling in large, representative subject groups. For example, in a study of sex differences in the peak $\dot{V}O_2$ of 164 prepubescent children, a mass exponent of 0.66 was identified[23]. Similarly, a mass exponent of 0.65 was reported for 212 12-year-old girls and boys[24], further emphasising the inability of the simple ratio standard to normalise peak $\dot{V}O_2$ data for body mass in children and adolescents. In smaller subject groups, however, sample specific exponents may well deviate from theoretical values; in a sample comprising 16 boys and 16 girls we reported a mass exponent for peak $\dot{V}O_2$ of 0.52[25].

Therefore, when considerations of sample size and subject heterogeneity are considered with reference to the data presented in table 1, the lack of concordance between these exponents and the theoretical value is perhaps not surprising given that the majority of previous studies included relatively small subject groups ranging widely in age and therefore body size. Had stature been incorporated into these analyses mass exponents closer to 0.67 may well have been observed.

Peak oxygen uptake and maturity

Subsequent to our finding that the pattern of increase in peak $\dot{V}O_2$ may not be static in males and declining in females, an allometric approach was used to examine the proposed age/maturation interaction effect on the growth of aerobic fitness[26]. Consistent with an earlier investigation[1] Tanner's indices were used to classify subjects into maturity groups, but in this study chronological age was also controlled for by using subjects from the same year group (12 to 13 y)[24]. Mass-related peak $\dot{V}O_2$ was analysed by sex and maturity using two-way ANOVA. A two-way log-linear ANCOVA was used to investigate the allometric relationships between peak $\dot{V}O_2$ and mass with sex and maturity. The conventional analysis yielded results consistent with the original study although here comparisons were only possible across maturity stages I to IV. Significant main effects were obtained for sex but not for maturity; for example in boys, mass-related peak $\dot{V}O_2$ values for stages I and IV were 50 and 52 $mL \cdot kg^{-1} \cdot min^{-1}$ respectively compared with 45 and 46 $mL \cdot kg^{-1} \cdot min^{-1}$ in girls. However, the log-linear ANCOVA revealed significant main effects for both sex and maturity, indicating that maturity, per se, has a significant influence on the growth of aerobic fitness over and above the influence of age and body mass. Further work is now required to determine the precise hormonal, physiological or metabolic mechanisms responsible for this effect.

Peak oxygen uptake and thigh muscle volume

One intriguing finding of our recent research has been the observation of a significant difference in mass-related peak $\dot{V}O_2$ (13.3%) in prepubertal boys and girls[23] which remains (increasing to 16.2%) when data are scaled appropriately for body mass using allometric techniques. As this difference cannot be simply explained by differences in body composition (no differences in skinfold thicknesses), haemoglobin levels, or levels of habitual physical activity likely to improve peak $\dot{V}O_2$, it was of interest to investigate the relationship between peak $\dot{V}O_2$ and muscle volume. Previous studies with young people had indicated significant relationships between anthropometrically determined leg volume and peak $\dot{V}O_2$[27,28], but neither of these studies had attempted to partition out the confounding influence of body size in their heterogeneous subject groups.

In an initial pilot study, anthropometric[29] techniques were used to determine leg volume and conventional ratio standards applied to normalise peak $\dot{V}O_2$ for body mass[30]. No significant relationship was found between mass-related peak $\dot{V}O_2$ and leg volume in these 10 y old boys, but this was perhaps not surprising considering the limitations of both the leg volume assessment technique and the use of ratio standards in correlational analyses[6,10]. In order to achieve a more precise examination of these relationships, techniques were developed for calculating thigh muscle volume from sequential MRI scans of the upper leg and allometric techniques were employed to account for body size. The results of this study, which were presented to PWP XVIII in 1995[32], demonstrated an absence of correlation between leg volume and peak $\dot{V}O_2$ once body size was appropriately accounted for.

Having refined methodologies, the key question of sex differences in peak $\dot{V}O_2$ in 10-year-old children in relation to muscle volume was addressed. Allometric techniques were employed to examine the problem in two different ways[25]. Firstly treadmill-determined peak $\dot{V}O_2$ was scaled to body mass and the power function ratio (peak $\dot{V}O_2$ $mL \cdot kg^{-0.52} \cdot min^{-1}$) correlated with thigh muscle volume. No significant relationship was obtained for either boys or girls. Secondly, peak $\dot{V}O_2$ was scaled to thigh muscle volume itself and sex differences in the values of litres of oxygen per litre of muscle per min ($L \cdot L^{-0.55} \cdot min^{-1}$) compared. Again, no significant sex difference was observed. The results thus suggested that the male-female difference in peak $\dot{V}O_2$ in this sample was not related to thigh muscle volume.

Peak oxygen uptake and adiposity

A well-recognised limitation of per body mass ratios is that they penalise large individuals, whereas small individuals are advantaged[2,8]. Clearly overfat individuals are disadvantaged in physical activities which require the body mass to be carried, but it does not necessarily follow that this reflects impaired cardiorespiratory function in relation to body size. This question was examined using peak $\dot{V}O_2$ data from 253 boys and girls aged 10 to 11 y drawn from a representative sample of English children[32]. For the purposes of the study individuals were defined as overfat if they equalled or exceeded the 75th percentile for both body mass and triceps skinfold thickness. Peak $\dot{V}O_2$ expressed relative to body mass was significantly higher in the normal mass boys (15.4%) and girls (13.6%) compared with the overfat children. However when the comparison was based upon log-linear ANCOVA, the discrepancy was considerably reduced to 5.6% for boys and 5.2% for girls, indicating that the functional aerobic fitness of overfat children is considerably less impaired than suggested by ratio-based comparisons. Interestingly, the mass exponent, common to all sex and fatness groups was 0.61, confirming the inadequacy of the ratio standard to control for body size differences and suggesting that the expression of peak $\dot{V}O_2$ relative to $mass^{0.67}$ will provide a more appropriate estimation of functional aerobic fitness in both normal mass and overfat children.

Scaling submaximal oxygen uptake

Data from Eston et al.[33] appear to have been the first to challenge the use of per body mass ratios in the interpretation of submaximal $\dot{V}O_2$ responses. Their results sinhowed that differences in submaximal $\dot{V}O_2$ between boys and men disappeared when data were analysed using linear ANCOVA. Data from our laboratory, reported elsewhere in this volume[34], support this finding in a comparison of 11-year-old girls with adult women analysed using log-linear ANCOVA.

Data from both this latter study and our examination of submaximal $\dot{V}O_2$ in relation to sex and maturity in 12 to 13-year-old boys and girls[35] have demonstrated mass exponents for $\dot{V}O_2$ at treadmill speeds ranging from 8 to 10 $km.h^{-1}$ ranging from 0.85 to 0.93. However, in contrast to our findings for peak $\dot{V}O_2$, log-linear scaling did not reveal any maturational effects on submaximal $\dot{V}O_2$ once body size had been partitioned out.

Scaling ventilatory responses to exercise

In contrast to the volume of data describing young people's oxygen uptake responses to exercise, documentation of ventilatory responses is sparse, particularly for prepubertal children. Having explored size-related issues in peak and submaximal $\dot{V}O_2$ subsequent studies have investigated peak and submaximal ventilatory responses in children and adolescents using allometry as a tool to tease out age and maturity effects, particularly as variables such as minute ventilation ($\dot{V}E$) and tidal volume (TV) are known to be highly related to anthropometric characteristics[36].

In prepubertal children[37], log-linear ANCOVA demonstrated both stature and mass to be significant covariates for peak $\dot{V}E$ with respective exponents of 0.69 and 0.48. Corresponding exponents for peak TV were 1.71 for stature and 0.27 for mass. At submaximal exercise intensities exponents were also shown to deviate from the simple ratio standard. For example at 80 to 85% peak $\dot{V}O_2$, peak $\dot{V}E$ scaled to $mass^{0.73}$, but both stature and mass remained covariates for TV yielding exponents of 1.65 and 0.37 respectively. Although allometric scaling did not significantly change the interpretation of sex differences in ventilatory responses, the findings were revealing in demonstrating that, despite the relative homogeneity of the subject group, different ventilatory measures were predominantly related to different anthropometric characteristics, and these varied between peak and submaximal exercise.

In what appears to be the first study to have examined ventilatory responses to peak and submaximal exercise in relation to sex and maturity, significant main effects for both sex and maturity were found for peak $\dot{V}E$ adjusted for body size in 12-year-old boys and girls. At the same relative submaximal intensity, $\dot{V}E$ adjusted for body size was significantly higher in the boys than in the girls but, in contrast to peak exercise, maturation had no significant effect upon submaximal ventilatory responses. This study is described in more detail elsewhere in this volume[38].

Scaling anaerobic and strength performance

Following on from investigations of exercise responses to submaximal and peak exercise, allometric scaling techniques have been applied to the interpretation of other types of exercise notably anaerobic and strength performance. Once again, the results have provided some interesting insights.

In a recent publication[39] young people's performance on the Wingate anaerobic test (WAnT) was examined. Using a similar approach to that used to investigate aerobic fitness[25] both ratio standards and log-linear ANCOVA were used to investigate sex and maturity differences in peak and mean power. In contrast to peak $\dot{V}O_2$, the results demonstrated no significant sex differences in either peak or mean power whether expressed in absolute, mass-related or allometrically scaled terms. Mass exponents for peak power and mean power of 1.03 and 0.82 were identified respectively. When data were examined by maturity group in 90 boys and 79 girls, significant main effects for both sex and maturity were observed for mass-related peak and mean power and were confirmed for both power outputs adjusted for mass using log-linear ANCOVA.

The exponent derived for peak power in this analysis (b=1.02) warrants further discussion. As with peak aerobic power, theoretical arguments would propose a mass exponent of 0.67 for peak anaerobic power and this has been confirmed for adults during sprinting[6]. The deviation of this peak power exponent found for young people is particularly interesting as, in these subjects, an exponent of 0.65 was obtained for peak aerobic power[25]. Furthermore, in data from our laboratory we have identified a mass exponent of 0.72 for boys' peak power where this has been measured using a Force-Velocity test[Armstrong and Welsman, unpublished data].

The discrepancy in exponents perhaps relates to the WAnT methodology. For example it is recognised that the braking force often applied - 0.74 $N{\cdot}kg^{-1}$- is insufficient to elicit true peak power[5]. Furthermore, as the resistance is itself computed as a per body mass ratio larger (fatter) children are penalised and true mass/power relationships are likely to be distorted. This issue was examined in children by computing the WAnT resistance in relation to thigh muscle mass determined using MRI[26]. Expressed in N, the mean braking force applied was not significantly different in boys and girls (23.5 vs 26.5 N). However, when the resistance was computed relative to thigh muscle mass using log-linear ANCOVA, the girls' adjusted mean resistance was 19% greater than the value for the boys (27.0 vs 21.9 $N{\cdot}L^{-1}$, $p<0.01$). Individual resistances varied by up to 49%. Thus it is perhaps not surprising that the peak power values derived deviated from theoretical expectations.

With respect to strength, very few studies have described isokinetic strength performance in young people[40]. Relationships between leg muscle volume and isokinetic strength in boys and girls investigated using allometric techniques are described in detail elsewhere in this volume[41]. To summarise, the data support our findings for peak aerobic and anaerobic power in that, once scaled appropriately, leg strength is not significantly correlated with thigh muscle volume. Once again b exponents were derived for strength measures which, being less than 1.0, challenge the use of ratio standards to interpret children's strength data.

Conclusions

This review of some of the recent research from the Children's Health and Exercise Research Centre has demonstrated how alternative scaling techniques have influenced our interpretation of young people's exercise performance. Where allometric analyses have been used these have, almost without exception, produced size exponents which suggest that the simple ratio standard inadequately removes the influence of body size from exercise performance data. In particular, the data have repeatedly demonstrated that a mass exponent of 0.67 appropriately partitions body mass differences from peak $\dot{V}O_2$. The use of allometric models has revealed some exciting findings which have challenged conventional understanding of the growth and maturation of aerobic fitness and provided unique insights into relationships between leg volume and exercise performance. Allometric analyses have enabled a more refined approach to elucidating relationships between age, anthropometry and ventilatory responses and highlighted issues relating to the assessment of anaerobic performance. Thus, it is evident that allometry has become a useful tool for investigating the problem of body size. However, it can only provide indications of changes in exercise performance with body size during growth and maturation, the challenge is to elucidate some of the physiological or metabolic factors underlying these changes.

Acknowledgments

The academic guidance provided by Professor Neil Armstrong, Dr Brian Kirby, Dr Alan Nevill and Dr Edward Winter is gratefully acknowledged. The technical assistance of the Children's Health and Exercise Research Centre Team and the staff of the Somerset MRI Centre, Bridgwater has been greatly appreciated. The studies cited have been supported by the British Heart Foundation, the University of Exeter, the Northcott Devon Medical Foundation and the Healthy Heart Research Trust.

References

1. Armstrong, N., Williams, J., Balding, J., Gentle, P. and Kirby, B. (1991) The peak oxygen uptake of British children with reference to age, sex and sexual maturity. *European Journal of Applied Physiology*, Vol. 62, pp. 369-75.
2. Tanner, J.M. (1949) Fallacy of per-weight and per-surface area standards and their relation to spurious correlation. *Journal of Applied Physiology*, Vol. 2, pp. 1-15.
3. Winter, E.M., Brooks, F.B.C. and Hamley, E.J. (1991) Maximal exercise performance and lean leg volume in men and women. *Journal of Sports Sciences*, Vol. 9, pp. 3-13.
4. Armstrong, N. and Welsman, J. (1994) Assessment and interpretation of aerobic fitness in children and adolescents. *Exercise and Sport Sciences Reviews*, Vol. 22, pp. 435-76.

5. Armstrong, N. and Welsman, J. (1997) Young People and Physical Activity, Oxford University Press, Oxford.
6. Nevill, A., Ramsbottom, R. and Williams, C. (1992) Scaling physiological measurements for individuals of different body size. *European Journal of Applied Physiology*, Vol. 65, pp. 110-7.
7. Williams, J.R., Armstrong, N., Winter, E.M. and Crichton, N. (1992) Changes in peak oxygen uptake with age and sexual maturation in boys: physiological fact or statistical anomaly?, in *Children and Exercise XVI* (eds. J. Coudert and E. Van Praagh), Masson, Paris, pp. 35-7.
8. Winter, E.M. (1992) Scaling: partitioning out differences in size. *Pediatric Exercise Science*, Vol. 4, pp. 296-301.
9. Nevill, A.M. and Holder, R.L. (1995) Scaling, normalizing and per ratio standards: an allometric modeling approach. *Journal of Applied Physiology*, Vol. 79, pp. 1027-31.
10. Welsman, J.R., Armstrong, N., Winter, E.M. and Kirby, B.J. (1993) The influence of various scaling techniques on the interpretation of developmental changes in peak $\dot{V}O_2$. *Pediatric Exercise Science*, Vol. 5, p. 485.
11. Welsman, J. R., Armstrong, N., Nevill, A. M., Winter, E.M. and Kirby, B.J. (1996) Scaling peak $\dot{V}O_2$ for differences in body size. *Medicine and Science in Sports and Exercise*, Vol. 28, pp. 259-65.
12. Schmidt-Nielsen, K. (1984). *Scaling: why is Animal Size so Important?* Cambridge University Press, Cambridge.
13. Astrand, P.O. and Rodahl, K. (1986) *Textbook of Work Physiology*. McGraw-Hill, New York.
14. McMiken, D.F. (1976) Maximum aerobic power and physical dimensions of children. *Annals of Human Biology*, Vol. 3, pp. 141-7.
15. Bailey, D.A., Ross, W.D. Mirwald, R.L. and Weese, C. (1978) Size dissociation of maximal aerobic power during growth in boys. *Medicine Sport*, Vol. 11, pp. 140-51.
16. Ross, W.D., Bailey, D.A., Mirwald, R.L., Faulkner, R.A., Rasmussen, R, Kerr, D.A. and Stini, W.A. (1991) Allometric relationship of estimated muscle mass and maximal oxygen uptake in boys studied longitudinally age 8 to 16 years, in *Children and Exercise, Pediatric Work Physiology XV*, (eds. R. Frenkl and I. Szmodis), National Institute for Health Promotion, Budapest, pp. 135-42.
17. Sjodin, B. and Svedenhag, J. (1992) Oxygen uptake during running as related to body mass in circumpubertal boys: a longitudinal study. *European Journal of Applied Physiology*, Vol. 65, pp. 150-7.
18. Paterson, D.H., McLellan, T.M. Stella, R.S. and Cunningham, D.A. (1987) Longitudinal study of ventilation threshold and maximal O_2 uptake in athletic boys. *Journal of Applied Physiology*, Vol. 62, pp. 2051-7.
19. Rogers, D.M., Turley, K.R., Kujawa, K.I., Harper, K.M. and Wilmore, J.H. (1995) Allometric scaling factors for oxygen uptake during exercise in children. *Pediatric Exercise Science*, Vol. 7, pp. 12-25.
20. Cooper, D.M. (1989) Development of the oxygen transport system in normal children, in *Advances in Pediatric Sports Sciences, Vol. 3* (ed. O. Bar-Or), Human Kinetics, Champaign, Il., pp. 67-100.

21. Nevill, A. (1994) The need to scale for differences in body size and mass: An explanation of Kleiber's 0.75 mass exponent. *Journal of Applied Physiology*, Vol. 77, pp. 2870-3.
22. Armstrong, N., Welsman, J. and Kirby, B.J. (under review) Allometric analysis of dynamic lung volumes in 10 to 16-year-olds.
23. Armstrong, N., Kirby, B., McManus, A. and Welsman, J. (1995) Aerobic fitness of prepubescent children. *Annals of Human Biology*, Vol. 22, pp. 427-41.
24. Armstrong, N., Welsman, J. and Kirby, B.J. (under review) Peak oxygen uptake and maturation in 12-year-olds.
25. Welsman, J.R, Armstrong, N. and Kirby, B.J. (1997) Exercise performance and magnetic resonance imaging determined thigh muscle volume in children, *European Journal of Applied Physiology*, Vol. 68.
26. Cunningham, D.A., Paterson, D.H., Blimkie, C.J.R. and Donner, A.P. (1984) Development of cardiorespiratory function in circumpubertal boys: a longitudinal study. *Journal of Applied Physiology*, Vol. 56, pp. 302-7.
27. Davies, C.T.M., Barnes, C. and Godfrey, S. (1972) Body composition and maximal exercise in children. *Human Biology*, Vol. 44, pp. 195-214.
28. Docherty, D. and Gaul, C.A. (1991) Relationship of body size, physique and composition to physical performance in young boys and girls. *International Journal of Sports Medicine*, Vol. 12, pp. 525-32.
29. Jones, P.R.M. and Pearson, J. (1969) Anthropometric determination of leg fat and muscle plus bone volumes in young male and female adults. *Journal of Physiology*, Vol. 204, pp. 63-6P.
30. Winsley, R., Armstrong, N, and Welsman, J. (1995) Leg volume is not related to peak oxygen uptake in 9-year-old boys, in *Children in Sport* (ed. F.J. Ring), Centre for Continuing Education, Bath, pp. 70-6.
31. Welsman, J.R, Armstrong, N., Winsley, R.J., Bell, M and Sharpe, P. (1996) Scaling the relationship between thigh volume, thigh muscle volume and peak $\dot{V}O_2$ in prepubertal girls. *Pediatric Exercise Science*, Vol. 8, pp. 177-8.
32. Welsman, J.R, Armstrong, N. and Kirby, B.J. (under review) Young people, physical activity, aerobic fitness and body fatness.
33. Eston, R.G, Robson, S. and Winter, E.W. (1993) A comparison of oxygen uptake during running in children and adults, in *Kinanthropometry IV*, (eds. W. Duquet and J. Day), E and FN Spon, London, pp. 236-41.
34. Armstrong, N., Kirby, B., Welsman, J and McManus, A. (1997) Submaximal exercise in prepubertal children, in *Children and Exercise XIX*, (eds. N. Armstrong, B. Kirby and J. Welsman), E and FN Spon, London.
35. Armstrong, N., Welsman, J. and Kirby, B.J. (under review) Submaximal exercise and maturation in 12-year-olds.
36. Mercier, J., Varray, A., Ramonatxo, Mercier, B. and Préfaut, C. (1991) Influence of anthropometric characteristics on changes in maximal exercise ventilation and breathing pattern during growth in boys. *European Journal of Applied Physiology*, Vol. 63, pp. 235-41.
37. Armstrong, N., Kirby, B., McManus, A. and Welsman, J. (in press) Prepubescents' ventilatory responses to exercise with reference to sex and body size. *Chest*.

38. Armstrong, N., Kirby, B., Mosney, J.R., Sutton, N.C. and Welsman, J. (1997) Ventilatory responses to exercise in relation to sex and maturation, in *Children and Exercise XIX*, (eds. N. Armstrong, B. Kirby and J. Welsman), E and FN Spon, London.
39. Armstrong, N., Welsman, J. and Kirby, B.J. (1997) Performance on the Wingate anaerobic test and maturation. *Pediatric Exercise Science*, Vol. 9.
40. De Ste Croix, M.B.A., Armstrong, N., Welsman, J.R. and Winsley, R.J. (1997) Muscle strength and MRI determined thigh muscle volume in young girls. *Medicine and Science in Sports and Exercise*, Vol. 29 (Suppl.).
41. De Ste Croix, M.B.A., Armstrong, N., Welsman, J.R., Winsley, R.J., Parsons, G. and Sharpe, P. (1997) Relationship of muscle strength with muscle volume in young children, in *Children and Exercise XIX*, (eds. N. Armstrong, B. Kirby and J. Welsman), E and FN Spon, London.

VENTILATORY RESPONSES TO EXERCISE IN RELATION TO SEX AND MATURATION

Ventilatory responses to exercise

N. ARMSTRONG, B.J. KIRBY, J.R. MOSNEY, N.C. SUTTON and J.R. WELSMAN

Children's Health and Exercise Research Centre, Institute of Clinical Science, University of Exeter, Exeter, UK

Keywords: Allometric scaling, exercise, maturation, minute volume, respiratory frequency, sex, tidal volume, ventilatory equivalent

Introduction

Recent studies have demonstrated that ratio standards, i.e. the simple division of a performance variable by an anthropometric measure, do not adequately partition out body size differences from young people's peak oxygen uptake (peak $\dot{V}O_2$) and that allometric scaling techniques are preferable[1,2]. Studies describing allometric relationships between young people's body size and ventilation ($\dot{V}E$) at peak $\dot{V}O_2$ are sparse[3,4] and allometric studies of ventilatory responses to submaximal exercise appear to be non-existent. No previous investigation has explored ventilatory responses in relation to maturation, with body size controlled for using allometric techniques.

The influence of both body size and maturation on physiological responses to exercise are important issues in paediatric exercise science. The purposes of this study were therefore, to examine ventilatory responses to exercise, and to explore any influence of maturation with body size controlled for using the allometric relationship specific to the data set.

Subjects

The subjects were drawn from a longitudinal study of a representative sample of children attending state schools in Exeter. Subject selection has been described in detail elsewhere[1]. The data reported here are from the 97 boys and 105 girls who

Children and Exercise XIX. Edited by Neil Armstrong, Brian Kirby and Joanne Welsman.
Published in 1997 by E & FN Spon, 2–6 Boundary Row, London, SE1 8HN.
ISBN 0 419 22100 X.

satisfactorily completed the procedures described below during the second year of the study.

Method

Age was computed from date of birth and date of testing. Sexual maturity was visually assessed, by the same nurse, using the pubic hair indices described by Tanner[5]. Stature and body mass were measured using a calibrated Holtain stadiometer (Crymych, Dyfed, UK) and an Avery beam balance (Avery, Birmingham, UK).

Ventilatory data were determined during a discontinuous, incremental treadmill test to voluntary exhaustion. The children were habituated to both the general environment and the specific experimental procedures and then warmed up by running on the treadmill (Woodway, Cranlea, Birmingham, UK) at a speed of 1.67 ms for 3 min. The test commenced with four 3 min periods at belt speeds of 1.94 $m{\cdot}s^{-1}$, 2.22 $m{\cdot}s^{-1}$, 2.50 $m{\cdot}s^{-1}$ and 2.78 $m{\cdot}s^{-1}$. For the remainder of the test the belt speed was held constant at 2.78 $m{\cdot}s^{-1}$ and the gradient elevated by 2.5% at the end of each 3 min period. A 1 min rest was allowed between stages with the children continuing to exercise to the point of voluntary exhaustion. If the child showed signs of intense effort and if his/her heart rate (HR) had levelled off prior to the final exercise intensity, or had reached a value near or above 200 $beats{\cdot}min^{-1}$, or if is his/her respiratory exchange ratio (RER) was at least unity, peak $\dot{V}O_2$ was accepted as a maximal index[6]. All subjects reported here satisfied these criteria.

Throughout the test ventilatory data were monitored continuously using an Oxycon Sigma on-line analysis system (Cranlea, Birmingham, UK) which was recalibrated prior to each test. Heart rate was monitored using an electrocardiograph (Rigel, Morden, UK).

Data analyses

Data were stored and analysed using SPSS-PC+ (SPSS Inc, Chicago, USA) statistical package. Descriptive statistics were computed for age, stature, mass, ventilatory data at peak $\dot{V}O_2$, and ventilatory data running at 2.22 $m{\cdot}s^{-1}$ (8 $km{\cdot}h^{-1}$). In addition, descriptive statistics were computed for ventilatory variables from children who exercised within the specific range 75-80% of peak $\dot{V}O_2$. Sex differences were examined using one way analysis of variance (ANOVA).

We have discussed in detail elsewhere the theoretical principles underlying the use of log-linear allometric models to partition out the effect of body size from measures of physiological function[7,8]. For $\dot{V}E$ and tidal volume (V_T) at peak $\dot{V}O_2$, at 75-80% of peak $\dot{V}O_2$, and at 2.22 $m{\cdot}s^{-1}$, analysis of covariance (ANCOVA) was initially computed with both stature and mass as covariates. In cases where the term for one anthropometric variable was not significant, a second ANCOVA was computed with a

Table 1. Physical characteristics and exercise data at peak oxygen uptake by sex

	Boys (n=97)	Girls (n=105)
Age (y)	12.2 ± 0.4	12.2 ± 0.4
Stature (m)	1.51 ± 0.08	1.52 ± 0.08
Body mass (kg)	41.4 ± 7.6*	43.8 ± 8.4
$\dot{V}O_2$ ($L{\cdot}min^{-1}$)	2.12 ± 0.34***	1.91 ± 0.28
$\dot{V}E$ ($L{\cdot}min^{-1}$)	67.4 ± 12.0**	62.5 ± 9.8
Adjusted $\dot{V}E$ ($L{\cdot}min^{-1}$)	67.3***	61.0
V_T (L)	1.35 ± 0.26*	1.27 ± 0.28
Adjusted V_T (L)	1.34***	1.22
Respiratory frequency (Rf) ($breaths{\cdot}min^{-1}$)	51 ± 8	51 ± 9
Ventilatory equivalent ($\dot{V}E/\dot{V}O_2$)	29.6 ± 2.6*	30.4 ± 2.9
Ventilatory equivalent ($\dot{V}E/\dot{V}CO_2$)	28.4 ± 2.0	29.0 ± 2.3
RER	1.05 ± 0.05	1.05 ± 0.05
HR ($beats{\cdot}min^{-1}$)	202 ± 7	202 ± 7

Values are mean ± SD
Level of significance *p <0.05, **p <0.01, *** p<0.001

single covariate. Adjusted means are reported from the model which represented the best fit for the ventilatory variable under investigation.

Two way (sex by maturity) ANOVA and ANCOVA were used to examine sex and maturational differences in ventilatory variables at peak $\dot{V}O_2$ and at 75-80% of peak $\dot{V}O_2$.

Results

Physical characteristics and exercise data at peak $\dot{V}O_2$ are presented in table 1 with significant sex differences indicated.

Eighty seven boys and 83 girls were classified according to Tanner's indices for pubic hair and descriptive data are presented in table 2. No significant ($p > 0.05$) interaction effects were detected. Significant main effects for both sex ($p < 0.01$) and maturity ($p < 0.001$) were demonstrated for $\dot{V}E$ and V_T. Significant main effects for both sex ($p < 0.001$) and maturity ($p < 0.05$) were demonstrated for adjusted $\dot{V}E$. Significant main effects for sex ($p < 0.001$) but not for maturity ($p > 0.05$) were demonstrated for adjusted V_T.

Table 2. Exercise data at peak oxygen uptake by maturity

Boys	Tanner Stage I (n=28)	II (n=32)	III (n=18)	IV (n=9)
$\dot{V}E$ (L·min^{-1})	61.8 ± 8.1	66.0 ± 10.5	71.4 ± 8.2	79.6 ± 19.6
Adj $\dot{V}E$ (L·min^{-1})	65.8	67.8	68.1	70.5
V_T (L)	1.19 ± 0.21	1.34 ± 0.26	1.50 ± 0.13	1.52 ± 0.30
Adjusted V_T (L)	1.28	1.38	1.41	1.33
Rf (breaths·min^{-1})	53 ± 9	50 ± 8	48 ± 6	53 ± 10
$\dot{V}E/\dot{V}O_2$	30.2 ± 2.6	29.3 ± 2.4	29.3 ± 2.0	29.8 ± 3.1
$\dot{V}E/\dot{V}CO_2$	28.8 ± 2.1	28.4 ± 1.9	28.0 ± 1.7	28.6 ± 2.4
Girls				
	(n=19)	(n=25)	(n=25)	(n=14)
$\dot{V}E$ (L·min^{-1})	53.3 ± 8.0	61.4 ± 9.6	61.4 ± 6.6	69.1 ± 5.1
Adj $\dot{V}E$ (L·min^{-1})	57.2	61.2	60.0	65.6
V_T (L)	1.10 ± 0.32	1.21 ± 0.23	1.28 ± 0.23	1.43 ± 0.34
Adjusted V_T (L)	1.18	1.20	1.24	1.31
Rf (breaths·min^{-1})	51 ± 11	52 ± 8	49 ± 10	50 ± 9
$\dot{V}E/\dot{V}O_2$	29.1 ± 2.9	30.7 ± 3.6	30.6 ± 2.8	30.9 ± 1.9
$\dot{V}E/\dot{V}CO_2$	27.9 ± 2.4	29.1 ± 2.7	29.2 ± 2.2	29.0 ± 1.6

Values are mean ± SD

Exercise data at 2.22 m·s^{-1} and at 75-80% of peak $\dot{V}O_2$ are presented in tables 3 and 4 respectively with significant sex differences indicated.

Ninety two of the children exercising in the range 75-80% of peak $\dot{V}O_2$ were classified according to Tanner's indices for pubic hair and descriptive data are presented in table 5. No significant ($p > 0.05$) interactions or main effects for maturity were detected. $\dot{V}E$ demonstrated the only significant ($p < 0.05$) main effect for sex.

Discussion

The boys' significantly higher $\dot{V}E$ and V_T at peak $\dot{V}O_2$ reflects their higher peak $\dot{V}O_2$, is independent of body size, and is consistent with the literature[9,10,11]. In accord with peak $\dot{V}O_2$[12], $\dot{V}E$ and V_T at peak $\dot{V}O_2$ increase with maturation but, unlike $\dot{V}E$ and peak $\dot{V}O_2$, the maturational effect on V_T is not independent of body size. Our finding that girls demonstrate a significantly higher $\dot{V}E/\dot{V}O_2$ at peak $\dot{V}O_2$ is in general agreement with previous studies[3,9,11] although conflicting evidence is available[10].

Table 3. Exercise data at 2.22 m·s^{-1} (8 km·h^{-1}) by sex

	Boys	Girls
$\dot{V}E$ (L·min^{-1})	37.0 ± 7.5*	39.6 ± 8.9
Adjusted $\dot{V}E$ (L·min^{-1})	37.2	37.7
V_T (L)	1.15 ± 0.31	1.15 ± 0.27
Adjusted V_T (L)	1.13	1.09
Rf (breaths·min^{-1})	34 ± 8	36 ± 9
$\dot{V}E / \dot{V}O_2$	22.8 ± 2.2***	24.2 ± 2.6
$\dot{V}E / \dot{V}CO_2$	25.4 ± 2.0*	26.0 ± 2.0
% peak $\dot{V}O_2$	70.4 ± 8.6***	78.0 ± 8.4
HR (beats·min^{-1})	167 ± 15***	179 ± 13

Values are mean ± SD
Level of significance *p <0.05, ***p <0.001

Table 4. Exercise data at 75-80% of peak oxygen uptake by sex

	Boys (n=56)	Girls (n=49)
$\dot{V}E$ (L·min^{-1})	41.7 ± 7.6	39.4 ± 7.8
Adjusted $\dot{V}E$ (L·min^{-1})	41.1*	38.6
V_T (L)	1.13 ± 0.30	1.11 ± 0.23
Adjusted V_T (L)	1.09	1.08
Rf (breaths·min^{-1})	39 ± 9	36 ± 7
$\dot{V}E / \dot{V}O_2$	23.5 ± 2.3	24.3 ± 2.7
$\dot{V}E / \dot{V}CO_2$	25.9 ± 2.2	26.0 ± 1.8
% peak $\dot{V}O_2$	77.2 ± 1.7	77.6 ± 1.7
HR (beats·min^{-1})	176 ± 10	178 ± 9

Values are mean ± SD
Level of significance * p <0.05

The girls' generally higher ventilatory responses when exercising submaximally, by running at 2.22 m·s^{-1}, can be explained by the higher relative intensity at which they were exercising, as reflected by % peak $\dot{V}O_2$ and heart rate. When exercising at the same relative submaximal intensity the sex differences in $\dot{V}E / \dot{V}O_2$ and $\dot{V}E / \dot{V}CO_2$ were no longer significant and the boys' $\dot{V}E$, with body size controlled for, was significantly higher (6.5%) than the girls'. Maturation does not appear to influence ventilatory responses to submaximal exercise in 12-year-olds.

Table 5. Exercise data at 75-80% of peak oxygen uptake by maturity

Boys	Tanner Stage I (n=18)	II (n=18)	III (n=7)	IV (n=7)
$\dot{V}E$ (L·min^{-1})	38.0 ± 5.6	40.0 ± 6.6	48.4 ± 5.6	49.2 ± 9.2
Adj $\dot{V}E$ (L·min^{-1})	41.7	41.5	43.1	41.6
V_T (L)	0.98 ± 0.25	1.09 ± 0.29	1.34 ± 0.19	1.32 ± 0.24
Adjusted V_T (L)	1.07	1.12	1.18	1.11
Rf (breaths·min^{-1})	41 ± 11	39 ± 10	37 ± 8	37 ± 4
$\dot{V}E / \dot{V}O_2$	24.1 ± 2.6	23.1 ± 2.0	24.6 ± 1.8	23.4 ± 2.8
$\dot{V}E / \dot{V}CO_2$	26.3 ± 2.7	25.7 ± 1.6	26.7 ± 2.0	26.1 ± 2.3
% peak $\dot{V}O_2$	77.3 ± 1.4	76.6 ± 1.5	78.7 ± 1.5	76.3 ± 2.0
Girls	(n=10)	(n=11)	(n=12)	(n=9)
$\dot{V}E$ (L·min^{-1})	33.5 ± 6.1	38.8 ± 9.0	38.1 ± 2.9	45.2 ± 6.4
Adj $\dot{V}E$ (L·min^{-1})	38.0	39.1	38.3	41.9
V_T (L)	0.94 ± 0.22	1.13 ± 0.14	1.03 ± 0.21	1.22 ± 0.21
Adjusted V_T (L)	1.07	1.16	1.02	1.12
Rf (breaths·min^{-1})	37 ± 8	35 ± 8	38 ± 8	38 ± 6
$\dot{V}E / \dot{V}O_2$	23.6 ± 2.3	25.4 ± 3.6	23.9 ± 2.3	25.1 ± 1.8
$\dot{V}E / \dot{V}CO_2$	25.7 ± 1.6	26.6 ± 2.4	25.7 ± 1.6	26.1 ± 1.6
% peak $\dot{V}O_2$	76.8 ± 1.5	77.3 ± 1.9	78.3 ± 1.6	78.3 ± 1.8

Values are mean ± SD

In summary, boys demonstrate higher peak $\dot{V}O_2$ than girls and this is supported by a higher $\dot{V}E$ and V_T even when the influence of body size is accounted for using allometric principles. Girls' ventilatory efficiency appears to be less than boys' at peak exercise. $\dot{V}E$ and V_T at peak $\dot{V}O_2$ are positively influenced by maturation in both sexes. However, other ventilatory responses at both peak exercise and at the same relative submaximal intensity appear to be generally independent of sex and maturity in this age group.

Acknowledgements

We gratefully acknowledge the technical assistance of Jenny Frost, Alison Husband, Teresa Smith and Sue Vooght. The work was supported by the British Heart Foundation and the Healthy Heart Research Trust.

References

1. Armstrong, N., Kirby, B.J., McManus, A.M. and Welsman, J.R. (1995) Aerobic fitness of pre-pubescent children. *Annals of Human Biology*, Vol. 22, pp. 427-41.
2. Welsman, J.R., Armstrong, N., Kirby, B.J., Nevill, A.M. and Winter, E.M. (1996) Scaling peak $\dot{V}O_2$ for differences in body size. *Medicine and Science in Sports and Exercise*, Vol. 28, pp. 259-65.
3. Rowland, T.W. and Cunningham, L.N. (in press) Development of ventilatory responses to exercise in normal Caucasian children: a longitudinal study. *Chest*.
4. Mercier, J., Varray, A., Ramonatxo, M., Mercier, B. and Prefaut, C. (1991) Influence of anthropometric characteristics on changes in maximal exercise ventilation and breathing pattern during growth in boys. *European Journal of Applied Physiology*, Vol. 63, pp. 235-41.
5. Tanner, J.M. (1962) *Growth at Adolescence (2nd edition)*, Blackwell Scientific Publications, Oxford.
6. Armstrong, N. and Welsman, J.R. (1994) Assessment and interpretation of aerobic fitness in children and adolescents. *Exercise and Sport Sciences Reviews*, Vol. 22, pp. 435-76.
7. Armstrong, N. and Welsman, J.R. (1997) *Young People and Physical Activity*, Oxford University Press, Oxford, pp. 46-55.
8. Welsman, J.R. and Armstrong, N. (1996) The measurement and interpretation of aerobic fitness in children: current issues. *Journal of the Royal Society of Medicine*, Vol. 89, pp. 281-5.
9. Andersen, K.L., Seliger, V., Rutenfranz, J. and Messel, S. (1974) Physical performance capacity of children in Norway. Part III. Respiratory responses to graded exercise loadings - population parameters in a rural community. *European Journal of Applied Physiology*, Vol. 33, pp. 265-74.
10. Rutenfranz, J., Andersen, K.L., Seliger, V., Klimmer, F., Ilmarinen, J., Ruppel, M. and Kylian, H. (1981) Exercise ventilation during the growth spurt period: comparison between two European countries. *European Journal of Pediatrics*, Vol. 136, pp. 135-42.
11. Åstrand, P.O. (1952) *Experimental Studies of Physical Work Capacity in Relation to Sex and Age*, Copenhagen, Munksgaard.
12. Armstrong, N., Welsman, J.R. and Kirby, B.J. (under review) Peak oxygen uptake and maturation.

EXERCISE INDUCED HYPOXAEMIA IN CHILDREN AT ALTITUDE

Exercise induced hypoxaemia in children

R.R. WOLFE and P.L. McCOOL
Section of Pediatric Cardiology, The Children's Hospital-University of Colorado Health Sciences Centre, Denver, Colorado, USA

Keywords: Children at altitude, exercise induced hypoxaemia, oxyhaemoglobin saturation distribution, relative hypoventilation

Introduction

The distribution of oxyhaemoglobin saturation in exercising children at sea level is not well described. The available data suggest that, similar to adults, young individuals with superior cardiopulmonary conditioning have a greater tendency to desaturate with exercise[1-4]. It appears that increasing age potentiates the occurrence of exercise induced hypoxaemia (EIH) in master athletes[5-7].

EIH has not been evaluated in normal children or in children with congenital heart disease at altitude. A hypobaric-hypoxic environmental influence is added to the matrix of possible mechanisms of EIH including arteriovenous shunts, alterations in the ventilation/perfusion ratio[8], diffusion defects[2,7], and relative or absolute alveolar hypoventilation[4]. The primary objective of this study was to describe the oxyhaemoglobin saturation distribution at rest and in response to maximum voluntary exercise in children chronically residing at altitude in normals and in children with and without several types of chronic cardiopulmonary disease. Measures of work capacity, aerobic fitness and ventilation were correlated with the difference between resting pulsed oxyhaemoglobin saturation ($rSpO_2$) and peak exercise pulsed oxyhaemoglobin saturation ($eSpO_2$). $rSpO_2$-$eSpO_2$ was defined as ΔSpO_2.

Methods

Paediatric normals (n=102, mean age 13.2 ± 5.2 y) and patients with cardiopulmonary disease (n=193, mean age 13.7 ± 4.8 y) performed the progressive protocol of James using an electronically braked cycle ergometer (SensorMedics 800, Yorba Linda, CA)

Children and Exercise XIX. Edited by Neil Armstrong, Brian Kirby and Joanne Welsman.
Published in 1997 by E & FN Spon, 2–6 Boundary Row, London, SE1 8HN.
ISBN 0 419 22100 X.

at an altitude of 5280 feet. $rSpO_2$ and $eSpO_2$ were measured with a pulse oximeter (Nellcor RS-10, Hayward, CA) and a reflectance oxygen transducer (Nellcor N-200, Hayward, CA). The test was assessed for maximum effort by either an experienced exercise physiologist or a paediatric cardiologist. Submaximal tests were not included in the study. Peak oxygen consumption (peak $\dot{V}O_2$) normalized for body weight ($mL \cdot kg^{-1} \cdot min^{-1}$) and end tidal carbon dioxide partial pressure ($PETCO_2$) were measured with a metabolic measurement cart (SensorMedics 2900Z). Total work (TW), mean power (MP), percent predicted peak mean power (%MP), O_2 pulse and VE/peak $\dot{V}O_2$ were calculated. Ventilatory anaerobic threshold (VAT) was determined by inspection of the ventilatory equivalent slope method and $\dot{V}O_2$ max at VAT (AT $\dot{V}O_2$) and percent exercise time at VAT (%ET) were noted. ΔSpO_2 of -3%, -4%, -5% and absolute SpO_2 $\leq$92%, SpO_2 $\leq$90% were correlated with parameters of work: TW, MP, %MP; parameters of aerobic fitness: peak $\dot{V}O_2$, AT $\dot{V}O_2$, %ET, %peak $\dot{V}O_2$ AT, and O_2 pulse; and parameters of ventilation: $PETCO_2$, peak ventilatory equivalent ($\dot{V}E$ /peak $\dot{V}O_2$), in the normal and patient population using 2-factor ANOVA for statistical significance. Of the 102 normals, 65 were males and 37 were females. The 193 patients were divided into five groups: obstructive lesions (postoperative coarctation of the thoracic aorta, pre and postoperative valvar aortic stenosis and postoperative valvar pulmonic stenosis) n=72; low cardiac output ($\dot{Q}$) (cardiomyopathy and postoperative Fontan procedures for univentricular heart variants) n=64; postoperative left-to-right shunt (ventricular and atrial septal defects) n=27; surgically corrected right-to-left shunt (tetralogy of Fallot, total anomalous pulmonary venous return) n=21; and chronic lung disease (cystic fibrosis) n=9.

Results

The mean $rSpO_2$ for the entire group was 96.6 ± 1.8% with range of sub group means from 96.2-97.2% (excluding chronic lung disease patients) (table 1). The mean $eSpO_2$ for the study group was 94.3 ± 4.2% with a range of 93.6 - 95.4% (table 1). The ΔSpO_2 for the study group was -2.2 ± 3.4% with a range of -1.5% to -2.8%.

The percent of patients demonstrating exercise induced desaturation in the total group at levels of $\geq$-3%, $\geq$-4%, $\geq$-5%, $\leq$92%, was 33.8%, 20.6%, 13.8%, 21% and 10.5% respectively (table 2). In the normal study group, 6.8% desaturated $\leq$90% with the low cardiac output and chronic lung disease groups having the highest proportion of desaturators (19.1% and 66.6% at $\leq$90%) (table 2).

Exercise parameters (TW, MP, %MP) and fitness parameters (peak $\dot{V}O_2$, AT $\dot{V}O_2$, %ET, %peak $\dot{V}O_2$ AT, O_2/pulse) in the four patient sub groups of cardiac disease were evaluated by 2-factor ANOVA at each level of ΔSpO_2 for statistical significance at the $p \leq 0.05$ level (table 3). The strongest correlations between work and ΔSpO_2 (six each) were in the normal and obstructive lesion groups. The strongest number of

Table 1. Resting SPO_2, exercise SpO_2, and ΔSpO_2 by group

	Total Group	Norm Pts	Obs Lesions	Low $\dot{Q}$	LR Shunts	RL Shunts	Lung In
Rest SpO_2	96.6 ± 1.8	96.7 ± 1.3	96.9 ± 1.4	96.2 ± 2.6	97.2 ± 1.1	96.4 ± 1.5	94.2 ± 2.7
Ex SpO_2	94.3 ± 4.2	94.7 ± 3.0	95.4 ± 2.9	93.7 ± 2.9	95.2 ± 2.5	93.6 ± 6.1	84.6 ± 7.7
ΔSpO_2	-2.2 ± 3.3	-1.9 ± 2.5	-1.5 ± 2.7	-2.5 ± 3.1	-2.0 ± 2.4	-2.8 ± 5.8	-9.6 ± 5.6

Values are mean ± SD

Table 2. Percentage of patients indicated by degree of desaturation

	Total Group	Norm Pts	Obs Lesions	Low $\dot{Q}$	LR Shunts	RL Shunts	Lung In
≥ Δ3%	33.8	34.3	22.2	41.4	33.3	29.4	77.7
≥ Δ4%	20.6	20.5	12.5	26.4	11.1	17.6	77.7
≥ Δ5%	13.8	10.7	9.7	19.1	7.4	11.7	66.6
≥92%	21.0	18.6	13.8	27.9	18.5	11.7	77.7
≥90%	10.5	6.8	2.7	19.1	7.4	5.8	66.6

Table 3. Number of significant correlations by ANOVA of exertional-induced hypoxaemia with work and fitness parameters ($p \leq 0.05$).

	Norms Pts	Obs Lesions	Low $\dot{Q}$	LR Shunts	RL Shunts
≥3%					
Work	2	2	0	0	0
Fitness	1	4	0	2	0
Ventilation	0	0	0	1	0
≥4%					
Work	2	2	0	0	0
Fitness	4	2	0	1	0
Ventilation	0	1	0	0	0
≥5%					
Work	0	2	0	2	0
Fitness	0	1	0	3	1
Ventilation	0	1	0	0	0
≥92%					
Work	2	0	0	0	3
Fitness	0	3	0	0	0
Ventilation	0	1	0	0	0
≥90%					
Work	0	0	0	0	1
Fitness	0	0	0	0	0
Ventilation	0	1	0	0	0
Total	11	20	0	9	5

Table 4. $\dot{V}E$/peak $\dot{V}O_2$ and $PETCO_2$ by group

	Total Group	Norm Pts	Obs Lesions	Low CO	LR Shunts	RL Shunts	Lung In
$\dot{V}E$ / p$\dot{V}O_2$	46.5 ± 7.9	45.2 ± 6.1	44.9 ± 7.3	48.6±10.2	48.5 ± 7.7	46.7 ± 7.0	48.6 ± 9.4
PET CO_2	34.6 ± 13.2	36.5 ± 22.4	35. 0 ± 5.2	32.3 ± 4.2	33.3 ± 3.2	33.4 ± 6.2	35.8 ± 6.6

correlations between fitness and ΔSpO_2 were found in the obstructive lesions[10] postoperative left-to-right shunts[6] and normals[5].

$PETCO_2$ as a possible index of relative hypoventilation at peak exercise demonstrated a significant correlation in the obstructive lesion group at the ≥-4%, and ≥-5% ΔSpO_2 levels and at the ≤92%, ≤90% $eSpO_2$ levels (table 3). No other patient group demonstrated significant correlations at these levels. VE/PVO_2 as an indicator of hypoventilation was correlated with EIH (defined as ΔSpO_2 ≤90%) in the four heart disease groups and only the obstructive lesion group demonstrated statistical significance (table 4) ($p \leq 0.04$ by 2-tail unpaired student t-test).

Discussion

The purpose of this study was to describe the resting and peak exercise oxyhaemoglobin saturation of normal children and adolescents and those with congenital heart disease at altitude. There is sparse paediatric data for peak exercise oxyhaemoglobin saturation at sea level and none at altitude. The $rSpO_2$ of 96.6 ± 1.8% of the entire study group does not vary significantly from the normal group value of 96.7 ± -1.3% nor is it significantly different from the $rSpO_2$ of any of the groups of heart disease (table 1). It is also similar to values reported for children and young adults at sea level[2]. Only the small group of patients with chronic lung disease had a lower $rSpO_2$ (94.2 ± 2.7%). The ΔSpO_2 of -2.2% for the entire study group and -1.9% for the normal group suggests that a ΔSpO_2 of ≥-3% be the threshold value for an unusual or abnormal response to exercise. For the entire study group the majority of subjects had a ΔSpO_2 of 0% to -2%, the next commonest ΔSpO_2 response was -3% to -5%, and the least common ΔSpO_2 responses were +1% to +3% or -5% to -15% (including EIH).

The definition of EIH remains somewhat arbitrary. Prior investigators[2,3] have chosen an SpO_2 of 91% or lower as the critical range at sea level. EIH has largely been associated with elite athletes or highly fit individuals and appears to be potentiated by advancing age. None of the participants in this study qualify as elite athletes. Respectively, 6.8% and 2.7% of the normal and obstructive lesion group desaturated to an SpO_2 ≤90%. An SpO_2 ≤90% would appear to be a reasonable definer of EIH in children and adolescents at 5280 feet.

The correlations between EIH and parameters of exercise fitness in the three "healthiest" groups, i.e. normals, obstructive lesions and postoperative left-to-right shunts, are intriguing but not surprising. Previous studies have emphasized the relationship between fitness and EIH. Our group has previously reported that children with mild to moderate aortic valvar stenosis have normal to above average exercise fitness profiles[9]. This was also true for the current study group. They would be expected to be "more fit" than Fontans, cardiomyopathies, postoperative tetralogy of Fallots and patients with chronic lung disease.

The mechanism of EIH remains speculative and multifactorial. Recent studies in healthy young subjects at sea level have tended to discount pulmonary diffusion capacity as a major contributor[10-12]. Relative hypoventilation seems to be gaining credibility as a significant mechanism in EIH. The hypothesis of relative hypoventilation at peak exercise as a mechanism of EIH is consistent with the observation of the highest $PETCO_2$ at ≤90% in the obstructive lesion group. In addition, the ventilatory equivalent for oxygen at peak exercise ($\dot{V}E$/peak $\dot{V}O_2$) was correlated with EIH ($eSpO_2$ ≤ 90%) to further assess the contribution of hypoventilation in the obstructive lesion patients (table 4). That a statistically significant relationship was found in only this group further suggests relative hypoventilation as a mechanism of EIH in children with aortic stenosis, pulmonic stenosis and coarctation of the thoracic aorta. The three other groups of heart disease and the chronic lung patients had even greater exercise induced hypoxaemia (table 1) but did not show statistically significant relationships with indicators of relative hypoventilation (table 4). This is not surprising as other mechanisms of exercise induced desaturation would be expected. The postoperative tetralogy of Fallot patients would likely have residual pulmonary collateral vessels (arteriovenous shunts). The Fontan and cardiomyopathy patients would be expected to have either pulmonary collaterals, diffusional abnormalities or ventilation-perfusion mismatch secondary to chronic left ventricular diastolic dysfunction.

Summary

1. Resting oxyhaemoglobin saturation in children and adolescents at 5,280 feet in 96.6 ± 1.8% and is similar to sea level values.
2. A change in oxyhaemoglobin saturation ≥-3% is unusual and may be abnormal.
3. It is suggested that exercise induced hypoxaemia (EIH) be defined as ≤90% in children living at 5280 feet.
4. EIH is most correlated with work fitness parameters in the obstructive lesion group. This sub group demonstrated the highest level of work fitness (peak $\dot{V}O_2$, VAT, etc) among the patients with heart disease.
5. The obstructive lesion group has the lowest VE/peak $\dot{V}O_2$ and the highest $PETCO_2$ of the cardiac lesions suggesting relative hypoventilation as the mechanism of the EIH. Statistical correlation between these two parameters and EIH further strengthens that probability.

References

1. Dempsey, J.A., Hanson, P.G. and Henderson, K.S. (1984) Exercise induced arterial hypoxaemia in healthy persons at sea level. *Journal of Physiology,* Vol. 355, pp. 161-75.
2. Williams, J.H., Powers, S.K. and Stuart, M.S. (1986) Haemoglobin desaturation in highly trained athletes during heavy exercise. *Medicine and Science in Sports and Exercise,* Vol. 18, pp. 168-73.
3. Powers, S.K., Dodd, S., Lawler, J., Landrey, G., Kirtley, M., McKnight, T. and Grinton, S. (1988) Incidence of exercise induced hypoxaemia in elite endurance athletes at sea level. *European Journal of Applied Physiology,* Vol. 58, pp. 298-302.
4. Miyachi, M. and Tabata, I. (1992) Relationship between arterial oxygen desaturation and ventilation during maximal exercise. *Journal of Applied Physiology,* Vol. 73 pp. 2588-91.
5. Johnson, B.D. and Dempsey, J.A. (1991) Demand vs capacity in the aging pulmonary system. *Exercise and Sport Sciences Reviews,* Vol. 19, pp. 171-210.
6. Prefault, C., Anselme, F., Caillaud, C. and Masse-Biron, J. (1994) Exercise induced hypoxaemia in older athletes. *Journal of Applied Physiology,* Vol. 76, pp. 120-6.
7. Aguilaniu, B., Flore, P., Perrault, H., Page, J.E., Payan, E. and Lacour, J.R. (1995) Exercise induced hypoxaemia in master athletes: effects of polyunsaturated fatty acid diet. *European Journal of Applied. Physiology,* Vol. 72, pp. 44-50.
8. Todaro, A., Leonardi, L.M., Desi, M., Faccini, P., Sardella, F., Menchinelli, C. and Gallozzi, C. (1995) Pulmonary gas exchange in athletes with exercise induced hypoxaemia. *Journal of Sports Medicine and Physical Fitness,* Vol. 35, pp. 114-23.
9. Wolfe, R.R., Wiggins, J.W., Daberkow, E.D., Mahoney, L.T. and Brammel, H.P. (1980) Exercise performance in children with moderate valvar aortic stenosis. *Pediatric Cardiology,* Vol. 1, pp. 321-2.
10. Miles, D.S., Enoch, A.D. and Grevey, S.C. (1986) Interpretation of changes in DLCO and pulmonary function. *Respiratory Physiology,* Vol. 66, pp. 135-45.
11. Miles, D.S. and Schaefer, R.S. (1988) Running induced changes in lung function are not altered by acute moderate hypoxia. *Aviation Space and Enviromental Medicine,* Vol. 59, pp. 234-8.
12. Manier, G., Moinard, J. and Stoicheff, H. (1993) Pulmonary diffusing capacity after maximum exercise. *Journal of Applied Physiology,* Vol. 75, pp. 2580-5.

ACQUISITION OF STABLE TREADMILL WALKING MECHANICS IN YOUNG CHILDREN

Acquisition of stable walking mechanics

D.W. MORGAN, W TSEH, J.L. CAPUTO, I.S. CRAIG and D.J. KEEFER
Department of Exercise and Sport Science, The University of North Carolina at Greensboro, Greensboro, USA
P.E. MARTIN
Department of Exercise Science and Physical Education, Arizona State University, Tempe, USA

Keywords: Accommodation, biomechanics, gait, treadmill walking, variability

Introduction

In order to obtain valid information regarding the walking mechanics of young children, clinicians and researchers must be confident that the variables being measured are stable and reproducible. Without this assurance, the interpretation of data obtained from gait testing or the use of a particular training stimulus or therapeutic regimen may be confounded, in part, by accommodation of the child to the treadmill[1].

The limited data available have shown that after 30 to 60 min, adult distance runners settle into a stable treadmill running pattern[2,3,4]. Little is known, however, about the length of time needed for young, prepubescent children to demonstrate a consistent biomechanical response to treadmill exercise. To address this question, we determined the period of time necessary for young, able-bodied boys and girls to exhibit stable gait mechanics during level treadmill walking. Data analysed in this paper were gathered as part of an on-going, 5 y longitudinal study examining the influence of physical growth on gait efficiency in young children. In an attempt to expand the current database, a variety of temporal and kinematic variables used typically to characterise the walking pattern were measured.

Methods

After obtaining written informed consent from parents, 31 6-year-old boys and girls with no cardiovascular or orthopaedic limitations (mean height = 117.5 ± 4.4 cm; mean body mass = 21.9 ± 2.6 kg) completed two testing sessions. In Session 1, each subject was familiarised with the laboratory environment and shown a video of a young child walking on a treadmill. After learning how to mount the treadmill, subjects practiced

Children and Exercise XIX. Edited by Neil Armstrong, Brian Kirby and Joanne Welsman.
Published in 1997 by E & FN Spon, 2–6 Boundary Row, London, SE1 8HN.
ISBN 0 419 22100 X.

walking at speeds slightly slower than the test speed of 1.34 $m \cdot s^{-1}$ (3 mph). This session culminated by having each subject walk for 5 min at 1.34 $m \cdot s^{-1}$.

Within approximately one week of Session 1, subjects returned to the laboratory to complete a second testing session. In this session, subjects completed three 10 min level treadmill walking bouts at 1.34 $m \cdot s^{-1}$. During the first minutes of each bout, a photoelectric cell mounted above the treadmill belt and connected to an electronic timer counted the elapsed time required for eight belt revolutions to establish and verify treadmill speed. A rest period of 10 min separated each walking trial. Prior to exercise, footswitches were taped to the underside of the heel and the anterior portion of the sole of each shoe to enable acquisition of the biomechanical variables of interest. Wires attached to the footswitches were taped to the back of each leg and connected to a belt that subjects wore while walking. During the last 2 min of each 10 min trial, voltage signals emanating from the footswitches were captured by an analog-to-digital board sampling at a rate of 200 Hz. To ensure that the footswitches were operating properly, light-emitting diodes registered heel contact and toe-off events.

Biomechanical indices chosen for analysis included step length, stance time, swing time, stride time and double-support time. Step length was calculated by multiplying treadmill velocity and step time, or the time interval between successive heel contacts. Stance time was defined as the time from heel contact of one foot to toe-off of the same foot and swing time was taken as the time interval between toe-off of one foot and heel contact of the same foot. Stride time was determined by adding stance time and swing time. Double-support time was defined as the time during which both feet were in contact with the ground.

A doubly multivariate repeated measures analysis of variance (MANOVA) design was used to ascertain whether the collective set of biomechanical factors differed across time. Univariate analysis and Tukey's Honestly Significant Difference post-hoc test were employed to identify the location of statistically significant differences ($p < 0.05$).

Table 1. Measures of step length, stance time, swing time, stride time, and double-support time obtained after 10, 20, and 30 min of treadmill walking

Variable	Walking time (min)			Univariate F
	10	20	30	
Step length (cm)	53.84 ± 2.55	54.46 ± 3.04	54.56 ± 2.95	13.34*
Stance time (ms)	458.8 ± 30.6	463.6 ± 32.5	465.3 ± 31.9	10.83*
Swing time (ms)	345.7 ± 21.2	349.5 ± 23.6	349.6 ± 24.1	4.65*
Stride time (ms)	804.4 ± 39.6	813.1 ± 45.7	814.9 ± 44.5	10.40*
Double-support time (ms)	57.5 ± 19.1	58.1 ± 17.2	57.6 ± 17.6	0.17

Values are mean ± SD
Level of significance $^*p < 0.05$ (20 min >10 min)

Results

Gait descriptors measured in Session 2 are displayed in table 1. MANOVA demonstrated that the time main effect was significant (Wilks' lambda = 0.59, F (10, 112) = 3.37, p <0.01). Univariate F-tests indicated that all biomechanical measures except double-support time varied across the 30 min testing session. Post-hoc analyses revealed that increases in step length, stance time, swing time, and stride time occurred between the first (minutes 8 to 10) and second (minutes 18 to 20) walking trials. No changes in any of these variables were observed between the second and third (minutes 28 to 30) trials.

Discussion

Our findings demonstrate that in young children, stable walking mechanics during level treadmill walking can be obtained within 20 min if data collection is preceded by exposure to the testing environment and a short amount of treadmill walking practice. These results differ from those obtained by Frost et al.[5], who observed no within-day variation in stride length or hip amplitude in 11 children who performed six 6 min level treadmill walking trials (speed range = 1.18 to 1.70 $m \cdot s^{-1}$) on each of 2 d. Consistent with our findings, however, these authors noted a tendency for stride length to increase during the first day of testing and for hip amplitude to increase during both testing sessions. In contrast, Rogers et al.[6] reported that among 42 7- to 9-year-old children who ran for 10 min at 2.23 and 2.68 $m \cdot s^{-1}$ on two separate days, stride length was shorter and stride frequency was greater on day 2. Based on these results, which were obtained from timed counts of foot falls, Rogers and colleagues[6] suggested that extended treadmill accommodation might be necessary for children to establish baseline values for stride length and stride frequency. Although this statement may have merit when evaluating variability in running mechanics, results from the current investigation support the notion that young children can produce a consistent walking pattern on the treadmill in 20 min. The lack of agreement between our findings and those reported by other investigators may reflect differences in sample size, mode of exercise, the extent of treadmill accommodation, and methodological procedures used to acquire biomechanical data.

While differences in step length, stance time, swing time, and stride time were observed across the first two testing trials, relative changes in these gait variables were quite small (range = 1.0 to 1.2 %). This implies that the majority of gait adjustments occurred during the initial 10 min walking bout or the familiarisation session. Although not evaluated formally in this study, future research in this area might be directed toward quantifying biomechanical accommodation during the first minutes of treadmill walking. Additionally, since walking patterns were analysed at a single velocity, it is not known whether treadmill accommodation would proceed in a similar fashion across a broader range of speeds.

In conclusion, data from this study indicate that acceptably stable measures of gait function can be obtained in 6-year-old boys and girls after 20 min of level treadmill walking. This consistency in response was observed after subjects were introduced to the laboratory setting and given an opportunity to briefly practice walking on the treadmill prior to data collection. From a practical standpoint, offering adequate exposure to the methodology and equipment used in biomechanical data collection may help young children feel more comfortable about the testing environment, thus facilitating the attainment of a stable and representative treadmill walking pattern.

Acknowledgment

This study was supported by funding from the National Institute of Child Health and Human Development (HD 30749).

References

1. Morgan, D.W. and Craib, M.W. (1992) Physiological aspects of running economy. *Medicine and Science in Sports and Exercise,* Vol. 24, pp. 456-61.
2. Cavanagh, P.R. and Williams, K.R. (1982) The effect of stride length variation on oxygen uptake during distance running. *Medicine and Science in Sports and Exercise,* Vol. 14, pp. 30-5.
3. Schieb, D.A. (1986) Kinematic accommodation of novice treadmill runners. *Research Quarterly for Exercise and Sport,* Vol. 57, pp. 1-7.
4. Morgan, D.W., Martin, P.E., Krahenbuhl, G.S. and Baldini, F.D. (1991) Variablity in running economy and mechanics among trained male runners. *Medicine and Science in Sports and Exercise,* Vol. 23, pp. 378-83.
5. Frost, G., Bar-Or, B., Dowling, J. and White, C. (1995) Habituation of children to treadmill walking and running: metabolic and kinematic criteria. *Pediatric Exercise Science,* Vol. 7, pp. 162-75.
6. Rogers, D.M., Turley, K.R., Kujawa, K.I., Harper, K.M. and Wilmore, J.H. (1994) The reliability and variability of running economy in 7-, 8-, and 9-year-old children. *Pediatric Exercise Science,* Vol. 6, pp. 287-96.
7. Tseh, W., Caputo, J.L., Craig, I.S., Keefer, D.J. and Morgan, D.W. (1997) Metabolic accommodation of young children to treadmill walking. *Medicine and Science in Sports and Exercise*, Vol. 29, (suppl).

SUBMAXIMAL EXERCISE IN PREPUBERTAL CHILDREN

Submaximal exercise in prepubertal children

N. ARMSTRONG, B.J. KIRBY and J.R. WELSMAN
Children's Health and Exercise Research Centre, Institute of Clinical Science, University of Exeter, Exeter, UK
A.M. McMANUS
Physical Education and Sports Science Unit, University of Hong Kong, Hong Kong
Keywords: Allometric scaling, oxygen uptake, prepubescents, submaximal exercise, women

Introduction

In comparison to adults and adolescents, relatively little is known about the responses of prepubescent children to submaximal exercise and the data are often difficult to interpret due to the confounding influence of body mass[1,2]. Most studies of children's exercise responses have "controlled for body mass" using the conventional ratio standard (exercise response ÷ body mass), but there is a growing conviction that per body mass ratios do not necessarily render performance measures independent of body mass[1]. The use of allometric models ($y = a \cdot x^b$) to derive size-independent exercise performance measures has been demonstrated to be theoretically and statistically superior to the simple ratio standard in analysing size-related function[3,4].

As part of an on-going longitudinal study we have collected submaximal exercise data on a large, well-defined sample of prepubescent children. The purpose of this paper is to use these data to enhance understanding of the responses of prepubescent children to submaximal exercise using allometric modelling, as well as the conventional ratio standard, to control for body mass. The girls' data will also be compared with those from a group of adult women.

Subjects

The children were drawn from a longitudinal study of a representative sample of children attending state schools in Exeter. Subject selection has been described elsewhere[4]. The data reported here are from the 105 boys and 77 girls who were classified as prepubertal and successfully completed the procedures described below

Children and Exercise XIX. Edited by Neil Armstrong, Brian Kirby and Joanne Welsman.
Published in 1997 by E & FN Spon, 2–6 Boundary Row, London, SE1 8HN.
ISBN 0 419 22100 X.

during the first year of the study. The 18 women were subjects in a parallel study carried out in the Centre during the same period of time.

Methods

Age was computed from dates of birth and examination. Sexual maturity was visually assessed using Tanner's[5] indices of pubic hair and stature, body mass and triceps and subscapular skinfolds were measured using standard techniques. The skinfolds were summed to provide a descriptor of body fatness. Submaximal and peak exercise variables were determined during a discontinuous, incremental treadmill test. Following habituation and a standardised warm-up the children completed four 3 min runs at treadmill speeds of 7, 8, 9 and 10 $km{\cdot}h^{-1}$ (1.94-2.78 $m{\cdot}s^{-1}$), the women started the test at 8 $km{\cdot}h^{-1}$. Subsequently, the treadmill speed was held constant at 10 $km{\cdot}h^{-1}$ and the gradient elevated by 2.5% at the end of each 3 min period. The test was terminated at the point of voluntary exhaustion and peak $\dot{V}O_2$ was accepted as a maximal index if established criteria[1] were satisfied. Throughout the test respiratory gases were monitored continuously using an Oxycon Sigma analysis system which was recalibrated prior to each test. Heart rate (HR) was monitored electrocardiographically. The children returned to the Centre the following morning and repeated the run at 8 $km{\cdot}h^{-1}$.

Data analyses

Data were stored and analysed using SPSS-PC+. Descriptive statistics were computed for anthropometric variables and peak and submaximal exercise responses. Sex differences and differences between girls and women were analysed using analysis of variance (ANOVA). Multivariate ANOVA was used to investigate differences in exercise data at submaximal intensities. Analysis of covariance (ANCOVA) on log transformed data was used to partition out the effects of body mass from peak and submaximal measures of $\dot{V}O_2$ and to obtain appropriately adjusted means for $\dot{V}O_2$. We have discussed in detail elsewhere the theoretical principles underlying the use of log-linear models to partition out body size from measures of physiological function[1,3]. Repeated measures ANOVA and ANCOVA were used to investigate sex differences and differences between girls and women in the response of $\dot{V}O_2$ to increases in exercise intensity. The standard deviation of the differences between two measures of $\dot{V}O_2$ at 8 $km{\cdot}h^{-1}$ was computed to assess the repeatability of the children's submaximal $\dot{V}O_2$ [6]. Relationships between peak and submaximal $\dot{V}O_2$ were explored using Pearson product moment correlation coefficients.

Results

Descriptives for the children's anthropometric characteristics and peak exercise data are presented in table 1. There were no significant differences ($p > 0.05$) in age, stature, mass, skinfold thickness, or peak HR between boys and girls. Peak $\dot{V}O_2$ was significantly higher in the boys ($p < 0.001$) whether expressed in $L \cdot min^{-1}$, in ratio with body mass ($mL \cdot kg^{-1} \cdot min^{-1}$), or adjusted for body mass using log-linear ANCOVA. The ANCOVA yielded a mass exponent of 0.70 (SE 0.04) which was common to both boys and girls and not significantly different ($p > 0.05$) from the theoretical exponent of 0.67[1]. The respiratory exchange ratio (RER) at peak $\dot{V}O_2$ was significantly higher ($p < 0.01$) in boys although in both sexes it exceeded unity.

The children's exercise responses at 7, 8, 9, and 10 $km \cdot h^{-1}$ are summarised in tables 2 and 3. At 7 $km \cdot h^{-1}$ absolute $\dot{V}O_2$ was significantly higher ($p < 0.01$) in boys but when values were expressed in $mL \cdot kg^{-1} \cdot min^{-1}$ or allometrically scaled differences became non-significant ($p > 0.05$). At this intensity girls were exercising at a significantly higher ($p < 0.001$) %peak $\dot{V}O_2$ and consequently demonstrated significantly higher HR ($p < 0.001$) and RER ($p < 0.01$). At speeds of 8, 9, and 10 $km \cdot h^{-1}$ boys demonstrated significantly higher ($p < 0.05$ to $p < 0.001$) values for absolute, mass-related, and adjusted $\dot{V}O_2$ than girls but mean values for %peak $\dot{V}O_2$, HR and RER were consistently higher in girls ($p < 0.01$). The allometric exponents common to both boys and girls were 0.93 (SE 0.05), 0.85 (SE 0.04), 0.93 (SE 0.04) and 0.92 (SE 0.04) at 7, 8, 9, and 10 $km \cdot h^{-1}$ respectively. The repeated measures analyses yielded no significant interaction terms ($p > 0.05$) (sex by treadmill speed) for absolute, mass-related or adjusted $\dot{V}O_2$.

Table 1. Physical characteristics and peak exercise responses

Variable	Boys	Girls
Age (y)	11.1 ± 0.4	11.0 ± 0.4
Stature (m)	1.45 ± 0.06	1.44 ± 0.08
Mass (kg)	36.3 ± 6.1	34.6 ± 5.2
Skinfolds (mm)	19.2 ± 8.8	21.0 ± 7.2
$\dot{V}O_2$ ($L \cdot min^{-1}$)	1.81 ± 0.26***	1.51 ± 0.22
$\dot{V}O_2$ ($mL \cdot kg^{-1} \cdot min^{-1}$)	50.4 ± 5.8***	43.9 ± 3.8
Adjusted $\dot{V}O_2$ ($L \cdot min^{-1}$)	1.76***	1.51
RER	1.07 ± 0.07**	1.04 ± 0.07
HR ($beats \cdot min^{-1}$)	200 ± 7	201 ± 7

Values are mean ± SD
Level of significance **$p < 0.01$, ***$p < 0.001$

Table 2. Submaximal exercise responses of boys

Variable	7 $km \cdot h^{-1}$	8 $km \cdot h^{-1}$	9 $km \cdot h^{-1}$	10 $km \cdot h^{-1}$
$\dot{V}O_2$ ($L \cdot min^{-1}$)	1.21 ± 0.23	1.30 ± 0.22	1.42 ± 0.26	1.54 ± 0.26
$\dot{V}O_2$ ($mL \cdot kg^{-1} \cdot min^{-1}$)	33.5 ± 3.7	36.1 ± 3.4	39.2 ± 3.8	42.6 ± 3.6
Adjusted $\dot{V}O_2$ ($L \cdot min^{-1}$)	1.16	1.26	1.37	1.48
%peak $\dot{V}O_2$	66.9 ± 8.7	72.4 ± 8.6	78.4 ± 9.9	85.1 ± 8.8
HR ($beats \cdot min^{-1}$)	160 ± 16	161 ± 16	179 ± 13	187 ± 12
RER	0.90 ± 0.06	0.92 ± 0.05	0.95 ± 0.05	0.98 ± 0.06

Values are mean ± SD

Table 3. Submaximal exercise responses of girls

Variable	7 $km \cdot h^{-1}$	8 $km \cdot h^{-1}$	9 $km \cdot h^{-1}$	10 $km \cdot h^{-1}$
$\dot{V}O_2$ ($L \cdot min^{-1}$)	1.13 ± 0.18	1.21 ± 0.17	1.32 ± 0.19	1.40 ± 0.22
$\dot{V}O_2$ ($mL \cdot kg^{-1} \cdot min^{-1}$)	32.8 ± 3.2	35.2 ± 2.8	38.2 ± 2.9	41.2 ± 2.8
Adjusted $\dot{V}O_2$ ($L \cdot min^{-1}$)	1.14	1.22	1.33	1.43
%peak $\dot{V}O_2$	74.7 ± 7.1	80.2 ± 7.8	87.2 ± 7.8	94.3 ± 7.1
HR ($beats \cdot min^{-1}$)	171 ± 13	180 ± 11	189 ± 11	196 ± 9
RER	0.93 ± 0.05	0.94 ± 0.04	0.99 ± 0.05	1.01 ± 0.06

Values are mean ± SD

Mass-related and peak $\dot{V}O_2$ raised to the mass exponent 0.70 were significantly correlated ($p < 0.001$) with $\dot{V}O_2$ expressed as $mL \cdot kg^{-1} \cdot min^{-1}$ or $\dot{V}O_2$ expressed as $mL \cdot kg^{-0.70} \cdot min^{-1}$ respectively at 7, 8, 9 and 10 $km \cdot h^{-1}$ in boys. Coefficients ranged from 0.35 to 0.55. In girls, significant coefficients ($p < 0.05$ to $p < 0.001$) ranged from 0.26 to 0.46 but the relationships between peak $\dot{V}O_2$ ($mL \cdot kg^{-0.70} \cdot min^{-1}$) and $\dot{V}O_2$ ($mL \cdot kg^{-0.70} \cdot min^{-1}$) at 8 and 9 $km \cdot h^{-1}$ were not significant ($p > 0.05$).

The mean ± SD values for $\dot{V}O_2$ at 8 $km \cdot h^{-1}$ on the second visit were 1.28 ± 0.21 $L \cdot min^{-1}$ for boys and 1.20 ± 0.16 $L \cdot min^{-1}$ for girls. These were not significantly different from the first measurement ($p > 0.05$). Repeatability coefficients were 0.23 and 0.16 $L \cdot min^{-1}$ for boys and girls respectively.

The mean ± SD age, stature, mass and skinfold thickness of the women were 21.7 ± 2.6 y, 1.69 ± 0.07 m, 61.2 ± 6.9 kg, and 27.9 ± 7.4 mm respectively. All values were significantly higher ($p < 0.001$) than those of the girls. The women's peak and submaximal exercise responses are presented in table 4. At peak exercise the women demonstrated significantly higher $\dot{V}O_2$ ($p < 0.001$) and adjusted $\dot{V}O_2$ ($p < 0.05$) than

Table 4. Peak and submaximal exercise responses for adult women

Variable	8 km·h^{-1}	9 km·h^{-1}	10 km·h^{-1}	Peak
$\dot{V}O_2$ (L·min^{-1})	2.02 ± 0.27	2.18 ± 0.29	2.36 ± 0.27	2.54 ± 0.26
$\dot{V}O_2$ (mL·kg^{-1}·min^{-1})	33.2 ± 3.8	36.3 ± 4.1	39.2 ± 3.6	41.8 ± 4.3
Adjusted $\dot{V}O_2$ (L·min^{-1})	1.58	1.68	1.81	2.04
%peak $\dot{V}O_2$	79.1 ± 6.9	87.1 ± 7.0	92.8 ± 5.9	100
HR (beats·min^{-1})	182 ± 9	191 ± 7	195 ± 9	201 ± 9
RER	0.94 ± 0.06	0.97 ± 0.07	1.00 ± 0.05	1.03 ± 0.06

Values are mean ± SD

the girls. There were no significant differences ($p > 0.05$) in HR, RER or mass-related $\dot{V}O_2$. The women demonstrated significantly higher ($p < 0.001$) $\dot{V}O_2$ but the girls' mass-related $\dot{V}O_2$ was significantly higher ($p < 0.05$) in all submaximal exercises. There were no significant differences ($p > 0.05$) in HR, RER, % peak $\dot{V}O_2$, or adjusted $\dot{V}O_2$. The allometric exponents common to both girls and women were 0.82 (SE 0.06), 0.89 (SE 0.06) and 0.92 (SE 0.05) at 8, 9, and 10 km·h^{-1} respectively. The girls' ventilatory equivalent ($\dot{V}E/\dot{V}O_2$) was significantly higher than women's at 8 km·h^{-1} (24.7 ± 2.2 vs 22.7 ± 3.7) but there were no significant differences ($p > 0.05$) at 9 km·h^{-1} (26.7 ± 2.8 vs 25.7 ± 4.0) or 10 km·h^{-1} (28.2 ± 2.7 vs 26.8 ± 4.7).

Discussion

The peak $\dot{V}O_2$ data are in accord with the literature[1] and will not be discussed in detail as we have recently examined prepubescents' peak $\dot{V}O_2$ using data drawn from the present population[4]. The common mass exponent of 0.70 reinforces the view[1,3,4] that both boys' and girls' peak $\dot{V}O_2$ increases relative to mass raised to the power of 0.67 rather than in direct proportion with body mass i.e. mass$^{1.0}$.

Several studies have investigated young people's running economy (ie the $\dot{V}O_2$ per kg body mass at a given treadmill speed and/or slope[2, p. 174]) in relation to their peak $\dot{V}O_2$ [7,8]. The results presented here are consistent with earlier studies and provide no evidence to support the view that a superior running economy optimizes peak $\dot{V}O_2$.

It is well-documented that "steady state" appears to be effectively achieved in children by 3 min, at least at low and moderate exercise intensities[2]. The repeatability coefficients reported here compare favourably with the extant literature and confirm the stability of submaximal $\dot{V}O_2$ in children[9].

The submaximal $\dot{V}O_2$ responses (mL·kg^{-1}·min^{-1}) of the children are in general agreement with previous reports[10,11]. The data indicate that girls demonstrate slightly, but significantly, lower $\dot{V}O_2$ with body mass controlled for than boys in the range 8-10 km·h^{-1}. It may be that as the girls were exercising at a higher %peak $\dot{V}O_2$ and demonstrating a higher RER the contribution of anaerobic metabolism may have been higher than in the boys. However, this finding is consistent with previous reports on children[2] although the evidence indicating differences in running economy between adult males and females is equivocal[12]. The reason why girls appear to be more economic than boys may be related to their lower basal metabolic rate[2] but the issue invites further study.

In an excellent review Rowland[2] identified potential contributors to adult-child differences in running economy as, resting energy expenditure, muscular efficiency, gait kinematics, elastic recoil forces, body composition, less efficient ventilation, substrate utilization, anaerobic energy, stride frequency and mass-speed imbalance. Differences in resting energy expenditure are too small to account for adult-child differences in running economy and the case for a contribution from adult-child differences in muscular efficiency, gait kinematics, elastic recoil forces and body composition remains to be proven. As there were no significant differences between girls and women in RER and % peak $\dot{V}O_2$ at all submaximal stages and $\dot{V}E/\dot{V}O_2$ at 9 and 10 km·h^{-1} it is unlikely that less efficient ventilation, substrate utilization or contribution of anaerobic energy can explain the girls-women differences in the present study. It has been demonstrated that the $\dot{V}O_2$ per kg per stride is not significantly different in adults and children[13,14] and this indicates a possible role for stride frequency in explaining adult-child differences in running economy. However, the explanation may lie in a mass-speed imbalance between children and adults. Several studies[15,16] have demonstrated that applications of external loads, of 5 to 10% body mass, decrease the oxygen cost of running in children when the $\dot{V}O_2$ is "corrected" for total mass (ie body mass plus the external load).

Eston et al.[17] appear to have been the first to challenge the use of the ratio-standard in comparing adult-child submaximal exercise performance. They demonstrated that, although the ratio standard indicated that young boys were less economic than adults during submaximal running[13], if linear ANCOVA was used to compare the regression lines of $\dot{V}O_2$:mass between the groups there were no significant differences between the boys and the men. Using log-linear ANCOVA to control for body mass we have demonstrated the same phenomenon in prepubertal girls and adult women. Once again, in comparison to analysis using the conventional ratio standard, the allometric approach has revealed intriguing differences in the interpretation of young people's responses to exercise[1,3] and physiological explanations need to be explored.

Acknowledgements

This work was supported by the British Heart Foundation and the Healthy Heart Research Trust.

References

1. Armstrong, N. and Welsman, J.R. (1997) Young People and Physical Activity, Oxford University Press, Oxford.
2. Rowland, T.W. (1995) *Developmental Exercise Physiology,* Human Kinetics, Champaign, Il.
3. Welsman, J.R., Armstrong, N., Kirby, B.J., Nevill, A.M. and Winter, E.M. (1996) Scaling peak $\dot{V}O_2$ for differences in body size. *Medicine and Science in Sports and Exercise*, Vol. 28, pp. 259-65.
4. Armstrong, N., Kirby, B.J., McManus, A.M. and Welsman, J.R. (1995) Aerobic fitness of prepubescent children. *Annals of Human Biology*, Vol. 22, pp. 427-41.
5. Tanner, J.M. (1962) *Growth at Adolescence*, Blackwell Scientific, Oxford.
6. Bland, J.M. and Altman, D.G. (1986) Statistical methods for assessing agreement between two methods of clinical measurement. *Lancet*, i, pp. 307-8.
7. Rowland, T.W., Auchinachie, J.A., Keenan, T.J. and Green, G.M. (1988) Submaximal running economy and treadmill performance in prepubertal boys. *International Journal of Sports Medicine*, Vol. 9, pp. 201-4.
8. Rowland, T.W. and Cunningham, L.N. (1992) Oxygen uptake plateau during maximal treadmill exercise in children. *Chest*, Vol. 101, pp. 485-9.
9. Unnithan, V.B., Murray, L.A., Timmons, J.A., Buchanan, D. and Paton, J.Y. (1995) Reproducibility of cardiorespiratory measurements during submaximal and maximal running in children. *British Journal of Sports Medicine*, Vol. 29, pp. 66-71.
10. Maliszewski, A.F. and Freedson, P.S. (1996) Is running economy different between adults and children? *Pediatric Exercise Science*, Vol. 8, pp. 351-60.
11. Rowland, T.W. and Green, G.M. (1988) Physiological responses to treadmill exercise in females: adult-child differences. *Medicine and Science in Sports and Exercise*, Vol. 20, pp. 474-8.
12. Morgan, D.W., Martin, P.E. and Krahenbuhl, G.S. (1989) Factors affecting running economy. *Sports Medicine*, Vol. 7, pp. 310-30.
13. Unnithan, V.B. and Eston, R.G. (1990) Stride frequency and submaximal treadmill economy in adults and children. *Pediatric Exercise Science*, Vol. 2, pp. 149-55.
14. Rowland, T.W., Auchinachie, J.A., Keenan, T.J. and Green, G.M. (1987) Physiological responses to treadmill running in adult and prepubertal males. *International Journal of Sports Medicine*, Vol. 8, pp. 292-7.
15. Davies, C.T.M. (1980) Metabolic cost of exercise and physical performance in children with some observations on external loading. *European Journal of Applied Physiology*, Vol. 45, pp. 95-102.
16. Thorstensson, A. (1986) Effects of moderate exercise loading on the aerobic demand of submaximal running in men and 10 year old boys. *European Journal of Applied Physiology*, Vol. 55, pp. 569-74.
17. Eston, R.G., Robson, S. and Winter, E.W. (1993) A comparison of oxygen uptake during running in children and adults, in *Kinanthropometry IV*, (eds. W. Duquet and J. Day), E and FN Spon, London, pp. 236-41.

OXYGEN UPTAKE DURING CONTINUOUS AND DISCRETE STEADY STATE RUNNING

Discrete and continuous running protocols

K. J. MELDRUM, J. S. CARLSON and G. A. NAUGHTON
Pediatric Exercise Research Unit, Victoria University, Melbourne, Australia
Keywords: Accumulated oxygen deficit, oxygen uptake, running protocols, steady state

Introduction

The use of submaximal steady state exercise is critical for the measurement of the accumulated oxygen deficit(AOD)[1,2]. The method requires linear regression equations to be constructed from the relationship between exercise intensity and submaximal oxygen uptake to predict exercise intensities representing relative supramaximal demands[1,2].

The method for evaluating the AOD requires the assessment of a series of submaximal steady state oxygen uptakes at various submaximal running speeds. Traditionally these tests have been conducted using discrete determinations of data points (i.e. 20 min rest between steady state performances and no more than 3 determinations per day).

The AOD method has recently been measured in preadolescent males utilising treadmill running as the mode of exercise[3]. The use of the AOD method with this population has been subjected to many criticisms. One of the major criticisms relates to the submaximal economy of children which is known to be poor when compared to that of adults during weight-bearing exercise[4]. A second criticism relates to the reliability of oxygen uptake kinetics of children over the testing period. A further disadvantage of the use of the AOD method with children, has been the need for separate and discrete determinations of steady state oxygen uptakes for subsequent AOD prediction, time consuming protocols and relatively large numbers of visits to the laboratory. Less time consuming, but reliable alternative protocols need to be developed.

Therefore the aim of this study was to compare the steady state oxygen uptake values of preadolescent males determined during continuous and discrete submaximal treadmill running protocols.

Children and Exercise XIX. Edited by Neil Armstrong, Brian Kirby and Joanne Welsman.
Published in 1997 by E & FN Spon, 2–6 Boundary Row, London, SE1 8HN.
ISBN 0 419 22100 X.

Subjects

Pre adolescent male subjects (n = 10) volunteered to participate in the exercise study. The subjects were recruited from a local school. Prior to the commencement of testing, parental consent and health risk forms were collected. Health risk forms were evaluated for potential medical conditions that may have precluded participation.

All procedures were approved by the Ethics Committee of Victoria University. Prior to the conduct of the testing the subjects attended the laboratory for familiarisation of the laboratory surrounds and instruction in treadmill running.

Methods

The first test involved a peak oxygen uptake test on a motorised treadmill. The initial speed was set at 6 km·h^{-1} with a gradient of 6%. Increments of 1 km·h^{-1} were imposed until the subject volunteered his exhaustion, and/or the criteria for peak oxygen uptake were reached[5]. Heart rate was recorded every min using a POLAR™ heart rate monitor during the peak oxygen uptake test.

In subsequent visits to the laboratory subjects undertook a series of submaximal steady state exercise tests. Sessions two and three required the subjects to participate in the discrete submaximal running tests. These running tests were of 4 to 6 min in duration at a constant grade of 6%. There was a recovery interval of at least 20 min between each run. No more than three submaximal tests were conducted on any one day. For both discrete and continuous protocols, steady state oxygen uptake was denoted as a difference in the $\dot{V}O_2$ in the last two min of each speed of the test of no greater than ± 2 mL·kg^{-1}·min^{-1}. The steady state test was terminated when the criteria for steady state oxygen uptake was met.

Session four consisted of the continuous submaximal steady state test with the subject running at identical speeds to those adopted for the discrete measures. In the continuous test however, these speeds were applied incrementally without stopping the treadmill. The oxygen uptake of the subject was required to reach steady state before the next incremental submaximal speed was imposed (3-4 min).

In order to determine each subject's relationship between steady state oxygen consumption and treadmill speed individual linear regression equations were calculated from the submaximal treadmill speeds, and their corresponding oxygen uptake values. Individual linear regression equations were calculated for both the continuous and discrete methodologies. These equations [y = a + b (x)] were subsequently used to predict running speeds which represented energy expenditure equivalent to 120% of peak oxygen uptake (supramaximal work) for AOD measurement.

Data analyses

Descriptive data were expressed as mean ± standard errors (M ± SEM). One way analysis of variance (ANOVA) was used to examine the differences in submaximal oxygen uptake between the protocols and whether significant differences existed in the prediction of the supramaximal treadmill speeds from the continuous and discrete submaximal tests. A linear regression was conducted to determine the significance of the slope of the regression line. The alpha level of 0.05 was adopted for all testing.

Results

Mean age (y), height (cm) and weight (kg) of the subjects were 10.38 ± 0.31, 152 ± 2 and 40.46 ± 2.17, respectively. The mean absolute peak oxygen uptake of the subjects was 1.66 ± 0.1 ($L\cdot min^{-1}$) and in relative terms, 64.32 ± 2.29 ($mL\cdot kg^{-1}\cdot min^{-1}$).

Table 1 represents the mean oxygen uptake values for the discrete and continuous protocols. Statistical analysis of the oxygen uptakes from the continuous and discrete protocols indicated that they were not significantly different.

Figure 1 shows the results of the linear regression equations constructed for the mean continuous and discrete oxygen uptakes. These equations were used to predict the supramaximal treadmill speeds necessary for the determination of the AOD. Mean supramaximal treadmill speeds were 11.79 ± 0.55 $km\cdot h^{-1}$ for the continuous protocol and 12.63 ± 0.44 $km\cdot h^{-1}$ for the discrete protocol. The two speeds were not different, ($p > 0.05$). There were no differences in the oxygen uptake of the subjects at the same speeds between experimental methods, ($p > 0.05$).

Discussion

There were no significant differences in the oxygen uptake of the subjects between the continuous and discrete protocols. The implications of these results with respect to the AOD method suggest that the use of a continuous protocol to determine the supramaximal exercise intensity is possible with children. The continuous method for determining supramaximal exercise intensity has been used with the adult population in the past[7,8].

Table 1. Mean oxygen uptake for continuous and discrete protocols

Speed ($km\cdot h^{-1}$)	$\dot{V}O_2$ ($mL\cdot kg^{-1}\cdot min^{-1}$)	
	Continuous	Discrete
6	30.57 ± 0.77	31.27 ± 0.76
7	39.19 ± 1.26	35.04 ± 3.94
8	45.54 ± 1.07	44.79 ± 1.16
8.5	49.02 ± 0.81	47.47 ± 1.10

Values are mean ± SEM

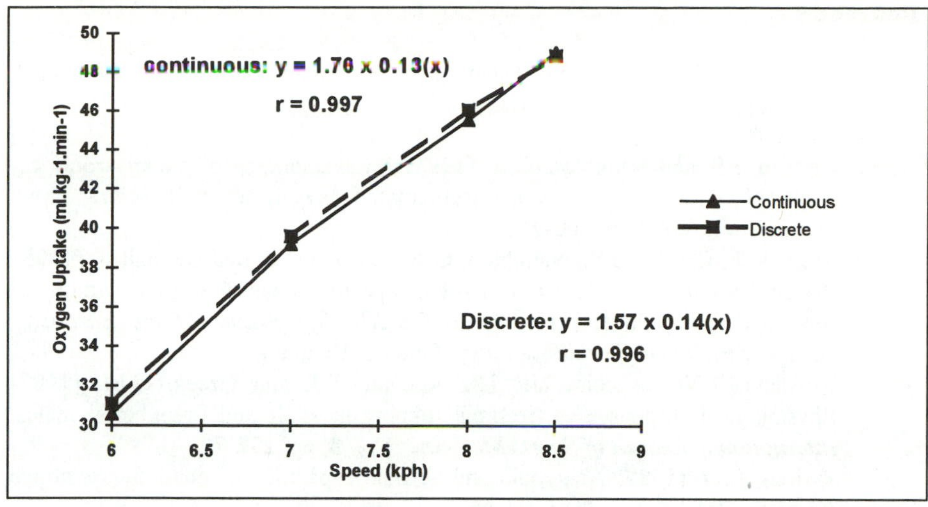

Fig. 1. Mean continuous and discrete oxygen uptake

The oxygen uptake kinetics of children when compared to those of adults have been suggested to be faster[9,10]. The authors[10] reported a shorter half time to steady state in young children with a mean age of 10.2 y. The subjects in this study reached steady state within 2-3 min. The criterion for steady state was ± 2 $mL{\cdot}kg^{-1}{\cdot}min^{-1}$ over four consecutive 15 s data points. This criterion was achieved by 98% of subjects before 3 min in the continuous steady state test. One hundred percent of subjects had reached the requirements for steady state within 4 min, under both protocols.

The use of a continuous steady state protocol, with children, may make the oxygen uptake data more acceptable for the AOD method. Studies examining the reliability of oxygen uptake in children[11] have found that the individual range of variability can be up to 8.4% between two treadmill tests at the same speed on different days. This intra-individual variability may influence the determinations of the relationship between oxygen uptake and treadmill speed in the AOD method, when a discrete protocol is used for steady state submaximal performances. When the relationship between oxygen uptake and treadmill speed from a continuous test can be conducted in one session the use of this protocol may decrease the impact of daily variation.

The use of a continuous protocol for AOD measurement would be more time efficient and decrease the average number of laboratory visits from 6 to 3. This is especially important in paediatric research where a smaller time request may result in greater motivation and programme adherence.

Future directions require an examination of the reliability of methods of measurement of submaximal oxygen uptake at various treadmill speeds.

References

1. Medbo, J.I., Mohn, A.C. and Tabata, I. (1988) Anaerobic capacity determined by maximal accumulated O_2 deficit. *Journal of Applied Physiology,* Vol. 64, pp. 50-60.
2. Carlson, J.S. and Naughton, G.A. (1993) An examination of the anaerobic capacity of children using maximal accumulated oxygen deficit. *Pediatric Exercise Science*, Vol. 5, pp. 60-71.
3. Stear, K.J., Carlson, J.S., Naughton, G.A., Buttifant, D. and Birchall, J. (1995) Pre adolescent and adolescent anaerobic capacity as measured by accumulated oxygen deficit. Paper presented to the *XIX Symposium of the European Group of Pediatric Work Physiology*, Odense, Denmark.
4. Rowland, T.W., Auchinachie, J.A. Keenan, T.J. and Green, G.M. (1987) Physiological responses to treadmill running in adult and prepubertal males. *International Journal of Sports Medicine*, Vol. 8, pp. 292-7.
5. Zwiren, L.D. (1989) Anaerobic and aerobic capacities of children. *Pediatric Exercise Science,* Vol. 1, pp. 31-44.
6. Tanner, J M. (1962) *Growth at Adolescence*, Blackwell, Oxford.
7. Gastin, P.B. and Lawson, D.L. (1994) Influence of training status on maximal accumulated oxygen deficit during all-out cycle exercise. *European Journal of Applied Physiology*, Vol. 69, pp. 321-30.
8. Gastin, P.B. and Lawson, D.L.(1994) Variable resistance all-out test to generate accumulated oxygen deficit and predict anaerobic capacity. *European Journal of Applied Physiology,* Vol. 69, pp. 331-6.
9. Sady, S. (1981) Transient oxygen uptake and heart rate responses at the onset of relative endurance exercise in prepubertal boys and adult men. *International Journal of Sports Medicine,* Vol. 2, pp. 240-4.
10. Freedson, P.S., Gilliam, T.B., Sady, S.P. and Katch, V.L. (1981) Transient $\dot{V}O_2$ characteristics in children at the onset of steady-rate exercise. *Research Quarterly for Exercise and Sport*, Vol. 52, pp. 167-73.
11. Rogers, D.M., Turley, K.R., Kujawa, K.I., Harper, K.M. and Wilmore, J.H. (1994) The reliability and variability of running economy in 7-, 8-, and 9 -year - old children. *Pediatric Exercise Science,* Vol. 6, pp. 287-96.

DEVELOPMENTAL ASPECTS OF OXYGEN UPTAKE KINETICS IN CHILDREN

Oxygen uptake kinetics in children

B.J. WHIPP
Department of Physiology, St George's Hospital Medical School, London, UK

Keywords: Excess oxygen uptake, exercise intensity domains, high-energy phosphates, oxygen deficit

Introduction

The bulk of the information regarding the control of physiological function relies in its transient, or non-steady state, response to a particular forcing regime. In the steady state of dynamic muscular exercise, for example, the oxygen uptake ($\dot{V}O_2$) response as a function of work rate is largely independent of physical "fitness" or training status, at least over the work-rate range within which there is not a sustained metabolic acidaemia (i.e. below the lactate threshold). The transient behaviour, however, is often appreciably different. In response to a square-wave or constant-load exercise bout, $\dot{V}O_2$ increases faster in "fit" or endurance-trained subjects, whereas the transient response is slower in sedentary subjects. Even at this simplified level, this response behaviour provokes two important questions:

(a) What are the physiological control mechanisms which produce the pattern of response in the non-steady state and which account for it varying with sedentarity or training?

(b) What are the consequences of the different response profiles for the demands on the energy stores which supplement the aerobic energy yield?

Kinetics

It is useful, in this regard, to consider the oxygen equivalent of the energy which was utilised during the exercise but which did not derive from reactions fuelled by atmospheric O_2 (i.e. that taken into the body after the start of the exercise). This has been termed the oxygen deficit (O_2 def), and is schematized in fig 1 with respect to both constant-load

Children and Exercise XIX. Edited by Neil Armstrong, Brian Kirby and Joanne Welsman.
Published in 1997 by E & FN Spon, 2–6 Boundary Row, London, SE1 8HN.
ISBN 0 419 22100 X.

and ramp-incremental exercise - the two most common exercising-forcing regimes used to characterise the dynamics of the $\dot{V}O_2$ response behaviour.

The ramp test offers the advantage of providing four parameters of aerobic function from a single exercise test[1]. As the test is typically performed to the limit of tolerance, it allows the maximum attainable (or at least attained) $\dot{V}O_2$ to be established, along with the estimated lactate threshold. But two other features of the ramp response prove useful and informative. The work efficiency can be estimated from the slope of the $\dot{V}O_2$ - work rate response - if an assumption is made regarding the substrate utilisation profile. This is because, for such first-order kinetics, $\dot{V}O_2$ will increase at the same rate as the steady-state response ($\dot{V}O_2 ss$)[1], as schematized in fig 1, but will lag it by the time constant of the system response (τ, which, for such a process, is the time to reach 63% of the final steady-state value), i.e.

$$\Delta \dot{V}O_2(t) = \Delta \dot{V}O_2 ss \quad \text{at} \quad (t - \tau) \tag{1}$$

where $\dot{V}O_2(t)$ is the current instantaneous $\dot{V}O_2$ value. This $\dot{V}O_2$ profile is the expected response for the moderate intensity domain. Why these response features are typically retained during heavy and severe exercise remains to be elucidated, as the response to constant-load exercise is so fundamentally different at these intensity domains.

It should be noted that quantifying the O_2 deficit requires both a precise characterisation of the non-steady-state $\dot{V}O_2$ response, and also a major assumption. In constant-load exercise the assumption is that the energy demands early in the non-steady state are precisely equivalent to those which obtain during the aerobic steady state. For the ramp, the assumption is that the steady-state O_2 demand (which can be determined rigorously under steady-state conditions over the lower work-rate range) continues to increase at the same rate throughout the entire work-rate range under consideration (usually up to maximum attainable levels).

With respect to constant-load exercise, as the muscle consumption (QO_2) is controlled by dynamic features of the high-energy phosphate pool utilisation, QO_2 expected to increase exponentially in proportion to the decrease in creatine phosphate (PCr) concentration (details of the competing theories for this control process can be found in refs[2] and[3]). This results in an exponential profile of change of $\dot{V}O_2$, i.e. its instantaneous rate of change ($d\dot{V}O_2/dt$) will be proportional to the difference between the steady-state requirement and the current instantaneous $\dot{V}O_2$ value. The proportionality constant for this relationship may be represented as k (the rate constant) or, more commonly, $1/\tau$; i.e.:

$$\Delta \dot{V}O_2(t) = \Delta \dot{V}O_2 ss(1 - e^{-t/\tau}) \tag{2}$$

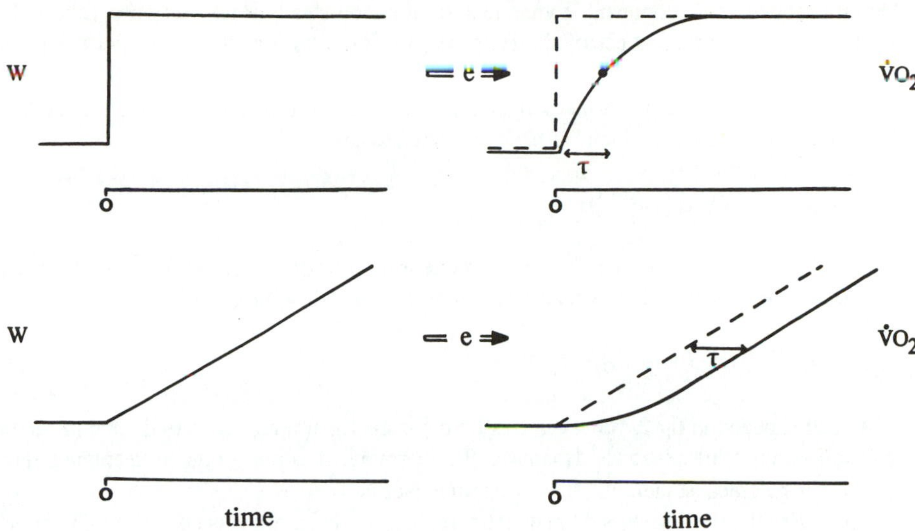

Fig. 1. Predicted first-order $\dot{V}O_2$ response profiles to constant-load exercise (upper panel) and ramp-incremental exercise (lower panel).

For a system with these response characteristics the O_2 deficit for constant-load exercise has two important features with respect both to quantitation and to plausible inferences which may be drawn from the response profile. Over the range in which steady states may be attained:

$$O_2 \text{ def} = \Delta \dot{V}O_2 \text{ ss} \cdot \tau \tag{3}$$

That is, the O_2 deficit is exclusively defined by the steady-state increment of $\dot{V}O_2$ and its time constant of response.

If, however, this profile is maintained up to a limiting $\dot{V}O_2$ value (i.e. a steady state cannot be obtained as the response is truncated by the maximum $\dot{V}O_2$ ($\dot{V}O_2$ max) being attained), then:

$$O_2 \text{ def} = \dot{V}O_2 \text{max} \cdot \tau \tag{4}$$

That is, in one intensity domain the O_2 deficit may be expected to increase as a linear function of work rate and then, in the higher-intensity domain (i.e. with $\dot{V}O_2$ requirements above $\dot{V}O_2$ max), it becomes constant, i.e. independent of further increases in work rate.

In reality, however, $\dot{V}O_2$ during constant-load exercise does not change with the simple exponential characteristics described above (fig 2). Rather, there is an early phase of $\dot{V}O_2$ (phase I) which is coupled to the increase in cardiac output prior to blood with greater O_2 extraction (as a result of the muscle contraction) reaching the lungs. During this period, $\dot{V}O_2$ is therefore predominantly a function of the cardiac output or pulmonary blood flow.

The subsequent and dominant component of the non-steady-state response (phase II) results from the further effect of the increased O_2 extraction in the blood perfusing the contracting muscles.

This two-phased feature of the non-steady-state $\dot{V}O_2$ response introduces, therefore, a delay-like component (δ) which has been characterized as:

$$\dot{V}O_2(t) = \Delta\dot{V}O_2 ss \, (1-e^{(t-\delta)/\tau}) \quad (5)$$

Eq. (5) not only provides a "better" characterisation of the response dynamics than eq. (2), but also allows an accurate quantification of the O_2 deficit, i.e.:

$$O_2 \text{ def} = \Delta\dot{V}O_2 ss \cdot (\tau + \delta) \quad (6)$$

As schematized in fig 2, however, this time constant is not an accurate depiction of the real non-steady-state response dynamics. Furthermore, it is important to recognise that, from a physiological standpoint, this δ is entirely factitious.

Consequently, those interested in quantifying the O_2 deficit may use either eq. (3) or eq. (6) for accurate quantification. Those interested in the control of the non-steady state $\dot{V}O_2$ dynamics, however, need a more precise characterisation of the response as eqs. (3) and (6) are misleading. Two approaches have been made to this problem. Hughson and his associates[4] have attempted to characterise the entire non-steady response with a model requiring six parameters (i.e. two delay terms, two time constants and two proportional gains). However, Whipp et al.[5] have proposed the strategy of deleting the "cardio-dynamic" phase I $\dot{V}O_2$ component from the exponential fit, as there is no sufficiently-sound evidence to support the exponentiality of the phase I component. Both these approaches, however, support the important concept that inferences for the control of $\dot{V}O_2$ during the non-steady state of muscular exercise require fitting procedures that appropriately characterise the time constant of the phase II $\dot{V}O_2$ response. The O_2 deficit, on the other hand, can be rigorously quantified by simpler strategies such as characterized by eqs. (3) and (6).

The sum of τ + δ in eqs. (5) and (6) has been termed the mean response time (MRT) or the "effective" time constant (τ). As discussed below, the distinction between the actual τ and the τ' or MRT for the entire response has major implications for the inferences which can be drawn from the dynamics.

The O_2 deficit may be computed as the steady-state increment in $\dot{V}O_2$ required for the task, multiplied by the effective time constant, i.e.:

$$O_2 \text{ def} = \Delta\dot{V}O_2 ss \cdot \tau' \quad (7)$$

And as $\Delta\dot{V}O_2 ss$ as a function of work rate is not appreciably different between children and adults (at least at work rates which do not engender a metabolic acidaemia), the O_2 deficit for a given work rate and the kinetics of the dynamic response are inextricably linked. It is therefore instructive to consider the source and potential magnitude of the physiological determinants of the O_2 deficit. Over the moderate work-rate range in which

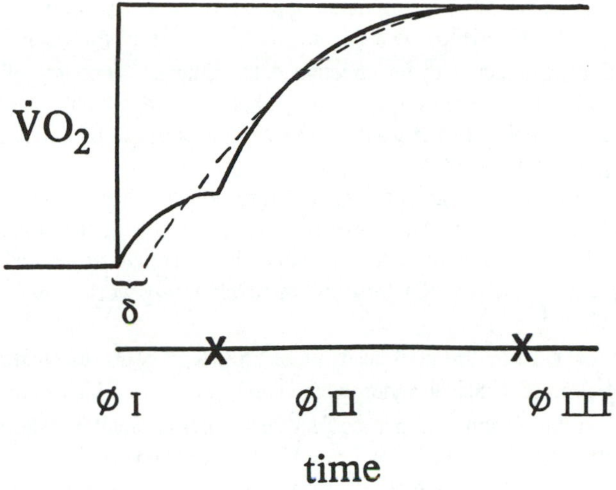

Fig. 2. Schematic of the measured $\dot{V}O_2$ response profile to moderate constant-load exercise (solid line) and the best-fit monoexponential with delay.

arterial blood [lactate] does not increase appreciably, the O_2 deficit is determined by the available high-energy phosphate stores and the usable O_2 stores.

Firstly, consider an adult: the intramuscular PCr stores are some 20-22 mmol·kg^{-1} (wet wt) which, at maximum exercise, may fall to levels as low as 2 mmol·kg^{-1}. Taking the muscle mass of the knee extensors to be some 5 kg (double that estimated in the one-legged knee-extensor exercise experiments of Andersen and Saltin[6]), a value double this for the muscle mass utilised during cycle ergometry would be reasonable. Consequently, 10 kg muscle mass with a PCr pool being depleted by some 20 mmol·kg^{-1} results in approximately 200 mmol of high-energy phosphate being available for the deficit. (ATP concentrations, which are normally only one-quarter that of PCr in human muscle, do not decrease appreciably until extremely high work rates.) Consequently, as $\sim P:O_2 = 6$, this results in approximately 33 mmol of O_2 equivalent and, as each mmol of O_2 is equivalent to 22.4 mL, then the O_2 equivalent of the total depletable high-energy phosphate pool is approximately 750 mL. The other alactic source of the O_2 deficit is the O_2 taken from the O_2 stores. As the O_2 solubility is low in plasma and muscle water (approximately 0.6 mL·L^{-1} muscle water · 20 mm Hg reduction in muscle tissue PO_2). This can be considered to be a trace quantity compared with the amount of O_2 used in the transient that is manifest as the reduction in mixed venous O_2 content.

Considering an adult with a 3 L venous blood volume, and a reduction in mixed venous O_2 content from 150 mL·L^{-1} at rest to some 50 mL·L^{-1} during high-intensity exercise, then the deficit equivalent of the usable O_2 stores will be (3 L x 100 mL·L^{-1}), giving a total of 300 mL. The myoglobin in the red muscle fibres, with its P_{50} of 2.5-3.0 mm Hg at physiological temperatures[7], is unlikely to contribute to this value until high levels of exercise. And then, assuming that half of the total available myoglobin, at 25 $mg{\cdot}g^{-1}$ dry wt[8], in 10 kg of skeletal muscle (being liberal and assuming the mass all to be "red") is depleted of its O_2, this would only contribute approximately 40 mL of O_2 to the deficit. Consequently, the total O_2 deficit available for such exercise in the adult is only of the order of 1 L. For a subject with an effective $\dot{V}O_2$ time constant (τ') of 30 s, this is equivalent to a work rate of approximately 200 W before the depletable alactic sources of O_2 deficit are, in fact, depleted. For a subject with a time constant of 1 min, naturally, this would occur at approximately 100 W.

In a child, the available high-energy phosphate stores are less than the adult as a result of the smaller muscle mass, and the O_2 stores are less as a result of the smaller blood and hence venous pool blood volume. The depletable alactic deficit stores will therefore be smaller, making anaerobiosis obligatory at relatively low work rates unless τ' is appropriately small.

Establishing τ or τ' from the non-steady-state profile of $\dot{V}O_2$ in children, however, demands a high degree of technical rigour, as the confidence with which τ can be estimated depends, in part, on the response amplitude ($\Delta \dot{V}O_2 ss$): this is small in children, especially within the intensity domain for which first-order kinetics are likely to obtain.

Cooper and his associates[9] attempted to provide a complete profile of the aerobic parameters of exercise as a function of body size during growth in children using ramp-incremental exercise. They utilised 109 healthy children in the age range 6-17 y, of whom 51 were girls and 58 boys. In addition to determining the peak $\dot{V}O_2$ and lactate threshold and estimating the work efficiency, they also determined the effective time constant of the $\dot{V}O_2$ response. They determined that the lactate threshold, estimated from pulmonary gas-exchange variables, as a fraction of the peak $\dot{V}O_2$ was independent of body weight in both boys and girls (fig 3). Others, however, have proposed that this ratio is high in young children and decreases with age[10-12].

With respect to the kinetics of $\dot{V}O_2$, Cooper et al.[9] found that the mean response time (estimated from ramp-incremental exercise) was independent of body weight in the children and adolescents, with a mean value of 43 ± 15 s. This is not significantly different from that of healthy young adults [4,5].

These authors further investigated the kinetics of the $\dot{V}O_2$ response in children[13]. In this study, they established the actual, rather than the effective, time constant of response (i.e. by deleting the first 20 s of the $\dot{V}O_2$ response from their model fit) utilising multiple repetitions of identical constant-load exercise bouts to improve the confidence of the estimate of exponentiality and also constraining the bout to be below the subjects' lactate threshold. They were able to show that there was no difference between the kinetics of $\dot{V}O_2$ during the on-transient of exercise between the 7-9-year-old children and the 15-18 year-old teenagers, having $\tau \dot{V}O_2$ values of 27 and 28 s, respectively (fig 4) - although the older girls had significantly longer time constants than did the other groups. But, as this group had a significantly lower peak $\dot{V}O_2 \cdot kg^{-1}$, this suggested to the authors that the longer time constants were reflective of lower "fitness" than the other groups[13], as fitness and endurance training are both known to result in faster $\dot{V}O_2$ kinetics.

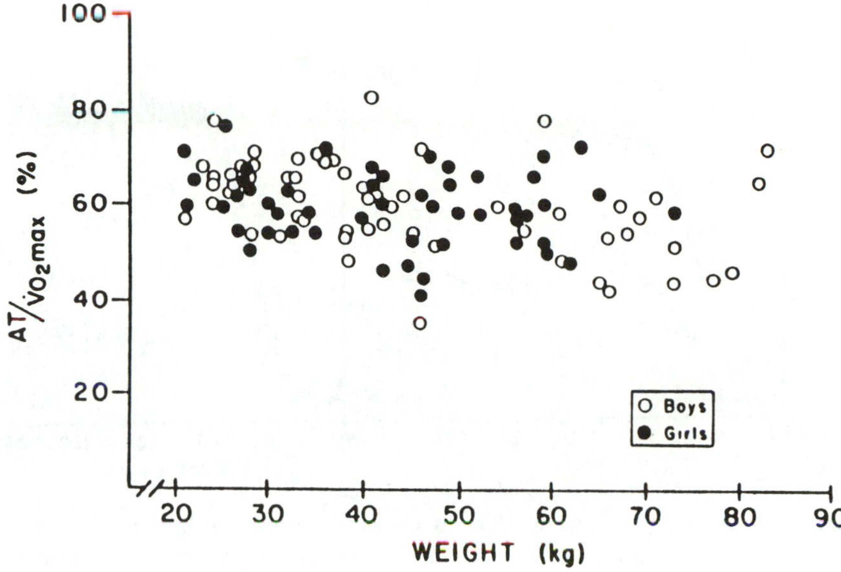

Fig. 3. Ratio of lactate (anaerobic) threshold to maximal $\dot{V}O_2$ (AT/$\dot{V}O_2$max) expressed as a function of body weight in a group of normal children (n = 109). Reproduced from Ref.[9], with permission.

The results of Cooper et al.[13] are similar to those of Sady et al.[14], who found that the half-time (t½) value for $\dot{V}O_2$ for exercise at approximately 40% of peak $\dot{V}O_2$ (i.e. plausibly below the lactate threshold) was not significantly different between children and adults. The values averaged 18.5 and 17.4 s, respectively. And as τ = 1.44 x t½ for a mono-exponential process, this would be equivalent to 26.6 and 25 s for the time constants.

These values agree closely with the values of 26.5 and 28 s reported by Cooper et al. [13] for their "youngest" subjects (8.6 $\pm$ 0.9 y) and "older" subjects (17.4 $\pm$ 1.1 y), respectively. Freedson et al.[15] also studied the dynamics of the $\dot{V}O_2$ response in 28 children (mean age 10.2 y) using constant-load exercise at 59 W. This represented 60.8%of the peak $\dot{V}O_2$ for the entire group; the intensity, however, is likely to have varied among individual subjects. This is at, or close to, the expected lactate threshold for this age group (see fig 3, for example). These authors could also discern no difference in the dynamics of the response in their children compared to other data for adults exercising at similar intensities.

However, while the results of Cooper et al.[13], Sady et al.[14] and Freedson et al.[15] support the hypothesis that the kinetics of $\dot{V}O_2$ for sub-threshold exercise are independent of size and age during growth, it is important to recognise that their results appear to differ from those of Macek and Vavra[16] who demonstrated that the $\dot{V}O_2$ transient during constant-load exercise was faster in 10-11 year-old boys than in 20-22 year-old men. There is, however, an important procedural difference in these studies. The study of Macek and

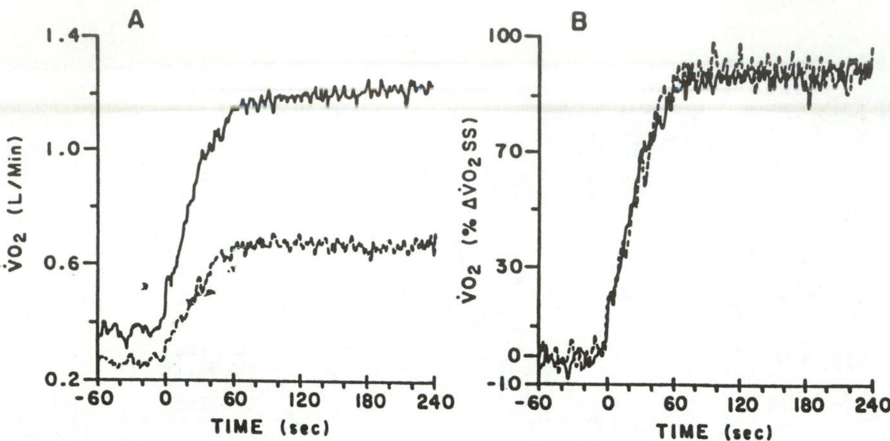

Fig. 4. Group mean response of $\dot{V}O_2$ to moderate constant-load exercise in young subjects (7-9 y) (dashed lines) and older subjects (15-18 y) (solid lines): absolute responses (A), normalized responses (B). Reproduced from Ref.[13], with permission.

Vavra[16] utilised work rates of 90-100% peak $\dot{V}O_2$, resulting in exhaustion in 4-5 min. These results are therefore similar to those of Sady[17] who demonstrated that 10 year-old boys had a quicker $\dot{V}O_2$ response at the onset of exercise than adult men (mean age 30 y) exercising at work rates requiring supra-maximal $\dot{V}O_2$. In contrast, Zanconato et al.[18] reported no differences in the t½ of the $\dot{V}O_2$ response to 1 min of exercise between 10 children (7-11 y) and 13 adults (26-42 y).

However, the t½ or τ of the $\dot{V}O_2$ response to a system-limited (i.e. peak $\dot{V}O_2$) value is fraught with complexities regarding the model assumptions. The asymptotic requirement for $\dot{V}O_2$ naturally increases progressively with increasing work rate: if the on-transient $\dot{V}O_2$ kinetics were independent of work rate, as was evident at the off transient[13], then the t½ (to the peak $\dot{V}O_2$) would necessarily increase with increasing work rate. In fact, for low work rates (requiring an increment of steady-state $\dot{V}O_2$ which is less than half the peak increment), the actual $\dot{V}O_2$ would never attain the t½ value.

The off-transient data of Zanconato et al.[18] demonstrated that $\tau\dot{V}O_2$ was less in children than in adults (but only, significantly, in response to a supra-maximal work rate) although with the cumulative O_2 cost of the 1 min exercise bout and subsequent recovery (mL $O_2 \cdot J^{-1}$) was higher. This was a consequence of the higher relative $\Delta\dot{V}O_2$ss values in the children, at this intensity. Paterson and Whipp[19] and Gerbino et al.[20] have demonstrated dynamic asymmetries of the $\dot{V}O_2$ kinetics between the on- and off-transient in adults. Whether this also obtains in children remains to be determined. But, regardless, inferences for the on-transient from the off-transient response therefore should be made with caution.

In comparing the results of studies on children, therefore, it is important to consider the role of the intensity domain within which the $\dot{V}O_2$ kinetics are determined. On careful analysis of the dynamics, there is general agreement (for adults, at least) that first-order kinetics for $\dot{V}O_2$ are only manifest at work rates which do not engender a sustained lactic acidaemia. At higher work rates, the steady state for $\dot{V}O_2$ in response to constant-load exercise is delayed as a consequence of the addition of a slow phase of the kinetics (fig 5).

The supra-threshold work-rate range within which steady states of $\dot{V}O_2$ can be attained appears to correlate with the work-rate range over which blood [lactate] and [H^+] do not continue to increase throughout the work rate. This is sometimes termed the maximum lactate steady state (MLSS). The data of Poole et al.[21] suggest that the work-rate equivalent of the MLSS coincides with the asymptote of the subject's power-duration curve (this has been termed the "critical power" or "fatigue threshold"). Little is known about this in children, however.

At even higher work rates, steady states of O_2 uptake are not attained; $\dot{V}O_2$ typically continues to increase to its peak or maximum value (fig 5).

As the kinetics of $\dot{V}O_2$ are likely to be different in these work-intensity domains in children (as they have been demonstrated to be in adults), resolving these kinetic control issues presents a formidable technical challenge. As the ratio of the lactate threshold to peak $\dot{V}O_2$ has been shown to be largely independent of size and growth [9] or is even higher in children[10,22], the absolute difference (Δ) will be progressively less the younger and smaller is the child. The absolute work-rate equivalents of these intensity domains, therefore, will be very small, presenting a challenge to the technique for discriminating the kinetic features. Elucidating finer details of the dynamic $\dot{V}O_2$ response to muscular exercise may therefore require precise placement of the particular work rate in a given intensity domain (small in children), and also require confidence limits on the estimated dynamic parameters to ensure that a statistically justifiable discrimination is used to justify apparent differences.

Several features of the dynamics of the $\dot{V}O_2$ response at high work rates are emerging, however. Beneke et al.[23], for example, have carefully determined the MLSS throughout the second decade of life. Their results show that the MLSS appeared to be independent of age and occurred at a value of approximately 4 $mmol{\cdot}L^{-1}$. This is similar to the average value found in adults - although marked individual differences are apparent in both groups. The work rate at which MLSS occurred, however, increased as a linear function of age [23].

Other authors have found that a 4 $mmol{\cdot}L^{-1}$ value is too high for a representative MLSS in children. Williams and Armstrong[24] propose that 2.5 $mmol{\cdot}L^{-1}$ is a better value for children, i.e. consistent with the previous demonstration by Williams et al. [25] that the 4 $mmol{\cdot}L^{-1}$ value occurred, on average, at greater than 90% of peak $\dot{V}O_2$ in 103 children (53 boys, 50 girls) aged 11-13 y. These issues underscore the importance of the intensity domain within which the $\dot{V}O_2$ kinetics are considered for a particular, rather than the mean or modally-representative subject (child or adult).

Asano and Hirakoba[26], Macek and Vavra[16] and Rowland and Rimany[27] have all considered the slow phase of the $\dot{V}O_2$ kinetics. At work rates equivalent to some 60-65% of peak $\dot{V}O_2$, there was no difference in the magnitude of the slow phase (sometimes

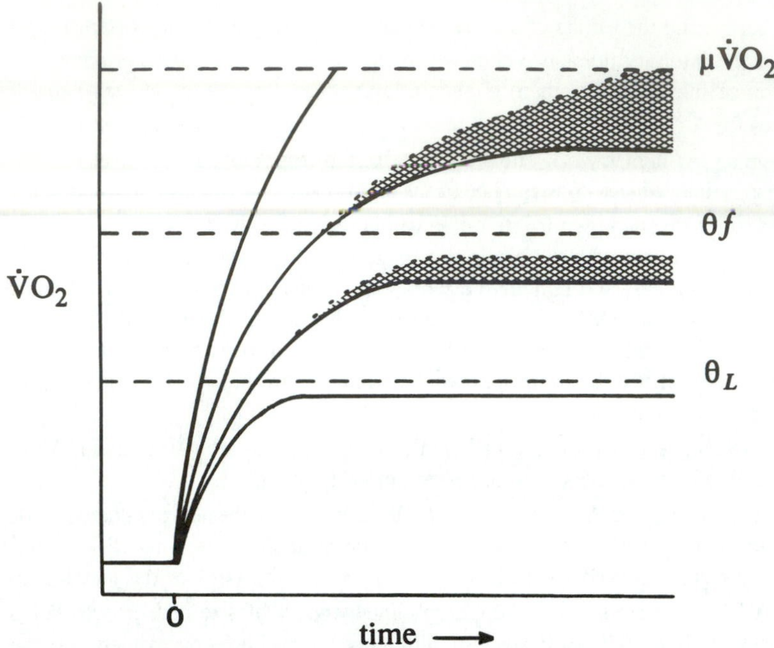

Fig. 5. Schematic representation of the temporal response of peak $\dot{V}O_2$ to constant-load exercise at different work intensities (from below, upwards): moderate, below the lactate threshold (θL); heavy, above θL, with $\dot{V}O_2$ reaching a steady state but with a delayed time course because of a component of "excess" $\dot{V}O_2$ (stippled area); very heavy, above the critical power or "fatigue threshold" (θf), with a component of "excess" $\dot{V}O_2$ that leads $\dot{V}O_2$ to attain the maximum $\dot{V}O_2$ ($\mu\dot{V}O_2$) despite the steady state value predicted from a first-order response being sub-maximal; and severe, a supra-maximal work rate where fatigue occurs so rapidly that the excess $\dot{V}O_2$ component has not had time to develop discernibly.

termed O_2 "drift") between boys (age range 10-14 y) and adult males, and between premenarcheal girls (mean age 11.4 y) and adult women. The mean increase in $\dot{V}O_2$ between boys aged 10 y and men aged 40-60 y was 8-11% among the studies, with no differences between the children and adults.

In contrast, however, Armon et al.[28] have demonstrated that the amplitude of the early exponential increase in $\dot{V}O_2$ during high-intensity exercise is actually greater in children than in adults. However, this was associated with the additional increment in $\dot{V}O_2$ ("excess" $\dot{V}O_2$) being less than in the adult (fig 6). Their finding of the high O_2 cost of the work in children supports the previous results of Zancanato et al [18].

Zancanato et al.[29] also recently addressed the issue of the changes in the intramuscular determinants of $\dot{V}O_2$ during exercise by establishing the profiles of [inorganic phosphate] (Pi) to [PCr] (Pi/PCr) and pH in the calf muscle of children and adults performing progressive (plantar flexion) exercise using ^{31}P magnetic resonance (MR) spectroscopy.

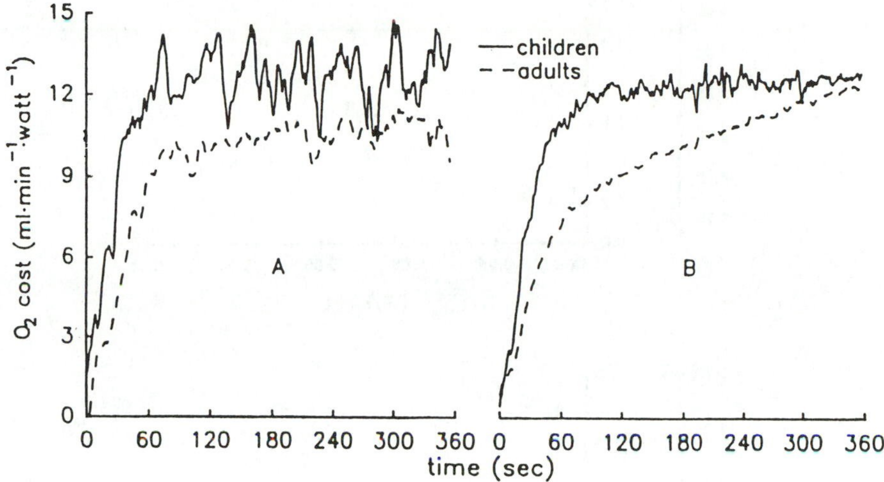

Fig. 6. Group mean O_2 cost of constant-load exercise below the lactate threshold (A) and above the lactate threshold (B) in children (solid lines) and adults (dashed lines). Reproduced from Ref.[28], with permission.

As shown in fig 7, these authors demonstrated a slow and a fast phase of both the Pi/PCr increase and the pH decrease in 75% of the adults and 50% of the children. The initial linear slopes, however, were not different between the children and adults. This is consistent with the determinants of the early $\dot{V}O_2$ kinetics not being discernibly different between the children and the adults. However, the subsequent more-rapid rate of change was appreciably greater in the adults than in the children. The intramuscular pH was higher, and the Pi/PCr ratios lower, in children compared with adults. This is consistent with the numerous reports of the relatively low blood lactate response to high-intensity exercise in children. Kuno and his associates[30] have also presented evidence of a reduced muscle glycolytic ability during exhaustive exercise in children compared with adults, using ^{31}P MR spectroscopy.

Cooper and Barstow[31], in recent review of the available evidence on both gas-exchange dynamics and intramuscular high-energy phosphate kinetics during high-intensity exercise, have concluded that: "Muscle high-energy phosphate kinetics during high-intensity exercise is different between children and adults. In this range of work children seem to rely less on anaerobic glycolytic metabolism than adults do".

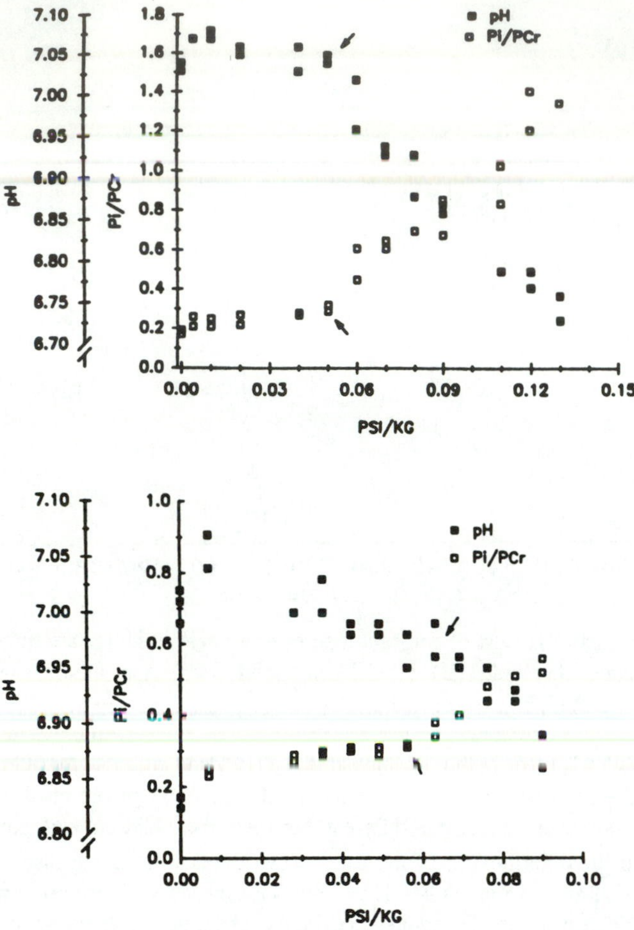

Fig. 7. Responses of intramuscular Pi/PCr and pH to incremental exercise in an adult (above) and a child (below), measured by MR spectroscopy. Reproduced from Ref.[29], with permission.

Conclusion

While there appears to be no reason to suppose that the fundamental mechanisms which control the O_2 utilisation dynamics in response to moderate muscular exercise are different in children than in adults, the control mechanisms at higher work rates are by no means as clear. There is evidence, for example, to suggest that the slow phase of the $\dot{V}O_2$ kinetics which induces an "excess $\dot{V}O_2$" (i.e. above that projected from the sub-threshold steady-state $\dot{V}O_2$ - work rate relationship or inferred from the ramp response slope) is similar in children and adults. The detailed kinetic analysis of Armon et al.[28] is consistent with children having an unusually small proportional range between their "critical power" or MLSS and their $\dot{V}O_2$ max, compared with adults (e.g. compare figs 5 and 6). This would be compatible with the reports of relatively low maximal lactate values during exercise in children and the suggestion that anaerobic potential exhibits maturational features. Further advances in understanding the control of $\dot{V}O_2$ kinetics at high work rates in children seem therefore to require careful attention to the intensity domain under consideration. Group mean response profiles of children exercising at a range of different intensities are likely to distort the particular patterns of $\dot{V}O_2$ from which control inferences are drawn.

References

1. Whipp, B.J., Davis, J.A., Torres, F. and Wasserman, K. (1981) A test to determine the parameters of aerobic function during exercise. *Journal of Applied Physiology*, Vol. 50, pp. 217-21.
2. Kushmerick, M.J., Meyer, R.A. and Brown, T.R. (1992) Regulation of oxygen consumption in fast- and slow-twitch muscle. *American Journal of Physiology*, Vol. 263, pp. C598-606.
3. Chance B., Leigh, J.S. Jr., Clark, B.J., Maris, J., Kent, J., Nioka, S. and Smith, D. (1985) Control of oxidative metabolism and oxygen delivery in human skeletal muscle: a steady-state analysis of the work/energy cost transfer function. *Proceedings of the National Academy of Sciences*, Vol. 82, pp. 8384-8.
4. Hughson, R.L. (1990) Exploring cardiorespiratory control mechanisms through gas exchange dynamics. *Medicine and Science in Sports Exercise*, Vol. 22, pp. 72-9.
5. Whipp, B.J., Ward, S.A., Lamarra, N., Davis, J.A. and Wasserman, K. (1982) Parameters of ventilatory and gas exchange dynamics during exercise. *Journal of Applied Physiology*, Vol. 52, pp. 1506-13.
6. Andersen, P. and Saltin, B. (1985) Maximal perfusion of skeletal muscle in man. *Journal of Physiology (London)*, Vol. 366, pp. 233-49.
7. Schenkman, K.A., Marble, D.R., Burns, D.H. and Feigl, E.O. (1997) Myoglobin oxygen dissociation by multiwavelength spectroscopy. *Journal of Applied Physiology*, Vol. 68, pp. 2369-72.
8. Terrados, N., Jansson, E., Sylven, C. and Kaijser, L. (1990) Hypoxia as a stimulus for synthesis of oxidative enzymes and myoglobin? *Journal of Applied Physiology*, Vol. 68, pp. 2369-72.
9. Cooper, D.M., Weiler-Ravell, D., Whipp, B.J. and Wasserman, K. (1984) Aerobic parameters of exercise as a function of body size during growth in children. *Journal of Applied Physiology*, Vol. 56, pp. 628-34.
10. Kanaley, J.A. and Boileau, R.A. (1988) The onset of the anaerobic threshold at three stages of physical maturity. *Journal of Sports Medicine and Physical Fitness*, Vol. 28, pp. 367-74.
11. Girandola. R.N., Wisewell, R.A., Frische, E. and Wood, K. (1981) $\dot{V}O_2$ and anaerobic threshold in pre- and post-pubescent girls. *Medicine and Sport*, Vol. 14, pp. 151-61.

12. Rowland, T.W. and Green, G.M. (1988) Physiological responses to treadmill exercise in females: adult-child differences. *Medicine and Science in Sports and Exercise*, Vol. 20, pp. 4474-88.
13. Cooper, D.M., Berry, C., Lamarra, N. and Wasserman, K. (1985) Kinetics of oxygen uptake and heart rate at onset of exercise in children. *Journal of Applied Physiology*, Vol. 59, pp. 211-7.
14. Sady, S.P., Katch, V.L., Villanacci, J.F. and Gilliam, T.B. (1983) Children-adult comparisons of oxygen uptake and heart rate kinetics during submaximum exercise. *Research Quarterly*, Vol. 54, pp. 55-9.
15. Freedson, P.S., Gilliam, T.B., Sady, S.P. and Katch, V.L. (1981) Transient $\dot{V}O_2$ characteristics in children at the onset of steady-rate exercise. *Research Quarterly*, Vol. 52, pp. 167-73.
16. Macek, M. and Vavra, J. (1980) The adjustment of oxygen uptake at the onset of exercise: a comparison between prepubertal boys and young adults. *International Journal of Sports Medicine*, Vol. 1, pp. 75-7.
17. Sady, S.P. (1981) Transient oxygen uptake and heart rate response at the onset of relative endurance exercise in prepubertal boys and adult men. *International Journal of Sports Medicine*, Vol. 2, pp. 240-4.
18. Zanconato, S., Cooper, D.M. and Armon, Y. (1991) Oxygen cost and oxygen uptake dynamics and recovery with one minute of exercise in children and adults. *Journal of Applied Physiology*, Vol. 71, pp. 993-8.
19. Paterson, D.H. and Whipp, B.J. (1991) Asymmetries of oxygen uptake transients at the on- and off-set of heavy exercise in humans. *Journal of Physiology (London)*, Vol. 443, pp. 575-86.
20. Gerbino, A., Ward, S.A. and Whipp, B.J. (1996) Effects of prior exercise on pulmonary gas exchange kinetics during high-intensity exercise in humans. *Journal of Applied Physiology*, Vol. 80, pp. 99-107.
21. Poole, D.C., Ward, S.A., Gardner, G.W. and Whipp, B.J. (1988) Metabolic and respiratory profile of the upper limit for prolonged exercise in man. *Ergonomics*, Vol. 31, pp. 1265-79.
22. Vanden Eynde, B., Van Gerven, D., Vienne, D., Vuylsteke-Wauters, M. and Ghesquiere, J. (1989) Endurance fitness and peak height velocity in Belgian boys, in *Children and Exercise*, (eds, S. Oseid and K.-H. Carlson), Human Kinetics, Champaign, Il, pp. 19-26.
23. Beneke, R., Heck, H., Schwarz, V. and Leithauser, R. (1996) Maximal lactate steady state during the second decade of age. *Medicine and Science in Sports and Exercise*, Vol. 28, pp. 1474-8.
24. Williams, J.R. and Armstrong, N. (1991) Relationship of maximal lactate steady state to performance at fixed blood lactate reference values in children. *Pediatric Exercise Science*, Vol. 3, pp. 333-41.
25. Williams, J.R., Armstrong, N. and Kirby, B.J. (1990) The 4mM blood lactate level as an index of exercise performance in 11-13 year old children. *Journal of Sport Science*, Vol. 8, pp. 139-47.
26. Asano, K. and Hirakoba, K. (1984) Respiratory and circulatory adaptation during prolonged exercise in 10-12 year old children and in adults, in *Child and Sport*, (eds, J. Ilmarinen and I. Valimaki), Springer-Verlag, Berlin, pp. 119-28.

27. Rowland, T.W. and Rimany, T.A. (1990) Physiological responses to prolonged exercise in premenarcheal and adult females. *Pediatric Exercise Science*, Vol. 7, pp. 183-91.
28. Armon, Y., Cooper, D.M., Flores, R., Zanconato, S. and Barstow, T.J. (1991) Oxygen uptake dynamics during high-intensity exercise in children and adults. *Journal of Applied Physiology*, Vol. 26, pp. 841-8.
29. Zanconato, S., Buchtal, S., Barstow, T.J. and Cooper, D.M. (1993) ^{31}P-magnetic resonance spectroscopy of leg muscle metabolism during exercise in children and adults. *Journal of Applied Physiology*, Vol. 74, pp. 2214-8.
30. Kuno, S., Takahashi, H., Fujimoto, K., Akima, H., Miyamaru, M., Nemoto, I., Itai, Y. and Katsuta, S. (1995) Muscle metabolism during exercise using phosphorus-31 nuclear magnetic resonance spectroscopy in adolescents. *European Journal of Applied Physiology*, Vol. 70, pp. 301-4.
31. Cooper, D.M. and Barstow, T.J. (1996) Magnetic resonance imaging and spectroscopy in studying exercise in children. *Exercise and Sport Sciences Reviews*, Vol. 24, pp. 475-99.

RESPONSE OF CHILDREN AND ADOLESCENTS TO ONSET OF EXERCISE

Children's transient oxygen uptake response

W.F. RINER, M. McCARTHY, L.V. DeCILLIS and D.S. WARD
Centre for Developmental Exercise and Nutrition Research, University of South Carolina, Lancaster, USA
Keywords: Oxygen transients, peak oxygen uptake

Introduction

During the years of growth and development, the respiratory gas exchange system of children is required to meet varying metabolic demands, as is the adult system. The exact cellular events and cardiorespiratory adjustments that affect this adaptation in children are, however, less well understood than the adult mechanisms. The short duration activity patterns typical of children's play do suggest that the maturing metabolic system is capable of rapidly accommodating work of high intensity. Previous studies have investigated the response of children during the initial stage of exercise. Some suggest that the time course of oxygen uptake ($\dot{V}O_2$) at the onset of constant load work is similar for children and adults[1,2]. Cooper and colleagues[3] also demonstrated no apparent difference in $\dot{V}O_2$ at the onset of constant load work in prepubescent children compared to adolescents. In contrast, other investigators[4,5] have reported a faster $\dot{V}O_2$ response in children at the onset of maximal exercise when compared to adults. Macek and Vavra[4] have speculated that this observed difference between children and adults may mean that children have fewer available glycolytic enzymes, resulting in lower anaerobic capability, or that the rapid onset of aerobic adaptation makes an anaerobic response less critical.

Previous studies of the response of children to the initial stages of exercise have not compared the effect of various levels of exercise intensity. Most have utilized submaximal exercise intensities[1,3,4]. The studies that involved maximal or supramaximal exercise intensities[2,5] did not compare lower intensities. All previous investigations have been conducted using cycle ergometers, which generally elicit lower levels of $\dot{V}O_2$ than treadmill exercise.

Children and Exercise XIX. Edited by Neil Armstrong, Brian Kirby and Joanne Welsman.
Published in 1997 by E & FN Spon, 2–6 Boundary Row, London, SE1 8HN.
ISBN 0 419 22100 X.

Table 1. Subject characteristics

Group	n	Age (y)	Height (cm)	Weight (kg)	Peak oxygen uptake ($mL{\cdot}kg^{-1}{\cdot}min^{-1}$)
Prepubescent Boys	5	9.2 ± 2.6	137.2 ± 14.7	37.86 ± 16.44	49.64 ± 4.90
Prepubescent Girls	8	8.5 ± 1.6	135.2 ± 11.6	35.92 ± 12.02	44.20 ± 4.25
Adolescent Boys	6	14.2 ± 0.9	174.1 ± 8.8	62.23± 11.24	58.33 ± 5.90*
Adolescent Girls	6	17.2 ± 1.0	165.1 ± 2.7	57.37 ± 10.80	43.20 ± 4.96

Values are mean ± SD
Level of signficance *$p < 0.05$ (significantly greater than the other groups)

The current study was designed to describe the response of $\dot{V}O_2$ to the onset of constant load treadmill walking at exercise intensities equivalent to approximately 85 and 100 percent of aerobic capacity in prepubescent and adolescent boys and girls.

Subjects

Twenty-five children and adolescents volunteered to participate in this investigation. Assignment to the adolescent groups was contingent upon the occurrence of menarche in girls and on the basis of Tanner's[6] indices in the boys. Informed consent was obtained from both the participants and their respective parent/guardian. The study was approved by the USC Lancaster Ethics/Human Subjects Committee. No compensation was provided to the subjects for their participation. The descriptive characteristics of the subjects are provided in table 1.

Methods

Peak oxygen uptake (peak $\dot{V}O_2$) was determined by standard open circuit spirometric methods using Applied Electrochemistry oxygen and carbon dioxide analyzers, a data processing system (Fitness Industries Technologies, Inc) and the 3 min treadmill protocol of Skinner et al.[7] (constant 3.5 mph, beginning at 10% grade with 2.5% increase every 2 minutes until volitional exhaustion). A 3 min warm-up period at 2.5 mph/5% grade preceded the protocol. Subjects were encouraged to continue until they could no longer maintain the treadmill pace. A second test was conducted, within 2 wk of the first, for the purpose of establishing the reliability of the protocol.

Subsequently, two visits to the laboratory involved a 5 min treadmill effort intended to elicit either 100% (max) or 85% (submax) of the previously determined peak $\dot{V}O_2$. Treadmill speed was constant at 3.5 mph, while the grade was adjusted to a level corresponding to the appropriate $\dot{V}O_2$ from the subject's peak $\dot{V}O_2$ determination. The test was preceded by a 5 min period of data collection while sitting quietly to establish resting $\dot{V}O_2$ level. During both tests the open circuit spirometric system was used to collect 10 s samples of expired air and ventilatory volumes, providing data for the assessment of the subjects response to the onset of exercise. A final laboratory visit was for the purpose of completing a randomly selected repeat of either the 100 or 85% exercise intensities in order to test the reliability of the protocols.

Results

Maximal treadmill test

Table 1 contains the results of the determination of peak $\dot{V}O_2$. Mean peak heart rate was 200.4 ± 1.7 beats·min^{-1}, with no significant difference between groups. Mean peak respiratory exchange ratio (RER) was 1.02 ± 0.01, again with no difference between groups. It was therefore concluded that valid measures of peak $\dot{V}O_2$ were obtained. Test-retest results revealed no significant differences, indicating reliability of the measurement methods.

Response to onset of exercise

The steady state $\dot{V}O_2$ values and the respective exercise intensities achieved are presented in table 2. The steady state value was taken as the average of five 10 s samples following the point at which the response curve plateaued.

Table 2. Steady state oxygen uptake and relative exercise intensity

Group	Steady State ($\dot{V}O_2$) mL·min^{-1} Max	Steady State ($\dot{V}O_2$) mL·min^{-1} Submax	Relative Intensity % Peak Max	Relative Intensity % Peak Submax
Prepubescent Boys	1936.4 ± 662.4 [1]	1455.2 ± 697.2[1]	102.1 ± 5.9	84.1 ± 15.9
Prepubescent Girls	1628.9 ± 502.4	1293.0 ± 393.3	102.2 ± 9.2	88.4 ± 9.1
Adolescent Boys	3584.6 ± 685.1 [1,2]	3027.3 ± 574.2[1,2]	103.1 ± 6.1	84.9 ± 4.1
Adolescent Girls	2534.5 ± 439.5[2]	2147.5 ± 477.8[2]	100.3 ± 9.1	84.7 ± 11.1

Values are mean ± SD

[1]Values for boys significantly greater than those for girls ($p < 0.05$)

[2]Values for adolescent boys and girls significantly greater than those for children ($p < 0.05$)

Table 3. Characteristics of response to onset of exercise

Group	Load	Linear Regression Slope $\dot{V}O_2$ mL·min^{-1}	Linear Regression $T_{1/2}$ to Steady State (s)	Exponential Regression $T_{1/2}$ to Steady State (s)
Prepubertal	85%	14.22 ± 4.92[1,2]	39.04 ± 3.05[1]	42.58 ± 3.50[1,3]
Boys	100%	14.79 ± 4.82[1]	37.56 ± 2.76[1]	39.69 ± 3.05[1,2,3]
Prepubertal	85%	9.47 ± 4.41[1,2,3]	38.99 ± 4.87[1]	41.19 ± 5.08[1]
Girls	100%	14.94 ± 5.86[1,3]	41.23 ± 6.54[1]	44.24 ± 7.13[1,2]
Adolescents	85%	28.88 ± 8.18[1,2,3]	45.97 ± 7.94[1,2]	49.58 ± 8.75[1,2]
Boys	100%	35.44 ± 8.53[1,2,3]	43.14 ± 9.06[1,2]	47.19 ± 9.42[1,2]
Adolescents	85%	18.58 ± 4.93[1,2]	55.25 ± 7.26[1,2]	61.38 ± 8.25[1,2]
Girls	100%	22.24 ± 6.43[1,2]	59.04 ± 9.06[1,2]	66.00 ± 10.37[1,2]

Values are mean ± SD

[1] Differences between children and adolescents statistically significant ($p<0.05$)

[2] Differences between boys and girls within maturation groups significant ($p<0.05$)

[3] Differences between exercise intensities significant ($p<0.05$)

Linear and exponential regression analyses of the time course of $\dot{V}O_2$ during the first 120 s of each subject's test at each exercise intensity provided the results presented in table 3, which allowed for comparison of the response among the four groups. The slope of the linear regression line and the time required to reach an oxygen uptake rate (mL·min^{-1}) equal to one half the difference between the oxygen uptake rate at the onset of work and the steady state level $T_{1/2}$ were noted. The time course data were fit to both linear and exponential models for analysis.

Discussion and conclusions

The results of this investigation, unlike some previous studies[2,3], showed significantly faster responses ($t_{1/2}$) of $\dot{V}O_2$ in the children when compared to the adolescents. This finding is congruent with the observations of Sady[5] and Macek et al.[4] that children adapt more rapidly than adults. The effect of gender was more obvious in the adolescent group than among the younger children. This observation of greater disparity between males and females after puberty has both biological and sociological explanations. The influence of exercise intensity on the responses to the onset of exercise was not consistently prevalent among the groups.

It was concluded therefore that the older girls appear less proficient in accommodating physical effort than their male counterparts, while prepubescent boys and girls are similar in their ability to adapt rapidly to exercise challenge. Furthermore, the level of exercise intensity did not have a significant effect on the ability to adapt to the onset of exercise.

References

1. Freedson, P.S. (1981) Transient $\dot{V}O_2$ characteristics in children at the onset of steady-rate exercise. *Research Quarterly for Exercise and Sport*, Vol. 52, pp. 167-73.
2. Zanconato, S., Cooper, D.M. and Armon, Y. (1991) Oxygen cost and oxygen uptake dynamics and recovery with 1 min of exercise in children and adults. *Journal of Applied Physiology*, Vol. 71, pp. 993-8.
3. Cooper, D.M., Berry, C., Lamarra, N. and Wasserman, K. (1985) Kinetics of oxygen uptake and heart rate at onset of exercise in children. *Journal of Applied Physiology*, Vol. 59, pp. 211-6.
4. Macek, M. and Vavra, J. (1980) Oxygen uptake and heart rate with transition from rest to maximal exercise in prepubertal boys, in *Children and Exercise IX*, (eds. K. Berg and B.O. Eriksson), University Park Press, Baltimore, pp. 64-8.
5. Sady, S.P. (1981) Transient oxygen uptake and heart rate responses at the onset of relative endurance exercise in prepubertal boys and adult men. *International Journal of Sports Medicine*, Vol. 2, pp. 240-4.
6. Tanner, J.M. (1962) *Growth at Adolescence (2nd edition)*, Blackwell Scientific, Oxford.
7. Skinner, J. S., Bar-Or, O., Bergsteinova, V., Bell, C.W., Royer, D. and Buskirk, E.R. (1971) Comparison of continuous and intermittent tests for determining maximal oxygen intake in children. *Acta Paediatrica Scandinavica*, Vol. 217 (suppl), pp. 24-8.

RATINGS OF PERCEIVED EXERTION IN PREPUBESCENT GIRLS AND BOYS

RPE in prepubertal children

A.M. McMANUS
Physical Education and Sports Science Unit, University of Hong Kong, Hong Kong
N. ARMSTRONG, B.J. KIRBY, and J.R. WELSMAN
Children's Health and Exercise Research Centre, Institute of Clinical Science, University of Exeter, UK

Keywords: Blood lactate, peak oxygen uptake, perceived exertion, prepubescents

Introduction

Perceived exertion has been defined as the ability to detect and respond to sensations that arise as a result of physiological adaptations to exercise[1]. This cognitive assimilation of physiological parameters is a form of biofeedback, in which information about central, peripheral and metabolic changes during exercise are generated. Such a feedback system involves complex neuronal and hormonal integration, which eventually make up subjective experience and may facilitate continuation or discontinuation of the activity. Ratings of perceived exertion, most commonly made in children by the 6-20 scale (RPE) proposed by Borg[2], provide an assessment of perceptual recognition of combinations of physiological responses to exercise.

Borg's[2] 15-point RPE scale was designed with adult men to give an overall psychological predictor of physiological markers of exertion, and in particular was suitable for those variables which share a linear relationship with increases in exercise intensity such as heart rate (HR) and oxygen uptake ($\dot{V}O_2$). Indeed, each of the 15 levels in the RPE scale is thought to correspond directly to a heart rate value calculated by multiplying the scale point by 10 (± 10 beats·min^{-1}).

The potential of a perceptual measure which could provide reliable and valid recognition of physiological exertion in children for the prescription of appropriate exercise for health and fitness, has resulted in much interest being generated in the RPE scale. Few studies however, have investigated RPE with young (<12y) children [3,4,5,6,7,8], and of those available none report data on girls formally classified as prepubertal.

Children and Exercise XIX. Edited by Neil Armstrong, Brian Kirby and Joanne Welsman.
Published in 1997 by E & FN Spon, 2–6 Boundary Row, London, SE1 8HN.
ISBN 0 419 22100 X.

Studies with children under 12 y have generally focused upon the relationship between RPE and heart rate at a given absolute exercise intensity[3,4,5,7,8]. With regard to the ability of RPE to provide a valid perceptual cue for heart rate, results have been varied. Using the Borg 6-20 scale, Nystad et al.[4] noted that 10-12-year-old children tend to over-estimate their perceived exertion in relation to the actual heart rate indicated. Bar Or[3] observed 7-9-year-old children's perceptual recognition of heart rate was the least accurate in comparison with adolescents and adults. Whilst Miyashita et al.[5] reported only modest correlation coefficients between heart rate and RPE for 7-9-years-old children (r = 0.55-0.74). More recently a study by Lamb[7] found correlation coefficients between HR and RPE over two identical exercise tests of r = 0.93 and 0.95 in boys aged 9.6 y, and similarly high correlation coefficients (r = 0.88 and 0.94) for girls aged 9.6 y. However, the HR measured at each exercise intensity was much higher than that predicted using the corresponding RPE scores. A later study by the same author[8] reported correlation coefficients between RPE and HR over two identical exercise tests of r = 0.73 in the same group of boys and only r = 0.47 and 0.57 in the same group of girls.

When related to other physiological markers of exertion such as % peak $\dot{V}O_2$, RPE in prepubertal boys has been found to provide differing perceptual recognition of similar levels of exertion in comparison to adolescents or adults[6]. These authors compared RPE at 70, 80 and 85% peak $\dot{V}O_2$ between prepubescents, pubescents and adult males. The prepubescents gave consistently higher RPE scores for each % peak $\dot{V}O_2$ in comparison to the other groups.

The reliability of RPE scores with prepubescents has, to date, only been investigated by Lamb[7,8]. Using a test-retest design in both studies, RPE scores either differed significantly between tests in both sexes[7], or provided inconsistent test-retest correlation coefficients for each exercise stage[8].

The ability of Borg's 6-20 RPE scale to provide a reliable, valid estimation of physiological markers of exertion in prepubertal children remains questionable, with few data available for boys and girls formally classified as prepubertal. This study was therefore designed to examine the ability of RPE to provide valid perceptual recognition of various physiological responses to absolute and relative exercise intensities in prepubertal girls and boys.

Subjects

The children were drawn from a longitudinal study of a representative sample of children attending state schools in Exeter. Subject selection has been described elsewhere[9]. The data reported here are from the 111 boys and 79 girls who were classified prepubertal, according to Tanner's[10] indices for pubic hair and breast or genitalia development, and successfully completed the procedures described below.

Methods

Stature was measured to the nearest 0.001 m using a Holtain stadiometer (Crymych, Dyfed, UK) and body mass was measured to the nearest 100g using a beam balance (Avery, Birmingham, UK).

All exercise tests were performed following habituation, running on a Woodway motorized treadmill. An incremental, discontinuous treadmill run to voluntary exhaustion was used to collect submaximal and maximal exercise data. The children warmed up for 3 min running at a speed of 1.67 $m \cdot s^{-1}$. Each subsequent stage of the test lasted 3 min commencing at a speed of 1.94 $m \cdot s^{-1}$, and increasing to 2.22 $m \cdot s^{-1}$, 2.50 $m \cdot s^{-1}$, and 2.78 $m \cdot s^{-1}$. After 2.78 $m \cdot s^{-1}$ the speed remained constant whilst the gradient was increased by increments of 2.5% until the children reached voluntary exhaustion. Peak $\dot{V}O_2$ was accepted as a maximal index if the child had a HR which leveled off prior to the final exercise stage, or was near or above 200 $beats \cdot min^{-1}$; a respiratory exchange ratio of at least unity and signs of intense effort (profuse sweating, an unsteady gait, dyspnoea).

At the end of each 3 min stage there was a 1 min rest during which the child was asked to rate his/her perceived exertion using Borg's 6-20 RPE scale[2]. The RPE scale was explained to all the children during habituation. Finger tip capillary blood samples were taken during the rest period for blood lactate analysis (YSI 2300 Stat Plus, Yellows Springs Instruments, Ohio, USA).

Throughout the exercise test inspired and expired gases were monitored continuously using an Oxycon Sigma on-line gas analysis system (Cranlea, Birmingham, UK) which was recalibrated prior to each test. Heart rate was monitored continuously from an electrocardiogram using a bipolar lead (Rigel, Morden, UK).

Data analyses

The data were stored and analysed using SPSS-PC+ (SPSS Inc., Chicago, USA). Differences between the girls and boys were examined using analysis of variance (ANOVA). Relationships were explored using Pearson product moment correlation. In all analyses a significance level of $p < 0.05$ was accepted.

Results

There was no significant ($p > 0.05$) difference between boys and girls in age (11.1 ± 0.4 vs 11. 0 ± 0.4 y), stature (1.45 ± 0.06 vs 1.44 ± 0.08 m), or mass (35.7 ± 6.1 vs 34.7 ± 5.3 kg). A significant ($p < 0.05$) sex difference in RPE was detected only at exercise stage 3. Blood lactate, HR and % peak $\dot{V}O_2$ were significantly ($p < 0.05$ to $p < 0.010$) higher in the girls at all exercise stages (table 1). The only significant ($p < 0.05$) correlations between physiological variables and RPE were between HR and RPE during exercise stages 2-4 in both sexes. Significant correlation coefficients ranged from $r = 0.20$ to $r = 0.28$.

Table 1. RPE and physiological variables during exercise in prepubertal children by sex

Stage (TM speed)	1 (1.94 m·s^{-1})		2 (2.22 m·s^{-1})		3 (2.50 m·s^{-1})		4 (2.78 m·s^{-1})	
	Boys	Girls	Boys	Girls	Boys	Girls	Boys	Girls
RPE	11 ± 2	11 ± 2	12 ± 2	12 ± 2	13 ± 3	14 ± 2*	14 ± 3	15 ± 3
HR (beats·min^{-1})	0 ± 15	170±13**	168 ± 14	180 ± 11**	178 ± 13	188 ± 11**	187 ± 12	196 ± 9**
La (mmol·L^{-1})	2.3 ± 0.7	2.6 ±0.7*	1.5 ± 0.6	2.2 ± 0.8**	1.9 ± 0.9	2.8 ± 1.0**	2.4 ± 1.2	3.6 ± 1.3**
% peak $\dot{V}O_2$	67 ± 8	75 ± 7**	72 ± 8	80 ± 8**	78 ± 10	87 ± 8**	85 ± 9	94 ± 7**

Values are mean ± SD
Level of significance *p <0.05, **p <0.01

Table 2. RPE and physiological variables at 70-75% and 80-85% peak $\dot{V}O_2$ by sex

% peak $\dot{V}O_2$	RPE		HR (beats·min^{-1})		Blood La (mmol·L^{-1})		% peak $\dot{V}O_2$	
	Boys	Girls	Boys	Girls	Boys	Girls	Boys	Girls
70-75%	12 ±2	12 ± 2	172 ± 13	172 ± 12	1.8 ± 0.8	2.3 ± 1.0*	73 ± 2	72 ± 2
80-85%	13 ± 2	13 ± 2	181 ± 12	179 ± 13	2.1 ± 0.8	2.4 ± 0.7	83 ± 2	82 ± 2

Values are mean ± SD
Level of significance *p <0.05
n = 66 boys and 34 girls at 70-75% peak $\dot{V}O_2$; n = 63 boys and 43 girls at 80-85% peak $\dot{V}O_2$

To compare girls' and boys' responses at the same relative exercise intensities similar analyses were performed using data from children who exercised within the specific ranges 70-75% and 80-85% peak $\dot{V}O_2$ (table 2). No significant (p >0.05) relationships between RPE and physiological variables were detected.

Discussion

A central issue in the study of RPE in children has been whether Borg's 6-20 scale[2] provides an accurate perceptual assessment of physiological changes associated with increasing exercise intensity. When these data are compared to previous studies with similarly aged children, there is much inconsistency. In this study both girls and boys appeared to underestimate their physical exertion, in relation to HR, using the RPE scale. This underestimation was more pronounced in prepubertal girls, who despite similar RPE scores at absolute exercise intensities to the boys, exhibited increased physiological responses. In contrast Nystad et al.[4] found that similarly aged children over-estimated their perceived exertion. In addition, the present study found very weak correlations between RPE and HR in both boys and girls, in contrast to the much higher correlation coefficients reported by Lamb[7]

When prepubertal boys and girls were compared at relative exercise intensities using % peak $\dot{V}O_2$, there were no differences in RPE corresponding with no significant differences in various physiological markers of exertion. The only difference detected, in blood lactate at 70-75% peak $\dot{V}O_2$, is most likely an artifact of nervousness at the beginning of the test, since for many of the girls stage 1 corresponded to 70-75% peak $\dot{V}O_2$. Previous data reporting RPE at specified % peak $\dot{V}O_2$ have identified similar RPE scores at 70% peak $\dot{V}O_2$ [6]. However, at the higher 80-85% peak $\dot{V}O_2$ Tolfrey and Mitchell[6] reported much higher RPE scores in similarly aged boys (14 and 15 for 80 and 85% peak $\dot{V}O_2$ respectively) in comparison with a rating of 13 found amongst the prepubertal boys in this study.

In conclusion, the present study does not support the ability of the RPE scale to provide accurate recognition of physiological exertion during absolute or relative exercise intensities in prepubertal children. It would seem that ratings of perceived exertion made using the RPE scale should be used with caution as descriptors of prepubescents' exertion during submaximal exercise.

References

1. Noble, B.J. and Robertson, R.J. (1996) *Perceived Exertion,* Human Kinetics, Champaign, Il.
2. Borg, G. (1986) Psychophysical basis of perceived exertion. *Medicine and Science in Sports and Exercise,* Vol. 14, pp. 371-81.
3. Bar-Or, O. (1977) Age-related changes in exercise prescription, in *Physical Work and Effort,* (ed. G. Borg), Pergamon Press, Oxford, pp. 255-6.
4. Nystad, W., Oseid, S. and Mellbye, E.B. (1989) Physical education for asthmatic children: the relationship between changes in heart rate, perceived exertion, and motivation for participation, in *Children and Exercise XIII,* (eds. S. Oseid and K. Carlson), Human Kinetics, Champaign, Il., pp. 369-77.
5. Miyashita, M., Onedera, K. and Tabata I. (1986) How Borg's RPE scale has been applied to Japanese, in *The Perception of Exertion in Physical Work,* (eds. G. Borg and D. Ottoson), Macmillan Press, Basingstoke, pp. 27-34.
6. Tolfrey, K. and Mitchell, J. (1996) Rating of perceived exertion at standard and relative exercise intensities in prepubertal, teenage and young adult males. *Journal of Sports Science,* Vol. 14, pp. 101-2.
7. Lamb, K.L. (1995) Children's ratings of effort during cycle ergometry: an examination of the validity of two effort rating scales. *Pediatric Exercise Science,* Vol. 7, pp. 407-21.
8. Lamb, K.L. (1996) Exercise regulation during cycle ergometry using CERT and RPE scales. *Pediatric Exercise Science,* Vol. 8, pp. 337-50.
9. Armstrong, N., Kirby, B.J., McManus, A.M. and Welsman, J.R. (1995) Aerobic fitness of prepubescent children. *Annals of Human Biology,* Vol. 22, pp. 427-41.
10. Tanner, J.M. (1962) *Growth at Adolescence* (2nd edition), Blackwell Scientific Publications, Oxford.

EFFORT PERCEPTION IN CHILDREN: A FOCUS ON TESTING METHODOLOGY

Effort perception in children

K.L. LAMB and S. TRASK
Department of Physical Education and Sports Science, University College Chester, Chester, UK
R.G. ESTON
Division of Health and Human Performance, University of Wales, Bangor, UK
Keywords: Effort perception, methodological issues, production protocols

Introduction

Interest in the concept and application of exercise-related effort perception amongst children has been obvious, yet rather erratic over the past 25 years. Whereas research with adults has yielded an abundance of published articles on the application of effort perception in an exercise environment, particularly with regard to the use of the Rating of Perceived Exertion (RPE) scale[1], relatively little sustained interest has been devoted to paediatric exercise. Within the last decade, however, concerns over the physical activity and fitness levels of children have provided the motivation for researchers to explore this area with more purpose. An obvious sign of this progress is the appearance of a child-specific perceived exertion scale, the Children's Effort Rating Table[2], and reports on its validation [3-5].

Most research to date has been fairly small-scale and conducted in a "laboratory" setting, partly because of the experimental control this allows, but primarily due to its practicality. As a consequence, the potential value of perceived exertion to physical educators and health promoters remains to be realized. Over 30 published studies have focused on how well children can use their perceptions to estimate and/or regulate exercise intensity, as reflected typically by recordings of heart rate and power output (or speed), during cycle or treadmill ergometry[6]. Yet, there appears to have been little or no attempt to standardise fundamental aspects of methodology[6], such as the structure of the exercise protocols, making it difficult to synthesize and interpret findings. For instance, when children are requested to regulate their exercise output to match experimenter-prescribed effort rating levels, their selection of loadings (resistances) and corresponding 'accuracy' is logically going to be influenced by factors such as the progression of the trial (continuous, or discontinuous with rest periods) and the order of load presentation (incremental or

Children and Exercise XIX. Edited by Neil Armstrong, Brian Kirby and Joanne Welsman.
Published in 1997 by E & FN Spon, 2–6 Boundary Row, London, SE1 8HN.
ISBN 0 419 22100 X.

random). No study so far has attended to these concerns. In addition, it has always been assumed that the heart rates recorded for each intensity level (usually after 4 min) reflect steady-state conditions. This may not be the case, especially during the highest prescribed levels[5]. Accordingly, the purpose of this investigation was to examine the effects of these protocol-related issues on children's exercise effort regulation during cycle ergometry.

Methods

Data were collected on 66 Year 5 (4th Grade) children of a primary school in Chester, England. Subject characteristics are shown in table 1. All subjects provided parental informed consent to participate in the study and were free of known contra-indications prior to testing. Ethical approval was granted by the University College Chester Ethics Committee.

Three weeks in advance of the testing, the children were introduced to the Children's Effort Rating Table (CERT) and the testing equipment by the experimenter. The CERT [2] is deemed to be more appropriate for children in terms of its language and numerical range, and has been offered as an alternative to the traditional RPE scale[3,4]. Following an explanation of how the verbal expressions for the CERT (fig 1) should be interpreted in numerical form, every child was given a copy of the table to keep and study.

The children were then randomly assigned to either a continuous protocol (CP) or a discontinuous protocol (DP) group (see table 1), and testing subsequently took place on the school premises, over a 2 wk period. All exercise tests used a mechanically braked (basket-loading) cycle ergometer (Monark 814, Sweden) fitted with wooden pedal blocks (to accommodate the shortest children) and a radio telemetry system for monitoring heart rates (Sports Tester PE4000, Polar Electronics, Finland).

Immediately prior to exercise, subjects were re-introduced to CERT and given standard instructions concerning its use and the purpose of the test. Common to both groups was the requirement to regulate exercise intensity to match a range of four effort rating levels (randomly presented for each child); 3, 5, 7, and 9. Furthermore, each so-called production trial began with a 3 min 25 W warm-up, followed by a 3 min rest, and continued with each

Table 1. Subject characteristics

Group	n	Age (y)	Stature (m)	Mass (kg)
Continuous				
All	33	10.30 ± 0.30	1.43 ± 0.05	35.08 ± 6.43
Boys	21	10.29 ± 0.30	1.44 ± 0.05	36.10 ± 6.06
Girls	12	10.33 ± 0.32	1.42 ± 0.05	33.29 ± 4.03
Discontinuous				
All	33	10.29 ± 0.33	1.45 ± 0.07	36.94 ± 6.74
Boys	20	10.30 ± 0.35	1.46 ± 0.06	38.38 ± 7.80
Girls	13	10.30 ± 0.32	1.44 ± 0.09	34.73 ± 4.03

Values are mean ± SD

1	VERY, VERY EASY
2	VERY EASY
3	EASY
4	JUST FEELING A STRAIN
5	STARTING TO GET HARD
6	GETTING QUITE HARD
7	HARD
8	VERY HARD
9	VERY, VERY HARD
10	SO HARD I'M GOING TO STOP

Fig. 1. The CERT scale[2]

child instructing the experimenter to adjust the cycling resistance (to add or subtract weights) in accordance with the specified perceived levels. A shield was in place throughout testing to hide from view the weights being applied by the experimenter.

The children were allowed 2 min to settle on an appropriate resistance, before cycling for a further 1 min at the chosen intensities. These intensities were recorded as power outputs, expressed in W. Heart rates were also recorded after 2 min, and again at the end of the 3rd. For subjects allocated to the discontinuous group, each exercise bout was interspersed with a 3 min rest period.

Data analyses

Exercise responses were analyzed with mixed factorial ANOVAs (Group x Levels x Time x Sex) with repeated measures on the second and third factors, using the MANOVA procedure in SPSS for Windows[7]. This procedure for repeated measures designs does not jeopardize the important pre-requisite of sphericity[8]. Alpha was set at 0.025 in order to reduce the risk of inflating the experimenter wise error associated with analysing more than one dependent variable (heart rate and power output) belonging to the same data set. Post-hoc comparisons of specific factor levels were analyzed, where appropriate, with the Tukey test.

Additionally, and in accordance with previous research, interclass correlations (Pearson's r) were calculated to assess the relationship between the measures of objective and perceived effort for each group (CP and DP). A two-tailed Fisher *z* transformation[9] was employed to test whether the correlation coefficients differed significantly ($p < 0.05$) between groups and across time periods.

Results

For heart rates, mean values were consistently lower across the exercise levels (see tables 2 and 3), particularly those recorded after 2 min, though the main effect for Group was not

Table 2. Heart rates (beats·min^{-1}) after 2 min

Group	Level	All 2 min	Boys 2 min	Girls 2 min
Continuous	3	152.5 ± 21.4	148.9 ± 16.5	158.8 ± 27.7
	5	157.8 ± 20.6	155.9 ± 20.2	161.2 ± 21.9
	7	168.4 ± 16.5	164.6 ± 14.4	175.1 ± 18.3
	9	174.0 ± 16.3	171.4 ± 14.3	178.7 ± 19.2
	Overall	163.2 ± 20.5	160.2 ± 18.4	168.4 ± 23.1
Discontinuous	3	137.9 ± 15.8	135.0 ± 14.3	142.5 ± 17.4
	5	152.1 ± 15.7	152.0 ± 15.5	152.3 ± 16.7
	7	162.8 ± 16.2	160.3 ± 14.5	166.8 ± 18.4
	9	171.4 ± 13.6	168.6 ± 13.4	175.7 ± 13.3
	Overall	156.1 ± 19.7	154.0 ± 18.9	159.3 ± 20.6

Table 3. Heart rates (beats·min^{-1}) after 3 min

Group	Level	All 2 min	Boys 2 min	Girls 2 min
Continuous	3	153.8 ± 20.9	150.6 ± 16.1	159.5 ± 27.3
	5	161.4 ± 20.5	158.1 ± 19.5	167.2 ± 21.7
	7	173.8 ± 16.0	167.9 ± 14.3	184.0 ± 13.7
	9	178.5 ± 16.9	175.2 ± 16.1	184.2 ± 17.5
	Overall	166.8 ± 20.9	162.9 ± 18.8	173.7 ± 22.8
Discontinuous	3	141.0 ± 18.2	138.0 ± 16.4	145.7 ± 20.5
	5	159.2 ± 18.7	158.5 ± 16.7	160.2 ± 22.1
	7	170.8 ± 16.6	168.6 ± 15.7	174.2 ± 18.1
	9	181.8 ± 14.2	178.5 ± 13.9	186.9 ± 13.7
	Overall	163.2 ± 22.6	160.9 ± 21.5	166.8 ± 24.0

significant ($F_{1,62} = 3.08$; $p = 0.084$). Post-hoc analysis of the significant Group x Levels interaction ($F_{3,186} = 3.87$; $p = 0.01$) identified the heart rates at CERT 3 to be significantly different ($T = 12.7$; $p < 0.05$), but not elsewhere (fig 2).

Values recorded after 2 min exercise were found to be generally lower than those after 3 min ($F_{1,62} = 174$; $p < 0.001$), but were also influenced by Group ($F_{1,62} = 13.8$; $p < 0.001$) and Levels ($F_{3,186} = 12.8$; $p < 0.001$). Lastly, post-hoc analysis of the highly significant ($p < 0.001$) Levels factor confirmed that heart rates increased stepwise with increases in prescribed CERT ratings ($T = 6.9$; $p < 0.05$).

For power output data (see table 4), the most notable finding was a Group x Sex interaction ($F_{1,62} = 8.2$; $p < 0.01$), accounted for principally by a mean difference of 12.4 W between the girls in the two groups ($T = 10.7$; $p < 0.05$). Likewise, the significant Group x Levels interaction ($F_{3,186} = 3.9$; $p = 0.01$) was mainly due to a 13.5 W between-groups difference in power outputs at the lightest CERT level ($T = 13.4$; $p < 0.01$).

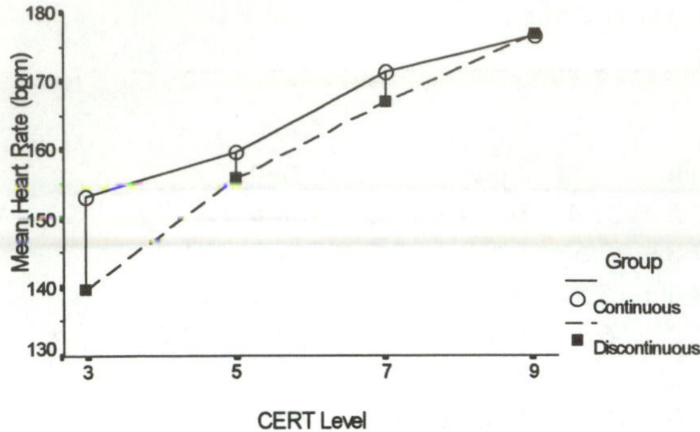

Fig. 2. Group x levels interaction

Correlation coefficients between heart rates and CERT levels were consistently and significantly ($p < 0.05$) larger in the DP group than the CP group (table 5), whereas those for power output and CERT levels only differed significantly for boys.

Discussion

The present data have demonstrated that children's use of perceived effort to regulate exercise intensity during cycle ergometry is, to some extent, protocol-dependent. Both the nature of the exercise protocol and the point at which data is recorded have an important bearing on the heart rate responses at specific perceived effort levels. In particular, the provision of recovery periods between exercise bouts seems to enhance their ability to utilize a scale such as the CERT, as does the duration of each bout. However, on a cautionary note, in studies of this kind it remains extremely difficult to separate the variance due to these factors from that due simply to individual differences.

Table 4. Power outputs (W) after 2 min

Group	Level	All	Boys	Girls
Continuous	3	52.1 (16.2)	52.9 (21.3)	55.8 (17.6)
	5	68.2 (17.0)	66.4 (17.1)	71.3 (16.9)
	7	89.4 (17.7)	87.9 (20.6)	92.1 (11.2)
	9	99.6 (15.0)	99.5 (16.8)	99.6 (12.0)
	Overall	77.2 (24.6)	76.0 (25.8)	79.7 (22.5)
Discontinuous	3	38.6 (14.4)	41.5 (14.5)	34.2 (13.5)
	5	70.5 (20.8)	75.0 (15.1)	63.5 (26.6)
	7	89.4 (21.4)	94.3 (16.2)	81.9 (26.5)
	9	102.7 (20.2)	111.3 (15.5)	89.6 (13.3)
	Overall	75.3 (30.9)	80.5 (30.1)	67.3 (30.5)

Values are mean ± SD

Table 5. Correlations between perceived effort ratings and objective measures of exercise intensity.

Relationship	Group Continuous 2 min	3 min	Discontinuous 2 min	3 min
All				
Perceived Effort and Heart Rate	0.41	0.46	0.63*	0.66*
Perceived Effort and Power Output	0.74	-	0.77	-
Boys				
Perceived Effort and Heart Rate	0.47	0.50	0.65*	0.69*
Perceived Effort and Power Output	0.74	-	0.85*	-
Girls				
Perceived Effort and Heart Rate	0.36	0.45	0.62*	0.65
Perceived Effort and Power Output	0.76	-	0.68	-

All correlations significant ($p < 0.01$)

* Significantly different ($p < 0.05$) to corresponding Continuous Group coefficient.

The findings that the children in this study had some success in using their perceptions of effort to increase or decrease exercise intensity corroborate existing knowledge acquired using discontinuous[5,10,11] and continuous[3,12] cycling. No previous effort production studies have compared these two conditions. Of note in the present study, therefore, are the significant interactions involving the Group factor. Whilst the lower heart rates (and power outputs) recorded for CERT 3 in the DP group are striking, being isolated they are difficult to interpret. This is especially true since loadings were randomly applied for each group. Also, that the mean heart rates recorded for the CP (176.3 beats·min^{-1}) and DP (176.6 beats·min^{-1}) groups were no different at the hardest prescribed level (CERT 9), implies nothing was gained by the rest periods in the DP. Similarly, an explanation for the Group x Time interaction in which the 2 min heart rates were disproportionately lower in the DP group than the CP group, is not obvious. The simple main effect of Time on heart rates, is, however, probably due to the non-attainment of steady-state conditions after 2 min of exercise. Whether this status was reached even after 3 min is not known.

Clearer evidence for the impact of the type of protocol on effort regulation is provided by the bivariate correlational analysis. The discontinuous protocol produced a consistently stronger relationship between perceived effort and heart rate levels, hinting that recovery periods may assist children in their perceptions of physiological strain. Conversely, the lower correlations in the CP group may simply reflect an inaccuracy of perception due as much to fatigue as error of judgement.

In conclusion, we would advise future investigations into children's effort perception not to disregard the manner in which the exercise stimulus is applied, nor indeed, the duration of the stimulus, since these two factors seem to modify the outcome measures.

References

1. Borg, G. (1985) *An Introduction to Borg's RPE-Scale*, Mouvement Publications, Ithaca, New York.
2. Williams, J.G., Eston, R.G. and Furlong, B. (1994) CERT: a perceived exertion scale for young children. *Perceptual and Motor Skills*, Vol. 79, pp. 1451-8.
3. Eston, R.G., Lamb, K.L., Bain, A., Williams, A.M. and Williams, J.G. (1994) Validity of a perceived exertion scale for children: a pilot study. *Perceptual and Motor Skills*, Vol. 78, pp. 691-7.
4. Lamb, K.L. (1995) Children's ratings of effort during cycle ergometry: an examination of the validity of two effort rating scales. *Pediatric Exercise Science*, Vol. 7, pp. 407-21.
5. Lamb, K.L. (1996) Exercise regulation during cycle ergometry using the children's effort rating table (CERT) and rating of perceived exertion (RPE) scales. *Pediatric Exercise Science*, Vol. 8, pp. 337-50.
6. Lamb, K.L. and Eston, R.G. (1997) Effort perception in children. *Sports Medicine*, Vol. 23, pp. 139-48.
7. SPSS (1994). *SPSS for Windows (Release 6.0)*, SPSS Inc., Chicago.
8. Schutz, R.W. and Gessaroli, M.E. (1987) The analysis of repeated measures designs involving multiple dependent variables. *Research Quarterly for Exercise and Sport*, Vol. 58, pp. 132-49.
9. Morehouse, C.A., and Stull, G.A. (1975) *Statistical Principles and Procedures with Applications for Physical Education*, Lea & Febiger, Philadelphia.
10. Ward, D.S. and Bar-Or, O. (1990) Use of the Borg scale in exercise prescription for overweight youth. *Canadian Journal of Sports Sciences*, Vol. 15, pp. 120-5.
11. Ward, D.S., Jackman, J.D. and Galiano, F.J. (1991) Exercise intensity reproduction: children versus adults. *Pediatric Exercise Science*, Vol. 3, pp. 209-18.
12. Williams, J.G., Eston, R.G. and Stretch, C. (1991) Use of rating of perceived exertion to control exercise intensity in children. *Pediatric Exercise Science*, Vol. 3, pp. 21-7.

PART IV

ANAERORIC PERFORMANCE AND MUSCULAR STRENGTH

DEVELOPMENTAL ASPECTS OF ANAEROBIC FUNCTION

Anaerobic performance during growth

E. VAN PRAAGH

Université Blaise Pascal, Clermont-Ferrand, France

Keywords: Anaerobic function, assessment of anaerobic performance, fibre type, genetics, muscle mechanics, muscle power, muscle strength, muscular energetics

Introduction

Anaerobic function during growth has not received the same attention from researchers, as aerobic function. This is a little surprising with respect to the anaerobic energy used daily during childhood and adolescence. Activity patterns in children are characterized by short bursts of exercise and therefore this pattern, perhaps, optimises the anabolic effects of exercise in the growing child[1]. During leisure-time activities or sport events, the child is spontaneously more attracted to short-burst movements, than to long-term activities. The fact, that anaerobic function is more performance-related and less health-related than aerobic function, might be a possible explanation for the relative disinterest from the paediatric exercise science community. The ability of muscle to generate power depends on its force capacity and shortening velocity. Because, both anaerobic adenosine triphosphate (ATP) turnover and muscle cross-section vary during growth and maturation, this paper will review some developmental aspects on energetic- and mechanical factors involved in anaerobic performances.

I. The anaerobic function: fundamental aspects

Definitions

The terminology used in the literature to define muscle anaerobic function is rather confusing. Biochemical, physiological and mechanical concepts like: alacticid, lactacid, anaerobic capacity, anaerobic work capacity, instantaneous power, peak power, mean power are often indiscriminately used, even in high-standard scientific journals. Power refers to the ability of the neuromuscular system to produce the greatest possible

Children and Exercise XIX. Edited by Neil Armstrong, Brian Kirby and Joanne Welsman.
Published in 1997 by E & FN Spon, 2–6 Boundary Row, London, SE1 8HN.
ISBN 0 419 22100 X.

impulse in a given time period. The time period depends on the resistance or the load against which the subject has to work and on the organisation of the acceleration. In some physical activities and sports it is necessary to overcome resistance with the greatest possible speed of muscle action at the beginning of the movement (sprinting, jumping or throwing). In others, the maximal acceleration should be delayed to reach a maximal velocity for the engine, the body or parts of the body. Power production is therefore limited by the rate at which energy is supplied (ATP production) for the muscle contraction (ATP utilisation), or in other words the rate at which the myofilaments can convert chemical energy into mechanical work.

ATP supply

Anaerobic Power: is the maximal anaerobic ATP per second yield by the whole organism, during a specific type of short duration, maximal exercise[2]. Considering the brevity of muscle contractions during short-term whole-body exercises (ballistic movements), some assumptions must be made with respect to the anaerobic energy turnover. It is therefore impossible today to measure directly this metabolism during exercise. Anaerobic power is characterized by the generation of very high power outputs (from about 1.2 kW in 11 year-old untrained children[3] to about 6.0 kW in elite adults[4].

Anaerobic Capacity: is the maximal amount of ATP resynthesised via anaerobic metabolism (by the whole organism) during a specific type of short-duration, maximal exercise[2]. The anaerobic ATP yield during exercise can be estimated and provides a direct measure of anaerobic capacity[5]. Short-term anaerobic muscle metabolism can also be investigated during exercise by the use of phosphorus magnetic resonance spectroscopy (^{31}P NMR). This promising method will be discussed later.

Mechanical work

Using work output to estimate or to reflect anaerobic capacity, is less difficult than attempting to quantify the ATP yield using 'direct methods' (e.g. needle biopsy-; ^{31}P NMR- or Accumulated Oxygen Deficit techniques). However, interpreting the physiological implications of work outputs is probably more difficult. This is especially true as the mechanical work estimates not only reflect anaerobic ATP supply, but also reflect the contribution of oxidative sources of ATP, as well as the various factors involved in the transduction of chemical- to mechanical energy (or work done).Thus, factors which influence work estimates of anaerobic capacity may not be completely anaerobic in nature[6,7].

Assessment of muscle energetics

In adults

In the intact human, making direct measurements of either the rate or the capacity of anaerobic pathways for energy turnover provokes several ethical and methodological difficulties. Bangsbo et al.[5] using needle muscle biopsies and arterial and venous catheterization have demonstrated that direct quantitative measurements of anaerobic energy turnover can be made during short-term high intensity exercise. However, the high invasiveness of these multiple techniques must be emphasised and the latter are certainly not suitable for healthy children investigations or large scale population studies. The measurement of the accumulated oxygen deficit (AOD) at the onset of exercise has been used as an alternative method in order to estimate the anaerobic capacity of the individual[8]. Due to the assumptions that need to be made with respect to mechanical efficiency and the energy equivalence of O_2 in supramaximal exercise, some caution is needed in interpreting the experimental results obtained[9,10].

In children

Because it is a highly invasive technique, needle biopsy of muscle cannot be ethically justified in the case of children. Moreover, the classical studies of Eriksson et al.[11, 12] were done and discussed only on the basis of the results of phosphofructokinase activity at rest. The use of phosphorus nuclear magnetic resonance (^{31}P NMR) spectroscopy offers an alternative indirect technique. ^{31}P NMR has proved to be a valuable non-invasive unique technique for investigating muscle metabolism during exercise in children. However, because of several methodological shortcomings, the measurement of short-term power during growth and maturation still offers a suitable alternative. One must keep in mind, that even though one may be measuring the power output of leg- or arm muscles, the constituent muscle will be submitted to the fundamental laws of muscle mechanics.

Assessment of muscle mechanics

As was pointed out by Hill[13] and afterwards by Wilkie[14], it is important to realise that for the production of maximal power output in humans, force and velocity must be matched. The relationship between the force that a muscle can generate and its velocity of contraction is described by an inverse linear relationship. The mathematical consequence of this relationship is that power (which is force times velocity) has a parabolic relation with velocity (or force). In in vitro animal experiments, maximal power is attained at an optimal velocity (Vopt), which is about one third of the maximum velocity of shortening. In whole-body exercise it is important to know at which 'force' (constant force ergometer) or 'velocity' (constant velocity ergometer) the exercise is being performed and how it relates to the 'general' power-force or power-velocity for that specific exercise. In short-term supramaximal cycling, maximal cycling power was attained at an optimal force (Fopt) of 50% of the maximum leg force (Fo). These values were found in adults[15], as in children[16]. The force that a muscle can generate depends upon its length as described by the length-tension relationship. The importance of the length effect is clearly seen in human experiments. For example in measurements of maximum torque generated on isokinetic ergometers, great care must be taken to standardise the range of length excursion in measurements of muscle power[17]. During growth, muscle can be increased in length by adding sarcomeres. However, little is known of the changes that occur in the passive elastic elements during that period. As a measure of the rate of work performance, power is a scalar quantity that is measured in watts (W). 1 kW (mechanical power) corresponding

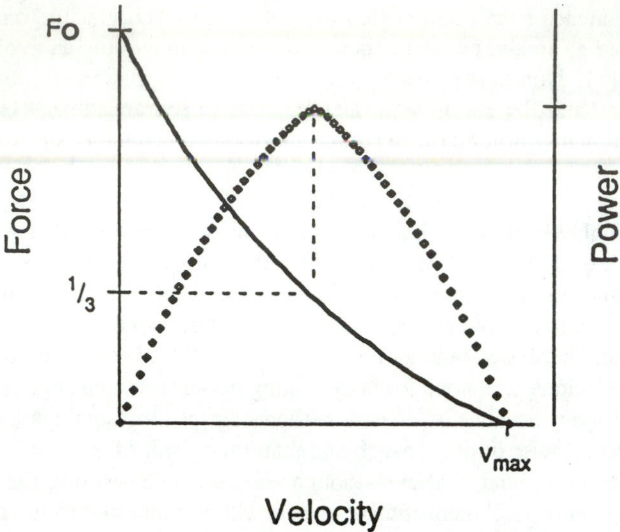

Fig. 1. The force-velocity relationship (solid line) based on data from an isolated-muscle preparation. The power curve is derived from the product of force and velocity (Adapted from Enoka, 1994)

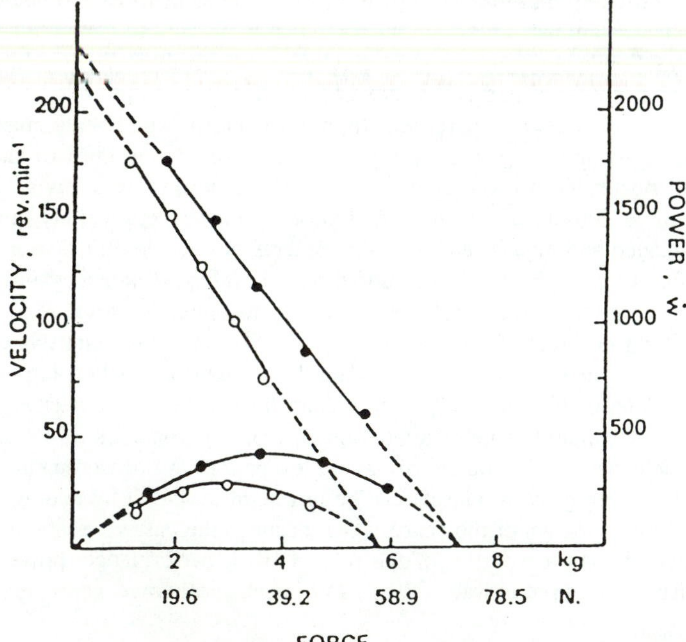

Fig. 2. Force-velocity and force-power relationships in 12-year-old girls (o) and boys (.) (Adapted from Van Praagh et al. 1990)

to an O_2 consumption of about 48 $mL \cdot s^{-1}$ (metabolic power) (for further information the reader is directed to Enoka[18])

II. The child's anaerobic potential

Potential = ' available for development or use'. In other words, what are the inherent anaerobic capabilities of the organism during growth ?

Energy supply

Anaerobic ATP production in skeletal muscle is determined primarily by PCr hydrolysis and La- accumulation. The following physiological correlates of the potential for muscle anaerobic ATP production are:

Substrate availability and utilisation

- Muscle storage of phosphagens

  A few studies[11,12] have shown that the content of the peripheral energy-delivering substrates is the same for both children and adults. From table 1 it can be observed that PCr unlike ATP, increases with age.

In adults, the rate of ATP turnover for running sprints or high jumping has been approximated as 2.7 $mmol \cdot kg^{-1}$ and 7 $mmol \cdot kg^{-1}$ respectively. To my knowledge no data are available for children. Because of the extremely fast kinetics of the chemical reactions, the available techniques (muscle biopsies) take too much time to sample the chemical events.

- Muscle storage of glycogen

  A limited number of reports have found low glycolytic ability in pre-pubescent children when compared to adults (see table 1). However, the exact underlying mechanism for relatively low anaerobic function is still unclear. It was suggested that the rate of anaerobic glycolysis is limited in children, because of their lower phosphofructokinase (PFK) activity[11]. In contrast to Eriksson's results, the pre-pubertal children studied by Berg et al.[20] did not show the expected lower activit-

Table 1. Resting values for muscle ATP, PCr and glycogen of boys and adults[19]

	ATP	PCr	Glycogen
Adults	5	17	80
Children			
12 years	4	15	55
13 years	5	20	70
14 years	5	17	70
16 years	5	24	85

Values are $mmol \cdot L^{-1}$ wet mass (from Eriksson, 1980[19])

ies of glycolytic enzymes. Furthermore it must be emphasised that these observations are discussed only on the basis of the results of glycolytic enzymes activity at rest and thus do not investigate muscle metabolism during exercise.

Post-exercise blood lactate [La-]b

The assumed lower glycolytic response to maximal and supramaximal exercise during childhood is manifested by a lower post-exercise lactate concentration in muscle[12] or blood[21], and by a lower post-exercise blood acidosis[22]. However, blood lactate reflects all those processes by which lactate is produced and eliminated[23]. Therefore, post-exercise [La-] b provides only a qualitative indication of the degree of stress placed on anaerobic metabolism by a particular bout of exercise, rather than a quantitative measure of glycolysis. It cannot be assumed, therefore that the children's post-exercise [La-] b are simply the result of a lower intramuscular lactate production. There has been a long-standing hypothesis that the increase of glycolytic ability is somehow dependent upon hormonal changes occurring during maturation. In boys, several studies have observed significant relationships between post-exercise lactates and testosterone levels[21,24]. However, testosterone levels are highly correlated with height and body mass and therefore they should be partialled out when relationships between testosterone and glycolytic capacity or anaerobic performance are established. In recent studies, which separated the influence of body size, no significant relationship between salivary testosterone level and post-exercise lactates following a maximal test or a supramaximal test was found[25,26]. The opinion on the validity of maximal blood lactate as an estimate of anaerobic (lactic) capacity is divided[27,28]. Besides, a number of methodological issues regarding lactate determination can significantly influence blood levels. In paediatric exercise research, these problems were recently reviewed[29].

Mechanical power

To obtain more insight into how mechanical output, produced by many different muscles, changes during growth, we must review jointly the development of muscle force and the velocity of muscle contraction. Indeed, given an adequate neural input to muscle, the principal determinants of power production are the number of in-parallel activated muscle fibres and the rate at which the myofilaments can covert energy into mechanical work.

Developmental aspects of muscle strength

Determinants of muscle force

- Heritability

  Physical performance is determined by environmental and genetic influences, and their interaction. Based on limited studies, there appears to be a low to moderate degree of heritability for isometric muscle force[30,31,32]. However, a strong genetic effect has been reported for dynamic force[33] and power[34]. The results of the latter study indicate that intrapair differences for maximal arm muscle power are greater between dizygotic twins than monozygotic twins.

- Muscle fibre characteristics

 Number of muscle cells: Postnatal muscle growth is frequently considered to be due primarily to muscle hypertrophy, in contrast to prenatal muscle growth which is characterized as the period of muscle fibre hyper-plasia[35].

 Fibre differentiation: The human skeletal muscle is comprised primarily of two muscle fibre types: slow-twitch (ST) or type I and fast-twitch (FT) or type II. The distribution of fibre types varies across different muscle groups. Type II fibres have been further differentiated into three sub-types: type IIa, IIb and IIc fibres. Type II fibres are better fitted to brief bursts of anaerobic activity at high-power output, than type I fibres where metabolic characteristics give them a capacity for sustained fatigue-resistant activity. It seems that this typology, based on conventional histochemical staining, is somewhat misleading since there exists a *continuum* in most, if not all contractile and metabolic properties. In human skeletal muscle this is found in three main isoforms: Type I (slow); Type IIA (fast); and a third type IIX (the fastest). This last type is associated with the human fibre type previously designated as type IIb[36]. Muscle fibre type differentiation seems to be largely complete a few years after birth. Bell et al.[37] demonstrated that by the age of 6 y, the histochemical profile is similar to that of a young adult. However, the percent distribution of type II fibres is lower in early childhood than in adulthood[38] and attains adult proportions during late adolescence[39,40]. In most studies[41], but not all[37] there was a greater prevalence of type IIa than type IIb fibres during childhood and adolescence. However, there does not appear to be any clear gender difference in fibre type distribution during childhood.

 Fibre size: Fibre diameter increases by about 75 % from birth to 1 y of age. From early childhood to adolescence this increase continues by a magnitude of about 3.5 fold in girls and 4.5 fold in boys[38,42]. The lower limb muscle fibre area has been reported to increase about 20 fold, while the upper limb muscle fibre area increases by about 7-12 fold during the same period[43]. In girls, the fibre diameter reaches its peak during adolescence, while boys only achieve their peak size during early adulthood[42]. In the study of Jansson and Hedberg[41], adolescent boys had larger average fibre areas than girls ($p<0.05$). The authors suggested, that these results were due to a combined effect of strength training among boys and a genetically determined larger muscle growth during puberty. Moreover, boys exhibit relatively greater size increase in type II fibres, and more specifically type IIb fibres, than girls[44]. Simoneau et al.[45] showed the same type of gender difference in 25-year-old subjects.

- Muscle mass

 Skeletal muscle, is the tissue responsible for force generation. During growth, one might predict a strong association between muscle mass and muscle force. Growth in muscle from foetus to adult is accompanied by changes in biochemical composition. There are important changes in the muscle protein content . For example, the myofibrillar fraction increases by about 3.4 times between the 14th week of gestation and adulthood. At the same time, the sarcoplasmic proteins show only a two-fold increase. The greater relative increase in the myofibrillar proteins during maturation probably reflects the stage of development and the need for enhanced muscle activity[46]. Muscle mass increases from about 42% to 54% of body mass in males from 5 to 18 y (from 7.5 kg to 37 kg, about a five-fold increase). Comparative values for females range from about 40% to 42.5% of body mass in the same age range (from 7 kg to 24 kg, about three-fold increase). After 6-7 years of age, boys have a larger absolute and relative (kg muscle per kg body mass) amount of muscle than girls [47]. These patterns of muscle mass development account for a large extent of the age- and gender-associated variations in strength during childhood and adolescence.

- Muscle size

  Saltin and Gollnick[48] demonstrated that muscle circumference growth can best be measured by increases in fibre cross-sectional area (CSA). Figure 4, shows a direct relationship between fibre area and age in human subjects. Correlation coefficients of 0.85 were found between age and fibre area for the lower limb muscles. The relationship between CSA and force production has been described for isolated animal muscle[49] and for various human skeletal muscles under both maximal voluntary contractions[50] and electrically evoked contractions[51]. Although increases in muscular strength are closely related to changes in CSA, there are numerous cases where increases in force occur without any increase in muscular bulk. This can be explained by an increase in their capacity to recruit and activate more motor units (see neural adaptation). In children, correlations between muscle CSA , determined either by anthropometry, ultrasound, or computerised tomography, and maximal voluntary force have recently been reviewed[52], and are generally moderate to strong in both sexes across a variety of muscle groups. The gender difference in muscle size is small until mid-puberty, and reaches its peak difference during early adulthood[53]. With advancing age, the sex-related difference becomes more marked in upper limbs than lower limbs. After adolescence, girls only have about 50 % of the upper limb, but about 70 % of the lower limb muscle size of boys[54]. However, when absolute muscle force is normalised for muscle CSA, the age- and gender-associated differences in muscle force disappear[39,51]. Blimkie[52] concludes, that muscle CSA, rather than age and gender per se, is the most important factor influencing muscle force during growth.

- Hormonal effects

  Age- and sex-related changes in muscle mass and muscle strength have been largely attributed to hormonal influences[55]. Testosterone is believed to be the most active stimulator of anabolic processes in muscles. However, growth hormone, thyroid hormones, somatomedins and insulin are known to be important effectors in muscle growth[56]. In boys, testosterone increases about 4 fold during early puberty and then increases by another 20 fold between mid- and late puberty. In girls, testosterone increases only 4 fold between early and late puberty[57]. If testosterone and other androgenic hormones are responsible for the dramatic increase in muscle mass and force in boys during puberty, one should expect that early-maturing children would exhibit higher muscle force, at each age during puberty, than those maturing late. This seems be true for static force[58].

Age and gender differences

During childhood and adolescence, strong positive correlations have been reported between calendar age and various measures of maximal voluntary strength in boys[59]. However, in pre-pubertal girls only moderate positive correlations have been

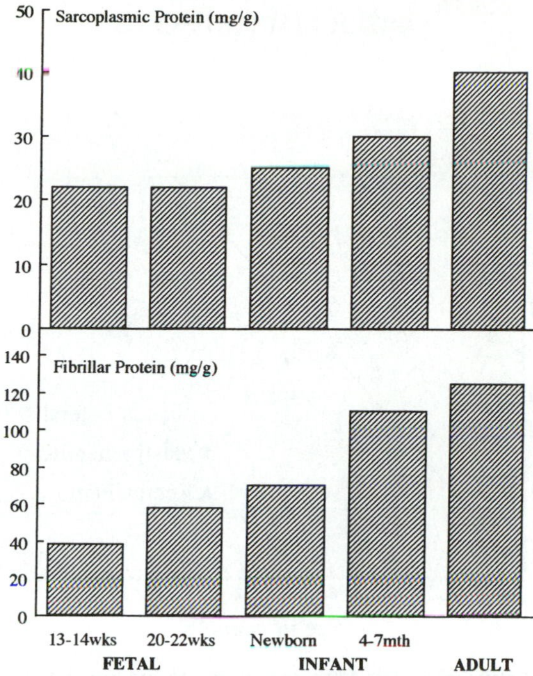

Fig. 3 Changes in percentage of sarcoplasmic and myofibrillar protein fractions during growth (Taken from Saltin and Gollnick, 1983 as adapted from Dickerson and Widdowson, 1960)

reported between age and muscle force, while the correlations are generally low and sometimes negative during adolescence[60]. Age might exert an independent influence on force development through the mechanism of enhanced neuro-motor maturation [61]. For boys, there exists a curvilinear increase in muscle force from early childhood until the onset of puberty. Muscle force increases rapidly during the pubertal period and still increases, but at a slower rate, during adolescence. A similar pattern can be observed in girls until the onset of puberty (about age 12 y), but in contrast to boys, there is only a slight increase during puberty. Boys have a consistently higher average muscle force than girls between 3 and 18 years of age[52]. However, sex-related differences are small, with a considerable overlap between girls and boys, before the pubertal growth spurt in boys. From the onset of boys' pubertal growth spurt, there is a dramatic increase of their muscle force compared to girls.

Developmental aspects of contractile velocity

- Genetic factors

  Recent research[62,63] shows that a complex set of genes is controlling the expression of contractile properties and that these are closely linked to those determining metabolic properties. Of the contractile proteins, it is the (iso-)form of the myosin heavy chain (MHC) that is expressed, which seems to be the primary determinant of

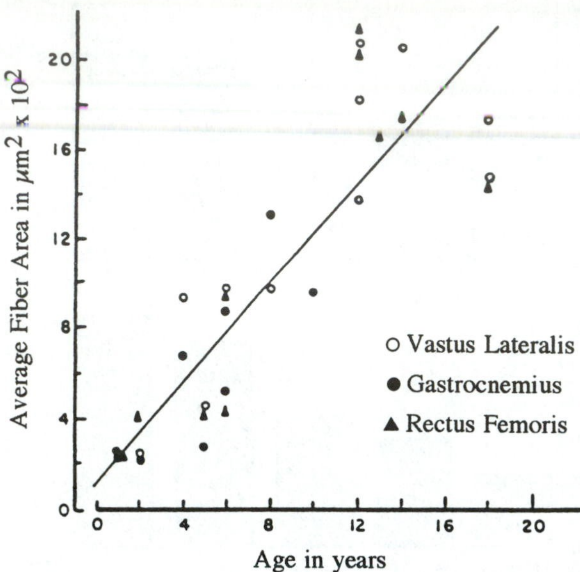

Fig. 4 Relationship between muscle fibre area and age for lower limb muscles (Taken from Saltin and Gollnick, 1983 using data from Aherne et al. 1971).

the muscle fibre's maximum velocity of shortening and hence power. Thus, to be successful in explosive events, large amounts of fast MHC (IIa/IIx(b)), often found in sprinters' muscle, are a necessity. Saltin[64] reported, that runners from East and West Africa had a different leg muscle fibre composition. Runners from East Africa presented 70% of slow-twitch fibres (distance runners), while only 25% slow-twitch fibres were found in West African runners (sprinters). Surprisingly, youngsters from the two regions had similar muscle fibre compositions to their senior counter parts, further supporting the notion that there is a strong genetic component in the contractile characteristics of skeletal muscle in man.

- Fibre type composition

  In the quadriceps of adult humans, type IIb fibres had 10 times greater maximum shortening velocity than type I fibres. The type IIa fibres were only 3 times more rapid than the type I fibres[65]. Difference at this level in shortening velocity might be expected to influence the velocity-dependent force and power relationships. If these contractile characteristics are present at all maturity stages, then the increase in type II fibre type distribution might give an advantage to older, compared with younger children, in short-term high intensity performances. Because of their significant higher type IIb areas, boys seem to have a potential advantage compared with girls, during the adolescent period.

- Length of myofibrils

  Physiologically, the maximum isometric force that a muscle can generate under any given conditions, will depend on the number of sarcomeres in parallel. Similarly, the maximum velocity of contraction of a muscle will depend only on the number of sarcomeres in series. Thus power, which is the resultant of force and velocity will depend upon the total number of sarcomeres both in parallel and in series. As muscle fibres increase in length, growth occurs as a consequence of an increase in the number of sarcomeres, which appear to be added to the ends of the myofibrils. Goldspink[66] has indicated that extra long sarcomeres are important, since the myofibrils are able to develop more force as a result of having a greater number of cross-bridges per sarcomere. Adaptation in sarcomere numbers in growing animals is of physiological significance, since the degree of muscle force depends on the degree of overlap of the thick and thin filaments. The optimum sarcomere length is that which allows the maximum amount of interaction between the myosin cross-bridges and the actin filaments. Since the length of both the thick and thin filaments are fixed, the only mechanism by which the muscle fibre can adjust its sarcomere length is to regulate the number of end-to-end sarcomeres. It seems probable then that each muscle can sense when its mechanical output decreases and add or remove sarcomeres to maintain the maximum functional overlap of the thick and thin filament.
- Neural factors

  Whether increased muscle force during puberty is due to muscle hypertrophy still remains a matter of debate[57]. This is especially true as the morphological adaptation is small in comparison with adults' data. Therefore, other factors besides change in muscle size must be taken into account. Among the suggested developmental neurological changes that might influence muscle force are, the process of myelinisation; the increased coordination of muscle synergists and antagonists[54]; and the increased ability to fully activate the muscles. Only the last hypothesis has been tested. Using the interpolated twitch technique[67], researchers from Mc Master University reported evidence that children have almost the same motor unit activation ability as adults[57]. It is also likely, that part of the muscle force gain may be attributed to improved motor coordination. Improved movement coordination is probably a more important contributor to muscle force gains in more complex, multi-joint exercises (vertical jump, arm- or leg cycling, sprint running, etc). It is during puberty that the pyramidal system attains full functional maturity and the subject becomes capable of developing the fine coordinated movements based on the integration of nervous activity from various levels of the central nervous system and the impact from all peripheral receptors[68]. Davies[51] argued that objective measurements of a muscle's ability to generate force should be independent of the subject's motivation. They used, therefore, electrically evoked twitch and tetanic tension at supramaximal voltages to measure contractile properties of the triceps surae muscle in pubescent girls and boys. In comparison, with young adults, no differences were observed, in specific muscle force (per cross-sectional area), fatiguability, contractile velocity and relaxation. It is suggested, that changes in muscle force as children grow do not appear to be explained by developmental alterations in the contractile mechanism. The study did not detect gender differences in contractile properties. Davies' findings agree with the study of Bäckmann and Henriksson [69] which observed that maximal contractile velocity is the same in children as in adults. This supports the conclusion that differences in muscle force between girls and boys are related to differences in body composition and hormonal stimulation, rather than to gender-related influences on the contractile properties of muscle[70].

III. Testing of developmental anaerobic function: issues, limitations and challenges

There is strong evidence, that the exercising child spends most of his/her daily activities fuelled by anaerobic rather than aerobic metabolism. However, until now, there has been a lack of an accurate, non-invasive method of measuring the anaerobic metabolism during exercise (for review see[28]). In the laboratory, most standard 'anaerobic' protocols used tests of relatively long-term duration. However, direct observations on prepubertal children show that the median duration of high-intensity activities was only of about 6 s. The median 'recovery' interval between these short bursts of activity was about 3 times longer[1].

Therefore, the aims of this section are, firstly to review if accurate and non-invasive methods exist, which are able to quantify the anaerobic ATP production during growth and maturation. Secondly, to see if the measurement of short-term mechanical work during the paediatric years is a relevant alternative to estimating indirectly the ATP energy turnover.

Instantaneous muscle power (< 1 s)

In numerous physical activities, games and sports, the child must activate and synchronise his/her motor units in order to displace his/her body mass for acceleration (e.g. sprints), against gravity (e.g. high jump) or throw a mass (e.g. shotput). These activities need a burst of muscular contractions of very short duration (< 1 s). Such instantaneous activity reflects the ability of the body to transform adenosine triphosphate (ATP) splitting into external power. If 'true' peak power output is to be measured, the duration of the test must be as short as possible, considering that power output decreases as a function of time. Moreover, anaerobic glycolysis and aerobic contribution are limited during instantaneous power exercises or tests. Since power is the product of force and velocity, the measurement of 'true' maximal anaerobic power requires measurements of instantaneous values of force and velocity. This condition is only satisfied in whole-body exercises (e.g. vertical jump) using a force platform or several monoarticular force-velocity tests[71].

Biochemical characteristics

Biochemical measurements on muscle biopsies[11] and nuclear magnetic resonance spectroscopy[72] data obtained in human muscles show that the phosphocreatine (PCr) and to a lesser extent the ATP levels, are reduced with increasing short-term high intensity exercise. Consequently, the maximal anaerobic muscular power of a subject is expected to be lower when a supramaximal exercise is performed on a much longer time basis. For example, during 4-6 s staircase running[73], because of the relatively long time basis, a substantial fraction of the overall ATP needed for performing

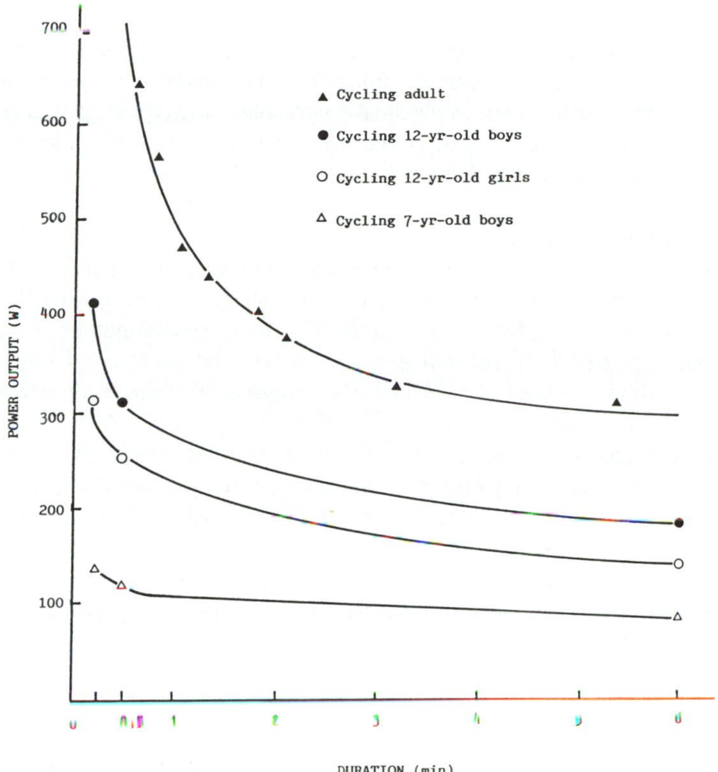

Fig. 5 Maximal external power as a function of exercise duration (Adult data from Wilkie, 1960; Children's data from Van Praagh et al. 1989, 1990)

the test was likely provided via ATP resynthesis by simultaneous PCr splitting. Ferretti et al.[74] were able to monitor maximal instantaneous muscular power on a time basis of only 4 ms, i.e., 1,000-1,500 times shorter than that for the Margaria's test. Recently, 13 children aged 8 to 13 y were matched against a group of sedentary subjects aged 20 to 50 y and a group of top level volleyball players[75]. The instantaneous power was calculated from instantaneous force measurements during a maximal vertical jump of both feet on a force platform[76]. The authors hypothesized that, at the moment during which the maximal instantaneous power is attained, the mechanical energy should derive exclusively from ATP splitting, without interference of ATP resynthesis from PCr.

Child/adult comparisons

Lower peak power values in children compared with adults is well documented[71,77]. However, the underlying mechanisms are still a matter of debate. The study of Ferretti et al.[75] provides more insight. They observed, absolute peak power values were 65% less in children than in young sedentary adults. At the same time, the cross-sectional areas (CSA) of lower limb muscles were 45% less in children than in young adults. Thus, the difference observed cannot simply be attributed to differences in muscle mass. Neither, can this discrepancy be attributed to differences in microscopic muscle structure, as the fibre composition does not seem to be different between children and adults[37]. Furthermore, no functional age-related changes could be observed: neither in [ATP][75] nor in maximal contractile velocity[69]. It was suggested, that hormonal changes occurring at puberty and neural factors may play a key role during developmental peak muscle power.

Short-term power (>1s-60s)
The issue is: can we consistently measure the 'anaerobic capacity' of children? Most of the traditional methods for testing anaerobic characteristics during growth have focused on power output[71,77]. The purpose of a more recent method: the accumulated oxygen deficit (AOD) method[8] was to assess the capacity of the anaerobic system. The method was used in paediatric populations by Carlson and Naughton[78].

Limitations of current short-term power- or muscle endurance tests
In children, direct measurements of anaerobic energy turnover cannot be done for ethical and (or) methodological reasons. Moreover, the exercise must be of sufficient duration to evoke the largest anaerobic ATP yield. For example, the total amount of ATP resynthesised during a 10s or 30s work period can be referred to as the anaerobic ATP yield, not to anaerobic capacity[2]. Therefore, several studies have focused on measuring the corresponding mechanical power output .

- Wingate 30-s cycling test
  This test has been evaluated more extensively than any other anaerobic performance test, and found to be highly reliable and valid in both normal and disabled populations. However, as was pointed out by Bar-Or[77], one disadvantage of this very popular test is that a 30-s cycling exercise is too short to sufficiently exhaust the organism and thus to extract all anaerobic work. Longer protocols would yield more work, but also require a higher percentage of aerobic participation[6,7].
- Force-velocity cycling test
  The aim of this test is to evaluate peak power during short-term (5-10s) leg cycling or arm cranking. Several 'all-out' exercise bouts are performed against different, but constant braking forces. The higher the braking-force, the lower the corresponding velocity (determined as pedalling rate). A 'quasi' linear force-velocity relationship is obtained in adults[79] and in children[80]. Recently, the main advantages of this test were reviewed[77]. However, more data are needed to establish the reliability and reproducibility of the force-velocity test.
- The accumulated oxygen deficit (AOD) method
  AOD is measured as the difference between the predicted (theoretical) oxygen demand and the actual oxygen uptake of a supramaximal exercise bout. The term 'accumulated' refers to measurements predicted or taken over the duration of the test. The prediction is calculated by an extrapolation from the linear regression of power and O_2 within a series of submaximal oxygen uptake exercise bouts. The number of submaximal tests depends on the range of workloads at which the subject can maintain a steady state. Carlson and Naughton[81] reported that one of the prob-

lems encountered with children is the small range of work capacity in which to establish a series of steady state values. This is not a problem with adults, as their range of work capacity is likely to be much higher. The power-O_2 relationship is calculated from the steady state tests. Saltin[28] criticised the method and argued that energy costs could not be extrapolated from submaximal to supramaximal conditions. Given that supramaximal conditions are more inefficient than submaximal conditions, Saltin postulated that any extrapolation of supramaximal energy demands from submaximal conditions would underestimate the true oxygen costs of high-intensity exercises. In adults, AOD is maximised within 1 min during an 'all - out' exercise, as opposed to a constant load exercise[82,83]. In children, Carlson and Naughton[81] reported AOD values for supramaximal cycling, for times ranging from 45 to 102 seconds at intensities representing work ranging from 150 to 110% of maximal aerobic power. The AOD method, as a measure of anaerobic capacity, has not gained complete international acceptance. For example, in well trained male cyclists, Green et al.[10] found that the AOD method was not related to muscle anaerobic ATP production ($r = -0.38$, $p > 0.05$). Despite some methodological difficulties, this method seems promising and suitable, especially for untrained- and paediatric populations (for recent review see[81]). More investigations are needed in this field.

New methods and challenges

In the near future, one of the main goals for paediatric exercise scientists is to conceive valid, reliable and minimally invasive methods to study the muscle metabolism on a cellular level. Amazing progress is actually being made in the development of molecular biology tools that can be used in for example, the genetic dissection of human performance phenotypes. Non-invasive power tools like: magnetic resonance imaging (MRI) and magnetic resonance spectroscopy (MRS) are still used with children. As an example, and related to the study of anaerobic function during growth, I would like to give the reader a short summary with respect to this promising field.

Genetic variation

Conflicting results have been reported with respect to the total genetic effect on short-term power[84]. The values ranging from just above zero to almost 100 % of the variance. Only two types of studies have been reported: a) Comparison of the phenotype in sibships of brothers and sisters by adoption or descent, b) The classical twin study

Simoneau et al.[45] investigated a total of 328 subjects belonging to adopted sibships; biological sibships of brothers and sisters; dizygotic twin sibships and monozygotic sibships were tested for supramaximal cycling during 10 s. The intraclass correlations for these types of sibships are summarised in Figure 6. Adopted children living together did not exhibit similarity in short-term cycling power (intraclass coefficient: R close to 0). Significant resemblances in short-term performance were found in pairs of sisters and brothers living together ($R = 0.46$). In a study of sibling similarities in sprint running (35-yd dash), Malina and Mueller[85] did not find differences in sibling correlations by race, but greater sibling similarities among brothers than sisters. Intraclass correlations between biological sibs and dizygotic twins ($R = 0.58$) were quite similar, suggesting that increased environmental similarity does not translate into in-

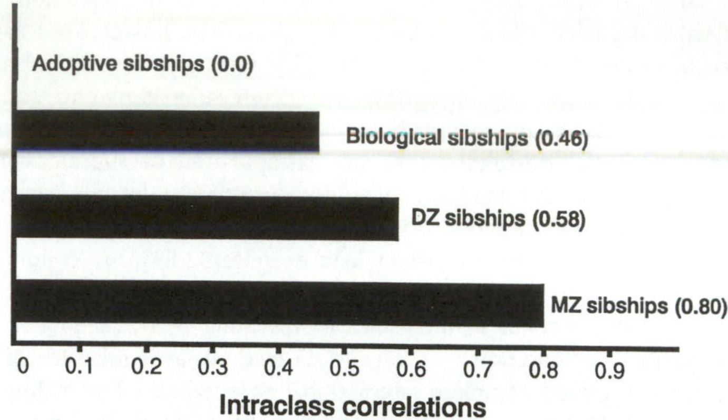

Fig. 6 Intraclass coefficients for maximal anaerobic power in adoptive, biological, dizygotic twin, and monozygotic twin sibships (Adapted from Simoneau et al., 1986)

creased phenotypic resemblance for short-term performance[45]. For monozygotic sibships, R reached 0.80. The latter results were fairly similar to those obtained by Komi et al.[86]. Simoneau and Bouchard[84] concluded that considerable variation exists in the ability to perform short-term power. This heterogeneity can to a large extent be attributed to genetic factors. Considering the small body of knowledge available, it is suggested that genetic factors account for approximately 50% of the total variance in short-term performance phenotype.

Magnetic resonance spectroscopy

Children's glycolytic ability which is presumed to be lower than adults was until now only discussed on the basis of the results of PFK activity at rest[11]. Using Magnetic resonance spectroscopy it is now possible to assess the anaerobic energy turnover during exercise in children. This technique provides a non-invasive means of monitoring intracellular inorganic phosphate (Pi), PCr, ATP and pH. Recently, it has been shown that during high-intensity exercise muscle Pi/PCr ratio increases to a smaller extent in children (untrained or trained) compared with adults[72,87]. The child/adult difference persisted even when the results were corrected for body size. In addition, children showed a smaller drop in end- exercise intramuscular pH than adults. It was suggested that the differences in metabolic responses during short-term intensity exercises between children and adults may be due to a maturational change in muscle fibre type distribution (percentage area of FT fibres increases with growth). The use of phosphorus nuclear magnetic resonance spectroscopy offers an alternative non-invasive indirect technique for investigating human muscle metabolism[88]. There are no apparent health risks and this technique seems suitable for use in children. However, as with all techniques it has its own limitations. The type of exercise (and the muscles involved) depends on the diameter of the bore magnets available. Cost and maintenance of the MR units are expensive and require highly skilled technicians. Furthermore, the time required for recording the spectra and the averaging of a number

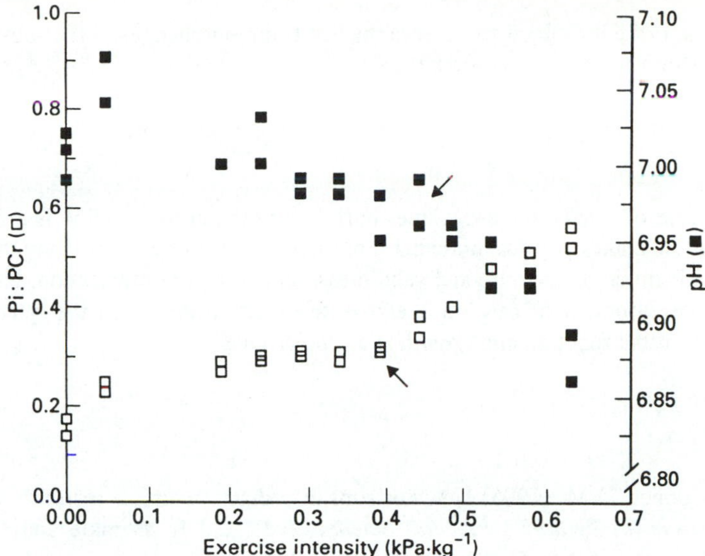

Fig. 7. Pi:PCr (□) and pH(■) at rest and during incremental exercise in a 9-year-old girl. The arrows indicate the transition points between the slow and fast phases of Pi:PCr and pH changes (From Zanconato et al., 1993)

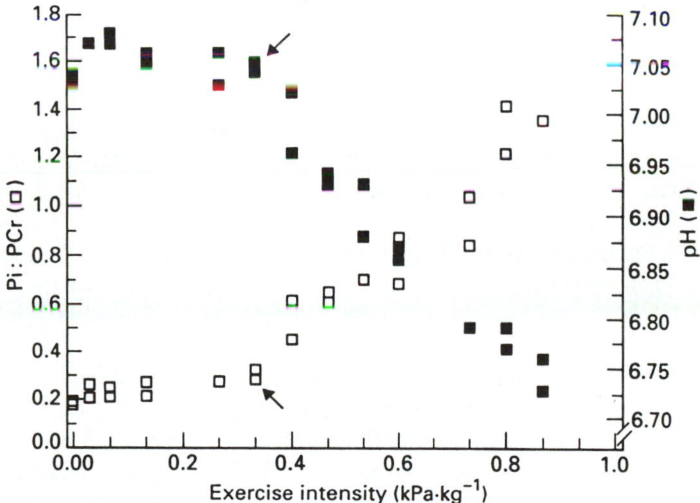

Fig. 8. Pi:PCr (□) and pH(■) at rest and during incremental exercise in a 33-year-old man. The arrows indicate the transition points between the slow and fast phases of Pi:PCr and pH changes (From Zanconato et al., 1993)

of spectra, make it difficult to observe the fast transient changes in the substrates being studied. (for a recent review see[89]).

Conclusion

The increase of anaerobic capabilities during growth and maturation is a fundamental aspect of the child's physical potential. For many years, this area of study was hindered by the difficulties of accurate and valid measurement and interpretation. However, today the development of new tools allows scientists to approach the relationship between anaerobic function and growth at a cellular level.

References

1. Cooper, D.M. (1995) New horizons in pediatric exercise research, in *New Horizons in Pediatric Exercise Science*, (eds. C.J R. Blimkie and O. Bar-Or), Human Kinetics, Champaign, Il., pp. 1-24.
2. Green, S. (1994) A definition and systems view of anaerobic capacity. *European Journal of Applied Physiology*, Vol. 69, pp. 168-73.
3. Davies, C.T.M. and Young, K. (1984) Effects of external loading on short-term power output in children and young male adults. *European Journal of Applied Physiology*, Vol. 52, pp. 351-4.
4. Grassi, B., Cerretelli, P., Narici, M.V. and Marconi, C. (1991) Peak anaerobic power in master athletes. *European Journal of Applied Physiology*, Vol. 62, pp. 394-9.
5. Bangsbo, J., Gollnick, P.D., Graham, T.E., Juel, C., Kiens, B., Mizuno, M. and Saltin, B. (1990) Anaerobic energy production and O_2 deficit-debt relationship during exhaustive exercise in humans. *Journal of Physiology*, Vol. 422, pp. 539-59.
6. Van Praagh, E., Bedu, M., Falgairette, G., Fellmann, N. and Coudert, J. (1991) Oxygen uptake during a 30-s supramaximal exercise in 7- to 15-year-old boys, in *Children and Exercise XV*, (eds. R. Frenkl and I. Szmodis), Nevi, Budapest, pp. 281-7.
7. Hebestreit, H., Mimura, K. and Bar-Or, O. (1993) Recovery of anaerobic muscle power following 30-s supramaximal exercise: comparison between boys and men. *Journal of Applied Physiology*, Vol. 74, pp. 2875-80.
8. Medbo, J.I., Mohn, A.C., Tabata, I., Bahr, R., Vaage, O. and Sejersted, O.H. (1988). Anaerobic capacity determined by maximal accumulated O_2 deficit. *Journal of Applied Physiology*, Vol. 64, pp. 50-60.
9. Bangsbo, J. (1996) Efficiency in repeated high intensity exercise, in *Human Muscular Function During Dynamic Exercise*, (eds. P. Marconnet, B. Saltin, P. Komi and J. Poortmans), Karger, Basel, Vol. 41, pp. 21-31.
10. Green, S., Dawson, B.T., Goodman, C. and Carey, M.F. (1996) Anaerobic ATP production and accumulated O_2 deficit in cyclists. *Medicine and Science in Sports and Exercise*, Vol. 28, pp. 315-21.

11. Eriksson, B.O., Karlsson, J. and Saltin B. (1971) Muscle metabolites during exercise in pubertal boys. *Acta Paediatrica Scandinavica*, Vol. 217 (suppl), pp. 154-7.
12. Eriksson, B.O., Gollnick, P.B. and Saltin, B. (1973) Muscle metabolism and enzyme activity after training in boys 11-13 years old. *Acta Physiologica Scandinavica*, Vol. 87, pp. 485-7.
13. Hill, A.V. (1938) The heat of shortening and the dynamic constraints of muscle. *Proceedings of the Royal Society of Belgium*, Vol. 126, pp. 136-95.
14. Wilkie, D.R. (1950) The relation between force and velocity in human muscle. *Journal of Physiology*, Vol. 110, pp. 249-80.
15. Vandewalle, H., Pérès, G. and Monod, H. (1987) Standard anaerobic exercise tests. *Sports Medicine*, Vol. 4, pp. 268-89.
16. Van Praagh, E., Falgairette, G., Bedu, M., Fellmann, N. and Coudert, J. (1989) Laboratory and field tests in 7-year-old boys, in *Children and Exercise XIII*, (eds. S. Oseid and K-H. Carlsen), Human Kinetics, Champaign, Il., pp. 11-7.
17. Sargeant, A.J. (1992) Problems in, and approaches to, the measurement of short term power output in children and adolescents, in *Pediatric Work Physiology XVI, Children and Exercise*, (eds. J. Coudert and E. Van Praagh), Masson, Paris, pp. 11-7.
18. Enoka, R.M. (1994) *Neuromechanical Basis of Kinesiology* (2nd edition), Human Kinetics, Champaign, Il.
19. Eriksson, B.O. (1980) Muscle metabolism in children: a review. *Acta Paediatrica Scandinavica*, Vol. 283 (suppl), pp. 20-7.
20. Berg, A., Kim, S.S. and Keul, J. (1986) Skeletal muscle enzyme activities in healthy young subjects. *International Journal of Sports Medicine*, Vol. 7, pp. 236-9.
21. Fellmann, N., Bedu, M., Spielvogel, H., Falgairette, G., Van Praagh, E., Jarrige, J-F. and Coudert, J. (1988) Anaerobic metabolism during pubertal development at high altitude. *Journal of Applied Physiology*, Vol. 64, pp. 1382-6.
22. Kindermann, V.W., Huber, G. and Keul, J. (1975) Anaerobe kapazität bei kindern und jugendlichen in beziehung zum erwachsenen. *Sportartz und Sportmedizin*, Vol. 6, pp. 112-5.
23. Brooks, G.A. (1985) Anaerobic threshold: Review of the concept and directions for future research. *Medicine and Science in Sports and Exercise*, Vol. 17, pp. 22-31.
24. Mero, A. (1988) Blood lactate production and recovery from anaerobic exercise in trained and untrained boys. *European Journal of Applied Physiology*, Vol. 57, pp. 660-6.
25. Welsman, J.R., Armstrong, N. and Kirby, B.J. (1994) Serum testosterone is not related to peak $\dot{V}O_2$ and submaximal lactate responses in 12- to 16-year-old males. *Pediatric Exercise Science*, Vol. 6, pp. 120-7.
26. Armstrong, N., Welsman, J.R. and Kirby, B.J. (in press) Performance on the Wingate anaerobic test and maturation. *Pediatric Exercise Science*.
27. Green, S. and Dawson, B. (1993) Measurement of anaerobic capacities in humans - definitions, limitations and unsolved problems. *Sports Medicine*, Vol. 15, pp. 312-27.

28. Saltin, B. (1990) Anaerobic capacity: past, present, and prospective, in *Biochemistry of Exercise VII,* (eds. A.W. Taylor, P.D. Gollnick, H.J. Green, C.O. Ianuzzo, E.G. Noble, G. Metivier and J.R. Sutton), Human Kinetics, Champaign, Il., pp. 387-412.
29. Welsman, J.R. and Armstrong, N. (in press) Blood lactate levels, in *Pediatric Anaerobic Fitness,* (ed. E. Van Praagh), Human Kinetics, Champaign, Il.
30. Kimura, K. (1956) The study on physical ability of children and youths: on-twins in Osaka City. *Jinrui Idengaku Zasshi*, Vol. 64, pp. 172-96.
31. Komi, P.V. and Karlsson, J. (1978) Skeletal muscle fibre types, enzyme activities and physical performance in young males and females. *Acta Physiologica Scandinavica*, Vol. 103, pp. 210-8.
32. Kovar, R. (1983) *Human Variation in Motor Abilities and its Genetic Analysis*, Charles University, Prague.
33. Kovar, R. (1975) Motor performance in twins. *Acta Geneticae Medicae et Gemellologiae*, Vol. 24, p. 174.
34. Jones, B. and Klissouras, V. (1986) Genetic variation in the force-velocity relation of human muscle, in *Sport and Human Genetics*, (eds. R.M. Malina and C. Bouchard), Human Kinetics, Champaign, Il., pp. 155-63.
35. Allen, R.E., Merkel, R.A., and Young, R.B. (1979) Cellular aspects of muscle growth: Myogenic cell proliferation. *Journal of Animal Science*, Vol. 49, p. 115.
36. Ennion, S., Sant'Ana Pereira, J. A., Sargeant, A.J., Young, A. and Goldspink, G. (1995) Characterisation of human skeletal muscle fibres according to the myosin heavy chains they express. *Journal of Muscle Research and Cell Motility*. Vol. 16, pp. 35-43.
37. Bell, R.D., MacDougall, J.D., Billeter, R. and Howald, H. (1980) Muscle fibre types and morphometric analysis of skeletal muscle in six-year-old children. *Medicine and Science in Sports and Exercise*, Vol. 12, pp. 28-31.
38. Colling-Saltin, A-S. (1980) Skeletal muscle development in the human foetus and during childhood, in *Children and Exercise*, (eds. K. Berg and B.O. Eriksson), University Park Press, Baltimore, pp. 193-207.
39. Hedberg, G. and Jansson, E. (1976) Skeletal muscle fibre distribution, capacity and interest in different physical activities among students in high school. *Pedagogiska Rapporter*, No. 54, Umea. (in Swedish with English abstract).
40. Fournier, M., Ricca, J., Taylor, A.W., Ferguson, R.J., Montpetit, R.R. and Chairman, B.R. (1982) Skeletal muscle adaptation in adolescent boys; sprint and endurance training and detraining. *Medicine and Science in Sports and Exercise,* Vol. 14, pp. 453-6.
41. Jansson, E. and Hedberg, G. (1991) Skeletal muscle fibre types in teenagers: relationship to physical performance and activity. *Scandinavian Journal of Medicine and Science in Sports*, Vol. 1, pp. 31-44.
42. Oertel, G. (1988) Morphometric analysis of normal skeletal muscles in infancy, childhood and adolescence. An autopsy study. *Journal of Neurological Sciences*, Vol. 88, pp. 303-13.

43. Aherne, W., Ayyar, D.R., Clarke, P.A., and Walton, J.N. (1971) Muscle fibre size in normal infants, children and adolescents: an autopsy study. *Journal of Neurological Sciences,* Vol. 14, pp. 171-82.
44. Glenmark, B., Hedberg, G. and Jansson, E. (1992) Changes in muscle fibre type from adolescence to adulthood in women and men. *Acta Physiologica Scandinavica,* Vol. 146, pp. 251-9.
45. Simoneau, J-A., Lortie, G., Leblanc, C. and Bouchard, C. (1986) Anaerobic alactacid work capacity in adopted and biological siblings, in *Sport and Human Genetics,* (eds. R.M. Malina and C. Bouchard), Human Kinetics, Champaign, Il., pp. 165-71.
46. Pearson, A.M. (1990) Muscle growth and exercise. *Critical Reviews in Food Science and Nutrition,* Vol. 29, pp. 167-96.
47. Malina, R.M. (1969) Quantification of fat, muscle and bone in man. *Clinical Orthopaedics and Related Research,* Vol. 65, pp. 9-38.
48. Saltin, B. and Gollnick, P.D. (1983) Skeletal muscle adaptability: Significance for metabolism and performance, in *Handbook of Physiology,* (ed. L.D. Peachy), American Physiological Society, Bethesda, p. 555.
49. Close, R.I. (1972) Dynamic properties of mammalian skeletal muscles. *Physiological Reviews,* Vol. 52, pp. 129-97.
50. Ikai, M. and Fukunaga, T. (1968) Calculations of muscle strength per unit cross-sectional area of human muscle by means of ultrasonic measurement. *Internationale Zeitschrift für angewandte Physiologie einschliesslich Arbeitsphysiologie,* Vol. 26, pp. 26-32
51. Davies, C.T.M. (1985) Strength and mechanical properties of muscle in children and young adults. *Scandinavian Journal of Sports Science,* Vol. 7, pp.11-5.
52. Blimkie, C.J.R. (1989) Age- and sex-associated variation in strength during childhood: Anthropometric, morphologic, neurologic, biomechanical, endocrinologic, genetic and physical activity correlates; in *Perspectives in Exercise Science and Sports Medicine. Vol. 2. Youth,* *Exercise and Sport,* (eds. C.V. Gisolfi and D.R. Lamb), Benchmark Press, Indianapolis, pp. 99-163.
53. Hettinger, T.H. (1958) Die trainierbarkeit menschlicher muskeln in abhängigkeit vom alter und geschlecht. *Internationale Zeitschrift für angewandte Physiologie einschliesslich Arbeitsphysiologie,* Vol. 17, pp. 371-7.
54. Sale, D.G. (1989) Strength training in children. in *Perspectives in Exercise Science and Sports Medicine. Vol. 2. Youth,* *Exercise and Sport,* (eds. C.V. Gisolfi and D.R. Lamb), Benchmark Press, Indianapolis, pp. 165-222.
55. Preece, M.A. (1986) Prepubertal and pubertal endocrinology, in *Human Growth,* Vol. 2, *Postnatal Growth Neurobiology,* (eds. F. Falkner and J.M. Tanner), Plenum Press, New York, pp. 211-24.
56. Florini, J.R. (1987) Hormonal control of muscle growth. *Muscle and Nerve.* Vol. 10, pp. 577-98.
57. Blimkie, C.J.R. and Sale, D.G. (in press) Strength development and trainability during childhood, *in Pediatric Anaerobic Fitness,* (ed. E. Van Praagh), Human Kinetics, Champaign, Il.

58. Beunen, G. and Malina, R.M. (1996) Growth and biological maturation: relevance to athletic performance, in *The Encyclopaedia of Sports Medicine: The Child and Adolescent Athlete.* (International Olympic Committee), (ed. O. Bar-Or), Blackwell Science, London, pp. 3-24.
59. Carron, A.V. and Bailey, D.A. (1974) Strength development in boys from 10 through 16 years. *Monographs of the Society for Research in Child Development.* Vol. 4.
60. Faust, M.S. (1977) Somatic development of adolescent girls. *Monograph Society For Research In Child Development.* Vol. 42, pp. 1-90.
61. Asmussen, E. (1973) Growth in muscular strength and power, in *Physical Activity, Human Growth and Development,* (ed. G.L. Rarick), Academic Press, New York, pp. 60-79.
62. Sant'Ana Pereira, J.A., Sargeant, A.J., de Haan, A., Rademaker, A.C.H.J. and van Mechelen, W. (1996) Myosin heavy chain isoform expression and high energy phosphate content of human muscle fibres at rest and post-exercise. *Journal of Physiology,* Vol. 496, pp. 1-6.
63. Sargeant, A.J. (in press) Fundamental considerations in the measurement of anaerobic muscle function in children, in *Pediatric Anaerobic Fitness,* (ed. E. Van Praagh), Human Kinetics, Champaign, Il.
64. Saltin, B. (1996) Values of Sport: A Biological Perspective, in *Frontiers in Sport Science*, (Book of Abstracts), Nice, pp. 18-9.
65. Larsson, L. and Moss, R.L. (1993) Maximum velocity of shortening in relation to myosin isoform composition in single fibres from human skeletal muscles. *Journal of Physiology*, Vol. 472, pp. 595-614.
66. Goldspink, G. (1983) Alterations in myofibril size and structure during growth, exercise and changes in environmental temperature, in *Handbook of Physiology*, (ed. L.D. Peachy), American Physiological Society, Bethesda, p. 539.
67. Belanger, A.Y. and McComas, A.J. (1989) Contractile properties of human skeletal muscle in childhood and adolescence. *European Journal of Applied Physiology*, Vol. 58, pp. 563-7.
68. Astrand, P.O. (1992) Children and adolescents: performance, measurements, education, in P*ediatric Work Physiology XVI, Children and Exercise*, (eds. J. Coudert and E. Van Praagh), Masson, Paris, pp. 3-7.
69. Bäckmann, E. and Henriksson, K.G. (1988) Skeletal muscle characteristics in children 9-15 years old: force, relaxation rate and contraction time, *Clinical Physiology*, Vol. 8, pp. 521-7.
70. Rowland, T.W. (1996) *Developmental Exercise Physiology,* Human Kinetics, Champaign, Il.
71. Van Praagh, E. (1996) Testing of anaerobic performance, in T*he Encyclopaedia of Sports Medicine: The Child and Adolescent Athlete*. (International Olympic Committee), (ed. Bar-Or. O.) Blackwell Science, London, pp. 602-16.
72. Zanconato, S., Buchtal, S., Barstow,T.J. and Cooper, D.M. (1993) 31P-magnetic resonance spectroscopy of leg muscle metabolism during exercise in children and adults. *Journal of Applied Physiology*, Vol. 74, pp. 2214-18.
73. Margaria, R., Aghemo, P. and Rovelli, E. (1966) Measurement of muscular power (anaerobic) in man. *Journal of Applied Physiology*, Vol. 21, pp.1662-4.

74. Ferretti, G., Gussoni, M., di Prampero, P.E. and Cerretelli, P. (1987) Effects of exercise on maximal instantaneous muscular power of humans. *Journal of Applied Physiology,* Vol. 62, pp. 2288-94.
75. Ferretti, G., Narici, M.V., Binzoni, T., Gariod, L., Le Bas, J.F., Reutenauer, H. and Cerretelli, P. (1994) Determinants of peak muscle power: effects of age and physical conditioning. *European Journal of Applied Physiology,* Vol. 68, pp. 111-5.
76. Davies, C.T.M. and Rennie, R. (1968) Human power output. *Nature*, Vol. 217, p. 770.
77. Bar-Or, O. (1996) Anaerobic performance, in *Measurement in Pediatric Exercise Science*, (ed. D. Docherty), Human Kinetics, Champaign, Il., pp. 161-82.
78. Carlson, J.S. and Naughton, G.A. (1992) Determination of the maximal accumulated oxygen deficit in male children, in *Pediatric Work Physiology XVI, Children and Exercise*, (eds. J. Coudert and E. Van Praagh), Masson, Paris, pp. 23-5.
79. Sargeant, A.J., Hoinville, E. and Young, A. (1981) Maximum leg force and power output during short-term dynamic exercise. *Journal of Applied Physiology*, Vol. 51, pp. 1175-82.
80. Van Praagh, E., Fellmann, N., Bedu, M., Falgairette, G. and Coudert, J. (1990) Gender difference in the relationship of anaerobic power output to body composition in children. *Pediatric Exercise Science,* Vol. 2, pp. 336-48.
81. Carlson, J.S. and Naughton, G.A. (in press) Assessing the accumulated oxygen deficit as a measure of anaerobic characteristics in children, in *Pediatric Anaerobic Fitness,* (ed. E. Van Praagh), Human Kinetics, Champaign, Il.
82. Gastin, P., Krzeminski, K., Costill, D.L. and McConnell, G. (1991) Accumulated oxygen deficit during isokinetic all-out and constant load supramaximal exercise. *8th Biennial Conference on Cardiovascular and Respiratory Responses to Exercise in Health and Disease*, University of Sidney.
83. Withers, R.T., Sherman, W.M., Clark, D.G., Esselbach, P.C., Nolan, S.R., Mackay, M.H. and Brinkham, M. (1991) Muscle metabolism during 30, 60 and 90 s of maximal cycling on a air-braked ergometer. *European Journal of Applied Physiology*, Vol. 63, pp. 354-62.
84. Simoneau, J-A. and Bouchard, C. (in press) Genetic variation of anaerobic performance, in *Pediatric Anaerobic Fitness,* (ed. E. Van Praagh), Human Kinetics, Champaign, Il.
85. Malina, R.M. and Mueller, W.H. (1981) Genetic and environmental influences on the strength and motor performance of Philadelphia school children. *Human Biology,* Vol. 53, pp. 163-79.
86. Komi, P.V., Klissouras, V. and Karvinen, E. (1973) Genetic variation in neuromuscular performance, *Internationale Zeitschrift für angewandte Physiologie einschliesslich Arbeitsphysiologie*, Vol. 31, pp. 289-304.
87. Kuno, S., Takahashi, H., Fujimoto, K., Akima, H., Miyamaru, M., Nemoto, I. Itai, Y. and Katsuta, S. (1995) Muscle metabolism during exercise using phosphorus-31 nuclear magnetic resonance spectroscopy in adolescents. *European Journal of Applied Physiology*, Vol. 70, pp. 301-4.

88. Chance, B., Sapega, A., Sokolow, D., Eleff, S., Leigh, J.S., Graham, T., Armstrong, J. and Waenell, R. (1983) Fatigue in retrospect and prospect 31P NMR studies of exercise performance, in *Biochemistry of Exercise,* (eds. H.G. Knuttgen and J. Poortmans), Human Kinetics, Champaign, Il., Vol. 13, pp. 895-908.
89. Cooper, D.M. and Barstow, T.J. (1996) Magnetic resonance imaging and spectroscopy in studying exercise in children, in *Exercise and Sport Sciences Reviews,* Vol. 24, pp. 475-99.

COMPARISON OF MUSCLE POWER BETWEEN LEGS

Single-legged muscle power

H. HEBESTREIT, S. HILPERT and V. STRASSBURG
Universitäts-Kinderklinik, Würzburg, Germany

Keywords: Leg volume, muscle power, peak $\dot{V}O_2$, single-legged cycling, thigh volume, Wingate anaerobic test

Introduction

The Wingate anaerobic test (WAnT) is commonly used to assess muscle power in children and adolescents with neuromuscular diseases[1]. The test has been shown to be feasible, reliable, and informative in these patients[2,3,4]. However, the WAnT only measures muscle performance of both legs combined. In some patients with neuromuscular disease such as cerebral palsy, meningomyelocele, or tethered cord syndrome one side is often more affected than the other. In these cases, small changes in muscle power of a single leg may reflect a worsening of the disease and necessitate further evaluation and treatment.

Single-legged muscle power has usually been assessed using dynamometers[5]. The overall costs for these tests are high due to the need of expensive equipment and long testing sessions requiring skilled personal. Sporadically, a single-legged cycling test following the protocol of the Wingate anaerobic test has been employed in the assessment of hemiplegic patients[6]. However, information on the normal range of power differences between one side and the other using a modified, single-legged WAnT are lacking.

The aim of this study was, therefore, to compare muscle power between legs in healthy and active postpubertal subjects. This age was chosen to minimize variation due to asymmetric body development. A second objective of the study was to examine the relationship between single-legged power and anthropometric measures.

Subjects

Eight women and 5 men, aged 17-20 y, volunteered to participate in this study.

Children and Exercise XIX. Edited by Neil Armstrong, Brian Kirby and Joanne Welsman.
Published in 1997 by E & FN Spon, 2–6 Boundary Row, London, SE1 8HN.
ISBN 0 419 22100 X.

Subjects´characteristics are summarized in table 1. All subjects were healthy and active, but none trained for more than 3 $h \cdot wk^{-1}$. All subjects were right-handed, all used their right leg more than or equally to the left leg for kicking a ball (kicking leg), but 7 subjects used the left leg for take-off in long-jump (jumping leg).

Methods

Each subject came to the laboratory twice for testing. During the first visit the study was explained to the subject and informed consent was obtained. Height and weight were determined and fat free body mass was calculated based on measurements of skinfold thickness and the equations of Slaughter et al.[7]. Subjects then performed a WAnT and, after 30 min rest, a progressive incremental cycling task to determine peak $\dot{V}O_2$. During the second visit various measurements of skinfold thickness, girth, and the length of multiple segments of the leg were taken on both legs[8]. Then subjects performed two single-legged, 30-s, all-out cycling tasks, one with each leg, administered in random order. At least 45 min of rest were scheduled between the tests.

All cycling tasks were performed using the Cardi O_2-Cycle ergometer (MedGraphics, Düsseldorf, Germany). Power and cycling cadence were transmitted on-line to a computer for further analysis using commercially available software (MedGraphics, Düsseldorf, Germany).

Wingate anaerobic test (WAnT)

The warm-up consisted of 4 min cycling at 50-60 $rev \cdot min^{-1}$ and at 15% of the predetermined resistance of the WAnT and included 4 short sprints of 3-5 s duration each. Then subjects rested for 4 min. Following another 2 min cycling at 15% of the applied resistance subjects were asked to accelerate and pedal as fast as possible for 30 s. Resistance during these 30 s was set to 5.05 $J \cdot kg^{-1} \cdot rev^{-1}$ for the women[9] and 5.76 $J \cdot kg^{-1} \cdot rev^{-1}$ for the men[10]. The test results are expressed as average power over the 30 s.

Single-legged cycling task (SLC)

For the SLC one foot was taped to a pedal while the other was resting on a chair with the leg stretched to avoid involvement in power generation. Subjects then performed a 2 min warm-up at 15% of the resistance calculated for the SLC using only the leg to be tested. Then they rested for 4 min. Following 1 further min cycling at 15% of the applied resistance they pedaled at maximum speed for 30 s. The resistance was set to 2.78 $J \cdot kg^{-1} \cdot rev^{-1}$ for the females and 3.17 $J \cdot kg^{-1} \cdot rev^{-1}$ for the males. In a pilot experiment, these settings were shown to induce the highest mean power during the test. The mean power over the 30 s was used for further analysis.

Data analyses

Based on the anthropometric data lean thigh volume and lean leg volume (total leg volume without the foot) were calculated for each leg separately[8]. The relationships between WAnT mean power and SLC mean power in the right and left leg were examined using

Table 1. Subject characteristics

	Women n=8	Men n=5
Height (cm)	167.1 ± 1 3.8	181.0 ± 5.6
Weight (kg)	60.2 ± 3.3	74.6 ± 5.0
Body Fat (%)	22.0 ± 4.2	11.4 ± 2.7
Lean Leg Volume right (L)	6.04 ± 0.50	8.00 ± 0.53
Lean Thigh Volume right (L)	3.96 ± 0.37	5.24 ± 0.37
Lean Leg Volume left (L)	6.01 ± 0.55	8.22 ± 0.58
Lean Thigh Volume left (L)	3.89 ± 0.34	5.42 ± 0.38
Peak $\dot{V}O_2$ ($mL{\cdot}kg^{-1}{\cdot}min^{-1}$)	45.36 ± 4.46	54.32 ± 3.54
WAnT Peak Power (W)	560.3 ± 44.1	860.0 ± 74.8
WAnT Mean Power (W)	470.4 ± 36.9	747.8 ± 49.3
WAnT Peak Power ($W{\cdot}kg^{-1}$)	9.31 ± 0.55	11.53 ± 0.53
WAnT Mean Power ($W{\cdot}kg^{-1}$)	7.82 ± 0.50	10.03 ± 0.31

Values are mean ± SD

correlation coefficients. Likewise, correlation coefficients were calculated for the SLC mean power and the thigh or leg volume, for the right and left side, respectively.

The percent difference between legs in power (ΔSLC) was calculated by dividing the difference of power of the right leg minus the power of the left leg by the average power of both legs, and multiplying by 100. Likewise, the percent difference in leg volume was computed (ΔVolume). Correlation analysis was performed to identify the relationship of differences in power and differences in size between the legs.

Results

Mean power of the right leg during the SLC averaged 268.1 ± 31.4 W in the females and 418.2 ± 22.4 W in the males. Respective values for the left leg were 260.5 ± 32.4 W and 394.0 ± 28.8 W. Power output tended to be higher in the right leg, but was not significantly different between legs in the females, males, and the total group combined ($p > 0.05$). The power of each leg correlated highly with the power of the other leg for the entire sample. Analysing each gender group separately, however, correlations were only low to moderate and not statistically significantly different from zero (table 2).

The sum of mean power in the two SLC combined was 529 ± 56 W in the females and 812 ± 47 W in the males. In all subjects except one girl the sum of SCL mean power was higher then the mean power in the WAnT (12.4 ± 8.0% in females, 8.8 ± 4.9% in males).

Tight correlations were observed between one-legged power of either side and the WAnT mean power in females, males, and the total group (table 2). Only when both gender groups were combined were thigh volume and leg volume correlated significantly with power of the respective side (table 2).

Table 2. Relationships between power in the SLC, power in the WAnT, and leg volume measures

	Total Group		Women		Men	
	SLC_{left} (W)	SLC_{right} (W)	SLC_{left} (W)	SLC_{right} (W)	SLC_{left} (W)	SLC_{right} (W)
SLC_{left} (W)	-	0.92*	-	0.36	-	0.64
WAnT Mean Power (W)	0.94*	0.96*	0.72*	0.58	0.91*	0.98*
Thigh $Volume_{left/right}$ (L)	0.85*	0.84*	0.37	0.21	-0.06	0.18
Leg $Volume_{left/right}$ (L)	0.83*	0.86*	0.15	0.08	0.16	0.46
	ΔSLC (%)		ΔSLC (%)		ΔSLC (%)	
ΔThigh Volume (%)	0.23		0.66		-0.93*	
ΔLeg Volume (%)	0.26		0.26		0.03	

Level of significance *$p<0.05$

The differences in average power during the SLC between legs ranged from -18.5% to 19.8% in the females (mean ± SD: 3.0 ± 11.4%) and from -3.6% to 11.8% in the males (6.1 ± 5.5%). Respective values for thigh volume differences were -3.7% to 6% (1.6 ± 2.8%) and -4.7% to -1.5% (-3.2 ± 1.0%), and for leg volume differences -3.9% to 3.2% (0.7 ± 2.5%) and -3.8% to -1.4% (-2.7 ± 0.9%). Correlations of power differences between legs and thigh volume differences were low for the entire group but moderate to high for each gender group. However, while the correlation was positive in the females, it was negative in the males (table 2). Using multiple regression analysis, only 11% of the variance in mean power differences between legs could be explained with thigh volume differences and sex as independent variables. Including the jumping leg as an independent variable did not increase the explained variance.

Discussion

The average power during a 30 s, all-out cycling exercise performed with one leg was not significantly different between the right and left leg. This finding is in agreement with Sargeant and Davies[11] who did not see significant differences in maximal power between the preferred and non-preferred leg during a single-legged, progressive incremental cycling task. Likewise, Smith[12] and Mohtadi et al.[13] detected no differences between the left and right legs in knee or hip torque during isokinetic dynamometry.

However, in the present study individual differences between the legs ranged from -18.5% to 19.8%. To our knowledge no other study has attempted to evaluate the inter-individual differences in power between legs during single-legged cycling tasks. Furthermore, little information is available on leg power determined with other methods. In preadolescent males a somewhat smaller variation of differences in peak quadriceps torque between legs has been reported ranging from -10.3% to +11.5% during concentric exercise and from -27.7% to +15.0% during eccentric exercise[13]. Asmussen[14] and later Sunnegårdh et al.[5] have suggested that children have lower differences between legs in power output because leg dominance has not developed fully.

It could be argued that the considerable individual differences in power between the legs reported in this study could be attributed to a high test-to-test variation. However, the performance of each side correlated well with the performance in the two legged WAnT, indicating a good reliability of power measurements during single-legged cycling. Furthermore, a high reliability of isokinetic single-sided peak torque measurements has been reported during flexion and extension knee exercise[13,15]. However, even in one of these studies considerable differences in torque were observed between legs[13].

In the present study, average power output during single-legged cycling was strongly related to lean thigh volume and lean leg volume in the group of females and males combined. This is in line with previous studies on short-term power output during two-legged cycling spanning a large range of volume measures[e.g. 14]. However, if the gender groups were analyzed separately, correlation coefficients were not significantly different from zero indicating that the interindividual variance in single-legged power could not be explained by inter-individual differences in thigh volume in these homogenous groups.

A surprising finding of this study was that the differences in power output between the legs were negatively related to differences in thigh volume in the men. Even when two additional young men were included in the analysis to increase n to 7 the relationship remained negative and significant ($r = -0.77$). In contrast, the females tended to have a higher power output with their larger leg. One possible explanation for this finding could be that performance in the SLC might be limited by cycling skill/coordination in the males whereas muscle mass might be limiting in the females. Further studies are necessary to assess this hypothesis.

In conclusion, performance in a single-legged 30-s, all-out cycling task was highly related to performance in the WAnT. However, considerable differences in average power were found between the legs which could not be explained by leg-dominance (kicking leg, jumping leg) or by differences in lean volume or leg volume. Further studies are necessary to better understand the mechanisms underlying the intra-individual differences in power output between the legs during single-legged cycling.

References

1. Bar-Or, O. (1996) Role of exercise in assessment and management of neuromuscular disease in children. *Medicine and Science in Sports and Exercise,* Vol. 28, pp. 421-7.
2. Parker, D.F., Carriere, L., Hebestreit, H. and Bar-Or, O. (1992) Anaerobic endurance and peak muscle power in children with spastic cerebral palsy. *American Journal of Diseases of Children,* Vol. 146, pp. 1069-73.
3. Parker, D.F., Carriere, L., Hebestreit, H., Salsberg, A. and Bar-Or, O. (1993) Muscle performance and gross motor function in children with spastic cerebral palsy. *Developmental Medicine and Child Neurology,* Vol. 35, pp. 17-23.

4. Tirosh, E., Rosenbaum, P. and Bar-Or, O. (1990) A new muscle power test in neuromuscular disease: feasibility and reliability. *American Journal of Diseases of Children,* Vol. 144, pp. 1083-7.
5. Sunnegårdh, J., Bratteby, L.-E., Nordesjö, L.-O. and Nordgren, B. (1988) Isometric and isokinetic muscle strength, anthropometry and physical activity in 8 to 13 year old Swedish children. *European Journal of Applied Physiology,* Vol. 58, pp. 291-7.
6. Bar-Or, O. (1993) Noncardiopulmonary pediatric exercise testing, in *Pediatric Laboratory Exercise Testing,* (ed. T.W. Rowland), Human Kinetics, Champaign, Il., pp. 165-85.
7. Slaughter, M.H., Lohman, T.G., Boileau, R.A., Horswill, C.A., Stillman, R.J., van Loan, M.D. and Bemben, D.A. (1988) Skinfold equations for estimation of body fatness in children and youth. *Human Biology,* Vol. 60, pp. 709-23.
8. Jones, P.R.M. and Pearson, J. (1969) Anthropometric determination of leg fat and muscle plus bone volume in young male and female adults. *Journal of Physiology,* Vol. 204, pp. 63-6P.
9. Dotan, R. and O. Bar-Or (1983) Load optimization for the Wingate anaerobic test. *European Journal of Applied Physiology,* Vol. 51, pp. 409-17.
10. Evans, J.A. and Quinney, H.A. (1981) Determination of resistance settings for anaerobic power testing. *Canadian Journal of Applied Sports Sciences,* Vol. 6, pp. 53-6.
11. Sargeant, A.J. and Davies, C.T.M. (1977) Limb volume, composition, and maximum aerobic power output in relation to habitual 'preference' in young male subjects. *Annals of Human Biology,* Vol. 4, pp. 49-55.
12. Smith, D.J. (1987) The relationship between anaerobic power and isokinetic torque outputs. *Canadian Journal of Sport Sciences,* Vol. 12, pp. 3-5.
13. Mohtadi, N.G.H., Kiefer, G.N., Tedford, K. and Watters, S. (1990) Concentric and eccentric quadriceps torque in pre-adolescent males. *Canadian Journal of Sport Sciences,* Vol. 15, pp. 240-3.
14. Asmussen, E. (1973) Growth in muscular strength and power, in *Physical Activity Human Growth and Development*, (ed. G.L. Rarick), Academic Press, London, pp. 50-79.
15. Lagassé, P.-P., Katch, F.I., Katch, V.L. and Roy, M.A. (1989) Reliability and validity of the Omnitron Hydraulic resistance exercise and testing device. *International Journal of Sports Medicine,* Vol. 10, pp. 455-8.
16. Katch, V. (1974) Body weight, leg volume, leg weight and leg density as determiners of short duration work performance on the bicycle ergometer. *Medicine and Science in Sports and Exercise,* Vol. 6, pp. 267-70.

WINGATE ANAEROBIC TEST PERFORMANCE IN RELATION TO THIGH MUSCLE VOLUME

Anaerobic performance of children

M. CHIA, N. ARMSTRONG, J.R. WELSMAN and R.J. WINSLEY
Children's Health and Exercise Research Centre, Institute of Clinical Science, University of Exeter, Exeter, UK
G. PARSONS and P. SHARPE
The Somerset MRI Centre, Bridgewater, UK
Keywords: Allometric scaling, magnetic resonance imaging, thigh muscle volume, Wingate anaerobic test

Introduction

Performance in the Wingate Anaerobic Test(WAnT) is often described in relation to a body size descriptor (e.g. body mass, fat-free mass). In exercise which involves moving and carrying the entire body mass such as during treadmill running, it is logical to express the performance in relation to body mass for ease of comparison between groups. However, in seated sprint cycling exercise where the body mass is supported, it may be more appropriate to relate the performance to some indicator of leg or thigh size. Some researchers have described young people's exercise performance in relation to leg muscle volume[1,2] but their results are equivocal, perhaps because the estimations of leg muscle volume are derived from anthropometric methods that may not be suitable for use with children. However, estimations of thigh muscle volume (TMV), employing magnetic resonance imaging (MRI), may be a more valuable approach in the study of young subjects. Researchers commonly use ratio standards to address differences in body size but there is a growing conviction that the ratio method may not appropriately normalise exercise data for differences in body size[3,4]. Allometric (log-linear) methods are recommended as more appropriate in accounting for body size effects, but these methods have not been widely used to describe young people's exercise performance in relation to TMV. Therefore, the purpose of this study was to examine the WAnT performance of young people in relation to TMV using both ratio and allometric models.

Children and Exercise XIX. Edited by Neil Armstrong, Brian Kirby and Joanne Welsman.
Published in 1997 by E & FN Spon, 2–6 Boundary Row, London, SE1 8HN.
ISBN 0 419 22100 X.

Methods

Twenty-four boys and 24 girls with appropriate consent participated in the study. Anthropometric variables were determined, and the sexual maturity[5] of the children was assessed by an experienced nurse.

Subjects completed a 30 s WAnT on a cycle ergometer (Monark 814E), from a rolling start of 60 rev·min^{-1}, with the applied force set at 0.74 N·kg^{-1} body mass. Inertia-adjusted 1 s peak power (PP) and mean power over 30 s (MP) were computed[6]. TMV was determined using MRI with a 0.5 Tesla scanner (Phillips Gyroscan T5II). The thigh was scanned medial to lateral in 6 mm thick longitudinal slices. Each scan was analysed from top to bottom of the femur and the areas of interest were traced using a mouse that was interfaced with the computer. TMV was obtained by multiplying the muscle area of each slice by its thickness and summing all the component slices.

Data analyses

Descriptive statistics of the subjects were generated. Gender differences in descriptive characteristics and WAnT performances were analysed using one-way analysis of variance (ANOVA). Allometric scaling factors for PP and MP were identified from log-linear analysis of covariance (ANCOVA), with TMV entered as the covariate. Subsequently, the appropriate power function ratios were computed. The level of statistical significance was set at $p < 0.05$.

Results

The physical and anthropometric characteristics of the children are presented in table 1. Sixty-seven percent of the boys and 75% of the girls were Tanner stage 1 for sexual maturity status. The rest of the subjects were either Tanner stage 2 for pubic hair and/or genitalia development for boys, or pubic hair and/or breast development for girls. Boys were significantly older and taller and had greater TMV than the girls. Log-transformed data describing allometric relationships between WAnT performance and TMV, revealed common b exponents for PP (b = 1.29 [SE 0.15]) and MP(b = 1.22 [SE 0.15]). Despite the boys being taller than the girls, the inclusion of stature and/or body mass into the log-linear model, did not make a significant additional contribution to b exponent. WAnT performances in absolute values and analysed in relation to TMV in ratio and allometric terms are summarised in table 2.

Discussion

The MRI data demonstrated that boys had greater TMV than girls, in contrast to previous anthropometrically determined data, albeit with older children that reported no

Table 1. Anthropometric and descriptive characteristics of the subjects

Variable	Boys	Girls
Age (y)	10.1 ± 0.3	9.9 ± 0.2 *
Stature (m)	1.37 ± 0.05	1.33 ± 0.06 *
Body mass (kg)	32.9 ± 4.1	31.5 ± 7.6
TMV (L)	1.98 ± 0.23	1.78 ± 0.32 *

Values are means ± SD
Level of significance *$p < 0.05$

Table 2. WAnT performances in absolute values and in relation to TMV

Variable	Boys	Girls
Peak power (W)	269 ± 45	220 ± 58 *
Peak power ($W \cdot L^{-1}$)	136 ± 15	122 ± 20 *
Peak power ($W \cdot L^{-1.29}$)	112 ± 12	103 ± 16
Mean power $_{30s}$ (W)	192 ± 33	168 ± 41 *
Mean power $_{30s}$ ($W \cdot L^{-1}$)	97 ± 12	93 ± 13
Mean power $_{30s}$ ($W \cdot L^{-1.22}$)	84 ± 10	82 ± 11

Values are means ± SD
Level of significance *$p < 0.05$

gender difference in TMV[7]. Inter-study subject differences and the limitations of anthropometric techniques to estimate TMV can account for the dissimilar results. In the present study, boys were significantly taller than girls and this could have accounted for the greater TMV of the boys. PP and MP allometrically modelled to TMV, were similar for boys and girls (see table 2), in agreement with the results of a recent study by Welsman et al[8]. In the present study, common b exponents identified for WAnT performance in relation to TMV (see table 2) were significantly different from 1.0. This supports the view that the conventional ratio technique inadequately adjusts for the effects of body size, and the log-linear technique more appropriately adjusts for body size effects[3]. It is noted that the TMV exponents identified for anaerobic performances deviate from that predicted from geometric similarity theory (i.e. $b = 0.67$)[9]. Two explanations are plausible. Firstly, subjects in the study did not conform to an isometric pattern, that is, they did not grow as geometric entities, as demonstrated by the inflated b exponents identified for both PP and MP. If this explanation is true, then sample-specific allometric modelling of exercise data is recommended in order to obtain meaningful information[3]. Secondly, the limitations of the WAnT in its ability to measure anaerobic performance in young people[3,7] may also influence the size of the b exponents.

References

1. Docherty, D. and Gaul, C.A. (1991) Relationship of body size, physique and composition to physical performance in young boys and girls. *International Journal of Sports Medicine*, Vol. 12, pp. 525-32.
2. Winsley, R. Armstrong, N., and Welsman, J. (1995) Leg volume is not related to peak oxygen uptake in 9-year-old boys, in *Children in Sport* (ed. F.J. Ring), Centre for Continuing Education, Bath, pp. 70-6.
3. Armstrong, N. and Welsman, J. (1997) *Young People and Physical Activity*, University Press, Oxford.
4. Nevill, A., Ramsbottom, R. and Williams, C. (1992) Scaling physiological measurements for individuals of different body size. *European Journal of Applied Physiology*, Vol. 65, pp. 110-7.
5. Tanner, J.M. (1962) *Growth at Adolescence*, Blackwell Scientific Publications, Oxford.
6. Chia, M.Y.H., Armstrong, N. and Childs, D. (1997) The assessment of children's performance using modifications of the Wingate Anaerobic Test. *Pediatric Exercise Science*, Vol. 9, pp. 80-9.
7. Van Praagh, E., Fellman, N., Bedu, M., Falgairette, G., and Coudert, J. (1990) Gender difference in the relationship of anaerobic power output to body composition in children. *Pediatric Exercise Science*, Vol. 2, pp. 336-48.
8. Welsman, J.R., Armstrong, N., Winsley, R.J., Parsons, G. and Sharp, P. (in press) Exercise performance and magnetic resonance imaging determined thigh musle volume in children. *European Journal of Applied Physiology*.
9. Schmidt-Nielsen, K. (1984) *Scaling: why is animal size so important?* Cambridge University Press, Cambridge, pp. 7-20.

TEST-RETEST REPRODUCIBILITY OF A NEW ISOKINETIC CYCLE ERGOMETER

Reproducibility of isokinetic cycle ergometry

C.A. WILLIAMS and P. KEEN
Chelsea School Research Centre, University of Brighton, Eastbourne, UK
Keywords: Anaerobic power, cycle ergometer, optimum cadence, reproducibility

Introduction

Cycle ergometer tests, to measure short-term muscle power, have been used since the turn of the century[1,2] Since these early studies and despite the methodological problems of measuring short-term power, many protocols and tests have been devised. Studies into muscle power using stationary ergometers, have been divided into two groups. Those researchers who use a fixed braking force and those investigators who propose the use of a series of very short tests at different braking forces. Both tests are affected by such factors as not knowing the optimal braking force or the optimal cadence, and problems of deceleration and acceleration of the flywheel.

The use of isokinetic cycle ergometers can alleviate some of these methodological difficulties. However, the literature is sparse in relation to children's isokinetic short-term muscle power[3,4,5]. In one study Sargeant and Dolan[5] found that the optimal pedalling cadence did not differ between adults and children.

Further research and development of muscle power measurement will promote understanding of children's anaerobic power. A priority of any new test or protocol is to ensure the reliability or reproducibility of the measurement. Therefore, the purpose of this study was to investigate the reproducibility of a new isokinetic cycle ergometer using the test-retest method.

Subjects

Twelve boys (mean age 13.1 ± 0.3 y; body mass 52.9 ± 11.3 kg; height 1.65 ± 0.1 m) completed the study and all were volunteers from a local secondary school. Prior to

Children and Exercise XIX. Edited by Neil Armstrong, Brian Kirby and Joanne Welsman.
Published in 1997 by E & FN Spon, 2–6 Boundary Row, London, SE1 8HN.
ISBN 0 419 22100 X.

the start of the study parents and children completed a written consent form. The study was approved by the ethics committee of the Faculty of Health.

Methods

The isokinetic cycle ergometer used for this study was constructed from a conventional bicycle frame, which was bolted securely to the superstructure of a large motor driven treadmill. The rear wheel was placed in contact with the treadmill which, by virtue of its reduction gearing and power, offers an immense braking force. The pedalling cadence of the ergometer is thus determined by the belt speed selected and remains constant (<2% variation) regardless of the power input of the subject. Pedal cadences between 0 and 170 rev·min^{-1} can be generated.

Power output was measured using a commercially available instrumented bicycle crank system (SRM Powercrank, Julich, Germany). The unit is designed to measure and record the power output produced riding a bicycle, and can be easily incorporated into any ergometer system that utilises a chain drive and conventional bicycle crank bearings.

The torque generated between the crank axle and the drive chain is measured by 20 strain gauges mounted on an aluminium disc connecting the crank axle to the chain-wheel. This arrangement detects the net driving torque generated from the forces applied to both cranks. Strain is processed "on board" the crank unit and transmitted inductively as an analogue signal, the frequency of which is directly proportional to the torque generated. The mean angular velocity for each revolution of the crankshaft is measured by triggering a reed-switch circuit. Torque and velocity data from the powercrank is collected by a small data logger located on the bicycle. Mean data over intervals of 1s or longer can be stored and downloaded to a PC. For this study torque and velocity data was sampled by a PC directly from the data logger at a frequency of 250 Hz. Mean power output over each complete crank revolution was then calculated.

The precision of the SRM powercrank was checked by a series of static and dynamic calibration trials. Complete linearity was established up to a torque of 125 Nm and repeated comparisons with constant velocity power measurements on a Monark ergometer revealed a standard error of estimation of <5 W in the range 100 - 500 W.

Prior to the start of the study each subject was habituated by practising a number of short maximal pedal sprints. The boys visited the laboratory on two occasions, the second was separated by at least a 2 d rest but within 7 d of the first test. The boys' height and body mass were determined, as well as leg length for the assessment of saddle height. All testing was conducted on the same purpose built isokinetic cycle ergometer with adjustable handlebars and saddle stem. All subjects wore toe-clips and an adjustable waist harness to prevent subjects from rising up off the seat during the test. Subjects then performed seven maximal all out sprints at differing pedal cadences. The first pedal cadence started at 90 rev·min^{-1} followed by a 5 min rest period. The pedal cadences were then subsequently increased by 10 rev·min^{-1} to a maximum of 150 rev·min^{-1}. Subjects performed the sprints from a non-rolling start and on initiation of the pedal start, a digital clock was started to time for 6 s. The recording of the torque and velocity data began once the subject initiated the movement of the pedal cranks. All subjects were given verbal encouragement. On the second test subjects returned to the laboratory and repeated the identical protocol.

Data analyses

Descriptive statistics were computed for the subjects' physical characteristics and the dependent variables in tests 1 and 2 (T1 and T2). The two dependent variables measured were mean power output (MP) over each complete crank revolution and the optimal cadence (Copt) determined from the power cadence parabolic curve. Pearson product moment correlation coefficients were determined for the two indices studied. To assess the reproducibility between the two tests, the method error of repeated measurements (ME) was used. The ME is calculated by determining the standard deviation of the mean average power difference between the two test sessions[6]. The method error is then often expressed as a coefficient of variation (V). A paired t-test was also used to check that there was no statistically significant difference between the mean values for the two test sessions. Quadratic regression equations were also generated between T1 and T2 where y represents the MP and where x is the pedal cadence. The determination of the Copt was calculated by fitting quadratic equations to the seven data points of the MP scores. The maximum power scores during each of the seven sprints demonstrated a parabolic curve whose apex represents the optimum cadence.

Results

Table 1 presents the test-retest data for MP for one complete revolution and the prediction of optimal cadence. Table 2 presents the quadratic regression equations between the maximum MP and pedal cadence for T 1 and T 2.

Discussion

The reliability of any new test is important if the test results are to be interpretable, reliable and accurate. The reliability of the WAnT has been reported extensively in the paediatric literature[7]. However, the test-retest method using interclass correlations is not an appropriate statistical method to show the reliability of an instrument[8]. An appropriate statistic to use is the method error of repeated tests which provides a number in the unit of the instruments measurement. The numeral is usually expressed as a percentage so that readers, unfamiliar with the units of measure, can assess the amount of variability.

The first findings from this study showed that the reproducibility of the power and optimal velocity scores was within acceptable limits. Naughton et al.[9] investigated the variability of children's anaerobic performance during a number of WAnTs. The V during one test session for peak power (PP)(highest recorded power over 0.1 s) and MP (averaged power over 30 s) was 7.3% and 6.8% respectively. In adults, Winter [10] produced similar Vs to determine optimised peak power using friction braked

Table 1. Test-retest data

Power (W) for one complete revolution		r	ME	V
Test 1	736 ± 155 (45)	0.92*	40	5.4%
Test 2	743 ± 147 (42)			
Optimal cadence ($rev{\cdot}min^{-1}$) (n=11)				
Test 1	123 ± 11 (3.3)	0.60*	7	5.8%
Test 2	117 ± 12 (3.6)			

Values are mean ± SD (SEM)
Level of significance * $p < 0.05$; no signifcant difference between means ($p > 0.05$)

Table 2. Test-retest quadratic equations between MP and pedal cadence

Test 1	MP $y = -349 + 16.6x - 0.065x^2$	$r^2 = 0.97$	F-ratio = 66.9	$p < 0.05$
Test 2	MP $y = -88 + 13.3x - 0.055x^2$	$r^2 = 0.79$	F-ratio = 7.6	$p < 0.05$

ergometers. Providing that standardised protocols and calibration procedures are rigorously followed, the majority of variance can be attributed to biological variation.

In the present study the 5 min rest intervals between sprints and minimum of 48 h recovery before T 2 should have ensured that fatigue was avoided. Another common threat to anaerobic reproducibility is motivation. This is a particular problem as there are no objective criteria to ascertain whether a maximal test has been performed. Naughton et al.[9] have shown through an interactive computer game that the V for PP, MP, and the fatigue index can be reduced compared to when the game was not used during a WAnT.

The second main finding was that the formulation of the quadratic equations to predict the optimised cadence score was subject to wide variation. Despite this, the prediction of optimal cadence was robust to deviations in the power cadence relationship curves. The second quadratic equation correlation was not as high as the first equation, which may be a reflection of the difficulty in continuously motivating children maximally, particularly when seven sprints are required. Future studies could investigate the optimal number of sprints to maintain a good quadratic fit for the data.

In conclusion, the current data from this isokinetic study are in agreement with similar studies. The protocol for this new isokinetic test was reproducible and indicates that the test will vary within 5.4% for mean power and 5.8% for optimal cadence. The seven short sprints used in this study provided additional power output information on the subject. However, it may be possible to have fewer sprints without compromising the power cadence relationship.

Acknowledgements

This study was supported by a grant from the Nuffield Foundation. The authors acknowledge the technical assistance of Alison Holmes.

References

1. Krogh, A. (1913) A bicycle ergometer and respiration apparatus for the experimental study of muscular work. *Scandinavian Archives of Physiology*, Vol. 33, pp. 375-94.
2. Dickinson, S. (1929) The efficiency of bicycle pedalling as effected by speed and load. *Journal of Physiology*, Vol. 67, pp. 242-55.
3. Sargeant, A.J., Dolan, P. and Young, A. (1984) Optimal velocity for maximal short-term power output in cycling. *International Journal of Sports Medicine*, Vol. 5, pp. 124-5.
4. Sargeant, A.J., Dolan, P. and Thorne, A. (1985) Isokinetic measurement of maximum leg force and anaerobic power output in children, in *Children and Sport*, (eds. J. Ilmarinen and I. Valimaski), Springer Verlag, Berlin, pp. 93-8.
5. Sargeant, A.J. and Dolan, P. (1986) Optimal velocity of muscle contraction for short-term power output in children and adults, in *Children and Exercise*, (eds. J. Rutenfranz, R. Mochellin and F. Klimt), Human Kinetics, Champaign, Il, Vol. 12, pp. 39-42.
6. Sale, D.G. (1991) Testing strength and power, in *Physiological Testing of the High-Performance Athlete*, (eds. J.D. MacDougall, H.A. Wenger and H.J. Green), Human Kinetics, Champaign, Il, pp. 74-8.
7. Bar-Or, O. (1987) The Wingate anaerobic test. An update on methodology, reliability and validity. *Sports Medicine*, Vol. 4, pp. 381-94.
8. Bland, J.M. and Altman, D.G. (1985) Statistical methods for assessing agreement between two methods of clinical measurement. *Lancet*, Vol. 1, pp. 307-10.
9. Naughton, G., Carlson, J. and Fairweather, I. (1992) Determining the variability of performance on Wingate anaerobic tests in children aged 6-12 years. *International Journal of Sports Medicine*, Vol. 13, pp. 512-7.
10. Winter, E.M. (1989) *Indices of External Power Output in Men and Women*, unpublished PhD Dissertation, Loughborough University of Technology, UK.

LACTATE, AMMONIA AND CATECHOLAMINE METABOLISM AFTER ANAEROBIC TRAINING

Lactate, ammonia, catecholamines and training

L.S. PRADO
Department of Sport Sciences, University of Constance, Germany

Keywords: Adrenaline, ammonia, anaerobic training, lactate, noradrenaline

Introduction

Children show different physiological reactions during and after short-duration, high-intensity exercise when compared to adults[1]. Many authors have observed reduced muscle and blood lactate concentrations in children after maximal aerobic bouts or after progressive exercise until exhaustion[2,3]. Similarly the catecholamine concentrations in blood, after progressive exercise to exhaustion, seem to be lower in children than in adults[4,5]. However, the data describing differences in the sympathetic activity of children and adults during maximal exercise, is contradictory[6]. Little information is available concerning the adaptations in the purine nucleotide metabolism essential for transforming chemical energy into mechanical work, after specific anaerobic training[7]. Furthermore, as far as the author is aware, nothing is known about purine nucleotide metabolism and muscle ammonia formation during anaerobic activity in children.

Many studies have noted that improvements in anaerobic capacity occur during adolescence[8,9]. The aim of this study was to investigate differences between male children and adults in maximal lactate levels, ammonia and catecholamine metabolism and changes in these metabolites following sprint swimming training.

Subjects

Twelve healthy boys aged 10.8 ± 0.7 y and twelve healthy male adults aged 24.0 ± 5.7 y were investigated. Both groups were involved in regular swimming training (three times a week). All subjects and the parents of the investigated boys gave written con-

Children and Exercise XIX. Edited by Neil Armstrong, Brian Kirby and Joanne Welsman.
Published in 1997 by E & FN Spon, 2–6 Boundary Row, London, SE1 8HN.
ISBN 0 419 22100 X.

Table 1. Descriptive data for children and adults at rest before and after training

	Children	Adults
Age (y)	10.8 ± 0.7	24.1 ± 5.7
Height (cm)	154.0 ± 8.8	180.4 ± 4.4
Weight (kg)	43.6 ± 7.7	77.3 ± 10.1
Testosterone pre ($ng{\cdot}mL^{-1}$)	0.20 ± 0.9	4.06 ± 1.6
Testosterone post ($ng{\cdot}mL^{-1}$)	0.19 ± 0.8	4.33 ± 1.3

Values are mean ± SD

sent after being informed about the experimental procedures. Physiological data are displayed in table 1. Maturational status was assessed by the determination of resting blood testosterone concentrations (see table 1)[10].

Methods

The subjects performed four 25 m swimming (freestyle) sprints at maximal intensity, with 5 s rest between sprints. This series was repeated three times with 5 min rest between series. Training was performed three times a week for 6 wk. Strong verbal encouragement was given throughout the training sessions. Training consisted exclusively of the described anaerobic series to minimise alterations in aerobic capacity.

Subjects were tested immediately before and after the training period. They underwent three maximal anaerobic tests on different days. First, a 25 m sprint with the time taken to complete the last 20 m measured. Second, time taken to swim a 100 m sprint. Third, distance swum in 45 s at the individual subject's maximal intensity. All tests were performed in a 25 m pool. Subjects swam only freestyle. No block starts were allowed and only simple turns were performed. Subjects received strong verbal encouragement during the testing sessions.

Testosterone was determined at rest and after the 100 m test, either before and after the training period and always at the same time of day (between 1700-1830) to avoid circadian variations. Five mL of blood was sampled from an arm vein into a vacutainer with 5 pg EDTA and 9 pg glutathione. Blood was centrifuged at 4° C for 10 min. Plasma testosterone concentration was determined by radioimmunoassay. Blood was collected in the laboratory for determination at rest and at the swimming pool for determination after effort. The sampling occurred immediately after the 100 m test.

For adrenaline and noradrenaline determination blood was collected and treated in the same way as described for testosterone. Plasma was stored at -20° C and later analysed by high-performance-liquid-chromatography (HPLC) (Waters Millipore, Eschborn). Plasma adrenaline and noradrenaline were determined at rest and after the 100 m test, before and after the training period.

Blood lactate concentrations were determined 1 and 3 min after the 45 s test, 1 min after the 20 m test and 3 min after the 100 m test. Concentrations were also determined 1 and 3 min after the first and the last training series at the beginning and at the end of the training period. Twenty µL blood were sampled from a hyperaemised ear lobe and analysed with the Accusport BM Lactate Kit (Boehringer Mannheim).

Blood ammonia was determined 3 min after the 3 performance tests. It was also determined after the subjects had completed the first and the last training pre and post training, as described for lactate. Twenty µL blood was collected from the hyperaemised ear lobe and analysed with the Ammonia Checker II (Menarini-Nobis, Endingen).

Results

Differences between groups before and after training were analysed with a Student's t-test for independent variables. Training effects within the groups were assessed with Student's t-test for dependent variables.

Testosterone levels at rest were significantly higher in adults before and after training. No alteration was observed within the groups after training (table 1). Post-exercise concentration also did not differ from rest values for both groups.

Adults improved their swimming performance in the 100 m test and the 45 s test after training. The 6 wk training period had no effect on the swimming performance of the children investigated.

Maximal lactate concentrations were markedly lower in children than adults after all exercise tests, both before and after training (see table 2). Training caused no alteration in the maximal lactate concentrations.

Maximal ammonia concentrations in blood were significantly lower ($p < 0.05$) in children than adults after all tests. Training did not change this situation. However, in adults a significantly lower average ammonia concentration in blood was observed in the 45 s and 100 m tests after training. No alterations were observed in the children.

Table 2. Lactate concentrations ($mmol \cdot L^{-1}$) before and after training

Test	Children	Adults
100 m pre	5.25 ± 1.00	11.92 ± 4.19
100 m post	4.96 ± 1.89	12.47 ± 3.40
45 s pre (1 min)	5.81 ± 1.54	9.47 ± 3.23
45 s pre (3 min)	3.76 ± 1.17	11.01 ± 2.61
45 s post (1 min)	5.47 ± 1.67	7.64 ± 2.82
45 s post (3 min)	4.86 ± 1.83	10.07 ± 2.13
20 m pre	3.45 ± 1.47	6.24 ± 1.55
20 m post	3.47 ± 0.79	4.91 ± 1.26

Values are mean ± SD

Table 3. Ammonia concentrations (μmol/L) before and after training

Test	Children	Adults
100 m pre	48.17 ± 13.13	149.17 ± 37.62
100 m post	50.00 ± 8.67	125.58 ± 41.60
45 s pre	68.72 ± 25.80	158.00 ± 38.13
45 s post	49.58 ± 12.41	114.00 ± 43.71
20 m pre	46.81 ± 16.43	74.41 ± 33.75
20 m post	38.91 ± 8.16	62.67 ± 34.89

Values are mean ± SD

Table 4. Adrenaline and noradrenaline concentrations ($nmol \cdot L^{-1}$) before and after training

Test	Children	Adults
Adrenaline 100 m pre	0.44 ± 0.32	5.38 ± 3.08
Adrenaline 100 m post	0.55 ± 0.51	7.17 ± 4.01
Noradrenaline 100 m pre	7.37 ± 3.21	27.12 ± 11.96
Noradrenaline 100 m post	7.06 ± 4.23	33.13 ± 12.04

Values are mean ± SD

Exercise induced a significant increase in adrenaline and noradrenaline concentrations for both groups, and post exercise increases were greater in adults. Training caused no alteration in the rest values of adrenaline and noradrenaline for both groups. The post-exercise values of adrenaline and noradrenaline remained unaltered by the children after training. However, significantly higher post-exercise concentrations of adrenaline and noradrenaline were observed following training in the adult group.

Discussion

Maximal lactate concentrations in this investigation were, without exception, significantly lower in children. This observation is in agreement with previous studies that have indicated reduced activity of glycolytic enzymes, lower maximal lactate concentrations and lower peak power output in anaerobic tests.

There were also no significant differences between the pre- and the post-training lactate values for both groups, which was expected for the children but not for the adults. Some authors have reported an increase in the maximal lactate concentration following sprint training[11,12]. This effect remains unexplained, since there was enough specific stimulation during the training period to produce the expected alterations in the maximal lactate concentrations in adults. The achievement of lactate concentrations after anaerobic exercise of short-duration demands a high motivational level[13,14]. Subjects in this study received consistent verbal encouragement during all the testing activities. Therefore, lack of motivation or concentration during the post-training testing sessions may be excluded as a cause for the lack of increase in maximal lactate concentrations.

Major differences in the blood ammonia concentrations after all the investigated exercise bouts were observed between children and adults. There are no available data describing muscular ammonia production in children. Acidosis is believed to be a major triggering factor of enhanced AMP deamination with ammonia formation in the active muscle[15,16]. The lower ammonia concentrations in blood after exercise in this study are in agreement with lower acidosis levels after anaerobic exercise in children. Training had apparently no effect on ammonia formation in children. On the other hand, blood ammonia concentrations decreased significantly among adults after training. This observation may be explained by a better energy availability for ATP-resynthesis[17,18], since ADP accumulation during maximal exercise is also an important triggering factor of AMP deamination to IMP in the working muscle [16, 19]. An improved ATP resynthesis may be possible due to an enhanced glycolytic flow after training or even to increased glycogenolysis[11,20].

An important finding was the observed child-adult differences in plasma adrenaline and noradrenaline concentrations after exercise. Prior limited data have shown similar responses in pre-pubertal boys after progressive work[4]. On the contrary, Rowland et al.[6] could not observe any difference in the plasma noradrenaline concentrations between boys and male adults after submaximal and maximal cycle exercise. Differences between the results from this study and that of Rowland[6] might be explained by a different sympathetic stimulation due to the different modes of exercise[21]. Training had no significant effect on post-exercise adrenaline and noradrenaline concentrations in children. However, significantly higher post-exercise catecholamine concentrations were observed among adults after training. This was an expected adaptation, since these hormones are responsible for the physiological reactions to the high energy demand during anaerobic exercise and for the activation of glycogenolysis[22,23]. A higher rate of glycogen breakdown could also lead to enhanced ATP resynthesis. This is in agreement with the reported lower ammonia levels in adults, although the effect of specific anaerobic training on catecholamine metabolism is not well known[11].

Many authors have suggested that maturational adaptations during puberty play a central role in the development of anaerobic metabolism[8,24]. The results of the present study are in agreement with the reported data. However, the reason for the reduced anaerobic capacity in children remains unclear. Some studies have shown a relationship between maximal lactate concentrations following anaerobic exercise and testosterone at different maturational stages[8,9,24]. Longitudinal investigations have shown also a relationship between the improvement of anaerobic capacity during puberty and the increase of testosterone concentrations during this time period[8,9,24]. A testosterone-stimulated increase in muscle mass during puberty could be responsible for the higher lactate concentration and anaerobic capacity after puberty. Some authors have observed a positive relationship between lean body mass and anaerobic capacity during puberty [8,9,24]. Bar-Or[1] pointed out the importance of qualitative characteristics of muscles for the development of anaerobic capacity. As mentioned earlier, AMP deamination is regulated by acidosis and ADP accumulation[16,19]. Since children in this study were not able to achieve high lactate levels, lower ammonia concentration seems to be explained by this rather than being directly influenced by maturational aspects. Further investigation is needed to clarify the role of maturation in the sympathetic regulation during anaerobic exercise.

References

1. Bar-Or, O. (1984) The growth and development of children's physiologic and perceptional responses to exercise, in *Children and Sport,* (eds. J. Ilmarinen and I. Välimäki), Springer, Berlin.
2. Eriksson, B.O., Karlsson, J. and Saltin, B. (1971) Muscle metabolism during exercise in pubertal boys. *Acta Paediatrica Scandinavica,* Vol. 217(suppl), pp. 57-63.
3. Kuno, S., Takahashi, H., Fujimoto, K., Akima, H., Miyamaru, M., Nemoto, I., Itai, Y. and Katsuta, S. (1995) Muscle metabolism during exercise using phosphorus-31 nuclear magnetic resonance spectroscopy in adolescents. *European Journal of Applied Physiology,* Vol. 70, pp. 301-4.
4. Lehmann, M., Keul, J. and Korsten-Reck, U. (1981) Einfluß einer stufenweise Laufbandergometrie bei Kindern und Erwachsenen auf die Plasmakatecholamine, die anaerobe und die aerobe Kapazität. *European Journal of Applied Physiology,* Vol. 47, pp. 301-11.
5. Keul, J., Berg, A., Lehmann, M., Dickhuth, H.-H. and Korsten-Reck, U. (1982) *Biochemische Grundlagen des Kinderleistungssports*, Leistungssport Beiheft, Vol. 28, pp. 28-46.
6. Rowland, T.W., Maresh, C. M., Charkoudian, M., Vanderburgh, P. M., Castellani, J. W. and Armstrong, L. E. (1996) Plasma norepinephrine responses to cycle exercise in boys and men. *International Journal of Sports Medicine,* Vol. 17, pp. 22-6.
7. Terjung, R. L., Dudley, G. A., Meyer, R. A., Hood, D. A. and Gorski, J. (1986) Purine nucleotide function in contracting muscle, in *Biochemistry of Exercise VI,* (ed. B. Saltin), Human Kinetics, Champaign, Il.
8. Mercier, B., Mercier, J., Granier, P., Le Gallais, D. and Prefaut, C. (1992) Maximal anaerobic power: relationship to anthropometric characteristics during growth. *International Journal of Sports Medicine,* Vol. 13, pp. 21-6.
9. Falgairette, G., Bedu, M., Fellmann, N., Van-Praagh, E. and Coudert, J. (1991) Bio-energetic profile in 144 boys aged 6 to 15 years with special reference to sexual maturation. *European Journal of Applied Physiology,* Vol. 62, pp 151-6.
10. Falgairette, G., Duche, P., Bedu, M., Fellmann, N. and Coudert, J. (1993) Bio-energetic characteristics in prepubertal boys. Comparison with active and non-active boys. *International Journal of Sports Medicine,* Vol. 14, pp. 444-8.
11. Nevill, M.E., Boobis, L.H., Brooks, S. and Williams, C. (1989) Effect of training on muscle metabolism during treadmill sprinting. *Journal of Applied Physiology,* Vol. 67, pp. 2376-82.

12. Sharp, R.L., Costill, D.L., Fink, W. J. and King, D.S. (1986) Effect of 8 weeks of cycle ergometer sprint training on human muscle buffering capacity. *International Journal of Sports Medicine,* Vol. 7, pp. 13-7.
13. Sawka, M.N., Knowlton, R.G., Miles, D.S. and Critz, J.B. (1979) Post-competition blood lactate concentrations in collegiate swimmers. *European Journal of Applied Physiology,* Vol. 41, pp. 93-9.
14. Ueda, T. and Kurokawa, T. (1995) Relationships between perceived exertion and physiological variables during swimming. *International Journal of Sports Medicine,* Vol. 16, pp. 385-9.
15. Meyer, R.A. and Terjung, R.L. (1980) AMP deamination and IMP reamination in working skeletal muscle. *American Journal of Physiology,* Vol. 239, pp. C32-8.
16. Sahlin, K. and Katz, A. (1993) Adenine nucleotide metabolism, in *Principles of Exercise Biochemistry,* (ed. J.R. Poortmanns), 2nd, revised edition, Karger, Basel, Vol. 38, pp. 89-136.
17. Snow, R.J., McKenna, M.J., Carey, M.F. and Hargreaves, M. (1992) Sprint training attenuates plasma ammonia accumulation following maximal exercise. *Acta Physiologica Scandinavica,* Vol. 144, pp. 395-6.
18. Stathis, C.G., Febbraio, M.A., Carey, M.F. and Snow, R.J. (1994) Influence of sprint training on human skeletal muscle purine nucleotide metabolism. *Journal of Applied Physiology,* Vol. 74, pp. 1802-9.
19. Sahlin, K. and Broberg, S. (1990) Adenine nucleotide depletion in human muscle during exercise: causality and significance of AMP deamination. *International Journal of Sports Medicine,* Vol. 11 (suppl), pp. S62-7.
20. Thorstensson, A., Sjodin, B. and Karlsson, J. (1975) Enzyme activities and muscle strength after sprint training in man. *Acta Physiologica Scandinavica,* Vol. 94, pp. 313-8.
21. Obert, P., Falgairette, G., Bedu, M. and Coudert, J. (1992) Bioenergetic characteristics of swimmers determined during an arm-ergometer test and during swimming. *International Journal of Sports Medicine,* Vol. 13, pp. 298-303.
22. Chasiotis, D., Brandt, R., Harris, C. and Hultman, E. (1983) Effect of ß-blockade on glycogen metabolism in human subjects during exercise. *American Journal of Physiology,* Vol. E245, pp. E166-70.
23. Stainsby, W.N., Sumners, C. and Eitzman, P.D. (1985) Effects of catecholamines on lactic acid output during progressive working contractions. *Journal of Applied Physiology,* Vol. 59, pp. 1809-14.
24. Fahey, T. D., Valle-Zurris, A., Oehlsen, G., Trieb, M. and Seymour, J. (1979) Pubertal stage differences in hormonal and hematological responses to maximal exercise in males. *Journal of Applied Physiology,* Vol. 4, pp. 823-7.

A STUDY OF KNEE ISOKINETIC STRENGTH IN PREADOLESCENCE

Preadolescents' knee isokinetic strength

A. FARO, J. SILVA, A. SANTOS, P. IGLESIAS
University of Coimbra, Coimbra, Portugal
Z. NING
Macau Polytechnic Institute, Macau
Keywords: Isokinetic strength, knee extensors, knee flexors,

Introduction

Adults' muscular isokinetic strength has been widely studied in the last 20 y but data on isokinetic strength characteristics of children are sparse[1].

Weltman et al.[2] studied 29 prepubertal boys aged 6-11 y for concentric isokinetic strength at the knee, shoulder, and elbow joints to explore elbow and shoulder flexion and extension peak torque, they concluded that prepubertal males have similar patterns of concentric isokinetic strength measured at the knee, shoulder, and elbow joints compared to adults. Gilliam et al.[3] tested 56 active children aged 7-13 y for knee and elbow flexors and extensors to study the torque differences between boys and girls. The results revealed significant ($p < 0.05$) sex differences. More recently, Calmels et al.[4] studied nine young gymnasts and found that a significant increase of the flexor/extensor peak torque ratio was observed with increasing speed, due to the concentric ratios. Kanecisa et al.[5] examined 60 boys and girls, aged 6-9 y, with isokinetic measurement to investigate the influences of age and gender on the strength capabilities in relation to muscle size. The results of the study indicated that the ability to produce strength proportional to muscle size is lower in children than in young adults, regardless of gender, and lower in women than in men within the same age group. Burnie and Brodie[6] measured 18 prepubescent males using the Cybex II isokinetic system. The results indicated that an increase in limb velocity from 1.05 $rad \cdot s^{-1}$ to 4.2 $rad \cdot s^{-1}$ produced a significant decrease in the peak torque generated. The limb velocity was also shown to influence the peak torque, and the young boys showed velocity-related isokinetic strength characteristics similar to adults, although they had lower absolute levels, the children showed typical adult reciprocal muscle group ratios.

The purpose of this study was to analyse and compare characteristics of isokinetic

Children and Exercise XIX. Edited by Neil Armstrong, Brian Kirby and Joanne Welsman.
Published in 1997 by E & FN Spon, 2–6 Boundary Row, London, SE1 8HN.
ISBN 0 419 22100 X.

strength measurement of knee joint between adolescents and adults, and to study the influences of age on isokinetic knee strength.

Subjects

The subjects were 14 Chinese college male students and 14 Chinese primary school male students aged 8-10 y. Prior to the beginning of the tests, the weight, height, and leg lengths were measured. The anthropometric characteristics are given in table 1.

Methods

The subjects were tested in a sitting position, the hip was fixed at 120 degrees of flexion, both trunk and thigh were fixed by means of straps, the shin pad was positioned 2cm proximal to the internal malleolus. Strength of both extensors (quadriceps) and flexors (hamstrings) at the knee joint of dominant side was measured by means of an isokinetic dynamometer (Cybex II 6000, Lumex, Inc.) at angular velocities of 60 $deg \cdot s^{-1}$, 180 $deg \cdot s^{-1}$, 300 $deg \cdot s^{-1}$, 400 $deg \cdot s^{-1}$ and 500 $deg \cdot s^{-1}$ for concentric action. Each subject was given a practice bout with three repetitions in each test to allow muscles to warm up, to experience isokinetic exercises and to allow the subjects to become familiar with the test protocol. Three trials were done for each test at each velocity, the testing sequence started from 60 $deg \cdot s^{-1}$, 180 $deg \cdot s^{-1}$, 300 $deg \cdot s^{-1}$, 400 $deg \cdot s^{-1}$ until 500 $deg \cdot s^{-1}$ for concentric action. The rest period between each test was standardised to 1.5 min, and the best value of the trials was used for data analyses. All force values were corrected for influences of gravity. In total 90 variables of isokinetic strength measurement of the dominant leg were chosen for the study.

Data analyses

Descriptive statistics were computed for each group, and Student's t-test was used to assess group differences. A probability value of $p < 0.05$ was accepted for significance level.

Table 1 Anthropometric data of the subjects

Group	N	Age(y)	Height(cm)	Weight(kg)
School Children	14	9.36 ± 0.84	138.63 ± 4.34	30.6 ± 3.8
College Students	14	29.36 ± 6.11	168.36 ± 4.97	60.9 ± 6.7

Values are mean ± SD

Results and discussion

The results of the comparisons of peak torque of flexor of body weight % (PTFBW), peak torque of extensor of body weight % (PTEBW), peak torque of flexor (PTF), peak torque of extensor (PTE), peak torque ratio: flexors/extensors (PTR), total work of extensor of body weight percentage (TWEBW), total work of flexor of body weight percentage (TWFBW), angle for best peak torque of extensor (BAE), and angle for best peak torque of flexor (BAF) are presented in tables 2 and 3. These isokinetic variables have been considered as the most important isokinetic measurements in previous studies[2,4,7,8]. The results of comparisons show that prepubertal males demonstrate similar patterns of concentric isokinetic strength measured at the knee to adults, although they have lower absolute levels. This is consistent with previous studies[2,6]. The isokinetic parameters of both groups (tables 2 and 3) show a trend that strength of knee extensors and flexors decrease radically as the velocities of movement (shortening velocity of the muscles) increase, which is consistent with muscular mechanics according to the force-velocity curve of muscles for concentric action. By considering the relative strength values, for children, PTEBW decreases 45.01% while the velocity increases from 60 deg·s^{-1} to 300 deg·s^{-1}, and descends 34.88% from 300 deg·s^{-1} to 500 deg·s^{-1}, for adults, PTEBW also decreases 50.06% from 60 deg·s^{-1} to 300 deg·s^{-1} and 25.49% from 300 deg·s^{-1} to 500 deg·s^{-1}. PTFBW decreases 39.05% while the velocity increases from 60 deg·s^{-1} to 300 deg·s^{-1}, and there is a 28.88% drop from 300 deg·s^{-1} to 500% deg·s^{-1}, however, the adults' values also show a similar decreasing pattern. There is a decrease of 39.17% from 60 deg·s^{-1} to 300 deg·s^{-1} and a decrease of 25.37% from 300 deg·s^{-1} to 500 deg·s^{-1}. As seen in table 2, the decreasing velocities between children and adults are different from one another, especially between the decreasing rates of the PTEBWs while the velocity of the movement increases from 60 deg·s^{-1} to 300 deg·s^{-1}. However, there is a common point, where both groups demonstrate that isokinetic strength of knee extensors decreases much faster than knee flexors. It is believed that the rapid rate of decrease indicates a better ability of knee flexors in performance as the velocity of muscular contraction increases. It is concluded that adults have better performance of knee extensors while velocity of the movement ascends since the decreasing rate of PTEBW from 60 deg·s^{-1} to 300 deg·s^{-1} is positively correlated with jumping performance of the knee[7].

PTR represents the balance between hamstrings and quadriceps which has been studied in numerous studies because of the important role of both muscle groups in knee stability. The imbalance of the PTR not only influences athletic ability, but also may lead to muscular injuries[6,9,10]. Furthermore, it may also be used to assess muscular action and in particular inter-action and co-contraction of two-joint antagonist pairs of muscles. A PTR of 1 would indicate equal strength in both muscle groups, however, values ranging from 0.41 to 0.87 in adults have been reported. An overall trend of PTR can be observed: as limb velocity increases, so does the PTR [6,10]. In this study, there is a progressive increase of PTR as velocity increases, the children's

Table 2. Comparisons of Isokinetic Strength Variables between Children and Adults

Velocity	Group	PTEBW	PTFBW	PTE	PTF	PTR
60 deg·s^{-1}	Children	75.21± 2.40	48.29 ± 7.29	52.07 ± 11.01	33.57 ± 6.90	64.57 ± 7.74
	Adults	114.43 ± 11.88	62.00 ±6.10	153.14 ± 14.44	83.50 ± 9.33	54.58 ± 5.81
180 deg·s^{-1}	Children	51.50 ± 8.65	39.64 ± 5.57	35.64 ± 7.72	27.57 ± 5.32	77.43 ± 7.44
	Adults	74.79 ± 7.14	46.29 ± 7.81	100.71 ± 11.96	62.57 ± 11.47	62.00 ± 10.86
300 deg·s^{-1}	Children	41.36 ± 7.76	29.43 ± 3.92	28.86 ± 7.24	20.64 ± 3.99	72.07 ± 7.98
	Adults	57.14 ± 6.62	37.71 ± 5.95	77.14 ± 0.90	50.86 ± 7.76	66.41 ± 9.21
400 deg·s^{-1}	Children	34.93 ± 6.52	26.21 ± 4.93	24.29 ± 5.40	18.29 ± 3.97	75.36 ± 9.37
	Adults	50.07 ± 6.62	33.50 ± 5.26	67.71 ± 9.92	45.57 ± 8.42	67.36 ± 12.36
500 deg·s^{-1}	Children	26.93 ± 6.31	20.93 ± 4.57	18.86 ± 4.97	14.71 ± 3.75	79.29 ± 15.92
	Adults	42.57 ± 5.33	28.14 ± 6.71	57.86 ± 9.32	38.57 ± 10.01	66.00 ± 13.44

Values are mean ± SD
All adult-child measures are significantly different ($p < 0.01$)

PTR increases from 64.57% to 79.29%, it ascends 22.79%; for adults it increases gradually from 54.29% to 66.00% as the velocity ascends to 500 deg·s^{-1} it gains 21.62%, the largest ratios appear when the speed is 500 deg·s^{-1} in children and 400 deg·s^{-1} in adults. It implies that as the velocity increases, the force of the hamstrings decreases more slowly than the quadriceps, as seen in fig 1. It is noteworthy that the PTR of children is significantly higher than that of adults $p < 0.05$, which is consistent with some previous studies[2,4,6]. In Calmels' study, it was also found that a significant increase of the flexor/extensor PTR was observed with increasing speed, due to the concentric ratios. This indicates that strength of the flexors of propubertal males is accounting for more than that of the extensors. The reasons ratios in children are higher than those in adults may be related to the body size of children. Gilliam et al.[3] found that increases in body size (height and weight) and age had a significant effect on the ratio of flexor and extensor, and the ratio score decreases as age, height, and weight increase. On the other hand, the maximum rate of force production which is largely dependent on the amount and rate of neural activation is lower in children aged

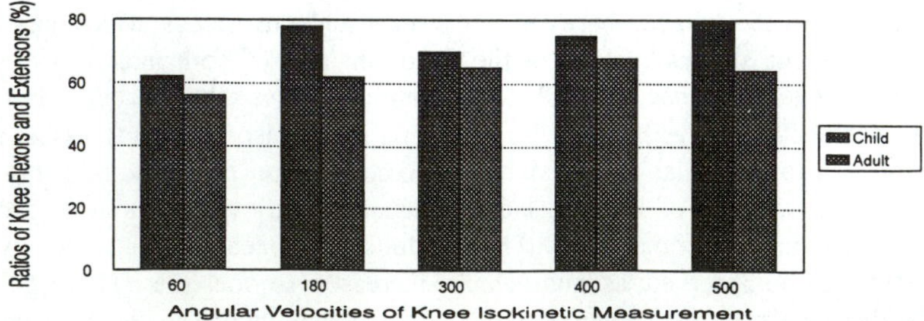

Fig. 1. Peak torque ratios of knee flexors and extensors between children and adults

8-11 y compared with college-aged men and women[5]. However, the relationship between hamstring and quadriceps strength of prepubescent children during the growth stage requires further study.

The same pattern of a decreasing trend was observed in the PTEWB and PTFWB (table 2). There is a big advantage of TWBW of knee flexor and extensor in adults. It shows that there are significant differences between adults and children in total work of body weight %. The values of these two variables in adults are significantly different from those in children as shown in table 3. Obviously the prepubescent children produce less total work than adults because of smaller values of peak torques produced by knee flexors and extensors. The other two variables examined in this study are the angles for maximal peak torque of extensors and flexors at five different velocities, which are BAE and BAF. The trend of BAE and BAF seems to be opposite from each other: that is, the BAF increases while the BAE decreases as the velocities of movement increase. The reason for this opposite trend is because 0 degree of the knee joint was defined as the full extension of the knee joint, that is, the increase of angle relative to extensor is equal to the decrease of angle relative to flexor. There is a similar pattern of these two variables, and no significant difference between adults and children. The angle for best peak torque of extensors decreases as the angular velocity increases, it decreases 35.34% for children and 31.23% for adults as the velocity ascends from 60 $deg{\cdot}s^{-1}$ to 500 $deg{\cdot}s^{-1}$. As to flexors, the angle for best peak increases 11.35% for children and 46.84% for adults in the same situation. The reason that the BAF of the children increases much less than that of adults may be related to absolute values of isokinetic strength measurement.

Conclusion

Isokinetic strength characteristics of the knee flexors and extensors are similar to those of adults, and children show lower absolute levels in almost all isokinetic

Table 3. Comparisons of means of main isokinetic variables

Velocity	Group	TWEBW	TWFBW	BAE	BAF
60 $deg{\cdot}s^{-1}$	Children	63.50 ± 12.91	47.86 ± 8.47	65.29 ± 5.77	43.43 ± 12.92
	Adults	98.14 ± 8.73**	67.10 ± 7.48**	61.50 ± 5.56	36.29 ± 6.83*
180 $deg{\cdot}s^{-1}$	Children	48.57 ± 8.69	42.21 ± 6.47	55.71 ± 7.22	46.07 ± 10.66
	Adults	76.86 ± 7.13**	50.14 ± 10.9**	49.93 ± 4.63*	42.36 ± 9.91
300 $deg{\cdot}s^{-1}$	Children	37.07 ± 8.12	29.07 ± 3.69	59.14 ± 4.19	37.86 ± 13.98
	Adults	56.29 ± 6.60**	37.50 ± 7.05**	54.07 ± 6.44*	38.57 ± 13.2
400 $deg{\cdot}s^{-1}$	Children	28.86 ± 5.84	22.57 ± 4.57	50.36 ± 5.43	39.93 ± 10.53
	Adults	45.36 ± 8.82**	29.07 ± 7.49**	48.00 ± 5.64	42.93 ± 5,65
500 $deg{\cdot}s^{-1}$	Children	21.14 ± 5.52	15.21 ± 4.26	42.21 ± 4.15	48.36 ± 5.02
	Adults	38.57 ± 6.22**	20.79 ± 5.91**	42.29 ± 5.61	53.29 ± 5.72

Values are mean ± SD

Level of significance between child and adult measures * $p < 0.05$, ** $p < 0.01$

strength parameters. Children demonstrated higher PTRs of flexors/extensors than adults, the reasons may be related to age, weight and other factors. and the relationship between hamstring and quadriceps strength of pre-pubescent children during growth requires further study.

Reference

1. Malina, R. and Bouchard, C. (1991) *Growth, Maturation, and Physical Activity*, Human Kinetics, Champaign, Il.
2. Weltman, A., Tippett, S., Janney, C., Strand, K., Rians, C., Cahill, B.R. and Katch, F.I. (1988) Measurement of isokinetic strength in prepubertal males. *Journal of Orthopedic and Sports Physical Therapy*, Vol. 9, pp. 183-6.
3. Gilliam, T.B., Villanacci, J.F. and Freedson, P.S. (1979) Isokinetic torque in boys and girls ages 7 to 13: effect of age, height, and weight. *Research Quarterly*, Vol. 50, pp. 599-609.
4. Calmels, P., Van Den Bourne, I., Nellen, M., Domenach, M., Minaire, P. and Drost, M. (1995) A pilot study of knee isokinetic strength in young, highly trained, female gymnasts. *Isokinetics and Exercise Science*, pp. 69-74.
5. Kanecisa, H., Ikagawa, S., Tsunoda, N. and Fukunaga, T. (1994) Strength and cross-sectional area of knee extensor muscles in children. *European Journal of Applied Physiology*, Vol. 65, pp. 402-5.
6. Burnie, J. and Brodie, D.A. (1986) Isokinetic measurement in preadolescent males. *International Journal of Sports Medicine*, Vol. 7, pp. 205-9.
7. Faro, A. and Ning, Z. (1995) Concentric and eccentric muscle function. *Biomechanics Seminar*, Vol. 9, pp. 148-53.
8. Ning, Z., Bouchard, C. and Faro, A. (1996) Isokinetic strength characteristics of four different event athletes. *The Proceedings of XIV International Symposium on Biomechanics in Sports*, Madeira, Portugal. June 24-28, 1996.
9. Baratta, R. (1988) Muscular coactivation. The role of the antagonist musculature in maintaining knee stability. *American Journal of Sports Medicine*, Vol. 16, pp. 113-22.
10. Westing, S.H. (1989) Eccentric and concentric torque-velocity characteristics, torque output comparisons. *International Journal of Sports Medicine*, Vol. 10, pp. 175-80.

RELATIONSHIP OF MUSCLE STRENGTH WITH MUSCLE VOLUME IN YOUNG CHILDREN

Muscle strength and muscle volume

M.B.A. DE STE CROIX, N. ARMSTRONG, J.R. WELSMAN and R.J. WINSLEY
Children's Health and Exercise Research Centre, Institute of Clinical Science, University of Exeter, Exeter, UK
G. PARSONS and P. SHARPE
The Somerset MRI Centre, Bridgewater, UK

Keywords: Allometry, isokinetics, muscle strength, muscle volume

Introduction

It is unclear whether gender differences in relative strength are due to differences in muscle mass or dissimilarity of use[1]. Davies[2] concluded that differences in absolute strength, ascribed to age and sex in young children, are a function of muscle mass and merely reflect differences in muscle development. This is supported by the work of Housh et al[3], who demonstrated with mature adolescents, moderate to high (0.61-0.70) correlations of total muscle mass to flexion and extension of the arm at 30, 180 and 300 $deg \cdot s^{-1}$. Their conclusions suggest that increases in peak torque across ages are fully accounted for by changes in muscle mass, and that there are no gender differences in peak torque per muscle and bone cross-sectional area.

No studies have related isokinetic leg muscle strength to magnetic resonance imaging (MRI) determined thigh muscle volume (TMV) in young children. Previous studies have determined peak torque per cross-sectional area (CSA) in adults, using both MRI[4,5] and anthropometric techniques[1]. The majority of research with children has focused upon the changes in CSA of muscle with strength training and has provided conflicting results[6,7]. However, few studies have examined the relationship between muscle size and strength. Early work[4] used ultrasonography to measure muscle mass of the arm, and demonstrated similar strength per unit of cross-sectional muscle between the sexes over the adolescent years. Others have noted that boys as young as 7 y have more muscle mass than girls and strength scores are not concomitant with increases in muscle mass[8]. This suggests that differences between the sexes in strength, from an early age, must be dependant on factors other than the quantity of muscle alone. Research has also demonstrated no significant differences in boys and girls of the same age in thigh muscle cross-sectional area, using anthropometric meas-

Children and Exercise XIX. Edited by Neil Armstrong, Brian Kirby and Joanne Welsman.
Published in 1997 by E & FN Spon, 2–6 Boundary Row, London, SE1 8HN.
ISBN 0 419 22100 X.

anthropometric measurements[9] or TMV using MRI[10]. It is generally acknowledged that there are limitations of using indirect measures of whole muscle mass and muscle CSA when determined anthropometrically and in relation to strength. Total muscle mass, or muscle plus bone cross-sectional area, using anthropometric equations taken from limb circumferences and skinfold measurements[11], were developed on adult subjects and remain to be validated for use with children.

Few studies have attempted to control for differences in body size, but where this has occurred it has been in simple ratio with body mass. Recent studies have demonstrated that the ratio standard does not adequately normalise data for body size[10,12]. Allometric (log-linear) models have been shown to be more appropriate for partitioning out body size effects, but have not been used in studies of children's muscle strength and muscle volume. Therefore, the relationship between strength and muscle mass or volume is at present unknown within the paediatric population.

This study was designed to investigate the relationship between isokinetic leg muscle strength and TMV determined by MRI, in young children, with the effects of body size controlled for using allometric scaling.

Subjects

The sample consisted of 42 healthy young children, 23 girls and 19 boys. Written informed consent was obtained from both the parents and the children. Prior to the start of the study all subjects spent a morning at the Centre to familiarise them with the testing procedure. Each child was examined by an experienced nurse to assess health status and to confirm that they were free of injuries to the lower extremities. Stature was measured using a Holtain standiometer (Crymych, Dyfed, UK) and body mass was measured using an Avery balance beam (Avery, Birmingham, UK).

Methods

Leg strength

Isokinetic concentric knee extension and flexion were measured using a calibrated Akron AIS dynamometer (Huntleigh Technology plc, Ipswich, UK). A specially designed chair was constructed which standardised the angle of hip flexion from the anatomical position to 120°, and which allowed for the various thigh lengths of the children. At all testing sessions a standardised procedure including a warm up of 2 min of stretching the hamstring and quadriceps muscles and 3 to 4 submaximal trials at each testing velocity was followed. Subjects were placed in a seated position with the lever arm of the dynamometer lined with the lateral epicondyle of the knee, and the force plate pad placed approximately 3 to 5cm superior to the medial malleolus with the foot in a plantigrade position. Range of motion during testing was set using the goniometer from 90° knee flexion to 180° extension with the range stop control set at soft. Testing occurred at 0.52, 1.04, 1.56, 2.09 and 3.15 $rads \cdot s^{-1}$ velocity modes, which were randomly assigned. At the start of each test session the subject was asked to relax their leg whilst it was held in an extended position by the examiner, so that a gravity correction reading could be established. Both limb and lever arm were allowed to fall passively against the resistance of the dynamometer (speed of velocity set at 5.24 rads·s^{1}) and corrections made[13]. Subjects were instructed to push the lever arm up, and pull it down, as hard and fast as possible for three maximal efforts, with extension always undertaken first. Maximal encouragement was given to each subject and a 90s rest period allowed between testing velocities.

Muscle volume

Evaluation of total TMV was determined by MRI, using a Philips Gyroscan T5 II with a field strength of 0.5 Tesla. The right thigh was scanned from medial to lateral, in 6mm thick longitudinal slices. The region of interest was measured from the head to the base of the femur. Subsequent analysis was conducted using a Phillips Gyroview computer. For each scan slice, total muscle area was measured by tracing around the relevant areas with a mouse interfaced with the computer. Volumes for each slice were obtained by multiplying the area of each component by the slice thickness (6mm). Individual slice volumes were summed to obtain total TMV.

Data analyses

All data were corrected for gravity and analysed using SPSS-PC^{+} (SPSS Inc., Chicago, USA). One-way analysis of variance (ANOVA) was performed to determine differences between boys and girls. Allometric scaling factors (b exponents) were identified from log linear analysis of covariance (ANCOVA) used to compute power function ratios (power/mass^{b}). Common b exponents relating mass to TMV generated from the allometric analysis were 0.69 (SE 0.14) (extension) and 0.88 (SE 0.15) (flexion) respectively. Pearson product-moment correlations were performed to determine the relationship of muscle strength, in absolute and body size adjusted terms, to TMV (table 2). Statistical significance was accepted at the $p < 0.05$ level.

Results

The physical characteristics of the children are presented in table 1.

Table 1. Physical characteristics by sex

Variable	Boys (n = 19)	Girls (n = 23)
Age (y)	10.2 ± 0.3 *	9.9 ± 0.2
Stature (m)	1.38 ± 0.05 *	1.33 ± 0.06
Mass (kg)	33.5 ± 4.2	31.8 ± 7.6
TMV (L)	1.97 ± 0.24 *	1.78 ± 0.32

Values are mean ± SD

Level of significance, *p<0.05

Table 2. Pearson product moment correlation coefficients between thigh muscle volume (L) and isokinetic leg muscle strength (highest peak torque, 0.52 rads·s^{-1})

Variable	Boys	Girls
Extension torque (Nm)	0.56*	0.78*
Flexion torque (Nm)	0.65*	0.67*
Extension torque (Nm·kg^{-1})	0.20	-0.18
Flexion torque (Nm·kg^{-1})	0.40	-0.18
Extension torque (Nm·$kg^{-0.69}$)	0.26	0.22
Flexion torque (Nm·$kg^{-0.88}$)	0.33	-0.05

* Level of significance, $p<0.05$

The boys were significantly older, taller and had greater TMV than the girls ($p<0.05$) but there were no significant differences in body mass.

Discussion

It is difficult to relate our data to those who have estimated CSA due to the limitations in anthropometic estimations of muscle mass, and due to the fact that we have determined TMV. However, others have shown no difference between young boys and girls in CSA of the thigh muscles[9].

There was no significant difference between the boys and girls when relating isokinetic leg muscle strength to TMV whether expressed in absolute, mass related terms, or as a power function ratio. This is in agreement with both adult and child studies, using CSA[1,2,3,4], as there appears to be no qualitative differences in the muscle function of the boys and girls in this study. TMV was significantly related to absolute isokinetic leg muscle strength over the range of velocities, supporting the notion that muscle strength is a direct function of muscle mass. This is in accord with much of the extant literature[2,3,14] but conflicting data are available[6,9]. The relationship between torque values recorded on the Akron and other isokinetic dynamometers has not been established so care must be taken when comparing results between studies.

We found no significant relationship between mass-related leg muscle strength and total TMV. The negative coefficients obtained in the present study for girls illustrate a well documented limitation of the ratio standard (Nm·kg^{-1}), in that it may 'overscale' by turning a positive correlation into a negative one[12]. The b exponents of less than 1 demonstrated in this study show that the ratio standard does not appropriately partition out body size differences from leg muscle strength. Others attempting to address the limitations of using the ratio standard have attempted to correlate muscle strength to lean body weight[15].

Data describing the allometric relationship between body mass and isokinetic leg muscle strength in children appear to be non-existent. The mass exponent of 0.69 for extension torque is close to the theoretical value of 0.67[10]. The slightly higher exponent of 0.88 for flexion torque identified in the present group of children may be explained partly by the small sample size. Our results demonstrate that TMV was not significantly related to peak extension and flexion torques once the effects of body mass had been partitioned out using appropriate allometric modelling. This is in agreement with research using absolute strength data[6], in which increases in strength were independent of changes in muscle size. Our data support the argument that expression of strength may be more dependant on neurological and mechanical factors (motor unit activation, motor skill co-ordination, individual moment arms), than muscle size, in young children[6].

In conclusion, this study has demonstrated that in young boys and girls there are no differences in isokinetic leg strength related to TMV. Data also show that absolute values for isokinetic peak extension and flexion torque are significantly related to TMV. However, these relationships became non-significant when the effect of body mass was controlled using appropriate allometric scaling techniques, suggesting that factors other than TMV contribute towards isokinetic leg muscle strength in young children.

References

1. Castro, M., McCann, D., Shaffrath, J. and Adams, W. (1995) Peak torque per unit cross -sectional area differs between strength trained and untrained young adults. *Medicine and Science in Sports and Exercise,* Vol. 27, pp. 397-403.
2. Davies, C.T.M. (1985) Strength and mechanical properties of muscle in children and young adults. *Scandinavian Journal of Sports Science,* Vol. 7, pp. 11-5.
3. Housh, T.J., Stout, J., Weir, J., Weir, L., Housh, D., Johnson, G. and Evans, S. (1995) Relationships of age and muscle mass to peak torque in high school wrestlers. *Research Quarterly for Exercise and Sport,* Vol. 66, pp. 256-61.
4. Narici, M.V., Roi, G.S. and Landoni, L. (1988) Force of knee extensor and flexor muscles and cross-sectional area determined by magnetic resonance imaging. *European Journal of Applied Physiology,* Vol. 57, pp. 39-44.
5. Conley, K.E., Cress, M.E., Jubrias, S.A., Esselman, P.C. and Odderson, I.R. (1995) From muscle properties to human performance, using magnetic resonance. *Journal of Gerontology,* Vol. 50A, pp. 35-40.
6. Ramsey, J.A., Blimkie, C.J.R., Smith, K., Garner, S., MacDougall, J.D. and Sale, D.G. (1990) Strength training effects in prepubescent boys. *Medicine and Science in Sports and Exercise,* Vol. 22, pp. 605-14.
7. Vrijens, J. (1978) Muscle strength developments in the pre and post-pubescent age. *Medicine Sport,* Vol. 11, pp. 152-8.
8. Rarick, G.L. and Thompson, J.A. (1956) Roentogenographic measures of leg muscle size and ankle extensor strength of seven year old children. *Research Quarterly for Exercise and Sport,* Vol. 29, pp. 200-3.
9. Sunnegardh, J., Bratteby, L.E., Nordesjo, L.O. and Nordgren, B. (1988) Isometric and isokinetic muscle strength, anthropometry and physical activity in 8 and 13 year old Swedish children. *European Journal of Applied Physiology,* Vol. 58, pp. 291-7.

10. Welsman, J.R., Armstrong, N., Kirby, B.J., Winsley, R.J., Parsons, G. and Sharp, P. (in press) Exercise performance and magnetic resonance imaging determined thigh muscle volume in children. *European Journal of Applied Physiology*.
11. Jones, P.R.M. and Pearson, J. (1969) Anthropometric determination of leg fat and muscle plus bone volume in young male and female adults. *Proceedings of the Physiological Society,* Vol. 204, pp. 63-6.
12. Nevill, A., Ramsbottom, R. and Williams, C. (1992) Scaling physiological measurements for individuals of different body size. *European Journal of Applied Physiology,* Vol. 65, pp. 110-7.
13. Nelson, S.G. and Duncan, P.W. (1983) Correction of isokinetic and isometric torque recordings for the effects of gravity. *Physical Therapy,* Vol. 63, pp. 74-6.
14. Docherty, D. and Gaul, C.A. (1991) Relationship of body size, physique, and composition to physical performance in young boys and girls. *International Journal of Sports Medicine,* Vol. 12, pp. 389-92.
15. Tabin, G.C., Gregg, J.R. and Bonci, T. (1985) Predictive leg strength values in immediately prepubescent and postpubescent athletes. *American Journal of Sports Medicine,* Vol. 13, pp. 387-9.

ASSESSMENT OF MATURITY STATUS AND ITS RELATION TO STRENGTH MEASUREMENTS

Maturity status and strength measurement

L. HANSEN and K. KLAUSEN
Laboratory of Human Physiology, August Krogh Institute, University of Copenhagen, Denmark
J. MÜLLER
Department of Growth and Reproduction, Rigshospitalet, Copenhagen, Denmark
Keywords: Isometric and functional strength, maturation, soccer, training

Introduction

During the latest decade the focus on sport for children has increased and so have public and scientific interests in training effects during childhood and adolescence. In studies concerning training effects on children and adolescents the assessment of pubertal maturation has been made from a variety of parameters such as chronological age, bone age, peak height velocity, Tanner stages, serum testosterone, age of menarche and testicular volume. However, one cannot be sure that these indicators measure the same kind of biological maturity nor that they have the same timing of appearance, although a high correlation is seen across studies[1]. In adults, substantial information about factors which determine strength and the trainability of strength is available[e.g. 2,3]. It has been suggested from early studies that prepubescent boys were incapable of increasing strength or muscle cross-sectional area[4]. Insufficient quantities of circulating androgens have been suggested as a rationale for the ineffectiveness of strength training in prepubertal boys[4]. A number of more recent studies have shown strength gains in prepubescent children following appropriate resistance training programmes[5, 6]. Strength is related to body size and muscle mass but it increases more than predicted from height alone[7].

In this study relations between maturation, growth, isometric strength and training were evaluated based on cross-sectional data from an ongoing longitudinal study.

Subjects

Ninety-eight boys, aged 10-13 y volunteered as subjects, and all participants and their parents gave their informed consent. The study was approved by the local ethical

Children and Exercise XIX. Edited by Neil Armstrong, Brian Kirby and Joanne Welsman.
Published in 1997 by E & FN Spon, 2–6 Boundary Row, London, SE1 8HN.
ISBN 0 419 22100 X.

committee of Copenhagen, Denmark. All subjects were soccer players, but at different levels: 47 boys were characterized as elite players, selected by the coach to be the best team in the age category and 51 boys were non-elite players matching the elite boys by playing in the same clubs and being in the same age category, but in the lowest rated teams. Seven successful clubs in the area of Copenhagen, at the highest level in their age category, participated in the study. Height and body weight were measured and BMI was calculated as weight (kg) divided by height (m) squared.

Methods

Puberty

Maturity status of all boys was assigned by the same experienced paediatric endocrinologist based on assessment of secondary sex characteristics using the criteria of Tanner[8] and from testicular volume estimated from measurements of the size of the testes using a Prader orchidometer. Blood samples were drawn from an antecubital vein between 1600-1730 and centrifuged. Serum was stored at -20° C and later analysed for levels of testosterone and IGF-1 (insulin like growth factor 1).

Strength measurements

All subjects had a standardised warm up period (stretching of the knee extensor muscles and 5 min exercise on a Monark cycle ergometer) before the strength measurements. All subjects started with the dynamic strength measurements.

Dynamic strength (functional strength) was evaluated from performance in vertical jump and in broad jump. Vertical jump was performed from standing position with hands on the hips and without shoes. A maximal counter movement jump was performed and the best of three attempts was accepted as maximal. The ability to lift the body was assessed by a tape-measure attached to the back by a belt around the waist of the subject. At the floor the tape-measure was held in a device which allowed it to slide as the subjects pulled it upwards, the distance moved was then read in cm. Standing broad jump was performed according to Eurofit[9]. The distance from the take-off to the point where the back of nearest heel touched the mat was measured and the best of three recorded trials was used as the performance score (cm).

Isometric strength

The maximal voluntary isometric strength (MVC) of the hip and knee extensors was measured using a strain gauge dynamometer in a standardised seated position with support of the back[10]. The boys were all encouraged to the highest effort by the test leader and the best of three attempts was accepted as maximal.

Data analyses

Data were analysed using Student's t-test and Pearson's correlation coefficient.

Results

The elite group was significantly ($p < 0.05$) older (12.1 ± 0.6 vs 11.7 ± 0.9 y) significantly ($p < 0.001$) taller (153.2 ± 7.8 vs 148.1 ± 7.4 cm), and significantly ($p < 0.05$) heavier (41.6 ± 6.5 vs 38.3 ± 6.9 kg) than the non-elite group. There was no significant ($p > 0.05$) difference in BMI (17.7 ± 1.7 vs 17.4 ± 2.2 kg·m^{-2}) between the two groups. The results from the assessment of sexual maturation are presented in table 1. Although there are strong correlations between the assessment of secondary sex characteristics, using the G and PH criteria of Tanner, and testicular volume ($r = 0.8$-0.9), testosterone ($r = 0.8$) and IGF-1 ($r = 0.6$) for the whole group (not presented), we could not separate the two groups according to their maturation evaluated from these criteria. However, the groups differ significantly when testicular volume and serum testosterone were compared (table 1). No significant ($p > 0.05$) difference between the groups was seen in IGF-1.

The isometric strength results are presented in table 2. The elite group was stronger in the dominant leg, the non dominant leg, and in both legs together (15-17%). Both groups were about 35% stronger when results from each leg were added compared to both legs together. The elite group performed significantly ($p < 0.001$) better in functional strength, ie vertical jump 30.3 ± 5.1 vs 26.6 ± 3.7 cm and broad jump 163.5 ± 15.0 vs 148.3 ± 17.3 cm, respectively. Correlations between strength and height, weight, testicular volume and IGF-1 were computed (table 3). In the non-elite group correlations between dimensions (height and weight) as well as IGF-1 and MVC were found, these correlations were weaker in the elite group especially for IGF-1 where no significant correlations were found. In the non-elite group only one significant correlation between testicular volume or testosterone to MVC was found but a consistent weak correlation between testosterone levels and functional strength was present. In the elite group a weak but significant correlation between MVC and both testicular volume and testosterone was found.

Table 1. Assessment of sexual maturation

	Elite	Non-Elite
Genitals	2.0 ± 0.9	1.8 ± 0.7
Pubic Hair	1.6 ± 0.9	1.2 ± 0.6
Axil Hair	1 ± 0	1 ± 0.1
Right testicular vol (mL)	6.5 ± 4.6 *	4.6 ± 2.7
Testosterone (nmol·L^{-1})	1.8 ± 3.1 *	0.63 ± 1.3
IGF-1 (ng·mL^{-1})	264.7 ± 77.9	252.1 ± 92.6

Values are mean ± SD
Level of significance * $p < 0.05$

Table 2. Isometric strength

	Elite	Non-Elite
Non-dominant leg (N)	1554 ± 319 ***	1329 ± 298
Dominant leg (N)	1555 ± 311 ***	1350 ± 246
Both legs (N)	2323 ± 732 **	1988 ± 475

Values are mean ± SD
Level of significance ** p <0.01 *** p <0.001

Discussion

From this study it is evident that one has to select the criteria from which pubertal status is evaluated. It is common to determine pubertal status in children from Tanner's indices when performance in children and adolescents is investigated[eg. 6]. If the two groups studied had been evaluated using these criteria, then no difference in pubertal status would have been found though significant differences in testicular volumes and in serum testosterone were present. Increase in testicular size is usually the first sign of impending puberty, and volume of the testis before puberty is seldom greater than 3 mL[11], therefore measurements of testicular volume may be a better way to assign whether a group is prepubertal or not when boys are studied. The use of circulating levels of testosterone as a maturity indicator has limited utility due to the diurnal variations of the hormone and because of the fact that the responsiveness of hormone receptors also play a role[11]. Serum IGF-1 increases with increasing age and pubertal stages, but a pronounced variation within Tanner stages is found[12], accordingly it is not possible to separate the effects of age and puberty on serum IGF-1 in a cross sectional study[12].

From a theoretical point of view one should expect that muscle strength is correlated to the linear dimensions in the second power. However, Asmussen[7] found that muscle strength in the leg extensors is correlated with length to the 2.89th power, indicating influence from factors other than the dimensions of the body alone. In the present study the isometric muscle strength is shown to correlate with height and weight of the non-elite boys and with weight in the elite boys, indicating dependency between muscle strength and the dimensions of the body. The elite group is stronger than the non-elite group which could partly be explained by height and weight. Since the correlation between height and strength in the elite group is weaker than in the non-elite group, the difference in strength could be due to qualitative and/or quantitative changes in the muscles caused by circulating androgen hormones. This is supported by correlations between isometric strength and both testicular volume and testosterone levels. Age itself could also affect the strength development, partly attributed to maturation of the central nervous system (CNS), but the difference in age between the two groups in this study was only 0.4 y, and hence the difference in MVC could be due to a possible training effect on the CNS.

Table 3: Correlations between strength (isometric and functional) and height, weight, testicular volume and IGF-1

Non-Elite Boys	Height	Weight	Right tes. vol	Testosterone	IGF-1
Non-dominant leg	0.56 ***	0.68 ***	0.36	0.20	0.54 ***
Dominant leg	0.51 ***	0.64 ***	0.22	0.06	0.36 *
Both leg	0.32 *	0.49 ***	0.11	0.09	0.28
Vertical jump	0.12	-0.04	0.15	0.28	0.22
Broad jump	0.20	-0.15	0.27	0.46 ***	0.21
Elite Boys					
Non-dominant leg	0.33 *	0.54 ***	0.37 **	0.30 *	0.01
Dominant leg	0.25	0.46 **	0.30 *	0.27	0.14
Both legs	0.28	0.49 ***	0.32 *	0.23	0.17
Vertical jump	0.06	-0.01	-0.02	-0.09	0.15
Broad jump	0.07	-0.04	0.15	0.24	-0.01

Level of significance * p <0.05 ** p <0.01 *** p <0.001

Functional strength is not correlated to the dimensions but still the elite group performs better compared to the non-elite group. The better performance in functional strength in the elite group is neither correlated to isometric strength nor dimensions. This could possibly indicate a better neuromuscular coordination due to training. However, the possibility of a selection of boys to the elite group, with a genetic potential for early maturation explaining the better performance in this group, cannot be excluded .

References

1. Malina, R.M. and Bouchard, C. (1991) *Growth, Maturation and Physical Activity,* Human Kinetics, Champaign, Il., pp. 243-4.
2. Klausen, K. (1990) Strength and weight-training, in *Physiology of Sports,* (ed. T. Reilly), E. and F.N. Spon, London, p. 41-67
3. Komi, P.V. (ed) (1992) *Strength and Power in Sport. The Encyclopaedia of Sports Medicine Vol.3*. Blackwell Scientific Publications, Oxford.
4. Vrijens, J. (1978) Muscle strength development in the pre- and post-pubescent age. *Medicine and Sport,* Vol. 11, pp. 152-8.
5. Ramsey, J., Blimkie, C., Smith, K., Garner, S., Macdougall, J. and Sale, D.G. (1990) Strength training effects in prepubescent boys. *Medicine and Science in Sports and Exercise,* Vol. 22, pp. 605-14.

6. Ozmun, J.C., Mikesky, A.E. and Surburg, P.R. (1994) Neuromuscular adaptations following prepubescent strength training. *Medicine and Science and Sports and Exercise,* Vol. 26, pp. 510-4.
7. Asmussen, E. and Hebøll-Nielsen, K. (1955) A dimensional analysis of physical performance and growth in boys. *Journal of Applied Physiology,* Vol. 7, pp. 593-603.
8. Tanner, J.(1962) *Growth at Adolescence*, Blackwell Scientific Publications, Oxford.
9. Handbook for the Eurofit Test of Physical Fitness. (1988) Rome, Italy.
10. Asmussen, E., Heebøll-Nielsen, K. and Mobech, S. (1959) Methods for evaluation of muscle strength. *Communication No. 5, Danish Polio-Institute, Denmark.*
11. Brook, C.G.C. (ed) (1989) *Clinical Paediatric Endocrinology*, Blackwell Scientific Publications, Oxford.
12. Juul, A., Bang, P., Hertel, N.T., Main, K., Dalgaard, P., Jørgensen, K., Müller, J., Hall, K. and Skakkebæk, N.E. (1994) Serum insulin-like growth factor-1 in 1030 healthy children, adolescent, and adults. *Journal of Clinical Endocrinology and Metabolism*, Vol. 78, pp. 744-52.

EXTENSION AND HYPEREXTENSION OF THE KNEE JOINT AMONG YOUNG CHILDREN

Knee joint mobility of children

V. HEIN
Institute of Sport Pedagogy, University of Tartu, Tartu, Estonia
Keywords: Extension, hyperextension, knee joint

Introduction

A distinction is made between the terms "extension" and "hyperextension". Extension is used when the motion opposite to flexion, at the zero starting position, is a natural motion. As the motion opposite to flexion at the zero starting position is an unnatural one, it is referred to as hyperextension[1]. However, the problem is how to determine which range of motion (ROM) is unnatural and which is natural, specially in joints with restricted extension ROM as the knee joint.

Young children typically have some degree of knee extension. Wynne-Davies[2], in a study of 3000 Edinburgh children, noted that 15% of the 3-year-old children could extend their knee beyond 10°, but this degree of extension was observed in <1% at age 6 y. Cheng et al.[3] reported a greater degree of knee extension in a study of 2360 Chinese children, but again, extension decreased as the children became older, averaging 16° ± 9 at age 3 y compared to a mean of 7° ± 9 by age 10 y. Daniel and Anderson[4] have evaluated the knee extension ROM for the same age group at 3° or lower as normal and 3-5° as nearly normal. The value higher than 6° was observed as abnormal. From this point most of the children at age of 10 y according to the results reported by Cheng et al.[3] have hypermobility of the knee joint.

Goniometry is a technique commonly used in physical therapy for assessing the limitation of a patient's joint motion. The reliability of goniometer measurements has been found by Boone et al.[5] to be with intratester variation of 4°. According to the results of Rothstein et al.[6] intertester reliability of goniometer measurements of passive motion of knee extension is low (r = 0.63 to 0.70). A little bit higher reliability values (r = 0.85) for measurements of active motion of knee extension have been recorded by Clapper and Wolf[7]. The measurement of knee extension ROM using the

Children and Exercise XIX. Edited by Neil Armstrong, Brian Kirby and Joanne Welsman.
Published in 1997 by E & FN Spon, 2–6 Boundary Row, London, SE1 8HN.
ISBN 0 419 22100 X.

linear measurement method by the special constructed instrument[8] showed higher intratester and intertester reliability r = 0.95 and r = 0.96, respectively. Axe et al.[9] measured the hyperextension of the knee joint, when the patient was in a supine position, the knee maximally extended, and the foot in a neutral position. The distance from the posterior border of the heel to the table in centimeters after the knee extension performance was recorded. Repeated testing of the knee hyperextension of 20 injured and healthy knees demonstrated an intraclass correlation coefficient of r = 0.94. The results of this study[9] demonstrated that individuals with anterior cruciate ligament injuries whose knees hyperextended 3 cm or more sustained significantly more joint damage at the time of injury than in those whose knees hyperextended less than 3 cm. So, hypermobility may be the risk factor for knee injuries.

The purpose of this study was to evaluate using the linear measurement procedure the knee extension ROM from the point of hyperextension, i.e. possible borderline between the hyperextension and the normal one among young children.

Methods

A hundred and fifty seven children at the age of 8-14 y participated in this investigation. Informed consent was obtained from each subject beforehand. No subjects had limitation of knee joint movement due to injury.

The knee extension ROM was measured using the special instrument constructed in Tartu University[8]. The design enabled recording the ROM of knee extension on a linear scale with an accuracy of 1 mm. The measurement plate was placed into a special box, fixed to the edge of the measurement table, on the same level. The subject was in sitting position, feet extended and heels on the measurement plate. The up-movement of the measurement plate during the knee extension performance takes place due to the pressure of the springs constructed inside the instrument. The knee extension ROM was read from the scale on the uplift measurement plate and expressed the distance between the heel support (measurement plate in zero position) and maximally uplifted heels. The fixing screw enabled the height of the measurement plate at the end of the knee extension performance to be fixed.

Calf length was measured as the projected length, which was vertical distance from the proximal surface of the tibia to the sole of the foot, according to the method of Martin et al.[10].

All measurements were taken in the same conditions: temperature, time, warm-up exercises including two initial practice attempts for each measurement procedure. No external force was used in any measurements.

The appropriate procedures in the Statgraphics package were used. The results were expressed by the mean ± SD. Z value was used to estimate the means of the range of motion at 95% levels of confidence interval. Pearson product moment correlations between test scores were established. The Mann-Whitney U test was used to determine the significant differences between age and sex groups. The $p < 0.05$ level was selected as the criteria of statistical significance.

Table 1. Knee extension ROM and calf length of young children

	Girls			Boys		
Age (y)	8-9	11-12	13-14	8-9	11-12	13-14
	n=30	n=29	n=27	n=25	n=17	n=29
Calf length (mm)	419.7±21.4	502.1±45.1	511.5±24.2	423.0±13.8	493.5±24.9	523.4±28.4
ROM (mm)	12.6 ± 6.8	13.5 ± 9.2	15.2 ± 11.8	9.2 ± 2.9	14.2 ± 10.5	14.3 ± 7.1
95% CI	10-15	10-17	11-20	8-10	9-20	12-17

Values are mean ± SD and 95% confidence interval (CI)

Results

The values of the range of motion of knee extension recorded by the constructed instrument in mm and the calf length of the observed age and sex groups are presented in table 1.

A weak relationship between calf length and knee extension ROM in mm of all the subjects was $r = 0.16$ ($p < 0.05$). Age related changes in knee extension ROM occurred only in boys groups, where statistically significant differences were followed by the group at the age of 8-9 y and older groups.

Discussion

The limitation of linear measurement is its dependence on segment length[11]. The mean calf length of all the subjects (n = 157) in this study varied only about 10 cm and therefore the correlation found between the ROM of knee extension and segment length was weak ($r = 0.16$, $p < 0.05$). Comparison of knee extension ROM in mm of young children with previous literature is difficult as the ROM has previously been determined in degrees. However, the values of calf length in mm and ROM of knee extension in mm allow the calculation of theoretical angle in degrees and to compare to some extent these with the results obtained previously by other authors. The calculation of knee extension ROM in degrees by the formula tan α of the rectangular triangle, where one of the two sides of the triangle was the distance from the bottom of the upraised heels to the initial position of the measurement plate and the other calf length, gives the angle about 1° 38′. It is 5 times lower than the values recorded by Cheng[3] but consistent to some extent with values offered by Danile and Anderson[4], who have evaluated the knee extension ROM at 3° or lower as normal at this age.

The upper limits of 95% confidence interval for all groups did not exceed the value of 20 mm. Therefore the value of knee extension ROM over 20 mm may be observed as hyperextension among children at age of 8-14 y. On the basis of these values the calculated angle of the hyperextension of knee is equal to the 2° 24′. It is inconsistent with values stated by Danile and Anderson[4]. They reported the knee extension ROM higher than 6° as abnormal. From this statement most of the children at age of

10 y according to the results reported by Cheng et al.[3] would have hypermobility of the knee joint. The investigation of Axe et al.[9] showed that subjects at age of 24 ± 9 years with knee extension ROM over 30 mm had sustained significantly more joint damage at the time of injury than those whose knees hyperextended less than 30 mm. The greater values in the adult group may be explained by their greater calf length. On the basis of this study knee extension ROM greater than 20 mm may be assumed to be a risk factor of knee joint injury for children at age of 8-14 y.

Conclusion

The values over 20 mm of knee extension ROM for young children at age of 8-14 y may be observed as hypermobility of the knee joint.

References

1. Greene, W.B. and Heckman, J.D. (1994) *The Clinical Measurement of Joint Motion*, Rosemont, Il.
2. Wynne-Davies, R. (1971) Familial joint laxity. *Proceedings of the Royal Society of Medicine,* Vol. 64, pp. 689-90.
3. Cheng, J.C., Chan, P.S. and Hui, P.W. (1991) Joint laxity in children. *Journal of Pediatric Orthopedics,* Vol. 11, pp. 752-6.
4. Daniel, D.M. and Anderson, A.F. (1992) Evaluation of treatment results, in *Biology and Biomechanics of the Traumatized Synovial Joint,* (eds. G.A.M. Finerman and R. Noyes), Rosemont, Il., pp. 573-84.
5. Boone, D.C., Azen, S.P., Lin, C-M., Spence, C., Baron, C. and Lee, L. (1978) Reliability of goniometer measurement. *Physical Therapy,* Vol. 58. pp. 1355-60.
6. Rothstein, J.M., Miller, P.J. and Roettger, R.F. (1983) Goniometric reliability in a clinical setting: elbow and knee measurements. *Physical Therapy,* Vol. 63, pp. 611-5.
7. Clapper, M.P. and Wolf, S.L (1988) Comparison of the reliability of the orthoranger and the standard goniometer for assessing active lower extremity range of motion. *Physical Therapy,* Vol. 68, pp. 214-8.
8. Hein, V. (1995) Knee extension range of motion: limits to sit- and- reach test. *Biology of Sport,* Vol. 12, pp. 189-93.
9. Axe, M.J., Lindsay, K. and Snyder-Mackler, L. (1996) The relationship between knee hyperextension and articular pathology in the anterior cruciate ligament deficient knee. *Journal of Sport Rehabilitation*, Vol. 5, pp.120-6.
10. Martin, A.D., Carter, L.J.E., Hendy, K.C. and Malina, R.M. (1988) Segment lengths, in *Anthropometric Standardization Reference Manual,* (eds. T.G. Lohman, A.F. Roche and R. Martorell), Human Kinetics, Il., pp. 9-26.
11. Hubley-Kozey, C.L. (1991) Testing flexibility, in *Physiological Testing of the High-Performance Athlete* (eds. J.D. MacDougall and H.A. Wenger), Human Kinetics, Il., pp. 330-51.

PART V

CARDIOVASCULAR FUNCTION IN HEALTH AND DISEASE

WHAT "JUST DOING IT" REVEALED - A PERSONAL STORY FOR YOUNG CLINICIANS AND RESEARCHERS

Clinical exercise testing

W. B. STRONG

Georgia Prevention Institute, Medical College of Georgia, Augusta, USA

Keywords: Blood pressure, cardiovascular reactivity, exercise testing, preventive cardiology, racial responses to exercise, sickle cell disease

During my fellowship years, 1967-1969, a year of research was not required as it is now. The tools of paediatric cardiology were limited. However, it was expected that a paediatric cardiologist would go to an academic centre or large general hospital with a residency programme. Therefore, it was expected that the paediatric cardiologist would be able to conduct research, at least on the clinical level. My chief and mentor Dr. Jerry Liebman insisted that the Fellow learn how to do research and publish the findings. Since his interests were primarily related to electrocardiography and vectorcardiography, that is the area that I directed my efforts toward. During my fellowship my primary project was to measure 95 different components of the adolescent EKG. This was performed on the EKG's of 114 adolescents judged to be normal by history and physical examination. Therefore, I made 11,730 measurements, manually, without any summer student help. That paper was finally finished and published in the American Heart Journal in January, 1972[1]. However, Dr. Liebman always insisted that whatever one does for research should arouse the researcher's curiosity and the researcher should enjoy the quest. In the second year of my fellowship he allowed me to spend three months in the laboratory of Dr. Herman Hellerstein, the pioneer of rehabilitative cardiology. Dr. Hellerstein exposed me to the clinical research exercise laboratory and what it could provide. Until he began to report that the clinical exercise test was much more useful than just to look at the J point and the ST segment for ischaemia, the test was under-used (the cycle ergometer was nothing more than an extension of the Master's Two-Step test). Dr. Hellerstein advocated the multiple facets of exercise testing for the evaluation of the patient and for progressive rehabilitation. His rehabilitation programme at the Cleveland Heights Jewish Community Centre was the prototype and model for all cardiovascular rehabilitation programmes.

Children and Exercise XIX. Edited by Neil Armstrong, Brian Kirby and Joanne Welsman.
Published in 1997 by E & FN Spon, 2–6 Boundary Row, London, SE1 8HN.
ISBN 0 419 22100 X.

Under Dr. Hellerstein's tutelage I was exposed to some basic aspects of clinical exercise testing. Because of my enjoyment of sports and of exercise, doing clinical exercise research was a natural relationship and one which would provide many branches including that of my early involvement in the clinical practice of paediatric preventive cardiology and subsequent involvement in sports medicine. Dr. Hellerstein promoted exercise testing because of the multiple cardiovascular measures that could be acquired to define an individual's functional status. This information could not always be predicted by their haemodynamic status, e.g. heart size or end diastolic pressure. Besides using the test to evaluate ischemia, Dr. Hellerstein incorporated the measurements of aerobic power (physical working capacity), blood pressure response to exercise, the response of arrhythmias to exercise and exercise to provoke arrhythmias in the clinical setting. Measuring the blood pressure response to exercise led to our proposal of exercise as an evaluation of cardiovascular reactivity. The only publication that I obtained from my work in Dr. Hellerstein's laboratory was not published until the mid 1970's and had to do with the differences of the Exercise EKG (Ex EKG) in trained and untrained adolescents who attended a private boarding school in University Heights, OH[2].

When I was recruited to the Medical College of Georgia the only request that I made was for an exercise laboratory. The promise was not fulfilled because the Chairman of Paediatrics who recruited me, Dr. Jerry Holman, took another position before I arrived. Therefore, our first exercise laboratory was not funded until we received our initial sickle cell grant from the National Institutes of Health (NIH).

It was very apparent after I arrived in Augusta that we were never going to compete with the larger programmes for large clinical studies of patients with congenital heart disease. Augusta is in the East Central region of Georgia (Southeastern USA) and the population density is low. However, the opportunity for clinical research was provided by the regions demographics i.e. a large Black population with a high prevalence of hypertension and sickle cell disease. In the early 1970s the National Heart Lung and Blood Institute (NHLBI) of the NIH was developing an interest in the manifestations of sickle cell disease and its natural history.

Because of our relatively large Black population and the increased prevalence of hypertension and sickle cell disease in the Black population it seemed reasonable for us to begin to evaluate the cardiovascular implications of these diseases in the young. Dr. Titus Huisman was and is one of the giants of haemoglobinopathy research and he was able to obtain NIH funding for a Sickle Disease Centre to be located at the Medical College of Georgia. As a part of that centre grant there was a component dedicated to the natural history of the disease beginning in childhood. With Dr. Huisman's help as well as the support of the Acting Chairman of Paediatrics (Dr. Audrey Brown) we began to evaluate the cardiovascular effects of sickle cell disease in children using exercise testing and M-mode echocardiography. In order to accomplish this it would first be necessary to determine what the normal responses to exercise were in a healthy population of children, in this case, healthy Black children since we could not use White children as our control group. There had been many exercise studies of children in the European literature as a matter of fact, too many to cite (the European Pediatric Work Physiology Group had already conducted at least two symposia) but there were few studies of healthy children in the USA literature and to our knowledge there were none related to Black children. Dr. Forrest Adams published data on healthy Scandinavian and White California children in 1961[3,4] and Drs. Kramer and Lurie studied healthy White children at the University of Indiana in the early 1960s[5]. Dr. Gordon Cumming, at Winnipeg, Canada published some of the early North American studies[6]. Dr. Stanley Goldberg, while at UCLA, compared healthy children with children who had congenital heart disease[7]. Our studies[8-10] begun in 1974 with paediatric cardiology fellows Salehbhai and Thapar, medical students Leatherbury (now my faculty associate) and Spencer and Dr. Max Miller were published at about the same time that the studies of Riopel[11] and James[12] were in press. In addition to aerobic power ("physical working capacity") this cohort of studies also investigated blood pressure and electrocardiographic responses to exercise in youth. These initial studies were conducted with children participating in a summer enrichment programme conducted at Paine College, a predominantly Black institution. These studies provided us with the normative data and the experience that we needed before proceeding to study the children with sickle cell disease. It also provided us with the experience of working in less than ideal environments. That summer we worked in the basement of the gymnasium and in two non-air conditioned Black community centres. We initially tested 250 children 6 to 16-years-old, but only 184 of the tests were deemed complete and of peak performance. One hundred and seventy of the children who were in the original publication were six to 15 y of age. The methods used to encourage the children to achieve their maximum (peak) effort were verbal encouragement by the researcher, cheerleading by other children and the threat that if they didn't continue we would have to have our "Big Dog" come and chase the exercising child. This last "threat" was accompanied by a good deal of laughter and a final burst of pedalling by the child to reach his/her peak effort, which was generally in the range of 190-200 beats·min^{-1}. The cooperation we had that summer, and the children, were excellent and I think that everyone thoroughly enjoyed the experience. For me it was fun being with the children and personally conducting and doing the testing. All of the faults and deficiencies of the studies were mine, I could never blame others. This first hand experience was very educational. It taught me the sites where various obstacles occurred in the conduction of a research project; it taught what hurdles had to be jumped and most of all, the necessity for safeguarding the quality of the acquired data. By being present and doing the studies it became obvious what data was "good data" and what data had been obtained in less than optimal conditions and was likely to be unreliable.

The protocol that we devised was a continuous, graded cycle ergometer test with 3 min intervals. The workloads were those reported by Adams[3] and added to sequentially in order to exhaust the child. The highest workload was calculated by adding the loads during the last 2 min of exercise and dividing by two (see table 1). Succeeding workloads were increased in increments of 75-300 kgm·min^{-1} according to the subjects' size and prior performance. Our intent was to do a clinical test that would help us assess the child's physical performance. We did not measure oxygen consumption or carbon dioxide production so that we have never been able to "categorically" state that the child had reached a plateau of oxygen consumption and hence "maximum" effort. Regardless, it was our belief that our children had certainly approached their maximum effort but we substituted the term "maximum voluntary effort" for "maximum".

Table 1. Work load required to produce anticipated heart rate

	Work load in kgm·min^{-1}			
Subject weight (kg)	1	2	3	4
<30	75	150	300	450
30-40	150	300	450	600
41-60	300	450	600	750
>60	450	600	750	900
Anticipated heart rate, beats·min^{-1}	120	150	170	Maximum

Those summer studies first appeared in the American Journal of Diseases of Children in a series of three articles in 1978[8-10]. It was in the second of the papers that we hypothesised that the blood pressure (BP) response to exercise might be predictive of future hypertension or of the individual who was at increased risk of future hypertension[8]. The theory being that at rest BP could be elevated either because of an elevation of resistance or of cardiac output or both. We believed that at maximum exercise, the cardiac index would be relatively similar in an otherwise healthy, untrained population. Therefore, if the BP response was unusually high it would more likely be due to an increase of systemic vascular resistance, i.e. the arterioles would not dilate as much as an individual whose maximum BP was, let us say, less than 200 mm Hg. To my knowledge this was the first description, at least in children, of what has become recognized as the study of cardiovascular reactivity. We arbitrarily assigned a value of 220 mm Hg as the cut-off point for a hypertensive response to exercise testing. This was approximately 20-25 mm Hg higher than the 95th percentile. Dr. David Fixler, in Dallas, refuted our hypothesis but on careful analysis of his data the children in his study, whose systolic BPs exceeded 220 mm Hg, were more likely to have subsequently higher BPs[13]. It should be noted that our early studies only reported systolic BP responses. I did not believe, and continue not to believe, that diastolic BP can be measured accurately by auscultating the fourth or fifth Korotkoff sounds during maximum exercise, neither the fourth or fifth Korotkoff sounds accurately reflect diastolic BP. This observation was well documented by Drs. Moss and Adams in 1963[14]. In order to facilitate the measurement of BP during exercise we constructed an adjustable arm rest that stabilized the subject's arm at heart level allowing the measurement to be made more readily without as much motion. Figure 1 illustrates the device. We chose the cycle ergometer as our exercise device because it would enable us to measure BP with greater ease than the treadmill would.

The results of our studies of healthy children's aerobic power (PWC_{170}) are shown in fig 2(girls) and 3(boys); for BP response in tables 2 and 3 and for ECG responses in fig 4 and 5 and tables 4 and 5. We initially had some difficulty in explaining why our healthy Black children from the Southeastern USA had lower physical working capacity than the Swedish or the White California children studied by Dr. Adams[3]. Identifying the reasons were obvious but not to us exercise testing neophytes. The answer

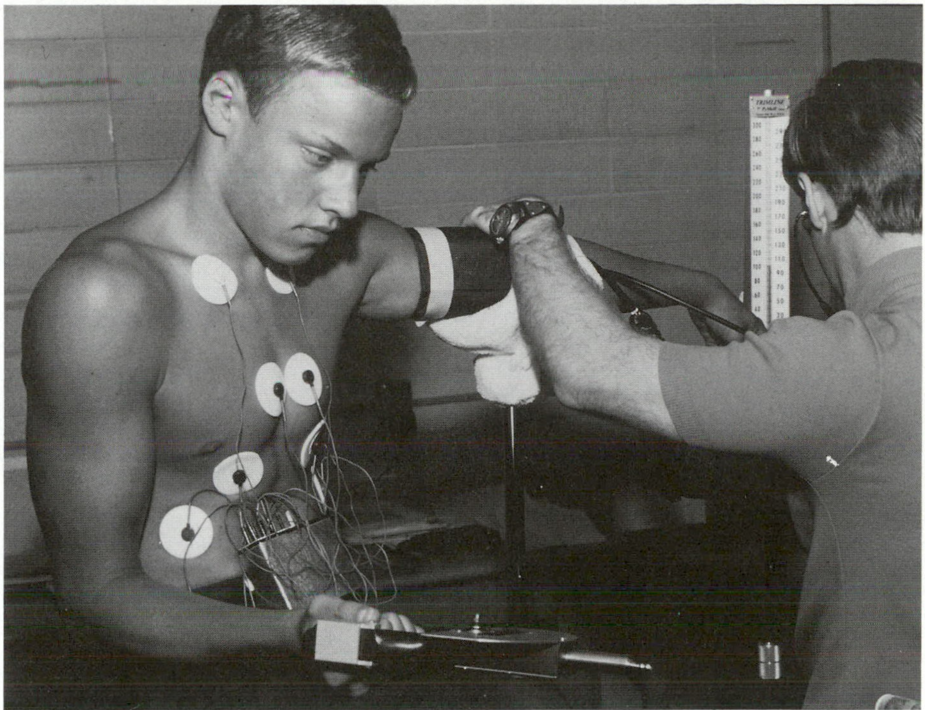

Fig. 1. The arm rest device is shown. It is an adjustable intravenous pole with a padded arm rest attached to the top.

lay in the fact that our studies which used similar workloads to those of Adams were formatted on a mechanically braked cycle ergometer whereas their studies were performed on an electronically braked cycle ergometer. Also we used a continuous test whereas they used 6 min intervals with an intermittent protocol. Calculating for the differences in protocol could account for the observed differences in physical working capacity. This observation made us critically aware of the need to compare apples with apples and not to overextend the results of our research. It also raised the issue of comparability of studies performed in different laboratories as well as studies performed in the same laboratory by different personnel.

Using exercise provided a more naturalistic setting to evaluate a child's functional abilities and to assess their response to a stressful stimulus. The purposes for which we wished to use the test were to measure the child's aerobic power (at that time we were using the term "physical working capacity"), BP response and electrocardiographic responses, i.e. J point depression and ST segment slope as well as the

Table 2. Blood pressures - by age and sex (A) at rest (B) isometric exercise (C) heart rate 170 (D) heart rate maximum

SUBJECTS			Blood Pressures, mm Hg (A) Resting Systolic Blood Pressure (BP_{rest})		(A) Resting Diastolic Blood Pressure		(B) Systolic Blood Pressure Response to Isometric Exercise (BP_{Iso})		(C) Systolic Blood Pressure Response to Dynamic Exercise-Heart Rate 170 (BP_{170})		(D) Systolic Blood Pressure Response to Dynamic Exercise - Maximum (BP_{max})	
	No of Subjects											
Age, y	Male	Female	Male	Female	Male	Female	Male	Female	Male	Female	Male	Female
7	6	5	102 ± 10	99 ± 5	65 ± 7	69 ± 8	124 ± 9	126 ± 6	139 ± 9	128 ± 6	139 ± 17	142 ± 9
8	11	15	97 ± 13	95 ± 11	60 ± 9	61 ± 10	114 ± 14	109 ± 16	139 ± 15	130 ± 14	151 ± 11	140 ± 15
9	8	12	99 ± 10	97 ± 8	67 ± 6	58 ± 7	116 ± 9	114 ± 9	135 ± 7	139 ± 17	150 ± 13	145 ± 16
10	19	17	102 ± 10	104 ± 11	64 ± 9	67 ± 9	123 ± 11	118 ± 10	140 ± 22	142 ± 15	163 ± 17	156 ± 14
11	9	20	111 ± 9	107 ± 12	68 ± 10	66 ± 11	129 ± 11	121 ± 12	144 ± 14	144 ± 13	166 ± 17	159 ± 16
12	15	8	104 ± 13	106 ± 10	67 ± 12	63 ± 9	121 ± 12	128 ± 10	156 ± 13	141 ± 17	167 ± 12	154 ± 21
13	7	12	115 ± 7	109 ± 7	74 ± 11	67 ± 11	128 ± 15	128 ± 10	146 ± 7	149 ± 10	167 ± 12	163 ± 12
14	1	5	...	122 ± 10	...	82 ± 10	...	132 ± 15	...	152 ± 6	...	167 ± 10

Values are means ± SD

Only one 14-year-old boy in the study.

Table 3. Systolic blood pressures - by body surface area (A) at rest (B) isometric (C) heart rate 170 (D) heart rate maximum

SUBJECTS			Blood Pressures, mm Hg							
			(A) Resting Blood Pressure (Bp_{rest})		(B) Blood Pressure Response to Isometric Exercise (BP_{Iso})		(C) Blood Pressure Response to Dynamic Exercise - Heart Rate 170 (BP_{170})		(D) Blood Pressure Response to Dynamic Exercise - Maximum (BP_{max})	
Body Surface	No of Subjects									
Area sq m	Male	Female	Male	Female	Male	Female	Male	Female	Male	Female
0.8	6	6	89 ± 7	89 ± 3	110 ± 5	105 ± 8	126 ± 10	122 ± 8	139 ± 10	126 ± 11
0.9	12	18	95 ± 11	98 ± 9	113 ± 11	112 ± 14	136 ± 7	132 ± 13	140 ± 10	144 ± 14
1.0	6	14	102 ± 8	100 ± 12	122 ± 18	117 ± 14	142 ± 13	143 ± 16	159 ± 20	149 ± 15
1.1	20	15	104 ± 11	101 ± 12	122 ± 12	119 ± 12	142 ± 17	134 ± 12	163 ± 14	147 ± 17
1.2	16	9	109 ± 8	104 ± 12	126 ± 12	121 ± 13	152 ± 14	146 ± 14	167 ± 12	163 ± 13
1.3	5	16	103 ± 14	110 ± 10	121 ± 16	125 ± 11	156 ± 9	145 ± 9	168 ± 11	160 ± 15
1.4	7	10	105 ± 10	112 ± 7	120 ± 13	128 ± 9	144 ± 11	152 ± 10	153 ± 16	167 ± 13
1.5	5	6	113 ± 11	114 ± 12	128 ± 7	130 ± 11	151 ± 17	151 ± 7	175 ± 12	162 ± 9
1.6	3	3	117 ± 10	115 ± 5.0	133 ± 19	127 ± 13	152 ± 10	150 ± 5	178 ± 3	162 ± 16

Values are mean ± SD
One subject omitted due to incomplete data.

Table 4. Children with elevation of J point, using PQ - PQ and P - R isoelectric lines

Method	No. (%) With Elevation of J Point		
	At Rest	At Heart Rate of 170 beats·min^{-1}	During Maximum Exercise*
PQ - PQ			
Boys (N = 76)	35 (42)	0 (0)	0 (0)
Girls (N = 94)	25 (25)	0 (0)	0 (0)
R - R			
Boys (N = 76)	26 (46)	2 (2.6)	1 (1.3)
Girls (N = 94)	25 (25)	2 (2.1)	1 (1.0)

*p values for boys vs girls during maximum exercise were not significant.

Table 5. Healthy children with depression of J point, using PQ - PQ and P - R isoelectric lines

Method	No. (%) With Depression of J Point			
	At Rest	At Heart Rate of 170 beats·min^{-1}	During Maximum Exercise	p, Boys vs Girls, During Max Exercise
PQ - PQ				
Boys (N = 74)	1 (1.2)	7 (8.1)	7 (8.1)	< 0.01
Girls (N = 96)	1 (0.9)	19 (13)	19 (18)	
R - R				
Boys (N = 74)	1 (1.2)	2 (2.3)	2 (2.6)	NS*
Girls (N = 96)	1 (0.9)	1 (0.9)	2 (2)	

* NS indicates not significant.

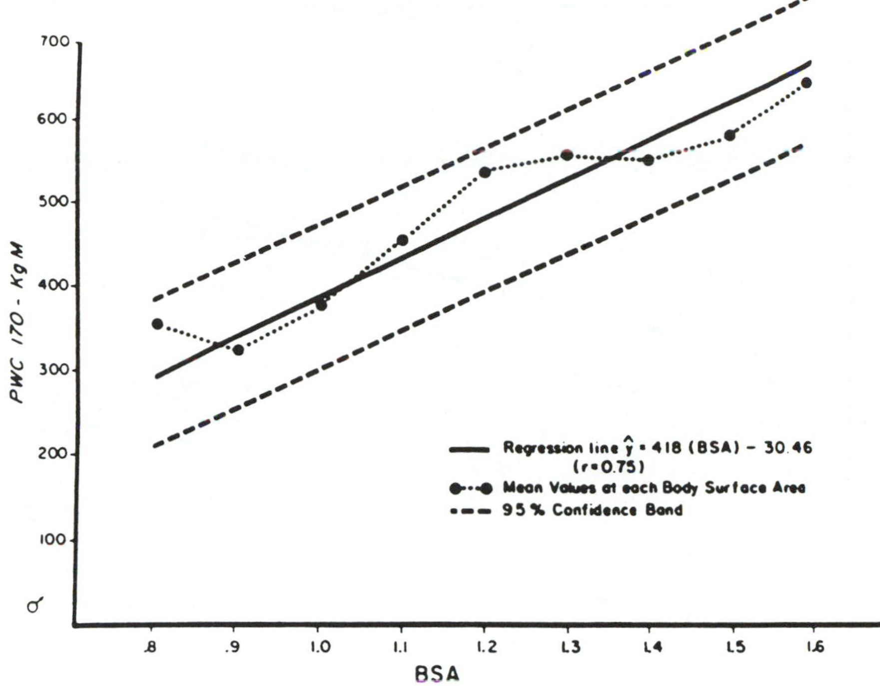

Fig. 2. Relationship between physical working capacity... and body surface area for healthy black boys. Dashed lines represent 95% confidence bands.

provocation of an arrhythmia or response of an arrhythmia after therapy had been initiated. Having begun our studies with healthy Black children it was our desire to eventually extend them to populations of children with chronic diseases, especially congenital heart disease.

With the healthy Black normative data it was then possible to begin to assess the children with haemoglobins SS, SA, SC, and S Beta thalassemia using exercise. Drs. Alpert and later Dr. Covitz were instrumental in moving these studies ahead. We were able to demonstrate significant differences in the response to exercise of children with SS compared to the healthy Black children. Electrocardiographically, 15% of the children with SS haemoglobin had evidence of overt ischemia with J point depression and J point flattening or downsloping during exercise testing. Another 35% had borderline changes, generally a flat or down sloping ST segment from an isoelectric J point: or a negative J point with an upsloping ST segment. Only 2% of the healthy children had the borderline changes and none had a definitely ischaemic pattern. No arrhythmias were provoked in either the healthy or the SS children. Peak heart rates in the healthy children were approximately 191 beats·min^{-1}, compared to 180 beats·min^{-1} in the SS group. The children with SS had lower physical working capacity and their maximum

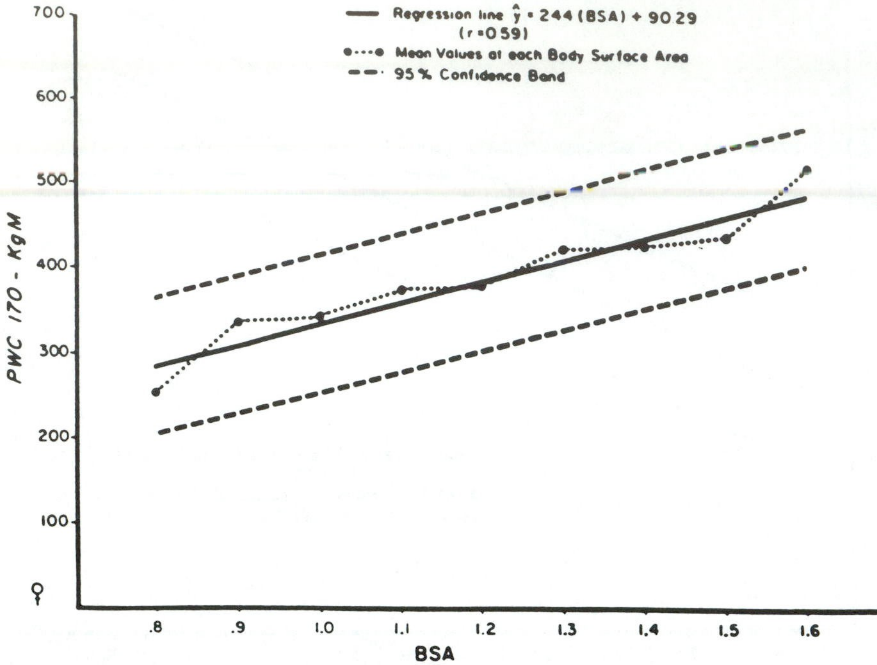

Fig. 3. Relationship between physical working capacity... and body surface area for healthy black girls. Dashed lines represent 95% confidence bands.

BP responses were also lower than the healthy suggesting that they had lower systemic vascular resistance in order to deliver their higher cardiac output[15]. Table 6 presents the results of the early studies with these children. These data were first presented at the 1983 PWP meeting. The results of the children with SA were significantly better than those with SS but less than their healthy peers[16]. The total number of maximum exercise tests that we performed on children with SS Hgb or its variants, in order to evaluate them cross sectionally or longitudinally was in the range of 600 to 700 studies. To my knowledge only one late-adolescent girl had a minor pain crisis and one had mild nonspecific symptoms following their maximum voluntary effort stress test. It was on the basis of these data that we believed it prudent and in the child's best interest not to arbitrarily restrict their physical activities. I believed that this was in the child's best interest and provided them with the ability to determine what they could and could not do and gave them the opportunity to test their own limits and achieve their fullest potential.

Dr. Covitz extended the research by incorporating radionuclide exercise studies and echocardiographic measurements, further defining the cardiovascular and haemodynamic abnormalities in the child and young adult with SS[17]. The radionuclide studies demonstrated, in 22 youths with SS haemoglobin, that cardiac contractility was normal at rest, but cardiac output and end diastolic volume were increased. At peak

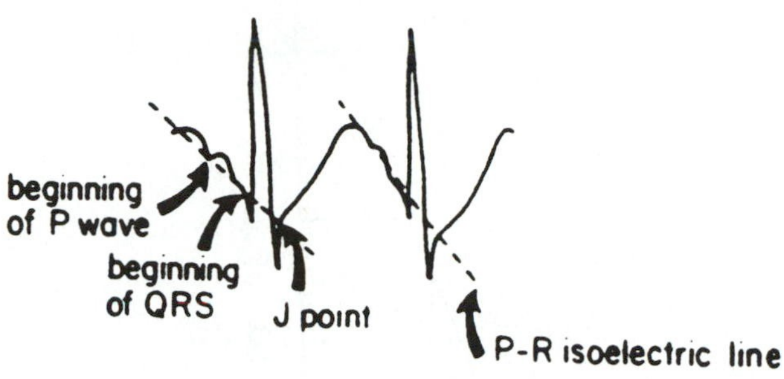

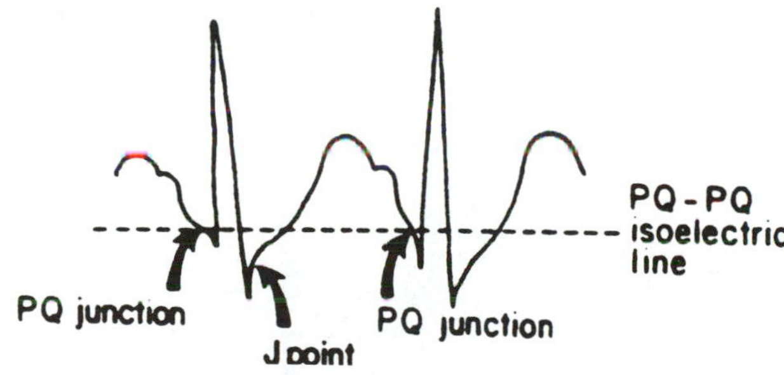

Fig. 4. Two methods of estimating isoelectric line. Top, P-R isoelectric. Line is drawn from beginning of P wave to beginning of QRS complex. This method tends to avoid artifact of J-point depression caused by Ta. Bottom, PQ-PQ isoelectric, more conventional procedure for measuring isoelectric line. Line is drawn from beginning of one QRS complex to beginning of next.

exercise, heart rate, cardiac output response and aerobic power were reduced; the reduction being related to the degree of anaemia. Left ventricular end diastolic volume decreased most markedly in patients with ischaemia exercise electrocardiograms. An abnormal ejection fraction occurred in four patients and each had evidence of ischaemia on their EKG. Two of these individuals had wall motion abnormalities. Cardiac dysfunction was manifested by an abnormal ejection fraction response, wall motion

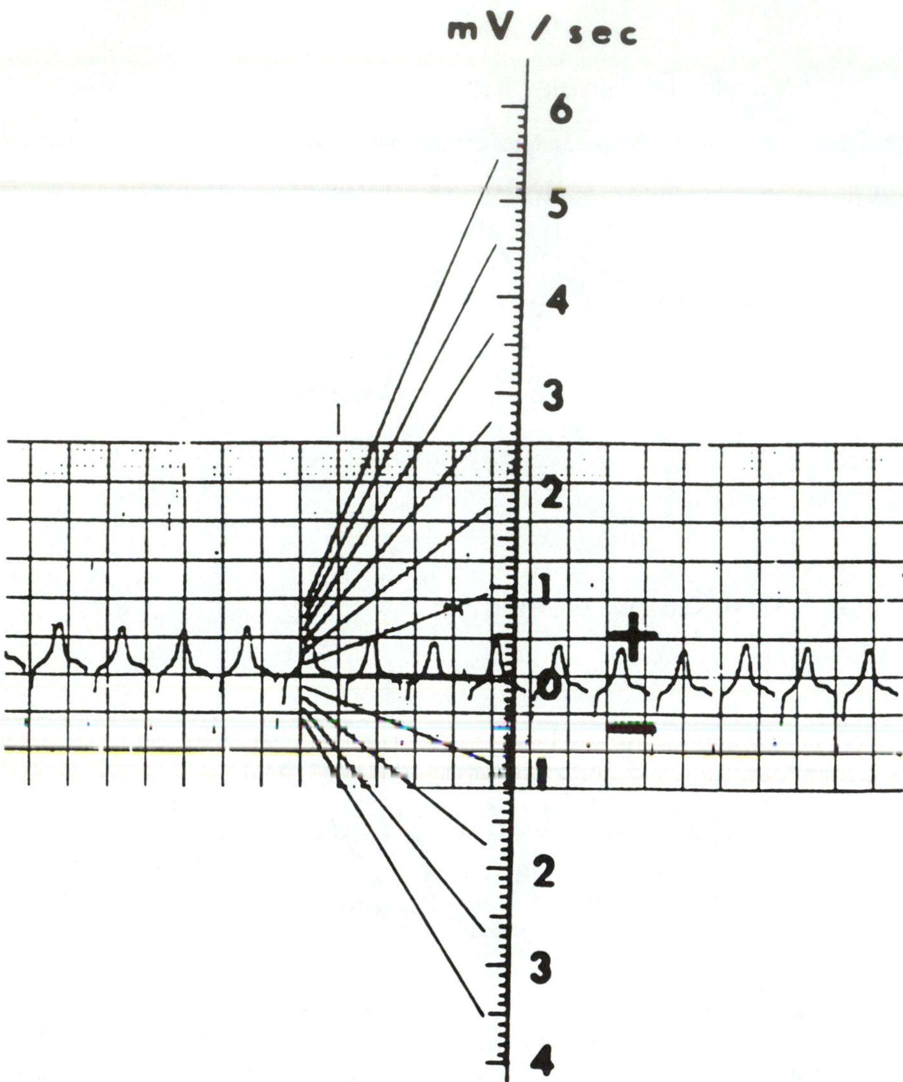

Fig. 5. This was a clear acrylic overlay that was used to measure the slope of the ST segment 80 msec after the QRS.

abnormalities and incomplete left ventricular filling during exercise. With one of our fellows, Dr Ian Balfour and Dr Casmir Eubig a model for the progression of the cardiovascular effects of SS were put forth using echocardiography as well as exercise and radionuclide measures[18].

Table 6. Response to exercise testing in children with SS haemoglobin

Results:		Heart Rate		Blood Pressure		PWCI	ECG Response		
Group	N	Rest	Max	Rest	Max	kgm/min/kg	Isch	Border	Normal
H8b AA	170	91 ± 16	191 ± 10	103 ± 13	158 ± 20	15.6 ± 3.5	--	2	168
Hgb AS	48	87 ± 16	181 ± 14	115 ± 16	163 ± 26	12 ± 2.3	--	4	44
Hgb SS	47	93 ± 14	180 ± 10	99 ± 17	122 ± 40	11.8 ± 2.4*	7	16	24
						11.1 ± 3.3**	Hemoglobin Levels		
						9.5 ± 2.6***	7.2 ± 0.4	8.2 ± 1.1	8.1 ± 1.0

*Normal
**Borderline
***Ischaemia

The exercise EKG not only permitted the evaluation of inequalities of myocardial oxygen supply and demand (ischaemia response) but also assisted in the evaluation of possible dysrhythmia. In 1978 Monarrez, Rees and I described the use of the exercise EKG in evaluating children with symptoms suggestive of dysrhythmia (e.g. palpitation, chest pain, syncope). We suggested that the stress of exercise was a useful tool for provoking dysrhythmias. It could also be used to evaluate the patients response to medication[19].

These works established the Section of Pediatric Cardiology's research abilities at the Medical College of Georgia. They also led to my participation with Dr. James Moller and other paediatric cardiology committee members of the American Heart Association to develop standards for exercise testing in children and adolescents with heart disease[20].

In the summer of 1980, with Dr. Alpert and two medical students, David Booker and Alfred Martin we studied a group of healthy white children at the Augusta Jewish Community Centre and the Boy Scout camp. These healthy children provided us with the ability to begin to look at racial differences in the haemodynamic responses to a physical stressor, exercise. These comparative data were first published in 1982[21]. We observed that the major differences were related to the BP response. Peak heart rate, physical working capacity and the EKG responses were not significantly different figs 6 to 9 present that early information. Figures 10 and 11 demonstrate the ethnic differences in BP response to exercise by age. These studies were the impetus for us to begin to develop our behavioural studies and to introduce other stressors into the protocols in order to assess cardiovascular reactivity[22].

To backtrack slightly, Dr. Hellerstein had piqued my interest in the potential for preventing premature cardiovascular disease in adults. Dr. Liebman also had something to do with this interest. Early in his career he had studied the dietary production of atherosclerosis in the white carneau pigeon. My other stimulus was personal, my father had his first myocardial infarction at the age of 36 y. Although he was physically active as a semiprofessional basketball player, he smoked three packs of cigarettes per day. Both his mother and father died before the age of 50 y of "acute indigestion" (often misdiagnosed for myocardial infarction in the early twentieth century). This led me to research the early antecedents of coronary heart disease in the young and to begin to publish on that subject in the mid 1970s. I was also able to get a super cast of authors to write chapters for the first text on the Pediatric Aspects of Atherosclerosis[23]. These scientists were my heroes and subsequently formed a network of experts that were willing to provide advice. Dr. Martin Reisman deserves special recognition. This Los Angeles clinician was the first paediatrician to call attention to this in the North American paediatric literature[24]. Dr. Russell Holman, at Louisiana State University, was the first American to identify the potential paediatric precursors[25]. In the early 1900s European pathologists had described atherosclerotic lesions in the young[26,27]. In the mid 1950s Dr. Holman began to assemble a team of researchers who would truly lay the ground work for all subsequent studies on the early manifestations and antecedents of atherosclerosis. McGill, Newman, J.C. Strong and Berenson are recognized as the pioneers of the paediatric aspects of atherosclerosis research.

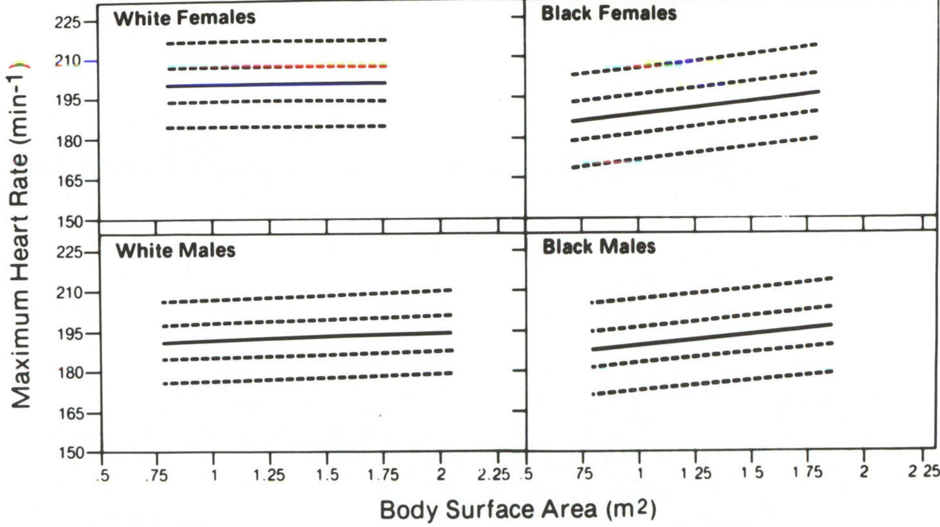

Fig. 6. Maximum heart rate values for healthy black children and white children 6 to 15 years old. Solid line is 50th percentile; extreme dashed lines represent the 5th percentile and 95th percentile levels.

This interest enabled Dr. Levy and me to receive one of the initial Preventive Cardiology Academic Awards from the NHLBI. With this grant we would develop the Students for Community Involvement programme known as SCI[28]. The SCI was predicated on the thesis that the best way to teach medical students preventive cardiology would be to have them become teachers of the subject. With the cooperation of Dr. John Strelec, Superintendent of the Richmond County Schools , we were able to teach 6th grade students throughout the county and at the same time educate our medical students about preventive measures. They also learned the importance of giving something back to their own community beyond their clinical practice. This probing into prevention gave Dr. Levy and me the concept to develop a broader prevention programme and thus the Georgia Institute for the Prevention of Human Disease and Accidents (GPI) was founded in November, 1981. This provided another avenue in which to study exercise response in a different population of children. It also enabled us to research the interaction of physical fitness and cardiovascular risk factors in the young.

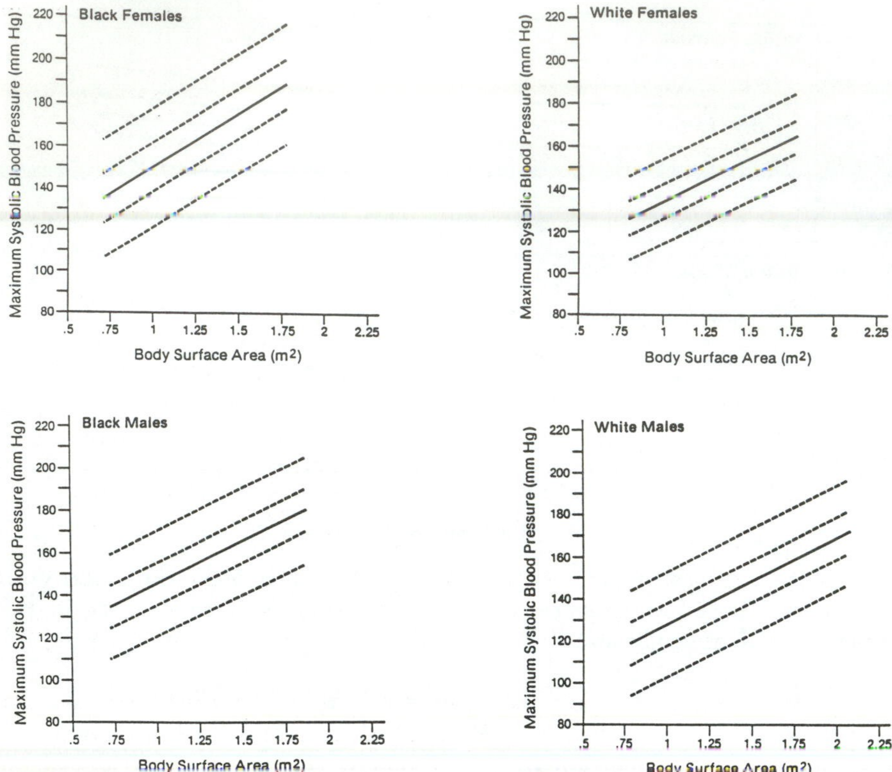

Fig. 7. Maximum systolic blood pressure levels for healthy black children and white children 6 to 15 years old. Solid line is 50th percentile; extreme dashed lines represent the 5th percentile and 95th percentile levels.

As the GPI was birthing we continued our clinical studies relating to assessment of BP by exercise and also developed automated methodologies. Being a paediatric car diologist with easy access to the cardiac catheterisation laboratory provided the opportunity to validate the accuracy of two non invasive technologies. The first was the accuracy of the automated BP device[29]. This instrument made it possible to measure diastolic BP during exercise quite accurately. With these data we could better assess systemic vascular resistance. The second instrument that we validated in the catheterisation laboratory was the thoracic bioimpedance device which measured cardiac output[30]. The incorporation of these two instruments into our methodological armamentarium gave us the ability to measure changes in systemic vascular resistance to various stressors. As part of the SCI lectureship we asked Dr. Robert Haggerty of the William T. Grant Foundation to visit with us. It was Dr. Haggerty's insight that provided us, specifically Dr. Alpert, with the means to obtain our first behavioural study grant to observe ethnic difference in cardiovascular reactivity. To illustrate the phenomenon of serendipity and the importance of "networking" Dr. Haggerty and I were both participating in a paediatric symposium at Bowman Gray School of Medicine. On our departure we were sitting at the Greensboro, NC airport awaiting our respective

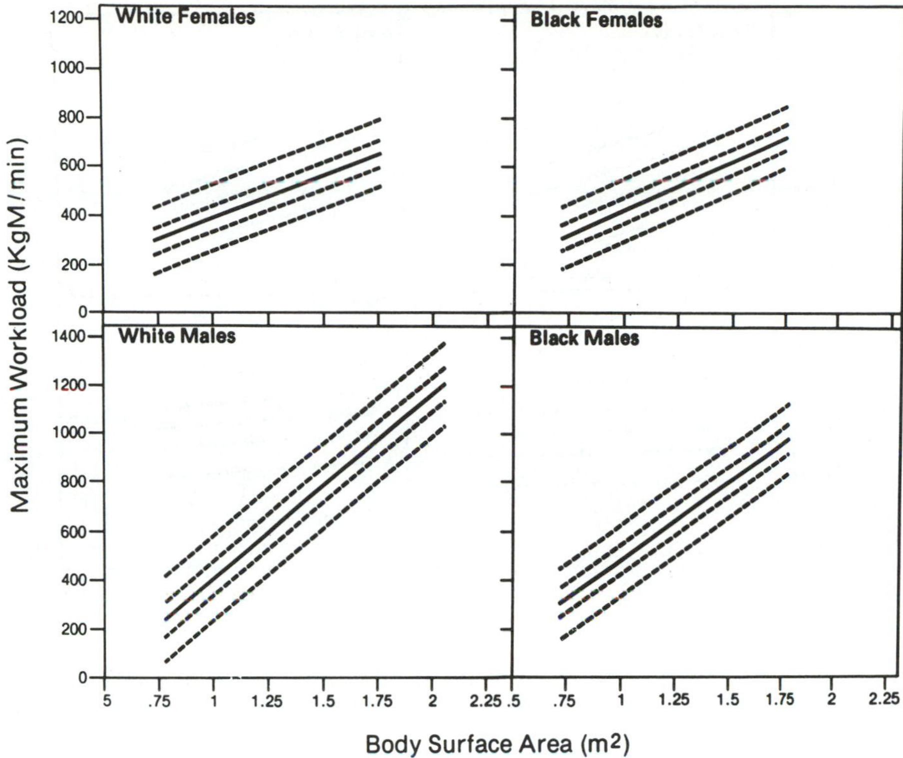

Fig. 8. Maximum workload (aerobic power) for healthy black children and white children 6 to 15 years old. Solid line is 50th percentile; extreme dashed lines represent the 5th percentile and 95th percentile levels.

flights when we initiated a discussion of the subject and it obviously caught his fancy and initiated a very productive line of research.

By 1983 we had performed enough exercise tests in various conditions including left ventricular volume overload studies to be able to write about the complications of exercise testing in children and the safety of the test[31]. The overall prevalence of complications was 1.79%. No deaths occurred. The frequency of complications were chest pain 0.69%, dizziness or syncope 0.29%, decreased BP 0.35% and hazardous arrhythmias 0.46%. We concluded that exercise testing of children with cardiovascular disease had a low associated morbidity and mortality. Reflecting on our experience we were able to advance guidelines for children with cardiac defects and take exercise prescription to another plane by utilizing objective measures and reducing the likelihood of developing psychological cardiac cripples[32]. A number of our successfully

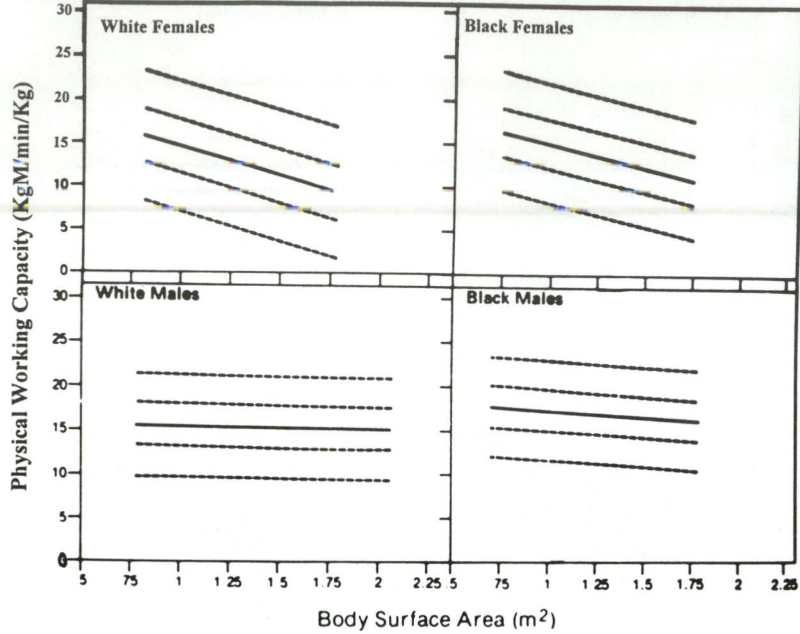

Fig. 9. "Physical working capacity" (kgm·min^{-1}) indexed by body weight in kg (PWCI) for healthy black children and white children 6 to 15 years old. Solid line is 50th percentile; extreme dashed lines represent the 5th percentile and 95th percentile levels.

operated children with congenital heart disease have become exceptionally good athletes. A young man who had tetralogy of Fallot repaired in early childhood is shown in fig 12. He is 16 years old, 190.5 cm tall and weighs 140.9 kg. He bench presses 160 kg. The young woman on the right was an all-star softball player after she was operated for a complete atrioventricular canal and had her mitral valve replaced with a mechanical valve. She performed at the 75th percentile of aerobic power without ischaemia or arrhythmia. The first woman who had a Fontan Procedure and then became pregnant, carried to term and delivered a normal baby...now that's exercise... was one of our "children". A. G. is shown in fig 14 with her baby who is now a 45.5 kg 10-year-old. Prior to becoming pregnant, using a supine ergometer protocol A.G. was able to achieve the 50th to 75th percentile of aerobic power, in spite of having only a single ventricle.

In 1984, together with Dr. Rao, who had collected the data before he moved to Saudi Arabia, we published data on left ventricular mass of children[33]. This was a forerunner of our studies of almost a decade later relating LV mass to ethnicity, family history, obesity and cardiovascular reactivity. It was in 1984 that the last of our SS papers was published even though there is still a great deal of data to be analysed[34].

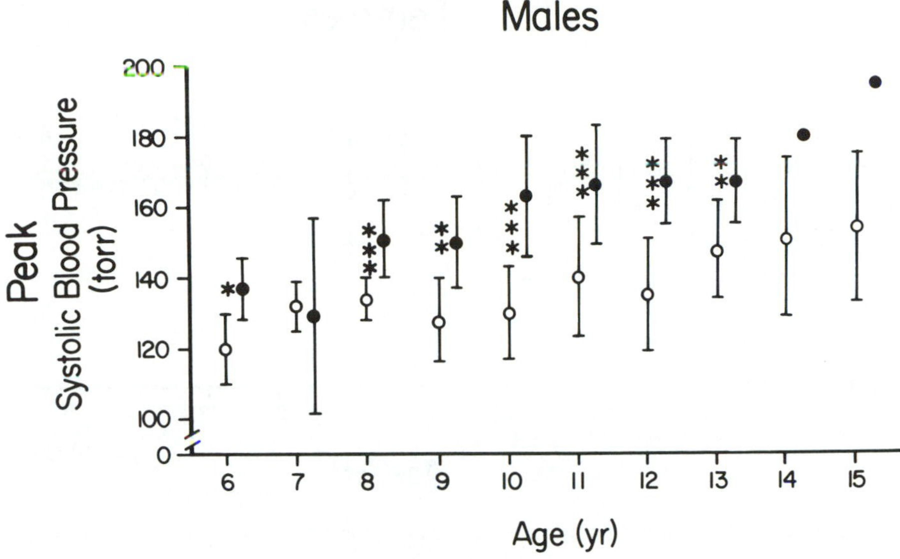

Fig. 10. Peak systolic blood pressure response for healthy black boys and white boys 6 to 15-years-old. Solid circles are the blacks, open circles are the whites.
Level of significance * = $p < 0.05$; **= $p < 0.01$; ***= $p < 0.001$

Dr. Covitz, who is now chief of paediatric cardiology at Bowman Gray School of Medicine recently reviewed the multicentre SS haemoglobin studies[35]. Together with David Braden, a former fellow, now at the University of Mississippi School of Medicine, they have just published the results of our SS thalassemia studies[36].

In 1985, Dr. Frank Treiber joined the GPI faculty and together we received our first major grant "Survey of Children's Activity and Nutrition" (SCAN). This grant would now lead us down another trail, a trail initiated by our observations of different racial responses to exercise. The early studies supported by that grant were more methodological and enabled us to be able to demonstrate that certain functions could be measured accurately both in the laboratory and in the field. Evaluation of the heart rate monitor as an effective and valid instrument was accomplished[37] as well as defining the limitation of such instruments as the Caltrac. Much of what we originally did has been abandoned because the relationships with laboratory stressors or tests was less than adequate although statistically significant, e.g., how many bites of food a child takes vs how many chews before swallowing. However, it was this 5 y grant that enabled us to validate the instruments described previously. Serendipitously research at

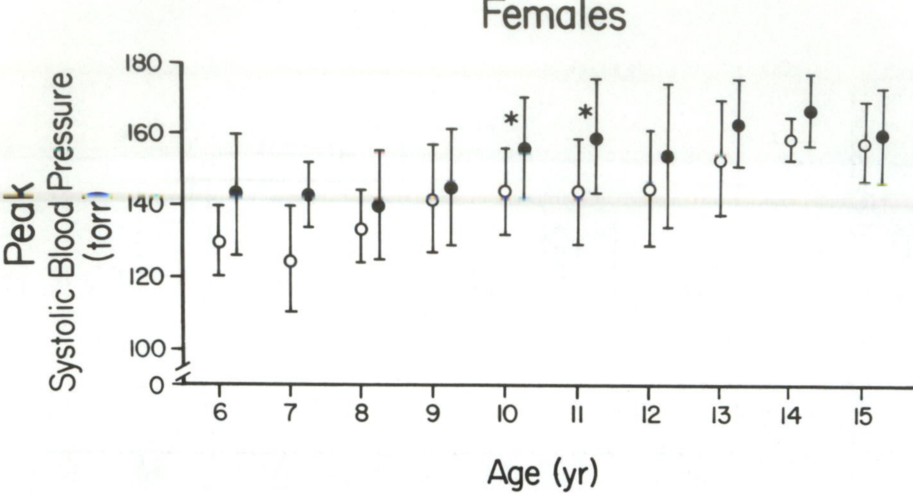

Fig. 11. Peak systolic blood pressure responses for healthy black girls and white girls 6 to 15-years-old. Solid circles are the blacks, open circles are the whites.
Level of significance * = $p < 0.05$;

the GPI first demonstrated systemic vascular resistance was different by race. The study was initially designed to demonstrate the ability to perform cardiac output studies during exercise using 2D echocardiography and Doppler techniques. Dr. Fred Arensman adapted the methodology[38] for the study and Dr. Frank Treiber[39] was able to analyse the data in 10-year-old boys. This study, probably more than any other, was the impetus to assess, in children, what was actually happening in the systemic vascular bed. By being able to measure cardiac output and incorporate it into the equation

$$\text{systemic vascular resistance} = \frac{\text{blood pressure (mean)}}{\text{cardiac output}}$$

we became able to evaluate the vascular response to exercise as well as other stressors, both physical and psychological[39-41]. Table 7 presents the haemodynamic variable measured and calculated in that study.

Treiber extended the studies to a younger population of children, 4 to 6 y of age, and demonstrated that the black children had higher BP responses at a submaximum work load than white children[42]. This further advanced the hypothesis that there

Fig. 12. A 16-year-old, young man who had been operated for tetralogy of Fallot.

Fig. 13. A 17-year-old, young lady operated for a complete atrioventricular canal with a mechanical mitral valve.

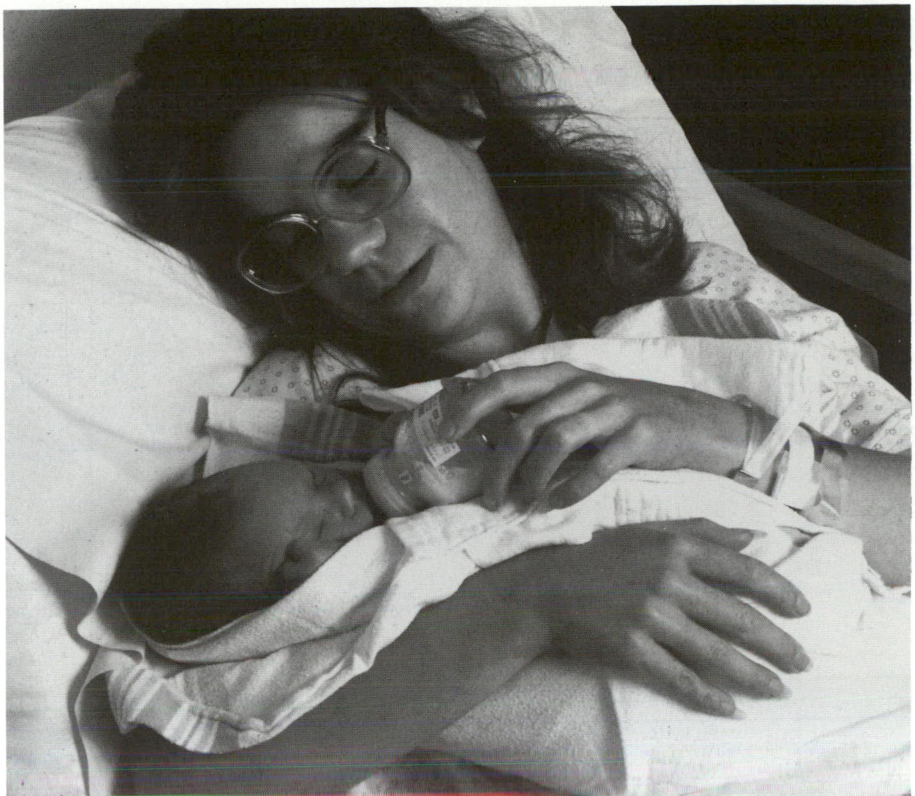

Fig. 14. A 20-year-old woman with tricuspid atresia, operated at 14 years of age with an atrial pulmonary conduit. The first woman to be described to go to full term and deliver a healthy baby after such a procedure.

were racial differences in systemic vascular reactivity identifiable at a very early age. This suggested a genetic basis for the differences and led him to recruit a cohort of twins in order to assess this observation. These studies have just begun.

Dr. Bernard "Bob" Gutin joined our faculty in 1991 and his interest in exercise and body composition continued to extend our research into the effects of exercise and physical activity into the metabolic domain. His studies relating insulin, visceral adiposity and other risk factors to obesity and physical fitness and activity are providing important and interesting insights[43-44]. Both of these colleagues and their associates will expand on their areas of research during the XIX International Pediatric Work Physiology Symposium.

The SCAN project has been renewed three times providing Dr. Treiber with the ability to longitudinally evaluate these changes and determine their ability to predict future clinical manifestations of hypertension[45]. The SCAN cohort was recruited on

Table 7. Haemodynamic variables for each exercise stage by race

	Exercise Stage Pre-exercise		Maximum		Initial Recovery		Final Recovery	
	White	Black	White	Black	White	Black	White	Black
Work capacity, kgm/kg	NA	NA	16.30 ± 72.75	16.20 ± 66.26	NA	NA	NA	NA
HR, beats/min	80.69 ± 14.98	76.22 ±11.73	177.50 ± 16.97	166.72 ± 17.17	119.16 ± 19.64	107.88 ± 13.40	103.04 ± 16.20	101.41 ± 16.20
SBP, mmHg	101.00 ±10.11	106.72 ± 11.62	147.49 ± 23.48	158.51 ± 19.66	138.76 ± 20.48	147.29 ± 19.58	111.04 ± 12.07	107.59 ± 12.35
DBP, mmHg	62.46 ± 9.58	68.48 ± 9.74	76.35 ± 16.94	83.46 ± 10.98	64.12 ± 16.94	69.65 ± 12.40	63.40 ± 6.92	65.24 ± 7.58
MAP, mmHg	75.31 ± 7.47	81.23 ± 8.68	100.06 ± 15.87	108.49 ± 11.74	89.00 ± 14.57	95.53 ± 13.55	79.28 ± 6.27	79.35 ± 6.92
Ejection time, ms	287.42± 31.91	281.11 ± 41.89	189.35 ± 20.44	196.56 ± 21.87	237.96 ± 26.96	246.35 ± 35.62	259.40 ± 34.02	259.59 ± 37.64
dV/dT	1.84 ± 0.77	1.87 ± 0.47	3.26 ± 1.02 ***	2.45 ± 0.68	2.93 ± 1.28	2.43 ± 0.79	2.53 ± 1.24	2.17 ± 0.36
Time to peak ejection, ms	71.69 ± 19.64	64.28 ± 9.07	52.23 ± 14.61*	61.78 ± 10.33	58.88 ± 17.80	59.53 ± 10.89	61.92 ± 15.00	61.71 ± 12.28
CI,CO/BSA, L/min/m^2	2.89 ± 0.75**	2.24 ± 0.55	5.77 ± 1.31	4.47 ± 1.11	4.75 ± 1.17**	3.38 ± 0.83	4.07 ± 1.02**	3.24 ± 0.81
SVR, MAP/CI, mmHg/L/min/m^2	24.10± 7.05**	31.20 ± 8.67	15.28 ± 3.20**	20.05 ± 6.68	17.20± 4.82***	24.43 ± 6.63	18.03 ± 5.28*	22.04 ± 7.59
Flow velocity integral	17.21 ± 3.59	16.48 ± 3.36	15.01 ± 2.85	14.35 ± 2.54	18.37 ± 3.82	16.83 ± 3.51	18.19 ± 3.46	17.06 ± 3.81
Rate-pressure product	8195 ± 2004	8177 ± 1432	26233 ± 5205	26357 ± 3815	16534 ± 3242	15756 ± 2765	11534 ± 2595	10975 ± 2423

Legend to table 7.
All values are mean ± SD. Differences between white and black subjects are not significant ($p > 0.05$) except where otherwise indicated. BPM indicates beats per minute; dV/dT, change in velocity over time; CI, cardiac index; CO, cardiac output; BSA, body surface area; SVR, systemic vascular resistance; MAP, mean arterial pressure; and NA, not applicable.
Level of significance * $p < 0.05$; ** $p < 0.01$; *** $p < 0.001$

the basis of a family history of coronary artery disease (CAD) being positive or negative for two generations. Children 7 to 10 y of age who had a positive family history for CAD have demonstrated a greater rise in their systolic BP and less attenuation of their systemic vascular resistance when exercised[46,47]. This suggested a reduced effect of endothelial derived relaxing factor (EDRF) in the children who had a positive family history. On the basis of these observations, Dr. Gutin and his colleagues at the GPI have begun to assess the effect of fitness and body composition on vascular responses. Their symposium will focus on these particular aspects of their research.

Based upon the observations of our clinical and epidemiologic studies we have come to the belief that it is time to take our work to the cellular, subcellular and molecular, and genetic levels. Collaboration with the MCG Centres of Vascular Biology and Institute of Molecular Medicine and Genetics is now underway to further define mechanism of the pathophysiology and gene control of our clinical observations.

Finally, a renewed interest in Sickle Cell disease has emerged at MCG and NHLBI. In collaboration with the MCG Sickle Cell Center, Dr. Gutin and associates have initiated a study to determine the physical trainability of women with SS haemoglobin.

In conclusion, the cardiovascular responses to exercise have provided a wonderful opportunity to evaluate a number of pathological processes and come to a better understanding of the mechanisms and interactions underlying cardiovascular disease processes .

I wish to acknowledge my colleagues and express to them my deepest appreciation of their support over the past three decades.

References

1. Strong, W.B., Liebman, J., Downs, T.D. and Liebowitz, R. (1972) The normal adolescent electrocardiogram. *American Heart Journal*, Vol. 83, pp. 115-28.
2. Rogers, J.H., Strong, W.B. and Hellerstein, H.K. (1977) The exercise electrocardiogram in trained and untrained adolescent males. *Medicine and Science in Sports*, Vol. 9, pp. 164-7.
3. Adams, F.H., Line, L.M. and Miyake, H. (1961) The physical working capacity of normal school children I California. *Paediatrics*, Vol. 28, pp. 55-64.
4. Adams, F.H., Bengtsson, E., Berven, H. and Wegelius, C. (1961) The physical working capacity of normal school children II Swedish City and Country. *Paediatrics*, Vol. 28, pp. 243-57
5. Kramer, J. and Lurie, P. (1964) Maximal exercise tests in children. *American Journal of Diseases of Children,* Vol. 108, pp. 283-97.
6. Cumming, G.R., Everatt, D. and Haskman, L. (1978) Bruce treadmill test and children's normal values in a clinic population. *American Journal of Cardiology*, Vol. 41, pp. 69-78.
7. Goldberg, S.J., Weiss, R. and Adams, F.H. (1966) Comparison of work required by normal children and those with congenital heart disease to participate in childhood activities, *Journal of Pediatrics*, Vol. 69, pp. 56-60.
8. Strong, W.B., Spencer, D., Miller, M.D. and Salehbhai, M. (1978) The physical working capacity of healthy black children. *American Journal of Diseases of Children*, Vol. 132, pp. 244-8.
9. Strong, W.B., Miller, M.D., Striplin, M. and Salehbhai, M. (1978) Blood pressure response to dynamic exercise in healthly black children. *American Journal of Diseases of Children*, Vol. 132, pp. 556-60.
10. Thapar, M., Strong, W.B., Miller, M.D., Leatherbury, L. and Salehbhai, M. (1978) Exercise electrocardiogram of healthy black children. *American Journal of Diseases of Children*, Vol. 132, pp. 592-5.
11. Riopel, D.A., Taylor, A.B. and Hohn, A.R. (1979) Blood pressure, heart rate, pressure rate product and electrocardiographic changes in healthy children during treadmill exercise. *American Journal of Cardiology*, Vol. 44, pp. 697-704.
12. James, F.W., Kaplan, S., Gulieck, C.J., Tsay, J.V., Knight, M.J.S. and Sarwar, C.J. (1980) Response of normal children and young adults to controlled bicycle exercise. *Circulation*, Vol. 61, pp. 902-12.
13. Fixler, D.E., Laird, W.P., Browne, R., Fitzgerald, V., Wilson, S. and Vance, R. (1979) Response of hypertensive adolescents to dynamic and isometric exercise stress. P*ediatrics*, Vol. 75, pp. 1071-5.
14. Moss, A.J. and Adams, F.H. (1963) Index of indirect estimation of diastolic blood pressure. *American Journal of Disease of Children,* Vol. 106, pp. 74-7.
15. Alpert, B.S., Gilman, P.A., Strong, W.B., Ellison, M.T., Miller, M.D., McFarlane, J. and Hayashidera, T. (1981) Hemodynamic and electrocardiographic responses to exercise in children with sickle cell anemia. *American Journal of Diseases of Children*, Vol. 135, pp. 362-6.

16. Alpert, B.S., Flood, N.L., Strong, W.B., Blair, J.R., Walpert, J.B. and Levy, A.L. (1982) Responses to exercise in children with sickle cell trait. *American Journal of Diseases of Children*, Vol. 136, pp. 1002-4.
17. Covitz, W., Eubig, C., Balfour, I.C., Jerath, R., Alpert, B.S., Strong, W.B. and Durant, R.H. (1983) Exercise induced cardiac dysfunction in sickle cell anemia: a radionuclide study. *American Journal of Cardiology*, Vol. 51, pp. 570-5.
18. Balfour, I.C., Covitz, W., Davis, H., Rao, P.S., Strong, W.B. and Alpert, B.S. (1984) Cardiac size and function in children with sickle cell anemia. *American Heart Journal*, Vol. 108, pp. 345-50.
19. Monarrez, C., Rees, A.H. and Strong. W.B. (1978) The use of the exercise electrocardiogram in the evaluation of dysrhythmia in children. *Pediatrician*, Vol. 7, pp. 116-25.
20. James, F.W., Blomqvist, C.G., Freed, M.D., Miller, W.W., Moller, J.G. and Nugent, E.W. (1982) Standards for exercise testing in the paediatric age group. American Heart Association, *Circulation*, Vol. 66, pp. 1377-97A.
21. Alpert, B.S., Flood, N.L., Strong, W.B., Dover, E.R., Durant, R.H., Martin, A.M. and Booker, D.L. (1982) Responses to ergometer exercise in a healthy biracial population of children. *Journal of Pediatrics*, Vol. 101, pp. 538-45.
22. Alpert, B.S., Dover, E.R., Booker, D.L., Martin, A.M. and Strong, W.B. (1981) Blood pressures response to dynamic exercise in healthy children - black vs white. *Journal of Pediatrics*, Vol. 99, pp. 556-61.
23. Strong, W.B. (ed.) (1978) *Atherosclerosis: Pediatric Aspects*, Grune and Stratton, New York.
24. Reisman, M. (1965) Atherosclerosis and pediatrics. *Journal of Pediatrics*, Vol. 66, pp. 1-7.
25. Holman, R. (1961) Atherosclerosis - a pediatric nutrition problem? *American Journal of Clinical Nutrition,* Vol. 9, pp. 565-9.
26. Saltykov, S. (1915) Jugendliche und beginnende atherosclerose, in *Korrespondenzblatt für Schweizer Aertze Basel,* XLV, 1057. Cited by R.D. Voller and W.B. Strong (1981). Pediatric aspects of atherosclerosis. *American Heart* Journal, Vol 101, pp. 815-36.
27. Monckeberg, J.G. (1921) Das gefassysten und seine erkrankunger. Hdb. D arztlichen erfabringen im Wellkreige ed v sbyerring Bd VIII.
28. Wilcox, L.S., Teaford, P.A., Levy, M. and Strong, W.B. (1981) Students for community involvement - a medical school project. *Journal of the Medical Association of Georgia*, Vol. 70, pp. 409-12.
29. Alpert, B.S., Flood, N.L., Balfour, I.C. and Strong, W.B. (1982) Automated blood pressure measurement during ergometer exercise in children. *Catheterization and Cardiology Diagnosis*, Vol. 8, pp. 525-33.
30. Braden, D.S., Leatherbury, L., Treiber, F.A. and Holland, G.J. (1990) Noninvasive assessment of cardiac output in children using impedance cardiography. *American Heart Journal*, Vol. 120, pp. 1166-72.
31. Alpert, B.S., Verrill, D.E., Flood, N.L., Boineau, J.P. and Strong, W.B. (1983) Complications of exercise testing in children. *Pediatric Cardiology*, Vol. 4, pp. 91-6.

32. Strong, W.B. and Alpert, B.S. (1982) The child with heart disease: play, recreation, and sports, in *Current Problems in Pediatrics*, (ed. L. Gluck), Year Book Medical Publishers, Inc., Chicago, Il, Vol. XIII, No. 2.
33. Rao, P.S., Thapar, M.K., Haggard, R.J. and Strong, W.B. (1983) Left ventricular muscle mass by M-mode echocardiography in children. *Journal of Cardiovascular Ultrasonography*, Vol. 2, pp. 381-9.
34. Alpert, B.S., Dover, E.V., Strong, W.B. and Covitz, W. (1984) Longitudinal exercise haemodynamics in children with sickle cell anemia. *American Journal of Diseases of Children*, Vol. 138, pp. 1021-4.
35. Covitz, W., Espeland, M., Gallagher, D., Hellenbrand, W., Leff, S. and Talner, N. (1995) The heart in sickle cell anemia. The cooperative study of sickle cell disease. *Chest*, Vol. 108, pp. 1214-9.
36. Braden, D.S., Covitz, W. and Millner, P.F. (1996) Cardiovascular function during rest and exercise in patients with sickle cell anemia and coexisting alpha thalessemia - 2. *American Journal of Hematology*, Vol. 52, pp. 96-102.
37. Treiber, F.A., Musante, L., Arensman, F., Hartdagen, S., Levy, M. and Strong, W.B. (1989) Validation of a portable heart rate monitor in young children. *Medicine and Science in Sports and Exercise*, Vol. 21, pp. 338-42.
38. Arensman, F.W., Treiber, F.A., Gruber, M. and Strong, W.B. (1989) Exercise induced differences in cardiac output, blood pressure and systemic vascular response in healthy biracial population of ten year old boys. *American Journal of Diseases of Children*, Vol. 143, pp. 212-6.
39. Treiber, F.A., Musante, L., Levy, M. and Strong, W.B. (1989) Racial differences in young children's cardiovascular reactivity to dynamic exercise. *American Journal of Diseases of Children*, Vol. 143, pp. 720-3.
40. Treiber, F.A., Musante, L., Braden, D.S., Arensman, F., Strong, W.B., Levy, M. and Leverett, S. (1990) Racial differences in hemodynamic responses to the cold face stimulus in children and adults. *Psychosomatic Medicine*, Vol. 52, pp. 286-96.
41. Treiber, F.A., Strong, W.B., Arensman, F., Davis, H., Musante, L. and Forrest, T. (1991) Family history of myocardial infarction and hemodynamic responses to exercise in young black boys. *American Journal of Diseases of Children*, Vol. 145, pp.1029-33.
42. Treiber, F.A., Davis, H., Musante, L., Raunikar, R.A., Strong, W.B., McCaffrey, F., Meeks, M.C. and Vandernoord, R. (1993) Ethnicity, gender, family history of myocardial infarction and hemodynamic responses to laboratory stressors in children. *Health Psychology*, Vol. 12, pp. 6-15.
43. Islam, S., Gutin, B., Manos, T., Smith, C. and Treiber, F.A. (1994) Low density lipoprotein cholesterol/apolipoprotein B-100 ratio: interaction of family history of premature atherosclerotic coronary artery disease with race and gender in 7 to 11 year olds. *Pediatrics*, Vol. 94, pp. 494-9.
44. Gutin, B., Islam, S., Treiber, F., Smith, C. and Manos, T. (1995) Fasting insulin concentration is related to cardiovascular reactivity to exercise in children. *Paediatrics,* Vol. 96, pp. 1123-5.

45. Treiber, F.A., Turner, J.R., Davis, H., Levy M. and Strong, W.B. (1996) Young children's cardiovascular stress responses predict resting cardiovascular functioning 2 ½ years later. *Journal of Cardiovascular Risk*, Vol. 3, pp. 95-100.
46. Treiber, F.A., Papavassiliou, D.P., Gutin, B., Malpass, D., Yi, W., Islam, S., Davis, H. and Strong, W.B. (in press) Determinants of endothelium-dependent femoral artery vasodilation in youth. *Psychosomatic Medicine*.
47. Musante, L., Turner, J.R., Treiber, F.A., Davis, H. and Strong, W.B. (in press) Moderators of ethnic differences in vasoconstrictive reactivity in youth. *Ethnicity and Disease*.

CARDIOVASCULAR STRESS RESPONSES PREDICT CARDIOVASCULAR FUNCTIONING: A FOUR-YEAR FOLLOW-UP

Longitudinal cardiovascular stress responses

F. TREIBER, J. DEL ROSARIO, H. DAVIS, B. GUTIN and W.B. STRONG
Georgia Prevention Institute, Medical College of Georgia, Augusta, USA

Keywords: Cardiovascular reactivity, essential hypertension, prediction, stress

Introduction

Exaggerated cardiovascular (CV) responsivity to stress has been proposed as a possible risk factor for the development of CV diseases including essential hypertension (EH)[for recent reviews see 1,2]. Although not entirely consistent [e.g. 3], several longitudinal studies have found CV stress responses to be predictive of increased resting blood pressure (BP) levels and EH[4-7].

Since the pathogenesis of CV diseases begins in childhood[8], CV responsivity to stress has been receiving increasing attention in paediatric CV preventive medicine research[9]. However, relatively few longitudinal CV stress responsivity studies have been conducted in youth, especially within the context of ethnicity and sex[9,10].

The purpose of the present study was to assess the independent contributions of children's CV responsivity to laboratory stressors as a predictor of resting CV function 4 y later. This was done after accounting for the contributions of standard CV risk factors (e.g. height, weight, adiposity, resting CV measures, socioeconomic status). The sample comprised normotensive children with family histories of EH[11]. Such prospective evaluations are particularly needed with such individuals since family history of EH has been associated with exaggerated BP stress responsivity and with an increased risk for development of EH later in life[12].

Subjects

Subjects were 217 children who were assessed on two separate occasions separated by an average of 4.0 ± 0.7 y. There were 132 Blacks (65 males) and 85 Whites (45 males). Subjects were aged 12. 7 ± 0.6 y on the first evaluation. All had a positive

Children and Exercise XIX. Edited by Neil Armstrong, Brian Kirby and Joanne Welsman.
Published in 1997 by E & FN Spon, 2–6 Boundary Row, London, SE1 8HN.
ISBN 0 419 22100 X.

Table 1. Descriptive characteristics of sample at baseline and follow-up evaluations

Characteristics	Baseline Evaluation	Follow-up
Age (y)	11.8 ± 2.5	15.8 ± 2.4
Height (cm)	150.8 ± 15.2	165.9 ± 9.9
Weight (kg)	51.7 ± 20.9	69.8 ± 22.3
Sum of Skinfolds (mm)	51.1 ± 34.0	58.6 ± 36.3
Conicity (m/{kg/m}) [a]	1.15 ± 0.08	1.18 ± 0.09
Resting CV Parameters		
SBP (mmHg)	107.9 ± 11.4	112.4 ± 11.5
DBP (mmHg)	59.0 ± 6.4	59.3 ± 6.6
HR (beats·min^{-1})	75.2 ± 10.6	71.5 ± 11.5

Values are mean ± SD

All means significantly different (p <0.001) between baseline and follow-up except DBP

[a] conicity=waist circumference(m)/[0.109 wt(kg)/ht(m)]

family history of EH (defined as having one or both biological parents and one or more grandparents with EH, which was verified by physician reports or hospital records). All subjects were nondiabetics and were normotensive for age and sex on both evaluations. Descriptive characteristics of the sample at the baseline and follow-up evaluations are presented in table 1.

Methods

On each evaluation measurements of height, weight and subscapular, suprailiac and triceps skinfolds measurements were obtained using established protocols. Conicity, a measure of central adiposity, was also obtained[13]. Following this, CV parameters were evaluated including systolic (SBP) and diastolic (DBP) blood pressure and heart rate (HR). Right arm blood pressure was assessed with a Dinamap model 1846SX (Critikon, Inc., Tampa, Florida, USA) during all evaluations except the exercise stressor. A Quinton 410 exercise BP monitor was used during the exercise test (Quinton Instrument Co., Seattle, Washington, USA). A Quinton Q4000 stress electrocardiograph was used with a Lead II electrocardiograph configuration to provide gating signals for the Quinton 410. The Quinton 410 BP monitor has been validated for use during exercise[14] and the Dinamap 1846SX has been validated for use at rest and during reactivity evaluations[15].

Following the anthropometric measurements, the subject was placed in a supine position and rested for 15 min. All CV parameters were simultaneously measured during minutes 11, 13 and 15 of the rest period (hereafter termed baseline). A minimal 5 min supine prestressor period preceded each stressor with CV parameters assessed every other minute. Prior to presentation of each stressor the subject's BP had to return to within 5mmHg of the mean baseline level.

Following the baseline resting assessment, the postural change task was conducted. The subject stood and placed his/her right arm at a 90° angle across the trunk. CV parameters were assessed during minutes 1, 2 and 3. The subject then participated in the exercise task which consisted of a maximal voluntary effort using a standard Bruce protocol[16] using a Quinton 645 treadmill (Quinton Instrument Co., Seattle, Washington, USA). The CV parameters were assessed during the last minute of each exercise intensity and immediately upon cessation of exercise. Following the exercise task, the subject rested a minimum of 20 min and then engaged in the forehead cold stressor which consisted of a plastic bag containing 6 cups of crushed ice and 1 ½ cups of water placed on the forehead for 1 min. One set of CV measurements were recorded during the last 30-40 seconds of the task. During the follow-up visit 4 y later, resting BP and HR were assessed using the same procedures as described in the baseline evaluation above.

Data analyses and results

Mean values for each CV parameter were calculated for the baseline and follow-up resting evaluations and peak CV responses were used as measures of stress responsivity. Initial univariate repeated measures analyses of variance examined changes in descriptive characteristics from baseline to follow-up. Significant increases were observed in height, weight, sum of skinfolds, conicity and SBP while a decrease was noted for HR (all p values < 0.001).

Anthropometric, demographic, resting baseline CV and CV stress responses from the first evaluation were related to the follow-up resting CV parameters using Pearson product moment correlations. Interaction effects for the above variables were also evaluated at the univariate level. As depicted in table 2, a number of significant relationships were observed. At follow-up Blacks were found to have higher resting SBP ($p <0.05$) and DBP ($p <0.01$) while males exhibited higher SBP and lower HR (both ps <0.001). Each baseline resting parameter was significantly related to its respective follow-up resting parameter (all ps <0.001). The measures of body habitus and adiposity were all significantly positively related to follow-up SBP (all ps <0.01) while only age and height were related to follow-up DBP and HR (all ps <0.001). SBP (all ps <0.001) responses to each stressor were significantly related to follow-up resting SBP while DBP and HR responses to postural change and forehead cold were related to the follow-up resting parameters (all ps <0.01).

To determine which of the parameters significant at the univariate level were independent predictors of follow-up resting CV values, a series of stepwise hierarchical multiple regressions were conducted using blocks of predictor variables. The first block consisted of the pertinent baseline CV value. The second block included race

Table 2. Univariate relationships of follow-up resting CV parameters with data from baseline evaluation four years earlier

Baseline Variable	Follow-up Resting Variable SBP (mmHg)	DBP (mmHg)	HR (beats·min^{-1})
Demographics			
Sex (male = 1; female =2)	-0.33***	0.06	0.27***
Race (White = 1; Black=2)	0.15*	0.18**	-0.12
Anthropometrics			
Age (y)	0.28***	0.15*	-0.31***
Height (cm)	0.35***	0.20***	-0.29***
Weight (kg)	0.34***	0.09	-0.13
Waist (cm)	0.33***	0.01	-0.05
Sum of skinfolds (mm)	0.18**	0.01	0.09
Conicity (m/{kg/m})	0.22***	-0.07	0.12
Respective CV Parameters			
Baseline Resting	0.59***	0.50***	0.37***
Postural Change Response	0.50***	0.37***	0.18***
Forehead Cold Response	0.54***	0.18**	0.28***
Treadmill Response	0.37***	0.13	0.01
Treadmill Duration (min)	0.09	0.03	-0.15**

Level of significance *p <0.05, **p <0.01, ***p <0.001

and sex, the third was comprised of anthropometric parameters and the fourth block consisted of the pertinent CV stress responses. The final block consisted of the two-way interactions involving CV stress responses with demographic and anthropometric variables found to be significant at the univariate level. Interaction terms were tested only in the presence of their main effects. This statistical approach ensured that CV stress responses were only considered as possible predictors after controlling for the significant contributions of other standard risk factors from the initial evaluation.

Follow-up resting SBP was predicted by baseline resting SBP (R^2 = 0.35) followed by sex (additional R^2 = 0.06) and finally forehead cold SBP responsivity (additional R^2 = 0.04, total model R^2 = 0.45, $p < 0.001$). After accounting for baseline resting DBP (model R^2 = 0.25), the only other significant predictor was height (additional R^2 = 0.02; total model R^2 = 0.27, $p < 0.001$). Follow-up resting HR was predicted by baseline resting HR (model R^2 = 0.14) followed by sex, height and weight (additional R^2 =

Table 3. Interrelationships of CV stress responses by task

	Treadmill Exercise			Postural Change		
	SDP	DBP	HR	SBP	DBP	HR
Forehead Cold						
SBP	0.35**			0.65**		
DBP		0.17*			0.23*	
HR			0.31**			0.31**
Postural Change						
SBP	0.38**					
DBP		0.25**				
HR			-0.06			

Level of significance * p <0.05, ** p <0.001, ***p <0.0001

0.10), and finally, forehead cold HR responsivity (additional $R^2 = 0.04$; total model $R^2 = 0.28$, $p < 0.001$).

Several other series of regressions were also conducted. In the first series, baseline parameters significant at the univariate level were all entered simultaneously. This approach usually results in the "best combination" of predictors, meaning the combination that accounts for the highest total amount of variance with p <0.05 for each variable in the model. A second approach involved the use of aggregated CV stress responsivity scores in the hierarchical block regressions rather than entry of all three stress responses. The CV responses were standardised separately for each stressor and then averaged across the three stressors. In this way an aggregated stress responsivity score was calculated for each CV parameter and used in the block for entry of CV responsivity.

The simultaneous entry approach and the hierarchical block approach using the aggregate standardised stress responses yielded models comparable to those observed in the original hierarchical block regressions for SBP and DBP (± 1% total variance accounted for). However, for HR the aggregated stress response was not a significant predictor.

Discussion

The current findings indicated that children's CV responses to laboratory stressors were significantly related to their resting CV function 4 y later. That is, univariate comparisons found SBP peak responses to all three stressors related to follow-up resting SBP while DBP and HR responses to postural change and forehead cold were related to their respective follow-up resting measures. In many cases the correlation coefficients were comparable or higher than those observed with standard risk factors such as height, weight, age, and indices of adiposity.

Most importantly, after accounting for the significant contributions of standard risk factors via regression analyses, SBP and HR responses to forehead cold stimulation added significant predictive power to their respective follow-up resting measures. These findings are consistent with long term prospective studies in adults in which BP responses to cold pressor tasks were predictive of EH[5,7]. Further, they replicate and extend a recent finding involving this cohort in which DBP forehead cold responsivity was predictive of resting DBP 1 y later[4].

Although SBP responsivity to dynamic exercise has been shown to be an independent predictor of future SBP levels in children[17] and of EH in adults[4], it was not an independent predictor of CV function in the current study. Responses which are dependent on vasodilator activity (e.g. dynamic exercise) may not be as useful in the prediction of future EH in individuals with such strong family histories of EH. This may in part be attributed to the fact that individuals with a family history of EH are more prone to exhibit exaggerated BP responses to stressors which are vasoconstrictor mediated[7,12]. The low intertask consistency in SBP responses between treadmill exercise and the two vasoconstrictive stressors of forehead cold and postural change and the relatively high consistency in SBP responsivity to the two predominant vasoconstrictive stressors provides partial support for this hypothesis. However, whether vasoconstrictor and/or vasodilator related BP responsivity in childhood will be predictive of future BP or early onset EH in adulthood in this cohort remains to be determined.

References

1. Manuck, S.B. (1994) Cardiovascular reactivity in cardiovascular disease: "Once more unto the breach". *International Journal of Behavioral Medicine*, Vol. 1, pp. 4-31.
2. Sherwood, A. and Turner, J.R. (in press) Hemodynamic responses during psychological stress: implications for studying disease processes. *International Journal of Behavioral Medicine*.
3. Eich, R.H. and Jacobsen, E.C. (1967) Vascular reactivity in medical students followed for 10 years. *Journal of Chronic Diseases*, Vol. 20, pp. 484-90.
4. Jackson, A.S., Squires, W.G., Grimes, G. and Beard, E.F. (1983) Prediction of future resting hypertension from exercise blood pressure. *Journal of Cardiac Rehabilitation*, Vol. 3, pp. 263-8.
5. Kasagi, F., Akahoshi, M. and Shimaoka, K. (1995) Relation between cold pressor test and development of hypertension based on 28-year follow-up. *Hypertension*, Vol. 25, pp. 71-6.
6. Light, K.C., Dolan, C.A., Davis, M.R. and Sherwood, A. (1992) Cardiovascular responses to an active coping challenge as predictors of blood pressure patterns 10 to 15 years later. *Psychosomatic Medicine*, Vol. 54, pp. 217-30.
7. Menkes, M.S., Matthews, K.A., Krantz, D.S., Lundberg, U., Mead, L.A., Oaqish, B., Liang, K., Thomas, C.B. and Pearson, T.A. (1989) Cardiovascular reactivity to the cold pressor test as a predictor of hypertension. *Hypertension*, Vol. 14, pp. 524-30.

8. Newman, W.P., Freedman, D.S., Voors, A.W., Gard, P.D., Srinivasan, S.R., Cresanta, J.L., Williamson, G.D., Webber, L.S. and Berenson, G.S. (1986) Relation of serum lipoprotein levels and systolic blood pressure to early atherosclerosis: The Bogalusa Heart Study. *New England Journal of Medicine*, Vol. 314, pp. 138-44.
9. Alpert, B.S., Murphy, J.K. and Treiber, F.A. (1994) Essential hypertension: approaches to prevention in children. *Medicine, Exercise, Nutrition and Health*, Vol. 3, pp. 296-307.
10. Murphy, J.K. (1992) Psychophysiological responses to stress in children and adolescents, in *Advances in Pediatric Psychology: Stress and Coping with Pediatric Conditions*, (eds. P.M. La Greca, L.J. Siegal, J.L. Wallander and C.E. Walker), Academic Press, New York, pp. 44-71.
11. Treiber, F.A., Raunikar, R.A., Davis, H., Fernandez, T., Levy, M. and Strong, W.B. (1994) One year stability and prediction of cardiovascular functioning at rest and during laboratory stressors in youth with family histories of hypertension. *International Journal of Behavioral Medicine*, Vol. 1, pp. 335-53.
12. Fredrikson, M. and Matthews, K.A. (1990) Cardiovascular responses to Behavioral stress and hypertension: a meta-analytic review. *Annals of Behavioral Medicine*, Vol. 12, pp. 30-9.
13. Valdez, R., Seidell, J.C., Ahn, Y.I. and Weiss, K.M. (1992) A new index of abdominal adiposity as an indicator of risk for cardiovascular disease. A cross-population study. *International Journal of Obesity*, Vol. 16, pp. 77-82.
14. Treiber, F.A., McCaffrey, F., Strong, W.B., Davis, H. and Baranowski, T. (1991) Automated exercise blood pressure measurements in children: a preliminary study. *Pediatric Exercise Science*, Vol. 3, pp. 290-9.
15. Rosner, B.A., Appel, L.J., Raczynski, J.M., Hebert, P.R., Whelton, P.K., Murphy, J.K., Miller, S.T. and Oberman, A. (1990) A comparison of two automated monitors in the measurement of blood pressure reactivity. *Annals of Epidemiology*, Vol. 1, pp. 57-69.
16. Cumming, G.R., Everatt, D. and Hastman, L. (1978) Bruce treadmill test in children: Normal values in a clinic population. *American Journal of Cardiology*, Vol. 41, pp. 69-75.
17. Mahoney, L.T., Schieken, R.M., Clarke, W.R. and Lauer, R.M. (1988) Left ventricular mass and exercise responses predict future BP. The Muscatine Study. *Hypertension*, Vol.12, pp. 206-13.

RELATIONSHIP OF TOTAL AND VISCERAL ADIPOSE TISSUE TO CARDIOVASCULAR HEALTH

Body composition and cardiovascular health

S. OWENS, B. GUTIN, W. KARP, M. FERGUSON, S. MOOREHEAD and J. ALLISON
Georgia Prevention Institute, Department of Pediatrics, Medical College of Georgia, Augusta, USA
N-A. LE
Lipid Research Laboratory, Emory University, Atlanta, USA
Keywords: Blood lipids, body composition, fat distribution, left ventricular mass, visceral fat

Introduction

Adult studies indicate that the relationships between body composition and cardiovascular risk (CV) factors such as dyslipidemia, hypertension, and hyperinsulinemia vary with body fat distribution[1-3]. Fat deposited centrally tends to be more deleterious than peripheral fat[4,5]. In addition, computed tomography (CT) and magnetic resonance imaging (MRI) have shown visceral adipose tissue (VAT) to be more highly correlated with CV risk factors than subcutaneous abdominal adipose tissue (SAAT)[6-8].

The literature is less extensive regarding visceral obesity and CV risk factors in children. In a group of obese 10 to 15-year-old boys and girls, significant correlations were observed between VAT and triglycerides (TG), total cholesterol (TC), and low density lipoprotein cholesterol (LDLC)[9]. A study involving obese and non-obese adolescent girls found VAT to be significantly correlated with TG, HDLC, and insulin in the obese girls only[10]. A study of non-obese, black and white girls 7-10 years of age found no significant relationship between VAT and TG, HDLC or insulin[11]. It appears, therefore, that the VAT-risk factor relationship may be more pronounced in obese as opposed to lean children.

Given the evidence that the underlying processes for CV disease begin in childhood [12] and evidence of a relationship between VAT and some CV risk factors in obese youths in the 10 to 16-year-old age range[9,10], the present study was conducted to examine these and several other CV risk factor relationships in a multi-ethnic group of obese children younger than previously investigated.

Children and Exercise XIX. Edited by Neil Armstrong, Brian Kirby and Joanne Welsman.
Published in 1997 by E & FN Spon, 2–6 Boundary Row, London, SE1 8HN.
ISBN 0 419 22100 X.

Methods

Subjects were 64 apparently healthy obese children aged 7 to 11 y. Children were recruited using promotional flyers distributed through selected public and private schools in Augusta, Georgia. Ethnicity was determined by self-designation by the parents. The subjects were part of a larger study of the effects of physical training on body fatness and CV risk factors. Children and their parents attended an orientation session and both gave informed consent in accordance with procedures of our Human Assurance Committee.

Total body composition was measured with dual x-ray absorptiometry (DXA) using the Hologic QDR-1000 (Waltham, MA). DXA segments the body into three compartments (fat, bone, fat-free soft tissue) and provides values for percent body fat (%BF), total body fat mass (TFM) and total body fat free mass (FFM). The reliability and validity of DXA measurements of body composition in children have been established[13].

VAT and SAAT were determined at the Medical College of Georgia Biomedical Imaging Laboratory using a 1.5 Tesla MRI system (General Electric Medical Systems, Milwaukee, WI). A series of five transverse images was acquired from the lumbar region of the abdomen with the image corresponding to L4 being used for data analysis. Images were obtained with the patient in the supine position. VAT and SAAT were segmented by simple thresholding. VAT was quantified as adipose tissue within a region of interest defined by a line drawn through the middle of the abdominal and back muscles. Values for VAT and SAAT from the L4 image were calculated in terms of surface area (cm^2). To eliminate inter-observer variability, all images were analysed by the same technician.

For blood measures, subjects reported to the laboratory between 0800 and 0900 following a 12 h fast on a day when no other lab measurements were taken (to prevent anxiety about the venipuncture from influencing the other lab measures). A 20 mL blood sample was obtained from an antecubital vein into vacutainers containing ethylenediaminetraacetate (EDTA). Samples were separated by low speed centrifugation (6000 x g x 10 min) with plasma placed in plastic vials and stored at -70° C until analysis. Blood measures were analysed at certified laboratories (College of American Pathologists) at the Medical College of Georgia (first 22 samples) and at Emory University (final 40 samples). All lipids were analysed using enzymatic methods. HDLC was obtained after precipitating apo B containing lipoproteins with phosphotungstic acid and magnesium chloride (first 22 samples) or Dextran sulfate and magnesium chloride (final 40 samples). LDLC was calculated using the Friedewald equation (first 22 samples) and by ultracentrifugation (final 40 samples)[14]. Apolipoproteins (apo) A-I and B were measured by nephelometry (first 22 samples)[15] and by immunoturbidimetric methods (final 40 samples)[16]. Insulin concentrations were determined by radio-immuno-assay[17,18]. LDL particle diameter was determined by nondenaturing polyacrylamide gradient gel electrophoresis as previously described[19]. When analysing the blood data, laboratory setting was included as a variable in the multiple regression analyses to account for measurement differences between laboratories.

Resting systolic blood pressure (SBP), diastolic blood pressure (DBP), and heart rate (HR) were measured with a Dinamap automated BP monitor (Critikon, Inc.,

Tampa, FL). Measurements were obtained after 10 min of rest in the supine position with an appropriately sized cuff placed on the right arm. Five readings were taken at 1 min intervals, and the last four were averaged.

Aerobic fitness was determined from heart rate during submaximal cycling (submaxHR) at a work rate of 49 W on a supine ergometer (Quinton 486T, Seattle, WA). The exercise intensity was increased gradually until it reached the 49 W level, after which the child maintained that power output for 8 min. SubmaxHR was the average HR over the last 5 min as measured with an ECG embedded in an echocardiograph (Hewlett-Packard Sonos 100, Andover, MA).

Pearson correlations were used to determine univariate relationships between measures of adiposity (VAT, SAAT, %BF, TFM) and the CV risk factors. Hierarchical stepwise multiple linear regression techniques were then used to evaluate the relative contributions of the demographic (age, gender, ethnicity), adiposity, and laboratory setting variables to the variance in CV risk factors. In this procedure[20], variables are entered in stepwise fashion within blocks. Block 1 variables included the demographic measures (age, gender, ethnicity). The block 2 variable was the laboratory setting used for analyzing blood samples (Medical College of Georgia or Emory University). Block 3 included the adiposity measures (VAT, SAAT, %BF, TFM) that were significantly correlated with the particular risk factor in question in the univariate analysis. ANOVA was used for the descriptive statistics to examine group differences related to gender and ethnicity and their possible interaction.

Results

Table 1 shows the descriptive statistics for the anthropometric variables. As none of the gender by ethnicity interactions was significant, data are presented as boys vs girls and whites vs blacks. The VAT measurements were log-transformed to normalise their distributions. Subsequent analyses involving VAT used the transformed values. For ease of comparison with other studies, however, the values in table 1 for VAT are shown in the original units. Body fat ranged between 27- 61% as determined by DXA. There were no significant differences in %BF between boys and girls or between blacks and whites. The only significant anthropometric differences between the genders involved VAT. Boys had significantly more VAT than girls. Boys and girls did not differ significantly in the VAT/SAAT ratio (0.19 ± 0.06 v 0.17 ± 0.05).

There were significant ethnic differences for several anthropometric variables, with blacks being taller and heavier than whites, and having greater TFM and fat free mass. Blacks and whites did not differ significantly on VAT, but blacks had significantly more SAAT than whites, resulting in a lower ratio of VAT to SAAT in blacks (0.15 ± 0.04 v 0.21 ± 0.05).

Table 2 shows the correlations between the adiposity measures and various CV risk factors. In general, VAT was more highly correlated with the lipid and lipoprotein risk factors than the other three measures of adiposity. In the case of LDL particle size, VAT was the only adiposity measure showing a significant (inverse) relationship. TC,

Table 1. Physical characteristics

	Boys n=21	Girls n=43	White n=29	Black n=35	Total n=64
Age (y)	9.7 ± 1.0	9.4 ± 1.0	9.4 ± 0.9	9.6 ± 1.1	9.5 ± 1.0
Height (cm)	142 ± 8	141 ± 8	139 ± 8	44 ± 8*	142 ± 8
Weight (kg)	63.8 ± 23.8	55.5 ± 13.9	50.3 ± 11.5	4.8 ± 19.8*	58.2 ± 18.0
VAT (cm^2)	75.4 ± 44.2	51.4 ± 18.7#	60.4 ± 25.1	8.3 ± 36.1	59.2 ± 31.4
SAAT (cm^2)	359 ± 183	298 ± 110	271 ± 103	57 ± 155*	318 ± 140
TFM (kg)	29.1 ± 15.5	24.7 ± 8.7	22.0 ± 8.6	9.5 ± 12.4*	26.1 ± 11.4
FFM (kg)	34.5 ± 9.9	30.5 ± 6.4	28.0 ± 4.5	5.0 ± 8.7*	31.8 ± 7.9
%BF	44.3 ± 7.8	44.0 ± 5.7	42.9 ± 6.3	5.0 ± 6.5	44.1 ± 6.4

Values are mean ± SD

Level of significance # boys different from girls ($p < 0.05$), *blacks different from whites ($p < 0.05$)

VAT=visceral adipose tissue, SAAT=subcutaneous abdominal adipose tissue, TFM=total body fat mass, FFM=total body fat free mass, %BF=percent body fat

LDLC, apo A-I, and diastolic blood pressure were not significantly related with any of the adiposity measures. Insulin was the only risk factor significantly correlated with all four adiposity measures. Four of the blood measures (TG, HDLC, TC/HDLC, apo B) were significantly correlated with the same three adiposity measures (VAT, SAAT, TFM).

Table 3 summarizes results from the hierarchical stepwise multiple regression procedure. For four of the lipid/lipoprotein measures (TG, HDLC, TC/HDLC, LDL particle size), VAT was the only variable to explain a significant proportion of the variance. In all cases, increased VAT was predictive of less favourable risk factor levels. For apo B, VAT explained an additional 7% of the variance after controlling for the variance explained by measurement differences between laboratories. For several of the non-lipid risk factors, TFM rather than VAT explained significant amounts of the variance. This was true for insulin, systolic BP, and LVM/$ht^{2.7}$. VAT and age were significant predictors of submax HR, but with negative regression coefficients in both cases. SAAT was not retained in any of the regression equations.

Discussion

This is the largest study to date (n = 64) utilizing MRI to examine VAT in children. We quantified VAT in obese black and white boys and girls and investigated relationships with a number of CV risk factors. Several previous studies have examined MRI-derived VAT in young people and its relationship to CV risk factors. However, they either studied children older than our subjects[9,10], were unable to investigate ethnic differences[9,10], or included only girls[10,11].

Table 2. Correlations between adiposity measures and CV risk factors

Variable	n	VAT	SAAT	%BF	TFM
Triglycerides	58	0.53**	0.32*	0.13	0.28*
Cholesterol	62	0.08	-0.03	0.01	-0.06
HDLC	60	-0.37**	-0.32*	-0.06	-0.26*
TC/HDLC	60	0.43**	0.34**	0.11	0.27*
LDLC	58	0.04	-0.01	0.05	-0.02
LDL size	41	-0.32*	-0.21	-0.01	-0.13
Apo A-I	62	-0.05	-0.09	-0.09	-0.09
Apo B	62	0.32*	0.32*	0.15	0.29*
Insulin	54	0.43**	0.46**	0.32*	0.52*
Systolic BP	64	0.24	0.30*	0.17	0.36**
Diastolic BP	64	-0.24	-0.15	-0.03	-0.10
LVM/ht$^{2.7}$	53	0.26	0.36**	0.25	0.37**
Submax HR	63	-0.37**	-0.17	0.13	-0.12

Level of significance *p <0.05, **p <0.01

We observed significant relationships between VAT and a number of CV risk factors. Consistent with the observations of most adult studies[6,7] and the child study of Caprio et al.[10] was our finding of a significant positive relationship between VAT and TG and a negative correlation between VAT and HDLC. Although SAAT and TFM were also correlated with these risk factors, the finding that VAT was the only significant predictor amongst the adiposity measures in hierarchical stepwise multiple regression underscores the relative importance of this fat depot for the lipid profile of obese children. By comparison, in non-obese 7 to 10-year-old girls, Yanovski et al. [11] did not find an association between VAT and TG or HDLC. They hypothesised that their findings may be due to the small absolute visceral adipose tissue levels in their normal-weight children.

We examined several VAT-lipoprotein relationships not previously reported in children and found they tended to coincide with the relationships reported for adults. That is, VAT was significantly related to TC/HDLC and apo B but not to apo A-I. Similar associations with VAT have been reported in adults for TC/HDLC[21,22] for apo B[22,23] and for apo A[8]. Again, VAT proved to be the lone adiposity measure retained in the stepwise multiple regression model for predicting TC/HDLC.

A suggested mechanism for the VAT-blood lipid/lipoprotein relationship emanates from the observation that visceral adipocytes have a high lipolytic nature, resulting in an increased free fatty acid (FFA) flux into the portal circulation[5]. Hepatic TG synthesis and VLDL secretion may be increased by the increased FFA exposure, both of which are negatively associated with HDLC concentrations[10]. Further investigation into the mechanisms responsible for these relationships are needed.

Table 3. Summary table for hierarchical stepwise multiple regression analyses for CV risk factors

Dependent Variable	Predictor Variables Retained	Block*	R^2	R^2 Increase
Triglycerides	VAT	3	0.29	
HDLC	VAT	3	0.14	
TC/HDLC	VAT	3	0.19	
LDL size	VAT	3	0.10	
Apo B	Lab	2	0.34	
	VAT	3	0.41	0.07
Insulin	Lab	2	0.22	
	TFM	3	0.40	0.18
Systolic BP	Age	1	0.13	
	TFM	3	0.20	0.07
$LVM/ht^{2.7}$	Gender	1	0.10	
	Ethnicity	1	0.17	0.07
	TFM	3	0.23	0.06
Submax HR	Age	1	0.13	
	VAT	3	0.24	0.11

*Block 1 variables = demographics (age, gender, ethnicity)
Block 2 variables = laboratory setting for blood analyses
Block 3 variables = adiposity measures (VAT, SAAT, %BF, TFM)

In the case of LDL particle size, we observed a strong, negative relationship between this variable and VAT. There is a growing body of evidence showing that small, dense LDL particles are relatively more atherogenic than larger, more buoyant particles[24,25]. There is some evidence, however, that the VAT-LDL particle size relationship may not be independent of other blood lipid parameters. A recent study of 79 men[26] found significant bivariate associations between VAT and LDL particle size ($r = -0.23$, $p < 0.05$), but even stronger associations between LDL particle size and TG ($r = -0.59$, $p < 0.01$), TC/HDLC ($r = -0.54$, $p < 0.01$), and LDL apo B/LDLC ($r = -0.54$, $p < 0.01$). In the multiple regression analysis from that study, TG, TC/HDLC, and LDL apo B/LDLC explained significant portions of the variance in LDL particle size, whereas VAT (and TFM) did not contribute significantly. In our children, in addition to its association with VAT ($r = -0.32$), LDL particle size was significantly correlated with TG ($r = -0.46$, $p < 0.01$) and TC/HDLC ($r = -0.53$, $p < 0.01$) and apo B/LDLC ($r = -0.35$, $p = 0.03$). In stepwise multiple regression, only TC/HDLC explained a significant proportion of the variance in LDL particle size ($R^2 = 0.45$) while the VAT, TG, gender and ethnicity terms fell out. Thus, it may be that VAT functions as a marker of LDL particle size rather than as the major causative agent.

For the non-lipid risk factors such as insulin, systolic blood pressure and LVM/ht$^{2.7}$, TFM proved to be a stronger predictor than VAT. In the case of insulin, our results appear to differ somewhat from Caprio et al.[27], who found that VAT was the only variable to account for a significant proportion of the variance in insulin levels in multiple regression equations that controlled for total abdominal fat, SAAT, body mass index, percent of ideal body weight, and waist-to-hip ratio (WHR). It may be that the use of DXA-derived TFM in our regression analyses as opposed to the surrogate measures of adiposity (BMI and percent of ideal body weight) used by Caprio et al.[27] contributed to the different findings. Also differing from our findings were those of Yanovski et al.[11] who did not see a relationship between VAT and insulin. The difference in this later case is likely related to the non-obese status of their subjects.

Some adult studies have reported significant VAT-systolic BP relationships[21,28]. It is also known that elevated systolic BP is predictive of elevated LVM/ht$^{2.7}$[20]. In our sample of children, however, we did not find evidence that VAT was a significant predictor of systolic BP or LVM/ht$^{2.7}$. This may be a case where length of exposure to the risk factor plays a role, with the exposure being relatively short in children.

Our finding that higher VAT was predictive of a lower submax HR, that is, better fitness, was unexpected. No physiological explanation immediately comes to mind as to why an increase in any fat depot, including VAT, would be predictive of a higher fitness level. This may be a chance finding.

In conclusion, for our sample of obese, 7 to 11-year-old children, VAT was a better predictor of the variation in blood lipid and lipoprotein parameters than were the other measures of adiposity or the demographic variables of age, gender, and ethnicity. TFM was more predictive than VAT for several non-lipid parameters. Elsewhere in this volume we report on the effects of controlled physical training on various aspects of body fatness, including VAT.

References

1. Gillum, R.F. (1987) The association of body fat distribution with hypertension, hypertensive heart disease, coronary heart disease, diabetes and cardiovascular risk factors in men and women aged 18-79 years. *Journal of Chronic Diseases,* Vol. 40, pp. 421-8.
2. Stern, M.P. and Haffner, S.M. (1986) Body fat distribution and hyperinsulinemia as risk factors for diabetes and cardiovascular disease. *Arteriosclerosis,* Vol. 6, pp. 123-30.
3. Thompson, C.J., Ryu, J.E., Craven, T.E., Kahl, F.R. and Crouse, J.R. (1991) Central adipose distribution is related to coronary atherosclerosis. *Arteriosclerosis and Thrombosis,* Vol. 11, pp. 327-33.
4. Despres, J.P., Allard, C., Tremblay, A., Talbot, J. and Bouchard, C. (1985) Evidence for a regional component of body fatness in the association with serum lipids in men and women. *Metabolism,* Vol. 34, pp. 967-73.

5. Kissebah, A.H. and Peiris, A.N. (1989) Biology of regional body fat distribution: relationship to non-insulin-dependent diabetes mellitus. *Diabetes-Metabolism Reviews,* Vol. 5, pp. 83-109.
6. Despres, J.P., Moorjani, S., Ferland, M., Tremblay, A., Lupien, P.J., Nadeau, A., Pinault, S., Theriault, G. and Bouchard, C. (1989) Adipose tissue distribution and plasma lipoprotein levels in obese women: importance of intra-abdominal fat. *Arteriosclerosis,* Vol. 9, pp. 203-10.
7. Pouliot, M.C., Despres, J.P., Nadeau, A., Moorjani, S., Prud'homme, D., Lupien, P.J., Tremblay, A. and Bouchard, C. (1992) Visceral obesity in men: associations with glucose tolerance, plasma insulin, and lipoprotein levels. *Diabetes,* Vol. 41, pp. 826-34.
8. Rissanen, J., Hudson, R. and Ross, R. (1994) Visceral adiposity, androgens, and plasma lipids in obese men. *Metabolism,* Vol. 43, pp. 1318-23.
9. Brambilla, P., Manzoni, P., Sironi, S., Simone, P., Del Maschio, A., diNatale, B. and Chiumello, G. (1994) Peripheral and abdominal adiposity in childhood obesity. *International Journal of Obesity,* Vol. 18, pp. 795-800.
10. Caprio, S., Hyman, L.D., McCarthy, S., Lange, R., Bronson, M. and Tamborlane, W.V. (1996) Fat distribution and cardiovascular risk factors in obese adolescent girls: importance of the intraabdominal fat depot. *American Journal of Clinical Nutrition,* Vol. 64, pp. 12-7.
11. Yanovski, J.A., Yanovski, S.Z., Filmer, K.M., Hubbard, V.S., Avila, N., Lewis, B., Reynolds, J.C. and Flood, M. (1996) Differences in body composition of black and white girls. *American Journal of Clinical Nutrition,* Vol. 64, pp. 833-9.
12. Zonderland, M.L., Erich, W.B.M., Erkelens, D.W., Kortlandt, W., Wit, J.M., Huisveld, I.A. and de Ridder, C.M. (1990) Plasma lipids and apoproteins, body fat distribution and body fatness in early pubertal children. *International Journal of Obesity,* Vol. 14, pp. 1039-46.
13. Gutin, B., Litaker, M., Islam, S., Manos, T., Smith, C. and Treiber, F. (1996) Body composition measurement in 9-11 year old children by dual x-ray absorptiometry, skinfolds and bioimpedance analysis. *American Journal of Clinical Nutrition,* Vol. 63, pp. 287-92.
14. Lipid and lipoprotein analysis. (1974) Manual for laboratory operations, Lipid Research Clinics Program. No. (NIH) 75-628 ed. Washington, D.C. U.S. Dept. of HEW.
15. Gutin, B., Islam, S., Manos, T., Smith, C., Cucuzzo, N. and Stachura, M. (1994) The relations of body fatness and aerobic fitness to the atherogenic and diabetogenic metabolic syndrome in black and white 7-11 year olds. *Journal of Pediatrics,* Vol. 125, pp. 847-52.
16. Le, A. (1996) Personal communication.
17. Gutin, B., Owens, S., Treiber, F., Islam, S., Karp, W. and Slavens, G. (in press) Weight-independent cardiovascular fitness and coronary risk factors. *Archives of Pediatrics and Adolescent Medicine.*
18. Tietz, N.W. (1990) editor *Clinical Guide to Laboratory Tests,* 2nd ed, WB Saunders , Philadelphia, p. 333.

19. Li, X., Innis-Whitehouse, W., Brown, W.V. and Le, N. (under review) Protocol for the preparation of a segmental linear gradient gel: Simultaneous determination of Lp(a), LDL and HDL particle sizes.
20. Treiber, F.A., McCaffrey, F., Pflieger, K., Raunikar, R.A., Strong, W.B. and Davis, H. (1993) Determinants of left ventricular mass in normotensive children. *American Journal of Hypertension,* Vol. 6, pp. 505-13.
21. Cigolini, M., Targher, G., Bergamo Andreis, I.A., Tonoli, M., Agostino, G. and De Sandre, G. (1996) Visceral fat accumulation and its relation to plasma hemostatic factors in healhty men. *Arteriosclerosis Thrombosis and Vascular Biology,* Vol. 16, pp. 368-74.
22. Lemieux, S., Prud'homme, D., Moorjani, S., Tremblay, A., Bouchard, C., Lupien, P.J. and Despres, J.P. (1995) Do elevated levels of abdominal visceral adipose tissue contribute to age-related differences in plasma lipoprotein concentrations in men? *Atherosclerosis,* Vol. 118, pp. 155-65.
23. Vohl, M.C., Tchernof, A., Dionne, F.T., Moorjani, S., Prud'homme, D., Bouchard, C., Nadeau, A., Lupien, P.J. and Despres, J.P. (1996) The ApoB-100 gene EcoRI polymorphism influences the relationship between features of the insulin resistance syndrome and the hyper-ApoB and dense LDL phenotype in men. *Diabetes,* Vol. 45, pp. 1405-11.
24. Chait, A., Brazg, R.L., Tribble, D.L. and Krauss, R.M. (1993) Susceptibility of small, dense, low-density lipoproteins to oxidative modification in subjects with the atherogenic lipoprotein phenotype, pattern B. *American Journal of Medicine,* Vol. 94, pp. 350-6.
25. Teng, B., Sniderman, A.D., Soutar, A.K. and Thompson, G.R. (1986) Metabolic basis of hyperapobetalipoproteinemia. Turnover of apolipoprotein B in low density lipoprotein and its precursors and subfractions compared with normal and familial hypercholesterolemia. *Journal of Clinical Investigation,* Vol. 77, pp. 663-72.
26. Tchernof, A., Lamarche, B., Prud'homme, D., Nadeau, A., Moorjani, S., Labrie, F., Lupien, P.J. and Depres, J. (1996) The dense LDL phenotype-association with plasma lipoprotein levels, visceral obesity, and hyperinsulinemia in men. *Diabetes Care,* Vol. 19, pp. 629-37.
27. Caprio, S., Hyman, L.D., Limb, C., McCarthy, S., Lange, R., Sherwin, R.S., Shulman, G. and Tamborlane, W.V. (1995) Central adiposity and its metabolic correlates in obese adolescent girls. *American Journal of Physiology,* Vol. 269, pp. E118-26.
28. Peiris, A.N., Sothmann, M.S., Hoffmann, R.G., Hennes, M.I., Wilson, C.R., Gustafson, A.B. and Kissebah, A.H. (1989) Adiposity, fat distribution, and cardiovascular risk. *Annals of Internal Medicine,* Vol. 110, pp. 867-72.

EFFECT OF PHYSICAL TRAINING ON CARDIOVASCULAR HEALTH IN OBESE CHILDREN

Physical training and cardiovascular health

B. GUTIN, S. OWENS, S. RIGGS, M. FERGUSON, S. MOOREHEAD, F. TREIBER, W. KARP, W. THOMPSON, J. ALLISON, M. LITAKER and K. MURDISON

Georgia Prevention Institute, Department of Pediatrics, Medical College of Georgia, Augusta, Georgia, USA

N-A. LE

Division of Arteriosclerosis and Lipid Metabolism, Emory University, Atlanta, Georgia, USA

Keywords: Body fatness, cardiovascular health, energy expenditure, obese children, physical activity, physical training

Introduction

Cardiovascular (CV) health may be conceived as a spectrum[1], at the left end of which is the unfit-obese child who has elevated risk factors for coronary artery disease (CAD) and non-insulin dependent diabetes mellitus (NIDDM). Although these diseases ordinarily come to full flower in the adult years, the underlying processes seem to begin during childhood in that risk factors measured during childhood predict adult morbidity[2]. Consequently, high levels of these risk factors in childhood suggest that the child is low in CV health.

If regular exercise moves an unfit-obese child toward the middle of the spectrum so he/she becomes only moderately overfat and does not have elevated risk factors, this might be termed disease prevention. In addition, regular exercise can help a child who is at the centre of the spectrum to move toward optimal well-being at the right extreme, which might be termed health promotion.

A number of studies, including some from our laboratory[3-5], have shown cross-sectional links of CAD/NIDDM risk factors to both total body percent fat and visceral adipose tissue (VAT). Moreover, a small-scale non-randomised pilot study suggested that physical training (PT) can reduce body fatness and favourably influence some other risk factors[6]. Adult studies have suggested that PT can reduce VAT[7,8]. However, no child studies have been reported of the effect of PT on VAT, and little is known about the effect of PT on some newly identified risk factors (e.g. LDL particle size, fibrinogen) in children.

The project described here was a randomised trial, in obese 7-11-year-old children, to determine if controlled PT would favourably influence total body percent fat, VAT, subcutaneous abdominal adipose tissue (SAAT), and an array of CAD/NIDDM risk

Children and Exercise XIX. Edited by Neil Armstrong, Brian Kirby and Joanne Welsman.
Published in 1997 by E & FN Spon, 2–6 Boundary Row, London, SE1 8HN.
ISBN 0 419 22100 X.

factors. Rowland[9] has pointed out that most previous studies of this topic have failed to provide evidence that PT improves CV health in children. However, we[1] have suggested that weaknesses in previous studies may provide a partial explanation for the null findings. For example, some studies used subjects who were not at the left of the CV health spectrum and who therefore did not have so much potential for improvement in CV health; thus, we recruited obese youths as subjects.

A second limitation of some studies concerns the degree to which the PT stimulus was controlled and documented to assure that a substantial dose of PT was imparted to the subjects. Since we wished to test the efficacy of PT, only those children who met pre-established criteria for exposure to the PT stimulus were included in the primary analyses. These criteria included a minimal rate of attendance of 3 $d \cdot wk^{-1}$ during which the average heart rate (HR) was >140 $beats \cdot min^{-1}$. Our provision of financial incentives for attendance and a high staff:child ratio were quite different from what might be typical in a field setting. The idea was to determine what happened (and what did not happen) to the various components of CV health in children who were exposed to a substantial "dose" of exercise. These efficacy data are a necessary step on the way to therapeutic effectiveness trials that are done in real-life settings and in which all subjects are included in the analyses, regardless of how well they adhere to the prescribed regimen.

Subjects and methods

We recruited, through flyers distributed at schools and newspaper advertisements, 81 children, 7-11-years of age, who were above the 85th percentile on triceps skinfold [10]. Ethnicity (white/black) was determined by self-designation. Subjects were randomly assigned, within gender and ethnicity, to the PT or control groups. Prior to the PT, two dropped out of the study due to medical problems and three dropped out before the posttesting. The control group included 38 children who completed pre and posttesting.

The PT program was offered 5 $d \cdot wk^{-1}$, children were paid $1 per session for each day of attendance, and given prizes for satisfactory participation (i.e. maintenance of HR >140 $beats \cdot min^{-1}$). Of the 38 children who completed the PT, two did not meet the criterion of at least 3 $d \cdot wk^{-1}$ attendance for inclusion in the primary statistical analyses. Therefore, 36 subjects were included in the PT group for the primary analyses. For these children, the average rate of attendance for the 5 $d \cdot wk^{-1}$ programme was 89%, or 4.45 $d \cdot wk^{-1}$.

Each 40 min PT session was divided into halves of 20 min each. During the first half, the children exercised on machines (treadmills, cycles, Nordic ski machines, mini-trampolines, rowers), spending about 5 min on each. During the second half, they played group games designed to assure that all children were continuously active. In addition to minimising any waiting to participate in the games, the children kept HRs elevated between activities by jumping on mini-trampolines, bench-stepping, rope-jumping, or running/jumping in place.

Each child wore a HR monitor (Polar Vantage, Port Washington, NY) during every session. After each session, the minute-by-minute values were down-loaded into a computer and displayed to the child. Points were earned for maintenance of the target HR and prizes were given after accumulation of specified numbers of points (approximately every 2 wk).

In order to estimate the energy expenditure during the PT sessions, each child underwent two multi-stage tests during the 4 mo PT period, in which oxygen consumption ($\dot{V}O_2$) and HR were measured. Oxygen consumption was measured with indirect calorimetry, using a FITCO (Farmingdale, NY) metabolic measurement cart and HR was measured with the Polar monitor. The test started at a power output of 30 W, and was incremented by 15 W every 2 min until a HR of approximately 180 beats·min^{-1} was reached. The regression of $\dot{V}O_2$ and $\dot{V}CO_2$ on HR was calculated for each child and the energy expenditure was calculated from the child's average HR during the PT sessions.

Most of the test protocols that were used before and after the 4 mo intervention period are described elsewhere in this volume[5]. Additional variables measured for the PT study included free-living physical activity (PA), as estimated from 7 d recalls using a semi-structured interview format[11]. The post-PT interview covered the last week of the intervention period. Total energy used was estimated from metabolic equivalents assigned to the five activity categories as follows: sleep (1.0 MET), light (1.5 METS), moderate (4.0 METS), hard (6.0 METS), and very hard (10.0 METS). Values from hard and very hard categories were condensed to derive vigorous PA.

We used submaximal supine exercise HR, at a power output of 49 W, as our primary index of CV fitness. This index was chosen for two reasons. Firstly, our baseline and post-PT test protocol was very long and involved (3-4 h) and we hesitated to impose a maximal VO_2 test in addition for fear that the overall experience might be perceived as unpleasant, thus jeopardising the willingness of the children to continue in the study. Secondly, we have found submaximal exercise HR to be a sensitive index of change in CV fitness due to PT[6]. We used supine exercise so that blood pressure (BP) could also be easily measured. These procedures are described in the companion chapter[5].

Because total body percent fat was our primary outcome variable, it should be noted that it was measured with dual x-ray absorptiometry.

Left ventricular mass (LVM), and associated parameters were measured with a Hewlett-Packard Sonos 100 echocardiograph (Andover, MA) as described by Feigenbaum[12].

Although this study investigated the influence of PT without dietary intervention, we did perform some diet assessments to help in the interpretation of the body composition changes. Prior to the PT period, a 2 d recall was completed; this was designed as an orientation to the process and these data were not used in the analysis. During the PT period, all subjects in both groups came in for a 2 d recall after 2 mo and after 4 mo. Thus we had 4 d of data for each subject during the intervention period that were used to compare the PT and control conditions. When the appointment for the visit was made, a reminder form was sent to the child/parent. To help the children remember what they ate, we asked them to write, with their parent's help, what they ate. We probed for serving sizes during the interview rather than asking the subjects to record this on their reminder forms. During the interview, the children recalled foods eaten from the time they awakened until going to sleep on the 2 d prior to the interview. Two dimensional food portion visuals were used to probe for information regarding portion sizes consumed. We utilised the Nutrition Data System of the Nutrition Coordinating Centre at the University of Minnesota[13]. Diet information was recorded on a computer and electronically stored on disks. The data were entered into the NCC nutrient data base 26 and food data base 11A. Values were expressed as total kcal and grams of fat, carbohydrate and protein.

To evaluate the effect of the PT, change scores were calculated by subtracting baseline values from the values obtained 4 mo later. Independent groups t-tests were used to compare the change scores, using one-tailed tests of significance to test the hypothesised differences between the PT and control groups. For the diet variables, the group means of the 4 d of assessment during the intervention period were compared with t-tests.

Results

Since this study was an efficacy trial, we assured that all youths used in the primary statistical analyses had been exposed to a substantial CV training stimulus. The mean HR during the sessions was 157 beats·min^{-1}, the average duration was 40 min, the mean energy expenditure was 228 kcal per session, the attendance rate was 4.45 d·wk^{-1}, and the intervention lasted for 4 mo. These values indicate that a substantial dose of PT was imparted to the subjects.

Table 1 shows the baseline means, the change scores and the results of the significance tests comparing the PT and control groups. Since we did not obtain complete data for all variables, the number of subjects for whom pre and post-PT values were available are also given.

Relative to the control group, the PT group reduced exercise HR significantly, suggesting that their CV fitness was influenced favourably. The difference between change scores in vigorous PA, as measured by the 7 d recall, was significant. It is noteworthy that the controls declined by 77 kcal·d^{-1}, perhaps because the baseline test was in the summer and the 4 mo test was during November-December, when they were in school and less active. This illustrates the importance of having a control group to account for seasonal variations. Thus, it seems reasonable to consider the net impact of the PT program to be the sum of the 66 kcal increase of the PT group and the 77 kcal decline of the controls, or 133 kcal·d^{-1}. If we assume that the PT subjects did no other vigorous PA beside that involved in the PT (228 kcal for 4.45-d·wk^{-1}), their vigorous PA for the week would be 1015 kcal·wk^{-1}, or 145 kcal·d^{-1}, a figure that is remarkably close to the 133 kcal·d^{-1} difference between the groups. Although the precision of the measurements is probably insufficient to draw conclusions about individuals, this result is consistent with the idea that the PT sessions themselves accounted for the group difference in vigorous PA.

Table 1. Baseline and change scores for physical training and control groups

	Baseline				Change	
	PT Group		Control		PT Group	Control
Variable	Mean	n	Mean	n		
Vigorous PA	121	35	200	38	+66	-77**
Percent fat	44	36	44	37	-2.1	-0.4**
Fat mass (kg)	26	36	26	37	-0.7	+0.8*
FFST (kg)	30	36	30	37	+1.8	+1.0*
BMC (kg)	1.4	36	1.3	37	+0.08	+0.09
VAT (cm^2)	59	28	59	31	+1.2	+1.7
SAAT (cm^2)	305	28	321	31	-3.8	+16.6*
Resting HR ($beats{\cdot}min^{-1}$)	79	36	80	38	-1.3	+1.2
Exercising HR ($beats{\cdot}min^{-1}$)	120	35	125	38	-3.7	+0.2*
Resting SBP (mmHg)	108	36	108	38	+0.5	+1.4
Resting DBP(mmHg)	58	36	60	38	+3.1	+1.5
Exercising SBP (mmHg)	129	31	122	34	-6.4	-1.5
Exercising DBP (mmHg)	72	30	71	35	-0.1	+2.0
TC/HDL	3.8	34	3.9	34	-0.23	-0.23
Insulin ($mU{\cdot}L^{-1}$)	22	28	30	31	-2.0	-2.0
Fibrinogen ($mg{\cdot}dL^{-1}$)	321	19	305	19	-30	-18
LVM/$ht^{2.7}$	36	32	37	34	+4.1	+4.8

Level of significance * $p < 0.05$, ** $p < 0.01$

Total body composition, specifically percent fat, was our primary outcome measure. As hypothesised, the PT subjects declined significantly in this variable. This was due to a significant decline in fat mass and a significantly greater increase than the controls in fat-free soft tissue (FFST); no significant difference was found for changes in bone mineral content. Although the PT group increased somewhat less than the controls in VAT, the group difference in change scores was not significant. For SAAT, the difference was significant; the PT group declined somewhat while the controls increased.

We had hypothesised that the index of BP that would be most sensitive to modification due to PT and reduction in percent fat was systolic BP during the standardised exercise stressor. Although the group difference was in the hypothesised direction, it was not significant; the group differences in the other BP changes also failed significance.

None of the other group differences in change scores achieved significance. For purposes of parsimony, only one variable from each other domain investigated is given in table 1. The lipids and lipoproteins are represented by the total cholesterol to high density lipoprotein cholesterol ratio, glycaemic control is represented by insulin, clotting/fibrinolysis is represented by fibrinogen, and left ventricular parameters are represented by LVM indexed to $height^{2.7}$.

Discussion

This study showed that it was possible to organise and administer an after-school programme that imparted a substantial dose of exercise to the obese children over a 4 mo period. We attribute our success in maintaining a high rate of attendance and participation in the PT to the reduction of barriers (e.g. provision of transportation to and from the classes), the high ratio of staff to students in the PT classes, and the financial incentives and prizes offered. Only two subjects failed to meet the pre-set 3 $d \cdot wk^{-1}$ criterion for inclusion in the primary analyses; as it turned out, when secondary analyses were conducted with these two children included, the conclusions concerning group differences were identical. Subjects accepted randomisation to either the PT or a control group and maintained participation in the project with very few dropping out from either group. This was attributable partly to the financial incentives we provided for returning for subsequent tests, partly because we maintained contact with them by scheduling mini-tests mid-way through the intervention period, and partly because after 4 mo the controls were then placed into a 4 mo PT program (the data from this last 4 mo period are not yet available).

The changes in CV fitness and total body composition were favourable for the exercising children, who showed significant decreases in percent fat and fat mass, and a significant increase in FFST. Since the energy densities of fat and FFST are approximately 9 $kcal \cdot g^{-1}$ and 1 $kcal \cdot g^{-1}$, respectively[14], the changes indicate that the PT group declined in energy stores. Since the group differences in energy and macronutrient intake during the 4 mo intervention period were not significant (data not shown), the group differences in body composition appear to be due to the differences in PA attributable to the PT.

This is the first child study to report the effects of PT on VAT and SAAT, as measured with magnetic resonance imaging (MRI). While adult PT studies that used computed tomography or MRI to measure VAT[7,8] found significant reductions in VAT, we did not provide evidence that the PT influenced this fat depot. The obese 7-11-year-olds in this study exhibited far more SAAT than VAT. Perhaps the developmental tendency to add to the VAT depot as the children matured overcame any tendency for the PT to mobilise fat from this depot. When the total body and abdominal measurements are considered together, we conclude that in these young children the PT tended to utilise fat from the depots that stored large amounts rather than from the VAT depot.

How can the absence of an effect on the other CAD/NIDDM risk factors be reconciled with the cross-sectional relationships on which we based our hypotheses? The simplest explanation is that the 4 mo period was too short to alter percent fat sufficiently to have an impact on the other risk factors, suggesting that a longer intervention period and/or restriction of energy intake is needed to elicit greater reductions in body fat. The importance of sustaining the PT over a longer period of time is illustrated by a study that found that after 3 mo of an exercise intervention the exercise and control groups did not differ significantly in fitness or BP. However, after 8 mo the exercise group had increased significantly in fitness and declined significantly in BP[15]. A related possibility is that changes in body composition must be retained over a longer period of time before they influence the other risk factors. If this is so, then longer follow-up periods after changes in body composition have been produced may alter the risk factors.

Another possibility is that VAT is the key component of body composition that drives CAD/NIDDM risk, and it is difficult to reduce this fat depot in growing children with exercise alone. However, the increase in VAT for the PT group was somewhat smaller than that of the controls, so even here a longer intervention period may be influential. Another factor to consider is that the technology and reliability of body composition measurement have improved markedly in recent years, perhaps making these variables more likely than the other variables to exhibit clear changes in response to stimuli such as PT. Of course, another possibility is that, even in obese children, the CAD/NIDDM risk factors are not so elevated that they are susceptible to reduction by PT at this early stage of life, in which case we might want to focus our attention on the many other reasons for children to be active[9]. However, it seems premature at this stage of knowledge to rule out the possible beneficial effects of regular exercise on CAD/NIDDM risk factors.

In summary, this study showed that a 4 mo PT program had a positive impact on the CV health of obese children, as indicated by favourable changes in total body composition, SAAT and CV fitness. However, no evidence was provided that the PT influenced VAT or the other CAD/NIDDM risk factors measured.

Acknowledgement

Supported by grants from the National Heart, Lung, and Blood Institute (HL49549) and the American Heart Association/Parke-Davis Company

References

1. Gutin, B. and Owens, S. (1996) Is there a scientific rationale supporting the value of exercise for the present and future cardiovascular health of children? The pro argument. *Pediatric Exercise Science*, Vol. 8, pp. 294-302.
2. Berenson, G. S., Wattingney, W.A., Tracy, R.E., Newman, W.P., Srinivasan, S. R., Webber, L.S., Dalferes, E.R. and Strong, J.P. (1992) Atherosclerosis of aorta and coronary arteries and cardiovascular risk factors in persons aged 6 to 30 years and studies at necropsy (The Bogalusa Heart Study). *American Journal of Cardiology*, Vol. 70, pp. 851-8.
3. Gutin, B., Islam, S., Manos, T., Smith, C., Cucuzzo, N. and Stachura, M. E. (1994) Relation of percentage of body fat and maximal aerobic capacity to risk factors for atherosclerosis and diabetes in black and white seven–to eleven–year–old children. *Journal of Pediatrics*, Vol. 125, pp. 847–52.
4. Gutin B., Owens, S., Treiber, F., Islam, S., Karp, W. and Slavens, G. (in press) Weight-independent cardiovascular fitness and coronary risk factors. *Archives of Pediatrics and Adolescent Medicine.*

5. Owens, S., Gutin, B., Karp, W., Ferguson, M., Moorehead, S., Allison, J. and Le, N-A. (1997) Relationship of total body composition and visceral adipose tissue to cardiovascular health, in *Children and Exercise XIX,* (eds. N. Armstrong, B.J. Kirby and J.R. Welsman), Spon, London.
6. Gutin, B., Cucuzzo, N., Islam, S., Smith, C. and Stachura, M. (1996) Physical training, lifestyle education and coronary risk factors in obese girls. *Medicine and Science in Sports and Exercise,* Vol. 28, pp. 19-23.
7. Schwartz, R., Shuman, W., Larson, V., Cain, K., Fellingham, G., Beard, J., Kahn, S., Stratton, J., Cerqueira, M. and Abrass, I. (1991) The effect of intensive endurance exercise training on body fat distribution in young and older men. *Metabolism*, Vol. 5, pp. 545-51.
8. Ross, R. and Rissanen, J. (1994) Mobilization of visceral and subcutaneous adipose tissue in response to energy restriction and exercise. *American Journal of Clinical Nutrition*, Vol. 60, pp. 695-703.
9. Rowland, T.W. (1996) Is there a scientific rationale supporting the value of exercise for the present and future cardiovascular health of children? The con argument. *Pediatric Exercise Science*, Vol. 8, pp. 303-9.
10. Must, A., Dallal, G.E. and Dietz, W.H. (1991) Reference data for obesity: 85th and 95th percentiles of body mass index (wt/ht^2) and triceps skinfold thickness. *American Journal of Clinical Nutrition*, Vol. 53, pp. 839-46.
11. Sallis, J.F., Buono, M. J., Roby, J.J., Micale, F.G. and Nelson, J.A. (1993) Seven-day recall and other physical activity self-reports in children and adolescents. *Medicine and Science in Sports and Exercise* Vol. 25, pp. 99-108.
12. Feigenbaum, H. (1994) *Echocardiography*, Lea and Febiger, Philadelphia.
13. Feskanich, D., Sielaff, B. H., Chong, K. and Buzzard, I.M. (1989) Computerized collection and analysis of dietary intake information. *Computer Methods and Programs in Biomedicine,* Vol. 3, pp. 47-57.
14. Jeejeebhoy, K.N. (1996) Body composition in weight loss and pathological states, in *Human Body Composition*, (eds. A.F. Roche, S.B. Heymsfield and T.D. Lohman), Human Kinetics, Champaign, Il., pp. 275-82.
15. Hansen, H., Froberg, K., Hyldebrandt, N. and Nielson, J.R. (1991) A controlled study of eight months of physical training and reduction of blood pressure in children: the Odense schoolchild study. *British Medical Journal*, Vol. 303, pp 682-5.

PSYCHOSOCIAL AND LIFESTYLE PREDICTORS OF CARDIOVASCULAR REACTIVITY IN YOUTH

Predictors of cardiovascular reactivity

L. B. WRIGHT
University of Kentucky, Lexington, USA
F. TREIBER, H. DAVIS and W.B. STRONG
Medical College of Georgia, Georgia Prevention Institute Augusta, USA

Keywords: Anger, cardiovascular reactivity, family environment, family history, hypertension, physical activity, youth

Introduction

Numerous epidemiological investigations have linked various psychosocial variables and lifestyle behaviours to increased risk of the development of cardiovascular diseases (CVD) including essential hypertension (EH). For example, coping styles such as anger suppression and expression have been associated with adverse health outcomes, including EH, coronary heart disease (CHD), and total CVD mortality[1-4]. Additionally, the inverse relationship of regular physical activity to CHD incidence and mortality has been extensively documented[5-7]. One pathway by which these various factors have been linked to CVD is via their impact upon cardiovascular (CV) reactivity to stress. That is, greater outward expression of anger and greater anger inhibition have been associated with increased CV reactivity in adolescents and adults[8-10]. Additionally, regular exercise and/or aerobic fitness have been related to reduced stress reactivity in youth and adults[11].

Another CV health-related psychosocial coping mechanism receiving increasing attention is family functioning. An underlying assumption of this approach is that an individual's CVD risk can be influenced by his or her own behavioural patterns as well as those with whom he or she closely interacts[12]. For example, several studies have observed the significant impact of spousal interactions upon marital partners' CV health (e.g. blood pressure, CHD, etc.)[13,14]. Few investigations, however, have assessed the impact of family functioning upon CV health of children[15-17]. To our knowledge, only one longitudinal study has assessed the relationship between children's family environments and their CV responses to stress[15]. Maternal reports of greater cohesion and expressiveness were associated with decreased reactivity in both systemic vascular resistance and systolic blood pressure to the forehead cold stressor.

Children and Exercise XIX. Edited by Neil Armstrong, Brian Kirby and Joanne Welsman.
Published in 1997 by E & FN Spon, 2–6 Boundary Row, London, SE1 8HN.
ISBN 0 419 22100 X.

Little is known with regard to the collective impact of individual coping styles, lifestyle behaviours and family functioning on children's CV health. Given that the pathologic processes of EH have their origin in childhood[18,19] and that CV reactivity has been associated with future EH[20-21], a need exists to explore further relationships between coping styles, lifestyle behaviours, and family environmental functioning upon children's CV functioning. The purpose of this study was to examine relationships between normotensive youths' self-reported anger coping styles, aerobic activity, physical activity, and maternal ratings of perceived family functioning with their CV reactivity to laboratory stressors 2 y later. Based upon previous findings, it was hypothesised that dimensions of anger-in, anger-out, and familial conflict would be associated with increased CV reactivity whereas increased aerobic activity, physical activity and familial cohesiveness would be associated with decreased CV reactivity.

Subjects

Two hundred and sixty-eight children (161 African Americans and 107 Whites) with a mean age of 12.1 ± 2.6 y and their biological mothers participated in this study after they had given informed written consent. Maternal reports of each child's medical history and a brief physical examination indicated that all of the children were normotensive, healthy and free of chronic disease. The children are participants in a larger study assessing the development of biobehavioural risk factors of EH in youth with family history of essential hypertension[22]. All subjects have at least one biological parent and one or more biological grandparents with EH as verified by their personal physicians.

Methods

Anger expression

Dimensions of anger expression were assessed using the Spielberger Anger Expression Scale[23]. Subscales used were anger-in, and anger-out. Adequate evidence of internal consistency, test-retest reliability, and discriminant, convergent and predictive validity have been demonstrated in youth and adults[23].

Family environment

Domains of family environment were assessed using two subscales from the Family Environment Scale (FES) which were cohesion and conflict[24]. Cohesion assesses the level of support and help demonstrated to one another by family members. Conflict assesses how often aggressive behaviour is expressed among family members. Test-retest reliability scores for these subscales range from 0.42 to 0.91 over intervals from one year to three years[24,25]. The internal consistency for these subscales range from 0.61 to 0.78[24,25]. Adequate evidence of construct validity has been shown with these subscales[24,25].

Physical and aerobic activity

Levels of self-reported physical and aerobic activity were assessed using Likert Scale questions regarding how much physical activity or aerobic activity the child engaged in compared to other children of the same age and gender. On a scale from 1 to 5, responses could range from much less than others to much more than others. These questions have been successfully used in other CV health research in youth[26,27].

Cardiovascular functioning

CV measures evaluated were systolic blood pressure (SBP), diastolic blood pressure (DBP), cardiac output and calculated total peripheral resistance (TPR). Blood pressure (BP) was evaluated with a Dinamap Adult/Paediatric Vital Signs Monitor (Model 1846SX, Critikon, Inc., Tampa, FL), using an appropriately sized BP cuff. Cardiac output and HR were calculated by a thoracic bioimpedance monitor (NCCOM3 Bo Med Medical Manufacturing, Ltd., Irvine, CA) every successive 12 QRS intervals while the Dinamap was inflating and calculating blood pressures. Cardiac output values were divided by body surface area ($L \cdot min^{-1} \cdot m^{-2}$) to give cardiac index (CI). Total peripheral resistance (TPR) was derived using concurrently measured blood pressure and CI values (TPR = [SBP+(2XDBP)/3]/CI) and was expressed in Wood units ($mmHg \cdot L^{-1} \cdot min^{-1} \cdot m^{-2}$).

Procedure

During a lab evaluation, the mother completed a set of questionnaires that included the two scales from the FES. The child completed a small battery of questions which included the Spielberger Anger Expression Scale and the two questions that assessed physical and aerobic activity. During a follow-up lab visit, an average of 2 y later, the subject's height and weight were measured with a Healthometer medical scale that was calibrated daily. The NCCOM3 electrodes were applied and an appropriately sized blood pressure cuff attached to the right arm. The child was placed in a supine position and instructed to relax while baseline CV measures were assessed at 11, 13 and 15 min. Afterwards, the postural change stressor was administered in which the child stood with the right arm bent at a 90% angle at the elbow resting against the trunk. Three sets of CV responses were measured at 1 min intervals. Two 10 min behavioural stressors followed which assessed CV reactivity to stressful interpersonal conflicts. The parent-child discussion task[28] involved the mother and child discussing a recent conflict that they had encountered with one another (e.g. issues pertaining to poor school performance, allowance, dating or household chores). The social competence interview[29] involved a trained research assistant using a structured interview to help the subject discuss a recent stressful interpersonal event (e.g. dating problems, request for alteration of family rules). Each stressor was preceded by a minimum 5 min prestressor period designed to allow BP readings to return ± 5 mmHg of the average initial baseline level prior to presentation of a stressor.

Data analyses and results

The data were reduced for each CV measure by averaging the three values taken during the initial baseline and each prestressor period. Reactivity was evaluated in terms of change scores (i.e., peak CV response minus prestressor CV response).

In order to assess the extent to which there was a relationship between youths' anger coping styles, physical activity, aerobic activity and family environment and their CV reactivity to stress 2 y later, univariate correlations were conducted separately by ethnicity. These findings, in the form of Pearson correlation coefficients, are shown in table 1. Findings indicated that among African American children, higher ratings of anger-out and maternal perceptions of family conflict were related to greater TPR reactivity to postural change, the parent child discussion and the social stressor interview. Maternal ratings of greater family cohesion were associated with lower TPR increases to postural change. African-American youths reports of increased physical and aerobic activities were related to lower TPR reactivity to all three stressors.

Among Whites, there were fewer significant findings. Maternal ratings of greater family cohesion were related to less TPR reactivity to all three stressors. Higher self-reported physical activity was associated with less TPR reactivity to the parent child discussion stressor.

Discussion

This study examined the relationship between normotensive youths' dimensions of anger coping styles, levels of physical and aerobic activity and family environmental functioning upon their CV responses to several laboratory stressors 2 y later. Overall, the findings indicated that parental reports of family functioning and youths' self reported overt expressions of anger, and levels of aerobic exercise and physical activity were significantly associated with less TPR reactivity to all three laboratory stressors. A more consistent pattern was noted among the African American youth than among the Whites.

Among African American families, the greater maternal perception of warmth and emotional support in the family, (i.e. cohesion), the less vasoconstrictive reactivity the children exhibited to postural change 2 y later. On the other hand, maternal ratings of verbal and physical conflict in the family (i.e. conflict) were related to greater vasoconstrictive reactivity to all three stressors among the African-American youth. Among Whites, only maternal ratings of greater cohesion were significantly related to decreased TPR reactivity to all three stressors. Collectively, these findings corroborate and extend other recent findings related to family functioning and CV health in young children. In a sample of White and African-American 6 to 8 year olds, maternal report of greater family cohesion and expressiveness were related to less SBP and TPR reactivity to forehead cold stimulation and greater family expressiveness was related to decreased SBP reactivity to postural change[15]. Similarly, another study found that reported parental ratings of increased verbal and or physical conflicts among family

Table 1. Correlations of psychosocial and physical activity variables with TPR reactivity to laboratory stressors among African-American (AA) and White youth

	Postural change		Parent-Child discussion		Social stressor interview	
	AAs	Whites	AAs	Whites	AAs	Whites
Anger In	0.09	-0.12	0.04	-0.00	0.07	-0.00
Anger Out	0.26**	0.18	0.26*	0.22	0.23*	0.22
Aerobic Exercise	-0.31***	0.11	-0.28**	0.08	-0.30***	0.08
Physical Activity	-0.18*	0.11	-0.22*	-0.42***	-0.23*	0.05
Cohesion	-0.19*	-0.25*	-0.16	-0.33*	-0.15	-0.35**
Conflict	0.19*	0.11	0.20*	0.09	0.18*	0.09

Level of significance * p <0.05, **p <0.01, ***p <0.001

members (i.e. conflict subscale) were correlated with increased cholesterol levels in young boys[16].

Among African American youth only, self reported levels of aerobic exercise and physical activity were each significantly related to less TPR reactivity to all three stressors. Among White youth, only one significant association was noted. That is, self reported physical activity level was related to decreased TPR reactivity to the parent-child discussion. These findings are consistent with an earlier finding by Murphy et al.[11]. In that study, aerobic fitness, was related to decreased BP reactivity to a challenging video game in African American youth but not among Whites.

Only among African American youth were significant relationships noted with regard to self reported anger coping styles and CV reactivity two years later. Specifically, their reports of greater overt anger expression were related to greater TPR reactivity to all three stressors. Previous findings with youth and adults have been mixed with some studies finding overt expression while others finding suppression of anger associated with increased BP reactivity[10,30-32]. One reason for these disparate results may depend upon whether the task is likely to elicit overt expression of anger, which was the case with the two interpersonal conflict stressors used in the present study.

In the USA, prevalence of EH is approximately twice that in African Americans compared to Whites[33]. Reasons for this discrepancy are unknown although greater exposure to chronic environmental stress with concomitant greater vasoconstrictive mediated BP reactivity has been identified as one possible source[34,35]. Interestingly, in the current study, the majority of relationships between CV reactivity and lifestyle behaviours involved the African American youth. Reasons for this ethnicity disparity in relationships between CV reactivity and lifestyle behaviours and coping styles are unknown. Follow-up studies are needed to determine whether these findings are stable over time and whether other psychosocial (e.g. social support) and lifestyle behaviours (e.g. smoking, diet) are related to CV reactivity in youth.

Acknowledgements

Supported by NIH [HL 41781 & HL03532]

References

1. Siegman, A.W. (1993) Cardiovascular consequences of expressing, experiencing and repressing anger. Journal of *Behavioural Medicine*, Vol. 16, pp. 539-69.
2. Diamond, E.L. (1982) The role of anger and hostility in essential hypertension and coronary heart disease. *Psychology Bulletin*, Vol. 92, pp. 410-33.
3. Johnson, E.H., Spielberger, C.D., Worden, T.J. and Jacobs, G.A. (1987) Emotional and familial determinants of elevated blood pressure in black and whiteadolescent males. *Journal of Psychosomatic Research*, Vol. 31, pp. 287-300.
4. Barefoot, J.C., Dahlstrom, G. and Williams, R.B. (1983) Hostility, CHD incidence, and mortality: a 25-year follow-up study of 255 physicians. *Psychosomatic Medicine*, Vol. 45, pp. 59-64.
5. Paffenbarger, R.S., Hyde, R.T., Wing, A.I., and Hsieh, C.C. (1986) Physical activity all-cause mortality and longevity of college alumni. *New England Journal of Medicine*, Vol. 314, pp. 605-13.
6. Kannel, W. B., Belanger, A., D'Agostino, R. and Israel, I. (1986) Physical activity and demand on the job and risk of cardiovascular disease and death: the Framingham study. *American Heart Journal*, Vol. 112, pp. 820-5.
7. Eaton, C.B. (1992) Relationship of physical activity and cardiovascular fitness to coronary heart disease, part 1. A meta-analysis of the independent relationship of physical activity and coronary heart disease. *Journal of the American Board of Family Practitioners*, Vol. 5, pp. 31-42.
8. Groer, M., Thomas, S., Droppleman, P. and Younger, M.S. (1994) Longitudinal study of adolescent blood pressures, health habits, and stress and anger. *Journal of Health Behaviour, Health Values, Education and Promotion*, Vol. 18, pp. 25-33.
9. Burns, J.W., Friedman, R., and Katkin, E.S. (1992) Anger expression, hostility, anxiety, and patterns of cardiac reactivity to stress. *Behavioural Medicine*, Vol. 18, pp. 71-8.
10. Holroyd, K. A. and Gorkin, L. (1983) Young adults at risk for hypertension: effects of family history and anger management in determining responses to interpersonal conflict. *Journal of Psychosomatic Research*, Vol. 27, pp.131-8.
11. Murphy, J.K., Alpert, B.S., Willey, E.S., Christman, J.V., Sexton, J.E. and Harshfield, G.A. (1989) Modulation of pressor responses by fitness: Racial differences among children. *American Journal of Hypertension*, Vol. 2, p. 25A.
12. Carmelli, D., Swan, G.E. and Roseman, R.H. (1986) Cross-family correlates of blood pressure in Western Collaborative Group study. *Journal of Behavioural Medicine*, Vol. 9, pp. 325-40.

13. Carmelli, D., Swan, G.E., Hunt, S.C. and Williams, R.R. (1989) Cross-spouse correlates of blood pressure in hypertension-prone families in Utah. *Journal of Psychosomatic Research,* Vol. 33, pp. 75-84.
14. Carmelli, D., Swan, G.E. and Rosenman, R.H. (1985) The relationship between wives' social and psychologic status and their husband's coronary heart disease: a case-control family study from the Western Collaborative Group Study. *American Journal of Epidemiology*, Vol. 122, pp. 90-100.
15. Wright, L.B., Treiber, F.A., Davis, H. and Strong, W.B. (1993) Relationship of John Henryism to cardiovascular functioning at rest and during stress in youth. *Annals of Behavioural Medicine,* Vol. 19, pp. 115-21.
16. Weidner, G., Hutt, J. Conner, S. L. and Mendell, N.R. (1992) Family stress and coronary risk in children. *Psychosomatic Medicine*, Vol. 54, pp. 471-9.
17. Woodall, K.L. and Matthews, K.A. (1989) Familial environment associated with Type A behaviours and psychophysiological responses to stress in children. *Health Psychology*, Vol. 8, pp. 403-26.
18. Berenson, G.S., Frank, G.C., Hunter, S.M., Srinivasan, S.R., Voors, A.W. and Webber, L.S. (1982) Cardiovascular risk factors in children. *American Journal of Diseases of Children*, Vol. 136, pp. 855-62.
19. Voors, A.W., Sklow, M.C., Wolf, T.M., Hunter, S.M. and Berenson, G.S. (1985) Cardiovascular risk factors in children and coronary-related behaviour, in *Promoting Adolescent Health: a Dialogue on Research and Practice*, (eds. T.J. Coates, A.C. Peterson and C. Perry), Academic Press, New York, pp. 281-304.
20. Menkes, M.S., Matthew, K.A., Krantz, D.S., Lundberg, U., Mead, L.A., Oagish, B., Liang, K., Thomas, C.B. and Pearson, T.A. (1989) Cardiovascular reactivity to cold pressor as a predictor of hypertension. *Hypertension*, Vol. 14, pp. 524-30.
21. Sparrow, D., Tifft, C.P., Rosner, B. and Weiss, S.T. (1984) Postural changes in diastolic blood pressure and the risk of myocardial infarction: the normative aging study. *Circulation*, Vol. 70, pp. 533-7.
22. Treiber, F.A., Rauniker, R.A., Davis, H., Fernandez, T., Levy, M. and Strong, W.B. (1994) One year stability and prediction of cardiovascular functioning at rest and during laboratory stressors in youth with family histories of hypertension. *International Journal of Behavioural Medicine,* Vol. 1, pp. 335-53.
23. Spielberger, C.D. (1988) *State-Trait Anger Expression Inventory*, Psychological Assessment Resources, Odessa.
24. Moos, R.H. and Moos, B.S. (1986) *Family Environment Scale Manual*, 2nd ed., Consulting Psychologist Press, Palo Alto, California.
25. Moos, R.H. and Moos, B.S. (1986) Family environment scale, in *Handbook of Measurements for Marriage and Family Therapy*, (eds. N. Freedman and R. Sherman), Brunner/Mazel, New York, pp. 82-6.
26. Treiber, F.A., McCaffrey, F., Pflieger, K., Raunikar, R.A. Strong, W.B. and Davis, H. (1993) Determinants of left ventricular mass in normotensive children. *American Journal of Hypertension,* Vol. 6, pp. 505-13.

27. Sallis, J.F., Patterson, T.L., Burns, M.J. and Nader, P.R. (1988) Relation of CV fitness and physical activity to CV disease risk factors in children and adults. *American Journal of Epidemiology*, Vol. 127, pp. 933-4.

28. Matthews, K.A., Woodall, K. and Lassner, J. (1990) Family resources associated with psychophysical responses during conflict resolution. Presented to the *Eleventh Annual Meeting of The Society of Behavioural Medicine*, Chicago, Il.

29. Ewart, C.K. and Kolodner, K.B. (1993) Predicting ambulatory blood pressure during school: effectiveness of social and non-social reactivity tasks in Black and White adolescents. *Psychophysiology*, Vol. 30, pp. 30-8.

30. Suarez, E.C. and Williams, R.B. (1989) Situational determinants of cardiovascular and emotional reactivity in high and low hostile men. *Psychosomatic Medicine*, Vol. 51, pp. 404-18.

31. Diamond, E. (1982) The role of anger and hostility in essential hypertension and coronary heart disease. *Psychology Review*, Vol. 92, pp. 410-33.

32. Goldstein, H.S., Edelberg, R., Meier, C.J. and Davis, L. (1982) Relationship of expressed anger to forearm muscle vascular resistance. *Journal of Psychosomatic Research*, Vol. 33, pp. 497-504.

33. Coroni-Huntley, J., LaCroiz, A.Z. and Havlik, R.J. (1989) Race and sex differentials in the impact of hypertension in the United States. *Archives of International Medicine,* Vol. 149, pp. 780-8.

34. Anderson, N.B., McNeilly, M. and Myers, H. (1991) Automatic reactivity and hypertension in blacks: a review and proposed model. *Ethnicity and Disease*, Vol.1, pp. 154-70.

35. Anderson, N.B., McNeilly, M. and Myers, H. (1992) Toward understanding race differences in automatic reactivity: A proposed contextual model, in *Individual Differences in Cardiovascular Response to Stress*, (eds. J.R. Turner, A. Sherwood and K.C. Light), Plenum Press, New York, pp. 5441-56.

OBSERVATIONS ON HUMAN MICROVASCULAR FUNCTION IN HEALTH AND DISEASE

Microvascular function, health and disease

J.E. TOOKE
Department of Vascular Medicine, Institute of Clinical Science, University of Exeter, Exeter, UK

Keywords: Capillary haemodynamics, cardiac failure, diabetes mellitus, hypertension, microcirculation

Introduction

Although historically scientific attention has centred on the function of the heart and larger blood vessels the cardiovascular system exists to subserve the function of the microcirculation, those smallest blood vessels conventionally defined as arterioles, capillaries, venules and terminal lymphatics. The major generic functions of the microcirculation are summarised in table 1, knowledge of the determinants of which have been limited by the lack of technology to study processes which at the same time are often inaccessible, exquisitely sensitive to pernibation and involve minute structures. Nevertheless, in the last two decades techniques have been developed to register microvascular pressure, flow and certain aspects of permeability at least in superficial tissues (table 2).

The aims of this brief review are to summarise what has been learnt of normal human microvascular physiology through the applications of these new technologies and illustrate the potential of study of the microcirculation to provide insights into the pathogenesis of several common diseases. Particular attention is paid to diabetes, one form of which typically strikes in childhood and adolescence and results in characteristic damage to the microvasculature in several key organs.

Table 1. Major functions of the microcirculation

- Transport and exchange of nutrients and waste products between blood and tissue fluid.
- Maintenance of tissue fluid economy.
- Involvement in tissue defence, growth and repair.

Children and Exercise XIX. Edited by Neil Armstrong, Brian Kirby and Joanne Welsman.
Published in 1997 by E & FN Spon, 2–6 Boundary Row, London, SE1 8HN.
ISBN 0 419 22100 X.

Table 2. Major techniques available for studying the human microcirculation

- In vivo capillary microscopy (capillary morphology).
- Dynamic capillary microscopy (capillary flow estimation).
- Single point laser Doppler fluximetry.
- Laser perfusion imaging.
- Dynamic capillary pressure measurement.
- Terminal lymphatic pressure measurement.
- Fluorescence microscopy.
- Capillary filtration coefficient measurement.

Observations on human microvascular physiology

Microvascular flow

Using epiluminescence of appropriate wavelength and video technology it is possible to record the movement of blood cells and plasma gaps through single capillaries of superficial human organs most notably the skin[1]. Computer analysis techniques permit the dynamic registration of capillary flow velocity both on and off line. Using these methodologies the variability, reactivity and intrinsic rhythmicity (flow motion) of human microvascular flow has been confirmed. Capillary flow velocity may vary from zero to several millimetres per second and under conditions of moderate flow an inherent rhythm of 6 to 10 cycles per minute[2] as well as that related to cardiac pulsatility are evident.

The skin is a thermoregulatory organ and capillary flow is strongly positively correlated with skin temperature[3]. Flow also increases following a brief period of arterial occlusion[4] (reactive hyperaemia) and in response to local injury.

The development of laser Doppler fluximetry[5] has permitted the estimation of relative microvascular flux or flow in a hemisphere of tissue of approximately $0.5mm^3$. As well as the phenomena described above this methodology is particularly suited to the study of neurovascular responses. Specialised probes have enabled the endoscopic, intraoperative and intraorgan assessment of microvascular perfusion.

Laser perfusion imaging employs the same principle as single point laser Doppler fluximetry but provides a flow map of a much wider area of tissue (typically many square centimetres). This technique has confirmed the spatial heterogeneity of microvascular perfusion which accounts for some of the wide variances observed with single point fluximetry.

By using iontophoretic techniques to enable the passage of vasoactive mediators across the skin surface the control mechanisms governing microvascular flow can be interrogated using the perfusion imager[6].

Less familiar than functional and reactive hyperaemia is the venoarteriolar response about which much has been learnt using laser Doppler technology. In the face of a rise in venous pressure arteriolar vasoconstriction occurs in skin and subcutaneous tissue, a response that is thought to be largely mediated by a sympathetic axon reflex[7]. This response accounts for postural vasoconstriction, the reduction in extremity microvascular blood flow when a limb is placed below heart level and is felt to be an important oedema prevention mechanism, limiting the rise in capillary pressure and preventing the washout of concentrating plasma proteins the osmotic pressure of which balances the increased hydrostatic pressure when a new equilibrium is reached[8].

Several of these aspects of microvascular flow have been studied in childhood and adolescence and significant features include the fact that skin capillary flow is lower and postural vasoconstriction more profound with passage through puberty[9].

Capillary pressure

Using an electronic servonulling technique it is possible to measure capillary pressure dynamically in single nailfold capillaries with considerable accuracy[10]. In contrast to capillary flow, capillary pressure is remarkably stable and appears to be a tightly controlled variable[11]. Modest increases are observed during reactive hyperaemia, and a linear though lesser increase (due to the operation of the venoarteriolar response) with increases in venous pressure[12], yet no significant increase occurs with modest elevations of arterial pressure that are physiologically induced[13].

Capillary pressure has not been measured in childhood but increases with female sex hormone exposure either due to exogenous hormones[14] or pregnancy[15] have been demonstrated and on average capillary pressure is lower in women than men until the menopause.

Pathological studies

Hypertension

Conventionally it has been conceived that the increased peripheral vascular resistance associated with arterial hypertension is sited at arteriolar level which protects the capillary bed from a rise in pressure. Direct measurement of capillary pressure in subjects with essential hypertension reveals elevated values[16], from which it may be concluded that part of the increased peripheral vascular resistance must be sited at capillary or postcapillary level. Studies of capillary population density conform capillary rarefaction in hypertension[17] and recent studies suggest that such rarefaction is present in the normotensive offspring of parents with hypertension[18], raising the possibility that microvascular architecture may be formative in the expression of hypertension in later life.

Cardiac insufficiency

The clinical features of cardiac insufficiency whether they may be secondary to disturbances of rate, rhythm, valvular dysfunction or impaired myocardial contractility are due to impaired microvascular function at organ level[19]. Contrary to earlier studies recent work suggests that pump failure is not associated with early elevation of capillary pressure but rather an increased capillary filtration coefficient[20]. A plausible candidate mechanism is the increase in atrial natriuretic peptide which has been shown to increase CFC when infused[21], and is known to be elevated when atrial distension occurs. By measuring capillary filtration coefficient in patients with programmable pacemakers during - mode (resulting in synchronised atrioventricular activity) and- mode (when the ventricular is stimulated and there is atrioventricular asynchrony) support has been provided for this hypothesis, CFC and ANP being higher in the asynchronous state[22].

Diabetic microangiopathy in insulin dependent diabetes

Proportionately more studies have been performed in subjects with diabetes representing the clear impact this condition has on the microcirculation. Measures of organ blood flow led to the so called haemodynamic hypothesis[23] which proposes that early insulin dependent diabetes (IDDM) is characterised by increased microvascular pressure and flow.

The increased shear and pressure is transduced by the microvascular endothelium resulting in elaboration of extravascular matrix proteins and microvascular sclerosis. This in turn results in physical limitation of vasodilatation and autoregulatory failure.

The development of techniques to measure human microvascular pressure and flow has allowed the testing of the haemodynamic hypothesis. In a cross sectional study it was demonstrated that capillary pressure was indeed elevated in subjects with IDDM compared to age and sex matched controls[24]. Furthermore, pressure was higher in those with worse control of their diabetes and in subjects at high risk of microangiopathy. Improvements in diabetic control (at least in subjects of short disease duration) resulted in reduction in elevated capillary pressure.

Maximum microvascular blood flow does appear to be limited in young adults[25], the degree of impairment relating to the duration of diseases and in keeping with the haemodynamic hypothesis degree of impairment is also correlated with the degree of microvascular sclerosis (basement membrane thickening)[26].

The same limitation of maximum microvascular blood flow is observed in children with IDDM and again is correlated with disease duration[27]. An intriguing observation is that neither capillary flow nor postural vasoconstriction respond in the normal way with passage through puberty. Capillary flow remains relatively high in subjects with IDDM and postural vasoconstriction is blunted[9], suggesting that the haemodynamic stresses to which the microcirculation is exposed are proportionately greater following puberty. This may provide a partial explanation for the clinical observation that the rate of development of diabetic microangiopathy appears to accelerate after puberty.

Non insulin dependent diabetes and the insulin resistant state

Contemporary opinion holds that glucose intolerance in later life is one manifestation of the insulin resistant syndrome[28] which underlies much of the propensity of the western population to atherosclerotic cardiovascular disease. Other features include hypertension, dyslipidaemia, visceral adiposity and fibrinolytic impairment. It has been suggested that a common cellular mechanism may be endothelial cell dysfunction[29], a suggestion that has gained ground with the recognition that muscle disposal of a glucose load (a key determinant of insulin sensitivity/resistance) is in part mediated by endothelial dependent vasodilatation of the skeletal microcirculation[30].

An intriguing possibility is that endothelial dysfunction could underly the development of diabetes itself in some cases. Given that exercise induced functional hyperaemia is also mediated by endothelial dependent relaxation of the microcirculation obvious links between sedentary life style, glucose intolerance and cardiovascular risk may be drawn.

Conclusion

Over the last two decades techniques have been developed for the measurement of human microvascular function. Studies using these techniques have not only provided unambiguous information about microvascular physiology but have provided unique insights into the pathogenesis of several common diseases. Relatively few studies have been performed in childhood and adolescence and currently the capacity to study microvascular function in exercising muscle is extremely limited. Recent work suggesting that cardiovascular risk and exercise capacity may both be dependent on endothelial cell function provides a real stimulus to redress this deficiency.

Acknowledgements

Personal work was supported by the Wellcome Trust, British Heart Foundation and British Diabetic Association.

References

1. Flynn, M.D., Williams, S.A. and Tooke, J.E. (1989) Clinical television microscopy. *Journal of Medical Engineering and Technology*, Vol. 13, pp. 278-81.
2. Fagrell, B., Fronek, A. and Intaglietta, M. (1977) A microscopy-television system for studying flow velocity in human skin capillaries. *American Journal of Physiology*, Vol. 233, pp. 318-21.
3. Bollinger, A. and Fagrell, B. (1990) Dynamic capillaroscopy without dyes, in *Clinical Capillaroscopy*, (eds. A. Bollinger and B. Fagrell), Hogrefe and Huber, Toronto, p. 19.
4. Ostergren, J., Svedman, P. and Fagrell, B. (1983) The influence of venous and arterial occlusion on capillary blood flow and transcutaneous oxygen tension in fingers. *International Journal of Microcirculation Clinical and Experimental*, Vol. 2, pp. 315-34.
5. Wardell, K., Jakobsson, A. and Nilsson, G. E. (1993) Laser Doppler perfusion imaging by dynamic light scattering. *IEEE Transactions on Biomedical Engineering,* Vol. 40, pp. 309-16.
6. Morris, S.J., Shore, A.C. and Tooke, J. E. (1995) Responses of the skin microcirculation to acetylcholine and sodium nitroprusside in patients with non-insulin-dependent diabetes. *Diabetologia*, Vol. 38, pp. 1337-44.
7. Hassan, A.A.K. and Tooke, J. E. (1988) Mechanism of the postural vasoconstrictor response in the human foot. *Clinical Science*, Vol. 75, pp. 379-87.
8. Rayman, G., Williams, S.A., Gamble, J. and Tooke, J. E. (1994) The study of the factors governing fluid filtration in the feet of diabetic and normal subjects. *European Journal of Clinical Investigation*, Vol. 24, pp. 830-6.
9. Shore, A.C., Price, K.J., Sandeman, D.D., Tripp, J.H. and Tooke, J.E. (1994) Posturally induced vasoconstriction in diabetes mellitus. *Archives of Disease in Childhood*, Vol. 70, pp. 22-6.

10. Williams, S.A., Wassermann, S., Rawlinson, D.W., Kitney, R.I., Smaje, L.H. and Tooke, J.E. (1988) Dynamic measurement of human capillary blood pressure. *Clinical Science*, Vol. 74, pp. 507-12.
11. Tooke, J.E., Sandeman, D.D. and Shore, A.C. (1993) Normal variability of human capillary blood pressure. *Progress in Applied Microcirculation*, Vol. 20, pp. 81-6.
12. Mahy, I.R., Tooke, J.E. and Shore, A.C. (1995) Capillary pressure during and after incremental venous pressure elevation in man. *Journal of Physiology*, Vol. 485, pp. 213-9.
13. Shore, A.C., Sandeman, D.D and Tooke, J.E. (1993) Effect of an increase in systemic blood pressure on nailfold capillary pressure in humans. *American Journal of Physiology*, Vol. 265, pp. H820-3.
14. Tooke, J.E., Tindall, H. and McNicol, G.P. (1981) The influence of a combined oral contraceptive pill and menstrual cycle phase on digital microvascular haemodynamics. *Clinical Science*, Vol. 61, pp. 91-5.
15. Tooke, J.E., Tindall, H. and Hancock, K.W. (1982) Capillary pressure during pregnancy. *Microvascular Research*, Vol. 24, p. 238.
16. Williams, S.A., Boolell, M., MacGregor, G.A., Smaje, L.E., Wasserman, S.M. and Tooke, J.E. (1990) Capillary hypertension and abnormal pressure dynamics in patients with essential hypertension. *Clinical Science*, Vol. 79, pp. 5-8.
17. Williams, S.A., Tooke, J.E. (1986) Microvascular haemodynamics in hypertension, in *Clinical Investigation of the Microcirculation*, (eds. L.H. Smaje and J.E. Tooke), Kluwer-Nijhoff, Massachusetts, USA.
18. Noon, J.R., Walker, B.R., Webb, D.J., Shore, A.C., Holton, D.W., Edwards, H.V. and Watt, G.C.M. (in press) Impaired microvascular dilatation and capillary rarefaction in young adults with a predisposition to high blood pressure. *Journal of Clinical Investigation.*
19. Mahy, I.R. and Tooke, J.E. (1995) The peripheral microcirculation in human heart failure. *Clinical Science*, Vol. 88, pp. 717-28.
20. Mahy, I.R., Shore, A.C., Smith, L.D.R., Tooke, J.E. (1995) Disturbance of peripheral microvascular function in congestive heart failure secondary to idiopathic dilated cardiomyopathy. *Cardiovascular Research*, Vol. 30, pp. 939-44
21. Groban, L., Cowley, A.W. and Ebert, T.J. (1990) Atrial natriuretic peptide augmens forearm capillary filtration in humans. *American Journal of Physiology*, Vol. 259, pp. H258-63.
22. Mahy, I.R., Lewis, D.M., Shore, A.C., Penney, M.D., Smith, L.D.R. and Tooke, J.E. (1995) Disturbance of peripheral microvascular fluid permeability by the onset of atrioventricular asynchrony in subjects with programmable pacemakers. *Heart*, Vol. 75, pp. 509-12.
23. Tooke, J.E. (1986) Microvascular haemodynamics in diabetes mellitus. *Clinical Science*, Vol. 70, pp.119-25.
24. Sandeman, D.D., Shore, A.C. and Tooke, J.E. (1992) Relation of skin capillary pressure in patients with insulin-dependent diabetes mellitus to complications and metabolic control. *New England Journal of Medicine*, Vol. 327, pp. 760-4.
25. Rayman, G., Williams, S.A., Spencer, P.D., Smaje, L.H., Wise, P.H. and Tooke, J.E. (1986) Impaired microvascular hyperaemic response to minor skin trauma in type I diabetes. *British Medical Journal*, Vol. 292, pp. 1295-8.
26. Rayman, G., Malik, R.A., Sharma, A.K. and Day, J.L. (1995) Microvascular response to tissue injury and capillary ultrastructure in the foot skin of type 1 diabetic patients. *Clinical Science*, Vol. 89, pp. 467-74.

27. Shore, A.C., Price, K.J., Sandeman, D.D., Green, E.M., Tripp, J.H. and Tooke, J.E. (1991) Impaired microvascular hyperaemic response in children with diabetes mellitus. *Diabetic Medicine,* Vol. 8, pp. 619-23.
28. Reaven, G.M. (1988) Role of insulin resistance in human disease. *Diabetes,* Vol. 37, pp.1595-607.
29. Tooke, J.E., Morris, S.J. and Shore, A.C. (1996) Microvascular functional abnormalities in diabetes: the role of the endothelium, *Diabetes Research and Clinical Practice*, Vol. 31 (suppl), pp. S127-32.
30. Steinberg, H.O., Chaker, J., Leaming, R., Johnson, A., Brechtel, G. and Baron, A.D. (1996) Obesity/insulin resistance is associated with endothelial dysfunction. *Journal of Clinical Investigation*, Vol. 97, pp. 260-1.

A YOUNG TO ADULT COMPARISON OF EXERCISE PLASMA VOLUME DECREASE

Maturation and plasma volume

J. MÉSZÁROS, A. PRÓKAI, J. MOHÁCSI and R. FRENKL
Department of Health Sciences and Sports Medicine, Hungarian University of Physical Education, Budapest, Hungary
T. SZABÓ
Central School of Sports, Budapest, Hungary
Keywords: Athletes, decrease in exercise, graded laboratory exercise, relative plasma volume

Introduction

A more or less marked decrease in relative plasma volume (RPV) during physical exercise of different intensity and duration has been described by various research teams[1,2,3]. The mechanisms of this kind of plasma volume decrease are not fully understood.

Wilmore and Costill[4] and Nieman[5] interpreted the changes in plasma volume during exercise as an imbalance caused by blood redistribution arising from Starling forces acting across capillary walls, changes in capillary pressure and transcapillary osmotic gradient. Wilmore and Costill[4] stressed also the importance of a changed metabolism in the working muscle. Ng and associates[6] found peak-exercise RPV to be independent of fluid loss and identified a low but significant correlation between RPV and weight-related muscle mass in male university students.

The relevant literature clearly shows that many factors contribute to a decrease in RPV during exercise, and that a comprehensive explanation and its exercise physiology consequences need further investigation. Data describing changes in RPV during exercise in young athletes are scarce[7]. One reason for this is that the procedure requires venous blood whilst exercise physiology investigations tend towards non-invasive or micro methods.

The aims of the investigation were:

- To compare RPV decreases estimated by the haemoglobin concentration and haematocrit of venous and capillary blood samples;
- To compare the RPV decrease during graded exhaustive laboratory exercise in physically active youngsters and qualified adult athletes.

The exercise-induced regulatory responses of adults and children differ markedly.

Children and Exercise XIX. Edited by Neil Armstrong, Brian Kirby and Joanne Welsman.
Published in 1997 by E & FN Spon, 2–6 Boundary Row, London, SE1 8HN.
ISBN 0 419 22100 X.

RPV decrease during exercise is assumed to depend on an adaptive change in circulatory regulation. Children have less mature mechanisms of regulation, and tend often to overshoot, therefore the expected degree of exercise-induced RPV decrease was hypothesised to be greater in prepubertal children. Hence two separate studies were done.

Subjects

The subjects of both studies (athletes, university students and young athletes) were volunteers informed of the tasks and the possible risks of the investigation. Written consents were collected from all the participants or their parents.

Young adult male university students (n = 18, age, 19 to 23 y) were recruited for Study 1. They all were physically active, but were not qualified athletes. The adult subjects in Study 2 (junior vs adult comparison) had won medals in the past two European and World Championships in modern pentathlon or paddling (n = 16, age, 22 to 31 y). The comparison group (n = 14, age, 10.50 to 12.50 y) consisted of judoists. They also were successful athletes at Hungarian age-group competitions, participated in eight intense training sessions a week and had been training for a minimum of two years. None of them had had their first ejaculation.

Methods

Study 1

Blood was concurrently sampled from the antecubital vein (16 mL) and from the arterialised fingertip (after 3 min immersion in a water bath of 35 °C) of the same arm (capillary, 30 μL) both at rest, and after a walking/running treadmill exercise of different intensities. Heart rates at post-exercise blood sampling ranged between 89 and 192 beats·min^{-1}. Haematocrit and haemoglobin concentrations in venous blood were determined using a K-1000 Fisnex (Japan) apparatus, while capillary samples were analysed by the QBC Autoreader (USA) technique. Exercise-induced RPV decrease was calculated[8] by:

$$\Delta PV\% = 100 - 100 \times [HGB_b \times HGB_a{}^{1} \times (1 \quad HCT_a) \times (1 \quad HCT_b{}^{1})],$$

where ΔPV%=RPV as a decrease of initial volume, HGB=haemoglobin (g·100mL^{-1}), HCT=haematocrit (%), b=before exercise, a=after exercise.

Differences between means and standard deviations (SD) of haematocrit, haemoglobin and estimated RPV decrease determined from venous and capillary samples were tested by two-tailed t -tests for dependent samples. Agreement between venous and capillary parameters was analysed using linear correlation and regression.

Study 2

All the subjects had previously practised treadmill running and all tests were carried out under standardised conditions (ambient temperature: 22 24°C, relative air humidity: 55 70%). After individual warming up (callisthenics, 2 min each of 5 $km \cdot h^{-1}$ walk and 10 $km \cdot h^{-1}$ running), the test began at a belt speed of 12 $km \cdot h^{-1}$ with no gradient. Belt incline was increased by 3% every second minute until exhaustion. Heart rate was recorded continuously, and blood lactate concentration was determined using a Lange (Germany) miniphotometer in 10 µL blood samples taken immediately after the subject stopped. In Study 2 RPV decreases were estimated by the haematocrit and haemoglobin concentrations of arterialised capillary blood samples taken sitting at rest, after warming up and within 5–10 s after the exercise. Differences between the compared parameters were tested by two-tailed t -tests for independent samples.

Results

Study 1

Statistics are shown in table 1. Haematocrit and haemoglobin means and SD were minimally but consistently greater in venous blood. The extent of this agreement enabled the generation of a prediction equation.

The equation predicting venous conditions from capillary values is as follows:

$$Y = 0.337 + 1.005X;\ r_{yx}=0.98,\ s_a=0.05;\ s_b=0.005;\ s_{yx}=0.09$$

where X=RPV decrease in arterialised capillary blood, Y=RPV decrease in venous blood, r_{yx}=correlation coefficient, s_a=sd of intercept, s_b=sd of slope, s_{yx}=sd around the line.

The less than 0.4% difference between the estimated sampling means of plasma volume decrease was significant at the 5% level of random error, the SD around the two means were similar. This observation indicates that RPV decreases estimated from capillary samples may minimally underestimate those obtained from venous samples. The relationship between the two estimates of RPV decrease was very close (r = 0.98) explaining 96 % of common variance.

It was concluded that RPV decrease can be reliably estimated from capillary blood samples provided that sampling is carried out with the necessary care, in particular at rest. Owing to the very consistent differences in, and very close relationship between, venous and capillary estimates of RPV decrease, even venous conditions can be calculated by the model equation, if necessary.

Study 2

The statistical differences between the groups in mean body height, peak-exercise heart rate, running distance, and blood lactate concentration reflect the age difference (table 2).

The RPV decrease was significantly smaller in young athletes both after warming up and at the end of the exercise. An observation of importance is that about 60% of the total RPV decrease occurred by the end of the warming-up period in both of the groups compared, independently of age.

Table 1. Comparison of the parameters measured in venous and capillary blood samples

	Venous	Capillary	Δven − cap	r
HCT rest (%)	45.78 ± 0.35	45.67 ± 0.33*	0.25 ± 0.05	0.88
HGB rest ($g \cdot 100mL^{-1}$)	15.03 ± 0.12	14.84 ± 0.09*	0.19 ± 0.03	0.96
HCT post ex (%)	47.69 ± 0.42	47.38 ± 0.42*	0.34 ± 0.05	0.97
HGB post ex ($g \cdot 100mL^{-1}$)	15.96 ± 0.22	15.70 ± 0.18*	0.26 ± 0.04	0.97
ΔRPV (%)	8.92 ± 1.07	8.54 ± 1.07	0.38 ± 0.07	0.98

Values are mean ± SEM
Level of significance * $p < 0.05$

Table 2. Young-to-adult comparison of the studied variables

	Adult medalists (n=16)	Young judoists (n=14)
Age (y)	24.82 ± 3.50*	11.49 ± 0.63
Height (cm)	178.52 ± 4.44*	145.60 ± 6.78
Peak exercise HR ($beats \cdot min^{-1}$)	189.86 ± 6.01*	195.07 ± 6.22
Post exercise blood lactate ($mmol \cdot L^{-1}$)	15.93 ± 1.64*	9.26 ± 2.58
Distance run on treadmill (m)	2899 ± 211*	1575 ± 145
ΔRPV% after warm-up	7.49 ± 1.85*	5.66 ± 0.78
ΔRPV% peak exercise	12.48 ± 2.24*	9.11 ± 0.78

Values are mean ± SD
Level of significance * $p < 0.05$

Discussion

As shown by the correlation and regression analyses of Study 1, capillary blood samples can reliably estimate RPV decrease across a relatively wide (1.77 to 16.30%) range. In general, this range of validation may sufficiently describe RPV decrease induced by exercise in physically active youngsters and adults. The observed mean and SD of peak-exercise RPV decrease in the studied adults (although all of them are highly qualified athletes) were comparable to other published data[4,9,10,11]. This result indicates that the extent of peak-exercise RPV decrease does not depend on the quality and volume of individual habitual physical activity, provided that the latter exceeds the level we often call "that of the physically well-trained" since decreases in RPV were markedly larger in sedentary males than in peer-age athletes or PE students [6,7].

The decrease of RPV in the young judoists was significantly smaller than the response of the qualified adult athletes. Our working hypothesis of a larger decrease in youngsters thus became untenable.

One of the possible reasons might have been the dissimilar power output in the groups compared. Wilmore and Costill[4], and Ng et al.[6] reported that within an individual RPV decreases were significantly and positively related to the intensity of physical exercise whereas in a comparison of groups RPV decreases and physical performance were unrelated. However, in our study both adult and young athletes exercised at a similar intensity by reaching their momentarily attainable maximum. Stephenson and Kolka[2] stressed that the various effects influencing RPV decrease during the process of exercise were negligible if the subjects performed near or at their maximum intensity.

The observed difference could not be explained by the known differences in the physiological exercise responses of adult and young athletes (e.g. either smaller systolic blood pressure rise, smaller peak-exercise blood lactate and adrenaline levels, reduced heat tolerance during intense physical activity in the young, etc.[12,13]).

The present data and previous experience with children's responses to exhausting exercise only allow a tentative reasoning: a) plasma adrenaline level (smaller in children) is positively related to RPV decrease[13]; b) children display a smaller increase in core temperature[12] since the hypothalamic thermoregulatory centre disallows a continuation of exercising at a lower than adult level of core temperature, another attribute of a not fully developed regulation; c) the rate of passive transport processes depends on body temperature as well.

We have to note, however, the similarities of the timing of RPV decrease between the young and adult athletes. In agreement with other data[2], RPV decrease was a rapid process at the beginning of exercise. The dominant, and a similar part (about 60%), of the RPV change was observed to have occurred by the end of the warming-up period in the adult and young athletes alike.

RPV decrease during exercise is a consistent observation, although the mechanisms of how it develops remain unclear. Individual differences by age and level of regular physical activity are marked. Hopper and associates[14] report that plasma volume changes within the range of 400–700 mL significantly affect stroke volume, as does cardiac output. Thus, a smaller RPV decrease during exercise is preferable, because cardiovascular functions are less stressed.

The extent of RPV decreases during exercise need be interpreted from another point of view too. The blood concentration of various substances leaving the plasma slower than water during exercise might appear spuriously high because of the variable individual extent of RPV decrease, so also the latter should be estimated concomitantly.

Summary and conclusions

There were marked differences between the RPV responses of the differently aged subjects in agreement with other reports. Peak-exercise RPV decrease was significantly smaller in the children than in the adults, contrary to expectations. RPV decrease during exercise is a rapid process, about 60% of the total change taking place by the end of warming-up period. The decrease in RPV may affect the concentration estimates of various plasma substances measured during exercise so its knowledge is of importance. The exercise decrease of RPV can be estimated in capillary as well as from venous blood samples as the correlation between RPV decrease estimates in venous and capillary samples was r = 0.98.

References

1. Schmidt, W., Maassen, N., Tegtbur, U. and Braumann, K.M. (1989) Changes in plasma volume and red cell formation after a marathon competition. *European Journal of Applied Physiology*, Vol. 58, pp. 453–8.
2. Stephenson, L.A. and Kolka, M.A. (1988) Plasma volume during heat stress and exercise in women. *European Journal of Applied Physiology*, Vol. 57, pp. 373–81.
3. Zappe, D.H., Tankersley, C.G., Meister, T.G. and Kenney, W.L. (1993) Fluid restriction prior to cycle exercise: effects on plasma volume and plasma proteins. *Medicine and Science in Sports and Exercise*, Vol. 25, pp. 1225–30.
4. Wilmore, J.H. and Costill, D.L. (1994) *Physiology of Sport and Exercise*, Human Kinetics, Champaign, Il., pp. 184–5.
5. Nieman, C.D. (1995) *Fitness and Sports Medicine – A Health-Related Approach,* Bull Publishing Company, Palo Alto CA.
6. Ng, K.N., Mészáros, J. and Farkas, A. (1996) The relationship between relative blood plasma change and anthropometric and physiological variables during exercise. *Fiziologia – Physiology, Official Journal of the Romanian Society of Physiological Sciences,* Vol. 2, p. RE12.
7. Mészáros, J., Mohácsi, J., Frenkl, R., Farkas, A. and Petrekanits, M. (1996) Age dependence of plasma volume decrease during an all-out exercise in athletic boys. *Fiziologia – Physiology, Official Journal of the Romanian Society of Physiological Sciences*, Vol. 2, pp. RE12.
8. Greenleaf, J.E. and Hinghofer-Szalkay, H. (1985) *Plasma Volume Methodology: Evans Blue, Hemoglobin-hematocrit, and Mass Density Transformations.* NASA Technical Memorandum 86834. NASA, Moffet Field CA.
9. Brandenberger, G., Candas, V., Follenius, M., Libert, J.P. and Kahn, J.M. (1986) Vascular fluid shift and endocrine responses to exercise in the heat. *European Journal of Applied Physiology*, Vol. 55, pp. 123–9.
10. Senay, L.C. and Pivarnik, J.M. (1985) Fluid shift during exercise. *Exercise and Sport Sciences Reviews*, Vol. 13, pp. 335–87.
11. Mészáros, J., Petrekanits, M., Mohácsi, J. and Prókai, A. (1994) Change in relative plasma volume in short laboratory exercise (A relatív plazma-térfogat változása rövid ideig tartó laboratóriumi terhelés alatt, in Hungarian). *Kalokagathia,* Vol. 32, pp. 66–74.
12. Bar-Or, O. (1983) *Pediatric Sports Medicine for the Practitioner*, Springer-Verlag, Berlin.

13. Field, J.C., Gougeon, R. and Marliss, E.B. (1991) Circulating mononuclear cell numbers and function during intense exercise and recovery. *Journal of Applied Physiology*, Vol. 71, pp. 1089–97.
14. Hopper, M.K., Coggan, A.R. and Coyle, E.F. (1988) Exercise stroke volume relative to plasma-volume expansion. *Journal of Applied Physiology,* Vol. 64, pp. 404–8.

PERIPUBERTAL PERIOD DECREASES INSULIN SENSITIVITY AND GLUCOSE UTILISATION DURING EXERCISE

Insulin sensitivity and exercise.

N. BOISSEAU, F. RANNOU, P. DELAMARCHE, M. MONNIER and A. GRATAS DELAMARCHE
Laboratoire de Physiologie et de Biomécanique de l'exercice Musculaire,UFR. APS, Université de Rennes II, Rennes, France
Keywords: Glucose utilisation, insulin sensitivity, prolonged exercise

Introduction

Several studies have emphasized that glucose tolerance is reduced during puberty in normal children[1,2]. Indeed, a decrease in insulin sensitivity has been demonstrated at rest from the beginning of the peripubertal period[3]. As exercise is associated with an increase in glucose uptake by the working muscles we can question whether the peripubertal period might affect the insulin responses and plasma glucose utilisation during exercise.

Then to investigate glucose tolerance and insulin sensitivity during exercise according to age, we compared the plasma glucose and glucose versus insulin ratio between two groups of boys and men performing a 60% $\dot{V}O_2$ max ergocycle-test after a glucose charge test (0.5 $g{\cdot}kg^{-1}$).

Subjects

Nine boys (9.8 ± 0.4 y) in Tanner stage 1 and 10 men (22 ± 0.3 y) participated in this experiment. The children, their parents and adults were fully informed about this study and its design and their written consent was obtained following the guidelines approved by the Ethical Committee University of Rennes I on Human Experimentation. Studies took place at 0930 on two different days (1 and 2) separated with a maximum interval of 15 days.

Children and Exercise XIX. Edited by Neil Armstrong, Brian Kirby and Joanne Welsman.
Published in 1997 by E & FN Spon, 2–6 Boundary Row, London, SE1 8HN.
ISBN 0 419 22100 X.

Methods

On day 1: height (cm), and weight (kg) were determined and percentage of body fat estimated from skinfolds[4,5]. Sexual maturation of the boys was evaluated using Tanner's indices[6]. All were judged free of cardiopulmonary disease based on medical examination including a resting electrocardiogram. Then $\dot{V}O_2$ max was determined using a Monark type ergometer[7].

The prolonged exercise was performed on day 2 and started about 2.5 h after a standardized breakfast composed of 50% carbohydrates, 35% lipids and 15% proteins for an average caloric amount of 40 $kJ \cdot kg^{-1}$. On arrival in the laboratory an intravenous catheter was inserted into an antebrachial vein of each subject for blood sampling. In order to decrease the stress as far as possible a supine position was maintained for about 20 min. The ambient temperature remained between 21 and 23° C. Then each subject performed a 30 min cycling exercise at 60% $\dot{V}O_2$ max. Heart rate (HR) was recorded using an electrocardiograph (Cardiofax type from Trophy). Gas exchanges were measured every 5 min during exercise. Between mins 2 and 3 of the exercise, the subject ingested a solution of pure glucose (0.5 $g \cdot kg^{-1}$). The dilution was realized in 150 mL of water for children and 300 mL for adults to obtain a same glucose dilution (11-12 $g \cdot 100mL^{-1}$) in both groups. Blood samples of 5 mL were withdrawn into a vacutainer just before the test on the cycle and at mins 3, 5, 10, 15 and 30 of the exercise.

Glucose/Insulin ratio was calculated to compare glucose for a same plasma insulin concentration. This ratio was used as index of the insulin sensitivity.

Haematocrit was immediately measured after a microcentrifuge. Then plasma was separated by centrifugation at 3000 g and the supernatant stored at -80° C for subsequent chemical analysis. The plasma glucose concentration was measured with a Boehringer kit (Meylan, France). Plasma insulin was determined by Radio Immunology Assay (R.I.A) with a CEA-SORIN kit. As the exercise induced a slight yet significant haemoconcentration (2.23 ± 0.23%) in adults but not in boys (0.16 ± 0.53%), all the blood parameters were corrected using haematocrit.

Data analyses

After verification of a normal distribution, a two-way analysis of variance (group-time by ANOVA) was used to determine significant differences at various times between both groups. The limit for statistical significance was always set at $p < 0.05$. Values are reported as mean ± standard error (SEM).

Results

Plasma glucose

The onset of the exercise induced a slight decrease of plasma glucose but was only significant in men between times 0 and 3 min ($p < 0.05$). The glucose charge induced a

Table 1. Morphological and physiological data for the two groups

Subject	Age (y)	Height (cm)	Mass (kg)	Fat (%)	$\dot{V}O_2$ max ($mL \cdot kg^{-1} \cdot min^{-1}$)
Men (n=10)	22 ± 0.3	178 ± 2	72.5 ± 2.0	13.8 ± 1.2	51.0 ± 1.8
Boys (n=9)	9.8 ± 0.4	145 ± 3	34.1 ± 1.9	12.9 ± 0.3	51.8 ± 1.9

Values are mean ± SEM

Table 2. Plasma glucose ($mmol \cdot L^{-1}$) and insulin ($\mu U \cdot mL^{-1}$) at rest and during exercise in both groups.

Time (min)	0	3	5	10	15	30
Glucose						
Men	5.37 ± 0.28	4.43 ± 0.24	4.30 ± 0.20*	5.00 ± 0.32	5.24 ± 0.24	5.52 ± 0.27
Boys	4.94 ± 0.18	4.65 ± 0.36	4.98 ± 0.26*	5.08 ± 0.38	5.98 ± 0.56	6.24 ± 0.33
Insulin						
Men	30.94 ± 6.01	20.37 ± 2.20	17.82 ± 1.31	18.95 ± 2.56	21.36 ± 3.13	18.51 ± 2.42
Boys	33.3 ± 3.90	26.61 ± 2.31	21.96 ± 1.75	21.60 ± 2.06	21.28 ± 2.63	22.69 ± 4.30

Values are mean ± SEM
Level of signficance, * $p < 0.05$

rise of plasma glucose in both groups. Boys and men exhibited the same pattern but values remained higher in boys especially at the 5th min ($p < 0.05$.).

Insulin

In all subjects insulin concentrations decreased during the first 5 min of exercise and then remained at a constant level until the end of the exercise.

Glucose/insulin

Whereas no difference appeared at rest between both groups in glucose versus insulin ratio, higher values were observed in boys especially at the 5th min ($p < 0.01$.).

Discussion

These results clearly emphasize that a same relative glucose charge (0.5 $g \cdot kg^{-1}$) ingested by boys and men at the onset of a 60% $\dot{V}O_2$ max ergocycle-test induced an increase of plasma glucose in both groups. Whatever the time of the exercise, glycaemic levels were always higher in the younger subjects. The difference was statistically significant at the 5th min. Throughout exercise the ratio of glucose versus insulin was also greater in boys.

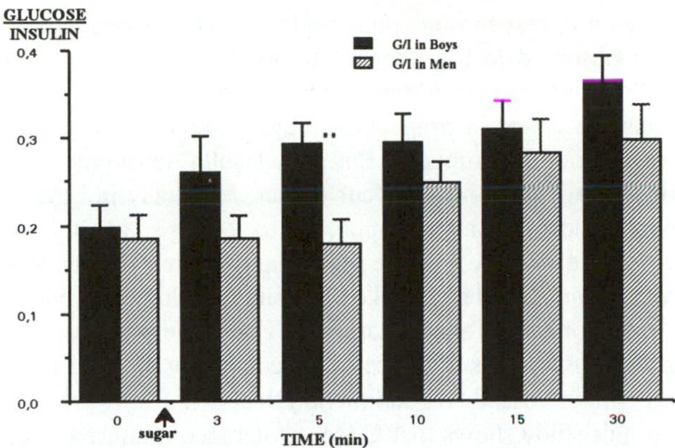

Fig. 1. Glucose versus insulin ratio (G/I) at rest and during the exercise in both groups.

Values are mean ± SEM
Level of significance, $^{**}p < 0.01$

Such results could not be explained by differences in the glucose diffusion between the gastrointestinal tract and the vascular bed, since we gave the glucose dilution according to the age of the subject. In these conditions how do we explain the higher values of plasma glucose and glucose versus insulin in boys?

First, two main factors are known to affect plasma glucose and insulin values during exercise: intensity of the exercise[8,9] and training status. Indeed hyperglycaemic values have been found in adults when the exercise is performed above 70% $\dot{V}O_2$ max [10]. On the contrary no change or a small increase was observed in children at 70% $\dot{V}O_2$ max[11,12]. Then we chose a 60% $\dot{V}O_2$ max ergocycle-test to avoid any hyperglycaemic effect induced by a too intense level of exercise. It is also well-known that endurance increases plasma glucose during exercise[13,14]. Here difference in the training status between both groups seemed not to be involved since the relative $\dot{V}O_2$ max values were the same in boys and men.

Consequently, our results supported strongly the hypothesis of differences in glucose tolerance during exercise according to age. As simultaneously the glucose and the glucose versus insulin values remained always higher in children, a reduced glucose tolerance seemed to be likely in boys compared to adults. The higher glucose versus insulin values in the younger subjects indicated that plasma glucose concentrations were always greater for a same insulin level. Therefore the reduced glucose tolerance in boys during exercise could be explained by a concurrent decrease in insulin sensitivity . This result is in agreement with studies which demonstrate an obvious insulin insensitivity at rest in normal and diabetic peripubertal subjects[1,2]. The decrease of insulin sensitivity during the peripubertal period seems to result from multifactorial factors. However, the main factor seems to be growth hormone (GH)[1,2,15]. GH is known to generate insulin resistance[16] and may also be responsible for the peripubertal decline in insulin sensitivity. In fact plasma GH levels increase as children progress through puberty[15,17]. However, in this study the lower insulin sensitivity observed in boys cannot be explained only by a direct GH effect. Indeed, boys in this study are all in stage 1 of Tanner's indices and it is known that the plasma GH levels are lower in prepubertal boys compared to pubertal children[17]. However, a recent study[3] suggests that the insulin sensitivity which is observed during the peripubertal period might occur earlier, especially in boys. The changes in insulin sensitivity follow a pattern opposite to changes in IGF-1, IGFBP-3 and testosterone. All these factors increase significantly from Tanner stage 1 to Tanner stage 2 whereas mean GH levels follow a slightly different pattern and become statistically elevated only in Tanner stage 4. For these authors[3] the peripubertal decrease in insulin sensitivity is not necessarily caused by an increase of GH secretion but is associated with increased GH peripheral effects.

In conclusion, this study shows that glucose tolerance is altered in peripubertal boys during exercise, in relation with a simultaneous decrease in insulin sensitivity.

References

1. Amiel, S., Sherwin, R., Simonson, D., Lauritano, A. and Tamborlane, W. (1986) Impaired insulin action in puberty a contributing factor to poor glycemic control in adolecents with diabetes. *New England Journal of Medicine,* Vol. 315, pp. 215-9.
2. Bloch, C., Clemons, P. and Sperling, M. (1987) Puberty decreases insulin sensitivity. *Journal of Pediatrics*, Vol. 110, pp. 481-7.
3. Cook, J., Hoffman, R., Stene, M. and Hansen, J. (1993) Effects of maturational stage on insulin sensitivity during puberty. *Journal of Clinical Endocrinology and Metabolism*, Vol. 77, pp. 725-30.
4. Parizkova, J. (1961) Total body fat and skinfold thickness in children. *Metabolism*, Vol. 10, pp. 794-807.
5. Durnin, J. and Rahaman, M. (1976) The assessment of the amount of fat in the human body from measurements of skinfold thickness. *British Journal of Nutrition,* Vol. 21, pp. 681-9.
6. Tanner, J.M. (1964) Physical and body composition, in *Fitness Health and Work Capacity,* (ed. L. Carlson), MacMillan, New-York.
7. Flandrois, R., Grandmontagne, M., Mayet, M.H., Favier, R. and Frutoso J. (1982) La consommation maximale d'oxygène chez le jeune français, sa variation avec l'âge, le sexe et l'entraînement. *Journal of Physiology (Paris),* Vol. 78, pp. 186-94.
8. Wahren, J., Felig, P., Ahlborg, G. and Jorfeld, L. (1971) Glucose metabolism during leg exercise in man. *Journal of Clinical Investigation*, Vol. 50, pp. 2715-25.
9. Ahlborg, G., Felig, P., Hagenfeld, L., Hendler, R. and Wahren, J. (1974) Substrate turnover during prolonged exercise in man: splanchnic and leg metabolism of glucose, free fatty acids, and amino acids. *Journal of Clinical Investigation,* Vol. 53, pp.1080-90.

10. Hermansen, L., Pruett, E.D.R., Osnes, J.B. and Giere, F.A. (1970) Blood glucose and plasma insulin response to maximal exercise and glucose infusion. *Journal of Applied Physiology*, Vol. 29, pp. 13-6.
11. Wirth, A., Träger, E., Scheele, K., Mayer, D., Diehm, K., Reischle, K. and Weicker, H. (1978) Cardiopulmonary adjustment and metabolic response to maximal and submaximal physical exercise of boys and girls at different stages of maturity. *European Journal of Applied Physiology*, Vol. 39, pp. 229-40.
12. Oseid, S. and Hermansen, L. (1971) Hormonal and metabolic changes during and after prolonged muscular work in prepubertal boys. *Acta Paediatrica Scandinavica*, Vol. 217 (suppl), pp.147-53.
13. Bloom, S.R., Johnson, R.H., Park, D.M., Rennie, M.J. and Sulaiman, W.R. (1976) Differences in the metabolic and hormonal response to exercise between racing cyclists and untrained individual. *Journal of Physiology (London)*, Vol. 258, pp. 1-18.
14. Coggan, A.R., Kohrt, W.M., Spina, R.J., Bier, D.M. and Hollozy, J.O. (1990) Endurance training decreases plasma glucose turnover and oxidation during moderate intensity exercise in man. *Journal of Applied Physiology*, Vol. 68, pp. 990-6.
15. Lindgren, F., Dahlquist, G., Effendic, S., Persson, B. and Skottner, A. (1990) Insulin sensitivity and glucose-induced insulin response changes during adolescence. *Acta Paediatrica Scandinavica*, Vol. 79, pp. 431-6.
16. Rizza, R., Miles, J. and Verdonk, C. (1980) Insulin sensitivity in man: a method for single day dose-response assessment using the euglycemic glucose-insulin clamp technique. *Clinical Research*, Vol. 28, pp. 409-14.
17. Rose, S.R., Municchi, G., Barnes, K.M., Kamp, G.A., Uriarte, M., Ross, J.L., Cassola, F. and Cutler, G.B. (1991) Spontaneous growth hormone secretion increases during puberty in normal girls and boys. *Journal of Clinical Endocrinology and Metabolism*, Vol. 73, pp 428-35.

ESTIMATES OF GLYCAEMIC CONDITION DURING EXERCISE IN CHILDREN WITH IDDM

Glycaemic control in diabetic children

G. STRATTON and N. HENDRY
Centre for Physical Education, Sport and Dance, Liverpool John Moores University, Liverpool, UK
C. SMITH and S. KERR
Royal Liverpool Children's Hospital, NHS Trust, Liverpool, UK
Keywords: Error grid analysis, estimating blood glucose, exercise, IDDM

Introduction

The three key factors in diabetes control are diet, insulin and exercise[1]. Patients with diabetes are also at greater risk of developing obesity, cardiovascular disease and low physical self esteem; all of which may be improved with regular exercise. The benefits of a physically active lifestyle for children and adolescents have been internationally promoted[2]. Exercise disturbs normal body homeostasis and the problem for children with IDDM is the recognition of symptoms of hyper or hypoglycaemia during or after exercise. Many parents express concern about their children taking part in vigorous physical activity especially when the activity is unsupervised[3]. These concerns seem well founded when 16% of children and adolescents reported hypoglycaemia after vigorous exercise or play[4]. Moreover, other investigators have reported that the majority of adolescents are not proficient at estimating their blood glucose (EBG) and that the relationship between estimated and actual blood glucose (ABG) is idiosyncratic[5,6]. There are a number of symptoms related to hyper or hypoglycaemia, such as hunger, pounding heart and sweaty palms that may be confused with the normal physiological responses to exercise. Rowland[7] has suggested that patients with IDDM who exercise often confuse the feeling of fatigue with hypoglycaemia, and that children in particular underestimate their blood glucose levels during exercise.

The ability to accurately estimate blood glucose before, during and after exercise is of prime importance if children with IDDM are to gain health benefits from regular physical activity. It is essential that children make clinically correct estimations of their glycaemic condition and do not perceive themselves as hyperglycaemic ($\geq$ 10 mM)

Children and Exercise XIX. Edited by Neil Armstrong, Brian Kirby and Joanne Welsman.
Published in 1997 by E & FN Spon, 2–6 Boundary Row, London, SE1 8HN.
ISBN 0 419 22100 X.

when they are hypoglycaemic (≤ 3.85 mM) or vice-versa. The error grid analysis (EGA) developed by Cox and co-authors[8] enables an accurate clinical analysis to be made of children's ability to EBG. Statistical analyses determine the degree to which EBG is related to ABG, they do not address the clinical significance of accuracy or the type of estimation error made. Conversely the EGA accounts for the absolute deviation of EBG from ABG as well as the ABG. In addition the EGA considers the clinical implications of any self treatment decisions based on EBG. Clinically accurate zone A estimates deviate ≤ 20% from the ABG. All other zones are based on the assumptions that when ABG is >10 mM or <3.85mM they will take corrective action to lower or raise ABG respectively. Zone B represent benign errors in EBG, Zone C leads to overcorrecting acceptable ABG, Zone D is dangerous "failure to treat" errors in EBG whereas Zone E reflects errors in EBG that would lead to opposite treatment than that required to correct ABG. To our knowledge EGA has not yet been validated or used with a controlled exercise protocol.

This study examined children's accuracy in EBG before, during and after a 30 min period of submaximal exercise at an intensity recommended for promoting health[2].

Subjects

Twenty-seven children 13.2 ± 1.9 years of age, diagnosed as having IDDM for 5.6 ± 3.9 y consented to participate in the study. The children's body mass (53.0 ± 18.4 kg) and stature (1.57 ± 0.12 m) were comparable to healthy children of a similar age range.

Methods

Glycosylated haemoglobin (HbA1c) concentrations were 9.41 ± 2.02%. Subjects were advised to follow normal dietary and insulin dosage patterns prior to their arrival at the laboratory. Body mass and stature were measured using standardised anthropometric techniques[9]. Fingertip capillary blood samples were assayed using a reflolux reflectance meter (Boehringer Mannheim, UK). Heart rates were monitored using the SportTester heart rate telemetry system (Polar, Finland). Cycling exercise was undertaken on a friction braked, cycle ergometer.

Pre-exercise blood glucose was assayed at 0 min and the result given to the child. Cycle ergometers were adjusted to suit the needs of the child. Children then rested in a seated position. At 5 min children were asked to EBG. ABG was then measured and the result was not divulged to the child. Cycling commenced at 5 min.

Children completed a 30 min cycling task. Exercise intensities were initially set at 1.0 $W \cdot kg^{-1}$ and 1.5 $W \cdot kg^{-1}$ for girls and boys respectively. Throughout the exercise individual exercise intensities were adjusted to sustain a submaximal heart rate (HR) between 140 and 160 $beats \cdot min^{-1}$. Blood samples were collected once every 5 minutes and immediately assayed for blood glucose. Prior to the collection of blood, children were asked to estimate their blood glucose level. HR was recorded every 5 min and ABG and EBG were recorded after 15 and 30 min recovery.

Data analyses

Actual and perceived blood glucose results were split into before (rest), during and after exercise (recovery) categories. Individual accuracy indices between ABG and EBG were calculated using Pearson correlation coefficients. Alpha was set at $p < 0.01$. All subjects data were then plotted on an error grid and both accuracy and error in EBG were calculated. Children's ability to accurately estimate their blood glucose was measured by the percentage of successful results in the A sectors of the error grid, whereas the percentage of clinically dangerous errors in estimation were calculated from the total number of hits in sectors C, D and E. Graphic data reporting raw EBG results are illustrated in fig 1.

Results

Table 1 represents descriptive statistics for HR, ABG, and EBG before, during and after exercise. HR drifted steadily upwards from the start to end of exercise and the HR of 11 children had exceeded 160 beats·min^{-1} by the end of exercise. ABG concentrations decreased by 16% over the exercise period compared to a 33% decrease in EBG. Individual correlation coefficients between ABG and EBG (Accuracy index) ranged between -0.83 and 0.95. Eleven correlation coefficients exceeded the $p < 0.01$ significance level of 0.77. None of the three negative correlation coefficients were significant. These data also revealed an insignificant relationship between HbA1c and accuracy indices ($r = 0.12$; $p > 0.05$). During the rest period children were 92.6% accurate in EBG and there were no clinically dangerous errors. Over the exercise period the children's accuracy in EBG fell to 46.9%, clinically dangerous errors totalled 17.9%. During the recovery period accuracy dropped again to 38.9% and clinically dangerous errors decreased to 14.8%.

Twelve of the 27 participating children made at least one clinically dangerous error during the procedure, whereas five children made three or more clinically dangerous errors in EBG. All but one of the dangerous errors were made during the final 15 min of exercise. Six children made dangerous errors 15 min into the recovery period, three of these continued to make dangerous errors at the end of the recovery period. The majority of errors made were benign underestimations of ABG.

The pattern of estimation is illustrated in fig 1. Panel A illustrates clinically accurate (A) estimates, panel B benign errors (B) and panel D, clinically dangerous errors. Unfilled bars represent an overestimate of ABG, filled bars represent correct EBGs and underestimated EBGs.

Data in table 1 and fig 1 illustrate that the majority of children underestimated their ABG. The pattern of accuracy and error is not abundantly clear, but data also revealed an increase in the incidence of error (B and D) and a concomitant decrease in children's accuracy in EBG from the start to the end of the exercise period. From rest to the end of exercise, accuracy scores decreased in number from 25 to 7. Fifteen min after exercise there was a slight improvement to 13 accurate estimates, however this decreased again to 9 correct estimates 30 min after exercise.

Table 1. Heart rate, estimated blood glucose and actual blood glucose values, before during and after exercise.

Time (min)	Activity level	Heart rate (beats·min^{-1})	Estimated blood glucose (mmol·L^{-1})	Actual blood glucose (mmol·L^{-1})
0	Rest	99 ± 18	na	12.58 ± 5.77
5	Rest	100 ± 18	11.80 ± 5.18	12.71 ± 5.88
10	Exercise	127 ± 21	11.29 ± 4.79	12.67 ± 5.59
15	Exercise	137 ± 19	9.91 ± 4.54	12.23 ± 5.17
20	Exercise	141 ± 22	9.04 ± 4.61	11.81 ± 5.03
25	Exercise	148 ± 23	8.89 ± 4.23	11.40 ± 5.70
30	Exercise	150 ± 24	8.49 ± 4.46	11.27 ± 6.00
35	Exercise	154 ± 25	7.61 ± 4.36	10.58 ± 5.54
50	Recovery	107 ± 17	7.83 ± 3.77	10.60 ± 5.17
65	Recovery	104 ± 18	8.21 ± 3.31	10.64 ± 5.24

Values are mean ± SD

Discussion

Replicating children's behaviour by divulging their ABG at the start of the procedure clearly influenced children's accuracy in EBG 5 min into the rest period. The high accuracy score also reflected children's ability to recognise that their glycaemic condition remains relatively stable during short periods of inactivity. Nineteen out of 27 children sustained their accuracy in EBG after 5 min exercise with only 2 making dangerous "D" errors at this stage. Throughout the second half of the cycling exercise, an inability to recognise hyperglycaemia caused the majority of benign and dangerous errors. Even though the majority of errors were benign, exercise clearly affected children's ability to EBG. Benign errors during the recovery period may also have been caused by children's intake of sweet drinks after exercise. The consumption of sweet drinks also elevated the final ABG at 65 min and mimicked children's normal patterns of behaviour after exercise of this type, intensity and duration. The effect of increasing blood glucose causing a greater release of catecholamines at the onset of exercise may well have increased children's errors in EBG at the start of, and subsequently, throughout the exercise period. During short periods of exercise which typify children's behaviour, dangerous errors may not be significant, as long as corrections are made immediately after exercise. Three out of 27 children dangerously underestimated their ABG at the end of the procedure giving cause for concern.

The range in accuracy index scores found in this study support Nurick and Johnson's[6] belief that the ability to accurately estimate a glycaemic condition is highly idiosyncratic. A non-significant HbA1c accuracy index correlation coefficient

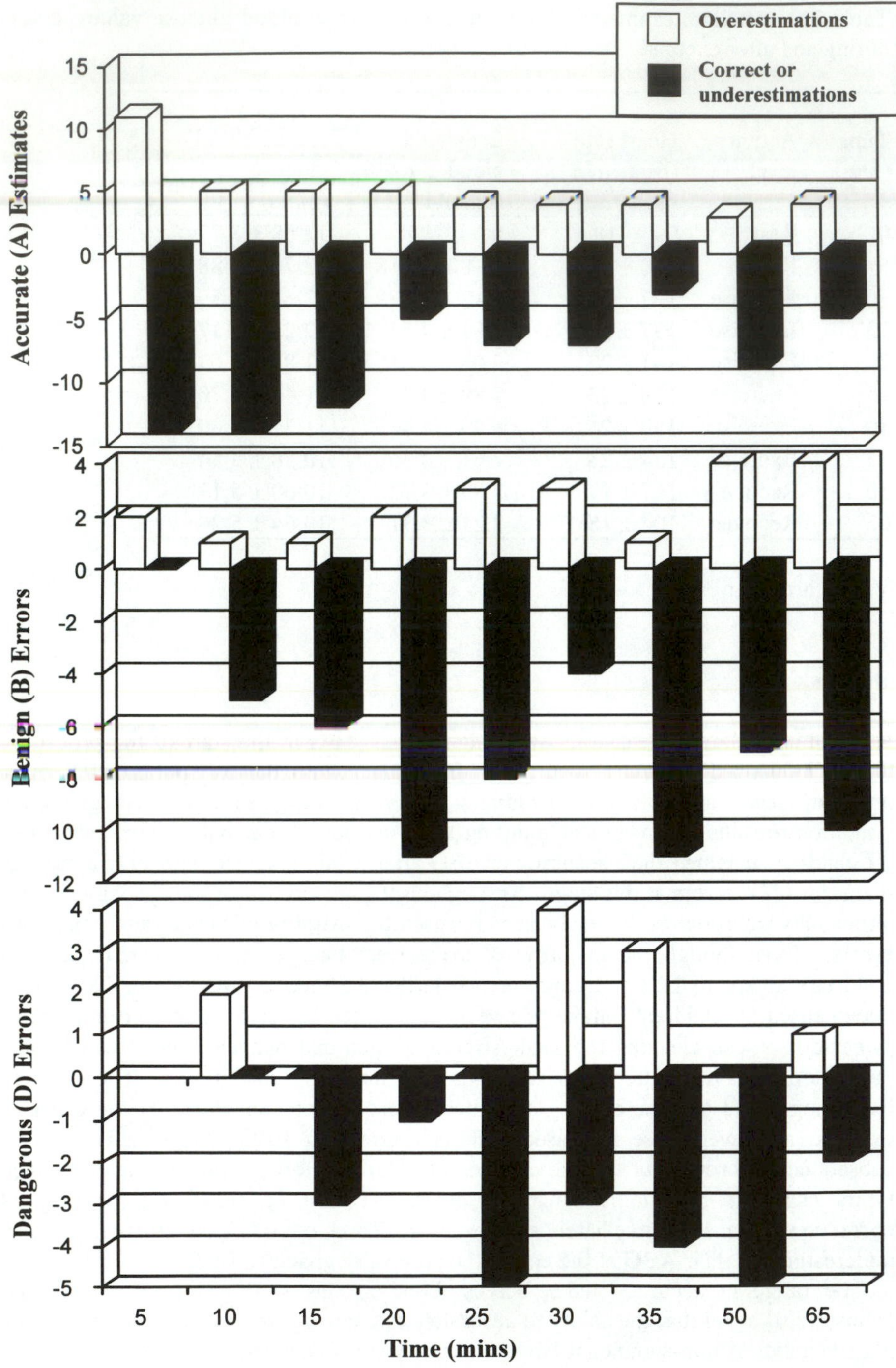

Fig.1. Error grid analyses accuracy charts

also suggests that accurate EBG is not related to glycaemic control. Perhaps the physiological responses to exercise override the normal sensations experienced during hyper or hypoglycaemia and idiosyncratic responses may be related to levels of fitness or ability to cope with similar amounts of exercise. Unfortunately the picture is unclear as many children found difficulty in maintaining a steady cycling rhythm for the entire 30 min, and this contributed to 11 children exceeding the 160 beats·min^{-1} threshold. Even though the majority of children's exercise heart rates were sub-maximal the upward drift in heart rate probably affected children's ability to accurately EBG during the latter parts of the exercise test. These data agree with Rowland[7] who found that fatigue affected children's ability to EBG.

Until now use of the EGA has not been reported during exercise, and although many of the benefits of the EGA are related to clinically correct decision making, it may be most effectively implemented as an educational tool for children with IDDM to use after exercise. Children's dangerous estimations of ABG occurred during exercise, although correction of these errors would only normally occur on cessation of exercise. Thus the use of the EGA may be most effectively used after varying bouts of controlled exercise.

References

1. Campaigne, B. N. and Lampman, R.M. (1994) *Exercise in the Clinical Management of Diabetes,* Human Kinctics, Champaign, Il.
2. Sallis, J.F. and Patrick, K. (1994) Physical activity guidelines for adolescents: consensus statement. *Pediatric Exercise Science,* Vol. 6, pp. 302-14.
3. Eastman, B.G., Johnson, S.B., Silverstein, J., Spillar, R.P. and McCallum, M. (1983) Understanding of hypo- and hyperglycaemia by children and their parents. *Journal of Pediatric Psychology*, Vol. 8, pp. 229-43.
4. McDonald, M.J. (1987) Post exercise late onset hypoglycaemia in insulin dependent diabetic patients. *Diabetes Care*, Vol. 10, pp. 584-8.
5. Freund, A., Johnson, S.B., Rosenbloom, A.L., Alexander, B. and Hanson, C.A. (1986) Subjective symptoms, blood glucose estimation, and blood glucose concentrations in adolescents with diabetes. *Diabetes Care,* Vol. 9, pp. 236-43.
6. Nurick, M.A and Bennet Johnson, S. (1991) Enhancing blood glucose awareness in adolescents and young adults with IDDM. *Diabetes Care,* Vol. 14, pp. 15-26.
7. Rowland, T.W. (1993) *Pediatric Laboratory Exercise Testing: Clinical Guidelines,* Human Kinetics, Champaign, Il.
8. Cox, D.J., Clarke, W.L., Gonder-Fenderick, L., Pohl, S., Hoover, C., Snyder, A., Zimbelman, L., Carter, W.R., Bobbitt, S. and Pennebaker, J. (1985) Accuracy of perceiving blood glucose in IDDM. *Diabetes Care*, Vol. 8, pp. 529-36.
9. Lohman, T.G., Roche, A.L. and Martorell, R. (Eds) (1988) *Anthropometric Standardisation Reference Manual,* Human Kinetics, Champaign, Il.

CARDIOVASCULAR ADJUSTMENT TO SUPINE VERSUS SEATED POSTURE IN PREPUBERTAL BOYS

Body position and cardiovascular adaptation

G. KOCH, J. MÖBERT and E-M OYEN
Department of Physiology, Free University, Berlin, Germany
Keywords: Blood pressure, cardiac output, cardiovascular adjustment, heart rate, left ventricular ejection time, pre-ejection period, stroke volume, total vascular resistance

Introduction

Despite the large number of studies of young people's aerobic power data on the physiological mechanisms that essentially determine maximal oxygen uptake ($\dot{V}O_2$ max) are sparse. Concerning the prepubertal growth period, only one study appears to yield a detailed analysis of the most important mechanisms such as central haemodynamics[1] and pulmonary gas exchange[2] including diffusing capacity[3] at rest and during submaximal and maximal exercise. The authors studied 9 boys aged 11-13 y using invasive methods at rest both in the supine and seated position, but only in the seated posture during exercise. The study thus does not allow any conclusion as to the effect of body position on the haemodynamic response to exercise. Concerning the adjustment of left ventricular (LV) contractility in relation to haemodynamic changes and to different body positions no information at all seems available. The purpose of the present study was to provide more detailed insight into the effects of body position on cardiovascular adaptation by comparing the adjustment of haemodynamics and of LV contractility at rest and during exercise in the supine versus seated posture.

Subjects and methods

Twelve healthy boys aged 13.7 ± 0.3 y (height 160.8 ± 9.0 cm, body weight 47.5 ± 9.7 kg) volunteered for the study with the informed consent of their parents. $\dot{V}O_2$ max was 2.52 ± 0.41 $L.min^{-1}$ corresponding to 54 ± 7 $mL\cdot kg^{-1}\cdot min^{-1}$ body weight.

Children and Exercise XIX. Edited by Neil Armstrong, Brian Kirby and Joanne Welsman.
Published in 1997 by E & FN Spon, 2–6 Boundary Row, London, SE1 8HN.
ISBN 0 419 22100 X.

Table 1. Means of haemodynamic variables and of systolic time intervals at rest and during exercise in the supine and seated posture

		Rest	50 W	100 W	150 W	Recovery
Heart rate	sup	81	123***	152***	175***	94***
(beats·min^{-1})	seat	90	122***	158***	181***	95***
Stroke volume	sup	69	73	75	74	72
SV, (mL)	seat	51+++	64***+	66++	68	67+
Cardiac output	sup	5.6	9.1***	11.6**	13.7*	6.8***
(L·min^{-1})	seat	4.6+	8.2***+	10.3**+	12.2	6.4
Syst. BP	sup	118	142***	160***	178***	122***
(mmHg)	seat	114	137***	152***	162***	128***
Diast. BP	sup	72	69	72	69	65
(mmHg)	seat	79	71	66	67	66
TVR	sup	17.4	11.7***	9.9**	9.3	13.7
(mmHg·L^{-1})	seat	21.6++	13.7***+	10.6*	9.6	14.9
PEP	sup	54	44***	38**	36	50
(ms)	seat	76+++	40***+	33**+	30+	49
PEP/LVET	sup	18	18	18	19	18
(%)	seat	29+++	16***+	17	18	18

*p <0.05, **p <0.01, ***p <0.001: change from preceding condition (e.g. 50 W vs rest)
+p <0.05, ++p <0.01, +++p <0.01: supine versus seated posture

They were studied at rest prior to and during steady state cycle ergometer exercise at 50 W, 100 W and 150 W as well as 4 min after cessation of exercise, both in the supine and the seated posture. Stroke volume (SV) and the systolic time intervals PEP (pre-ejection period) and LVET (LV ejection time) used as criteria of LV contractility[4] were determined by impedance cardiography. A transthoracic impedance cardiogram according to Kubicek et al.[5], an ECG and a phonocardiogram were continuously recorded on-line and processed using an OS9 system. The data given are the mean values obtained during the last 30 s of each measuring period. Details of the methods used, their validity and reproducibility, and of the calculation are given elsewhere[6,7]. Systolic (SBP) and diastolic (DBP) blood pressures were obtained by the Riva-Rocci-Korotkoff method. Cardiac output (CO) was derived from SV and heart rate (HR) as CO = SVxHR, total vascular resistance (TVR) from mean arterial blood pressure (MBP) and CO as TVR = MBP/CO, with MBP = ½ (SBP+DBP).

Results

HR, SBP and DBP were virtually identical in both the supine and seated postures under all conditions except for a tendency of HR and DBP towards higher values at rest (table 1).

Table 2. Haemodynamic variables and systolic time intervals at rest and percentage changes during 150 W exercise in the supine and seated posture (symbols as in table 1)

		Rest	% change 150 W			Rest	% change 150 W
HR	sup	81±8	116***	SBP	sup	118±11	51***
	seat	90±10	101***		seat	114±12	42***
SV	sup	69±13	7	DBP	sup	72±5	-4
	seat	51±15+++	33***+++		seat	79±6	-15*++
CO	sup	5.6±1.5	145***	PEP	sup	54±7	-33***
	seat	4.6±1.4+	165***+		seat	76±11+++	-60***+++
TVR	sup	17.4±3.9	-46***	PEP/	sup	18±3	5
	seat	21.6±5.5++	-55***+	LVET	seat	29±5+++	-38***+++

Values are mean ± SD

Under resting conditions, SV, CO and LVET were significantly lower, and TVR, PEP and PEP/LVET significantly higher in the seated than in the supine posture. During exercise, SV and CO remained significantly lower and TVR higher in the seated position at exercise intensities of 50 W and 100 W; at 150 W there was only a tendency towards lower values. In contrast to resting conditions, PEP and PEP/LVET were, or tended to be, lower during exercise in the seated compared with the supine position; LVET became identical.

Table 2 displays the total percentage change of the different variables during exercise at the highest level. All of them except SV, DBP and PEP/LVET in the supine posture showed significant changes with exercise. Except for HR and SBP the differences in the degree of change between the two body positions were highly significant and, except for LVET, more pronounced in the seated posture. Concerning SV, TVR and PEP the greatest changes occurred during 50 W exercise and were again more pronounced in the seated than the supine posture, namely +25% versus 6%, -55% versus -46% and +47% versus 19%. PEP/LVET decreased by 45% initially, in the seated posture, but was unchanged supine.

Discussion

Quite evidently, body position strongly affects cardiovascular adjustment both at rest and during exercise. At rest, SV is 26% lower in the seated than in the supine posture; it rises during exercise at the initial exercise intensity by 6% in the supine and by as much of 25% in the seated position. It is noteworthy that SV in the present study is nearly identical with the corresponding values obtained by Eriksson and Koch[1] with invasive methods underlining the validity of impedance cardiography. The increase of SV during exercise in these prepubertal boys appears significantly less pronounced than in adults. Bevegård and Shephard[8] found an increase by 12% and 67% in the supine and seated posture respectively in normal subjects and a rise of 17% and 50% in a group of well trained cyclists. Practically the same figures (6% and 51% respectively) were obtained by Buchberger and Koch[7] 100 s after onset of exercise at 150 W in moderately trained young adults. However, the difference between resting supine and seated SV appears to be significantly larger in the adult. It was 41% in the previous study using the same method[7] versus 26% in the present series. This difference may explain the weaker increase of SV at the transition from rest to exercise in the boys.

SV is closely correlated to the contractile state as shown by the changes of PEP which mainly reflects the isovolumetric contraction period.

The significantly smaller SV in the seated posture at rest corresponds to a 40% longer PEP, and a 61% higher PEP/LVET ratio, i.e. lower contractility in comparison to supine. Concomitantly with the 6% and 25% increase of SV at the onset of exercise in the supine and seated posture respectively, PEP decreases by 19% versus 47%; PEP/LVET does not change in the supine posture, but decreases by 45% in the seated position.

Quite obviously, the larger SV and enhanced contractility at rest in the supine compared with the seated posture are due to the Frank-Starling mechanism, i.e. the larger LV end diastolic volume present when the subject is supine. During exercise, both augmented end diastolic filling and increased adrenergic stimulation contribute to the enhancement of contractility, both probably from the very beginning of exercise. However, the pronounced increase of contractility and of SV particularly in the seated posture during the first seconds following the onset of exercise[6] suggest that under these conditions the exercise induced increase of venous return and thus enhanced end diastolic filling is the most important mechanism. During continued incremental exercise with increasing HR and decreasing diastolic filling time adrenergic activity probably plays the predominant role. Plasma noradrenaline has been shown to increase twofold from rest to low intensity exercise but by 12 to 16 times during near maximal exercise in boys 15-16-years-old[9]. In accordance with these observations, in the present study PEP continues to decrease by a further 25% and 18% in the seated and supine posture respectively between 50 W and 150 W while SV is mainly unchanged.

Final SV and CO attained at 150 W in the seated posture are only insignificantly lower than in the supine position, while contractility in terms of PEP is higher. Also TVR, significantly higher at rest and at 50 W exercise in the seated posture, attain the same levels as in the supine position. Obviously, the SV and CO deficit observed at rest in the seated compared to the supine posture tend to be compensated at significantly lower exercise intensities at prepuberty than later in life[7,8].

References

1. Eriksson, B.O. and Koch, G. (1973) Effect of physical training on haemodynamic response during submaximal and maximal exercise in 11-13 year old boys. *Acta Physiologica Scandinavica*, Vol. 87, pp. 27-9.

2. Koch, G. and Eriksson, B.O. (1973) Effect of physical training on pulmonary ventilation and gas exchange during submaximal and maximal work in boys aged 11 to 13 years. *Scandinavian Journal of Clinical and Laboratory Investigation,* Vol. 31, pp. 87-94.
3. Koch, G. and Eriksson, B.O. (1973) Effect of physical training on anatomical R-L shunt at rest and pulmonary diffusing capacity during near-maximal exercise in boys 11-13 years old. *Scandinavian Journal of Clinical and Laboratory Investigation,* Vol. 31, pp. 95-103.
4. Lewis, R.P., Rillgers, S.E., Forrester, W.F. and Boudonlas, H. (1977) A critical review of the systolic time intervals. *Circulation,* Vol. 56, pp.146-53.
5. Kubicek, W.G., Patterson, R.P. and Wilsoe, D.H. (1970) Impedance cardiography as a non-invasive method of monitoring cardiac function and other parameters of the cardiovascular system. *Annals of the New York Academy of Science,* Vol. 170, pp. 724-32.
6. Koch, G., Buchberger, D., Koralewski, H.E. and Perschel, F.H. (1992) Determination of stroke volume by impedance cardiography: variability, reproducibility and validity, in *Pediatric Work Physiology,* (eds. J. Coudert and E. Van Praagh), Masson, Paris, pp. 63-5.
7. Buchberger, D. and Koch, G. (1992) Adjustment of stroke volume and of left ventricular contractility during the initial phase of exercise in the supine versus seated posture, in *Pediatric Work Physiology,* (eds. J. Coudert and E. Van Praagh), Masson, Paris, pp. 67-9.
8. Bevegård, S. and Shepherd, J.T. (1967) Regulation of the circulation during exercise in man. *Physiological Reviews,* Vol. 47, pp. 178-93.
9. Koch, G., Johannsen, U. and Arvidsson, E. (1980) Radioenzymatic determination of epinephrine, norepinephrine and dopamine in 0.1 ml plasma samples. Plasma catecholamine response to submaximal and near maximal exercise. *Journal of Clinical Chemistry and Biochemistry,* Vol. 18, pp. 367-72.

CARDIOVASCULAR ADJUSTMENT TO SUPINE AND SEATED POSTURES: EFFECT OF PHYSICAL TRAINING

Haemodynamics, body posture and training

J. MÖBERT, G. KOCH, O. HUMPLIK and E-M OYEN
Department of Physiology, Free University, Berlin, Germany

Keywords: Haemodynamics, left ventricular contractility, posture, training

Introduction

Both haemodynamics and left ventricular (LV) contractility are significantly affected by body posture[1,2,3]. Due to the more favourable filling conditions in the supine posture, supine stroke volume (SV) and cardiac output (CO) at rest are significantly greater than in the seated posture[1,2,3,4]. At the onset of exercise SV, CO and contractility rise significantly, in particular in the seated posture[2,3]. However, SV and CO in the seated posture attain the supine levels, if ever, only at high intensity or maximal exercise[1,3]. Observations in sedentary and highly trained adult men[1] suggest that physical training may attenuate the differences in cardiovascular capacity between supine and seated posture both at rest and during exercise. The purpose of this study was to evaluate this aspect of the effect of physical training in prepubertal boys by comparing cardiovascular adaptation at rest and during exercise in supine and seated posture before and after physical training.

Subjects and methods

Twelve healthy boys aged 13.7 ± 0.3 y, height 160.8 ± 9.0 cm, body weight 47.5 ± 9.7 kg, $\dot{V}O_2$ max = 2.52 ± 0.41 $L{\cdot}min^{-1}$; 54 ± 7 $mL{\cdot}kg^{-1}{\cdot}min^{-1}$ volunteered for the study with the informed consent of their parents. After the initial study they attended a 7 mo training programme supervised and coordinated by an experienced physical education instructor. Training was performed for 90 min twice a week and mainly aimed at increasing aerobic capacity. However, only six boys participated regularly and efficiently in the training sessions; participation was irregular and drop-outs frequent in the other

Children and Exercise XIX. Edited by Neil Armstrong, Brian Kirby and Joanne Welsman.
Published in 1997 by E & FN Spon, 2–6 Boundary Row, London, SE1 8HN.
ISBN 0 419 22100 X.

six. It thus turned out that at the end of the training period two groups could be defined; the six boys who regularly participated displayed an increase in $\dot{V}O_2$ max from 2.45 ± 0.48 $L{\cdot}min^{-1}$ or 49 $mL{\cdot}kg^{-1}{\cdot}min^{-1}$ to 3.02 ± 0.40 $L{\cdot}min^{-1}$ or 55 $mL{\cdot}kg^{-1}{\cdot}min^{-1}$(group T), while in the other six $\dot{V}O_2$ max was unchanged implying a reduction of their relative $\dot{V}O_2$ max from 59 to 52 $mL{\cdot}kg^{-1}{\cdot}min^{-1}$ (group U).

Prior to and after the 7 mo training period, the boys were studied in an identical manner at rest and during steady state cycle ergometer exercise at 50 W, 100 W and 150 W in both the supine and seated posture. Stroke volume (SV) and the systolic time intervals PEP (pre-ejection-period) and LVET (left ventricular ejection time) were determined by impedance cardiography and used as criteria of LV contractility[5]. Details of the methods used, their validity and reproducibility, and of the calculations are given elsewhere[3,6].

Results

Except for a 10% increase in SV at rest, none of the variables studied in the supine posture (table 1) changed after the 7 mo training period in group U. Conversely, in the group displaying a favourable training effect (T), HR was lower; SV, contractility in terms of PEP and PEP/LVET, and diastolic blood pressure (DBP), were higher under

Table 1. Cardiovascular variables at rest and during exercise in the supine posture before (b) and (a) physical training

Supine		Rest		50 W		100 W		150 W	
		b	a	b	a	b	a	b	a
Heart rate	U	78	81	122	119	149	146	177	178
(beats·min^{-1})	T	84	77*	128	113**	159	143*	171	158*
Stroke volume	U	68	75**	70	75	72	73	67	69
SV, (mL)	T	67	77**	76	83**	77	88**	79	84*
Cardiac output	U	5.4	6.1	8.5	8.9	10.8	10.8	12.0	12.3
(L·min^{-1})	T	5.8	6.1	9.4	9.6	12.3	12.6	13.5	13.3
Diast. BP	U	72	74	70	70	71	80	70	78
(mmHg)	T	71	81*	69	83*	72	86*	68	86*
PEP	U	54	52	43	48	39	38	34	32
(ms)	T	53	52	45	37*	37	28***	37	26**
PEP/LVET	U	18	18	16	15	15	14	16	15
(%)	T	17	18	16	14*	18	14**	18	15*

U: group without, T: group with positive training effect
Level of significance of change from preceding condition (e.g. 50 W vs rest)
*$p < 0.05$, **$p < 0.01$, ***$p < 0.001$

Table 2. Cardiovascular variables at rest and during exercise in the seated posture before (b) and after (a) physical training (symbols as in table 1)

Seated		Rest		50 W		100 W		150 W	
		b	a	b	a	b	a	b	a
Heart rate	U	92	89	124	117	158	158	184	182
(beats·min^{-1})	T	88	83*	120	114*	159	154	178	171*
Stroke volume	U	47	49	65	66	63	65	62	62
SV, (mL)	T	55	66***	69	82***	69	81**	77	84*
Cardiac output	U	4.3	4.4	8.1	7.8	10.0	10.3	11.3	11.3
(L·min^{-1})	T	4.8	5.4*	8.3	9.3*	10.9	12.5*	13.7	14.3*
Diast. BP	U	77	84	69	76	63	79*	64	79*
(mmHg)	T	80	83	74	81*	69	78*	72	85*
PEP	U	73	69	39	37	31	29	28	26
(ms)	T	79	67*	40	33*	36	27**	34	26*
PEP/LVET	U	28	28	18	18	19	18	19	18
(%)	T	30	26*	18	15*	18	14*	18	14*

virtually all conditions. Systolic blood pressure (SBP), CO and total vascular resistance (TVR) were unchanged.

In the seated posture (table 2) only DBP at 100 W and 150 W exercise was significantly higher after the training period in group U. However, in the group displaying an increase in $\dot{V}O_2$ max, SV, CO and contractility in terms of PEP and PEP/LVET were significantly higher under all conditions. DBP was higher during exercise, HR lower at rest and during 50 W and 150 W exercise. SBP and TVR were reduced by 8% and 19% respectively at rest only.

Discussion

In spite of repeated encouragement and even remonstrance, only six of the 12 boys who volunteered for the study participated regularly and with enthusiasm in the training programme. They improved their relative $\dot{V}O_2$ max from 49 to 55 mL·kg^{-1}·min^{-1}, while the less active group displayed a reduction from 59 to 52 mL·kg^{-1}·min^{-1}. Interestingly, the initially less well trained boys were highly motivated, while those initially well trained turned out to be much less interested and failed to maintain or to further improve their aerobic capacity. The division of the whole group into these two subgroups allowed for examination of the pure effect of training since physical development was similar in both groups.

In the untrained group (U), the only significant changes observed after the 7 mo training period were a 10% increase of SV at rest supine and a slight rise of DBP during 100 W and 150 W exercise in the seated posture. In the trained group (T), SV increased by as much as 15% ($p < 0.001$) at rest supine; the difference ($p < 0.05$) suggests that physical development alone accounts for the SV increase in group U. The significant increase of DBP in group T under practically all conditions - supine and seated - and in group U during exercise in the seated posture is noteworthy; a similar increase has been observed when blood pressure was measured intraarterially[4]. Though the increase of SV and corporeal maturation might have contributed, they cannot entirely explain the rise in DBP.

The most consistent finding was the concomitant increase of SV and contractility in terms of PEP under all conditions in group T. PEP mainly reflects the isovolumetric contraction period, implying that the lower PEP the higher contractility. In the supine posture SV increases by 6% to 15% and PEP decreases by 18% to 30% under the various conditions, in the seated posture SV rises by 9% to 19% and PEP is reduced by 15% to 25%. The size of SV is mainly dependent on the end diastolic volume according to the Frank-Starling mechanism and on the intrinsic myocardial contractility modulated by adrenergic activity. Echocardiographic studies[7,8] suggest that the training induced increase of SV is due to both mechanisms: the widening of the end systolic-end diastolic diameter observed reflects a larger end diastolic volume; the reduction of the end systolic diameter and the increase of the velocity of circumferential fibre shortening (VCF) and of fractional fibre shortening (FS) reflect increased contractility. Training induced LV hypertrophy[8] most probably accounts at least partly for the enhancement of contractility.

Post-training HR was lowered under all conditions supine as well as seated in group T only. A training induced reduction of HR has been widely documented in adults and has also been reported in the circumpubertal age[4,7,9]. Despite the reduction of HR, CO in the seated posture was significantly larger at rest and during exercise in group T. Furthermore, CO in the seated posture attained the level of supine CO already at the lowest work load (50 W). Quite obviously, in the circumpubertal age group effective training attenuates under all conditions the differences in SV and CO persisting between seated and supine posture; during exercise SV and CO in the seated posture equal those in the supine position already at very low work levels.

References

1. Bevegård, S. and Shepherd, J.T. (1967) Regulation of the circulation during exercise in man. *Physiology Review,* Vol. 47, pp. 178-93.
2. Buchberger, D. and Koch, G. (1992) Adjustment of stroke volume and of left ventricular contractility during the initial phase of exercise in the supine versus seated posture, in *Pediatric Work Physiology*, (eds. J. Coudert and E. Van Praagh), Masson, Paris, pp. 67-9.
3. Koch, G., Möbert, J. and Oyen, E-M. (1997) Cardiovascular adjustment to supine versus seated posture in prepubertal boys, in *Children and Exercise XIX*, (eds. N. Armstrong, B.J. Kirby and J.R. Welsman), E and F.N. Spon, London.
4. Eriksson, B.O. and Koch, G. (1973) Effect of physical training on hemodynamic response during submaximal and maximal exercise in 11-13 year old boys. *Acta Physiologica Scandinavica,* Vol. 87, pp. 27-9.

5. Lewis, R.P., Rillgers, S.E., Forrester, W.F. and Boudonlas, H. (1977) A critical review of the systolic time intervals. *Circulation,* Vol. 56, pp.146-53.
6. Koch, G., Buchberger, D., Koralewski, H.E. and Perschel, F.H. (1992) Determination of stroke volume by impedance cardiography: variability, reproducibility and validity, in *Pediatric Work Physiology*, (eds. J. Coudert and E. Van Praagh), Masson, Paris, pp. 63-5.
7. Oyen, E-M., Schuster, S. and Brode, P.E. (1991) Echocardiographic evaluation of left ventricular functions in physically trained children compared to untrained healthy children, in *Children and Exercise, Pediatric Work Physiology XV*, (eds. R. Frenkl and T. Szabo), National Institute for Health Promotion, Budapest, pp. 212-6.
8. Oyen, E-M., Maas, W. and Koch, G. (1995) Left ventricular dimensions and systolic function at rest and during exercise in boys aged 12-14 years: an echocardiographic study. *Pediatric Exercise Science*, Vol. 7, p. 435.
9. Eriksson, B.O., Grimby, G. and Saltin, B. (1971) Cardiac output and arterial blood gases during exercise in pubertal boys. *Journal of Applied Physiology*, Vol. 31, pp. 348-52.

HEART RATE VARIABILITY IN 11- TO 16-YEAR-OLDS

Heart rate variability

B.J. KIRBY
Institute of Clinical Science, University of Exeter, Exeter, UK
R.M. KIRBY
Department of Psychology, University of Exeter, Exeter, UK
Keywords: Body fatness, heart rate variability, peak oxygen uptake

Introduction

Autonomic control of heart rate is determined by the interplay between the excitatory influences of the sympathetic nervous system and inhibition by the parasympathetic system. These are modulated by many influences notably activity, emotion, and absorptive state, yet, in spite of the diversity of these influences, heart rate variability has emerged as a reliable index of autonomic control. In adult life a reduction in heart rate variability can be a harbinger of coronary disease and it is associated with an increased hazard of sudden death. While this is well established in adults very little is known about heart rate variability in young people. What little information is available has been gained in infants[1] or in disease[2]; there are very few normative data.

Methods for assessing heart rate variability have been developing rapidly resulting in several different methods for deriving it. Where continuous beat-to-beat (R-R) recordings are available it is possible to analyse high frequency components which can be analysed using frequency-domain methods (spectral analysis). When heart rates are determined by taking the mean of several beats over a period of time, then any high frequency oscillations are filtered out. Other, time-domain, methods are more appropriate for deriving this lower frequency variability. Using the considerable amount of data we have accumulated using heart-rate averaging recorders, we have used these time-domain methods to examine children's heart rate variability. As we know obesity and poor physical fitness are associated in adults with a reduced heart rate variability, we examined whether these variables played any part in determining children's heart rate variability.

Children and Exercise XIX. Edited by Neil Armstrong, Brian Kirby and Joanne Welsman.
Published in 1997 by E & FN Spon, 2–6 Boundary Row, London, SE1 8HN.
ISBN 0 419 22100 X.

Subjects and methods

We re-analysed heart rate recordings in 472 11 to 16-year-old boys and girls who had participated in studies in which we used heart rate recordings as a surrogate for physical activity. This population of children is well-described, homogeneous, and representative of children living in the southern part of England. There were between three and six records containing 12 h of data. For this purpose we selected only one record per child with complete data. Peak oxygen consumption was measured in 295 of this group. The methods used for anthropometric measurements, lipids, physical activity, and aerobic fitness, have been described already in our previous work[3,4]. Heart rates were collected for a minimum of 12 h using a Polar Sports Tester – a lightweight heart rate monitor capable of recording 12 h or more of heart rates which could then be interfaced with a computer for storage and analysis. This method depends on averaging successive R-R intervals.

Data analyses and results

There was no statistical difference in heart rate data between boys and girls therefore, for the purposes of this study, the data for both sexes have been combined.

Mean, standard deviation, maximum, and minimum heart rate were computed for 12 h in the whole group. Three time domain methods were used to assess heart rate variability, namely, i) Standard Deviation (SD) for the heart rates in each individual participant; ii) The Mean Square of Successive Differences (MSSD) calculated by the formula:

$$\mathrm{MSSD} = \delta^2 = \frac{1}{n-1}\sum_{1}^{n-1}(x_{i+1} - x_i)^2$$

where x_i = a chronological value, i.e. x_{i+1} = next chronological value etc., and n = size of the sample; and iii) the 'Range of Variability 80%' (RV80) calculated by taking the range of heart rates for 80% of the 12 h period, thereby excluding extremes of the range. Multiple regression analyses were carried out using SPSS for PC Plus using standard statistical techniques.

Table 1. Physical characteristics

Age (y)*	12.6 ± 1.09 (12-16)
Stature (m)*	1.53 ± 0.10 (1.31 - 1.84)
Mass (kg)*	44.8 ± 10.7 (27.2 - 95.8)
Sum of Skinfolds (mm)**	22.81 ± 10.6 (9.4 - 72.0)
Peak $\dot{V}O_2$ ($L \cdot min^{-1}$)***	1.89 ± 0.45 (1.07 - 3.75)

Values are mean ± SD (min-max)
*n = 472, **n = 456, ***n =295

The mean heart rate was consistent with normative data for children of this age. There was a wide range of heart rate with, even during the waking hours, surprisingly low heart rates in some participants. We had scanned the data carefully for invalid recordings so we can be reasonably sure that these were correct observations. The descriptive statistics are shown in table 2.

There are no normative data for children of this age with which to compare our results but by extrapolation from adult data using SD, MSSD, and RV80, we found children had greater heart rate variability than young adults and much greater variability than the elderly.

We used Pearson correlation coefficients to examine possible factors influencing heart rate variability in all participants. We then used multiple regression analysis using age, body mass, and peak $\dot{V}O_2$ with those 295 youngsters in whom we had all of these measurements. As might be anticipated there was a significant overall inverse inverse relationship between heart rate and age and peak $\dot{V}O_2$ ($F = 4.28$; p 0.002). For two measures of heart rate variability – 'SD of 12 h recordings' and 'MSSD' – the regression equations were a poor fit with peak $\dot{V}O_2$ appearing to be the major influence on it (SD $t = 2.5$; $p < 0.01$, and, MSSD $t = 2.9$; $p < 0.003$). No such associations were found for RV80.

Discussion

Heart rate in mammals varies with age, body mass, body temperature, activity, and environment. For example, the resting heart rate is 25 to 41 in elephants and 600 beats·min^{-1} in mice[5]. Similar considerations apply to humans with resting heart rate decreasing from- infancy through to adult life although the narrow age range of those participating in this study would be unlikely to show it. Although the resting heart rate contains some useful physiological information, the practical difficulties of measuring truly basal heart rate outweigh its value. Heart rate variability has become increasingly more important with the realisation that it enables autonomic function to be assessed by non-invasional means and, moreover, that this has important implications in heart disease where it may be a determinant of sudden death.

Table 2. Children's heart rate (beats·min^{-1}) and heart rate variability (n = 472)

Mean	101.3 ± 9.7 (71.9 - 145.8)
Median	97.1 ± 9.8 (69.0 - 150.0)
Min	67.5 ± 9.5 (38.0 - 108)
Max	200.6 ± 28.5 (123.0 - 239.0)
SD*	20.1 ± 5.0 (9.8 - 52.5)
MSSD	266.8 ± 154.2 (24.0 - 1789.5)
RV80	45.8 ± 12.5 (23.0 - 162.0)

Values are mean ± SD (min-max)
*SD of total 12 h recordings

Studies of heart rate variability (HRV) in adults have shown that there are two components, namely, slow frequency variations reflecting sympathetic influences, and faster frequency components, indicating vagal, or parasympathetic, influences[6]. Hitherto determining the relative contribution of sympathetic and parasympathetic influences on the heart has required physical or pharmacological interventions that would not be ethically acceptable in normal youngsters; HRV offers an opportunity to investigate this field though methods for doing so are still being developed and debated. Higher frequency variability is measured using frequency domain methods (frequency spectrum and time-series) while lower frequency variability is more appropriately measured by time domain methods such as those we used. We used these methods as we were constrained by the method used to collect the data which, although accurate and prolonged, could not be analysed for high frequency components. Accordingly, our estimates of HRV are predominantly indicative of sympathetic nervous system influences on heart rate. Though this may seem a deficiency, use of certain spectral frequency methods has recently been criticised as during activity it may incorrectly attribute certain components to neural influences[7]. No exactly comparable data exist for young people of this age but, by comparison with data for children aged 0 to 6 y, and with normal adults, it is apparent that children show a diminishing HRV with age and that they have a much higher HRV than 30- year-old adults and it is even greater than 70-year-olds[8,9]. This implies that cardiac neural sympathetic activity decreases throughout childhood. This is an important observation as there has been a tendency to suggest that the decreasing HRV observed in adults is due to disease. Our observations suggest that it occurs long before the onset of disease. Much of the emphasis on HRV has centred on coronary disease and heart failure where it has been shown that decreased HRV is predictive of increased mortality and sudden death[10,11,12].

As a consequence of these observations there has been further exploration of factors that could influence HRV; in adults two have emerged, namely obesity[13] and exercise; the former decreases HRV and the latter increases it[14,15]. Plainly both could be modified though whether doing so would reduce risk is unknown[16,17]. Aerobic fitness as assessed by peak $\dot{V}O_2$ illustrates that in children too those who are fitter not only have a lower intrinsic heart rate during everyday activity but also show a greater degree of HRV. Body mass and indices of fatness appear to have far less influence in children when compared to adults. It is probably explained by the greater proportional degree of fatness encountered in adults. Our observations have two important implications. First, the HRV demonstrated in adults is already discernible in childhood long before the onset of heart disease, and secondly, and perhaps more importantly, those children who are more physically fit have the greater HRV with its potential in adult life for reducing sudden death. Once more it reaffirms the importance of encouraging children in the habit of regular exercise.

References

1. Oberlander, T.F., Berde, C.B. and Saul, J.P. (1996) Halothane and cardiac autonomic control in infants: assessment and quantitative respiratory sinus arrhythmia. *Pediatric Research*, Vol. 40, pp. 710-7.

2. Jartti, T.T., Tahvanainen, K.U.O., Kaila, T.J., Kuusela, T.A., Koivikko, A.S., Vanto, T.T. and Valimaki, I.A.T. (1996) Cardiovascular autonomic regulation in asthmatic children evidenced by spectral analysis of heart rate and blood pressure variability. *Scandinavian Journal of Clinical and Laboratory Investigation*, Vol. 56, pp. 545-54.

3. Armstrong, N., Balding, J., Gentle, P. and Kirby, B.J. (1992) Serum lipids and blood pressure in relation to age and sexual maturity. *Annals of Human Biology*, Vol. 19, pp. 447-87.

4. Armstrong, N., Kirby, B.J., McManus, A.M. and Welsman, J.R. (1995) Aerobic fitness of pre-pubescent children. *Annals of Human Biology*, Vol. 22, pp. 427-41.

5. Altman, P.L. and Dittermer, D.S. (eds)(1971) Biological Handbooks: Respiration and Circulation. *Federation of American Societies for Experimental Biology*, Bathesda, Maryland.

6. Pieper, S.J. and Hammill, S.C. (1995) Heart rate variability: technique and investigation applications in cardiovascular medicine. *Mayo Clinic Proceedings*, Vol. 70, pp. 955-64.

7. Casadei, B., Cochrane, S., Johnston, J. and Sleight, P. (1995) Pitfalls in the interpretation of spectral analysis of the heart rate variability during exercise in humans. *Acta Physiologica Scandinavica*, Vol. 153, pp. 125-31.

8. Finley, J.P. and Nugent, S.T. (1995) Heart rate variability in infants, children and young adults. *Journal of Autonomic Nervous System*, Vol. 51, pp. 103-8.

9. Craft, N. and Schwartz, J.B. (1995) Effects of age on intrinsic heart rate, heart rate variability, and AV conduction in healthy humans. *American Journal of Physiology*, Vol. 37, pp. H1441-52.

10. Barron, H.V. and Lesh, M.D. (1996) Autonomic nervous system and sudden cardiac death. *Journal of the American College of Cardiology*, Vol. 27, pp. 1053-60.

11. Fei, L., Copie, X., Malik, M. and Camm, A.J. (1996) Short- and long-term assessment of heart rate variability for risk stratification after acute myocardial infarction. *American Journal of Cardiology*, Vol. 77, pp. 681-4.

12. Tsuji, H., Larson, M.G., Venditti, F.J., Manders, E.S., Evans, J.C., Feldman, C.I. and Levy, D. (1996) Impact of reduced heart rate variability on risk for cardiac events: the Framingham Heart Study. *Circulation*, Vol. 94, pp. 2850-5.

13. Gao, Y.Y., Lovejoy, J.C., Sparti, A., Bray, G.A., Keys, L.K. and Partington, C. (1996) Autonomic activity assessed by heart rate spectral analysis varies with fat distribution in obese women. *Obesity Research*, Vol. 4, pp. 55-63.

14. Davey, K.P., Miniclier, N.L., Taylor, J.A., Stevenson, E.T. and Seals, D.R. (1996) Elevated heart rate variability in physically active postmenopausal women: a cardioprotective effect? *American Journal of Physiology*, Vol. 40, pp. H455-60.

15. Byrne, E.A., Fleg, J.L., Vaitkevicius, P.V., Wright, J. and Porges, S.W. (1996) Role of aerobic capacity and body mass index in age-associated decline in heart rate variability. *Journal of Applied Physiology*, Vol. 81, pp. 743-50.

16. Bernardi, L., Valle, F., Coco, M., Calciati, A. and Sleight, P. (1996) Physical activity influences heart rate variability and very-low frequency components in Holter electrocardiograms. *Cardiovascular Research*, Vol. 32, pp. 234-7.
17. Boutcher, S.H. and Stein, P. (1995) Association between heart rate variability and training response in sedentary middle aged men. *European Journal of Applied Physiology*, Vol. 70, pp. 75-80.

AN EXPLORATORY STUDY OF CARDIAC OUTPUT RESPONSES TO SUBMAXIMAL EXERCISE

Cardiac output during submaximal exercise

C. R. POTTER, N. ARMSTRONG, B. J. KIRBY and J. R. WELSMAN.
Children's Health and Exercise Research Centre, Institute of Clinical Science, University of Exeter, Exeter, UK

Keywords: Allometry, arteriovenous oxygen difference, cardiac output, heart rate, maturation, submaximal exercise, stroke volume

Introduction

Cardiac output (Q) plays a central role in the delivery of oxygen to the working muscles but, due to problems associated with its measurement[1], data describing the Q responses of children to exercise are sparse[2-4]. It appears that at any given level of oxygen consumption ($\dot{V}O_2$) Q may be as much as 1-2 L·min^{-1} lower in the young person than in the adult, largely due to the child's lower stroke volume (SV) during both submaximal and maximal exercise[4-6]. Few studies have sought to examine the effects of body size and maturation on Q and sex differences have rarely been explored[4,5,7]. The present study was designed to examine the influence of sex and maturation on cardiac responses to exercise with body size controlled using allometric scaling techniques.

Subjects

The subjects were drawn from a longitudinal study of a representative sample of children attending state schools in Exeter. Subject selection has been described elsewhere[8]. The data reported here are from the 216 subjects who successfully completed the appropriate tests during the second year of the study.

Methods

Age was calculated from date of birth and date of examination. Sexual maturity was

Children and Exercise XIX. Edited by Neil Armstrong, Brian Kirby and Joanne Welsman.
Published in 1997 by E & FN Spon, 2–6 Boundary Row, London, SE1 8HN.
ISBN 0 419 22100 X.

assessed from pubic hair using Tanner's indices[9]. All examinations were conducted by the same nurse. Stature and body mass were measured using a Holtain stadiometer (Crymych, Dyfed, UK) and an Avery balance beam (Avery, Birmingham, UK) respectively. Peak exercise responses were measured during a discontinuous, incremental treadmill test to voluntary exhaustion. Belt speed was incremented at 3 min intervals from 1.94 $m \cdot s^{-1}$ (6 $km \cdot h^{-1}$) to a maximum of 2.78 $m \cdot s^{-1}$ (10 $km \cdot h^{-1}$), and subsequently, the gradient was elevated by 2.5% every 3 min.

Both boys' and girls' Q was estimated by the indirect Fick method using carbon dioxide (CO_2) rebreathing at 2.22 $m \cdot s^{-1}$ (8 $km \cdot h^{-1}$). A subset of the boys had Q determined at two subsequent intensities (2.50 $m \cdot s^{-1}$ {9 $km \cdot h^{-1}$} and 2.78 $m \cdot s^{-1}$). The volume of gas in the rebreathing bag was calculated to be 1.5 times the mean of 3 tidal breaths, and the bag CO_2 concentration was calculated based on the $\dot{V}O_2$ and the end-tidal partial pressure of CO_2. The bag size was selected so that it could easily accommodate the volume of rebreathing gas. Gas exchange was measured using an Oxycon Sigma on-line analysis system (Cranlea, Birmingham, UK) which was calibrated with gases of known concentration prior to each test. Heart rate (HR) was monitored continuously using an electrocardiograph (Rigel, Morden, UK).

Data analyses

Data were stored and analysed using SPSS-PC+ (SPSS Inc., Chicago, USA) statistical package. Descriptive statistics were computed for age, stature, body mass and responses at peak and submaximal exercise. Sex differences were analysed using analysis of variance (ANOVA). The effects of body size (stature and/or mass) were partitioned out of $\dot{V}O_2$, Q and SV, and sex differences compared using log-linear analysis of covariance (ANCOVA). We have discussed in detail elsewhere the theoretical principles underlying the use of log-linear models to partition out the effect of body size from measures of physiological function[5].

Differences in exercise responses for boys who completed the Q protocol at 2.22, 2.50, and 2.78 $m \cdot s^{-1}$ were analysed using repeated measures ANOVA. Two way (sex by maturity) ANOVA was used to examine sex and maturational differences in exercise data.

Results

Anthropometric data, grouped by sex, are presented in table 1. There were no significant differences ($p > 0.05$) in age, stature, or mass between boys and girls.

Boys' and girls' Q and related data at 2.22$m \cdot s^{-1}$ are presented in table 2. No significant differences were found in $\dot{V}O_2$ ($p > 0.05$), whether expressed in $L \cdot min^{-1}$, $mL \cdot kg^{-1} \cdot min^{-1}$ or adjusted using ANCOVA. Both HR and % peak $\dot{V}O_2$ were significantly lower in boys ($p < 0.001$), as was RER ($p < 0.05$), while O_2 pulse was significantly higher ($p < 0.05$). There was no significant sex difference in Q whether expressed in

Table 1. Anthropometric and peak exercise responses by sex

Variable	Boys (n = 61)	Girls (n = 56)
Age (y)	12.2 ± 0.4	12.2 ± 0.4
Stature (m)	1.52 ± 0.07	1.52 ± 0.07
Mass (kg)	41.2 ± 7.2	42.4 ± 6.9

Values are mean ± SD
Level of significance $p > 0.05$

absolute terms or when adjusted for body size ($p > 0.05$). SV was significantly higher in boys, both in mL and when adjusted using ANCOVA ($p < 0.001$). No significant ($p > 0.05$) sex differences in arteriovenous oxygen difference (a-vO_2) were detected.

The exercise responses of the 31 boys who completed the Q protocol at 2.22, 2.50, and 2.78 $m{\cdot}s^{-1}$ are presented in table 3. The mean ± SD age, stature and body mass of this group were 12.3 ± 0.3 y, 1.53 ± 0.07 m, 40.7 ± 6.5 kg respectively. All exercise responses were significantly different ($p < 0.01$ to $p < 0.001$), showing higher values with increasing intensity, except for SV which did not change significantly ($p > 0.05$) from 2.22 to 2.78 $m{\cdot}s^{-1}$.

Fifty three boys and 44 girls were classified according to Tanner's indices and descriptive data are presented in table 4. No significant interaction effects were detected ($p > 0.05$). Significant ($p < 0.05$ to $p < 0.01$) main effects for maturity were demonstrated for $\dot{V}O_2$, O_2 pulse and a-vO_2 difference. Significant ($p < 0.05$ to $p < 0.01$) main effects for sex were demonstrated for SV, O_2 pulse, and HR.

Table 2. Exercise responses at 2.22 $m{\cdot}s^{-1}$ by sex

Variable	Boys	Girls
$\dot{V}O_2$ ($L{\cdot}min^{-1}$)	1.44 ± 0.25	1.45 ± 0.23
$\dot{V}O_2$ ($mL{\cdot}kg^{-1}{\cdot}min^{-1}$)	35 ± 3	34 ± 3
Adjusted $\dot{V}O_2$ ($L{\cdot}min^{-1}$)	1.44	1.42
Heart rate ($beats{\cdot}min^{-1}$)	163 ± 13	176 ± 12***
RER	0.88 ± 0.06	0.91 ± 0.05*
O_2 pulse ($mL{\cdot}beat^{-1}$)	8.9 ± 1.5	8.2 ± 1.3*
% peak $\dot{V}O_2$	68.7 ± 8.3	77.1 ± 9.0***
Cardiac output ($L{\cdot}min^{-1}$)	13.64 ± 2.02	13.37 ± 1.86
Adjusted cardiac output ($L{\cdot}min^{-1}$)	13.54	13.18
Stroke volume (mL)	84.2 ± 12.9	76.2 ± 10.7***
Adjusted stroke volume (mL)	83.0	75.4***
a-vO_2 difference ($mL{\cdot}100mL^{-1}$)	10.60 ± 1.31	10.95 ± 1.82

Values are mean ± SD
Level of significance * $p < 0.05$, *** $p < 0.001$

Table 3. Boys' submaximal exercise responses

Variable	2.22 m·s^{-1}	2.50 m·s^{-1}	2.78 m·s^{-1}
$\dot{V}O_2$ (L·min^{-1})	1.39 ± 0.24	1.54 ± 0.23	1.67 ± 0.26***
Heart rate (beats·min^{-1})	158 ± 15	169 ± 14	177 ± 13***
RER	0.89 ± 0.06	0.91 ± 0.05	0.92 ± 0.04***
O_2 pulse (mL·beat^{-1})	8.8 ± 1.4	9.1 ± 1.3	9.5 ± 1.4***
% peak $\dot{V}O_2$	64.6 ± 7.8	71.6 ± 7.4	77.7 ± 7.1***
Cardiac output (L·min^{-1})	13.27 ± 1.89	13.98 ± 2.25	14.72 ± 2.14***
Stroke volume (mL)	84.2 ± 11.9	82.7 ± 12.1	83.3 ± 12.2
a-vO_2 difference (mL·100mL^{-1})	10.50 ± 1.07	11.08 ± 1.21	11.37 ± 0.88**

Values are mean ± SD
Level of significance ** $p < 0.01$, *** $p < 0.001$

Discussion

Running at 2.22 m·s^{-1} the $\dot{V}O_2$, Q and a-vO_2 difference of boys and girls were not significantly different. However, the girls supported their Q with a higher heart rate and lower SV. The significant difference in SV persisted even with body size controlled for. It should, however, be noted that although there was no difference in $\dot{V}O_2$ the girls were working at a significantly higher % peak $\dot{V}O_2$. These findings are consistent with the literature[4,5,10].

The influence of maturation on $\dot{V}O_2$ and a-vO_2 difference but not on Q may be a reflection of a higher concentration of haemoglobin in the blood[11] but this clearly warrants further investigation.

Increases in exercise intensity were supported in the boys with significant increases in all cardiopulmonary variables except SV. Stroke volume appears to have reached a plateau at 2.22 m·s^{-1} and subsequent exercise demands were met with increases in HR and a-vO_2 difference. This is in accord with previous studies[4,5] and indicates that SV levels off before 65% of peak $\dot{V}O_2$ is achieved. It is noteworthy that, despite the apparent plateau in SV, O_2 pulse continued to rise with increasing exercise intensity. This brings into question the use of O_2 pulse as a surrogate for SV during moderate to vigorous exercise.

In summary, although during submaximal exercise the boys and girls in this study demonstrated similar Q and $\dot{V}O_2$ the girls supported the Q with a higher HR and lower SV than the boys. The boys' higher SV was independent of body size. In boys, at exercise intensities in the range 65-80% peak $\dot{V}O_2$ increases in Q are supported exclusively by increases in HR. The maturational effect on boys' $\dot{V}O_2$ appears to be due to increases in a-vO_2 difference rather than Q.

Table 4. Exercise responses at 2.22 m·s^{-1} by maturity

Maturity Group	I	II	III	IV
Boys	(n=12)	(n=22)	(n=13)	(n=6)
$\dot{V}O_2$ (L·min^{-1})**	1.36 ± 0.23	1.33 ± 0.18	1.61 ± 0.27	1.57 ± 0.19
Adjusted $\dot{V}O_2$ (L·min^{-1})	1.44	1.44	1.39	1.42
HR (beats·min^{-1})	165 ± 13	161 ± 13	167 ± 18	162 ± 10
$\dot{Q}$ (L·min^{-1})	13.45 ± 1.84	12.85 ± 1.38	14.17 ± 2.05	14.22 ± 2.14
Adjusted Q (L·min^{-1})	14.20	14.03	13.17	12.94
SV (mL)	80.8 ± 9.6	80.7 ± 10.3	85.0 ± 11.3	88.5 ± 16.2
Adjusted SV (mL)	84.6	77.6	82.1	72.3
O_2 pulse (mL·beat^{-1}) **	8.20 ± 1.09	8.33 ± 1.22	9.71 ± 1.45	9.72 ± 1.40
a-vO_2 diff (mL·100mL^{-1})*	10.1 ± 1.2	10.4 ± 1.4	11.4 ± 0.8	11.2 ± 1.0
Girls	(n=9)	(n=14)	(n=15)	(n=6)
$\dot{V}O_2$ (L·min^{-1})*	1.27 ± 0.16	1.44 ± 0.26	1.40 ± 0.16	1.63 ± 0.19
Adjusted $\dot{V}O_2$ (L·min^{-1})	1.47	1.41	1.44	1.45
HR (beats·min^{-1})	179 ± 11	181 ± 10	175 ± 12	167 ± 12
Q (L·min^{-1})	13.01 ± 1.47	12.99 ± 2.02	13.43 ± 1.39	13.88 ± 1.52
Adjusted Q (L·min^{-1})	13.28	13.44	13.18	12.95
SV (mL)	72.3 ± 8.8	71.9 ± 10.3	76.5 ± 8.0	83.8 ± 8.4
Adjusted SV (mL)	79.2	76.5	78.0	78.0
O_2 pulse (mL·beat^{-1})**	7.11 ± 0.88	7.97 ± 1.28	8.03 ± 0.89	9.76 ± 0.99
a-vO_2 diff (mL·100mL^{-1})*	9.8 ± 0.4	11.1 ± 1.5	10.5 ± 1.2	11.7 ± 0.5

Values are mean ± SD
Level of significance * $p < 0.05$, ** $p < 0.01$

Acknowledgements

We gratefully acknowledge the technical assistance of Jenny Frost, Alison Husband, Teresa Smith and Sue Vooght. The work was supported by the British Heart Foundation and the Healthy Heart Research Trust.

References

1. Driscoll, D., Staats, B.A. and Beck, K.C. (1989) Measurement of cardiac output in children during exercise: a review. *Pediatric Exercise Science*, Vol. 1, pp.102-15.
2. Sady, S.P., Freedson, P.S. and Gilliam, T.B. (1981) Calculation of submaximal and maximal cardiac output in children using the CO_2 rebreathing technique. *Journal of Sports Medicine*, Vol. 21, pp. 245-52.

3. Locke, J.E., Einzig, S. and Moller, J.H. (1978) Hemodynamic response to exercise in normal children. *American Journal of Cardiology*, Vol. 41, pp.1278-85.
4. Rowland, T.W. (1996) *Developmental Exercise Physiology*, Human Kinetics, Champaign, Il.
5. Armstrong, N. and Welsman, J.R. (1997) *Young People and Physical Activity*, Oxford University Press, Oxford.
6. Eriksson, B.O., Grimby, G. and Saltin, B. (1971) Cardiac output and arterial blood gases during exercise in pubertal boys. *Journal of Applied Physiology*, Vol. 32, pp. 348-52.
7. Åstrand, P.O. (1976) The child in sport and physical activity-physiology, in *Child in Sport and Physical Activity*, (eds. J.G. Albinson and G.M. Andrew), University Park Press, Baltimore, pp.19-33.
8. Armstrong, N., Kirby, B.J., McManus, A.M. and Welsman, J.R. (1995) Aerobic fitness of pre-pubescent children. *Annals of Human Biology*, Vol. 22, pp. 427-41.
9. Tanner, J.M. (1962) *Growth at Adolescence (2nd edition)*, Blackwell Scientific Publications, Oxford.
10. Shephard, R.J., Allen, C., Bar-Or, O., Davies, C.T.M., Degre, S., Hedman, R., Ishii, K., Kaneko, M., LaCour, J.R., diPrampero, P.E. and Seliger, V. (1969) The working capacity of Toronto schoolchildren. *Canadian Medical Association Journal*, Vol. 100, pp. 560-6.
11. Armstrong, N., Williams, J., Balding, J., Gentle, P. and Kirby, B.J. (1991) The peak oxygen uptake of British children with reference to age, sex and sexual maturity. *European Journal of Applied Physiology*, Vol. 62, pp. 369-75.

CARDIAC REHABILITATION IN CHILDREN. AN INTERDISCIPLINARY APPROACH

Cardiac rehabilitation

A. CALZOLARI
Sport Medicine Department, Ospedale Pediatrico Bambino Gesù, Rome, Italy
G. BIONDI
Psychosocial Department, Ospedale Pediatrico Bambino Gesù, Rome, Italy

Keywords: Cardiac rehabilitation, interdisciplinary approach, psychosocial and physiological aspects

Introduction

Since the beginning of the modern era of surgery for children with congenital heart disease, many patients have had operative procedures which while greatly improving their overall status, have left them with residual impairments in global function. This group of children in many ways parallels those adults who have had surgery for coronary artery disease. These adults have been found to have improved physical performance and increased longevity if they participate in a programme of cardiac rehabilitation. The extension of this type of rehabilitative therapy to children who have had cardiac surgery that has left them with impaired exercise tolerance has been a logical and beneficial progression. This paper reviews the interdisciplinary approach to this type of child followed in our centre as well as results from other centres and raises several points for future investigation.

Cardiac rehabilitation for children has been defined as the supervised process of progressive exercise training to improve aerobic fitness in patients with congenital heart disease. While this definition is correct, it is also incomplete because even when a patient's aerobic fitness needs no improvement, it may nonetheless be important to try to increase their physical activity and movement. Hence our programme has always recognised the need to develop along with the concept of training that of improving mobility. In addition, in defining the concept of cardiac rehabilitation in children, we cannot overlook the importance of improving these patients' quality of life by instilling in them a sense of enjoyment of physical activity.

When discussing the selection of paediatric patients who should receive cardiac rehabilitation, all investigators in the field have unanimously agreed that these programmes should be primarily for children who have been operated upon for

Children and Exercise XIX. Edited by Neil Armstrong, Brian Kirby and Joanne Welsman.
Published in 1997 by E & FN Spon, 2–6 Boundary Row, London, SE1 8HN.
ISBN 0 419 22100 X.

complex congenital heart disease and who have severe residual cardiac defects. Even the most expert heart surgeon cannot restore completely the anatomy of the heart to normal in these children. One must understand that they have indeed been "treated", but they have not been "cured". For example, infants born with the transposition of the great arteries and who have had an atrial switch operation may no longer be cyanotic but it is their anatomic right ventricles which must do the systemic work usually done by the better configured left ventricle. Children with a single functioning ventricle who have had a Fontan operation to divide their circulation may have a circulation in series but there is no ventricle to pump blood into the pulmonary circulation. Other children with tetralogy of Fallot, whose repair included a significant reconstruction of the right ventricular outflow tract always are left with residual impairment of their right ventricular function. Still more lesions may leave impairment in ventilation which may reduce oxygen consumption and others may produce reduced cardiac output or exercise intolerance from impairment in ventricular function. Reduced exercise tolerance therefore has a number of possible causes: reduced chronotropic response; poor fitness induced by a sedentary lifestyle due to the severity of the cardiac defect; reduced muscle mass; reduced left ventricular function; and respiratory insufficiency.

Cardiac rehabilitation has even stronger indications when the significant clinical deficit coexists with psychological problems. These psychological problems may have various causes, including overprotective parents who refuse to allow or are afraid of allowing their children to participate in physical activity, or from the child's own difficulty in adapting to daily life with healthy children in their age group. It is for these patients with multiple problems that rehabilitation professionals dedicate their efforts, endeavouring to improve the children's physical activity efficiency, their aerobic capacity and their quality of life.

As well as striving to improve exercise efficiency, aerobic capacity and quality of life, cardiac rehabilitation programmes aim at reducing the incidence of sudden death. Although adult rehabilitation programmes have been proven to reduce the risks of sudden death after myocardial infarction, it has yet to be proven that paediatric cardiac rehabilitation programmes influence the risk of sudden death in children with congenital heart disease. Cardiac rehabilitation by simulating the rigours of training in a protected environment should also establish whether young patients can take part safely and effectively in athletics. This is an extremely important question in Italy from a medical-legal point of view. In the long term, it should also help children with congenital heart disease to develop the various adaptive mechanisms that will enable them to lead a normal and fulfilling life. Although some may debate this wider concept, most investigators in the field believe that a rehabilitation programme can teach these children how to use their bodies more appropriately and advantageously. We believe that this implies using a learned adaptive mechanism.

The design of a paediatric rehabilitation programme

The consensus of investigators is that cardiac rehabilitation programmes must take place in protected environments, such as a hospital setting or in a specially equipped gymnasium. Only in special circumstances when patients live a long way from the hospital or have family problems that preclude coming to the hospital can training be performed at home. Although home therapy will often solve psychosocial problems, the work intensity must be lower to assure safety and thus such a programme cannot be expected to improve physical fitness.

Whereas psychological intervention including periodic follow-up visits can be arranged within an ordinary outpatient clinic setting, regular supervised physical activity requires specialised facilities. This need for a special facility within the hospital setting has certainly been a major drawback in putting paediatric cardiac rehabilitation programmes into practice in many centres.

In selecting patients for participation in a paediatric cardiac rehabilitation programme, we use the following criteria: time since surgery longer than 6 mo, no severe motor deficits; no severe cardiac arrhythmias; and no exercise-induced symptoms at mild exercise levels. Before starting the rehabilitation programme, all patients should undergo the following tests: clinical assessment with measurement of arterial blood pressure; a 12-lead resting electrocardiogram; maximal cycle ergometer or treadmill exercise testing with determination of the duration of testing, maximum heart rate, maximum systolic blood pressure, heart rate and oxygen consumption at rest and at peak exercise, arterial oxygen saturation, heart rhythm for the presence of arrhythmias; lung function testing; two-dimensional and Doppler echocardiogram; and a dynamic 24-h electrocardiograph recording. These assessments give the physician an accurate view of the individual subject's cardiorespiratory physiopathology. These tests are also used to determine the proper work load to use during the rehabilitation sessions.

Our rehabilitation sessions take place in a gymnasium within the hospital. Three sessions are held per week. Sessions are held in the afternoon after school and they last from 45 min to 1 h. The total programme lasts at least 3 mo. Each session is comprised of four phases: warm up; stretching, submaximal aerobic activity and "cool down". The time dedicated to submaximal aerobic activity increases from 15 min to 30 min as the programme advances and the child adapts to the work load. A heart-rate recorder (Sport-Tester 3000) attached to the body allows each patient's physical activity to be gradually increased from 60 to 70-80% of the maximum heart rate attained during the pre-participation exercise test. Staffing needs include a physician, a physical education instructor and a nurse. The type of patient being treated and the potential for problems makes it important to have an emergency kit available on site including oxygen, resuscitation drugs and a defibrillator.

When the programme ends after 3 mo, all patients undergo repeat testing to learn which of the areas that determine their functional capacity have improved. Recommendations for future physical activities are made to the patients and their families to assure that the gains achieved are not lost by a return to inactivity.

Psychosocial aspects

Cardiac rehabilitation must be planned as a multidisciplinary intervention. By working together as a team, the various specialists can best achieve their aim of providing their young patients with the maximal benefit. To ensure that the exercise sessions produce effective results, specialised paediatric physical education instructors who are used to motivating children to exercise must be used to lead the training sessions. Equally important is the collaboration provided by a team of psychologists.

If a psychology team succeeds in fitting their activities in with the work of the cardiologist and the instructor, this interaction not only benefits the children by providing a better insight into his or her motivation, but it also helps all concerned to better study the patient, to ensure that the children undertake their physical activity in safety, and thus aid them to integrate into the ordinary activities of childhood thus enhancing their quality of life.

As many others have noted, it is difficult to quantify in a scientific manner the effectiveness of psychosocial intervention. Whereas cardiorespiratory functional assessment yields objective data for assessing the results of physical training programmes, no similar precise indices are available for quantifying the results of psychosocial intervention. Psychosocial intervention is nonetheless of key importance because it provides the physicians with information about the patients that they would otherwise not acquire. This information can be used to tailor the instructional techniques used to motivate the child to achieve better physical performance and to increase their enjoyment of physical activity.

In the development of children with a chronic illness such as a complex heart condition that has been treated but not cured, psychosocial support along with the rehabilitation programme followed later by regular physical activities can help to improve the quality of life thus ensuring a better psychosocial outcome.

As part of their psychological assessment, our patients perform the Machover draw-a-person test, the Corman family drawing test, and the "Person in the Rain" drawing test. Their parents are also asked to answer a series of questions about the family sociocultural level, the child's physical activity and the quality of diagnosis communication.

The psychologist's participation studies may bring to the fore various shortcomings in a rehabilitation programme. Among the most important areas observed is the working relationship among the various staff members. If the staff fail to exchange their ideas about the individual patient frequently enough, optimal attention to important aspects of the child's development may be overlooked. This lack of internal cooperation may result in the interventions achieving less than satisfactory results. Other issues to emerge during team meetings may include uncovering practical difficulties owing to lack of suitable facilities, problems of organisation and questions concerning the proper approach to medico-legal problems that may arise. This cooperation may also bring to light specific information about the problems that parents, physicians and other staff have to cope with outside the hospital.

Psychological results

In a group of 14 patients, we observed that a programme of cardiac rehabilitation including psychosocial intervention achieved many worthwhile changes. It increased the children's trust in their own abilities in general and especially their ability to make plans. It improved their understanding of their own bodies. The programme made them less dependent upon their parents and it increased communication within the family.

The drawing tests in the 14 patients revealed major psychological problems, the most frequent being regression, anxiety and aggressive behaviour. In contrast, the drawing tests failed to detect a sense of inner security in the children.

Our net impression is that these psychosocial findings do not quantify a phenomenon but they do point out that problems exist and need to be dealt with to permit normal development. The findings also provide information that should cause the children's parents to reflect on their own attitudes toward their children with heart disease. Many parents have an overprotective, confused, unduly strict and poorly stimulating attitude towards their children. Only by involving the parents in the programme and having them collaborate fully can we hope to improve a child's performance at school and indeed during life. Fully committed parents are far more likely to allow their children to join in physical activities out of school. They are also more likely to agree to the type of activity best suited to the child's capabilities as found during physical training.

We must remember that the determinants of health belong in a general framework encompassing socio-economic, cultural and environmental conditions, the conditions of life and of work, the influences of the society and the community and the individual's lifestyle. These factors are linked to age, sex and obviously to upbringing. A proper understanding of all of these determinants can only help to produce adults more able to cope with their chronic problems.

Physiological results

Galioto and coworkers in the United States have published the results of various studies concerning hospital based paediatric cardiac rehabilitation. They described an average exercise-induced increase in oxygen uptake from 37.43 $mL \cdot kg^{-1} \cdot min^{-1}$ to 45.29 $mL \cdot kg^{-1} \cdot min^{-1}$ at peak exercise, a 21% improvement ($p < 0.001$) with a concomitant increase in maximal systolic arterial blood pressure and in the duration of exercise testing. In another study, Galioto has reported an increase in cardiac output at rest and at peak exercise following a programme of cardiac rehabilitation by using the rebreathing method and a mixture of acetylene-helium. Cardiac output values at rest were 2.9 $L \cdot min^{-1} \cdot m^{-2}$ before rehabilitation and increased to 3.1 $L \cdot min^{-1} \cdot m^{-2}$ after training ($p < 0.05$). Maximal cardiac output was 4.9 $L \cdot min^{-1} \cdot m^{-2}$ at the beginning of the programme and 6.05 $L \cdot min^{-1} \cdot m^{-2}$ at the end ($p < 0.05$). In addition to these results, their cardiac rehabilitation programme significantly increased the duration of the post training exercise test and maximal systolic arterial blood pressure.

Our experience agrees with that of Galioto. In particular, when we had every patient work on the treadmill at sub-maximal exercise by regulating the treadmill speed to achieve 70% of the maximal heart rate recorded during exercise testing, 90% of the patients increased the distance run in 6 min from 593 ± 113 m before the programme to 648 ± 129 m afterwards ($p < 0.002$).

Questionnaire

To determine the number and the activities of world wide centres offering regular paediatric cardiac rehabilitation programmes, we sent questionnaires to 110 centres. Eighty-six centres replied, but 31 in Europe and 37 in the USA, Canada, Guatemala and Hong Kong replied that they had no ongoing programmes. Of the European centres that stated that they offered programmes, only four centres seemed to hold them regularly. What struck us most in reading the replies was that there were similar reasons given for the difficulty in setting up these programmes: first the distance from the hospital, then traffic, and finally poor compliance by patients and their parents.

We have recently completed a project designed to assess the number of Italian rehabilitation centres offering paediatric cardiac rehabilitation and to find out whether it was perceived that the need for paediatric cardiac rehabilitation has reached the proportions of a social problem. The study involved 22 cardiology and paediatric cardiac surgery centres, the Italian Society of Cardiology, and the Italian Group of Functional Evaluation and Cardiac Rehabilitation. The results show that Italy has a steadily growing population of patients who have congenital cardiac disease, about 3000 every year. Yet even though the majority of persons interviewed consider the matter important, Italy currently has only two centres suitable for paediatric cardiac rehabilitation. Both of these centres treat only a very small number of patients.

Conclusions

We believe that emphasising the results of physical training alone as a measure of the success of a paediatric cardiac rehabilitation is a mistake. An effective programme of physical activity should undoubtedly improve a patient's cardiorespiratory response. Yet, despite its importance, this physiological achievement should not be considered in isolation. As we have underscored here, the purpose of cardiac rehabilitation in children is to help individuals in whom corrective cardiac surgery has left haemodynamic sequelae to integrate - as fully as possible and with minor risk of physical injuries - into the ordinary everyday life led by healthy children of their age.

A programme of this kind demands the cooperation of the rehabilitation team (physicians, psychologists, physical education instructors, physiotherapists and nurses), parents, families and school authorities. If cardiac rehabilitation programmes are to have a useful place in helping heart disease patients to lead a near normal life, then the programmes must conduct regular clinical follow-up observations that will allow the physicians to monitor the long term results that such a programme produces. Referring specifically to Italy, in our view, exercise centres need to be opened in the suburbs so that more of the entire population has an opportunity to benefit from these facilities.

In addition, case numbers need to be increased. This would increase the information feedback needed to solve unanswered problems about long term results of cardiac surgery and to reach more definitive conclusions. Organisational difficulties seem uppermost, not to mention the economic stresses for both the hospital and the parents. But the patients' enthusiasm, their manifest enjoyment of the exercise, and their parents' willingness to let their children join in this experience encourage us to continue our research in this field. We say this not because we merely seek to obtain valid scientific results but because we want to help these patients have a better future.

Acknowledgements

We wish to recognise the efforts of our colleagues in the preparation of the manuscript. We are especially indebted to Dr. Ugo Giordano, Dr. Salvatore Giannico, Dr. Enrica Pastore, Dr. Attilio Turchetta and Mrs Nadia Ciciani for their work in the establishment and conduct of the Paediatric Cardiac Rehabilitation Programme at Ospedale Paediatrico Bambino Gesù.

We wish to thank our master and friend FM Galioto MD, who helped us to make cardiac rehabilitation known in Italy.

References

1. Balfour, I.C., Drimmer, A.M., Nouri, S., Pennington, D.G., Hemkens, C.L. and Harvey, L.L. (1991) Pediatric cardiac rehabilitation. *American Journal of Diseases of Children,* Vol. 145, pp. 627-30.
2. Bar-Or, O. (1983) *Pediatric Sports Medicine for the Practitioner,* Springer-Verlag, New-York, pp. 1-66.
3. Barber, G., Danielson, G., Puga, F., Heise, C. and Driscoll, D. (1986) Pulmonary atresia with ventricular septal defect: preoperative and postoperative responses to exercise. *Journal of the American College of Cardiology,* Vol. 7, pp. 630-8.
4. Bradley, L.M., Galioto, F.M., Vaccaro, P., Hansen, D.A., Vaccaro, J. (1985) Effect of intense aerobic training on exercise performance in children after surgical repair of tetralogy of Fallot or complete transposition of the great arteries. *American Journal of Cardiology,* Vol. 56, pp. 816-8.
5. Buckenmeyer, P.J., Vaccaro, P., Vaccaro, J. and Galioto, F.M. (1986) Effect of a pediatric cardiac rehabilitation programme on isokinetic strength and power measures in children. *Journal of Cardiopulmonary Rehabilitation,* Vol. 6, p. 437.
6. Calzolari, A., Turchetta, A., Biondi, G., Drago, F., De Ranieri, C., Gagliardi, G., Giambini, I., Giannico, S., Kofler, A.M., Perrotta, F., Santilli, A., Vezzoli, P., Ragonese, P. and Marcelletti, C. (1990) Rehabilitation of children after total correction of tetralogy of Fallot. *International Journal of Cardiology,* Vol. 28, pp. 151-8.
7. Calzolari, A., Drago, F., Turchetta, A. and Marcelletti, C. (1991) *Rehabilitation of Children after Cardiac Surgery*, Tipografia Vaticana.
8. Calzolari, A., Drago, F., Gagliardi, G., Giambini, I., Giannico, S., Santilli, A., Turchetta, A., Ragonese, P. and Marcelletti, C. (1989) I protocolli di riabilitazione in bambini operati di cardiopatia congenita. *Cardiologia,* Vol. 34, pp. 587-92.

9. Calzolari, A., Drago, F., Pastore, E., Santilli, A., Turchetta, A. and Marcelletti, C. (1992) Functional evaluation and rehabilitation in children after cardiac surgery. *International Journal of Sport Cardiology,* Vol. 1, pp. 125-33.
10. Donovan, E.F., Mathews, R.A., Nixon, P.A., Stephenson, R.J., Robertson, R.J., Dean, F., Fricker, F.J., Beerman, L.B. and Fischer, D.R. (1983) An exercise programme for paediatric patients with congenital heart disease: psychosocial aspects. *Journal of Cardiopulmonary Rehabilitation,* Vol. 3, pp. 476-80.
11. Driscoll, D.J. (1990) Exercise rehabilitation programmes for children with congenital heart disease: a note of caution. *Pediatric Exercise Science*, Vol. 2, pp. 191-6.
12. Driscoll, D., Danielson, G., Puga, F., Schaff, H., Heise, C. and Statts, B. (1986) Exercise tolerance and cardiorespiratory response to exercise after the Fontan operation for tricuspid atresia or functional single ventricle. *Journal of the American College of Cardiology,* Vol. 5, pp. 1087-94.
13. Galioto, F.M. (1990) Exercise rehabilitation programmes for children with congenital heart disease: a note of enthusiasm. *Pediatric Exercise Science*, Vol. 2, pp. 197-200.
14. Galioto, F.M. (1990) Cardiac rehabilitation for children, in *The Science and Practice of Paediatric Cardiology*, (eds. A. Garson, W. Bricker and R. McNamara), Lea & Febiger, Philadelphia.
15. Galioto, F.M. and Tomassoni, T.L. (1992) Cardiac rehabilitation for children with heart disease. *Medicine, Exercise, Nutrition and Health,* Vol. 1, pp. 272-80.
16. Galioto, F.M. and Tomassoni, T.L. (1993) Exercise rehabilitation in congenital cardiac disease. *Programs in Pediatric Cardiology,* Vol. 2, pp. 50-4.
17. Goldberg, B., Fripp, R.R., Lister, G., Loke, J., Nicholas, J.A. and Talner, N.S. (1981) Effect of physical training on exercise performance of children following surgical repair of congenital heart disease. *Pediatrics,* Vol. 68, pp. 691-9.
18. Koch, B.M., Galioto, F.M., Vaccaro, P., Vaccaro, J. and Buckenmeyer, P.J. (1988) Flexibility and strength measures in children participating in a cardiac rehabilitation programme. *Physical and Sport Medicine,* Vol. 16, pp.139-47.
19. Longmuir, P.E., Turner, J.A., Rowe, R.D. and Olley, P.M. (1985) Postoperative exercise rehabilitation benefits children with congenital heart disease. *Clinical Investigators in Medicine,* Vol. 8, pp. 232-8.
20. Mathews, R.A., Nixon, P.A., Stephenson, R.J., Robertson, R.J., Donovan, E.F., Dean, F., Fricker, F.J., Beerman, L.B. and Fischer, D.R. (1983) An exercise programme for paediatric patients with congenital heart disease: organizational and physiologic aspects. *Journal of Cardiac Rehabilitation,* Vol. 3, pp. 467-75.
21. Mocellin, R., Bastanier, C., Hofacker, W. and Buhlmeyer, K. (1976) Exercise performance in children and adolescents after surgical repair of tetralogy of Fallot. *European Journal of Cardiology,* Vol. 4, pp. 367-74.
22. Montella, S., Massari, D., Pini, A. and Pozzoli, G. (1995) Cardiac rehabilitation in the paediatric age: state of the art and perspectives. *Giorniale Italiano di Cardiologia,* Vol. 25, pp. 457-62.

23. Perrotta, F., Calzolari, A., Drago, F., Giannico, S., Kofler, A.M., Ragonese, P., Santilli, A., Turchetta, A., Vezzoli, P. and Marcelletti, C. (1991) Esperienze di un protocollo di riabilitazione in bambini operati di cardiopatia congenita: aspetti organizzativi, riflessioni, problematiche. *Giorniale di Riabilitazione*, Vol. 2, pp. 131-4.
24. Pernot, C., Xenard, J. and Goeplert, P.C. (1974) Readaptation de l'enfant cardiaque. Adaptation à l'effort. *Coeur*, Vol. 5, p. 35.
25. Ruttenberg, H.D., Adams, T.D., Orsmond, G.S., Conlee, R.K., Fisher, A.G. (1983) Effects of exercise training on aerobic fitness in children after open heart surgery. *Pediatric Cardiology*, Vol. 4, pp. 19-24.
26. Ruttenberg, H.D., Moller, J.H., Strong, W.B., Fisher, A.G. and Adams, T.D. (1984) Recommended guidelines for graded exercise testing and exercise prescription for children with heart disease. *Journal of Cardiopulmonary Rehabilitation*, Vol. 4, pp.10-6.
27. Tomassoni, T.L., Galioto, F.M., Vaccaro, P. and Vaccaro, J. (1990) Effect of exercise training on exercise tolerance and cardiac output in children after repair of congenital heart disease. *Sports Training, Medicine and Rehabilitation*, Vol. 2, pp. 57-62.
28. Utens, E.M., Verhulst, F.C., Meijboom, F.J., Duivenvoorden, H.J., Erdman, R.A., Bos, E., Roelandt, J.T. and Hess, J. (1993) Behavioural and emotional problems in children and adolescents with congenital heart disease. *Psychological Medicine*, Vol. 23, pp. 415-24.
29. Utens, E.M., Verhulst, F.C., Erdman, R.A., Meijboom, F.J., Duivenvoorden, H.J., Bos, E., Roelandt, J.T. and Hess, J. (1994) Psychosocial functioning of young adults after surgical correction for congenital heart disease in childhood: a follow-up study. *Journal of Psychosomatic Research*, Vol. 38, pp. 745-58.
30. Vaccaro, P., Galioto, F.M., Bradley, L.M. and Vaccaro, J. (1987) Effect of physical training on exercise tolerance of children following surgical repair of d-transposition of the great arteries. *Journal of Sports Medicine and Physical Fitness*, Vol. 27, pp. 443-8.
31. Washington, R.L. (1992) Cardiac rehabilitation programmes in children. *Sports Medicine*, Vol. 14, pp. 164-70.
32. Wessel, H.U., Cunningham, W.J., Paul, M.H., Bastanier, C.K., Muster, A.J. and Idriss, F.S. (1980) Exercise performance in tetralogy of Fallot after intracardiac repair. *Journal of Thoracic and Cardiovascular Surgery*, Vol. 80, pp. 582-93.

EXERCISE TESTING AND 24h ABPM IN CHILDREN AFTER COARCTATION REPAIR

Blood pressure and aortic coarctation.

E. PASTORE, U. GIORDANO, A. TURCHETTA and A. CALZOLARI
Sport Medicine Department, Bambino Gesu' Children's Hospital, Rome, Italy
S. GIANNICO and P. RAGONESE
Pediatric Cardiology Department, Bambino Gesu' Children's Hospital, Rome, Italy
Keywords: Ambulatory blood pressure, aortic coarctation, exercise blood pressure, hypertension

Introduction

Despite successful surgical repair of coarctation of the aorta (CoA), resting hypertension and exercise-induced hypertension are common complications[1,2,3].

To evaluate blood pressure in these patients it is useful to perform ambulatory blood pressure monitoring (ABPM) in addition to exercise testing (ET)[4]. This permits blood pressure to be monitored continuously over 24 h, thus providing a more detailed profile of changes during the day and night. Appropriate therapy can then be determined if necessary, in terms of dosage and frequency of hypertension medication[5,6].

The purpose of this study was to investigate the behaviour of blood pressure and the correlation between the response of blood pressure to exercise and 24h ABPM in children after CoA repair.

Subjects

We studied 27 patients (Pt) after CoA repair, 9 female, 18 male, whose mean ± SD age was 9.9 ± 3.2 y, (range 4-18 y). Eighteen had subclavian flap, six had patch angioplasty and three had end-to-end anastomosis. Twelve patients had the surgical repair before the first year of life, five at 1 y, four at 4 y, five at 7 y and one at 14 y. Mean follow-up was 68 ± 32 mo. No patient was on antihypertensive treatment.

The control group consisted of 27 healthy children (C) matched for age and gender.

Children and Exercise XIX. Edited by Neil Armstrong, Brian Kirby and Joanne Welsman.
Published in 1997 by E & FN Spon, 2–6 Boundary Row, London, SE1 8HN.
ISBN 0 419 22100 X.

Methods

Clinical evaluation was performed in the two groups, before exercise with the measurement of systolic and diastolic blood pressure at rest (SBPr and DBPr); cuff size and reference values were consistent with Task Force criteria[7]. A 12-lead electrocardiogram was recorded at rest.

All subjects carried out an exercise test on a treadmill according to the Bruce protocol, in which the speed and slope of the treadmill were increased every 3 min until exhaustion. A 12-lead electrocardiogram (ECG) and heart rate were obtained each minute during the exercise test. At 1.5 min and at the end of each stage the SBP was measured with a Tycos aneroid sphygmomanometer.

Comparisons have been made between the patients and controls for: time of exercise (TE) in min, maximal heart rate (HR) in beats$\cdot$min^{-1} and maximal SBP (SBP) in mmHg. Only in the Pt have we measured the gradient between arm and leg both before and after exercise (ΔBPr\ΔBPm).

In the patients 24h ABPM was performed using an Oxford-Medilog ABP recorder. Measurements were taken at 15 min intervals throughout the day (0700 to 2300) and every 60 min at night (2300 to 0700). The following parameters were recorded, mean 24h SBP and DBP, mean daytime SBP and DBP, mean night time SBP and DBP. The patients were requested to compile a diary of their activities during monitoring, to better differentiate physical and sedentary activities.

Any readings that met the following criteria were discarded: SBP <70 mmHg; DBP <45 mmHg; pulse pressure (i.e. systolic-diastolic pressure) ≤20 mmHg. To define ABPM data as normal (<90th centile), high normal (90th - 95th centile) or hypertensive (>95th centile), we used data obtained from previous studies[8].

We also compared mean 24h SBP to maximal SBP.

Data analyses

Results are presented as means ± SD. Unpaired Student's t tests were used to compare patients and controls. Linear regression analysis was done using correlation coefficient r for mean 24h SBP and maximal SBP. The level of statistical significance for all comparisons was set at $p < 0.05$.

Results

Clinical evaluation

Physical examination was unremarkable in all subjects, except in two patients that presented SBPr as high-normal[7]. No abnormalities were detected on the ECG.

Exercise testing

Results of exercise testing are presented in table 1.

We found in all patients a reduced working capacity, a HR lower than in the controls and maximal SBP higher than controls.

Table 1. Exercise responses in patients and control subjects

Subjects	SBPr (mmHg)	DBPr (mmHg)	TE (min)	HR (beats·min^{-1})	SBP max (mmHg)
Patients	110 ± 11	66 ± 9	10.9 ± 1.8	181 ± 17	149 ± 26
Controls	105 ± 8	64 ± 8	13.7 ± 1.8	197 ± 20	135 ± 15
p value	ns	ns	$p < 0.001$	$p < 0.01$	$p = 0.01$

Values are mean ± SD

The gradient arm/leg increased significantly pre to post exercise ($p < 0.01$).

In patients, arm/leg gradient at rest (ΔBPr) was 9 ± 6 mmHg and ΔBP post-exercise, at first minute of recovery period, (ΔBPm) was 22 ± 15 mmHg.

Ambulatory blood pressure

Results of ABPM, only in patients, are presented in table 2.

We found normal mean values of ABPM data in comparison to data obtained from a healthy children group from a previous study[8]. However seven of the 27 patients had abnormal values of mean 24h SBP: four as high normal and three as hypertensive (one of them was high normal also at rest).

The correlation between mean 24h SBP and maximal SBP was significant ($p < 0.001$) with $r = 0.6$ (fig 1).

Discussion

Systemic hypertension is unfortunately a frequent finding following surgical repair of aortic coarctation. Our results support those from previous studies, which showed an exercise-induced hypertension and a residual obstruction with a positive arm/leg blood pressure gradient[2, 3, 9]. Therefore the reduced working capacity of these patients is probably due to detraining, and/or not enough blood flow to the legs.

In addition we confirm that the mean blood pressure parameters of 24h ambulatory monitoring do not differ between patients and normal subjects[4], although we found seven patients (26%) were abnormal.

Table 2. Ambulatory blood pressure in patients

SBP 24h (mmHg)	DBP 24h (mmHg)	SBP day (mmHg)	DBP day (mmHg)	SBP night (mmHg)	DBP night (mmHg)
116 ± 15	60 ± 7	118 ± 15	62 ± 7	110 ± 20	55 ± 9

Values are means ± SD

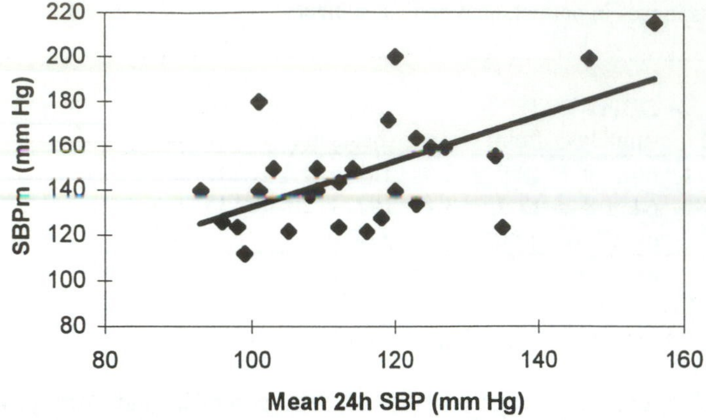

Fig. 1. Regression analysis of the patients mean 24h SBP vs maximal SBP ($y = 1.04\chi + 28.9$)

The positive correlation between the mean systolic blood pressure from ABPM and the maximal systolic blood pressure at exercise suggests that patients with a higher blood pressure response during exercise testing could have an abnormal profile during 24h blood pressure monitoring.

We find exercise testing and ABPM respectively useful, non-invasive methods in the follow-up of these patients; to predict blood pressure responses to physical activity and to detect the behaviour of blood pressure during normal life, and particularly to advise them about appropriate physical activity and possibly the need for antihypertensive therapy.

References

1. Daniels, S.R., James, F.W., Loggie, J.M.H. and Kaplan S. (1987) Correlates of resting and maximal exercise systolic blood presssure after repair of coartation of the aorta: a multivariable analysis. *American Heart Journal*, Vol. 113, pp. 349-53.
2. Free, M.D., Rocchini, A., Rosenthal, A., Nadas, A.S. and Castaneda, A.R. (1979) Exercise-induced hypertension after surgical repair of coarctation of the aorta. *American Journal of Cardiology*, Vol. 43, pp. 253-8.
3. Sigurardòttir, L.Y., Helgason, H. (1996) Exercise-induced hypertension after corrective surgery for coarcation of the aorta. *Pediatric Cardiology*, Vol. 17, pp. 301-7.
4. Parrish, M.D., Torres, E., Peshock, R. and Fixler, D.E. (1995) Ambulatory blood pressure in patients with occult recurrent coarctation of the aorta. *Pediatric Cardiology*, Vol. 16, pp. 166-71.
5. Mancia, G., Giannattasio, C. and Omboni, S. (1992) ABPM and antihypertensive treatment. *European Heart Journal*, Vol. 13 (suppl), pp. 43-7.

6. Reid, J.L., Bainbridge, A.D. and MacFayden, R.J. (1991) The contribution of ABPM to the evaluation of new antihypertensive drugs. *Journal of Hypertension*, Vol. 9 (suppl), pp. 54-6.
7. Report of the Second Task Force on Blood Pressure Control in Children. (1987) *Pediatrics*, Vol. 79, pp. 1-25.
8. Harshfield, G.A., Alpert, B.S., Pulliam, D.A., Somes, G.W. and Wilson, D.K. (1994) Ambulatory blood pressure recordings in children and adolescents. *Pediatrics*, Vol. 94, pp. 180-4.
9. Johnson, D., Bonnin, P., Perrault, H., Marchand, T., Vobecky, S.J., Fournier, A. and Davignon, A. (1995) Peripheral blood flow responses to exercise after successful correction of coarctation of the aorta. *Journal of the American College of Cardiology*, Vol. 26, pp. 1719-24.

EXERCISE HAEMODYNAMICS AND LEFT VENTRICULAR PARAMETERS IN CHILDREN

Haemodynamics and left ventricular paramaters

B. GUTIN, S. OWENS, F. TREIBER, and G. MENSAH
Georgia Prevention Institute, Medical College of Georgia, Augusta, USA

Keywords: Cardiac output, ethnicity, exercise, gender, left ventricular size and function, total peripheral resistance

Introduction

How the cardiovascular (CV) system responds to exercise provides insight into the fitness and health of the system. For example, exercise blood pressure (BP) is an independent predictor of future BP[1] and the heart rate (HR) at a standard power output is frequently used as a measure of CV fitness, either by itself or after being converted into another index, such as predicted maximal oxygen consumption[2]. It has been shown that even in the early years of life, boys have lower exercise HRs than girls, implying that boys have better CV fitness[3]. It is not clear whether this is due to the boys having greater left ventricular (LV) dimensions (i.e. wall thickness, cavity size) or a greater functional capacity of some kind. The LV mid-wall shortening fraction has been identified as a valid index of LV function[4]. Since some studies have shown black children to have greater LV mass and different haemodynamic responses to exercise than white children[5], it is possible that ethnicity may influence these relationships.

Measurement of cardiac output during exercise in children is a daunting task. Invasive techniques (e.g. direct Fick) involve a substantial subject and investigator burden, and non-invasive rebreathing methods require a good deal of cooperation from the child in carrying out the rebreathing manoeuvres. The recent development of the echo-Doppler technique allows cardiac output to be measured non-invasively during supine exercise without imposing any burden on the child, thus permitting easier exploration of cardiac dynamics. Performing the exercise in a supine position also allows the influence of weight and body fatness on the exercise responses to be minimized[6].

Children and Exercise XIX. Edited by Neil Armstrong, Brian Kirby and Joanne Welsman.
Published in 1997 by E & FN Spon, 2–6 Boundary Row, London, SE1 8HN.
ISBN 0 419 22100 X.

Thus, this study was designed to clarify the effects of gender, ethnicity, LV dimensions, and LV function on haemodynamic responses to supine exercise in children.

Subjects and methods

The subjects were 61 children, 7-13 y of age, recruited through school flyers and newspaper advertisements. A total of 26 boys and 35 girls were enrolled. Ethnicity (black/white) was determined by self-designation; there were 29 whites and 32 blacks. Children and parents gave informed consent in accordance with procedures of our Human Assurance Committee.

Body weight and height (without shoes) were measured with a Detecto scale and stadiometer. Percent bodyfat was measured with a Hologic QDR-1000 dual x-ray absorptiometer (DXA) (Waltham, MA). Whole body scan time was 10-12 min and the radiation dose was approximately 1.5 mRem, which is approximately the dose received in a trans-continental airplane flight. We have shown that DXA provides reliable and valid measures of body composition in children[7].

Echocardiographic measurements were made with a Hewlett-Packard Sonos 100 (Andover, MA). The parasternal long axis window was used for M-mode determination of end diastolic internal dimension, and posterior wall thickness. The results of five cardiac cycles were averaged. Echo-Doppler measurement of cardiac output and calculations of LV parameters were carried out as described by Feigenbaum[8]. LV mid-wall shortening fraction was calculated as described by de Simone et al.[4].

CV measurements were made at rest and during submaximal cycling at a power output of 49 W on a supine ergometer (Quinton 486T, Seattle, WA). After resting measurements, the power output was increased gradually until it reached the 49 W level and 3 min were then allowed for the child to achieve a steady state. The child then maintained that power output for approximately 5 min until the CV measurements were completed.

Resting and exercise BPs were measured with a Dinamap (model 1846 sx) automated BP monitor (Critikon, Tampa, FL) using an appropriately sized cuff on the right arm. Resting measurements were made after the child had lain quietly for 10-min. Five readings were taken at 1 min intervals, and the last four were averaged. During exercise, BPs were obtained at 1 min intervals throughout the steady state exercise period and averaged. Total peripheral resistance (TPR) was derived by dividing mean arterial BP by cardiac output.

Data analyses and results

Table 1 provides the descriptive statistics for the four gender-ethnicity subgroups and for all subjects combined. ANOVA revealed no significant age differences among groups. Age was correlated with many of the variables and it was therefore used as a covariate in ANCOVA comparisons of groups for the other variables. The boys were

Table 1. Mean values for ethnicity-gender groups

	Whites Boys (n=14)	Girls (n=15)	Blacks Boys (n-12)	Girls (n=20)	Total (n=61) Mean	SE	Significance
Age, y	11.5	10.7	11.2	10.4	10.9	0.23	ns
Height, cm	152	145	153	145	148	1.49	ns
Weight, kg	53.2	50.0	67.8	52.5	55.1	2.06	boys>girls, p = 0.020
Percent fat	31.5	37.0	35.2	37.7	35.6	1.70	ns
LVMWSF	22.2	21.2	20.6	21.3	21.4	0.27	ns
LVIDD, cm	4.66	4.27	4.62	4.40	4.47	0.05	boys>girls, p = 0.009
LVPWD, cm	0.73	0.71	0.77	0.72	0.73	0.01	ns
Rest HR, beats·min^{-1}	68	72	73	70	70	1.1	ns
Ex HR, beats·min^{-1}	111	121	113	120	117	1.4	girls>boys, p = 0.008
Rest SV, mL	82.2	72.0	83.7	72.9	76.9	2.0	boys>girls, p = 0.029
Ex SV, mL	87.6	74.8	88.4	77.1	81.2	2.2	boys>girls, p = 0.021
Rest CO, L	5.50	5.14	6.13	5.05	5.39	0.15	boys>girls, p = 0.022
Ex CO, L	9.68	9.03	9.83	9.25	9.41	0.22	ns
Rest SBP, mmHg	107	106	109	107	107	1.25	ns
Ex SBP, mmHg	136	136	137	124	132	2.34	ns
Rest DBP, mmHg	57	59	59	60	59	0.69	ns
Ex DBP, mmHg	72	73	80	73	74	1.22	ns
Rest MAP, mmHg	75	75	76	77	76	0.84	ns
Ex MAP, mmHg	94	96	101	92	95	1.57	ns
Rest TPR, mm·L^{-1}	13.9	14.7	13.1	15.7	14.5	0.39	ns
Ex TPR, mm·L^{-1}	10.0	10.9	10.9	10.2	10.5	0.33	ns

LVMWSF - LV mid-wall shortening fraction
LVIDD - LV internal diameter (diastole)
LVPWD - LV posterior wall (diastole)
Rest HR - resting heart rate
Ex HR - exercise heart rate
SV - resting stroke volume
SBP - systolic blood pressure
CO - cardiac output
MAP - mean arterial pressure
DBP - diastolic blood pressure
TPR - total peripheral resistance

significantly heavier than the girls, but the groups did not differ significantly in height or percent fat. With respect to the LV measurements, the groups did not differ significantly in mid-wall shortening fraction or posterior wall dimension, while the boys had significantly larger internal diameters.

The main effects and interactions involving exercise, gender and ethnicity for the CV measurements were assessed by repeated measures ANCOVA; the covariates were age, percent fat and the LV parameters. All of the factors were entered together. Thus, we determined the extent to which each factor explained variance in the CV parameter, after adjustment for all other factors and interactions in the model.

For HR, age was the only covariate that explained a significant proportion of the variance ($t = -2.38$, $p = 0.021$), with HR declining with older age. The t-ratio for percent fat ($t = 1.86$) approached significance ($p = 0.069$). There was a significant interaction of exercise and gender ($p = 0.001$), such that the HR of the girls increased more than the HR of the boys.

For stroke volume, significant proportions of the variance were explained by LV posterior wall dimension ($t = 4.48$, $p < 0.001$) and mid-wall shortening fraction ($t = 3.27$, $p = 0.002$), but not by age or LV internal diameter (for which $t = 1.77$, $p = 0.083$). The exercise effect was significant ($p < 0.001$) and there were no gender-ethnicity interactions.

For cardiac output, significant proportions of the variance were explained by LV posterior wall dimension ($t = 3.44$, $p = 0.001$) and mid-wall shortening fraction ($t = 2.44$, $p = 0.018$). There were no significant interactions of exercise with gender or ethnicity; only the exercise effect was significant ($p < 0.001$).

For systolic, diastolic and mean arterial BPs, the increases induced by the exercise were significant ($p < 0.001$). There were no gender-ethnicity interactions and none of the covariates explained significant proportions of the variance.

For TPR, none of the covariates explained a significant proportion of the variance. There was a significant three-way interaction of exercise, gender and ethnicity ($p = 0.008$), such that exercise caused a decline in TPR for all groups, with the black girls showing the greatest reduction and the black boys showing the smallest reduction.

Discussion

Our finding that the girls had higher HRs during submaximal exercise is consistent with other child studies showing that this gender difference shows up at an early age [e.g. 3]. Since the boys had larger LV internal diameters, this might be one factor explaining the gender difference in exercise HR.

As expected, both stroke volume and cardiac output were positively related to an index of LV size (i.e. posterior wall dimension) and contractile function (i.e. mid-wall shortening fraction). The absence of LV internal diameter in the multiple regression may be due to the fact that the equation already included LV posterior wall dimension, with which internal diameter was significantly correlated; the partial r, controlling for age, was 0.42, $p = 0.001$.

All indices of BP increased during the supine exercise, with the increase in systolic BP (25 mmHg) being greater than the increase in diastolic BP (15 mmHg); no interactions with gender or ethnicity were found. The finding that the black boys reduced their TPR least of all groups during exercise is consistent with a previous study from our institute that found black boys to have higher TPR during maximal exercise[5]. These and other findings in youths and young adults suggest that higher levels of vasoconstrictive activity in blacks is a factor responsible for their higher incidence of essential hypertension [9].

Acknowledgements

Supported by NIH (HL35073, HL49549) and the MCG Pediatrics Research Fund

References

1. Mahoney, L., Schieken, R., Clarke, W. and Lauer, R. (1988) Left ventricular mass and exercise responses predict future blood pressure. *Hypertension,* Vol.12, pp. 206-13.
2. McArdle, W., Katch, F. and Katch, V. (1991) *Exercise Physiology*, Lea and Febiger, Philadelphia, pp. 223-4.
3. Gutin, B., Basch, C., Shea, S., Contento, I., DeLozier, M., Rips, J. and Zybert, P. (1990) Blood pressure, fitness, and fatness in 5-6 year old children. *Journal of the American Medical Association*, Vol. 264, pp. 1123-7.
4. de Simone, G., Devereux, R., Koren, M., Mensah, G., Casale, P. and Laragh, J. (1996) Midwall left ventricular mechanics: an independent predictor of cardiovascular risk in arterial hypertension. *Circulation*, Vol. 93, pp. 259-65.
5. Arensman, F., Treiber, F., Gruber, M. and Strong, W. (1989) Exercise-induced differences in cardiac output, blood pressure, and systemic vascular resistance in a healthy biracial population of 10-year-old boys. *American Journal of Diseases of Children*, Vol. 143, pp. 212-6.
6. Gutin, B., Owens, S., Treiber, F., Islam, S., Karp, W. and Slavens, G. (in press) Weight-independent cardiovascular fitness and coronary risk factors. *Archives of Pediatrics and Adolescent Medicine.*
7. Gutin, B., Litaker, M., Islam, S., Manos, T., Smith, C., Treiber, F. (1996) Body composition measurement in 9-11 year old children by dual x-ray absorptiometry, skinfolds and bioimpedance analysis. *American Journal of Clinical Nutrition*, Vol. 63, pp. 287-92.
8. Feigenbaum, H. (1994) *Echocardiography* Lea and Febiger, Philadelphia, pp. 90-106.
9. Sherwood, A. and Turner, J. (1995) Hemodynamic responses during psychological stress: implications for studying disease processes. *International Journal of Behavioral Medicine*, Vol. 2, pp. 193-218.

CARDIOPULMONARY PERFORMANCE DURING EXERCISE AFTER PAEDIATRIC BONE MARROW TRANSPLANTATION

Exercise after paediatric BMT

A. N. HOGARTY, A. LEAHEY, N. BUNIN, H. ZHAO, A. CNAAN, A. CAREY, and S. M. PARIDON

Department of Pediatrics, Divisions of Cardiology, Oncology, and Biostatistics and Epidemiology, University of Pennsylvania School of Medicine, The Children's Hospital of Philadelphia, Philadelphia, USA

Keywords: Bone marrow transplantation, cardiovascular function, exercise performance, pulmonary fitness

Introduction

Bone marrow transplantation (BMT) has become an increasingly used treatment option for children and adolescents with high risk oncologic and haematologic diseases [1,2,3]. Medical regimens both before and as part of BMT, including treatments such as anthracycline administration and chest irradiation, may result in significant toxicity to the cardiovascular and pulmonary systems[4,5]. Not surprisingly, BMT has been acutely associated with significantly decreased exercise capacity[6,7,8]. To date, there have been no longitudinal studies of exercise capacity following BMT. It is unclear whether exercise responses remain abnormal for prolonged periods following BMT and what organ systems, if any, suffer long-term impairment. The purpose of this study was to evaluate serially cardiac, pulmonary and musculoskeletal function during exercise in a group of children and adolescents following BMT and assess changes in exercise performance in these organ systems.

Subjects

The study population consisted of 33 children, adolescents, and young adults. The group represented all patients followed at our institution who underwent BMT from 1988 to 1996 and had at least two post-BMT exercise tests.

Children and Exercise XIX. Edited by Neil Armstrong, Brian Kirby and Joanne Welsman.
Published in 1997 by E & FN Spon, 2–6 Boundary Row, London, SE1 8HN.
ISBN 0 419 22100 X.

Methods

Pulmonary function testing

Prior to exercise testing, subjects underwent measurement of maximal inspiratory and expiratory flow-volume loops. Testing was monitored graphically to ensure proper technique and reproducibility. Maximum voluntary ventilation (MVV) was calculated from the forced expiratory volume in one second (FEV_1) by the formula: MVV = FEV_1 x 40. Resting values were compared to healthy children and adolescents from data by Polgar, et al.[9].

Exercise testing

The patients were exercised to maximum volition using a ramp cycle protocol. Heart rate and electrocardiogram were monitored continuously throughout the study. Minute oxgyen consumption ($\dot{V}O_2$) and minute carbon dioxide production ($\dot{V}CO_2$) were monitored on a breath-by-breath basis. Ventilatory threshold (VT) was calculated by the V-slope method. Because of a high incidence of obesity in this population, $\dot{V}O_2$ was normalized to the ideal body weight for the subject's height if the actual body weight was greater than 110% of ideal weight[10]. The maximal $\dot{V}O_2$ and $\dot{V}O_2$ at VT were compared to normal data from Cooper, et al.[11] using a similar exercise protocol. Cardiac output was estimated from effective pulmonary blood flow using the helium-acetylene rebreathing method at rest and each 3 min of exercise. Cardiac output was indexed to ideal body surface area. Maximum cardiac index values were compared to data from healthy subjects by Miyamura, et al.[12]. Minute ventilation ($\dot{V}E$) was monitored continuously using a turbine flow meter or mass flow meter. Breathing reserve (BR) was calculated as BR = [1 - (MVV - max VE)/ MVV] x 100% and expressed as a percentage.

Data analyses

Means and standard deviations at baseline for pulmonary function tests and exercise test results were obtained. A linear mixed-effects model, with a linear relationship between the outcome variable and time, and a random intercept for each patient was assumed, to examine changes in exercise performance, such as MCI, $\dot{V}O_2$ max, $\dot{V}O_2$ - VT, and Max Work over time. All variables were used as percent predicted because the children are at different ages[13,14].

Results

Study population

A total of 96 exercise tests were performed on 33 patients (median: 3 tests/ patient, range 2 - 5). Demographic data from the study population are presented in tables 1A and 1B. Median time from BMT to the first exercise test was 1.6 y (range 0.33 to 9 y). Median time from BMT to the last test was 6.1 y (range 1.9 - 11.8 y).

Table 1A. Patient characteristics, reported as median and range

	Total	Male	Female
n	33	20	13
Age at BMT (y)	10.3 (2.2 - 30.7)	9.3 (2.2 - 30.7)	11.4 (2.6- 24.8)
Age at initial exercise test (y)	12.4 (6.1 - 32.7)	11.7 (6.1 - 32.7)	12.6 (7.9 - 25.7)
Time from BMT to initial test (y)	1.6 (0.3 -9.0)	1.6 (1.0 - 8.0)	2.2 (0.3 - 9.0)
Time from BMT to last test (y)	6.1 (1.9 - 11.8)	5.7 (2.0 - 10.9)	7.1 (1.9 - 11.8)

Table 1B. Diagnoses/ BMT

	Total	Male	Female
Acute Lymphocytic Leukemia	13	7	6
Acute Myelogenous Leukemia/ MDS	8	6	2
JCML; Non-Hodgkins Lymphoma	2	0	2
Neuroblastoma	8	5	3
Severe Aplastic Anemia	2	2	0
Autologous BMT	14	7	7
Allogeneic BMT	19	13	6

Pulmonary function tests

As a group the resting pulmonary mechanics at initial testing are within normal ranges with no significant change over the follow-up period. Breathing reserve was also in the normal range with no changes over the study period. This could indicate that pulmonary reserve does not limit exercise performance in these subjects.

Exercise performance

In terms of electrocardiographic findings, there were no significant episodes of arrhythmia observed during any of these exercise tests.

Four measurements of cardiovascular function are reported: maximum cardiac index (MCI), maximum $\dot{V}O_2$ ($\dot{V}O_2$ max), $\dot{V}O_2$ at ventilatory threshold ($\dot{V}O_2$ - VT), and maximum work (Max Work). Table 2 shows the mean and standard deviation values for these parameters at initial exercise test, reported as raw numbers and percent predicted. The mean values and standard deviation of the maximum heart rate (HR) and the maximum achieved respiratory exchange ratio (Max RER) are reported as well.

Table 2. Cardiac performance at initial exercise test, as mean and standard deviation

	n	Raw Values	Percent Predicted
MCI ($L \cdot min^{-1} \cdot m^{-2}$)	25	7.27 ± 1.60	62.4 ± 14.1
$\dot{V}O_2$ max ($mL \cdot kg^{-1} \cdot min^{-1}$)	32	24.7 ± 5.1	61.6 ± 14.7
$\dot{V}O_2$ - VT ($mL \cdot kg^{-1} \cdot min^{-1}$)	20	17.04 ± 4.28	74.9 ± 22.4
Max Work (W)	33	78.2 ± 47.7	63.3 ± 19.6
Maximum HR ($beats \cdot min^{-1}$)	33	181 ± 13	
Max RER	33	1.16 ± 0.16	

Values are mean ± SD

When MCI, $\dot{V}O_2$ max, $\dot{V}O_2$ - VT, and Max Work were modeled as linear functions in time, both $\dot{V}O_2$ max and Max Work showed increases over time, while MCI and $\dot{V}O_2$ - VT did not show a significant change over time within this group of patients and this duration of follow-up. In all models, percent predicted was used and not raw scores. Figs 1 and 2 show the estimated $\dot{V}O_2$ max and MCI as a function of years since BMT. $\dot{V}O_2$ max shows an increase of $4\% \cdot y^{-1}$ on average, while MCI shows no significant increase. At the end of 5 y, $\dot{V}O_2$ max is estimated to be 69.3% of predicted and Max Work is estimated to be 76.8% of predicted.

Despite improvement in some values over the course of this study, $\dot{V}O_2$ max, $\dot{V}O_2$ - VT, and maximum cardiac index all remain significantly impaired compared to values obtained from a healthy control population.

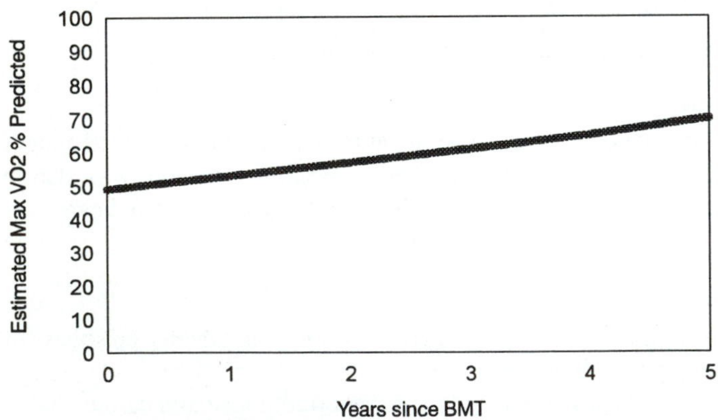

Fig. 1. $\dot{V}O_2$ max as a function of years since BMT

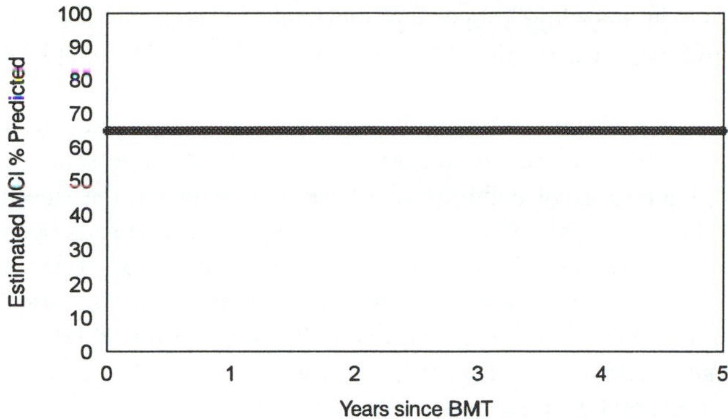

Fig. 2. MCI as a function of years since BMT

Discussion

This study is the first longitudinal assessment of exercise performance following BMT in the paediatric population. The most significant finding of this study is the failure of the maximum cardiac index to improve over the median follow-up time of 6 y after BMT. Although the acute cardiotoxic effects of anthracyclines and radiation are well known, the chronic effects in this young population remain relatively unknown. It would appear from this study that the cardiotoxic effects from BMT are both chronic and stable. There is no significant improvement or deterioration in maximum cardiac index over the study period. This would suggest that although the acute insult to the myocardium is significant, it does not result in further progressive chronic deterioration in function.

The effects of impaired myocardial function on exercise performance are significant. When compared to healthy control data, all parameters of exercise performance including maximum cardiac index, $\dot{V}O_2$ max, $\dot{V}O_2$-VT and maximal work rate are impaired. This supports the findings by Larsen, et al.[8] who examined subjects acutely after BMT and found similar exercise impairment. It would appear that decreased myocardial performance rather than other organ system abnormalities is primarily responsible for impaired exercise capacity after BMT. It should be noted that our study population included patients who were able and motivated to perform this exercise testing, and as such, may not represent an accurate spectrum of functional cardiovascular status of bone marrow transplantation survivors.

It is interesting that both $\dot{V}O_2$ max and maximum work rate improved significantly over the course of this study despite the lack of improvement in cardiovascular performance. There are several possible explanations for this finding. An increase in haemoglobin concentration may have resulted in increased oxygen delivery. This is unlikely, however, since the initial studies were on average over 1 y after BMT. The effects of BMT on haemoglobin concentration should have been therefore minimal during the study period. Both oncologic diseases as well as the BMT regimen are frequently associated with significant systemic toxicities acutely. It would be expected that these subjects would initially have significant musculoskeletal deconditioning due to both chronic inactivity and overall catabolic state. Recovery from BMT would be associated with improved nutrition and activity levels. This could presumably result in improved efficiency of oxygen extraction by the skeletal muscles. It appears likely that whatever that mechanism of the increased oxygen utilization, it represents a compensatory mechanism for an apparent inability of the heart to improve maximum cardiac output following BMT. This type of compensation by skeletal muscle has been seen in other types of chronic cardiac disease, such as adult survivors of large myocardial infarction. While it is at least somewhat reassuring that cardiac function did not deteriorate over the observation period of this study, the long-term outlook for these subjects must remain guarded. Routine, regular assessment of their cardiovascular status both at rest and exercise appears to be warranted.

References

1. Evans, A.E., August, C.S., Kamani, N., Bunin, N., Goldwein, J., Ross, A.J. and D'Angio, G.J. (1994) Bone marrow transplantation for high risk neuroblastoma at the Children's Hospital of Philadelphia: An update. *Medical and Pediatric Oncology*, Vol. 23, pp. 323-7.
2. Kamani, N., Bayever, E., August, C.S., Bunin, N. and Goldwein, J.W. (1995) Fractionated total-body irradiation preceding high-dose cytosine arabinoside as a preparative regimen for bone marrow transplantation in children with acute leukemia. *Medical and Pediatric Oncology*, Vol. 25, pp. 179-84.
3. Dinndorf, P. and Bunin, N. (1995) Bone marrow transplantation for children with acute myelogenous leukemia. *Journal of Pediatric Hematology/Oncology,* Vol. 17, pp. 211-24.
4. Lipshultz, S.E., Colan, S.D., Gelber, R.D., Perez-Atayde, A.R., Sallan, S.E. and Saunders, S.P. (1991) Late cardiac effects of doxorubicin therapy for acute lymphoblastic leukemia in childhood. *New England Journal of Medicine*, Vol. 324, pp. 808-15.
5. Jakacki, R.I., Goldwein, J.W., Larsen, R.L., Barber, G. and Silber, J.H. (1993) Cardiac dysfunction following spinal irradiation during childhood. *Journal of Clinical Oncology,* Vol. 11, pp. 1033-8.
6. Jenney, M.E.M., Faragher, E.B., Morris Jones, P.H. and Woodcock, A. (1995) Lung function and exercise capacity in survivors of childhood leukemia. *Medical and Pediatric Oncology*, Vol. 24, pp. 222-30.
7. Turner-Gomes, S.O., Lands, L.C., Halton, J., Hanning, R.M., Heigenhauser, G.J.F., Pai, M. and Barr, R. (1996) Cardiorespiratory status after treatment for acute lymphoblastic leukemia. *Medical and Pediatric Oncology*, Vol. 26, pp. 160-5.
8. Larsen, R.L., Barber, G., Heise, C.T. and August, C.S. (1992) Exercise assessment of cardiac function in children and young adults before and after bone marrow transplantation. *Pediatrics,* Vol. 89, pp. 722-9.
9. Polgar, G. and Promadhat, V. (1971) *Pulmonary Function Testing in Children: Techniques and Standards,* WB Saunders Co., Philadelphia, p. 254.

10. Hamill, P.V.V. Drizd, T.A., Johnson, C.L., Reed, R.B., Roche, A.F. and Moore, W.M. (1979) Growth charts for girls and boys, ages 2 to 18 years, Ross Growth and Development Program, *American Journal of Clinical Nutrition*, Vol. 32, pp. 607-29.
11. Cooper, D.M., Weiler-Ravell, D., Whipp, B.J. and Wasserman, K. (1984) Aerobic parameters of exercise as a function of body size during growth in children. *Journal of Applied Physiology,* Vol. 56, pp. 628-34.
12. Miyamura, M. and Honda, Y. (1973) Maximum cardiac output related to sex and age. *Japanese Journal of Physiology,* Vol. 23, pp. 645-56.
13. Diggle, P.J., Liang, K-Y. and Zeger, S.L. (1994) *Analysis of Longitudinal Data,* Oxford University Press, New York, pp. 126-30.
14. BMDP. (1991) *BMDP/ 386 User's Guide,* BMDP Statistical software, Inc., Los Angeles.

EXERCISE CAPACITY FOLLOWING SUCCESSFUL TREATMENT OF CHILDHOOD CANCER

Exercise limitations following childhood cancer

G. BARBER and C.T. HEISE
Pediatric Cardiology Program, New York University Medical Center, New York, USA
Keywords: Anthracyclines, exercise testing, late effects cardiotoxicity, oncology

Introduction

Tremendous advances have been made in the therapy of childhood cancer. It is now estimated that within the next 15 y 1 out of every 250 adults age 15 to 45 y will be a survivor of childhood cancer[1]. Therapy for most of these individuals will include the anthracycline antibiotics, a class of drugs known to have both acute and late cardiotoxicity. Previous exercise studies[2-10] have suggested that these survivors may have significant limitations of their exercise ability. However, several potential limitations occur in these earlier studies, such as small patient numbers, inclusion of patients during or shortly after completion of therapy, and inclusion of patients who received mediastinal irradiation, a confounding cardiotoxic agent. In an attempt to better assess exercise performance following cure of childhood malignancy, we evaluated patients at least 2 y following completion of therapy. All patients received anthracyclines as their only known cardiotoxic chemotherapeutic agent.

Subjects

The study population consisted of 84 cured oncology patients ("subjects") and 82 controls. Eligibility criteria for the subjects included diagnosis of cancer prior to age 18 y and treatment with anthracyclines. All subjects were a minimum of 2 y beyond completion of therapy and without evidence of residual malignancy. In order to avoid the confounding cardiotoxicity of radiotherapy, subjects who had received chest or mediastinal irradiation were excluded from this study.

Children and Exercise XIX. Edited by Neil Armstrong, Brian Kirby and Joanne Welsman.
Published in 1997 by E & FN Spon, 2–6 Boundary Row, London, SE1 8HN.
ISBN 0 419 22100 X.

Initial control data were obtained from a database of controls from prior studies. For the last 3 y, additional control data have been obtained by asking the oncology subject to bring a friend, when possible, to serve as his or her control. To be eligible, the "friend control" had to be of the same sex and close in age (within 2 y).

Methods

Treatment

Subjects had been treated with a variety of disease specific protocols. Cumulative anthracycline dosage ranged from 75 to 630 $mg \cdot m^{-2}$ (mean ± SD: 293 ± 105 $mg \cdot m^{-2}$). The subjects had completed chemotherapy between 2 and 17 y prior to the exercise evaluation (mean ± SD: 6.3 ± 3.3 y).

Controls had received no prior procedures or treatments with known cardiotoxic effects.

Evaluation

Resting spirometry was performed by all subjects and controls prior to the exercise test. Anthropometric measurements were then obtained. The subject or control was then connected to standard electrocardiographic, blood pressure, and pulse oximetry monitoring equipment. Exercise testing was performed using an electronically braked cycle ergometer. A James protocol was used for studies prior to 1990. A ramp protocol[11] was used for all subsequent studies.

Heart rate, respiratory rate, tidal volume, minute ventilation, oxygen consumption, and carbon dioxide production were measured on a breath-by-breath basis. Blood pressure, cardiac output, stroke volume, systemic vascular resistance, and lung diffusion capacity were measured at rest and every 3 min throughout exercise using an acetylene-helium-carbon monoxide rebreathing technique.

Data analyses

Chi-squared and t-tests were used for all data analyses. In order to control for possible size and sex effects, data were analyzed as percent of predicted corrected for size and sex where appropriate.

Results

There was no difference between subjects and controls with respect to age, height, weight, or body surface area. There was a sex bias ($p = 0.01$) with females comprising 51% of the subjects but only 32% of the controls.

Although subjects had not received any agents known to cause pulmonary or chest wall abnormalities, they tended to have a mildly restrictive ventilatory pattern at rest when compared to the controls. The mean FEV_1 was 91 ± 17% predicted and the mean FVC was 88 ± 17% predicted in the subjects compared to 97 ± 15% predicted

Table 1. Comparison of exercise tolerance between subjects and controls

Parameter	Subjects	Controls	Probability
Exercise time (% Predicted)	80 ± 24	104 ± 26	<0.00001
Peak Power (% Predicted)	81 ± 23	106 ± 26	<0.00001
Peak VO_2 ($mL \cdot kg^{-0.67} \cdot min^{-1}$)	85 ± 24	131 ± 33	<0.00001
Anaerobic Threshold ($mL \cdot kg^{-0.67} \cdot min^{-1}$)	53 ± 15	72 ± 17	<0.00001

Values are mean ± SD

Table 2. Comparison of exercise response between subjects and controls

Peak Exercise Parameters	Subjects	Controls	Probability
Heart Rate (% Predicted)	92 ± 7	97 ± 7	<0.0001
Systolic BP (% Predicted)	92 ± 12	97 ± 11	<0.005
Diastolic BP (% Predicted)	88 ± 14	87 ± 14	NS
Respiratory Rate (% Predicted)	88 ± 24	96 ± 20	< 0.05
Tidal Volume (% Predicted)	99 ± 27	105 ± 23	NS
VE (% Predicted)	84 ± 22	99 ± 20	< 0.00001
VE/MVV	0.54 ± 0.15	0.67 ± 0.14	< 0.00001
Respiratory Quotient	1.16 ± 0.11	1.17 ± 0.10	NS
Cardiac Index ($L \cdot min^{-1} \cdot m^{-2}$)	7.4 ± 1.7	9.2 ± 1.5	< 0.00001
SVI ($mL \cdot beat^{-1} \cdot min^{-1}$)	45 ± 11	51 + 8	< 0.0001
SVRI (Um^2)	14 ± 3	11 ± 2	< 0.00001
Lung Diffusion (% Predicted)	104 ± 19	108 ± 22	NS

Values are mean ± SD

Abbreviations:

VE Minute Ventilation

MVV Maximum Voluntary Ventilation

SVI Stroke Volume Index

SVRI Systemic Vascular Resistance Index

and 95 ± 15% predicted for FEV_1 and FVC, respectively, in the controls (both $p < 0.01$). Despite this, there were no significant differences in maximum voluntary ventilation between subjects (101 ± 26% predicted) and controls (93 ± 16% predicted).

The exercise tolerance data are summarized in table 1 and the cardiorespiratory parameters are summarized in table 2. Both subjects and controls performed maximum exercise tests and achieved similar respiratory quotients at peak exercise. When compared to controls, subjects had a significant reduction in their exercise performance with reductions in total exercise time, peak work achieved, peak oxygen consumption, and anaerobic threshold. Compared to controls, at peak exercise, subjects had a reduced heart rate, systolic blood pressure, cardiac index, and stroke volume index. At peak exercise, systemic vascular resistance was elevated in subjects compared to controls. Respiratory rate, minute ventilation, and minute ventilation as a ratio of maximum voluntary ventilation were reduced in the subjects at peak exercise compared to the controls. Tidal volume and lung diffusion capacity were similar for subjects and controls.

Discussion

This study demonstrates that anthracyclines, as the sole cardiotoxic agent, produce significant limitations of exercise performance years after completion of chemotherapy. The exact cause of this late cardiotoxicity is unknown.

Although pulmonary function parameters are abnormal at rest, cardiac abnormalities are the cause of the exercise limitations seen in this study. Anthracyclines have been shown previously to interfere with both the systolic and diastolic properties of the left ventricle[8]. Such abnormalities could explain the reduction in stroke volume and peak cardiac index seen in this study. The elevated systemic vascular resistance could be the result of the subject's attempt to maintain blood pressure, and hence cerebral perfusion, in the face of their diminished cardiac output response. A similar pattern of elevated systemic vascular resistance and diminished cardiac output is frequently seen following surgery for several types of congenital heart disease. While anthracyclines typically produce prolongation of the QT interval and both supraventricular and ventricular arrhythmias, sinus node dysfunction and chronotropic incompetence are not typically thought of as significant complications of this therapy. The blunting of the heart rate response to exercise, seen in this study, however, suggests that chronotropic abnormalities many be more significant in this group of patients than previously thought.

Pulmonary parameters were normal for the work performed and, at the end of exercise, the subjects still had significant respiratory reserve as indicated by their low minute ventilation relative to maximum voluntary ventilation.

Effective therapy for this exercise limitation is unknown. The elevation in systemic vascular resistance, however, does provide one avenue for research, namely, angiotensin converting enzyme inhibitors. Cardiac rehabilitation is another potential therapy. A prior rehabilitation study, in a small number of oncology patients[12], demonstrated an improvement in total exercise time but the crucial parameters of oxygen consumption, cardiac index, and stroke volume index were unchanged by the rehabilitation.

Conclusion

Following cure of childhood cancer, anthracyclines produce significant late cardiotoxicity as demonstrated by cardiac limitations in exercise performance. With the prevalence of childhood cancer survivors projected to reach 1 in 250 adults in the near future, this cardiotoxicity may have significant medical and economic ramifications.

References

1. Bleyer, W.A. (1990) The impact of childhood cancer on the United States and the world. *CA-A Cancer Journal for Clinicians,* Vol. 40, pp. 355-67.
2. Kadota, R.P., Burgert, E.O., Driscoll, D.J., Evans, R.G. and Gilchrist, G.S. (1988) Cardiopulmonary function in long-term survivors of childhood Hodgkin's lymphoma: a pilot study. *Mayo Clinical Proceedings,* Vol. 63, pp. 362-7.
3. Lipshultz, S.E., Colan, S.D., Gelber, R.D., Perez Atayde, A.R., Sallan, S.E. and Sanders, S.P. (1991) Late cardiac effects of doxorubicin therapy for acute lymphoblastic leukemia in childhood. *New England Journal of Medicine,* Vol. 324, pp. 808-15.
4. Yeung, S.T., Yoong, C., Spink, J., Galbraith, A. and Smith, P.J. (1991) Functional myocardial impairment in children treated with anthracyclines for cancer. *Lancet,* Vol. 337, pp. 816-8.
5. Larsen, R.L., Barber, G., Heise, C.T. and August, C.S. (1992) Exercise assessment of cardiac function in children and young adults before and after bone marrow transplantation. *Pediatrics,* Vol. 89, pp. 722-9.
6. Matthys, D., Verhaaren, H., Benoit, Y., Laureys, G., De Naeyer, A. and Craen, M. (1993) Gender difference in aerobic capacity in adolescents after cure from malignant disease in childhood. *Acta Paediatrica,* Vol. 82, pp. 459-62.
7. Silber, J.H., Jakacki, R.I., Larsen, R.L., Goldwein, J.W. and Barber, G. (1993) Increased risk of cardiac dysfunction after anthracyclines in girls. *Medical and Pediatric Oncology,* Vol. 21, pp. 477-9.
8. Fukazawa, R., Ogawa, S. and Hirayama, T. (1994) Early detection of anthracycline cardiotoxicity in children with acute leukemia using exercise-based echocardiography and Doppler echocardiography. *Japanese Circulation Journal,* Vol. 58, pp. 625-34.
9. Lang, D., Hilger, F., Binswanger, J., Andelfinger, G. and Hartmann, W. (1995) Late effects of anthracycline therapy in childhood in relation to the function of the heart at rest and under physical stress. *European Journal of Pediatrics,* Vol. 154, pp. 340-5.
10. Pihkala, J., Happonen, J.M., Virtanen, K., Sovijarvi, A., Siimes, M.A., Pesonen, E. and Saarinen, U.M.. (1995) Cardiopulmonary evaluation of exercise tolerance after chest irradiation and anticancer chemotherapy in children and adolescents. *Pediatrics,* Vol. 95, pp. 722-6.
11. Tanner, C.S., Heise, C.T. and Barber, G. (1991) Correlation of the physiologic parameters of a continuous ramp versus an incremental James exercise protocol in normal children. *American Journal of Cardiology,* Vol. 67, pp. 309-12.
12. Sharkey, A.M., Carey, A.B., Heise, C.T. and Barber, G. (1993) Cardiac rehabilitation after cancer therapy in children and young adults. *American Journal of Cardiology,* Vol. 71, pp. 1488-90.

PART VI

SPORT AND PHYSICAL EDUCATION

FUELS USED FOR DIFFERENT ATHLETIC EVENTS: QUANTITATIVE AND QUALITATIVE ANALYSIS

Fuels for exercise

E.A. NEWSHOLME
Merton College, University of Oxford, UK

Keywords: Aerobic metabolism, anaerobic metabolism, athletic events, fatigue, fuels for exercise

Introduction

Energy for the contractile unit in the muscle fibre (the myofibrils) is obtained from the hydrolysis of adenosine triphosphate (ATP) to adenosine diphosphate (ADP) and phosphate. However, the amount of ATP in the muscle is limited: the total amount of ATP in the muscles of the sprinter would support the energy requirement for about 2 s. To continue running, ATP must be regenerated from ADP and phosphate; this occurs due to the oxidation of fuels. Thus ATP is produced in energy-yielding reactions and is utilised in energy-requiring processes: this constitutes the ATP/ADP cycle (fig 1). Although the precise chemical details of the use of ATP by muscle and its production in the mitochondria interest many biochemists and physiologists, it is the fuels whose metabolism provides energy for the synthesis of ATP that are of much more relevance to the scientifically interested athlete, the health scientist and the physician.

This subject appears to be straightforward since only two major fuel reserves exist in the body - glycogen and triacylglycerol. For the 70 kg human, total musculature normally contains about 400-500 g glycogen. This fuel is used in all track events so that it is the most important fuel for the athlete. Glycogen is also stored in the liver (about 100 g) where its main purpose is to provide glucose to maintain the blood level, for example, between meals. A number of tissues require glucose. Paramount among these is the brain which uses about 5 $g{\cdot}h^{-1}$. Some of the glucose released from the glycogen in the liver can also be used by muscles and this is particularly important in prolonged endurance activity such as the marathon and ultramarathon runs. However, depletion of liver and muscle glycogen increases the risk of hypoglycaemia, which is common in ultramarathons[1]. Since small adults and also children have small livers, less glycogen is stored and, depending on the energy requirements for exercise, the

Children and Exercise XIX. Edited by Neil Armstrong, Brian Kirby and Joanne Welsman.
Published in 1997 by E & FN Spon, 2–6 Boundary Row, London, SE1 8HN.
ISBN 0 419 22100 X.

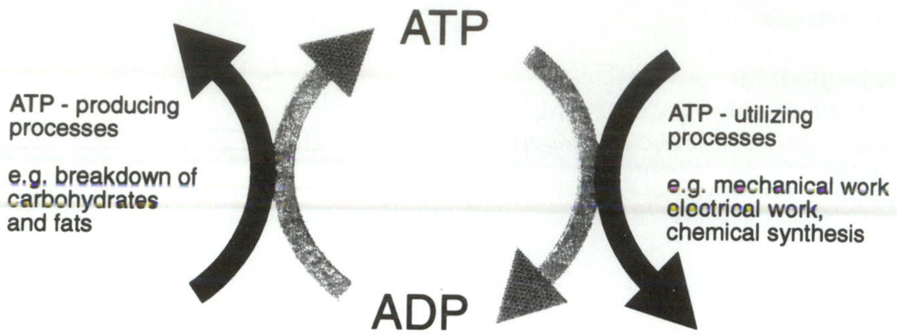

Fig.1. The ATP/ADP energy currency cycle.

liver glycogen stored might be used more quickly thereby increasing the risk of hypoglycaemia. Much more work is needed in this area.

Triacylglycerol is stored in special cells called adipocytes, each of which contains a droplet of triglyceride which occupies almost the whole cell. An adult male may contain 10^{11} such cells. These adipocytes cluster together to form discrete depots of adipose tissue, the primary function of which is to store chemical energy. Compared with glycogen, the quantities of triacylglycerol stored are large; on average, a 70 kg male stores about 8 kg triacylglycerol and an average woman of 60 kg stores nearly twice as much. The amount of triacylglycerol even in the male contains enough energy for 4-5 days of marathon running activity at an elite marathon runner's pace. Why then does fatigue in such events occur so early[2,3]? To be used by muscle, triacylglycerol must be hydrolysed in the adipocyte to fatty acids which are released into the bloodstream where they are carried to the muscle bound to albumin; the latter may restrict the rate at which they can be utilised[2].

There is one additional fuel, phosphocreatine, which acts as a short-term buffer for ATP in muscle. It is a particularly important fuel in the 100 and 200 m events and in sprinting to the tape in other races (see below).

Glucose, glucose-contained-in-glycogen, or fatty acids are, in a series of reactions, oxidised to carbon dioxide and water which regenerates ATP from ADP. The salient features of each pathway are listed below.

Glycolysis

- A glucose molecule arises from blood glucose or muscle glycogen (as glucose 6-phosphate) and is split into two pyruvate molecules. Under conditions of hypoxia, or in muscles which contain few mitochondria (type IIB fibres) most of the pyruvate will be converted to lactate plus protons[3];
- a small amount of ATP is regenerated from ADP.

Krebs cycle (tricarboxylic acid cycle)

- The pyruvate is oxidised to carbon dioxide and water in the Krebs cycle and the electron transfer chain;
- a large amount of ATP is regenerated from ADP.

Generally, this can be represented by two equations:

glucose + oxygen ⟶ carbon dioxide + water

phosphate + ADP ⟶ ATP + water

These two reactions are obligatorily coupled together. For each glucose unit originally in glycogen, that is oxidised in this way, 31 molecules of ATP are formed.

Beta-oxidation of fatty acids

The process of beta-oxidation breaks down fatty acids (formed from triacylglycerol) and the product, acetyl-CoA is fed into the Krebs cycle so that their oxidation too can generate ATP.

Each of these pathways consists of many enzymes and one of the benefits of aerobic training is to increase the amounts of these enzymes in muscle fibres.

Fuels - the rate of ATP production from them and how long they can last

When the amounts of fuel stored are compared with the maximum rates at which ATP can be regenerated from that fuel, an inverse relationship is observed (table 1). From work on muscles of male adult volunteers, the highest rate of ATP formation in muscle is provided from use of phosphocreatine, the smallest store of fuel, and the slowest is from fatty acid oxidation, whereas fat is the largest store of fuel in the body. The rates are approximately 5.0 and 0.3 μmol ATP g wet wt·s^{-1}, respectively. The maximum rate of ATP generation in different running events and the amount of fuel stored allow calculations to be made on how long the stores would last. [Phosphocreatine breakdown and glycogen degradation to lactate regenerate ATP without the use of oxygen (this is sometimes described as anaerobic but this does not mean that oxygen is absent - it is simply limiting: therefore it is described as 'anaerobically')].

- If phosphocreatine alone were to be used for maximum sprinting, it would provide ATP, at most, for about 10 s (since the amount stored in muscle is very small).
- Muscle glycogen, if completely broken down to lactate, would provide ATP for about 3.3 min of maximum activity - a theoretical value since fatigue sets in well before this time.
- Complete oxidation of muscle glycogen would provide ATP for about 90 min of running (or cycling) during activity involving about 70% of $\dot{V}O_2$ max.
- Triacylglycerol in muscle would last about 100 min in top marathon runners; adipose tissue triacylglycerol would last, however, about 5,000 min[2,3]. The latter is theoretical since fatigue will occur well before all the fat is utilised (see below).

Although useful for considering metabolic principles and possible limitations in the use of fuels, these rates are not very valuable for considering actual activity since more than one fuel is always used (see below).

Table 1. Approximate maximal rates of ATP formation from various fuels during exercise and the approximate amount stored in muscle (or adipose tissue) in humans Data from references[4,5]

Fuel	Approx. max rate ATP formation ($\mu mols^{-1}\cdot g$ wet wt^{-1}) at 37°C	Approx. store in muscle ($\mu mol\cdot g$ wet wt^{-1})	Theoretical time for complete depletion (min)
Phosphocreatine	5.0	30	6*
Glycogen (to lactate)	2.0**	100	2.5††
Glycogen (to CO_2)	0.6	100	90
Fat to CO_2	0.3	12† × 10^6	5000

*seconds and estimated for about 5 s, the maximal is probably higher for shorter periods when glycolysis will contribute less[5]. **This value is for mixed muscle; for type II fibres it is 2.7 and for type I fibres it is 1.5 $\mu mols^{-1}\cdot g$ wet wt^{-1}[6]. †Most of the fat is stored in adipose tissue. ††This is for mixed muscle; for type II fibres it is 1.6 min and for type I, 3.3 min since the activities of glycogen phosphorylase are about 64 and 30 $\mu mols^{-1}\cdot g$ wet wt^{-1} at 37° in type II and type I fibres respectively[6].
Note: since creatine phosphokinase catalyses a near-equilibrium reaction the rate of ATP rephosphorylation from phosphocreatine could be much higher than this but is probably limited not by the activity of this enzyme but by the maximum rate of ATP turnover in human muscle.

Aerobic versus 'anaerobic' metabolism

One extremely important facet of ATP generation in all sports is the balance between aerobic and anaerobic metabolism. The balance can be measured either from the changes in the contents in muscle of fuels such as phosphocreatine and glycogen and/or the accumulation of lactate, or from the oxygen deficit that occurs at onset of short-term exhaustive exercise (see below). A guesstimate of the proportion of ATP generated from aerobic metabolism in the various running events of the Olympic Games is given in table 2[4]. A simple guide is that in the 100 m, none of the energy is generated aerobically, in the 800 or 1500 m half of the energy is generated aerobically and in the half- or full marathon all of the energy is generated aerobically.

In fit individuals, at low exercise intensities, most if not all of the ATP is generated aerobically, that is from the Krebs cycle and electron transfer. However, as exercise intensity increases and oxygen is used at a faster rate by the mitochondria, the oxygen concentration within muscle decreases and becomes limiting for the aerobic system. More ATP can, however, be generated by conversion of glycogen to pyruvate and the latter converted to lactate. Since the latter process is independent of oxygen, it provides ATP additional to that which is produced from aerobic metabolism. Although it is only a small proportion of that required in the longer races, it allows a faster pace to be maintained, so that the athlete can compete more effectively.

Several important biochemical facts need to be appreciated.

- In adults and also probably in children, a major limitation in running performance is the supply of oxygen to the muscle.
- The amount of ATP that can be generated 'anaerobically' from glycogen degradation is very small compared with that which can be generated aerobically - 3 mol compared with about 31 mol, from a mole of glucose-in-glycogen.
- Only glucose, glycogen and phosphocreatine provide ATP under 'anaerobic' conditions.
- For events in which a considerable amount of the ATP is generated anaerobically glycogen, not blood glucose, is the fuel used. This is because the capacity to use glucose, indicated by the activity of hexokinase, in comparison with that for glycogen (indicated by the activity of phosphorylase) is very low (20 to 30-fold less)[2].
- Both aerobic and 'anaerobic' metabolism produce acidic end products, carbon dioxide and lactic acid, respectively, but it is the latter that poses a problem since the capacity for production of the lactic acid is very much greater (20-30-fold greater) than that for the production of CO_2. An increase in the concentration of protons in a muscle of <10-fold jeopardises the biochemical life of the cell. Hence it results in fatigue[2,3,4].

Fuels and their metabolism for track events and the marathon

The question as to what fuels are used during different competitive events is difficult to answer since it will depend upon a number of factors:

- age
- fibre composition of muscle
- previous diet
- fitness of the athlete
- elitism of the athlete.

It is difficult to carry out meaningful experiments on athletes who are actually participating in competition or in training (i.e. field experiments). Experiments are usually done in the laboratory and for running events these are usually done on a treadmill but it is easier to measure power output and how it declines (fatigue) during cycling activity so that cycle ergometers are frequently used. In addition, it is possible to do 'one-legged' cycling in which one leg is physically active but the other acts as a resting control. Finally, it is difficult to persuade a sufficient number of elite athletes to volunteer for scientifically-useful experiments so that they tend to be carried out on university students; caution must be exerted in extrapolation of these results to elite athletes.

In one particular study of endurance exercise, the techniques of isotope dilution, arteriovenous measurement and indirect calorimetry were used to provide information on the type of fuel used and the rate of utilisation by subjects exercising for 30 min at 25, 65 and 85% of their $\dot{V}O_2$ max, using well-trained competitive cyclists[8].

- At 25% $\dot{V}O_2$ max, most of the energy (>80%) was obtained from the oxidation of fatty acids (which were obtained via the blood from adipose tissue)

Table 2. An estimate of percentage contribution of different fuels to ATP generation in different events

Event	Percentage contribution to ATP generation				
	Phosphocreatine	Glycogen		Blood glucose (liver glycogen)	Triglyceride (fatty acids)
		anaerobic	aerobic		
100 m	50	50	-	-	-
200 m	25	65	10	-	-
400 m	12.5	62.5	25	-	-
800 m	*	50	50	-	-
1500 m	*	25	75	-	-
5000 m	*	12.5	87.5	-	-
10000 m	*	3	97	-	-
Marathon	-	-	75	5	20
Ultramarathon (52 miles)	-	-	35	5	60
24 h race	-	-	10	2	88
Soccer game	10	70	20	-	-

*In these events phosphocreatine will be used for the first few seconds and, if it has been resynthesised during the race, in the sprint to the tape. For source of data see reference[7].

- At 65% $\dot{V}O_2$ max, glycogen was the most important fuel but muscle triacylglycerol plus plasma fatty acids provided more than half of the energy
- At 85% $\dot{V}O_2$ max, >60% of the energy was obtained from glycogen: fatty acid oxidation now contributed 14%; not surprisingly, the latter was increased if a low carbohydrate diet had been consumed prior to the exercise (table 3).

These results suggest that fatty acids and glycogen are quantitatively the most important fuels even at high intensity exercise. However, the intensity of exercise in athletic events such as the 10,000 m is probably considerably greater than 85% $\dot{V}O_2$ max and likely to be at least 95%. The inference from this is that glycogen utilisation would provide even more of the energy under these conditions (table 3). One further reason for suggesting this is that the oxidation of fatty acids provides about 10% less ATP per mL of O_2 used than does glycogen (or glucose)[2]. Since, in middle distance events, oxygen supply to the muscle fibres limits performance, the use of fatty acid instead of glycogen, would, for the same rate of oxygen consumption, produce less ATP. Hence performance would suffer. The author predicts that elite middle distance runners would obtain most of the ATP from the oxidation of glycogen (table 3). This assumption is used in discussions below. Indeed, this may be one result of the intense training for middle distance events, that is, to ensure the utilisation of as much glycogen and as little fat as possible. However, the biochemical mechanism by which this is achieved is not known. It is possible to speculate but much further research is needed on elite athletes performing under competitive conditions. For example, measurement of respiratory exchange ratio in elite athletes during simulated competition could provide an answer to this question.

Fuel used to provide ATP in athletic races

Events in which 'anaerobic' metabolism dominates

There is no doubt that, for the sprints, fatty acid oxidation plays no role, and all of the ATP is generated from phosphocreatine plus glycogen. The question that is difficult to answer is how much ATP is produced from aerobic and how much from 'anaerobic' metabolism of glycogen? The values given in table 4 are for elite runners but they are guesstimates; no detailed studies have been done on elite athletes. The Wingate test has been used for many years to test the anaerobic capacity. The subject pedals on a cycle ergometer at all out supra-maximal exertion for 30 s against a frictional load depending on body mass. However, there is no doubt that aerobic metabolism plays some role in generating ATP during 30 s of exercise.

Two other methods, perhaps more accurate than the Wingate test, for measurement of ATP generation from anaerobic metabolism have been used.

Measurement of concentration change in energy intermediates in muscle

ATP is generated 'anaerobically' from breakdown of phosphocreatine and conversion of glycogen to lactate: if the change in muscle contents of phosphocreatine and lactate are measured during the exercise period, the amount of ATP generated can be calculated (1 mole phosphocreatine produces 1 mole ATP and 1 mole lactate produced from glycogen is equivalent to the production of 1.5 mole ATP). (See references 4, 5, 6 and 9.)

Measurement of oxygen deficit

When exercise is initiated, oxygen consumption increases to reach a new steady state level over several minutes. The difference between the oxygen actually used during this transient period and that which would have been used if oxygen consumption had reached its steady state value immediately, is known as oxygen deficit (fig 2). The maximal oxygen deficit can be measured by performing a $\dot{V}O_2$ max experiment and continuing the exercise to exhaustion. When exercise is carried out at this intensity until exhaustion is reached, the oxygen used and the oxygen deficit are quantitative indices of aerobic and anaerobic energy generation respectively. For these measurements, it is assumed that 1 mole of oxygen is equivalent to 5.2 mol of ATP. (The oxidation of 1 mole of glucose requires the oxidation of 6 moles of oxygen and produces 31 moles of ATP: therefore 1 mole of oxygen equals 31÷6 moles ATP.) Hence the contribution of aerobic and 'anaerobic' metabolism for some events can be calculated from these measurements[10,11].

100 metres: Of the standard track events, the 100m sprint is unique in that it is run almost entirely without oxygen (tables 2 and 4). Although there is enough phosphocreatine in leg muscles to account for most of the ATP needed, it has been shown that maximal sprinting performance can occur only when both phosphocreatine and glycogen are used simultaneously and it is shown that each contributes about half to the energy required[5,9]. Phosphocreatine contributes, probably, most to the formation of ATP in the first second or two of the sprint since increasing the rate of glycogen breakdown and glycolysis, which involves 12 enzymes, will take a little time. After this, both fuels are used[5,9]. Reliance on this form of metabolism means that providing blood for the muscle is much less important and hence the number and size of arteries and veins is reduced, so that there is more room for muscle fibres. Similarly, mitochondria are much less important and their volume can be reduced allowing more space within the muscle for myofibrils. More myofibrils in the fibre, more fibres in the muscle and bigger muscles means much more power - faster sprinting.

Table 3. Relative contribution from plasma glucose, muscle glycogen, plasma fatty acid and muscle triacylglycerol to energy production during 30 min cycling at 65 and 85% $\dot{V}O_2$ max.

	Approximate contributions to energy expenditure (%)			
Percentage $\dot{V}O_2$ max	Plasma glucose	Muscle glycogen	Plasma fatty acid	Muscle triacylglycerol
65	8	38	30	24
85	12	60	14	14
*95	*10	*90	-	-

Data from reference[8].

*Current author's speculation based on discussion in text and in[3]

Table 4. Calculated and measured contributions of anaerobic metabolism to energy generation in some Olympic running events

Olympic event	Anaerobic ATP generation (% of total)		Approx. world record time
	Biochemical assessment from calculation	Physiological assessment from O_2 deficit measurement	
100 m	100	-	<10 s
200 m	80	-	<20 s
400 m	70	80	>45 s
800 m	50	-	<1 min 40 s
1500 m	40	45	<3 min 30 s
5,000 m	12.5	-	<13 min
10,000 m	3	-	<27 min

For basis of calculations see references[2,3,7]; for those based on oxygen deficit measurements see reference[11].

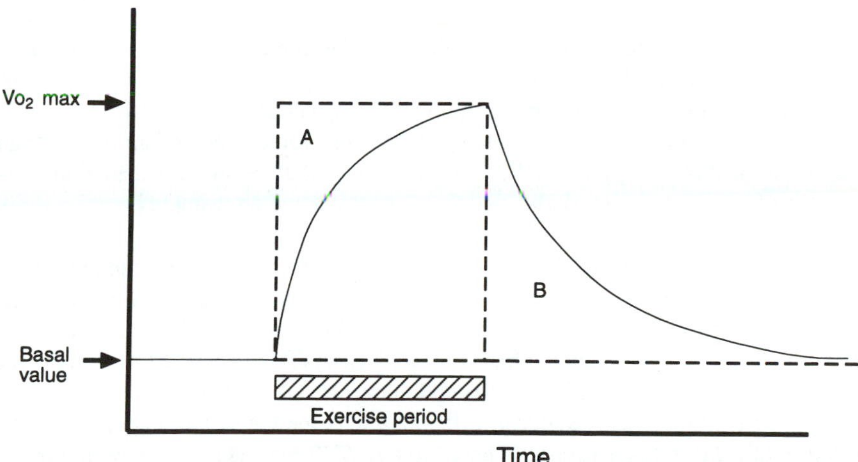

Fig. 2. Oxygen uptake before, during and after exercise: the relationship between deficit and debt. The cross-hatched rectangle shows the exercise period. the oxygen uptake increases to a steady-state value during the exercise period and declines asymp-

200 metres: As with the 100m sprint, both phosphocreatine and glycogen conversion to lactate will be used simultaneously. However phosphocreatine cannot be used at the same rate as in the 100m sprint, since muscle contains only about 30 $\mu mol \cdot g^{-1}$ (wet wt) of phosphocreatine so that it would be completely exhausted by <100 m of maximum sprinting and the pace would then need to fall. If the pace was slightly less than that in the 100m, phosphocreatine could be used over the whole 200m. If phosphocreatine was used at a rate of 1.5 $\mu mol \cdot s \cdot g^{-1}$ the total amount used over 20 s would be 30 $\mu mol \cdot g^{-1}$ phosphocreatine, the amount present in muscle (table 1). If 'anaerobic' glycogen metabolism provided about 5 μmol of $ATP \cdot s^{-1}$, this suggests a contribution of about 10-20% from aerobic metabolism of glycogen in this event.

400 metres: From a fuel point of view, the 400m is a specialised event. Calculations suggest that three modes of ATP generation contribute to the ATP generation required for this event; phosphocreatine breakdown, glycogen conversion to lactate and glycogen conversion to CO_2. Calculations suggest that less than 10% of the energy comes from phosphocreatine. Ideally, after the use of phosphocreatine in the first second or two, the remainder should be 'eked out' to supplement the other sources of ATP for the whole race. Inability to store sufficient phosphocreatine is one factor which may contribute to fatigue in this event, but a more important limitation is acid accumulation. To decrease this latter problem, it is estimated some 30% or more of the ATP needed is generated aerobically from the oxidation of glycogen. It has been shown experimentally that, for 30 seconds of intense exercise to exhaustion, about 80% of the energy is obtained from 'anaerobic' metabolism[11].

Events in which aerobic and 'anaerobic' metabolism of glycogen contribute about equally

800 and 1500 m: As the distance and hence the time for the event increases, phosphocreatine becomes less important. It will be used in the first couple of seconds and also in the sprint to the tape, if some of it has been 'saved' during the race. Aerobic metabolism now becomes much more important in generating ATP and, for races of 800 or 1500 m, aerobic provides as much ATP as 'anaerobic' metabolism (tables 2 and 4). It has been shown experimentally that for exercise that results in exhaustion in 3-4 min about 45% of the energy is obtained from anaerobic metabolism[11].

Events in which aerobic metabolism of glycogen dominates energy generation

Long distance track events: 3-10000 m: It is assumed that glycogen is the only fuel of significance and that most of the ATP is obtained from its aerobic metabolism in events longer than 3000 m; it is estimated that 87.5% of the ATP is generated by aerobic metabolism in the 5000 m and 97% in the 10000 m events (tables 2 and 4).

It is considered that oxygen supply to the muscle is the major limiting factor for the generation of ATP in these events. Therefore any ATP that can be generated without the use of oxygen would be enormously advantageous in permitting a faster pace and the calculated extra 3% ATP generated in the 10000 m, although small, could make the difference between winning or losing. The reason why the contribution cannot be greater than about 3% is interesting: it is calculated that, during the 30 min or so it takes to run the race, enough 'anaerobic' glycolysis to provide 3% of the ATP would cause the breakdown of almost 30% of the glycogen stored in the muscle (table 5). If the pace demanded more ATP to be produced from this process, or if glycogen stores were below normal at the start of the race, then this store would be depleted well before the end of the race, resulting in severe fatigue[3].

Marathon and ultramarathon races: These events must be run entirely aerobically. A full marathon needs about 700 g of carbohydrate - more than is stored even after rest and successful carbohydrate loading. And, although there is an additional store of about 100 g of glycogen in the liver, some (10-15 g) will be needed by the brain, which uses about 5 $g{\cdot}h^{-1}$. So marathon runners appear to have a fuel problem. The solution is to oxidise fatty acids to supplement the carbohydrate. How much fatty acid is used? It is speculated that 10 to 50% of the energy required to run the marathon is obtained from fatty acid oxidation. The lowest contribution will apply to the elite runner, whose running 'economy' is very good - that is, whose tendons are very effective in absorbing energy in the elastic recoil mechanism[3] and who has raised the muscle glycogen levels as high as possible by decreasing the intensity of training ('tapering') prior to the race and by eating an appropriate diet[3].

Fuel use and fatigue

It is possible to make important interpretations concerning the metabolic cause of fatigue based on quantitative knowledge of fuel utilisation rates by muscle. In the longer sprints (200-400 m), the amount of phosphocreatine is limiting. The power output falls as the phosphocreatine levels are depleted[5,9]. Hence increasing the phosphocreatine levels in muscle by increasing the level of creatine via supplementing the diet with large amounts of creatine has been shown to improve performance in explosive sports[12]. Dietary supplementation with creatine is now very popular with power athletes.

In short-term, intense physical activity and during isometric contraction to fatigue, glycogen is converted to lactic acid at a high rate and the muscle pH drops. The increase in proton concentration in the muscle is at least partially responsible for the fatigue. However, fatigue after prolonged exercise (e.g. 75 min of cycling at 75% $\dot{V}O_2$ max) results in fatigue, but there is no change in pH (table 6). Indeed, the levels of nucleotides and inorganic phosphate are similar in all these three fatigued states. In isometric contraction and intense short-term cycling, glycogen levels are high but pH is low. In endurance cycling pH is normal but glycogen levels are very low. It is lack of glycogen which results in fatigue[3] (table 6).

Muscle can obtain some energy during exercise by the oxidation of amino acids, especially the branched-chain amino acids. However, the calculation based on the maximum activity of the key enzyme involved in the oxidation of these amino acids suggests that it does not provide a great deal of ATP[2]. Together with tryptophan, it has been suggested that these amino acids play a role as a sensor that can result in mental fatigue during exercise.

Tryptophan and branched-chain amino acids enter the brain on the same carrier so that there is competition for entry. Tryptophan is converted to the important neurotransmitter 5-hydroxytryptamine (5-HT), which might have a role in mental fatigue. Tryptophan is unique amongst the amino acids in that it is bound to plasma albumin, so

Table 5. Estimation of the contribution of aerobic and anaerobic metabolism of glycogen to ATP provision for different track events

Distance of event (metres)	Percentage contribution to ATP generation from aerobic systems (approx.)	Calculated percentage glycogen used by:	
		aerobic metabolism	anaerobic metabolism
800	50	7	93
1500	65	20	80
5000	87	36	64
10,000	97	72	28
marathon	100	100	0

Data from reference[7]

that it exists as a bound and a free form, which are in equilibrium: it is considered that it is the free concentration that competes with branched-chain amino acids for entry into the brain. The plasma level of free tryptophan increases when the plasma fatty acid level is increased, since the binding of fatty acids to albumin decreases its affinity for tryptophan. It is predicted that an increase in the plasma concentration of free tryptophan without an increase in the plasma level of branched-chain amino acids, would increase the brain concentration of 5-HT (fig 3) and this would result in central fatigue[13].

The plasma concentration ratio, free tryptophan/branched-chain amino acids, is increased in man and in the rat after prolonged and exhaustive exercise. In exercise, either intermittent or continuous, there is elevation in the blood catecholamine level and a decrease in that of insulin which will result in fatty acid mobilisation from adipose tissue. This could result in an increase in the plasma fatty acid level. If there is precise control between the mobilisation of fatty acids from adipose tissue, the extent of vasodilation in muscle and the stimulation of fatty acid oxidation within muscle, the increased rate of fatty acid oxidation by muscle may occur without much, if any, of an increase in the plasma level of fatty acids. Hence, this will not influence the free tryptophan level. However, if the co-ordination between the increased rate of release of fatty acids and the increased rate of utilisation by active muscle is poor - due, for example, to lack of training - the blood fatty acid concentration could be increased sufficiently that the plasma concentration of free tryptophan is increased. Furthermore, in intermittent exercise in which there is usually a greater dependence upon 'anaerobic' exercise and, therefore, less opportunity to oxidise these fatty acids, the plasma level of fatty acid could rise and hence increase the concentration of free tryptophan. A large increase in the plasma fatty acid level could also occur in response to hypoglycaemia which will, via changes in hormone levels, encourage a greater rate of fatty acid mobilisation from adipose tissue.

Since branched-chain amino acids are not taken up by liver but by muscle, upon ingestion they are not removed by the liver so that their plasma concentration is rapidly increased. This can, therefore, maintain the resting plasma free tryptophan/branched-

Table 6. Effect of three different types of exercise on contents of glycogen, lactate, some energy-intermediates and pH in muscle of humans

	Intensity	Duration of exercise (min)	Glycogen content (% of initial concn.)	Contents ($\mu mol \cdot g$ wet wt^{-1})						Muscle pH
				Phosphocreatine	ATP	ADP	P_i	IMP	Lactate	
Rest	-	-	100	22	6.2	0.75	9.5	<0.1	0.75	7.1
Isometric contraction to fatigue	66% MVC	0.8	85	1.9	5.2	0.87	27	0.75	23	6.6
Intense short-term cycling to fatigue	100% $\dot{V}O_2$ max	6	81	4.2	5.0	0.90	22	0.87	28	6.6
Endurance cycling to fatigue	75% $\dot{V}O_2$ max	75	11	7.2	5.7	0.87	25	0.5	3.5	7.1

MVC is maximum voluntary contraction.
Data from reference[4].

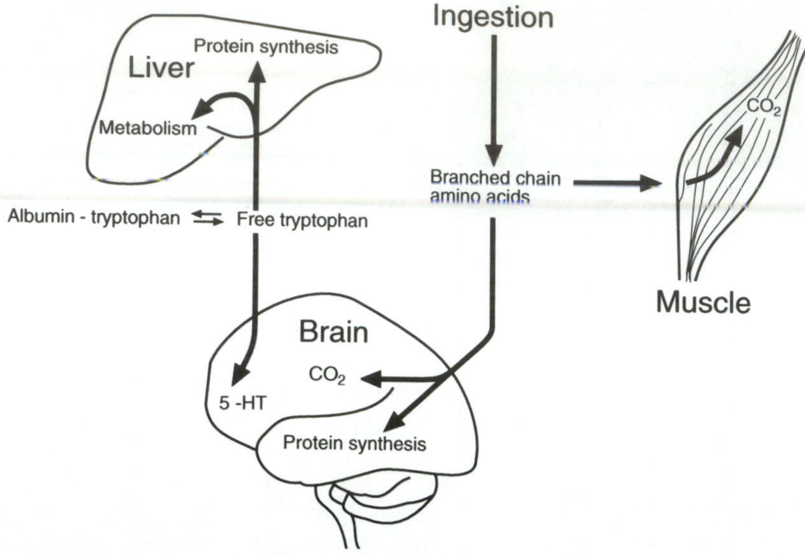

Fig. 3. Interrelationship between tryptophan and branched-chain amino acids. Tryptophan is metabolised by liver, as are most amino acids, but branched-chain amino acids are taken up by muscle. An increased uptake of branched-chain amino acids by muscle and an increased plasma level of fatty acids which would decrease the binding of tryptophan to albumin, could result in an increased concentration ratio, free tryptophan/branched-chain amino acids. This will favour the entry of tryptophan into the brain and possibly increase the neuronal level of 5-HT. Oral supplementation with branched-chain amino acids, since they are not metabolised by the liver, can maintain this ratio at resting levels.

chain amino acid concentration ratio during exercise. Thus administration of branched-chain amino acids may not be very important as a fuel for muscle but in their ability to delay mental fatigue in adult athletes. This they do by maintaining the plasma tryptophan/branched-chain amino acid ratio and hence decreasing central fatigue[13]. The importance of this mechanism in children is not, however, known.

References

1. Noakes, T.D. (1986) *The Lore of Running*, Oxford University Press, Cape Town.
2. Newsholme, E.A. and Leech, A. (1983) *Biochemistry for the Medical Sciences*, John Wiley, Chichester.
3. Newsholme, E.A., Leech, A.R. and Duester, G. (1994) *Keep on Running: the Science of Training and Performance*, John Wiley, Chichester.
4. Sahlin, K. (1992) Metabolic aspects of fatigue in human skeletal muscle. *Medicine and Sports Science*, Vol. 34, pp. 54-68.

5. Hultman, E., Greenhaff, P.L., Ren, J.-M. and Söderlund, K. (1981) Energy metabolism and fatigue during intense muscle contraction. *Biochemical Society Transactions*, Vol. 19, pp. 347-52.
6. Greenhaff, P.L., Söderlund, K, Ren, J.-M. and Hultman, D. (1993) Energy metabolism in single human muscle fibres during intermittent contraction and occluded circulation. *Journal of Physiology*, Vol. 460, pp. 443-53.
7. Newsholme, E.A., Blomstrand, E. and Ekblom, B. (1992) Physical and mental fatigue: metabolic mechanism and importance of plasma amino acids. *British Medical Bulletin*, Vol. 48, pp. 477-95.
8. Romlin, J.A., Coyle, E.F. and Sidossis, L.S. (1993) Regulation of endogenous fat and carbohydrate metabolism in relation to exercise intensity and duration. *American Journal of Physiology*, Vol. 265, pp. E381-91.
9. Hultman, E. and Sjöholm, H. (1986) Biochemical causes of fatigue, in *Human Muscle Power*, (eds. N.L. Jones, N. McCarney and A.J. McComas), Human Kinetics, Champaign, Il, pp.215-38.
10. Medbø, J.E. and Burgess, S. (1990) Effect of training on anaerobic capacity. *Medicine and Science in Sports and Exercise*, Vol. 22, pp. 501-7.
11. Bangsbo, J., Gollnick, P.D., Graham, T.E. and Saltin, B. (1990) Anaerobic energy production and O_2-deficit-debt relationship during exhaustive exercise in humans. *Journal Physiology*, Vol. 422, pp. 539-59.
12. Greenhaff, P.L., Casey, A., Short, A.H. and Hultman, E. (1993) Influence of oral creatine supplementation on muscle torque during repeated bouts of maximal voluntary exercise in man. *Clinical Science*, Vol. 84, pp. 565-71.
13. Newsholme, E.A., Blomstrand, E., Hassmén, P. and Ekblom, B. (1991) Physical and mental fatigue: do changes in amino acids play a role? *Biochemical Society Transactions*, Vol. 19, pp. 358-62.

CARDIAC STRUCTURE AND FUNCTION IN HIGHLY-TRAINED PREPUBERTAL GYMNASTS AND SWIMMERS

Cardiac parameters in prepubertal athletes

P. OBERT, D. COURTEIX, P. GERMAIN, A.M. LECOQ and P. GUENON
Laboratory of Muscular Exercise Physiology, Faculty of Sport Sciences, University of Orléans, France
F. STECKEN
Department of Cardiology, Hospital of "La Présentation", Fleury-Les-Aubrais, France

Keywords: Echocardiography, gymnastics, prepuberty, swimming, training

Introduction

In adults, changes in cardiac structure and function after aerobic training are well documented[1-4], with different adaptations occurring in endurance vs power athletes[4,5]. In children, far less information is available. Studies have shown that the cardiovascular systems of prepubertal children can adapt to aerobic training but the mechanisms (central and/or peripheral), responsible for these functional adaptations are not well established[6-8]. In particular, little is known about the influence of aerobic training during prepuberty on cardiac structure and function and conflicting results have been reported[6,9-14]. In addition, previous studies did not involve a great deal of anaerobic training. In a recent longitudinal study[15], we reported specific physiological adaptations (i.e. increase in $\dot{V}O_2$ max) in a group of prepubertal swimmers after a 1 y intensive training programme when compared to a control group. The purpose of the present study was to investigate the cardiac structure and function in this group of highly-trained swimmers. The same analysis was also applied to prepubertal gymnasts in order to evaluate the effect of aerobic vs anaerobic training.

Subjects

Subjects were 37 children classified as prepubertal using Tanner's indices. Nine belonged to a local youth swimming team (S), 15 to local gymnastic clubs (G) and 11 were recruited to serve as a control group (C). The swimmers had trained on average

Children and Exercise XIX. Edited by Neil Armstrong, Brian Kirby and Joanne Welsman.
Published in 1997 by E & FN Spon, 2–6 Boundary Row, London, SE1 8HN.
ISBN 0 419 22100 X.

10 to 12 h·wk^{-1} for at least 2 y. Further information regarding their training programme is available in a previous publication[15]. The gymnasts had also trained intensively (12-15 h·wk^{-1}) for at least 4 y. Their training programme was based principally on strength and power exercises involving anaerobic metabolism. The control group was untrained.

The study was described to the children and their parents and their written consent was obtained

Methods

All measurements and calculations were obtained according to standard procedures recommended by the American Society of Echocardiography[16]. The subjects were examined by M-mode, bi-dimensional and Doppler analyses at rest in a left lateral supine position. Measurements were carried out by the same cardiologist. The echocardiographic parameters measured or derived included left ventricular (LV) internal dimension at end-diastole (LVIDd) and at end-systole (LVIDs), posterior wall thickness at end-diastole (PWT), interventricular septal thickness at end-diastole (ST), LV shortening fraction (FS), and ejection fraction (EF). Left ventricular mass (LVmass) was calculated according to Devereux's formula. Doppler examinations of LV inflow were also performed and the following measurements and calculations were made: peak velocity of early diastolic rapid inflow (peak E), peak velocity of atrial contraction filling (peak A), ratio of peak E/peak A. Furthermore, for the early diastolic inflow curve, the mitral acceleration (mA, from baseline to peak E wave) and deceleration (mD, from peak E wave to baseline) were measured. The isovolumic relaxation time (IVRT) was quantified via a simultaneous pulsed Doppler recording of left ventricular output flow and mitral valve inflow. In addition, the cardiac output was evaluated from transaortic Doppler examinations[17]. For this, the time-velocity integral of aortic flow (Ao-TVI) was calculated. The aortic diameter was measured at the level of the aortic valve annulus and the cross-sectional area of the annulus (Ao-CSA) was then calculated. Finally, stroke volume (SV) was calculated as Ao-TVI x Ao-CSA. Heart rate (HR) was measured simultaneously with all echocardiographic and Doppler examinations. Cardiac output (Q) was calculated from SV and HR. All values are the average of a minimum of three technically adequate cardiac cycles and measurements were expressed relative to the individual subject's body surface area (BSA) according to the recommendation of Henry et al.[18]. In a preliminary study, two blinded observers independently analysed several random recordings on two occasions. The inter- and intra-observer variability were very low and values reported are those of the cardiologist who analysed all recordings.

Data analyses

Data are expressed as mean ± SD. Group differences were examined using factorial one-way analysis of variance (ANOVA). Where statistically significant differences were indicated ($p < 0.05$), a post-hoc PLSD Fisher multiple range test was used. For cardiac chamber dimensions (internal diameter and wall thicknesses), an univariate analysis of covariance (ANCOVA) was used, with lean body mass (LBM) being treated as the covariate measure.

Results

There were no significant differences (p >0.05) in age, stature and mass among the three groups. Highly-trained children exhibited a lower % fat mass than the control group and lower values for LBM were obtained between S and G, only (table 1).

Findings on cardiac examinations are presented in tables 2 and 3. Left ventricular internal dimensions measured at end-diastole were significantly higher in S than in the other two groups. Values for C and S were very similar. No significant differences among groups were observed in cardiac wall thicknesses. The enlargement of the left ventricle found in S resulted in greater left ventricular mass when compared to the other two groups. The parameters of left ventricular resting contractility were similar in all groups. There were also no significant differences between groups for peak E. However, the control group had significantly higher peak A than S and G. Consequently, lower values (not significant) were reported for the control group when compared to the other two groups for the peakE/peakA ratio. The isovolumic relaxation time as well as the mitral acceleration and deceleration were not different between groups. SV was higher in S than in the other groups, which is consistent with the higher left ventricular internal diameter reported above. Because of a bradycardia observed among S vs C, the resting Q was similar in the three groups.

Discussion

Few studies have investigated the effect of training on cardiac structure and function in children and results are conflicting[6,10-13,19]. The findings of the present study strongly support the idea that morphological and functional cardiac adaptations can occur in a prepubertal child as a result of daily intense training over a prolonged

Table 1. Biometric parameters of swimmers (S), gymnasts (G) and control group (C)

	Age (y)	Height (m)	Weight (kg)	Fat mass (%)	Lean body mass(kg)	Surface area (m^2)
S	10.7 ± 1.0	142 ± 9	35 ± 6	17.8 ± 4.2	28 ± 4	1.18 ± 0.14
C	10.9 ± 0.7	142 ± 9	34 ± 7	23 ± 3.1	26 ± 4	1.18 ± 0.13
G	10.2 ± 1.3	135 ± 10	29 ± 7	17.9 ± 1.9	24 ± 5	1.06 ± 0.17
	ns	ns	ns	S-C *** G-C ***	S-G *	ns

Values are mean ± SD
Level of significance * p<0.05, *** p<0.001, ns: non significant

Table 2. Echocardiographic data of the three groups indexed to body surface area (m^2)

	LVIDs ($mm/SA^{1/3}$)	LVIDd ($mm/SA^{1/3}$)	PWT ($mm/SA^{1/2}$)	ST ($mm/SA^{1/2}$)	Lvmass (g/SA)	Q (L/min/SA)	SV (mL/SA)	HR ($beats \cdot min^{-1}$)
S	25.6 ± 1.0	41.7 ± 1.6	5.3 ± 0.6	5.9±0.4	69.5±8.7	3.23±0.6	46.7±6.8	69 ± 7
C	23.4 ± 2.0	39.1 ± 2.1	5.4 ± 0.7	5.8±0.5	61.1±9.2	3.40±0.4	41.7±6.4	83 ± 13
G	23.8 ± 2.0	39.1 ± 2.2	5.5 ± 0.6	6.2±0.6	61.3±9.3	3.18±0.5	43.1±4.9	74 ± 14
	S-C **	S-C **	ns	ns	S-C *		S-C *	S-C **
	S-G *	S-G **			S-G *			

Values are mean ± SD
Level of significance * $p<0.05$, ** $P<0.01$

Table 3. Systolic and diastolic function of the 3 groups

	FS (%)	EF (%)	Peak E ($m \cdot s^{-1}$)	Peak A ($m \cdot s^{-1}$)	E / A	mA ($m \cdot s^{-2}$)	mD ($m \cdot s^{-2}$)	IVRT (ms)
S	38.5±3.0	76.7±0.3	1.04±0.12	0.45±0.10	2.4±0.4	12.7±2.0	7.5±1.2	61±5
C	40.1±4.2	78.2±0.4	1.07±0.16	0.55±0.11	2.0±0.3	14.2±3.6	7.6±0.8	60±12
G	39.0±4.5	77.0±0.5	1.00±0.13	0.46±0.10	2.3±0.6	13.6±2.2	7.7±1.4	56±9
	ns	ns	ns	S-C *	ns	ns	ns	ns
				G-C *				

Values are mean ± SD
Level of significance * $p<0.05$

period. They also highlight the fact that these adaptations are sport specific. In this population of highly trained swimmers and gymnasts enlarged internal cardiac dimensions and higher LVmass only were noted in the swimmers. Moreover, despite their intensive training, data obtained from the gymnasts were surprisingly close to those of the age-matched controls (table 2). These results are consistent with previous cross-sectional studies of highly-trained prepubertal swimmers[11,12]. They also agree with a longitudinal study[6] which reported, in 6-10 y old children after a 2 y training period, significantly higher echocardiographic LV size in the swimmers vs non-training controls. However, contrasting findings are available. Rowland et al.[13] did not report any cardiac morphological differences between competitive runners (4 $h \cdot wk^{-1}$) and untrained prepubertal boys of the same age. Geenen et al.[10] did not report any LV remodelling in young boys after 8 months of aerobic training (2 $h \cdot wk^{-1}$) either. It seems therefore that the quality (intensity, frequency) of an aerobic training programme determines the extent of morphological cardiac adaptations. The type of training also appears to be critical as no cardiac adaptations occur with anaerobic training. The increase in cardiac chamber size in the swimmers was not associated with an increase in the LV septal and posterior wall thicknesses. These parameters were also found to be

Table 4. Adjusted cardiac morphological values resulting from ANCOVA

	LVIDd (mm)	PWT (mm)	ST (mm)	LVmass (g)
S	43.2 ± 2.2	6.3 ± 0.6	5.6 ± 0.7	78.4 ± 10.0
C	41.1 ± 2.3	6.2 ± 0.6	5.8 ± 0.7	70.9 ± 9.2
G	40.7 ± 2.3	6.5 ± 0.6	5.6 ± 0.7	69.2 ± 9.7
	S-C *	ns	ns	S-C *
	S-G **			S-G (ns)

Values are mean ± SD
Level of significance *p <0.05, **p<0.01

normal for the gymnasts. In the previously mentioned studies, higher values for both these parameters have been reported in prepubertal highly-trained athletes, but Mayers[19] when comparing 6-14 y runners vs controls matched for height and weight, did not note any differences despite higher LV internal dimensions in the trained group. To our knowledge, there is no report on cardiac parameters in prepubertal children involved in anaerobic training. In adults, Wolfe et al.[20] did not observe any differences in LV internal diastolic dimensions but higher septal and posterior wall thicknesses in anaerobic-type athletes compared to non-athletes were noted. Differences in certain biometric parameters (table 1) especially LBM, which was lower in the gymnast group, might have led to misleading results since cardiac parameters are strongly related to LBM. However, we observed exactly the same results when an appropriate statistical analysis was performed using LBM as a covariate (table 4). The LV enlargement of the swimmers could probably be attributed to the chronic volume overloading obtained during endurance physical conditioning[1].

The morphological adaptations were associated with functional adaptations with lower HR and higher SV at rest shown in the swimmers vs the other 2 groups, supporting data from previous studies[21,22]. In adults, it seems that endurance training is associated with an increase in parasympathetic tone at rest[1] similar mechanisms also occur in prepubertal children in intensive aerobic training. Intensive swimming or gymnastic training did not alter LV systolic function and LV shortening fraction and ejection fraction were found to be of the same order as those of the control group. Other investigations have also shown that LV contractility is not modified by moderate to intensive training in children[5,10-12]. Similarly, the diastolic filling characteristics of both our swimmers and gymnasts were similar to those of the control group (table 3). To our knowledge, the effect of aerobic or anaerobic training on diastolic function parameters has not been reported in children. In adults, several studies have reported enhanced diastolic function in highly-trained endurance athletes, related to facilitated early diastolic filling due to better ventricular compliance[23-25]. This was not the case in our highly-trained swimmers.

In conclusion, the findings of the current investigation suggest that cardiac structure and function adaptations occur in prepubertal children as a result of prolonged intensive training if the training programme focuses on aerobic exercise. However, neither LV systolic nor diastolic functions are affected by either aerobic or anaerobic training.

Further investigations are needed to clarify diastolic function adaptations to intensive training in children. The duration and intensity of endurance training necessary to elicit cardiac adaptations in children are important questions which need to be addressed.

References

1. Fagard, R., Aubert, A., Staessen, J., Vanden Eynde, E., Vanhees, L. and Amery, A. (1984) Cardiac structure and function in cyclists and runners. Comparative echocardiographic study. *British Heart Journal,* Vol. 52, pp. 124-9.
2. George, K.P., Wolfe, L.A. and Burggraf, G.W. (1991) The "athletic heart syndrome". A critical review. *Sports Medicine,* Vol. 11, pp. 300-31.
3. Keul, J., Dickhuth, H.H., Lehmann, M. and Staiger, J. (1982) The athlete's heart - haemodynamics and structure. *International Journal of Sports Medicine*, Vol. 3, pp. 33-43.
4. Longhurst, J.C., Kelly, A.R., Gonyea, W.J. and Mitchell, J.H. (1980) Echocardiographic LV masses in distance runners and weight lifters. *Journal of Applied Physiology*, Vol. 48, pp. 154-62.
5. Gutin, B., Mayers, N., Levy, J.A. and Herman, M.V. (1988) Physiological and echocardiographic studies of age-group runners, in *Competitive Sports for Children and Youth,* (eds. E.W. Brown and C.F. Branta), Human Kinetics, Champaign, Il., pp. 117-28.
6. Hollmann, W., Rost, R., Meirleir, K., Liesen, H., Heck, H. and Mader, A. (1986) Cardiovascular effects of extreme physical training. *Acta Medica Scandinavica,* Vol. 711 (suppl), pp. 193-203.
7. Rowland, T.W. (1992) Aerobic responses to physical training in children, in *Endurance in Sport,* (eds. R.J. Shephard and P.O. Astrand), Blackwell Scientific Publication, Oxford, pp. 377-84.
8. Wenkai, J. (1990) Effects of specificity in training on cardiorespiratory functions and anaerobic thresholds in athletes. *Sports Science,* Vol. 10, pp. 50-6.
9. Allen, H.D., Stanley, M.D., Goldberg, J., Sahn, D.J., Schy, N. and Wojcik, R. (1977) A quantitative echocardiograhic study of champion childhood swimmers. *Circulation,* Vol. 55, pp. 142-5.
10. Geenen, D.L., Gilliam, T.B., Crowley, D., Morehead-Steffens, C. and Rosenthal, A. (1982) Echocardiograph measures in 6 to 7 year old children after an 8 month exercise program. *American Journal of Cardiology*, Vol. 49, pp. 1990-5.
11. Medved, R., Fabecic-Sabadi, V. and Medved, V. (1986) Echocardiographic findings in children participating in swimming training. *International Journal of Sports Medicine*, Vol. 7, pp. 94-7.
12. Rowland, T.W., Delaney, B.C. and Siconolfi, S.F. (1987) "Athlete's heart" in prepubertal children. *Pediatrics*, Vol. 79, pp. 800-4.
13. Rowland, T.W., Unninthan, V.B., Macfarlane, N.G., Gibson, N.G. and Paton, J.Y. (1994) Clinical manifestations of the "athletes's heart" in prepubertal male runners. *International Journal of Sports Medicine*, Vol. 8, pp. 515-9.

14. Telford, R.D., McDonald, I.G., Ellis, L.B., Chennells, M.H.D., Sandstrom, E.R. and Fuller, P.J. (1988) Echocardiographic dimensions in trained and untrained 12-year old boys and girls. *Journal of Sports Science*, Vol. 6, pp. 49-57.
15. Obert, P., Courteix, D., Lecoq, A.M. and Guenon, P. (1996) Effect of long-term intensive swimming training on the upper body peak $\dot{V}O_2$ of prepubertal girls. *European Journal of Applied Physiology*, Vol. 73, pp. 136-43.
16. Sahn, D.J., DeMaria, A., Kisslo, J. and Weyman, D. (1978) Recommendations regarding quantitation in M-mode echocardiographic measurements. *Circulation*, Vol. 58, pp. 1072-83.
17. Lewis, J.F., Kuo, L.C., Nelson, J.G., Limacher, M.C. and Quinones, M.A. (1984) Pulsed Doppler echocardiographic determination of stroke volume and cardiac output: clinical validation of two new methods using the apical window. *Circulation*, Vol. 70, pp. 425-31.
18. Henry, W.L., Ware, J., Gardin, J.M., Hepner, S.I., McKay, J., Weiner, M. (1978) Echocardiographic measurements in normal subjects. Growth-related changes that occur between infancy and early adulthood. *Circulation*, Vol. 57, pp. 278-85.
19. Mayers, N.S. (1983) *Cardiac Response in Endurance Trained Children*, Doctoral dissertation, Columbia University.
20. Wolfe, L.A., Cunningham, D.A. and Boughner, D.R. (1986) Physical conditioning effects on cardiac dimensions: a review of echocardiographic studies. *Canadian Journal of Sport Sciences*, Vol. 11, pp. 66-79.
21. Eriksson, B.O. and Koch, G. (1973) Effect of physical training on hemodynamic response during submaximal and maximal exercise. *Acta Physiologica Scandinavica*, Vol. 87, pp. 27-9.
22. Thoren, C.A.R. and Asano, K. (1984) Functional capacity and cardiac function in 10-year-old-boys and girls with high and low running performance, in *Children and Sport*, (eds. J. Ilmarinen and I. Välimäki), Springer-Verlag, Berlin, pp 183-8.
23. Martinez-Mas, M.L., Chorro, F.J., Sanchis, J., Asensi, J.F., Losada, J.A., Ruitz, R. and Loez-Merino, V. (1994) Doppler assessment of LV diastolic function in marathon runners. *Journal of Sports Medicine and Physical Fitness*, Vol. 34, pp. 50-5.
24. Matsuda, M., Sugishita, Y., Koseki, S., Ito, I., Akatsuka, T. and Takamatsu, K. (1983) Effect of exercise on LV diastolic filling in athletes and nonathletes. *Journal of Applied Physiology*, Vol. 55, pp. 323-8.
25. Yellin, E.L., Nikolic, S. and Frater, R.W.M. (1990) Left ventricular filling dynamics and diastolic function. *Progress in Cardiovascular Disease*, Vol. 32, pp. 247-71.

CARDIAC RESPONSES TO EXERCISE IN ELITE MALE JUNIOR CYCLISTS

Cardiac responses in junior cyclists

V.B. UNNITHAN
Department of Movement Science and Physical Education, University of Liverpool, UK
T.W. ROWLAND
Baystate Medical Centre, Springfield, USA
N.T. CABLE and N. RAINE
Centre for Sport and Exercise Science, Liverpool John Moores University, Liverpool, UK

Keywords: Elite junior cyclists, peak $\dot{V}O_2$, stroke volume, cardiac output

Introduction

A significant and major determinant for success in cycling is the ability of the athlete to generate high levels of cardiac output (Q) during exercise and hence high levels of aerobic power[1]. These increases in Q are thought to be sustained primarily through increases in stroke volume[2]. With the refinement of nuclear and Doppler echocardiography it is possible to determine more accurately cardiovascular responses during exercise. A growing number of young cyclists are involved in high level training and competition[3], hence, it is worthwhile to investigate the extent to which long-term training and/or genetic factors (i.e. pre-selection) can influence cardiovascular responses during exercise and attempt to determine the cardiovascular basis for the superior peak $\dot{V}O_2$ seen in these young athletes[4]. This study compared cardiorespiratory and echocardiographic findings at submaximal and peak exercise intensity in a group of elite junior cyclists to those of active, but non-trained, controls.

Methods

Fourteen male subjects volunteered for the study; 7 members of the Great Britain (GB) junior cycling team and 7 control (non-training) subjects. Pubertal status was determined through self-assessment of pubic hair development[5,6]. Physical characteristics of the two groups are presented in table 1.

Children and Exercise XIX. Edited by Neil Armstrong, Brian Kirby and Joanne Welsman.
Published in 1997 by E & FN Spon, 2–6 Boundary Row, London, SE1 8HN.
ISBN 0 419 22100 X.

Table 1. Physical characteristics of cyclists and control subjects

	Cyclists	Control	p
Age (y)	16.3 ± 6.9	15.6 ± 0.5	ns
Stature (m)	1.81 ± 0.09	1.73 ± 0.04	ns
Body Mass (kg)	68 ± 8.4	61.1 ± 11.1	ns
Sum of skinfolds (mm)	24.0 ± 4.3	34.4 ± 14.1	ns
Tanner stage	4.3 ± 0.49	3.4 ± 0.97	ns
Body surface area (m^2)	1.87 ± 0.16	1.72 ±0.15	ns

Values are mean ± SD

The cyclists had trained for an average of 5.2 y (range, 2.5-10). They trained 5 times per week (range, 4-6), training for 9.9 $h \cdot wk^{-1}$ (range, 6-17). Average weekly distance was 205.8 km (range, 80-320). The control subjects completed a physical activity questionnaire modified from Bar-Or[7]. They participated in cycling, swimming and football, but none were undergoing formal training. Of the seven control subjects two rated themselves as highly active, two as active and one as moderately active and two as sedentary. All perceived their fitness levels as moderate. All subjects completed a pre-test questionnaire regarding activity and food intake on the day of the test. Sum of skinfolds was determined from biceps, triceps, subscapular and suprailliac skinfolds.

A Monark 814E cycle ergometer modified with racing pedals, toe-clips, dropped handlebars and a racing saddle, was used for all testing. La Voie et al.[8] demonstrated that accurate metabolic information from competitive racing cyclists could be obtained from a cycle ergometer providing the above stated modifications were made. Gotshall et al.[9] demonstrated that increases in stroke volume are directly related to a higher pedal cadence. Hence, the submaximal pedal cadence for the current study was selected to be 60 rpm.

All subjects cycled at two, 3 min, submaximal exercise intensities (50 W and 100 W). Subsequently, the cyclists increased their pedalling cadence to 90 rpm[8]. The controls increased cadence to 70 rpm and the exercise intensity was increased by 50 W every 2 min until volitional exhaustion. Criteria for peak $\dot{V}O_2$ were; inability to maintain selected cadence, respiratory exchange ratio (RER) greater than 1.0, and heart rate (HR) over 190 $beats \cdot min^{-1}$.

Cardio-respiratory variables were measured every 30 s throughout the test using an on-line computerised system (ULTIMA) which was calibrated prior to each test. Exercise heart rates were determined from an electrocardiogram, by averaging R-R intervals over ten consecutive beats, and recorded during the final 30s of each work load and at peak effort.

Cardiac stroke volume (SV) at rest and during exercise was estimated as the product of the aortic diameter (measured at rest) and integral of ascending blood velocity and time using a standard Doppler echocardiographic technique[10]. Velocity of blood in the ascending aorta was recorded with a 2.0 Mhz continuous wave Doppler transducer (Pedof) directed from the parasternal notch. The outline contour of the velocity curve over time was traced both on-line and off-line, with automatic integration of the velocity time integral (VTI). The end of each VTI was taken as the observed closure of the aortic valve. Values for VTI were averaged from 3-10 curves with highest values which demonstrated crisp spectral envelopes. These measurements were obtained during the final minute of each workload and the final 30 s of exercise.

The maximal systolic diameter of the ascending aorta was measured at rest by two dimensional echocardiography (Hewlett Packard Sonos 1500, Andover, MA, USA) in the parasternal long axis view with the subject supine. Five to 10 measurements were recorded from inner edge to inner edge at the level just above the sinuses of Valsalva (sinotubular junction). The mean resting value was used for all resting and exercise SV calculations. The cross-sectional area of the ascending aorta was calculated from the mean diameter, assuming the aorta to be circular. Q was calculated as the product of Doppler estimated SV (VTI x aortic root diameter) and HR. Values were related to body surface area[11] to calculate cardiac index and stroke index. Peak and mean ejection velocity were recorded from the velocity-time envelope and systolic ejection time was determined as VTI/mean velocity.

Results

Differences between groups were examined using unpaired t-tests. The only significant ($p < 0.05$) between groups difference for submaximal cardio-respiratory variables was %peak $\dot{V}O_2$; Cyclists: 32.1 ± 3.54 vs Control: 44.9 ± 6.51 at 50 W and Cyclists: 47.6 ± 5.4 vs Control: 67.9 ± 11.3 at 100 W. Peak $\dot{V}O_2$ was significantly ($p < 0.05$) higher in the cyclists (absolute and relative) than the control subjects (Cyclists: 4.9 ± 0.47 vs Control: 3.41 ± 0.62 $L \cdot min^{-1}$ and Cyclists: 71.8 ± 3.2 vs Control: 55.8 ± 5.8 $mL \cdot kg^{-1} \cdot min^{-1}$). SV index (Cyclists: 65 ± 11 vs Control: 49 ± 5 $mL \cdot m^{-2}$)and cardiac index (Cyclists: 12.19 ± 1.89 vs Control: 9.53 ± 0.85 $L.min^{-1}.m^{-2}$) were significantly ($p < 0.05$) higher in the cyclists at peak exercise. Both maximal (Cyclists: 219 ± 33 vs Control: 175 ± 17 $cm \cdot s^{-1}$) and mean (Cyclists: 149 ± 22 vs Control: 122 ± 9 $cm \cdot s^{-1}$) blood velocities were significantly higher ($p < 0.05$) in the cyclists at peak exercise. No significant differences were noted for duration of systole and diastole at either rest or peak exercise. Left ventricular posterior wall thickness (LVPW) index was the only resting cardiac dimension that was significantly ($p < 0.05$) different (Cyclists: 6.1 ± 0.7 vs Control: 5.2 ± 0.8 $mm \cdot m^{-2}$). All other comparisons were non-significant.

Discussion

Although the cyclists tended to be taller, heavier, leaner and have greater body surface area than the control subjects, these differences were not significant. Hence, the use of body surface area (index) to "scale" the data did not penalise either group.

The mean values for mass-relative and absolute peak $\dot{V}O_2$ of the cyclists are consistent with other reports[12,13,14] In the only comparative study with junior cyclists,

Faria et al.[3] obtained mean peak $\dot{V}O_2$ values of 75.5 $mL \cdot kg^{-1} \cdot min^{-1}$ from the US Reebok Junior National cycling team.

No differences in SV index were found at rest. This finding is consistent with no differences in resting left ventricular shortening fraction (SF) and peak Doppler velocity, both of which are indicators of contractility. In addition, there was no significant difference in left ventricular end diastolic dimension (LVEDD) at rest. These results are consistent with previous findings[15,16], which demonstrated no significant differences in SV index, LVEDD and SF between elite adult male endurance and strength trained athletes, and controls. In contrast Obert et al.[17] found greater LVEDD in highly trained pre-pubertal swimmers but no differences in SF. Similar findings were reported in highly trained adult cyclists vs controls[18]. Fagard et al.[19] also demonstrated increased LVEDD at rest in elite cyclists (mean age 22 y), but cautioned that cardiac alterations have a minimum effect on the systolic function of the heart.

No significant differences were noted for SV index at 50W and 100W, but at peak exercise SV index was significantly higher in the cyclists. In conjunction with the lack of difference in $a - \bar{v}O_2$ difference, the superior peak $\dot{V}O_2$ in the cyclists is likely to be the result of the enhanced SV response at peak exercise. In athletes, this has been demonstrated at peak exercise[20]. Several studies[13,20,21] have demonstrated increases in SV only in trained adult cyclists at peak exercise. The possible reason for the greater SV index at peak exercise may result from a combination of factors; a) greater pre-load resulting from either increased left ventricular size[22] or enhanced filling at peak exercise due to superior systemic venous return[9], b) greater myocardial contractility, and or c) a greater fall in peripheral vascular resistance in the cyclists (less afterload). Maximal systolic velocity at peak exercise intensity was significantly ($p < 0.05$) higher in the cyclists, while the duration of systole remained similar to the control group. Therefore, the athletes were capable of ejecting a greater relative stroke volume in the same amount of time. This can only occur if contractility is greater or peripheral resistance falls more. There is evidence to support both theories. Schairer et al.[23] demonstrated in elite male cyclists (19 y) that shortening fraction increased significantly ($p < 0.01$) at maximal exercise and Oyen et al.[24] demonstrated increased LVEDD at the end of supine exercise in healthy normal children.

At rest only LVPW index was significantly greater than in the cyclists than in the controls and chamber sizes were not different. Thus, the elite cyclists did not show the mild left ventricular dilatation reported previously in older cyclists[19,25]. The present findings support the theory that the athlete's heart is acquired after many years of training[4]. They also suggest, as stated above that greater left ventricular size at rest is not the explanation for the greater relative SV in athletes. The increases in SV in cyclists during exercise possibly result from enhanced venous return and hence preload resulting from the superior muscle pump characteristics of the peripheral musculature.

Acknowledgements

Hewlett Packard Ltd for donating the HP Sonos 1500 Cardiovascular Imaging System. Isis Hreczuk-Hirst, Liu Xun and Kevin Jones for technical assistance.

References

1. Falsetti, H., Gisolfi, C. and Lemon, D. (1982) Non-invasive evaluation of left ventricular function in trained bicyclist. *Journal of Sports Medicine*, Vol. 22, pp. 199-205.
2. Coyle, E.F., Coggan, A.R., Hopper, M.K. and Walters, T.J. (1988) Determinants of endurance in well trained cyclist. *Journal of Applied Physiology*, Vol. 64, pp. 2666-70.
3. Faria, I.E., Faria, E.W., Roberts, S. and Yoshimura, D. (1989) Comparison of physical and physiological characteristics in elite young and mature cyclists. *Research Quarterly for Exercise and Sport*, Vol. 60, pp. 388-95.
4. Rowland, T.W., Unnithan, V.B., MacFarlane, N.G., Gibson, N.G. and Paton, J.Y. (1994) Clinical manifestations of the " Athlete's heart" in prepubertal male runners. *International Journal of Sports Medicine*, Vol. 15, pp. 515-9.
5. Tanner, J.M. (1962) *Growth and Adolescence*, Blackwell, Oxford.
6. Matsudo, S.M.M. and Matsudo, V.K.R. (1994) Physician assessment of sexual maturation in Brazilian boys and girls: concordance and reproducibility. *American Journal of Human Biology*, Vol. 6, pp. 451-5.
7. Bar-Or, O. (1983) *Pediatric Sports Medicine for the Practitioner: from Physiologic Principles to Clinical Applications*, Springer-Verlag, New York, pp.10-1.
8. LaVoie, N., Mercer, T.H. and Ciolfi, M.A. (1986) $\dot{V}O_2$ max of competitive cyclists using a conventional cycle ergometer test versus a sport specific bicycle test, in *Science of Cycling*, (ed. E. Burke), Human Kinetics, London, pp. 20-2.
9. Gotshall, R.W., Bauer, R.W. and Fahrner, S.L. (1996) Cycling cadence alters exercise hemodynamics. *International Journal of Sports Medicine*, Vol. 17, pp. 17-21.
10. Nishimura, R.A., Callahan, M.J., Schaff, H.V., Ilstrup, D.M., Miller, F.A. and Tajik, A.J. (1984) Noninvasive measurement of cardiac output by continuous-wave Doppler echocardiography: initial experience and review of the literature. *Mayo Clinical Proceedings*, Vol. 59, pp. 484-9.
11. Collins, W.E. (1967) *Clinical Spirometry*, Warren E. Collins Inc, Braintree, MA, USA.
12. Hagberg, J.M., Mullin, J.P., Bahrke, M. and Limburg, J. (1979) Physiological profiles and selected physiological characteristics of national class American cyclists. *Journal of Sports Medicine*, Vol. 19, pp. 341-6.
13. Di Bello, V., Talarico, L., Di Muro, C., Santoro, G., Bertini, A., Giorgi, D., Caputo, M.T., Bianchi, M., Cecchini, L. and Giusti, C. (1995) Evaluation of maximal left ventricular performance in elite bicyclists. *International Journal of Sports Medicine*, Vol. 16, pp. 498-506.
14. White, J.A., Quinn, G., Al-Dawalibi, M., Mulhall, J. (1982) Seasonal change in performance, Part 1. The British Olympic road race squad. *British Journal of Sports Medicine*, Vol. 15, pp. 4-12.
15. Ahmad, M. and Dubiel, J.P. (1990) Left ventricular response to exercise in regular runners and controls. *Clinical Nuclear Medicine*, Vol. 15, pp. 630-5.

16. MacFarlane, N., Northridge, D.B., Wright, A.R., Grant, S. and Dargie, H.J. (1991) A comparative study of left ventricular structure and function in elite athletes. *British Journal of Sports Medicine*, Vol. 25, pp. 45-8.

17. Obert, P., Stecken, F., Courteix, D., Germain, P., LeCoq, A.M. and Guenon, P. (1996) *Effect of Intensive Swimming Training on Left Ventricular Size and Function in Prepubertal Children*, in Proceedings of the European College of Sports Medicine: First Annual Congress, pp. 526-7.

18. Nishimura, T., Yamada, Y. and Kawai, C. (1980) Echocardiographic evaluation of long-term effects of exercise on left ventricular hypertrophy and function in professional bicyclists. *Circulation*, Vol. 61, pp. 832-40.

19. Fagard, R., Van den Broeke, C., Bieleu, E., Vanhees, L. and Amery, A. (1987) Assessment of stiffness of the hypertrophied left ventricle of bicyclists using left ventricular inflow doppler velocimetry. *Journal of American College of Cardiology*, Vol. 9, pp. 1250-4.

20. Gledhill, N., Cox, D. and Jamnik, R. (1994) Endurance athletes' stroke volume does not plateau: major advantage is diastolic function. *Medicine and Science in Sports and Exercise*, Vol. 26, pp. 1116-21.

21. Di Bello, V., Santoro, G., Talarico, L., Di Muro, C., Caputo, M.T., Giorgi, D., Bertini, A., Bianchi, M. and Giusti, C. (1996) Left ventricular function during exercise in athletes and in sedentary men. *Medicine and Science in Sports and Exercise*, Vol. 28, pp.190-6.

22. Levine, B.D., Lane, D.L., Buckey, J.C., Friedman, D.B. and Blomquist, C.G. (1991) Left ventricular pressure-volume and Frank-Starling relations in endurance athletes. *Circulation*, Vol. 84, pp.1016-23.

23. Schairer, J.R., Briggs, D., Kono, T., Alam, M., Keteyian, S., Fedel, F., Rosman, H., Kuznetsov, A. and Stein, P.D. (1991) Left ventricular function immediately after exercise in elite cyclists. *Cardiology*, Vol. 79, pp. 284-9.

24. Oyen, E.M., Ignatzy, K., Ingerfeld, G. and Brode, P. (1987) Echocardiographic evaluation of left ventricular reserve in normal children during supine bicycle exercise. *International Journal of Cardiology*, Vol. 14, pp. 515-9.

25. Fagard, R., Aubert, A., Lysens, R., Staessen, J., Vanhees, L., Amery, L. and Amery, A. (1983) Noninvasive assessment of seasonal variations in cardiac structure and function in cyclists. *Circulation*, Vol. 67, pp. 896-900.

CARDIOVASCULAR ADJUSTMENTS FOLLOWING MAXIMAL EXERCISE IN ELITE MALE JUNIOR CYCLISTS

Post-exercise hypotension in junior cyclists

N.T. CABLE and N.M. RAINE
Centre for Sport and Exercise Science, Liverpool John Moores University, Liverpool, UK
V.B. UNNITHAN
Department of Movement Science, University of Liverpool, Liverpool, UK
T.W. ROWLAND
Department of Pediatrics, Baystate Medical Centre, Springfield, USA
Keywords: Cardiovascular adjustments, calf blood flow, elite cyclists, post-exercise hypotension, stroke volume

Introduction

In adults, there is a decrease in both systolic (SBP) and diastolic (DBP) blood pressure immediately following an acute bout of muscular exercise. This hypotensive effect is well documented in both hypertensive[1,2] and normotensive[3,4] individuals and may persist for up to 12.7 h[5]. Several mechanisms have been proposed to account for this effect including the release of vasoactive metabolites from the exercising muscle[3], the resetting of baroreflex control of sympathetic tone[2], inhibition of sympathetic nervous activity[6] and thermoregulatory induced changes in peripheral blood flow following exercise[7]. However, despite these suggestions the underlying haemodynamic changes that occur immediately post-exercise remain unclear.

The cardiovascular adjustments that occur during cycling[8], and immediate post-exercise changes in cardiac dimensions and performance[9] have been investigated in elite young athletes. However, to our knowledge post-exercise blood pressure regulation and the associated haemodynamic changes have not been investigated in such an adolescent population. The present study therefore examined the recovery blood pressure response following maximal exercise in normally active adolescent boys and highly trained elite junior cyclists. In addition the relationship between blood pressure and peripheral blood flow was investigated in both groups of subjects.

Subjects

Six elite junior male cyclists and six age-matched non-training adolescent male control subjects gave their written and informed consent to participate in the following study.

Children and Exercise XIX. Edited by Neil Armstrong, Brian Kirby and Joanne Welsman.
Published in 1997 by E & FN Spon, 2–6 Boundary Row, London, SE1 8HN.
ISBN 0 419 22100 X.

The protocol and experimental procedures had been approved by the Human Ethics Committee of the University of Liverpool.

Subject characteristics are itemised in table 1. The control subjects were classified as normally active and participated in a range of activities including cycling, swimming and football, but none were undergoing formal training. The elite junior cyclists were highly trained. They had been competing for 4.9 ± 2.9 y and currently were training for 9.9 ± 3.48 $h \cdot wk^{-1}$ with a weekly training mileage of 205.8 ± 76.5 km.

Methods

On arriving in the laboratory subjects rested in the seated position for approximately 15 min during which time they completed subject consent forms. Following this period subjects adopted the supine posture whilst experimental apparatus was placed in position. Subjects then rested quietly in this position for 15 min to allow for the measurement of baseline blood pressures, heart rate, stroke volume and calf blood flow. Blood pressure and heart rate were measured continuously and sampled at 30 s intervals, SV at 10 min and CBF at 0 and 15 min of the baseline period.

Subjects then exercise on a Monark Ergomedic 814E ergometer modified to include racing pedals, toe clips, dropped handlebars and racing saddle. All subjects completed two, 3 min, submaximal workloads of 50 and 100W at a cadence of 60 $rev \cdot min^{-1}$. At the end of this period, the cyclists increased their cadence to 90 $rev \cdot min^{-1}$ in accordance with[8], and the control subjects increased their pedal frequency to 70 $rev \cdot min^{-1}$ and in both groups the work intensity was increased by 50W every 2 min until volitional exhaustion was attained. The criteria for test termination were: 1) an inability to maintain the selected cadence, 2) respiratory exchange ratio of greater than 1.0, and 3) heart rate greater than 190 $beats \cdot min^{-1}$. Oxygen consumption was measured every 30 s using a metabolic cart which was calibrated prior to each test. Heart rate was monitored continuously using an electrocardiograph.

Table 1. Physical characteristics of cyclists and control subjects following exercise

	Cyclists	Control
Age (y)	16.3 ± 0.3	15.6 ± 0.2
Stature (m)	1.81 ± 0.03	1.73 ± 0.02
Body Mass (kg)	68.0 ± 3.2	61.1 ± 4.2
Sum of Skinfolds (mm)	24.0 ± 1.6	34.4 ± 5.3
Tanner Stage	4.3 ± 0.2	3.4 ± 0.4
Body Surface Area (m^2)	1.87 ± 0.06	1.72 ± 0.06
Peak $\dot{V}O_2$ ($L \cdot min^{-1}$)	4.90 ± 0.18*	3.41 ± 0.23
Peak $\dot{V}O_2$ ($mL \cdot kg^{-1} \cdot min^{-1}$)	71.8 ± 1.2*	55.8 ± 2.2

Values are mean ± SEM
Level of significance *$p < 0.05$

Following exercise subjects returned to the supine position for 30 min of recovery measurements. Blood pressures and heart rate were again recorded continuously and stroke volume and calf blood flow measured at 5, 15 and 30 min of recovery.

Beat-by-beat systolic (SBP) and diastolic blood pressure (DBP) and heart rate were measured non-invasively from the digital artery using a photoplethysmographic device (Ohmeda Finapres 2300, Englewood, USA). This instrument has been shown to accurately track the arterial pressure waveform during a variety of blood pressure raising and lowering laboratory tests[10]. Throughout measurements the hand was maintained at heart level. The output voltage from the finapres was relayed to a personal computer comprising an 8-channel analogue-to-digital converter and displayed in real time. Mean arterial pressure (MAP) was calculated according to the formula; MAP = 1/3 (SBP - DBP).

Blood flow in the calf was measured non-invasively by venous occlusion plethysmography using calibrated mercury in silastic strain gauges (Parkes Medical Electronic, Oregon, USA). With the ankle and knee supported, a cuff above the knee was inflated to a pressure of 50 mmHg in a cycle of 10 s inflation - 5 s deflation for a total of 3 min using a rapid cuff inflator (Hokanson, Washington, USA). Blood flow to the foot was occluded for 1 min before each venous occlusion cycle commenced by inflating an ankle cuff to 200 mmHg. Calf blood flow was calculated [11] from the percentage change in limb circumference during venous occlusion and is expressed as blood flow in $mL \cdot 100mLtissue^{-1} \cdot min^{-1}$. Calf vascular resistance (CVR) and calf vascular conductance (CVC) were calculated using the following formulae:- CVR = MAP/CBF and CVC = CBF/MAP.

Cardiac stroke volume at rest and during recovery from exercise was estimated as the product of the aortic diameter (CSA) and integral of ascending blood velocity and time (VTI) using standard Doppler echocardiographic techniques[12]. Velocity of blood in the ascending aorta was recorded with a 2.0 Mhz continuous wave Doppler transducer (Pedof) directed from the parasternal notch, and maximal systolic diameter of the aorta measured by M-mode echocardiography (Hewlett Packard Sonos 1500, Andover, MA, USA). Stroke volume was calculated as CSA x VTI. All measurements were recorded in the supine position.

Data analyses

Results are expressed as means $\pm$ SEM. Changes from baseline and differences between subject groups in recovery variables were assessed using two way analysis of variance with repeated measures. Pearson's product moment correlation analysis was used to determine the strength of relationship between recovery measurements. Unpaired t-tests were used to compare differences between baseline values.

Results

Prior to exercise there were no significant differences in baseline SBP or heart rate between the groups. Diastolic (61 ± 1.9 vs 73 ± 2 mmHg) and MAP (81 ± 2 vs 92 ± 3 mmHg) were significantly lower ($p < 0.05$) in the control subjects than in the cyclists respectively. Stroke volume, cardiac output, CBF and CVC were not different between groups.

In the cyclists SBP, DBP and MAP were all significantly reduced ($p < 0.05$) below baseline values for 25 min of recovery and had not returned to pre-exercise levels after 30 min. In comparison recovery blood pressures had returned to pre-exercise values 20 min after exercise in the control subjects, and at no time were they significantly reduced below baseline ($p > 0.05$).

From table 2 it is apparent that there was an hypotensive effect of exercise in the cyclists, with MAP being reduced by 24 mmHg during the first 10 min of recovery compared with -2 to -6 mmHg in control subjects. The reductions in pressure from baseline were significantly greater in the cyclists than in the control subjects ($p < 0.05$) throughout the recovery period. Recovery heart rates were similarly elevated in both groups and remained 15 ± 6 and 19 ± 5 beats·min^{-1} above baseline values in controls and cyclists 30 min after exercise.

In recovery, SV was not different between groups and was unaltered relative to baseline (table 3). Following exercise CBF was significantly elevated above baseline levels in controls and cyclists. Although CBF tended to be greater in the cyclists during the recovery period, these differences were not significant (table 3). Similarly, CVC was significantly elevated throughout recovery in both groups and was greater in the cyclists although not significantly so ($p > 0.05$). However there was a significant group/time interaction suggesting that the pattern of recovery CVC was different between the subjects.

When all subject data were pooled there was a significant inverse relationship between MAP and CVC ($r = -0.68$; $p < 0.01$). Approximately 46% of the variation in MAP can be explained by the changes in CVC.

Table 2. The change in recovery SBP, DBP and MAP from baseline values following exercise in control subjects and elite cyclists

Recovery	SBP (mmHg)		DBP (mmHg)		MAP (mmHg)	
Time (min)	Controls	Cyclists	Controls	Cyclists	Controls	Cyclists
5	4 ± 10	-28 ± 8*	-4 ± 5	-22 ± 5*	-2 ± 6*	-24 ± 5*
10	-8 ± 11	-32 ± 7*	-5 ± 5	-20 ± 5*	-6 ± 6*	-24 ± 5*
15	-7 ± 9	-22 ± 7*	-3 ± 2	-14 ± 6*	-4 ± 4*	-17 ± 6*
20	-5 ± 9	-18 ± 4*	2 ± 4	-13 ± 4*	0 ± 6*	-15 ± 4*
25	4 ± 7	-14 ± 6*	7 ± 3	-12 ± 6*	6 ± 4*	-13 ± 6*
30	2 ± 6	-7 ± 5*	7 ± 2	-10 ± 5*	5 ± 3*	-9 ± 5*

Values are mean ± SEM

*Anova revealed significant group and time differences ($p < 0.05$) but no significant interaction effect for the response of each pressure.

Table 3. Stroke volume, calf blood flow and calf vascular conductance at baseline and following exercise in control subjects and elite cyclists

Time (min)	SV (mL)		CBF (mL·100mL^{-1}·min^{-1})		CVC (mLflow·mmHg^{-1})	
	Controls	Cyclists	Controls	Cyclists	Controls	Cyclists
Baseline	86 ± 10	94 ± 9	3.4 ± 0.5	3.4 ± 0.9	0.04 ± 0.01	0.04 ± 0.01
5 post-Ex	97 ± 9	90 ± 14	9.8 ± 1.8	12.7 ± 2.1	0.13 ± 0.02	0.20 ± 0.04
15 post-Ex	88 ± 7	81 ± 13	8.1 ± 1.1	10.0 ± 1.7	0.10 ± 0.01	0.13 ± 0.03
30 post-Ex	77 ± 4	85 ± 8	6.2 ± 0.7	7.2 ± 1.4	0.07 ± 0.01	0.09 ± 0.03

Values are mean ± SEM

Anova revealed no significant group or interaction effects ($p > 0.05$) but significant time effects for CBF and CVC ($p < 0.05$).

Discussion

The hypotensive effects of an acute bout of exercise have been described previously in an adult population[1,2,3,4]. In particular, following maximal exercise, there is a prolonged diastolic hypotension, suggesting that this response is mediated by a decrease in total peripheral resistance rather than a decline in cardiac contractility[4]. The present study was designed to investigate this phenomenon in adolescent boys of different training status, as this population has not previously been examined.

This study confirms the presence of post-exercise hypotension, but only in the highly trained group of elite cyclists. Mean arterial pressure was significantly reduced for the majority of the recovery period in the cyclists, and remained 9 mmHg below baseline values 30 min after the cessation of exercise. This arterial hypotension was characterised by a fall in both systolic and diastolic pressures, with MAP declining by 24 mmHg during the first 10 min of recovery. In the control subjects there was a transient reduction in MAP of up to 6 mmHg during the first 15 min of recovery. However, this reduction in arterial pressure was not significantly below pre-exercise levels. Indeed, after 20 min of recovery MAP had returned to baseline values and remained slightly elevated for the remainder of the recovery period. This difference in response pattern is confirmed by the significantly greater change from baseline observed for SBP, DBP and MAP in the junior cyclists than in control subjects (table 2).

Post-exercise hypotension is reportedly mediated via a decreased systemic vascular resistance rather than reduced cardiac contractility[4,13,14]. In the present study, stroke volume was slightly elevated or remained at baseline levels throughout recovery in both groups. Given that heart rate was significantly greater than before exercise during this period, cardiac output was augmented confirming the observations that the decline in MAP was mediated by a fall in vascular resistance[4,13,14].

The nature of the vasodilatory signal causing this reduction in peripheral resistance is not established. Mechanisms including resetting of the baroreflex[2], reduced sympathetic nervous activity[6] and thermoregulatory considerations[7] have been suggested. A further possibility relates to a persistent vasodilatation of the exercising limb. Calf blood flow was significantly elevated throughout the recovery period in both groups of subjects. Although CBF was not significantly greater in the cyclists than in control subjects, it tended to be higher, and indeed there was a significant group/time interaction effect for calf vascular conductance which indicates that there was greater vasodilatation in the lower limb of the trained subjects. This suggests that the greater hypotensive effect in the cyclists may be mediated by a more persistent vasodilatation in the exercised limb than in control subjects. This hypothesis is supported by the observation of a significant negative correlation between MAP and CVC when all subject data is pooled ($r = -0.68$; $p < 0.01$), indicating that the greater the calf blood flow the greater the reduction in MAP.

Although CBF is not significantly greater in the cyclists, the data are reported as blood flow per 100ml of tissue and is therefore a relative measure. Muscle mass was not assessed in this study. However, given the training status of the cyclists, their capacity to perform at far greater workloads at exhaustion and their significantly higher $\dot{V}O_2$ max, it is reasonable to assume that they had a much greater muscle mass. This would suggest that the whole limb or total blood flow to muscle in the immediate post-exercise period was greater in the cyclists than in control subjects, thereby reducing systemic vascular resistance further and preempting hypotension. The degree of hypotension observed in the cyclists is much greater than that reported previously [4,13] following this mode of exercise. This may be accounted for by the greater training status of the subjects in this study, again suggesting that the degree of hypotension is dependent on the capacity to generate high muscle blood flow. This hypothesis warrants further investigation.

In conclusion, this study has demonstrated the presence of a significant post-exercise hypotension in highly trained elite young cyclists. This is mediated by a reduction in systemic vascular resistance that is related to a persistent increase in calf vascular conductance relative to baseline values. This increase in CVC appears to compromise the regulation of blood pressure as it is not evident in normally active adolescent boys, suggesting that training alters blood pressure regulation. This requires further investigation.

References

1. Wilcox, R.G., Bennett, T., Brown, A.M. and MacDonald, I.A. (1982) Is exercise good for blood pressure? *British Medical Journal*, Vol. 285, pp.767-9.
2. Bennett, T., Wilcox, R.G. and MacDonald, I.A. (1984) Post-exercise reduction of blood pressure in hypertensive men is not due to impairment of baroreflex function. *Clinical Science*, Vol. 67, pp. 97-103.
3. Kaufman, F.L., Hughson, R.L. and Schaman, J.P. (1987) Effect of exercise on recovery pressure in normotensive and hypertensive subjects. *Medicine and Science in Sport and Exercise*, Vol. 19, pp. 17-20.

4. Coats, A.J.S., Conway, J., Isea, J.E., Pannarale, G., Sleight, P. and Somers, V.K. (1989) Systemic and forearm vascular resistance changes after upright bicycle exercise in man. *Journal of Physiology*, Vol. 413, pp. 289-98.
5. Pescatello, L.S., Fargo, A.E., Leach, C.N. and Scherzer, H.H. (1991) Short-term effect of dynamic exercise on arterial blood pressure. *Circulation*, Vol. 83, pp. 1557-61.
6. Floras, J.S., Skiney, C.A., Aylward, P.E., Seals D.R., Thoren, P.E. and Mark, A.L. (1989) Post-exercise hypotension and sympathoinhibition in borderline hypertensive men. *Hypertension*, Vol. 14, pp. 28-35.
7. Franklin, P.J., Green, D.J. and Cable, N.T. (1993) The influence of thermoregulatory mechanisms on post-exercise hypotension in humans. *Journal of Physiology*, Vol. 470, pp. 231-41.
8. Faria, I.E., Faria, E.W., Roberts, S. and Yoshimura, D. (1989) Comparison of physical and physiological characteristics in elite young and mature cyclists. *Research Quarterly For Exercise and Sport*, Vol. 4, pp. 388-95.
9. Rowland, T.W. (1987) Post-exercise echocardiography in pre-pubertal boys. *Medicine and Science in Sport and Exercise*, Vol. 19, pp. 393-7.
10. Parati, G., Casadei, R., Gropelli, A., DiRenzo, M. and Mancia, G. (1989) Comparison of finger and intraarterial blood pressure monitoring at rest and during laboratory testing. *Hypertension*, Vol. 13, pp. 647-55.
11. Whitney, R.J. (1953) The measurement of volume changes in human limbs. *Journal of Physiology*, Vol. 121, pp. 1-27.
12. Nishimura, R.A., Callahan, M.J., Schaff, H.V., Ilstrup, M., Miller, F.A. and Tajik, A.J. (1984) Non-invasive measurement of cardiac output by continuous-wave Doppler echocardiography: Initial experience and review of the literature. *Mayo Clinical Proceedings*, Vol. 59, pp. 484-9.
13. Piepoli, M., Coats, A.J.S., Adamopoulos, S., Bernardi, L., Feng, Y.H., Conway, J. and Sleight, P. (1993) Persistent peripheral vasodilatation and sympathetic activity in hypotension after maximal exercise. *Journal of Applied Physiology*, Vol. 75, pp. 1807-14.
14. Casiglai, E., Palatini, P., Bongiovi, S., Mario, L., Colangeli, G., Ginocchio, G. and Pessina, A.C. (1994) Haemodynamics of recovery after strenuous exercise in physically trained hypertensive and normotensive subjects. *Clinical Science*, Vol. 86, pp. 27-34.

DIETARY INTAKE IN ADOLESCENT ORIENTEERING ATHLETES IN SWEDEN

Dietary intake in adolescent athletes

A.K. YNGVE, U. M. EKELUND and M. SJÖSTRÖM
Dept of Medical Nutrition and Dept of Biosciences at Novum, Karolinska Institutet, Stockholm and Dept of Physical Education and Health, University of Örebro, Sweden
Keywords: Adolescence, activity assessment, dietary assessment, energy balance, energy expenditure, nutrient intake, orienteering, physical exercise

Introduction

Several studies of adolescents' eating habits in Sweden[1-3] and internationally[4-9] have shown that their intakes of zinc, iron, selenium and folic acid as well as other nutrients are lower than the recommended dietary allowances, especially for girls. It has been suggested that a higher energy expenditure with a subsequently higher energy intake would lead to greater essential nutrient intakes, whereby the problem would automatically be resolved[10]. The nutrient intake of those involved in orienteering has been questioned[11].

A recently published statement from the American Dietetic Association (ADA) emphasised the importance of ensuring children's and adolescents' nutrient needs are met and that they have adequate energy stores to fuel the growth spurt[12]. Sports-related expectations combined with an obsessive focus on weight and food intake may set the stage for eating disorders[12].

Risk for both undernutrition and overnutrition is present in adolescence, although the risk for undernutrition in particular, may be increased during the physiologic stress associated with athletic performance. It is therefore important to monitor eating habits as well as height and weight during this vulnerable period, particularly in active females.

This cross-sectional study assessed dietary intakes using a 7 d weighed record. Physical activity was recorded using a diary during the same period. This particular boarding school in Strängnäs, Sweden, accepts high school students who are 17-19 y and who qualify as elite orienteerers according to national standards. Each student lives in their own apartment, they come from all parts of Sweden and most are responsible for their own meals for the first time in their lives. On weekdays, lunch is served in school. Aside from one dinner per week which is prepared with the coach,

Children and Exercise XIX. Edited by Neil Armstrong, Brian Kirby and Joanne Welsman.
Published in 1997 by E & FN Spon, 2–6 Boundary Row, London, SE1 8HN.
ISBN 0 419 22100 X.

most meals are eaten in private. Weekends are often spent with family at home. Over one week in March 1996, 34 boarding school students' dietary intake as well as their physical activity level were investigated.

Subjects and methods

All elite orienteering students at the school, 15 boys and 19 girls, were thoroughly instructed how to weigh and register everything they ate and drank over the 7 d period. They were equipped with an electronic scale and a standardised registration form. The students were asked to describe the food items as thoroughly as possible, e.g. fat content of cheese and milk, type of bread, important ingredients in different dishes etc. Support was provided by facilitators who were present at the boarding school for the first 3 d of recording, as well as available via telephone for the last 4 d, if required.

Dietary data were analysed using the national Swedish food database and resulting nutrient intakes were then compared to relevant recommendations, namely the Nordic Nutrition Recommendations (NNR)[13].

Physical activity was registered in a diary which is to say that the students registered their subjectively perceived activity level at 15 min intervals. They did this using a scale from 1 to 10, where 1 was equivalent to Basal Metabolic Rate (BMR_{est}) and 10 was equivalent to ten times BMR_{est}, a modified model from Bouchard et al[14]. From these figures, Total Daily Energy Expenditure (TDEE) was estimated as well as Physical Activity Level (PAL), which was computed by comparing TDEE with the BMR_{est} according to Schofield[15].

Results

Physical characteristics and activity measures are given in table 1, and energy and nutrient intakes are summarised in table 2.

Mean total energy intakes (EI) were 14.4 ± 3.2 MJ for boys, 10.8 ± 2.6 MJ for girls. Data on mean energy intakes divided by BMR_{est} (EI/BMR_{est}) were similar to PAL levels. Seven of 19 girls showed lower mean data for EI compared to TDEE for the whole week (fig 1).

Breakfast and lunch were regularly distributed over the day during all weekdays. Weekend meals were more randomly distributed, and energy intakes were lower (fig 2). The girls' largest source of energy were snacks (boys 26%, girls 29%EI), followed by dinner (boys 32%, girls 28%E). Corresponding figures for energy contribution from lunch were 25% for boys 23%E for girls, and from breakfast 17% for boys, 20%E for girls.

The mean fat intake in percentage energy was higher than recommended and similar for both groups. Fibre density ($g{\cdot}MJ^{-1}$) was generally low, and lower for boys than for girls. Sugar intake was high. The boys had a greater intake of sugar than the girls which was also the case with percentage energy intake (table 2). Two of the boys had an intake of sugar of 20%EI on individual days. There were no vegetarians in the

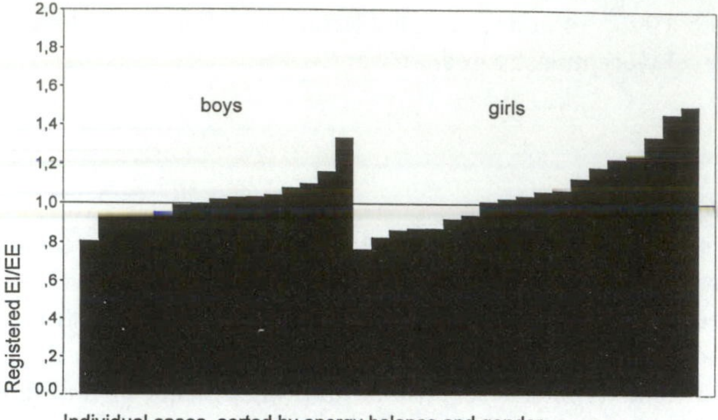

Fig. 1. Relative comparison of Energy Intake (EI) with Energy expenditure (EE) in boys and girls respectively, mean for the week

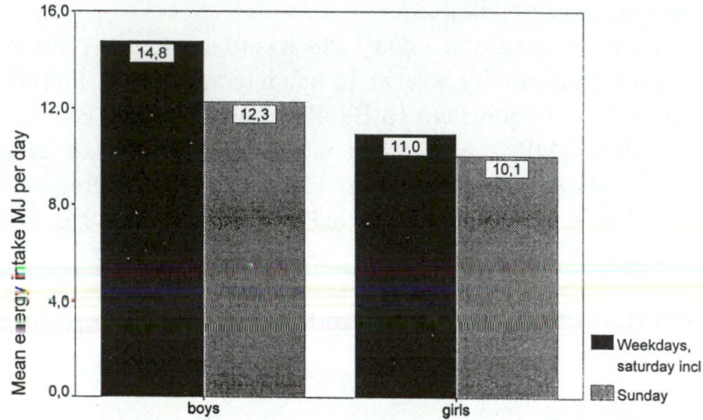

Fig. 2. Mean energy intake for boys and girls respectively, comparison weekdays with Sunday

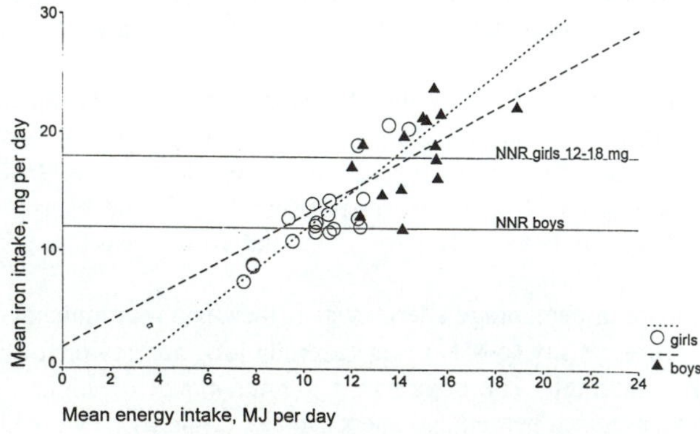

Fig. 3. Iron intake per day, mean for the week, shown by gender

Table 1. Physical characteristics of boys and girls and activity measures

	Boys (n=15)		Girls (n=19)	
Age (y)	17.7	±1.0	17.7	±0.9
Height (m)	1.80	±0.06	1.68	±0.06
Weight (kg)	68.2	±5.8	58.4	±6.7
BMI ($kg \cdot m^{-2}$)	21.1	±1.9	20.5	±1.5
BMR_{est} ($MJ \cdot d^{-1}$)	7.82	±0.40	6.22	±0.48
TDEE ($MJ \cdot d^{-1}$)	14.3	±1.1	11.0	±1.2
PAL	1.83	±0.10	1.77	±0.10
EI/BMR_{est}	1.84	±0.39	1.75	±0.43

Values are mean ± SD

group. Only three students reported any intake of alcohol.

Selenium intakes were low for both groups, some girls had low folic acid and iron intakes. Intakes of several micronutrients (e.g. iron) were closely correlated to energy intakes (fig 3).

Discussion

Macronutrients and energy

EI/BMR_{est} indicated that under-reporting of food intake was of minor importance. The mean EI in this study was higher than in several other studies that examined students from the same age group[1-3,5-9]. At this point, the athletes had not yet started their heavier training programme. The energy expenditure data are probably relatively low, compared to what they would be in summer when the orienteering season culminates. In spite of this, seven out of 19 girls seemed to have a TDEE that exceeded the EI. The girls also seemed to have a larger variation of EI over TDEE (fig 1).

In agreement with other findings[1,3], EIs decreased on weekends when many of the students spent time with their families and did not have to cook or plan meals themselves. The meal patterns over weekends were highly irregular and the time of day when lunch and/or dinner were served varied considerably.

The contribution of sugar to total EI was higher than recommended and higher in the present study than that from the national survey from 1989[1]. The contribution of energy from fat was considerably lower for both sexes than that seen in the national survey[1], although this may partly be due to this group's higher sugar intake.

Recommended intake of fibre is in NNR[13] related to EI, 3g per MJ. These students did not reach those levels, but their mean total dietary fibre intake in grammes sufficed according to the new US recommendation for children and adolescents: age in years plus 5 g[16]. The total grams dietary fibre intake was also considerably higher in this study when compared to corresponding data from the national survey[1].

Table 2. Daily energy and nutrient intakes and daily recommended intakes according to Nordic Nutrition Recommendations (NNR)

	Boys (n=15, 7 d)	*NNR*	Girls (n=19, 7 d)	*NNR*
Energy (MJ)	14.4± 3.2	*11.3**	10.8 ± 2.6	*9.0**
Fat (E%)	31.7± 6.4[1]	*< 30*	32.3 ± 7.1[2]	*< 30*
Fibre (g·MJ^{-1})	1.6 ± 0.5[2]	*3*	1.97 ± 0.60[2]	*3*
Fibre (g)	23 ± 8.7		21 ± 7.2	
Sugar (E%)	13.6 ± 6.5[2]	*< 10*	12.8 ± 5.2[2]	*< 10*
Sugar (g)	117 ± 64		81 ± 39	
Iron (mg)	18.0 ± 6.9	*12*	13.2 ± 6.0	*12-18*
Zinc (mg)	15.8 ± 4.8	*12*	11.7 ± 3.8	*9*
Vit A (RE, mg)	1.84 ± 1.3	*0.9*	1.65 ± 1.2	*0.9*
Carotene (mg)	4.38 ± 3.9		4.66 ± 4.1	
Vit E (mg)	10.2 ± 4.1	*10*	8.25 ± 3.2	*8*
Vit C (mg)	118 ± 96	*60*	131 ± 97	50
Folic acid (mcg)	317 ± 123	*300*	290 ± 117	300
Selenium (mcg)	37.8 ± 22.7[2]	*50*	25.5 ± 14.0[2]	*40*

Values are mean ± SD
* Also given as ranges from 6.7-15.1 and 6.2-11.3 for boys and girls respectively[13]
[1]Compared with NNR, p=0.007 [2]Compared with NNR, p=0.000

Micronutrients

Nutrient density for most vitamins and minerals was found to be lower than those from the national survey[1]. The athletes' total micronutrients intake appeared to be somewhat higher, in some cases much higher in comparison with the figures given in the national survey[1], such as was seen with folic acid intakes among the girls as a mean for the group, which was 100 microgrammes higher than the national average.

Betacarotene intake was also considerably higher than normal, with mean values approximately double those of the national survey.

On group level the recommended daily intakes in NNR was met for all micronutrients except for selenium intake, which was significantly lower (table 2). On individual level, the recommended daily intake for iron was not met by 7 of the 19 girls. The number of the 19 girls that did not meet the recommended daily intakes for various micronutrients through their mean daily intake over the week were as follows: 13 girls for folic acid, 9 vitamin E, 4 zinc and 18 for selenium. The corresponding numbers for the 15 boys were none for iron, 5 folic acid, 3 vitamin E, 1 zinc and 14 for selenium. It is important to note however, that the recommended daily intakes in NNR were not developed for this type of comparison. The figures given in the NNR as "lower limit of intake" are the ones to be used for this. When using mean daily intake over the week all nutrient intakes on group level reached the lower limit. On individual level this lower limit was not met for selenium intakes for 5 girls and 1 boy. No such lower limit is set for iron for women in the NNR. The reason for this is that assessment of individual iron status in women is considered to be more important, as needs can be very varied[13]. No individual assessment of iron status was made for these girls, which should perhaps take place on a regular basis.

There is no recommended daily intake level for betacarotene in NNR, although National Cancer Institute has suggested a level of 6 mg for this purpose. This level was not reached by the groups.

Concluding remarks

Since the daily intake levels in NNR were developed for population use, and not specifically for athletes, the levels might not fit this particular group. There may be increased needs for certain nutrients in athletes, due to their higher energy expenditure and increased losses.

What can be learned from these young athletes is that they have a higher intake for most nutrients than seen for individuals in the same age group in other studies, both in Sweden[1-3] and internationally[4-9]. Increased EI does appear to be correlated automatically to increased essential nutrient intakes, even though the nutrient density could be higher and the meal patterns and choice of foods could be better. We can ask ourselves whether the low nutrient density is a problem. Do adolescents with high energy expenditure have micronutrient needs that are correspondingly higher?

We can also conclude that we seem to have some girls who might be in negative energy balance here and that some problems can exist concerning micronutrient status of the females, especially iron. This requires further investigation.

The issue of eating, and not merely loading carbohydrates in a non-critical fashion, should be properly addressed in the boarding school as well as by coaches and school catering facilities.

References

1. Becker, W. (1994) *Befolkningens Kostvanor och Näringsintag i Sverige 1989*. Livsmedelsverkets förlag, Uppsala.
2. Lindholm, C., Hagenfeldt, K. and Hagman, U. (1995) A nutrition study in juvenile elite gymnasts. *Acta Paediatrica,* Vol. 84, p. 273-7.
3. Bergström, E., Hernell, O. and Persson, L.Å. (1993) Dietary changes in Swedish adolescents. *Acta Paediatrica,* Vol. 82, pp. 472-80.
4. Downey, B.L., Gordon, A.R. and Burghardt, J.A. (1995) Dietary intakes of students. *American Journal of Clinical Nutrition,* Vol. 61 (suppl), pp. 205-12.
5. Crawley, H.F. (1993) The energy, nutrient and food intakes of teenagers aged 16-17 years in Britain. *British Journal of Nutrition,* Vol. 70, pp. 15-26.
6. Bull, N. (1985) Dietary habits of 15-25 year olds. *Human Nutrition: Applied Nutrition,* Vol. 39A (suppl 1), pp. 1-68.
7. Gregory, J., Foster. K., Tyler, H. and Wiseman, M. (1990) *The Dietary and Nutritional Survey of British Adults*. H.M. Stationery Office, London.

8. Barker, M.E., McLean, S.I., McKenna, P.G., Reid, N.G., Strain, J.J., Thompson, K.A., Williamson, A.P. and Wright, M.E. (1989) *Diet, Lifestyle and Health in Northern Ireland.* Centre for Applied Health Studies, Colraine, University of Ulster.
9. Frost Andersen, L., Nes, M., Sandstad, B., Bjoerneboe, G.E.-Aa. and Drevon, C.A. (1995) Dietary intake among Norwegian adolescents. *European Journal of Clinical Nutrition,* Vol. 49, pp. 555-64.
10. Hallberg, L., Hulten, L., Lindstedt, G., Lundberg, P.-A., Mark, A., Purens, J., Svanberg, B. and Swolin, B. (1993) Prevalence of Iron Deficiency in Swedish Adolescents. *Pediatric Research,* Vol. 34, pp. 680-7.
11. Håglin, L. (1995) Näringsbrist kan ge plötslig hjärtdöd. *Läkartidningen,* Vol. 92, pp. 30-1, pp. 2809-12.
12. American Dietetic Association. (1996) Timely statement of the American dietetic association: nutrition guidance for adolescent athletes in organized sports. *Journal of the American Dietetic Association,* Vol. 96, pp. 611-2.
13. Nordic Council of Ministers. (1996) Nordic Nutrition Recommendations 1996. *Scandinavian Journal of Nutrition,* Vol. 40, pp. 161-5.
14. Bouchard, C., Tremblay, A., Leblanc, D., Lortie, G., Savara, R. and Theriau, G. (1983) A method to assess energy expenditure in children and adults. *American Journal of Clinical Nutrition,* Vol. 37, pp. 461-7.
15. Schofield, W.N. (1985) Predicting basal metabolic rate, new standards and review of previous work. *Human Nutrition and Clinical Nutrition,* Vol. 39C (suppl), pp. 5-41.
16. Williams, C.L., Bollella, M. and Wynder, E.L. (1995) A new recommendation for dietary fiber in childhood. *Pediatrics,* Vol. 96, pp. 985-8.

CALCIUM, IRON, VITAMINS AND CALORIC INTAKE AMONG FEMALE DANCERS

Young dancers and nutrition

M.A.VIOLAN, M.N. ZETARUK, E.W. SMALL and L.J.MICHELI
Division of Sports Medicine, Children´s Hospital, Harvard Medical School, Boston, USA

Keywords: Calcium, calorie intake, female dancers, fibre, iron, vitamins

Introduction

The aesthetic ideal may force dancers to have a control of body composition. Previous research has suggested that a desire to achieve or maintain the "ideal" performing body image may be a major factor motivating the high incidence of eating disorders observed among dancers[1,2]. Dance is basically non-aerobic, therefore weight control and a thin body are primarily achieved though dietary restriction rather than from endurance training. The energy expenditure during dancing is not more than 200 $kcal \cdot h^{-1}$ [2,3,4]. Some works suggest that female dancers tend to be undernourished when compared with reference women of similar age[3] and inadequate ingestion of certain minerals may contribute to a health risk. This is of particular concern among female athletes such as gymnasts, long distance runners and ballet dancers who restrict caloric intake to maintain low body weight[5]. The evaluation of calcium intake and vitamin D is important because of the strong relationship between low calcium intake and reduced bone mass and stress fractures[2,3,5,6,7,8]. It is beleived that ballet dancers eat less than the general population and may not make proper food choices in order to mantain a low body weight. The purpose of this study was to compare the characteristic eating habits of dancers with non-dancers in a performing arts boarding school and to examine their attitudes towards food selection.

Subjects

A total of 17 female students participated in the study. Nine of the subjects were ballet students, aged 4 - 18 (mean age $\pm$ SEM = 15.8 $\pm$ 0.5 y) with an average of practice

Children and Exercise XIX. Edited by Neil Armstrong, Brian Kirby and Joanne Welsman.
Published in 1997 by E & FN Spon, 2–6 Boundary Row, London, SE1 8HN.
ISBN 0 419 22100 X.

time in dance of 14 h. The second group consisted of eight performing arts students (4 drama students, 3 musicians and 1 painter), ages 13-17 (mean age ± SE = 16 ± 0.5 y) with a mean of 17 h of practice per week in performing arts. None of the second group did more than 3 h of physical exercise a week. They were properly informed about the purpose of the study and voluntarily participated. All participants were living in a boarding high school for performing arts. Both groups had the same academic schedule with similar practice times for dancers and non-dancers. They shared the same dining room and had the freedom of selecting food. Descriptive statistics of the subjects are in table 1.

Methods

Sum of skinfolds: six places were measured (biceps, triceps, subscapular, abdominal, suprailiac, thigh). The sites were tested three times using a Lange™ skinfold caliper and the mean value was calculated[9]. Height was recorded in cm, without shoes and having the subjects breathing a maximal inspiration. Weight was measured in kg using a scale with subjects wearing shorts, t-shirt and no shoes.

YAQ nutritional questionnaire (Young Adult Questionnaire), which has been tested qualitatively and quantitatively on children aged 10-18 y, was used in this study. Dietary assessment consisted of values obtained from the food frequency. Validation of this questionnaire has existed since September 1994 and results from this study were analysed by an expert senior research nutritionist.

Data analyses

Student´s t test and Chi square analyses were used to measure statistical significance with the α level set as $p < 0.05$. Data analysis was performed with Super ANOVA statistical package (Abacus Concept, Berkeley, CA).

Results

Seventeen female students completed the study, doing a nutritional questionnaire and anthropometric measurements on the same day. When baseline characteristics of both groups (table 1) were compared, the non-dancer group had a higher body weight and higher sum of six skinfolds. These anthropometric parameters were the only statistically significant ones.

The results of the nutritional questionnaire are reported in tables 2, 3 and 4. The mean caloric intake was 1851 $kcal \cdot d^{-1}$ for dancers, and 1536 $kcal \cdot d^{-1}$ for non-dancers. Although the caloric intake did not differ significantly between groups, it was above the RDA in both groups[10]. Non-dancers ate less protein ($g \cdot kg^{-1}$) and dietary fibre when statistically compared to dancers. The results of the data analysis of vitamins, calcium, iron, percent of proteins, fat and carbohydrate (CHO) showed no differences

Table 1. Characteristics of the subjects

	Dancers	Non-dancers
Age (y)	15.8 ± 0.5	16 ± 0.5
Weight (kg)	53.4 ± 1.5*	60.4 ± 2.5
Height (cm)	163.4 ± 1.7	165.9 ± 3.0
Sum of Skinfolds (mm)	73.8 ± 4.5*	98.3 ± 8.6

Values are mean ± SEM
Level of signficance * $p < 0.05$

between groups, but calcium and vitamin D were below RDA[10] in both groups. None of the subjects reported taking vitamin or mineral supplements, even though some studies have reported that about 40 - 65 % of Americans take such supplements[11].

Table 2. Caloric intake and fibre

	Dancers		Non-dancers	
Total calories	1851 ± 148.7	(985-2568)	1536 ± 225	(872-2677)
% Protein	14.5 ± 0.5	(12-17)	14.5 ± 0.6	(13-18)
% Fat	20.8 ± 1.8	(11-229)	22.8 ± 2.0	(13-34)
% Carbohydrates	66 ± 2.2	(59-80)	63.7 ± 2.4	(53-77)
Protein ($g \cdot kg^{-1}$)	1.2 ± 0.1*	(0.6-1.8)	0.9 ± 0.1	(0.5-1.5)
Dietary fibre (g)	27.2 ± 2.7*	(3-46)	18.2 ± 2.1	(6 - 24)

Values are mean ± SEM (range)
Level of significance * $p < 0.05$
RDA % proteins: 12-15 % ;proteins : 0.8 $g \cdot kg^{-1} \cdot d^{-1}$
RDA % fat: <30 %; % carbohydrates: 55-65 %
RDA total calories: 1900 - 2200; dietary fibre: 12 $g \cdot d^{-1}$

Table 3. Iron and Calcium intake

	Dancers	% RDA	Non-dancers	% RDA
Iron (mg)	23.2 ± 3 (11-38)	155.1	19.4 ± 4.5 (6-46)	129.8
Calcium (mg)	1047 ± 97.1 (585-1538)	87.2	856 ± 170.6 (315-1939)	71.4

Values are mean ± SEM (range)

Table 4. Vitamin intake

Vitamin	RDA	Dancers	% RDA	Non-dancers	% RDA
A (IU)	4000	12019.6 ± 2260.6	300.4	8792.5 ± 1419.4	219.8
C (mg)	50	213.8 ± 21	427.6	162.5 ± 19.9	325.1
B6 (mg)	1.5	2.4 ± 0.3	161.1	1.9 ± 0.2	126.6
D (IU)	400	374.9 ± 55.8	93.7	323.5 ± 89.8	80.8
B1 (mg)	1.1	2.4 ± 0.1	221	2 ± 0.3	187.1
B2 (mg)	1.3	2.6 ± 0.2	200	2.2 ± 0.3	170
Niacin (mg)	15	25.6 ± 2.3	171.2	22.7 ± 3.9	151.9
B12 (mcg)	2.0	5.4 ± 0.8	271.8	4.7 ± 1	237.8
E (mg)	8	16.1 ± 4.1	202.2	14.5 ± 4.3	181.8

Values are mean ± SEM

Discussion

The most significant finding in this study was that both groups had a lower intake of calories, calcium and vitamin D than would be expected for this particular age and gender. The RDA is reported as 2200 kcal·d^{-1}[10,12]. Of special importance for dancers is that dancing burns no more than 200 kcal·h^{-1}[2,3,4] and they tend to mantain their body weight between 6 and 12% below ideal weight[13]. This lower body weight is maintained by dietary restriction and not by extra practice[4] since weight reduction cannot be achieved through dance alone. From this study, it appears that both groups restrict intake, which results in calories, calcium and vitamin D being below the RDA (RDA of calcium is 1200 mg, RDA for vitamin D is 400 IU[8,10]). As well, we know that dancers are at increased risk of stress fractures and amenorrhea[2,6,7,8], which may be potentiated by the lower calcium and vitamin D intake. By achieving a higher peak bone mass during early years, the outcome of bone loss during ageing might not necessarily lead to osteoporosis and bone fractures[14]. We realize that the non-dance group is at a similar risk of osteoporosis due to levels of calcium intake <1200 mg·d^{-1} [12] and a more sedentary lifestyle. Percent intake of fat, CHO and protein was similar in both groups and adhered to the RDA for this age and gender[10,12]. Intake of vitamins A, C, B6, Niacin, B12 and E was higher among dancers, but no subject reached potentially toxic intake levels. Iron intake was correct in both groups (RDA of iron: 15 mg·d^{-1}).

Any reports of lower calcium, vitamin D and caloric consumption[7] among dancers as well as their higher risk of developing eating disorders than their non-dancing peers[15], have dealt with adult or professional populations. In our study we compared two groups of non professional performing artists at the beginning of their careers and we discovered that both groups have similar problems concerning knowledge about proper dieting and receive inadequate nutritional guidance[16]. It has been reported that variables such as age and school attendance seem to have a negligible influence on eating behaviour[17]. Furthermore, adolescent athletes are not at higher risk for developing eating disorders[17]. In summary, all performing arts students appear to need nutritional guidance as an integral part of the training programme. They must have the knowledge that food is not only fuel; it affects fitness level, athletic performance and optimizes health status.

References

1. Pierce, F.E., Daleg, M.L. and McGowan, R.W. (1993) Scores on exercise dependence among dancers. *Perceptual and Motor Skills,* No. 76, pp 531-6.
2. Hamilton, L.H., Brooks-Gunn, J., Warren, M.P. and Hamilton, W.G. (1986) The impact of thinness and dieting on the professional ballet dancer. *Journal of the Canadian Association for Health, Physical Education and Recreation,* Vol. 52, pp.117-22.
3. Hamilton, L.H., Brooks-Gunn, J. and Warren, M.P. (1986) Nutritional intake of female dancers: a reflection of eating problems. *International Journal of Eating Disorders,* Vol. 5, pp. 925-34.
4. Hamilton, L.H., Brooks-Gunn, J., Warren, M.P. and Hamilton, W.G. (1988) The role of selectivity in the pathogeninesis of eating problems in ballet dancers. *Medicine and Science in Sports and Exercise,* Vol. 20, pp. 560-5.
5. Clarkson, P.M. and Haymes, E.M. (1995) Exercise and mineral status of athletes: calcium, magnesium, phosphorus, and iron. *Medicine and Science in Sports and Exercise,* Vol. 27, pp. 831-43.
6. Micheli, L.J., Gillespie, W.J. and Walaszek, A. (1984) Physiologic profiles of female professional ballerinas. *Clinics in Sports Medicine*, Vol. 3, pp. 199-209.
7. Frusztajer, N.T., Dhuper, S., Warren, M.P., Brooks-Gunn, J. and Fox, R.P. (1990) Nutrition and the incidence of stress fractures in ballet dancers. *American Journal of Clinical Nutrition,* Vol. 51, pp. 779-83.
8. NIH Consensus Development Panel on Optimal Calcium Intake. (1994) Optimal Calcium Intake. *Journal of American Medical Association,* Vol. 272, pp. 1942-8.

9 Physical Fitness Testing. (1995) in *ACSM's Guidelines for Exercise Testing and Prescription,* 5th Edition, (ed. W.L. Kenney), Williams and Wilkins, Baltimore, pp. 55-8.

10. Recomended Dietary Allowances 10th Edition. (1989) National Academy Press, Washington, D.C.
11. Clark, N., Nelson, M. and Evans, W. (1988) Nutrition education for elite female runners. *The Physician and Sports Medicine,* Vol.16, pp.124-36.
12. Position of The American Dietetic Association and The Canadian Dietetic Association: Nutrition for physical fitness and athletic performance for adults. (1993) *Journal of The American Dietetic Association,* Vol. 93, pp. 691-6.
13. Calabrese, L.H. and Kirkendall, D.T. (1983) Nutritional and medical considerations in dancers. *Clinics in Sports Medicine,* Vol. 2, pp. 539-48.
14. Nelson, M.E., Fisher, E.C., Catsos, P.D., Meredith, C.N., Turksoy, R.N. and Evans, W. (1986) Diet and bone status in amenorrheic runners. *The American Journal of Clinical Nutrition,* Vol. 43, pp. 910-6.
15. Holderness, C.C., Brooks-Gunn, J. and Warren, M.P. (1994) Eating disorders and substance use: a dancing vs a nondancing population. *Medicine and Science in Sports and Exercise*, Vol. 26, pp. 297-302.
16. Sundgot-Borgen, J. (1994) Risk and trigger factors for the development of eating disorders in female elite athletes. *Medicine and Science in Sports and Exercise,* Vol. 26, pp. 414-9.
17. Rosen, L.W., McKeag, D.B., Hough, D.O. and Curley, V. (1986) Pathogenic weight-control behavior in female athletes. *The Physician and Sports Medicine,* Vol. 14, pp. 79-84.

BONE STATUS IN HIGHLY TRAINED PREPUBERTAL GIRLS : PRELIMINARY REPORT

Bone status in young girls

D. COURTEIX, P. OBERT and P. GERMAIN
Laboratoire de la Performance Motrice, Université d'Orléans, Orleans, France
E. LESPESSAILLES, S. LOISEAU PERES and C.L. BENHAMOU
Pôle d'Activité Rhumatologie, Centre Hospitalier Régional, Orleans, France
B. FERRY
Laboratoire de Médecine du Sport, Faculté des Sciences, Université, Limoges, France
Keywords: Bone status, gymnastics, prepubertal girls, swimming, training

Introduction

Physical activity is known to have an anabolic effect on bone tissue. It has been shown to increase the bone mineral density (BMD) in young and middle-age adults, as well as in teenagers[1]. The type, intensity and duration of exercise necessary to influence BMD in humans is well documented in adults. Thus, sport activities including heavy load, or producing impact loading on the skeleton, are associated with higher bone density than sports which do not generate stress on the skeleton. But few studies refer to human subjects involved in swimming, particularly in childhood, despite the attractiveness of swimming as a non-traumatic activity. However, some researchers have shown that physical activity in childhood was an important determinant of peak bone mass in women[2]. Moreover, the prepubertal period is an important stage of growing in children because the optimal period of bone turnover is, in female, over a period from 11 to 14 y of age[2-3]. Most of the studies have investigated BMD or bone mineral content (BMC) in female subjects. However, the resistance of bone tissue is influenced by bone density and by trabecular bone microarchitecture. The growing period, when the bone mineral acquisition is at the optimal phase, could be particularly sensitive to this phenomenon. Thus, studies dealing with the relationship between physical activity and bone metabolism have to investigate, not only bone mineralization parameters, but also bone architecture parameters. The purpose of this study was to compare the effects of 3 y of intensive sport training on the bone status (bone density and architecture) in a group of elite prepubertal girls, at the starting period of their peak bone mass acquisition. These girls were engaged either in sport requiring significant impact loading on the skeleton (gymnastics), or in sport without impact loading (swimming). These results are the first of a longitudinal study which will be conducted over the pubertal period.

Children and Exercise XIX. Edited by Neil Armstrong, Brian Kirby and Joanne Welsman.
Published in 1997 by E & FN Spon, 2–6 Boundary Row, London, SE1 8HN.
ISBN 0 419 22100 X.

Subjects

A total of 41 healthy prepubertal girls were recruited to participate in this study. The group included 10 swimmers and 18 gymnasts who have been involved in sport training during the last 3 y. Thirteen girls of the same age were recruited from primary schools, and served as a control group. None of the subjects had any disease or had ever used medication that might have affected bone. Informed written consent was obtained from the parents. This study was approved by the « Comité de Protection des Personnes Participant à la Recherche Biomédicale », Orléans, France.

Methods

Weight and height were measured in all subjects. Bone age was assessed by left wrist radiographs of all the subjects, and analysed, using Greulich and Pyle tables. Fat tissue mass, expressed as percentage of body weight, was measured by dual-energy x-ray absorptiometry (DEXA, Hologic QDR-1000/W; Hologic Inc., Waltham, MA) using assessed procedure[4]. All measurements were taken during the training season.

The swimmers had been engaged in an intensive training programme for 3 y. They trained, at the time of the study, 12 $h{\cdot}wk^{-1}$ (4 $d{\cdot}wk^{-1}$ plus two competitions per month). The gymnasts had performed an intensive training programme (10 to 15 $h{\cdot}wk^{-1}$, 5 $d{\cdot}wk^{-1}$ plus competitions) for 3 y. The control group was much less active than the athletes. Girls had only been engaged in various leisure activities about 2 or 3 $h{\cdot}wk^{-1}$.

Bone mineral density (BMD in $g{\cdot}cm^{-2}$) was measured in the whole body and at the following sites: lumbar vertebrae (L2-L4), femoral neck and Ward's triangle (non dominant), mid-radius and distal radius (non dominant). Measurements were made by DEXA. The reproducibility was based on two repeat measurements over 2 wk in three subjects. The in-vivo coefficient of variability, using this technique is less than 1% for lumbar spine, 2% for femoral neck and up to 5% for the whole body. This programme did not include any invasive procedure in this young healthy population.

Bone architecture was evaluated on calcaneus radiographs by fractal analysis of trabecular bone texture. This technique, previously validated[5-6], has been shown to be reproducible. The fractal analysis is based on the Fractional Brownian motion model. Results can be expressed by a single numeric evaluation representative of the image: H mean. H mean parameter is linked to the fractal dimension (D) by H mean = 2-D. The fractal dimension is determined in 36 different directions which can be, each one, reported on a polar diagram to characterise the anisotropy of the bone texture.

A 24 h period of urine collection was self-made by all the subjects. We evaluated the deoxypyridinoline (Dpyr) concentration, which is a reliable specific marker of bone resorption. The values of Dpyr were expressed as a ratio relative to urinary creatinine to allow for variations in body mass. Measurements of urinary calcium and creatinine excretions were done. Urine samples were dosed in aliquot which were previously stored at -20° C until analysed. Assays were performed by the departments of biological analysis and biochemical analysis at Orleans Regional Hospital, France.

Data analyses

The mean and standard deviations were calculated for subject characteristics, BMC and BMD data, H mean and bone markers measurements. Results of the groups were compared using a one-way analysis of variance. When the test indicated a significant difference ($p < 0.05$), Newman-Keul test was used as the post-hoc test.

Results

As shown in table 1, both groups were satisfactorily matched concerning body height, body weight, body composition and pubertal maturation assessed according to Tanner's stages[7]. The groups were very homogenous with a closed range of age. There was no significant difference between the groups for bone age, but there was a tendency to lower mean bone age in gymnasts in comparison with the other groups. Moreover, difference between chronological and biological age (tested with a paired t test) was close to the limit of the significance for gymnasts ($p = 0.057$), a phenomenon which is well-known for such a kind of practice.

Table 2 provides the distribution of bone mineral measurements, at the different sites, of the three groups. There was no statistically significant difference between swimmers and controls for all the measurements. Mean BMD in gymnasts, for all the measurements, were statistically higher than in other groups, except for whole body BMD. In gymnasts, BMD at radius and femoral neck was above normative values[8].

Table 3 shows the mean values of fractal analysis for the three groups. There was no statistical significant difference between the groups for both dominant and non-dominant calcaneus analysis.

As shown in table 3, there were no significant differences between the groups for urinary calcium and DPyr concentrations. The calcium values were consistent with normal range of values which is less than 3 $mg \cdot kg^{-1} \cdot d^{-1}$. The ratio calcium / creatinine observed in our subjects was in accordance with the normal value (below 0.5). Results of our analysis showed lower values for mean Dpyr/creatinine, compared to the

Table 1. Descriptive characteristics of the three groups

	Swimmers (n=10)	Δ_{G-S}	Gymnasts (n=18)	Δ_{G-C}	Controls (n=13)	Δ_{S-C}
Age (mo)	125.9 ± 16.7	NS	124.8 ± 16.2	NS	129.1 ± 11.8	NS
Bone age (mo)	128.7 ± 11.3	NS	118.6 ± 18.5	NS	127.9 ± 11.3	NS
Tanner stage	1		1		1	
Total body weight (kg)	36.3 ± 6.4	NS	31 ± 6.1	NS	35 ± 6	NS
Height (cm)	143 ± 8.6	NS	136.9 ± 9.5	NS	142.1 ± 7	NS
Percent body fat (%)	21.35 ± 6.24	NS	16.5 ± 2	NS	22.15 ± 5.6	NS
Fat-free mass (kg)	27.68 ± 4.8	NS	25.43 ± 4.8	NS	26.51 ± 2.9	NS

Values are mean ± SD
Level of significance NS $p > 0.05$

Table 2. Bone mineral density at the different sites in the three groups

Site of measurement	BMD ($g \cdot cm^{-2}$)					
	Swimmers (n=10)	Δ_{G-S}	Gymnasts (n=18)	Δ_{G-C}	Controls (n=13)	Δ_{S-C}
Whole body	0.827 ±0.04	NS	0.843 ±0.08	NS	0.831 ±0.05	NS
Mid radius	0.405 ±0.03	* * *	0.471 ±0.04	* * *	0.408 ±0.03	NS
Distal radius	0.311 ±0.03	* * *	0.406 ±0.05	* * *	0.305 ±0.03	NS
L2-L4	0.698 ±0.06	*	0.761 ±0.10	*	0.685 ±0.07	NS
Femoral neck	0.696 ±0.06	* * *	0.792 ±0.09	* * *	0.687 ±0.07	NS
Ward's triangle	0.627 ±0.09	* *	0.778 ±0.12	* *	0.677 ±0.11	NS

Values are mean ± SD
Level of significance * $p < 0.05$, ** $p < 0.01$, *** $p < 0.001$, NS $p > 0.05$

normal range[9] for a population of children (mean:31 $nmol \cdot mmol^{-1}$). Nevertheless, values of Dpyr were homogeneous for the groups. The coefficients of variation ranging from 23.4 to 26.1% could be a reflection of the considerable variability which exists in the amount of DPyr excreted from day to day in the same subject[9].

Discussion

The main result of our study was that intensive gymnastic training, contributes to enhance the mineral density within the skeleton in a group of prepubertal girls. The statistically higher BMD in the gymnastic group at most of the skeletal sites was in accordance with results of previous studies in adults which have shown that sports producing impact loading induced greater BMD[10] than sports which did not generate impact loading. Exercise exerts a local anabolic effect on the stressed part of the

Table 3. Bone architecture index values (H mean of calcaneus) and values of bone metabolism markers measured in urine samples

	Swimmers (n=10)	Δ_{G-S}	Gymnasts (n=18)	Δ_{G-C}	Controls (n=13)	Δ_{S-C}
H mean (calcaneus non-dominant)	0.8121 ± 0.027	NS	0.7761 ± 0.049	NS	0.7987 ± 0.026	NS
H mean (calcaneus dominant)	0.8076 ± 0.024	NS	0.7825 ± 0.043	NS	0.8028 ± 0.036	NS
Calcium ($mg \cdot kg^{-1} \cdot 24h^{-1}$)	1.676 ±0.92	NS	1.324 ±0.77	NS	1.916 ±1.02	NS
Calcium/creatinine	0.30 ± 0.16	NS	0.22 ± 0.10	NS	0.31 ± 0.21	NS
Deoxypyridinoline/ creatinine ($nmol.mmol^{-1}$)	20.66 ±5.1	NS	17.51 ±4.1	NS	17.25 ±4.5	NS

Values are mean ± SD
Level of significance NS $p > 0.05$

skeleton. During gymnastic practice, forearms and hips were highly stressed, and it was expected to find higher BMD at these sites in gymnasts than in non-gymnasts.

The swimming group had no significant difference versus the control group for all the BMD measurements, even though swimmers had performed an intensive training programme during three years. As regards the results in gymnasts, the specificity of swimming activity seemed to explain this phenomenon (activity which does not exert too much loading on the skeleton to influence bone metabolism). Another explanation could be suggested. We could suppose that, in such training conditions (body in water immersion), the water unloading, which suppresses limb-ground pounding on weight-bearing bones, induced a relative weightlessness situation, known to be a cause of decrease in bone[11]. This phenomenon could act in opposition to the intensive and long term training programme.

Evaluation of trabecular bone architecture showed no differences between the groups. Usually, the radiographic procedure, to obtain bone images, is very standardized. In this study, we have seen that, from one subject to another, there were important variations of calcaneus thickness (due to the period of maturation). Thus, we exposed the calcaneus of girls under non-identical conditions concerning the voltage. In order to correct variations of the fractal dimension (D) that could be linked to these different voltage conditions, we have always exposed a step wedge with the bone to be measured. Yet, we have not recorded the final corrected D results. Uncorrected results of D were not statistically different between the groups. Thus, we could not conclude, at the present moment, about the effect of training on bone texture.

The lack of significant difference in Dpyr and urinary calcium values between the groups, suggested that higher BMD values in the gymnasts were not a consequence of a decrease in bone resorption. The lower DPyr values observed in our population compared to normal range might be due to the technique of measurement which is different in our study (radioimmunoassay) than in the study of reference (HPLC technique)[9].

In conclusion, physical activity in childhood can be an important factor of bone mineral acquisition in prepubertal girls only if the type of sport induces bone strains during a long term programme. It should be interesting to measure a marker of bone formation (e.g. osteocalcin) to elucidate if an increase of bone formation is linked to an increase of physical activity. Long-term consequences of such a gymnastic training are not well known. Further prospective research needs to be conducted.

References

1. Smith, E.L. and Gilligan, C. (1991) Physical activity effects on bone metabolism. *Calcified Tissue International,* Vol. 49 (suppl), pp. S50-4.
2. Cooper, C., Cawley, M., Bhalla, A., Egger, P., Ring, F., Morton, L. and Barker, D. (1995) Childhood growth, physical activity, and peak bone mass in women. *Journal of Bone and Mineral Research*, Vol. 10, pp. 940-7.

3. Theintz, G., Buchs, B., Rizzoli, R., Slosman, D., Clavien, H., Sizonenko, P.C. and Bonjour, J.PH. (1992) Longitudinal monitoring of bone mass accumulation on healthy adolescents: evidence for a marked reduction after 16 years of age at the levels of lumbar spine and femoral neck in female subjects. *Journal of Clinical Endocrinology and Metabolism*, Vol. 75, pp. 1060-5.
4. Haarbo, J., Gotfredsen, A., Hassager, C. and Christiensen, C. (1991) Validation of body composition by dual energy X-ray absorptiometry (DEXA). *Clinical Physiology*, No. 11, pp. 331-41.
5. Benhamou, C.L., Lespessailles, E., Jacquet, G., Harba, R., Jennane, R., Loussot, T., Tourliere, D. and Ohley, W. (1994) Fractal organisation of trabecular Bone image on calcaneus radiographs. *Journal of Bone and Mineral Research*, Vol. 9, pp. 1909-18.
6. Benhamou, C.L., Lespessailles, E., Tourliere, D., Jacquet, G., Harba, R., and Jennane, R. (1993) Fractal characterization of trabecular bone microarchitecture: interset of a maximum likehood estimation. *Journal of Bone and Mineral Research*, Vol. 8 (suppl 1 S), p. 263.
7. Tanner, J.M. (1962) *Growth at Adolescence*, (2nd edition), Blackwell Scientific, Oxford.
8. Zanchetta, J.R., Plotkin, H. and Alvarez Filgueira, L. (1995) Bone mass in children: normative values for the 2-20-year-old population. *Bone*, Vol. 16 (suppl), pp. 393S-9S.
9. Shaw, N.J., Dutton, J., Fraser, W.D. and Smith, C.S. (1995) Urinary pyridinoline and deoxypyridinoline excretion in children. *Clinical Endocrinology*, No. 42, pp. 607-12.
10. Davee, A.M., Rosen, C.J. and Adler, A. (1990) Exercise patterns and trabecular bone density in college women. *Journal of Bone and Mineral Research*, Vol. 5, pp. 245-50.
11. Bourrin, S., Ghaemmaghami, F., Vico, L., Chappard, D., Gharib, C. and Alexandre, C. (1992) Effect of five-week swimming program on rat bone: a histomorphometric study. *Calcified Tissue International*, Vol. 51, pp. 137-42.

DELAYED GROWTH AND DECREASED ENERGY INTAKE IN FEMALE GYMNASTS

Energy intake in female gymnasts

M.L. ZONDERLAND
Department of Medical Physiology and Sports Medicine, Faculty of Medicine, Utrecht University, Utrecht, The Netherlands
A.L. CLAESSENS, J. LEFEVRE, R. PHILIPPAERTS and M. THOMIS
Department of Kinesiology, Faculty of Physical Education and Physiotherapy, Katholieke Universiteit Leuven, Leuven, Belgium
Keywords: Energy intake, growth, gymnasts

Introduction

In sports like gymnastics the physique is an integral part of the judgement of performance and leanness is unambiguously emphasised. Consequently female gymnasts tend to have a rather low energy intake[1,2]. Since in children a positive energy balance is critical to sustaining growth and health, the low energy intake of female gymnasts could result in retardation of growth and development. Most studies on this topic are cross-sectional and follow-up information is lacking. Therefore we studied energy intake and growth status of top-level Flemish gymnasts over a period of 3 to 4 y in order to find out whether the presumed low energy intake of the gymnasts was associated with growth retardation.

Subjects

In total 77 Flemish (Belgian) gymnasts, members of two clubs, participated in a longitudinal study of the growth and development of female gymnasts, after informed consent was obtained. The study was approved by the Medical Ethics Committee of the Faculty of Physical Education and Physiotherapy of the Katholieke Universiteit Leuven.

Three levels were distinguished: Top-level, which implies participation in national and international competitions and a training frequency of 15 h per week; sub-top level, participating in national and local competitions and a training frequency of 5 h per week and finally, the recreational level with 1-2 h training per week. This study deals with 13 top-level gymnasts (age, 10.2 ± 1.1 y) who completed (at least) three nutritional diaries in a 3 or 4 y follow-up. The period between two measurements was 1 or 2 y.

Children and Exercise XIX. Edited by Neil Armstrong, Brian Kirby and Joanne Welsman.
Published in 1997 by E & FN Spon, 2–6 Boundary Row, London, SE1 8HN.
ISBN 0 419 22100 X.

Methods

Anthropometric measurements were carried out according to Simons et al.[3]. To estimate skeletal age the Tanner Whitehouse II method was used[4].

The 7 d record method was used to assess energy intake. The gymnasts and one of their parents were instructed individually by a dietician who was familiar with Flemish products and nutritional habits. The completed diaries were checked by the same dietician. Energy intake was calculated using the GVOP computer programme[5] based on a nutrient file from the Dutch Food Table[6].

Results

During the 4 y of the investigation the gymnasts grew 13.0 ± 2.7 cm in height and 8.4 ± 2.6 kg in weight (table 1; RMANOVA, $p \leq 0.001$). For each individual gymnast, height and weight relative to the height and weight of the average Flemish girl of the same age[3] are reflected in the percentile scores. For height, this score decreased not significantly, for weight the decline was significant (RMANOVA, $p \leq 0.05$). At the first time of measurement, mean skeletal age was similar to mean chronological age while at the last measurement their skeletal age was 0.7 ± 1.2 y (range: -2.7 to 1.7) behind chronological age (RMANOVA, $p \leq 0.01$).

Total energy intake expressed in MJ per day did not change during the follow-up. At the first measurement, energy intake was 75% of the Dutch Recommended Daily Allowances (DRDA [7]). During the follow-up this percentage tended to decrease. When the energy intake was related to body weight the gymnasts ate increasingly less over the period of study (RMANOVA, $p \leq 0.001$). Energy intake expressed as percentage of the DRDA was almost 90% (range: 65-119%) at the first measurement and decreased to 80% (range: 51-92%) at the third measurement (RMANOVA, $p \leq 0.05$). There were no relationships between anthropometric measures and energy intake data.

The stability of the position of the subjects in the group is reflected by the unbiased estimate of reliability. All variables met the criteria for the parallel model (table 2). For the anthropometric measurements the estimate was very high, indicating that nothing had been changed in ranking from tall to small. The estimates for the energy intake were somewhat lower but still high enough to conclude that ranking also proved to be stable for these variables.

Discussion

The gymnasts in this study were much smaller and had lower body weight than the average Flemish girl of the same chronological age. During the follow-up the discrepancy with the reference group increased, in particular the difference in body weight. In addition, skeletal age increasingly lagged behind chronological age, indicating a delay in maturation. These

Table 1. Anthropometry and energy intake of top-level gymnasts (n=13) measured on three occasions

	Measurement Occasion 1	2	3	
Age (y)	10.2 ± 1.1	11.6 ± 1.1	12.8 ± 1.1	
Skeletal age (y)	10.2 ± 1.1	11.2 ± 1.6	12.1 ± 1.2	***
Height (cm)	136.4 ± 7.3	143.3 ± 6.2	149.3 ± 6.9	***
Weight (kg)	29.2 ± 4.5	33.2 ± 4.3	37.6 ± 6.0	***
Percentile score [3]				
Height	36 ± 22	32 ± 22	30 ± 22	n.s.
Weight	31 ± 21	25 ± 19	23 ± 20	*
Daily energy intake				
MJ	6.3 ± 1.0	6.5 ± 1.2	6.2 ± 1.1	n.s.
kJ·kg^{-1}	220 ± 42	196 ± 31	168 ± 35	***
Daily energy intake as percentage of DRDA				
MJ	75 ± 11	72 ± 12	67 ± 12	n.s.
kJ·kg^{-1}	89 ± 19	89 ± 18	80 ± 16	*

Values are mean ± SD
Level of significance *$p < 0.05$, ***$p < 0.001$

Table 2. Internal consistency of the measurements (unbiased estimate of reliability)

Height	0.98	percentile score height:	0.97
Weight	0.97	percentile score weight:	0.98
Skeletal age	0.96		
MJ	0.85	as % of recommendation:	0.77
kJ·kg^{-1}	0.80	as % of recommendation:	0.84

findings are in agreement with the results of the longitudinal study of Peltenburg et al.[8] which reported a delay in growth and development in similar Dutch female gymnasts.

The low energy intake in our gymnasts corroborates earlier reports[1,2]. The intake remained low and was reduced further during the follow-up. The reliability estimates indicate that the gymnasts kept their relative ranking with regard to energy intake within the group. Since the reliability estimates of the anthropometric characteristics were also high, the conclusion can be drawn that the pattern of energy intake in gymnasts during the follow-up is independent of whether the girls' height or weight is relatively high or low.

The decreasing percentile score for weight and the increasing discrepancy between chronological age and skeletal age indicate that growth advanced with a slower pace in these gymnasts than in the average girl of the same chronological age. In combination with the increasingly lower energy intake this might suggest that the low energy intake inhibited growth and development. However, gymnasts can be identified as constitutionally small children[8] who will grow less in height and weight and whose growth spurt is delayed and blurred and this explains the observed growth delay. Due to this it will be increasingly difficult for a gymnast to meet the DRDA for the energy intake since in the DRDA the extra energy need for growth is accounted for.

In conclusion, during a 3 to 4 y follow-up, the gymnasts showed a delay in growth and development with a concomitant decrease in energy intake but there was no evidence for a relationship between these two phenomena. However, the conclusion holds that low energy intake is related to body weight in female gymnasts. This might have consequences for the vitamin status of the girls, so the quality of the nutritional intake needs continuous concern.

References

1. van Erp-Baart, A.M.J., Saris, W.H.M., Binkhorst, R.A., Vos, J.A. and Elvers, J.W.H. (1989) Nationwide survey on nutritional habits in elite athletes. Part I. *International Journal of Sports Medicine*, Vol. 10, pp. S3-10.
2. Reggiani, E., Arras, G.B., Trabacca, S., Senarega, D. and Chiodini, G. (1989) Nutritional status and body composition of adolescent female gymnasts. *Journal of Sports Medicine and Physical Fitness*, Vol. 29, pp. 285-7.
3. Simons, J., Beunen, G.P., Renson, R., Claessens, A.L., van Reusel, B. and Lefevre, J. (eds) (1990) *Growth and Fitness of Flemish Girls. The Leuven Growth Study*, Human Kinetics, Champaign, Il.
4. Tanner, J.M., Whitehouse, R.H., Cameron, C., Marshall, W.A., Healy, M.J.R. and Goldstein, H. (1983) *Assessment of Skeletal Maturity and Prediction of Adult Height (TW2-method)*, Academic Press, London.
5. Elvers, J.W.H. (1980) *Food Coding Software Packet* (Dutch), GVO Reports (Health Education Project), University of Nijmegen.
6. UCV Food Table (Dutch) (1985) Stichting Nederlands Voedingsstoffenbestand, Zeist.
7. Nutritional Council. (1989) *Dutch Recommended Daily Allowances* (Dutch), Voorlichtingsbureau voor de Voeding, The Hague.
8. Peltenburg, A.L., Erich, W.B.M., Zonderland, M.L., Bernink, M.J.E., van den Brande, J.L. and Huisveld, I.A. (1984) A retrospective growth study of female gymnasts and girl swimmers. *International Journal of Sports Medicine*, Vol. 5, pp. 262-7.

THE ULNAR VARIANCE PHENOMENON: A STUDY IN YOUNG FEMALE GYMNASTS

Gymnastic training and ulnar variance

A.L. CLAESSENS, J. LEFEVRE, R. PHILIPPAERTS, M. THOMIS and G. BEUNEN
Department of Kinesiology, Katholieke Universiteit Leuven, Leuven, Belgium

Keywords: Female gymnasts, mixed longitudinal study, training load, ulnar variance

Introduction

Unlike most other sports, the upper extremities are often used as weight-bearing limbs in gymnastics, so that the wrist is a site of considerable physical loading. Hence, attention is often given to injuries of the hand and wrist[1,2]. Although wrist pain is often viewed as a pure consequence of the sport, e.g. gymnastics[3], other authors focus on epiphysial trauma and related changes caused by repetitive gymnastic loading mainly of the distal end of the radius at its interface with the carpals[4,5,6]. Further, some authors claim that repetitive injury to the radial epiphysis may inhibit normal growth of the radius resulting in "positive ulnar variance"[1,5,6,7], i.e. the distal end of the ulna exceeds the distal end of the radius. An opposite phenomenon is known as negative ulnar variance. Although ulnar overgrowth is often observed in gymnasts, most of the available studies are based on "patients" or "case" reports, i.e. those individuals who present themselves to a clinic with wrist pain. However, a 'normal' ulnar variance distribution was observed in a representative sample of outstanding female gymnasts, as studied by Claessens et al.[8] in 156 participants of the 24th World Championships in Artistic Gymnastics, held in Rotterdam, the Netherlands, in 1987. Up till now, ulnar variance results in gymnasts were only gathered based on cross-sectional data, so that the real influence of repetitive gymnastic training on this ulnar variance phenomenon is not known. The aim of this study is therefore to investigate the impact of gymnastic training on the ulnar variance in young female gymnasts longitudinally followed over a 4 year period.

Children and Exercise XIX. Edited by Neil Armstrong, Brian Kirby and Joanne Welsman.
Published in 1997 by E & FN Spon, 2–6 Boundary Row, London, SE1 8HN.
ISBN 0 419 22100 X.

Subjects

Between 1990 and 1994, in total 36 female gymnasts were followed annually for four or five occasions, with a total of 158 observations. At the first observation, in 1990, the age of the girls varied between 6 and 14 y. According to their training level, based on the total hours of gymnastic training/week, the total group could be divided in three subgroups: a) a "top-level" group (n = 13, with about 15 h training per week); b) a "subtop" group (n = 13, with about 5 to 7 h training per week); and c) a "recreational" group (n = 10, with about 1 to 2 h training per week).

Methods

Stature was measured with a Holtain wall stadiometer with an accuracy of 1 mm. Weight was measured with a beam balance (SECA) accurate to 0.1 kg. Because all girls were skeletely immature, ulnar variance was determined according to the method of Hafner et al.[9]. The distance from the most distal point of the ulnar metaphysis to the most distal point of the radial metaphysis (DIDI) was determined on a hand-wrist radiograph using a Graphic Digitizer (Numonics, Model 2200), accurate to 0.1 mm. A specially gridded glass plate with built-in illumination (which was placed upon the Graphic Digitizer) was designed in order to light up the radiographs. Positive results, i.e. the respective ulna point is more distally located relative to the respective radius point (ulnar overgrowth), while negative results indicate the opposite. All measurements were done by a single observer. Thirty X-rays were marked and measured twice. No significant difference between test - retest was observed, and the correlation between readings was very high, r = 0.98.

Data analyses and results

Means and standard deviations for stature, weight and the ulnar variance parameter DIDI were calculated for the whole group, arranged per age category, from 6 to 16 y. Numbers of gymnasts for each age group are given in table 1.

In order to investigate the impact of the level of gymnastic training on the ulnar variance phenomenon, the two extreme subgroups, i.e. the "top-level" (n = 13) and the "recreational" (n = 10) groups were compared (Students t-test), arranged per age category, ranging from 8 to 15 y. Probability values for stature, weight and DIDI, arranged per age category, are given in table 2.

Discussion

Compared to reference data for Flemish girls[10], the mean values for both stature and weight of the gymnasts' group as a whole, are situated below the 50th percentile value (= P50) for all age groups, except for the 6th, 15th, and 16th age categories. For stature, the mean values are situated between P35 and P76 of the reference data, and

Table 1. Stature, weight and ulnar variance (DIDI) in 36 female gymnasts (total observations = 158) per age category

Age Group (y)	N	Stature (cm)	Weight (kg)	DIDI (mm)
6	3	119.5 ± 0.6	20.8 ± 1.6	- 3.4 ± 0.4
7	10	121.9 ± 5.2	21.6 ± 2.5	- 3.6 ± 0.6
8	18	126.3 ± 4.2	23.8 ± 2.7	- 3.8 ± 1.1
9	21	132.4 ± 4.5	26.7 ± 2.8	- 3.8 ± 1.6
10	25	137.9 ± 4.4	29.8 ± 3.1	- 4.6 ± 1.7
11	23	142.5 ± 4.4	32.6 ± 3.2	- 4.5 ± 2.3
12	21	148.2 ± 5.7	36.6 ± 4.8	- 4.9 ± 2.7
13	14	155.1 ± 6.8	43.0 ± 6.3	- 5.4 ± 2.7
14	9	159.3 ± 6.5	48.6 ± 6.8	- 5.3 ± 2.3
15	10	163.5 ± 6.4	53.5 ± 8.1	- 5.9 ± 2.5
16	4	168.1 ± 4.4	61.0 ± 6.7	- 6.5 ± 6.5

Values are mean ± SD

for weight between P28 and P77, respectively for the age groups 12 and 16 years. This indicates that the gymnasts under study are, in general, smaller in stature and have a lower body weight, as compared to reference girls of the same chronological age. The observed differences in stature and weight are even more pronounced in comparing the top-level gymnasts with the recreational ones, as indicated in table 2. These observations are in correspondence with other studies on elite female gymnasts as compared to reference data[11], and with studies dealing with somatic differences between higher and lower performance gymnasts[12].

Focussing our attention on the ulnar variance phenomenon, it is demonstrated that for all age categories a negative ulnar variance (as indicated by the negative signs) is observed, which means that the distal end of the radius exceeds the distal end of the ulna. With increasing age, this negative ulnar variance becomes more pronounced, DIDI ranging from -3.4 mm at the age of 6 y to -6.5 mm at the age of 16 y (table 1). This is rather an uncommon outcome from two viewpoints. Firstly, compared to reference girls[9], where a relatively stable negative ulnar variance pattern can be observed throughout the growth period. As studied by Hafner and co-workers [9], ulnar variance varied between -2.5 mm at the age of 6 y and -2.8 mm at the age of 15 years in a representative sample of 259 girls aged 6 to 15 y[9]. Secondly, based on the available literature of ulnar variance in gymnasts, a rather "positive ulnar variance" was expected, especially with increasing age. This is not the case here, suggesting that gymnastic training has no negative impact on the relative positioning of the distal ends of the ulna compared to the radius, and resulting in ulnar overgrowth. In order to study this aspect in more detail, two extreme gymnastic groups with different training

Table 2. Stature, weight and ulnar variance (DIDI) in Recreational- (REC) and Top- (TOP) level gymnasts

Age group (y)	Number		Stature (cm)			Weight (kg)			DIDI (mm)		
	REC	TOP	REC	TOP	Prob.	REC	TOP	Prob.	REC	TOP	Prob.
8	4	7	130.2 ± 3.6	125.8 ± 4.0	0.11	26.5 ± 3.2	23.6 ± 2.4	0.12	- 4.0 ± 1.2	- 3.6 ± 1.3	0.59
9	4	8	136.7 ± 4.0	131.9 ± 4.3	0.09	29.5 ± 3.1	26.6 ± 2.7	0.12	- 3.9 ± 1.1	- 3.5 ± 2.5	0.76
10	5	9	140.9 ± 4.3	137.8 ± 4.2	0.21	32.0 ± 2.9	29.9 ± 3.1	0.24	- 5.0 ± 0.6	- 4.2 ± 2.3	0.36
11	5	11	144.8 ± 2.4	142.5 ± 4.4	0.31	33.9 ± 2.6	32.5 ± 3.6	0.47	- 3.2 ± 2.6	- 4.7 ± 2.2	0.27
12	7	11	152.0 ± 3.6	146.1 ± 6.4	0.04	39.7 ± 4.3	34.7 ± 4.4	0.03	- 4.1 ± 2.7	- 5.0 ± 2.3	0.47
13	4	6	159.0 ± 6.2	152.4 ± 8.4	0.22	46.2 ± 7.7	39.7 ± 5.6	0.16	- 6.1 ± 1.4	- 4.0 ± 2.5	0.18
14	3	4	163.7 ± 3.4	155.5 ± 8.1	0.16	51.3 ± 3.2	44.5 ± 7.7	0.21	- 4.1 ± 1.8	- 5.0 ± 1.1	0.42
15	4	4	168.1 ± 4.4	159.3 ± 7.1	0.08	57.7 ± 7.9	47.8 ± 6.5	0.10	- 5.5 ± 3.1	- 5.6 ± 1.2	0.94

Values are mean ± SD

levels, were compared. As seen from table 2, no significant differences in ulnar variance (DIDI) could be observed between groups within all age categories, the probability value ranging from $p = 0.18$ to $p = 0.94$. Within the limitations of this mixed-longitudinal investigation it can thus be concluded that gymnastic training does not inhibit the normal growth of the radius, resulting in a positive ulnar variance, as previously claimed by several authors[1,5,6,7].

References

1. Caine, D., Roy, S., Singer, K.M. and Broekhoff, J. (1992) Stress changes of the distal radial growth plate. A radiographic survey and review of the literature. *American Journal of Sports Medicine*, Vol. 20, pp. 290-8.
2. Weiker, G.G. (1992) Hand and wrist problems in the gymnast. *Clinics in Sports Medicine*, Vol. 11, pp. 189-202.
3. Aronen, J.G. (1985) Problems of the upper extremity in gymnasts. *Clinics in Sports Medicine*, Vol. 4, pp. 61-71.
4. Caine, D.J. (1990) Growth plate injury and bone growth: an update. *Pediatric Exercise Science*, Vol. 2, pp. 209-29.
5. Mandelbaum, B.R., Bartolozzi, A.R., Davis, C.A., Teurlings, L. and Bragonier, B. (1989) Wrist pain syndrome in the gymnast: pathogenetic, diagnostic, and therapeutic considerations. *American Journal of Sports Medicine*, Vol. 17, pp. 305-17.
6. Roy, S., Caine, D. and Singer, K.M. (1985) Stress changes of the distal radial epiphysis in young gymnasts: a report of twenty-one cases and a review of the literature. *American Journal of Sports Medicine*, Vol. 13, pp. 301-8.
7. Albanese, S.A., Palmer, A.K., Kerr, D.R., Carpenter, C.W., Lisi, D. and Levinsohn, M. (1989) Wrist pain and distal growth plate closure of the radius in gymnasts. *Journal of Pediatric Orthopedics*, Vol. 9, pp. 23-8.
8. Claessens, A.L., Lefevre, J., Beunen, G., De Smet, L. and Veer, A.M. (1996) Physique as a risk factor for ulnar variance in elite female gymnasts. *Medicine and Science in Sports and Exercise*, Vol. 28, pp. 560-9.
9. Hafner, R., Poznanski, A.K. and Donovan, J.M. (1989) Ulnar variance in children: standard measurements for evaluation of ulnar shortening in juvenile rheumatoid arthritis, hereditary multiple exostosis and other bone or joint disorders in childhood. *Skeletal Radiology*, Vol. 18, pp. 513-6.
10. Simons, J., Beunen, G.P., Renson, R., Claessens, A.L., Van Reusel, B. and Lefevre, J.A.V. (1990) *Growth and Fitness of Flemish Girls: the Leuven Growth Study,* Human Kinetics, Champaign, Il.
11. Claessens, A.L., Veer, F.M., Stijnen, V., Lefevre, J., Maes, H., Steens, G. and Beunen, G. (1991) Anthropometric characteristics of outstanding male and female gymnasts. *Journal of Sports Sciences*, Vol. 9, pp. 53-74.
12. Claessens, A.L., Beunen, G., Lefevre, J., Stijnen, V. Maes, H. and Veer, F.M. (1990) Relation between physique and performance in outstanding female gymnasts, in *Sports, Medicine and Health*, (ed. G.P.H. Hermans), Elsevier Science Publishers B.V., Amsterdam, pp. 725-31.

MORAL WELL-BEING: THE ROLE OF PHYSICAL EDUCATION AND SPORT

Moral well-being, PE and sport

M. LEE
Chelsea School Research Centre, University of Brighton, UK
Keywords: Moral well-being, physical education, sport

Introduction

It is a privilege to be invited to present a paper at this conference, the more so because this is a conference of paediatric physiologists! In such company I acknowledge that there is some risk in presenting an argument based upon data gathered by the rather "soft" techniques of interviewing and questionnaire administration. After all, how do we know whether our subjects are telling the truth, are consistent with it, or even know what it is! However, I hope to show that despite the difficulties of measurement, which are truly significant, consistencies about moral behaviour in a sporting context can be identified and that physical education and sport can, and possibly do, have an impact upon it.

In recent years a concern for the moral well-being of young people in Britain has been expressed among many sections of society. There have been frequent reports of violence among young people and a number of very high profile court cases such as those of the murders of 3-year-old James Bulger by two 10-year-old boys, of Philip Lawrence, a headmaster, by a group of youths, and the manslaughter of 13-year-old Louise Allen by two other girls of who kicked her to death when she attempted to stop a fight. However, whether the levels of violence in society are, in the long term, getting appreciably worse has been challenged by Pearson[1] who argued that successive generations have expressed fears of social breakdown and moral degeneration; longing for the security of a bygone age. He contends that the "golden age" for which people long appears to be, typically, 20 y previously, but is in fact mythical since people of all eras express a desire to return to it! In support of his argument he produces extensive historical evidence for the existence of antisocial behaviour in previous ages.

Children and Exercise XIX. Edited by Neil Armstrong, Brian Kirby and Joanne Welsman.
Published in 1997 by E & FN Spon, 2–6 Boundary Row, London, SE1 8HN.
ISBN 0 419 22100 X.

The debate in the United Kingdom has recently focused attention on what are popularly called "family values", though their definition has been implicit rather than explicit. The School Curriculum Assessment Authority(SCAA)[2] has demonstrated the difficulty of identifying "core values" and also brought to the fore questions about the location of responsibility for nurturing them and promoting moral development. There is a sense in which the values to be espoused are positive in that they identify forms of behaviour which are to the benefit of society, both collectively and individually, and are not merely designations of forbidden actions. Both the SCAA and other government agencies concerned with education consider that physical education and sport have a role to play in promoting values and moral well-being as has been traditional in education since the Greeks. However, despite the claims evidence has been rather thin and, indeed, a considerable body of research indicates the contrary[3].

This paper will address two major issues which define the topic of moral well-being. The first is: Do physical education and sport experiences promote the development of moral qualities? The second is: If so, are moral qualities developed in physical education and sport generalised to other life situations? In order to do this it is necessary to clarify the meaning of morality and moral well-being prior to examining evidence which informs the topic. I will outline some theoretical perspectives on the development of morality, describe some research findings in sport psychology, and present some of my own data on value systems among young athletes.

Nature of moral qualities: philosophical bases

For a clarification of morality we need to turn to philosophy. An important influence on recent thinking in moral philosophy has been John Rawls' A Theory of Justice[4], an extensive essay in political theory in which a view of justice as fairness is advanced. This view is dependent upon the application of two principles: (a) that each individual shall have equal access to liberties as far as is compatible with liberty for all, and (b) that inequalities should be arranged so that they are to the greatest benefit of the least advantaged, and attached to positions which are open to all. In sporting terms these principles may be interpreted in terms of the freedom to behave as one will to the extent that such behaviour does not restrict the freedoms of others, and that where there are inequalities they should operate to the advantage of the less able, as in a system of handicapping to equalise opportunities for competitive success. The principles denote morality as a characteristic of interpersonal rather than intrapersonal behaviour. Thus one can make moral decisions about behaviour in relationships with other people but not about one's duty to oneself, a view which is supported by psychological analyses. For example, as a result of empirical research Rokeach[5] identified a system of values, or conceptions of the desirable, which is characterised by two dimensions: (a) desirable goals or modes of behaviour, and (b) inter-personal or intra-personal concerns. Within this framework it is possible to identify four types of values (see table 1) of which moral values are identified as those which are concerned with inter-personal behaviour.

Table 1. Model of value types

	Goals	Behaviour
Intrapersonal	Personal/Achievement	Competence
Interpersonal	Social	Moral

Adapted from Rokeach[5]

Goals are terminal values, or objectives, which we try to reach in our lives, while behaviour represents instrumental values, exhibited in the ways in which we act. Both of the categories were applied to intrapersonal and interpersonal beliefs. Although later research has indicated that the terminal / instrumental distinction may be a linguistic artefact this model does reveal a distinction between inter- and intrapersonal values and provides a framework to distinguish self-focused competence and achievement on the one hand and prosocial values on the other.

The moral point of view

With these thoughts in mind moral well-being may be described as a state in which individuals act in accordance with a moral point of view and make decisions according to the characteristics associated with it. Thus Kurt Baier[6, p.194] suggests that, "If one has adopted the moral point of view, then one acts on principle and not merely by conforming to rules of thumb designed to promote one's aim. This involves conforming to the rules whether or not doing so favours one's own or anybody else's aim". However, merely to refer to principled behaviour seems to leave the door open to the principle of self-interest, which violates the principles advanced by Rawls[4]. Key characteristics of the moral principles are (a) prescriptiveness, they determine the ways in which people should behave, and (b) universality, moral rules apply to all parties at all times. In sport, behaviour is, for the most part, determined by the rules without favour to any of the contestants; to question the applicability of the rules to a particular competitor or circumstance is to invite ridicule[7]. However, there may also be a tacit agreement about how to operate a set of rules which is entered into by the competitors, e.g. the use of contact in basketball. This represents normative behaviour within the culture, but which, though unwritten, may be equally binding.

Moral well-being

To draw the analogy from notions of physical well-being the notion of moral well-being appears to imply the acquisition of a state of moral health. Let us consider it as a condition of moral maturity in which interpersonal decisions are made from the moral perspective, as a result of the application of broad principles of behaviour in all areas of life, unrestricted by the immediate demands of the situation. Such a state implies that those who achieve it respond for the greater good and not on the basis of self-interest. From this position moral well-being implies the internalisation of moral principles which are subsequently invoked in order to resolve moral conflicts. Physical education and sport can only make a contribution to moral well-being to the extent that they provide an avenue for this process.

The foregoing discussion has identified the importance of moral principles as universalisable, i.e. they are applicable in all situations. Where individuals make apparently inconsistent decisions in different situations the explanation may lie in the weight attached to different principles. For example, it may be that, in a given circumstance, the injunctions to preserve life and not to steal may come into conflict. The choice of the most appropriate action invokes the assignment of value to each option; hence it may be appropriate to steal in order to save a life, but it is not so otherwise. Lawrence Kohlberg, a pre-eminent scholar in moral development has commonly used such a problem to investigate levels of moral reasoning in both children and adults which he then judges on the basis of their reasoning[8].

Moral development: psychological approaches

There are a number of different positions on how people develop a conception of principled behaviour. Not surprisingly they represent the different schools of psychology. Hence there are positions drawn from psychoanalytic, personality trait, behaviourist, social learning, and cognitive developmental positions. Since it has been probably the most influential I will elaborate on the cognitive-developmental approach, however, it is appropriate also first to outline some of the other perspectives.

Psychoanalytic approach

Psychoanalytic theory was the first organised approach to the psychology of moral behaviour. In his theory of personality Freud's concept of the super-ego is a mechanism for mediating and controlling the chaotic driving forces of the id. It acts as the conscience and has a self-observation function which enables the individual to stand apart from himself in order to be self-critical. From this perspective children are considered to learn moral values from their parents' through a process of identification[9]. According to Freud children acquire their parents moral position by identification because they wish to be like them. Importantly it is the parents super-ego and not their behaviour which provides the model[10].

Trait approach

Among the earliest research into moral judgements was the seminal work of Hartshorne and May who conducted a series of studies into the nature of honesty and "character"[see 3,11,12 for discussions]. Essentially they studied the behaviour of children in a variety of situations, including athletic contests, where there were opportunities to cheat, lie and steal. Their efforts to identify a general predisposition towards dishonesty as a personality trait met with little success and they concluded that there was little evidence for a general trait of honesty[3]. Subsequent reanalyses of the data using more sophisticated statistical techniques have demonstrated modest evidence of a general factor in moral conduct which extracted 35-40% of the variance, but the most consistent conclusion, of this and subsequent research in the same vein, remains that children's behaviour is inconsistent and behaviour varies according to the demands of the situation[11,12].

Behaviourist approaches

Behaviouristic explanations of moral behaviour are extensions of learning theory which explains changes in behaviour as a product of the particular patterns of reward and punishment. The subsequent development of social learning theories resulted in an explanation of internalisation of moral values by processes of modelling and self-reinforcing events - those which bring their own reward. For example, if cheating in a game brings success then it will be repeated. Age related changes in moral judgements are accounted for by the interaction between changes in cognitive and behavioural competence and social learning variables, e.g. obedience to authority, response to reward and punishment[13]. Reviews from this perspective once again point to the specificity of behaviour and the need to consider the particular conditions of the situation in determining responses.

Cognitive developmental theory

The positions outlined above have been subject to the criticism that, while confirming the specificity of moral behaviour, they are unable to account adequately for principled behaviour. Psychoanalytic theory does not provide a good account of the integration of cognitive, affective and behavioural elements morality or the relations between predispositions and experience[10]. The Hartshorne and May studies failed to recognise the important role of moral reasoning by addressing only the content of moral beliefs and behaviour[3]. Hence the inconsistencies they found may be due in part to the failure to recognise that how children think about moral issues is different from how adults think. The perspective assumed that there was not only a right and wrong solution to the problems posed, but also that it was determined by adults. Behavioural perspectives address the issue of situational specificity rather well, but hold little hope for those who wish to establish the development of internalised moral principles. Moreover, they are unable to account for developmental patterns in the cognitive and affective dimensions of values or address the question of how children incorporate values in the control of actions. Furthermore, the preoccupation with behaviour inhibits any explanation of such cognitive events as moral reasoning or conscience and their development[10]. In the light of these criticisms we now turn to the cognitive-developmental perspective which has come to dominate the field.

Discussions of moral development owe a debt to the work of Piaget and Kohlberg who constructed stage theories of moral development which identified both the content of moral thought and its structure. They propose that moral development is a function of changes to the ways in which children think about moral issues; i.e. the content of the problem may be the same but the structure of reasoning may change. This is an extension of the proposition that changes in moral rules are a function of changes in children's perceptions of their relationships with each other[10]. Consequently, it is proposed that moral maturity is gained as people progress through a series of stages of thinking which are characterised by changes from concrete, context bound, to more abstract levels of judgement. According to this explanation moral development follows the pattern of cognitive development. Thus, as children become more capable of abstract thought the more sophisticated they become in making moral decisions. Unfortunately the argument does seem to suggest that unless you are clever you cannot be good!

Piaget

At about the same time as the Hartshorne and May studies Piaget made observations of what children considered to be fair or unfair[14]. Contrary to the predominant method of the time he developed a clinical interview technique in order to understand how children organised their thoughts about the world and the moral issues they faced. As a result he identified four types of unfair behaviour: (a) behaviour in contravention of adult instructions, e.g. lying, stealing etc., (b) behaviour against the rules of a game, e.g. cheating, (c) inequality, both in treatment and punishment, and (d) injustice in adult society, e.g. economic or political. Moreover, he demonstrated that the occurrence of these types varied with age.

On the basis of his observations he concluded that there were three significant periods of development of a sense of justice in children: (a) subordination to adult authority, (b) progressive equalitarianism, and (c) equity. In the first period, lasting until about 8 years of age, right requires conforming to adult rules, hence it is important for adults to be consistent. The second period appears at 7 to 8 years of age and is characterised by the development of autonomy and of equality; Piaget quotes an example of inequality given by a 12 year old as "a referee who takes sides."[14, p. 605]. By 11 or 12 years of age children moderate the criterion of equality in favour of equity in which the particular circumstances of individuals and situations are taken into account when deciding on a just course of action.

Kohlberg

Drawing upon the foundations laid by Piaget, Kohlberg[8,15] developed a more elaborate system which proposes that people pass through three increasingly abstract levels of moral reasoning: (a) egocentric morality, (b) social responsibility, and (c) independent morality. At each level there are two sub-stages characterised by slightly different orientations to moral problems. In the first, individuals take normative or consequence stances to the resolution of moral dilemmas. In the second, decisions are made on the basis of the higher level principles of justice. These include consideration of liberty, equality, and contract, in combination with the recognition of conscience and the presentation of an ideal image.

The first level is one of egocentric morality in which moral decisions are made on the basis of self-interest. The second level, social responsibility, is the conventional level of morality which recognises the predominance of the needs of the group or society as a whole and conforms to the principle of the Golden Rule; there is an emphasis on conformity, adherence to rules, and social maintenance. Decision making at the third level, independent morality, is characterised by independence from the normative demands of the group. It emphasises individual rights and universal ethical principles which lead to the development of a personal code of behaviour.

Evidence for the validity of the proposed stages has indicated that egocentric morality dominates during childhood. During mid-childhood moral decisions are made on the basis of self-interest and then fair exchange; during late childhood egocentric reasoning is still predominant, but from about 10 years of age it declines in favour of social responsibility. By the age of 14 y this becomes the dominant mode of moral reasoning and increases in importance throughout adolescence and adulthood. The incidence of independently principled judgements begins to appear in young adulthood but is limited even among mature samples[8]. Kohlberg investigated this sequence by analysing responses to a series of hypothetical moral dilemmas as in the example given above.

Haan

A student of Kohlberg, Norma Haan, has proposed an alternative model which draws upon the nature of daily negotiations to explain how we resolve moral dilemmas. She argued that Kohlberg's approach represented a formal logic drawn from a Kantian deontological perspective which bore little resemblance to common experience. Because there existed a difference in the conclusions of a formal logic and of a logic derived from interpersonal action she proposed that "... people engage in dialogues ... with the intents of achieving new or maintaining old moral balances, ..., in order to protect and enhance their sense of themselves as moral beings ... ."[16, p. 287]. Hence it would be better to investigate children's thinking in situations which were more meaningful to them and in which the principles of the need for moral balance and moral dialogue were called into operation. As a result of her investigations, and again in a Piagetian tradition, Haan proposed a framework of three phases giving rise to five stages of moral development (see table 2).

The principle of moral balance suggests that interpersonal negotiations include agreements and obligations between the parties which are demonstrated in the dialogue between them. Agreement is reached when both parties accept the existence of a moral balance between their respective needs and obligations. In sport there is a set of formal laws which govern the activity, but the players also agree to abide by a set of accepted norms of behaviour. Violations of this set of agreements may well lead to cries of "unfair!" or to retaliation. If the balance in a particular setting is tipped one way or another then a moral dialogue is initiated which may result in behavioural

Table 2. Haan's model of interactive morality

Phase	Level of Balance	Features
Assimilation	a) Power	Meeting the demands of self interest.
	b) Egocentric	Compromise made for self-interest.
Accommodation	a) Harmony	Balance based upon good faith.
	b) Common interest	Compromise to protect the group.
Equilibration	a) Mutual interest	Harmony achieved according to demands of the situation and personal interest.

Adapted from Haan[16]

changes to restore the moral balance. This does not mean that the parties necessarily sit down and discuss the problem, though indeed this may be part of the process. The negotiation may take the form of retaliation with a possible decline into a downward spiral of negative behaviour.

In an investigation of this model Haan subjected adolescents to both (a) Kohlberg type interviews and (b) moral problems in the form of ego involving games while under discreet observation. The results indicated that (a) formal morality as assessed by interview was a poor predictor of action morality, (b) higher levels of action morality occurred under pleasant conditions and lower levels under stressful conditions, (c) levels of formal morality were more affected by the nature of the situations encountered[16]. These results support the argument that the Kohlbergian perspective is too formal to account adequately for the moral decisions that children, and others, are required to make in everyday life. Haan's perspective acknowledges the complexity of moral decision making which people encounter on a daily basis and draws attention to the contextual limitations of those decisions.

An example of Haan's model in an informal setting was provided to me by a colleague some years ago. His wife taught at a middle school (ages 9-13 years) where, as is common with most schools in Britain, children played informal football at break-times. Since the games frequently overlapped and interfered with each other two boys organised a league in which all those who wished to could take part, teams were balanced as well as possible, a timetable was devised, and breaches of the rules were adjudicated by a conference of opposing captains (a sin bin being introduced for repeated offences). Such was the concern for fairplay that the side judged to be strongest in any contest was required to play up the hill! The processes involved in the negotiations seem to provide excellent examples of striving to achieve moral balance through moral dialogue - in the absence of adult input.

Critiques of cognitive developmental theory

Kohlberg's system has come under frequent criticism but continues to be most influential. Phillips, a philosopher of science, published a stringent attack on it on account of both the claims it makes, i.e. the credibility of stages themselves, invariance of the sequence, the logical necessity of the sequence; and methodological shortcomings, e.g. inaccessibility of the interview and scoring techniques, presentation of findings, and a strategy of seeking confirmation rather than disconfirmation of the theory. His conclusion was that the programme has little merit, but that there was nothing then available with which to replace it[17]. However, Lind[18], a psychologist and student of methodology, has also examined the theory and data submitted in its support and has concluded that "...we should regard the cognitive-developmental approach ... as a very 'courageous speculation' which has proved to be of great significance for progress in moral psychology, even where it fails." (p. 51). Haan's modification appears to provide a better explanation of moral development and of the associated behaviour by taking into account the actor's perceptions of the specific contextual demands while still providing a mechanism for the development of principled behaviour necessary for moral well-being.

Mechanisms for change

Having said that and, with reservations, accepted that the description of sequential stages is a reasonable representation of the progress of moral reasoning the perspective does not of itself address the issue of how such changes are brought about. Neither do trait or behaviourist approaches account for them. The former suggest that certain predispositions are constant within individuals; but they have only minimal support. The latter predict that moral behaviour is determined by the conditions pertaining at the time, which may include social influences, and do not address the issue of socially oriented principled judgement. However, Kohlberg has argued the importance of social situations in promoting movement from one stage to another. While cognitive stimulation is a necessary condition for moral development it is not sufficient and must be supplemented by opportunities for social interaction which includes moral decision making, moral dialogue, and moral interaction. He proposed that there are three mediating factors for moral development: (a) role taking opportunities, (b) institutional moral environment, and (c) opportunities for moral reflection. For Kohlberg, role-taking provides a bridge between the cognitive and moral levels of thought by placing children in situations where they must give due consideration to the perspective of others in the conflict. Such opportunities can be found in families and among peer groups where children are required to take on a variety of roles. The second factor draws attention to the level of moral reasoning in the institutions in which children find themselves. Here they may be exposed to levels of moral action, reasoning and rules which are perceived as a unified whole and bring about change to conform with it. Finally, the identification of cognitive-moral conflict in a social situation, once exposed, can bring about change through discussion with others and reflection[15]. The salient aspect of these propositions is the recognition of the importance of social influences upon development and that the "moral atmosphere" of a group is important in determining the course of moral decision making[19]. This position is of particular interest since sports and physical education involve groups and teams to a significant degree and provide an identifiable moral atmosphere which may facilitate the internalisation of moral principles.

Research in physical education and sport

So where does this leave physical education and sport? What do they offer to development of moral well-being? It can be argued that they are potentially fertile settings for the exertion of social influence; and provide situations in which moral judgement, moral action, and moral dialogue are required. Physical education frequently requires young people to work together either for a common cause or for the benefit of one of their number. This may be achieved during the learning of skills or during the practice of those skills in a contest. In contests, participants are called upon to operate within a set of constitutive rules and agree, if only tacitly, to those rules, not only as written but also in the spirit which they represent. Violations of the rules, or the spirit, destroy the balance which must then be restored. If this can be done positively then the game can continue amicably; if this is not possible it will deteriorate as opponents seek to establish an advantage. Moreover, given the degree of stress which athletes encounter it might be expected that participants would demonstrate lower levels of moral action when under the stress of competition.

We appear, therefore, to have a social situation which demands the demonstration of moral behaviour, at whatever level, and which is subject to the influence of significant others. In other words a potential forum for the transmission, or development, of moral principles. Schools, classes, clubs and teams each develop a set of norms, or behavioural expectancies, which can be expected to affect young athletes' moral decisions in sports situations. For example, some years ago a colleague and I were interviewing young soccer players about moral dilemmas with a view to identifying underlying values which guided their actions in sport. When faced with a dilemma which gave the option of cheating or allowing an opponent the opportunity to score one subject replied quite openly that his decision depended on whether he was playing for his school team or for his (professional) club youth team. If the former he would abide by the rules, if the latter he would break the rule. He went on to explain that that was what the respective coaches expected.

Let us now turn to research about morality in sport, specifically youth sport, which will inform the original questions. The positive view of sport as an agent for moral growth remains widespread yet research which supports the view remains sparse, though there are oases of hope! Possible approaches have examined attitudinal positions, behavioural tendencies (mostly related to aggressive behaviour), moral development, and, more recently, values.

Attitudes

The bulk of research into fairplay, or violations of its principles, have been attitudinal studies[e.g. 20,21,22,23,24,25]. The results suggest that instrumental, as opposed to moral, attitudes are more commonly associated with older athletes, competitive success, males rather than females, and élite rather than non-élite levels of participation. While this may sound somewhat negative, a study of 500 young athletes by Lee, Balchin and Whitehead found that subjects held significantly negative attitudes towards cheating and 'gamesmanship', the latter being defined as adopting strategies which seek to gain an unfair advantage without actually cheating (table 3)[23].

These data indicate positive attitudes towards fairplay among young athletes and negative attitudes towards winning at all costs. However, further analysis also indicated that there were small but reliable effects of gender, girls held more positive

Table 3. Differences of moral attitude scores from scale mid-points

	Mean	SD	x	t
Cheating	2.03	.66	-.97	-32.37**
Gamesmanship	2.57	.82	-.43	-11.60**
Keep winning in proportion	4.25	.58	1.25	48.13**
Winning is all that matters	2.80	.87	-.20	-5.18**

** p <0.001

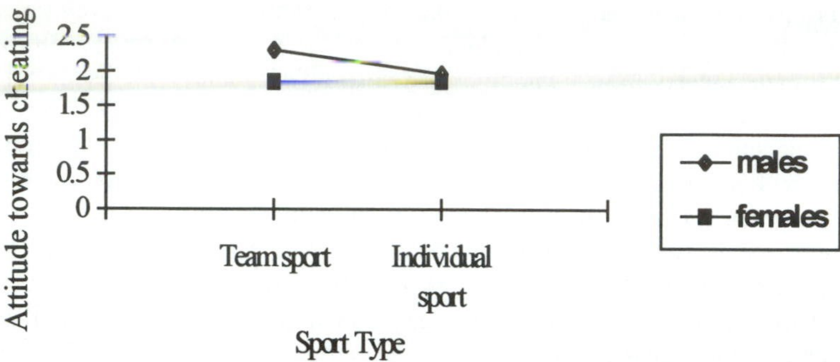

Fig. 1. Effect of sport type and gender on attitude towards cheating [23]

attitudes towards fairplay than boys; age, young athletes were more positive than older athletes, and level of performance, elite players are more likely to endorse instrumental attitudes. From the point of view of educational policy the data also question the much vaunted benefits of team sports by showing that, even though effects are small, male team sport players are more likely to endorse cheating than girls or male individual sport players (fig 1).

Vallerand and Losier[25] examined relationships between sportsmanship and motivation using a measure of sportsmanship which was developed by selecting and piloting a pool of items with a large sample of adolescent athletes. It consists of five scales which represent commitment to: (a) participation, (b) social conventions, (c) officials, (d) opponents, and (e) negative approach to participation. The last is exemplified by the item "If I make a mistake I get upset." and is scored with reverse polarity, though it is not immediately clear what it means. In a season long study of élite male adolescent ice-hockey players they found a decline in both sportsmanship scores and motivation and cross-lagged correlations and regression analyses indicated that motivational orientation has a greater influence on sportsmanship than the reverse. Other research has indicated that young players who adopt a predominantly comparative assessment of competence are more prone to unfair behaviour[24,26]. Attitudinal studies, therefore, suggest that, far from promoting moral attitudes within the activity, even if children hold high regard for moral attitudes they decline with continued participation.

Moral developmental research

During the 1980s Bredemeier and her co-workers conducted a series of studies which attempted to evaluate the claims for moral development in the sporting context [e.g. 27, 28, 29]. Shields and Bredemeier have summarised the work in a comprehensive book Character Development and Physical Activity and devoted a section to the evaluation of the character building claims for sport[3]. After a historical examination of the roots of the proposition itself and a recognition that a major problem lies in defining character, Shields and Bredemeier review literature concerned with the relations between sport participation and delinquency, aggression, value hierarchies, and moral development. They conclude that there is a negative relationship between sports participation and delinquency and a positive relationship between sports participation and the expression of aggression. There is limited evidence for a negative relationship between participation and moral maturity. In particular Bredemeier has shown that athletes demonstrate lower levels of moral reasoning in discussing athletic situations than everyday life situations[26].

These conclusions are depressing for the proponents of sport as a moral educator. However, Bredemeier and her colleagues have also shown that physical education settings, if not sport, can be used to promote moral development[28,30]. In the first study Bredemeier et al. examined the effect of instructional strategies in promoting moral growth among young children in a sports camp setting. Subjects aged 5 -7 y were randomly allocated to a control, a social learning, or a structural-developmental group. In the first group instructors used traditional physical education methods which encouraged conformity to teacher prescribed rules, obedience; in the second, instructors modelled and reinforced prosocial behaviour; and in the third, instructors used Haan's approach to facilitate moral dialogue to resolve moral conflicts as they arose. The data indicated that both social learning and moral dialogue techniques improved moral growth over a 6 wk period. This is encouraging in that it indicates that provided the context is structured appropriately physical education can be used to promote moral growth, within that setting. However, the caveat is that the study was carried out with very young children in a sports camp which has a predominantly recreational nature and hence does not adequately represent a setting comparable with competitive sport. Nevertheless, in support of these data, in a field experiment, Romance, Weiss, and Bockovan demonstrated that children's moral reasoning could be significantly improved by a specifically targeted intervention programme in physical education[31].

In another study Bredemeier examined moral reasoning in response to hypothetical moral dilemmas, two about sport and two about daily life, in order to test the veracity of Kohlberg's contention of cross-situational consistency of moral judgement. One hundred and ten children aged between 9 and 12 y and, again, enrolled in a summer sports camp programme took part in moral interviews which posed the hypothetical dilemmas and asked subjects to select, for example, between honesty and loyalty, or reactive aggression and indifference to cheating. The data indicated that children in the two younger age groups were consistent across situations but the oldest children (11-12 y) showed lower levels of moral reasoning in response to sports dilemmas than in life dilemmas (table 4)[29]. Bredemeier put these data together with an earlier study of older athletes, high school, and college[26], to show a consistent trend of increasing divergence beginning at 11 to 12 years of age. This, of course, is the time when young people begin to show a greater commitment to competitive sport. The data provide no support for the inter-context consistency hypothesis with increasing age. In explanation of the observed pattern Shields and Bredemeier invoke the concept of game reasoning which further emphasises the lack of cross-situational transfer of moral reasoning. Drawing upon Huizinga's[32] view that play involves stepping out of reality into a different sphere of activity which is bounded by time and space they argue that moral

Table 4. Differences in moral reasoning in sport and daily life situations for children

Age Group	n	Situation Life	Sport	t	p
9-10	41	2.39	2.39	0.00	ns
10-11	42	2.46	2.48	0.24	ns
11-12	27	2.58	2.42	3.91	<.05
Total	110	2.47	2.43	1.09	ns

Adapted from Bredmeier[30]

negotiations in sport form a bracketed morality which occurs within, but is separate from, a broader morality[3].

They argue that athletes perceive sport as a separate arena in which self-interest is dominant and in which personal interests can reasonably take precedence over interpersonal relations. Some support for this view is provided by Erikson who considers that "The playing adult steps sideward into another reality; the playing advances forward to new stages of mastery"[33, p. 222]. This implies that for children playing is a reality. If so, then Bredemeier's[29] observation that divergence in moral judgements occurs at about 12 y is consistent with the onset of puberty which heralds the passage to adulthood.

These studies go some way to providing answers to the questions posed at the beginning. It appears that, first, mere participation in sporting activities does not of itself increase moral reasoning or judgement, Indeed the evidence suggests that those who continue to participate and are successful tend to show greater tolerance for immoral attitudes. Secondly, however, it is possible to structure teacher-pupil interaction in a physical education setting to produce positive change in moral thinking. Thirdly, there is evidence that as young athletes enter adolescence their ability to discriminate the salient features of a given situation actually encourages the application of a different set of moral standards in sport and life and argues against the transfer of moral reasoning across contexts.

Social Influence

It has been shown that during adolescence moral reasoning in daily life is related to parental moral judgement, with girls being more strongly affected than boys[34]. Hence it is reasonable to propose that children learn sportsmanship through interaction with significant others in sport. Indeed there is some evidence to support this view. Smith reports a study of young players, aged 12 to 21 y, in the notoriously violent sport of ice-hockey in which parents, coaches, and team mates were all perceived as approving violent behaviour by players. Levels of approval increased with age and level of performance[35].

With a sample of basketball players aged 9 to 15 y Stuart and Ebbeck showed not only that social approval of morally undesirable intentions by significant others was related to level of moral development but also that the relationship changed with age.

For younger children mothers were the most influential, lower approval was related to higher levels of moral judgement and moral intentions, and for adolescents peers were most influential, higher approval was related to lower prosocial behaviour, reasoning, moral judgement and intent. However, the data also indicate generally benign attitudes in that levels of moral judgement, intent, and coach assessed behaviour were high[36].

Lee and Balchin also report the influence of significant others. A sample of 500 competitive athletes aged 12 to 16 y indicated that club environment, school, role models, and parents were all influential in determining their sporting values. The results provide further evidence to doubt the benign influence that simply playing sport has on sportsmanship and direct attention to the social environment in which sport is presented to young athletes in order to assess its potential for promoting desirable ethical standards[37].

Finally, an interesting study by Stephens and Bredemeier suggests that social influence is more important than personal motivational orientations in predicting aggressive intent among female soccer players aged 9 to 14 y. The study used a commonly used questionnaire to measure goal orientation, the Task and Ego Orientation in Sport Questionnaire (TEOSQ), and a specially designed instrument to assess Judgements about Moral Behaviour in Youth Sport (JAMBYSQ). Stephens and Bredemeier found that more players expressed aggressive tendencies than hypothetical players should; i.e. probable altruistic behaviour in response to a specific game situation was at a lower level of judgement than duty required. Endorsement of aggression was predicted by perceptions of social norms and perceptions of the coaches' ego orientation[38]. While these results are valuable in demonstrating that social influence on moral attitudes is important, they should be seen in conjunction with data which show that similar attitudes in boys may be more affected by their own goal orientations[24].

Values

Until very recently there have been fewer studies which explicitly used the concept of values despite there being a case to be made that value systems are fundamental to an adequate understanding of fairplay. Research which has explicitly adopted a values approach had been restricted to studies which, though useful in giving some initial insights, have not been thoroughly grounded in theory, drawn upon a clear conceptual analysis, or utilised a universe of concepts derived from the populations of interest [e.g. 39, 40, 41]. However, the research initiative of the Council of Europe and the Sports Council in the late 1980s stimulated an interest in this area [e.g. 42,43,44] and a suitable instrument has been developed to measure sports values in children[45].

Given the difficulties encountered in defining character and the variety of moral constructs a values approach is useful because the underlying motivation to behave in a prosocial or antisocial manner reflects the hierarchical value system of the individual in question. Furthermore, since there is a wish to promote the understanding and adoption of universalisable principles of moral judgement rather than situationally specific attitudes or behaviours then the study of values is appropriate. The argument is based upon a conception of values as beliefs that certain goals or behaviours are preferable to their alternatives and act as guides to the selection and evaluation of behaviour. Thus, individuals develop a value system in which values are arranged in order of importance; where they come into conflict a choice must be made[46]. The system is

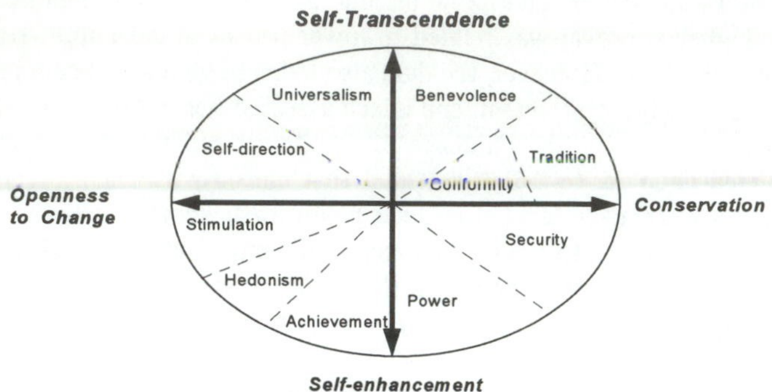

Fig 2. Model of relationship among motivational types of values[46]

considered to be universal in the sense that values guide behaviour across a variety of situations. Thence it is proposed that an individual's value system will guide his or her choice of behaviour in all settings, in this case both in sport and out of it. Such an argument, that values developed in a sport transfer to other contexts, provides a rationale for the proposal that 'sport develops character' - whether or not that 'character' is good or bad!

Schwartz has proposed a model of values which identifies two major motivational dimensions, (a) Openness to Change vs. Conservation and (b) Self-enhancement vs. Self-transcendence, which provide a framework for the location of 10 value types according to their compatibility and relationship to the basic dimensions. Each value type contains a number of specific values (fig 2). Values which are located in the same area constitute a higher order motivational domain. Adjacent domains, e.g. Universalism and Benevolence, are compatible in that selection and evaluation of behaviours resulting from them are not in conflict. Value domains which are diametrically opposed, e.g. Achievement and Benevolence, result in conflicting demands[46]. In sport, for example, the pursuit of achievement values in the form of an emphasis upon winning contests, ambition, and competence, conflicts with the moral behaviours implied by the domain of benevolence which emphasises such values as honesty, loyalty, forgiveness, and responsibility. Most importantly the model specifies the role of basic motivations which identify a continuum of self-transcendence to self-enhancement. As a competitive activity, sport is essentially an activity of self-enhancement - yet, rather paradoxically, a desirable outcome of sports participation for children is that of self-transcendence.

Schwartz' model highlights the moral conflicts inherent in sporting situations and which confront performers, teachers and coaches to varying degrees. Achievement, as represented by defeating others in a contest is an expression of self interest which conflicts with expressing concern for others, i.e. universal values; the reward structure of sport demands self-interested behaviour. However, Bardi and Schwartz present a cogent argument for the resolution of the conflict by arguing that achievement oriented behaviour may also derive from the value type Self-direction which is compatible with Universalism and Benevolence. They support their argument by pointing out that adolescent value systems are still at a formative stage and that personal achievement values are typically located in the Self-direction value type for adolescents, in cross-cultural research[47].

In pursuing the thesis that socio-moral behaviour in sport is a reflection of an individual's personal value system Lee[37,42,45] has, first, identified values which guide the behaviour of adolescent athletes and, second, examined the nature of the relationships between those values among adolescent athletes.

Broadly, the results indicate that:(a) young people's behaviour in sport is guided by a relatively limited set of 18 values (a selection is presented in Table 5), (b) a group of six socio-moral values can be identified (italicised), (c) two other groups of values concerned with competence and status have also been indicated, (d) socio-moral values collectively held an important position in the value hierarchy, all are ranked in the top half, (e) socio-moral values are negatively related to attitudes which indicated the acceptance of cheating, acceptance of gamesmanship, and winning at all costs.

In common with most research in this field children value Enjoyment most highly, followed by Personal Achievement. Socio-moral values all rank between 3 and 9 in order of importance and the average rating of the group, on a scale of -1 to 5, shows consistently high scores across age groups. There is evidence of a decline in early

Table 5. Rankings of selected values among young competitive athletes 12-16 y

Value	Descriptor	Rank
Enjoyment:	Experiencing feelings of satisfaction and pleasure	1
Achievement:	Being personally or collectively successful in play.	2
Sportsmanship	Being of good disposition, accepting bad luck with the good, demonstrating positive behaviours toward opponents, and accepting defeats.	3
Contract Maintenance:	Supporting the essence of agreeing to play the game, to play in the spirit of the game.	4
Being Fair:	Not allowing an unfair advantage in the contest/judgement.	5
Compassion:	Showing concern for other people.	6
Tolerance:	Being able to get along with others despite differences between each other	7
Obedience:	Avoiding punishment..	9
Health & Fitness:	Becoming healthy as a result of the activity, and in becoming fit to enhance performance.	13
Winning:	Demonstrating superiority in the contest.	18

Adapted from Lee and Balchin [45]

adolescence which is arrested later (see fig 3). Trend analysis of the data indicated significant linear and quadratic trends. Although the effects are small they are reliable. Of further interest, particularly to the advocates of team sports as specially valuable in promoting moral values, was the finding that small, but reliable differences, existed between team (mean = 3.68) and individual (mean = 3.89) sport athletes on ratings of moral values.

Two further points of interest are (a) the relatively low importance given to Health and Fitness, and (b) the bottom ranking of the value Winning. The former suggests that it may be better to encourage activity by emphasising its intrinsically enjoyable aspects rather than its health benefits. The second point may cause concern for those for whom sport is about élite performance. However, it points to the value of promoting self-referenced goals of personal improvement over comparative goals of competitive success in order to retain interest.

These data are, of course, only descriptive, providing a baseline of data for young British athletes, and no attempt has yet been made to compare the value systems of athletes with non-athletes. They are encouraging for those who believe that moral values are being sacrificed to competitive success and the finding that the athletes ranked their clubs and coaches, followed by teachers and schools as the most important influences upon their values suggests that not only do they have an influence but also that influence may be beneficial for promoting desirable moral values.

Conclusion

This paper set out to examine the premise that physical education and sport provide suitable settings for the development of moral well-being which was conceived of as a condition of internalised moral principles which the individual applies to interpersonal decision making in a variety of social situations. Specifically it addressed two major questions: do physical education and sport experiences promote the development of moral qualities? and, if so, are moral qualities developed in physical education and sport generalised to other life situations? These questions are important because they

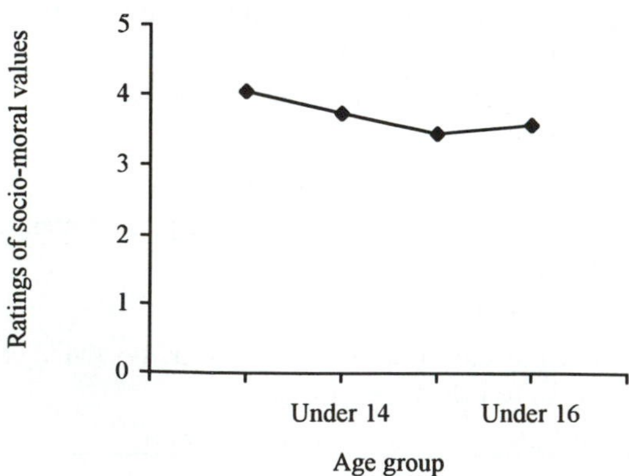

Fig. 3. Effect of age on importance of socio-moral values[45]

call into question national policy, at least in the United Kingdom, and the bases on which sport for young people is being promoted. As sport is increasingly seen as a commodity and commercial pressures grow, even upon the young, so the Corinthian ideals and educational values which sustained it in the past have come under further threat such that its use as vehicle for moral development is in doubt. Yet it may not necessarily be so, providing that sport providers are aware of the possibilities available.

The evidence suggests that because physical education and sport are part of young people's social experience they may be expected to impact upon moral development along with other experiences. However, reliance on simple participation to promote moral values is misplaced, indeed the likelihood is that adolescents operate at lower levels of moral reasoning in sport than out of it. The hypothesis of consistency of reasoning in sport and daily life lacks support. Indeed the evidence is that in sport settings athletes show increasing tendencies to regress to lower levels, so if sport did teach moral principles its effects are equally likely to be detrimental! However, clearly it is possible to so arrange things that, if moral development is an explicit objective of the programme, then physical education and sport can provide suitable, even valuable, settings for the transmission of moral values. But teachers and coaches need to be aware of the impact they have on children's moral judgements. Unfortunately the increasing commercialism within sport and its significance as a source of national pride places pressure on coaches and administrators to achieve competitive success for the few at the cost of more altruistic motives for the many. If sport is to be used successfully as an effective vehicle for moral development it is even more important that those entrusted with the future of youth sport make it explicit that moral values are part of life and are to be upheld both on and off the field.

Acknowledgements

The author would like to thank Jean Whitehead for her helpful comments during the preparation of this paper and to acknowledge the support of the Sports Council in funding aspects of the research.

References

1. Pearson, G. (1983) *Hooligan: a History of Respectable Fears*, Macmillan, London.
2. School Curriculum and Assessment Authority. (1996) *Education for Adult Life: the Spiritual and Moral Development of Young People*, SCAA Publications, Hayes, Mx.
3. Shields, D.L.L. and Bredemeier, B.J.L. (1994) *Character Development and Physical Activity*, Human Kinetics, Champaign, Il.
4. Rawls, J. (1971) *A Theory of Justice*, Harvard University Press, Cambridge, MA.
5. Rokeach, M. (1973) *The Nature of Human Values*, Free Press, New York.
6. Fraleigh, W.P. (1985) *Right Action in Sport*, Human Kinetics, Champaign, Il.

7. Rawls, J. (1955/1979) The practice conception of rules, in *Sport and the Body: a Philosophical Symposium*, (ed. E.W. Gerber and W.J. Morgan), Lea and Febiger, Philadelphia, pp. 294-6. Excerpted from Two Concepts of Rules, *The Philosophical Review*, Vol. 64 (1955), pp. 3-32.
8. Colby A. and Kohlberg, L. (1987) *The Measurement of Moral Judgement, Vol.1*, Cambridge University Press, Cambridge, England.
9. Chaplin, J.P. and Krawiec, T.S. (1970) *Systems and Theories of Psychology*, Holt, Rinehart and Winston, London.
10. Aaronfreed, J. (1976) Moral development from the standpoint of general psychology, in *Moral Development and Behaviour: Theory, Research and Social Issues*, (ed. T. Lickona), Holt, Rinehart, and Winston, New York, pp. 54-69.
11. Burton, R.V. (1976) Honesty and dishonesty, in *Moral Development and Behaviour: Theory, Research and Social Issues*, (ed. T. Lickona), Holt, Rinehart, and Winston, New York, pp.173-97.
12. Lickona, T. (1976) Critical issues in the study of moral development and behaviour, in *Moral Development and Behaviour: Theory, Research and Social Issues*, (ed. T. Lickona), Holt, Rinehart, and Winston, New York, pp. 3-27.
13. Mischel, W. and Mischel, H.N. (1976) A cognitive social learning approach to morality and self-regulation, in *Moral Development and Behaviour: Theory, Research and Social Issues*, (ed. T. Lickona), Holt, Rinehart, and Winston, New York, pp. 84-107.
14. Piaget, J. (1932/1972) The moral judgement of the child. Macmillan, London, excerpted in *Social Psychology: Experimentation, Theory, Research*, (ed. W.S Sahakian), Scranton, Penn, Intext, pp. 604-7.
15. Kohlberg, L. (1976) Moral stages and moralization: the cognitive developmental approach, in *Moral Development and Behaviour: Theory, Research and Social Issues*, (ed. T. Lickona), Holt, Rinehart, and Winston, New York, pp. 31-53.
16. Haan, N. (1978) Two moralities in action contexts: relationships to thought, ego regulation, and development. *Journal of Personality and Social Psychology*, Vol. 36, pp. 286-305.
17. Phillips, D.C. (1987) *Philosophy, Science, and Social Enquiry*, Pergamon, Oxford.
18. Lind, G. (1987) The theory of moral-cognitive development: a socio- psychological assessment, in *Moral Development and the Social Environment*, (ed. G. Lind, A. Hartmann and R. Wakenhut), Precedent, Chicago, pp. 21-53.
19. Higgins, A., Power, C. and Kohlberg, L. (1984) The relationship of moral atmosphere to judgements of responsibility, in *Morality, Moral Behaviour and Moral Development*, (eds. W. Kurtines and J. Gewirtz), Wiley, New York, pp. 74-106.
20. Blair, S. (1985). Professionalisation of attitude towards play in children and adults. *Research Quarterly*, Vol. 56, pp. 82-3.
21. Case, B.W., Greer, H.S. and Lacourse, M.G. (1987) Moral judgement development and perceived legitimacy of spectator behaviour. *Journal of Sport Behaviour*, Vol. 10, pp. 147-56.

22. Goncalves, C. (1990) Fair play and youth sport participants, in *Physical Education and Lifelong Activity: Reports of Physical Culture and Health 73* (eds. R. Telama, L. Laakso, M. Pieron, I. Ruoppila and V. Vihko), Foundation for the Promotion of Physical Culture and Health, Jyvaskyla, Finland, pp.137-43.
23. Lee, M.J., Balchin, N. and Whitehead, J. (1996) Ethical attitudes among youth sport participants in the United Kingdom. Paper presented to the *First Annual Congress of the European College of Sports Sciences*, Nice, France, May 30th.
24. Stephens, D.E. (1995) Lying, hurting, and cheating in youth sport: variations in patterns of predictors for female and male soccer players. Paper presented to the *Annual Conference of the Association for the Advancement of Applied Sport Psychology*, New Orleans, Sept. 30th.
25. Vallerand, R.J. and Losier, G.F. (1994) Self-determined motivation and sportsmanship orientations: an assessment of their temporal relationship. *Journal of Sport and Exercise Psychology*, Vol. 16, pp. 229-45.
26. Duda, J., Olson, L.K. and Templin, T.J. (1991) The relationship of task and ego orientation to sportsmanship attitudes and the perceived legitimacy of injurious acts. *Research Quarterly for Exercise and Sport*, Vol. 62, pp. 79-87.
27. Bredemeier, B.J. and Shields, D.L.L. (1984) Divergence in moral reasoning about moral reasoning about sport and life. *Sociology of Sport Journal*, Vol.1, pp. 348-57.
28. Bredemeier, B.J., Weiss, M.R., Shields, D.L. and Cooper, B. (1987) The relationships between sport involvement and with children's moral reasoning and aggression tendencies. *Journal of Sport Psychology*, Vol. 8, pp. 304-18.
29. Bredemeier, B.J., Weiss, M.R., Shields, D.L. and Schewchuk, B.A.B. (1987) Promoting moral growth in a summer sport camp: the implementation of theoretically grounded instructional strategies. *Journal of Moral Education*, Vol. 15, pp. 212-20.
30. Bredemeier, B.J.L. (1995) Divergences in children's moral reasoning about issues in daily life and sport specific contexts. *International Journal of Sport Psychology*, Vol. 26, pp. 453-63.
31. Romance, T., Weiss, M.R. and Bockovan, J. (1986) A program to promote moral development through elementary school physical education. *Journal of Teaching in Physical Education*, Vol. 5, pp. 126-36.
32. Huizinga, J. (1955) *Homo Ludens: A Study of the Play Element in Culture*, Beacon, Boston.
33. Erikson, E. (1950) *Childhood and Society*, Norton, New York.
34. Speicher, B. (1994) Family patterns of moral judgement during adolescence and early adulthood. *Developmental Psychology*, Vol. 30, pp. 624-32.
35. Smith, M.D. (1983) Social determinants of violence in hockey: a review, in *Children in Sport*, (eds. R.A. Magill, M.J. Ashy and F.L. Smoll), Human Kinetics, Champaign, Il, pp. 295-309.
36. Stuart, M.E. and Ebbeck, V. (1995) The influence of perceived social approval on moral development in youth sport. *Pediatric Exercise Science*, Vol. 7, pp. 270-80.

37. Lee, M.J. and Balchin, N. (1996) Social influences on values in young athletes. Paper presented to the *Annual Conference of the British Association of Sport and Exercise Sciences*, Lilleshall, England, Sept. 7th.
38. Stephens, D.E. and Bredemeier, B.J.L. (1996) Moral atmosphere and judgements about aggression in girls soccer: relationships among moral and motivational variables. *Journal of Sport and Exercise Psychology*, Vol. 18, pp.158-73.
39. Dubois, P.E. (1986) Gender differences in value orientation toward sports: a longitudinal analysis. Paper presented to the *7th Annual Meeting of the North American Society for the Sociology of Sport*, Las Vegas, Nevada, Oct. 29 - Nov. 1.
40. Dubois, P.E. (1986) The effect of participation in sport on the value orientations of young athletes. *Sociology of Sport Journal*, Vol. 3, pp. 29-42.
41. Simmons, D.D. and Dickinson, R.V. (1986) Measurement of values expression in sports and athletics. *Perceptual and Motor Skills*, Vol. 62, pp. 651-8.
42. Lee, M.J. and Cockman, M.J. (1995) Values in children's sport: spontaneously expressed values among young athletes. *International Review for the Sociology of Sport*, Vol. 30, pp. 337-52
43. Meilke, R. and Bahlke, S. (1995) Structure and preferences of fundamental values of young athletes. *International Review for the Sociology of Sport*, Vol. 30, pp. 419-37.
44. Telama, R. and Kahila, S. (1996) Adolescents participation in sport and its relation to their prosocial behaviour and moral judgements. Paper presented to the *First Annual Congress of the European College of Sports Sciences*, Nice, France, May 30th.
45. Lee, M.J. and Balchin, N. (1996) *Young People, Sport and Ethics: an Examination of Fairplay in Youth Sport.* Technical Report to the Research Unit, The Sports Council, London.
46. Schwartz, S. (1992) Universals in the content and structure of values: Theoretical advances and empirical tests in 20 Countries, in *Advances in Experimental Social Psychology,* (ed M. P. Zanna), Academic Press, London, Vol. 25, pp. 1-65,
47. Bardi, A. and Schwartz, S. (1994) Values and behaviour in sports: a theoretical framework. Paper presented to the *23rd International Congress of Applied Psychology*, Madrid, Spain, July 17-22.

AUTHOR INDEX

KEYWORD INDEX

This index has been compiled from the keywords assigned to the papers, edited and extended as appropriate. The page references are to the first page of the relevant paper.